Higher National Co

Higher National Computing

Bruce Hellingsworth
Patrick Hall
Howard Anderson

Newnes
OXFORD AUCKLAND BOSTON JOHANNESBURG MELBOURNE NEW DELHI

Newnes
An imprint of Butterworth-Heinemann
Linacre House, Jordan Hill, Oxford OX2 8DP
225 Wildwood Avenue, Woburn, MA 01801-2041
A division of Reed Educational and Professional Publishing Ltd

 A member of the Reed Elsevier plc group

First published 2001
Reprinted 2001

British Library Cataloguing in Publication Data
A catalogue record for this book is available from the British Library

ISBN 0 7506 52306

Composition by Genesis Typesetting, Laser Quay, Rochester, Kent
Printed and bound in Great Britain

Contents

Introduction

This book has been written to help you achieve the learning outcomes of the core units of Edexcel's new BTEC Higher National Computing programme. The three authors have many years' experience of teaching HNC and HND computing students and have worked with Edexcel in the team that produced the new HNC/HND computing units. In producing the book, the authors' principal aim has been that of capturing, within a single volume, the core knowledge required of all computing students at HNC/HND level.

The six core units covered in the book are: Hardware and Networks, Systems Analysis, Software Constructs and Tools, Computing Solutions, Quality Management Principles and Communication Technology. The book has been organized on a logical basis with each chapter devoted to a single core unit. We have, however, attempted to reduce duplication and some material is appropriate to more than one of the core units. Furthermore, to put supporting concepts into context, we have developed a number of topics within the individual chapters and in sections at the end of the book. You will also find that, where difficult concepts are introduced, we have included notes in the margin headed **Another View**. These will provide you with an alternative way of understanding them.

This book has been designed to provide you with a thorough introduction to each of the core units. Despite this, you are advised to make use of other reference books and materials wherever and whenever possible. You should also get into the habit of using all of the resources that are available to you. These include your tutor, your college or university library, computer centre, and other learning resources. Extensive use should be made of the Internet; to help you there are numerous URLs in the text. As this subject is perhaps the most fast changing of all technologies, the most up-to-date information is often only available from the Internet. You should also become familiar with selecting materials that are appropriate to the topics you are studying. In particular, you may find it useful to refer to materials that will provide you with several different views of a particular topic.

Throughout the book we have provided worked examples that show how the ideas introduced in the text can be put into practice. We have also included problems and questions at various stages in the text (solutions can be found on the publisher's website: www.newnespress.com). Depending on the nature of the topic, these questions take a variety of forms, from simple problems requiring short numerical answers to those that may require some additional research or that may require the use of an analytical software package in their solution. Your tutor may well ask you to provide answers to these questions as coursework or homework but they can also be used to help you with revision for course assessments.

The first chapter, **Hardware and Networks**, introduces the hardware of personal computers with the accent on component selection rather than specialized descriptions of the components themselves. **Systems Analysis** concentrates on what people actually need a computer for and how to translate these tasks into a solution before any consideration is made about programming. **Software Constructs and Tools** is intended to support these units with a description of problem-solving techniques and guidance on the kind of programming languages or software tools most suitable for given problems. The chapter **Computing Solutions** supports the ideas introduced in Systems Analysis with a wider view then presents other computer techniques that are considered for a range of problem types. **Quality Management Principles** presents the ideas that must underpin the whole subject of computing, the provision of systems whose quality and reliability are assured. Sufficient information on the subject of networks is presented in the **Communication Technology** chapter to allow meaningful collaboration with networking specialists.

Finally, we would like to offer a few words of practical advice to students. At the beginning of your HNC or HND course you will undoubtedly find that some topics appear to be more difficult than others. Sometimes you may find the basic concepts difficult to grasp (perhaps you haven't met them before), or you might have difficulty with things that you cannot immediately visualize.

No matter what the cause of your temporary learning block, it is important to remember two things: you won't be the first person to encounter the problem, and there is plenty of material available to you that will help you overcome it. All that you need to do is to recognize that it is a problem and then set about doing something about it. A regular study pattern and a clearly defined set of learning goals will help you get started. In any event, don't give up – computing is a challenging and demanding career and your first challenge along the road is to master the core knowledge, that is what you will find in this book.

May we wish you every success with your Higher National studies!

Bruce Hellingsworth
Patrick Hall
Howard Anderson

1 Hardware and networks

Summary

The aim of this chapter of the book is to provide sufficient technical information to enable users to make informed purchasing or specification decisions without becoming overinvolved with detail. Each heading will present the information from the user's point of view and, where necessary, ignore or gloss over the most technical details. For instance, no real attempt will be made to describe the precise working of a disk drive but the benefits of its performance will be outlined. No attempt has been made to cover other aspects of the use of microprocessors such as embedded systems, mobile communications devices, etc., nor to look at larger machines, mainframe computers or other specialized areas. The focus will be on how to buy a PC but with sufficient content to be at HNC level.

1.1 The basic components of a PC

This part of the book is intended to describe the basic parts of a computer ready to fulfil the requirements of Unit 1, i.e. how to buy a PC.

Students who have embarked on an HNC in Computing will not need to be told that there is a monitor, a system box, etc.; all will have used these items, but they will need the knowledge of how to specify each one or to communicate effectively with experienced technicians.

The system box

This contains the motherboard with the CPU or *Central Processing Unit*, storage devices such as hard drives or CD-ROM drive, the memory, a power supply and any add-on components such as a video card, modem, etc.

Motherboard

So called because older computers were made from a large number of components organized onto several circuit boards. These were plugged into one 'main' or motherboard that contained the CPU and the circuits that communicated with the add-on boards. Modern machines have most of the principal components on one board but the name has stuck. The motherboard will house the CPU, the *chipset*, the memory connectors or expansion buses for the circuits that are still separate and often the I/O (input/output) ports. The chipset controls DMA or *Direct Memory Access*, the *bus interface*, memory, disks, keyboard, I/O ports and timing.

CPU

The CPU is the circuit that is able to execute the instructions stored in the memory. Modern CPUs in the Intel Pentium series and others are able to execute these instructions at high speed and provide considerable computing power in a small component.

Storage

All the instructions and data that form *software* must at one point be stored. This data is all in the form of logical 1s or 0s and any physical property of any substance or device that will remain in one state or another can be used to store this software. Most hard disks are magnetic devices that store 1s and 0s as changes in the patterns of magnetic particles held on a surface. CD-ROMs hold 1s and 0s by optical patterns on the surface of a simple material. The only real reason why magnetic hard drives are common is that they are cheap, fast and reliable. When newer, faster devices with higher capacity are manufactured, magnetic hard drives may become a thing of the past; purely optical devices hold this promise. The point is, there is nothing special about a *hard drive*, it is simply a device that can store a large number of 1 s and 0 s and deliver them to another circuit at an acceptable speed.

Memory

The memory stores software, i.e. program instructions and data. There are two broad kinds with the rather confusing names RAM for *Random Access Memory* and ROM for *Read Only Memory.* The problem is that both may be randomly accessed and some kinds of ROM can be written to! The key point is that RAM is *volatile*, i.e. it loses its data when the power is turned off ROM does not, it is *non-volatile*.

Power supply

The power supply is another misleading name as the power to run the computer usually comes from the mains or from batteries. Its job is to provide 12 volts to run disk drive motors, etc. and 5 or 3.3 volts to run the digital circuits. It must be able to provide enough current to run everything in the machine without overheating and to ensure the voltage is constant with defined limits.

Display

The most commonly used desktop display device is the CRT or *Cathode Ray Tube*, a device first widely used in the sciences and defence in the 1940s and extremely expensive at the time; they were also very unreliable. Now CRTs are made cheaply by the million and are amongst the most reliable devices in common use. With the rise in use of laptop computers and the need to save desk space, etc., newer screen types have also become available and the marketplace has become extremely competitive with LCD screens currently being the most common. The common name for a CRT is a VDU or *Visual Display Unit.*

If you need to buy a PC or just one of the components, you need to know more about its *performance* than how it works. A knowledge of how it works will help with your understanding of the performance and some of the difficulties overcome by the maker but this knowledge does not need to be in great detail. The remaining sections in this chapter are intended to provide the required knowledge.

The hierarchy of design

You know that computers are binary devices often made with silicon circuits and they work with logical 1 s and 0 s. It is hard to imagine the connection between this statement and seeing a word processor in action with all the screen colours, text and clickable buttons, i.e. a program in action. To illustrate this, imagine you are given the task of explaining the idea of a 'city' to someone who has only ever lived on a desert island and never had need of permanent housing. If you started by describing 'what is a brick' and then immediately described the construction of a whole town using bricks, the connection between the small hard brick and the warm and comfortable rows of houses would be very difficult to follow. If you then took the view of a town planner and spoke of where the hospital should be in your town, any connections with bricks would be entirely lost. The trouble is, towns are made of bricks!

The connection between 1 s and 0 s and tasks such as installing Windows is of a similar nature. The way to overcome this is to think of 'layers' of knowledge. Using the brick and the town example, consider these layers:

of bricks and towns	*of computer hardware*	*of computer software*
Bricks. Study what a brick is made of, how it is made, how strong it is, what will it cost.	1 s and 0 s, simple digital circuits and how logical arithmetic can be performed with a circuit.	Boolean logic.
Walls. Study how to mix cement, how to lay bricks to make a wall, how strong a wall is.	How a sequence of logical operations can be achieved with a circuit, how to add, subtract, perform logical AND and OR operations, etc.	How to perform arithmetic with simple numbers.

of bricks and towns	*of computer hardware*	*of computer software*
How to make several walls into a building with spaces for windows and doors, etc. How to build a roof.	How to store many logical instructions and feed them in sequence to a circuit that can execute them.	How to perform arithmetic with multiple digit numbers.
How to install all the services a building needs, water, electricity, gas, heating, etc. and to move in the carpets, furniture, etc.	How to accept human inputs by devices such as a keyboard and to display outputs using devices like a colour monitor.	How to handle data such as text and how to edit it, i.e. move a sentence within a paragraph.
How to build a row of houses, provide street lighting, public access, etc.	How to provide a complete set of devices such as a mouse, keyboard, printer, CPU, etc. and, to make them all connect correctly.	How to present a complete set of facilities in a word processor.
How to plan a town, provide libraries, shops, hospital, bus station, etc.	A complete PC.	How to control the entire machine – the operating system.

In normal life, we expect different people to be expert at these different layers; a bricklayer is not a town planner. When studying for the HNC in Computing we do not expect you become expert in any one of the layers, rather to understand all the layers in the same way that you can imagine all the tasks required to build a town; specialization will come later in your studies.

What I am asking you to do here is to take on trust that descriptions of the 'bricks' will lead to an understanding of the 'town council'. It just takes some time.

1.2 Elements in the history of microprocessors

It is said that history is written by the victors. Although this really refers to political history and especially the result of political failure, war, it also applies to vast business areas like computing. Much of the history of computers has been written by the commercial 'victors', the Americans, but you should read it with care; often the rest of the world is left out. As an example, is it often quoted that the world's first computer was an American machine called ENIAC which came out in 1946. The problem is, this machine and others built around the same time were not like modern machines so we get into a discussion about what exactly *is* a computer. Amongst other computer projects around the world, in Britain, Germany and other countries, was a highly secret project that predates ENIAC. The design and use of this project was carried out with brilliant success in Britain during the Second World War; it was called the *Colossus* computer and was used at Bletchley

Park in the decryption of enemy cyphers. It was so secret that its very existence was not officially published until 1974, long after some of the history books were written.

Here is the real problem, some people only use other history books as their source so some 'facts' are propagated with time. If you research the history of microprocessors, you will find that different sources quote 'facts' that vary greatly one from another. As you advance in your studies, you must develop the ability to look critically at these facts and to decide what is the most accurate. The world is a complex place so simple claims are unlikely to be true. As an example, most people will consider it a fact that Isaac Newton discovered gravity when an apple hit him on his head whilst seated under an apple tree. The trouble is, this is a complete fiction but it is propagated as a fact. Beware!

The first Colossus computer, the Mark 1, was operational in January 1944. It was designed and built by the Post Office at Dollis Hill in London. Like ENIAC (Electronic Numerical Integrator and Computer), Colossus is not a stored programme machine, the 'program' was hard-wired and stored as switch settings. During the decryption process for which it was built, messages to be worked on were stored as a Baudot code (a 5 digit binary code) on a paper tape and these messages were read at 5000 characters a second. In the 200 microseconds it took between each character, Colossus could perform 100 Boolean calculations on each of the 5 binary digits of a character. It is difficult to compare exactly the speed difference between this kind of computer and a modern computer because Colossus did some of its work in parallel, but if you take 100 Boolean calculations, one for each of the 5 digits and do this 5000 times a second, you get $100 \times 5 \times 5000 = 2\,500\,000$ Boolean calculations per second. It would *not* be right to compare this directly with a speed of 2.5 MIPS (see page 59) but for the world's first computer it is a very respectable performance; this machine was not slow. See www.codesandciphers.org.uk/ for more information.

There is little doubt that the first commercial microprocessor was the Intel 4004 and that Intel has gone on to become a dominant force in the world of microcomputers, but other brilliant designs remain less well known. The ubiquitous PC uses Intel microprocessors but Apple machines use the Motorola MC680x0 series and most mobile phones use a British designed RISC chip called the ARM.

It is not the purpose of this book to describe in detail each of several hundred different microprocessors, but details can be seen directly from the makers' web pages:

Intel	www.intel.com/intel/product/index.htm
Intel past types	www.intel.com/intel/museum/25anniv/
Motorola	www.mot.com/SPS/MMTG/mp.html
ARM	www.arm.com (follow links to CPUs)
Cyrix	www.cyrix.com/products/cyrindex.htm
AMD	www.amd.com/products/cpg/cpg.html
IBM	www.chips.ibm.com/products/powerpc/
Sun	www.sun.com/microelectronics/products/microproc.html
Zilog	www.zilog.com/products/zx80.html
General	cpusite.examedia.nl/
	www.tme-inc.com/html/service/general.htm
	www.tme-inc.com/html/service/general.htm

Table 1.2.1 shows some important Intel microprocessors, the intention being to show the rapid development in terms of speed and complexity. (Intel actually produce many more types.)

Table 1.2.1 *Crude indicators for Intel microprocessors. Graph 1.14.1 was generated from this data*

Intel chip	*Date*	*MIPS*	*Width of data bus*	*Number of transistors*
4004	1971	0.06	4	2 300
8008	1972	0.06	8	3 500
8080	1974	0.64	8	6 000
8085	1976	0.37	8	6 500
8086	1978	0.33	16	29 000
8088	1979	0.33	16	29 000
80286	1982	1.2	16	134 000
80386SX	1985	5.5	16	275 000
80486DX	1989	20	32	1 200 000
80486SX	1991	13	32	1 185 000
80486DX2	1992	41	32	1 200 000
80486DX4	1994	52	32	1 600 000
Pentium P5	1993	100	64	3 100 000
Pentium P54C	1994	150	64	3 200 000
Pentium MMX	1997	278	64	4 500 000
Pentium Pro	1995	337	64	5 500 000

Beware!

(1) The table shows speed in Millions of Instructions Per Second or MIPS. As explained in section 1.13, this is a very crude means of testing microprocessor speed and is only included here with this warning. The speed in MIPS of these chips will change if the clock speed is changed and you will notice the clock speed has been left out. This is because comparing chips on clock speed is an even cruder means of evaluating performance. A 100 MHz 80486 is not four times slower than a 400 Mz Pentium, the speed difference is in fact a little tricky to pin down but it is certainly more than eight times slower.

(2) The width of the data bus can also be given an inappropriate level of importance when comparing microprocessor performance. An 8-bit microprocessor will take many times longer to perform a 16-bit by 16-bit multiplication with a 32-bit answer than a 16-bit microprocessor; the 8-bit machine will take dozens of instructions, the other will take 1 instruction. Couple this with the fact that the 16-bit machine will perform this instruction in fewer clock cycles and the clock is running faster and you can see the microprocessor speed is indeed tricky to pin down!

Nonetheless, the table shows the remarkable development over nearly 30 years.

Moore's law

In 1965, Gordon Moore was the Research Director of the electronics company Fairchild Semiconductor. Some 3 years later he was to become one of the founders of Intel. He made an interesting prediction based on what had happened up to that time with memory chips (not microprocessors). He noticed that memory capacity doubled in capacity every 18–24 months. He then predicted this would continue, leading to an exponential growth in size and hence computing power. Until now, with memory and with microprocessors, Market trends have shown it to have come true; there are predictions that it will fail in the future but these predictions have themselves failed in the past as they have been made many times.

Mathematics in action

What is exponential growth?

It is when the next value in a series is multiplied by a factor, not added to. So if you start with a number, say 1, and multiply it by a factor, say 2, you get an answer of 2. If you then repeat this, the number grows slowly at the start but very soon becomes very fast.

For instance: if you start with 1 and keep multiplying by 2, you get the series 1, 2, 4, 8, 16, 32, 64, 128, 256, 512, 1024 and so on. The speed of increase is best displayed as a graph.

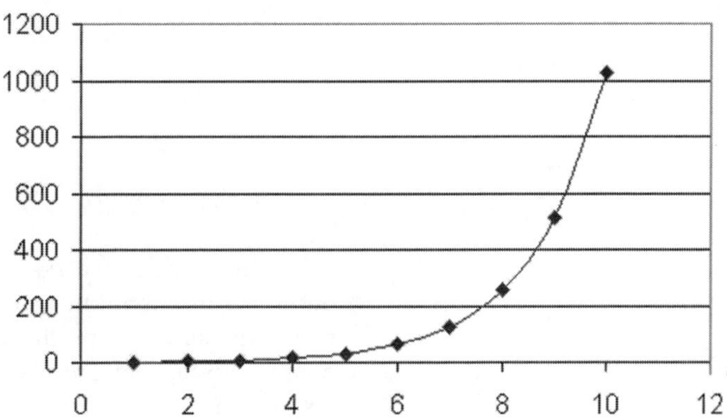

Figure 1.2.1 *Simple exponential growth*

Searching the internet

Much detailed information on current microprocessor specifications can be seen on the internet. The problem with giving too many URLs is that they are not guaranteed to exist after this book is printed. If you make good use of a search engine, will find them very quickly.

There are different types of search engine so:

You could use a *keyword search engine* such as Go (www.go.com), with a search string of

+microprocessor +history

The +signs show the word must be present (it is like the boolean AND operator).

You could also use a *subject-based search engine* such as Yahoo Advanced (search.yahoo.com/search/options) with the search string

microprocessor history

making sure the 'Matches on all words (AND)' box is checked.

Finally you could choose a *meta search engine* such as Metacrawler (www.metacrawler.com/). The search string will be

microprocessor history

make sure the 'all' box is checked.

Be *very* careful who you believe!

1.3 What is a microprocessor?

A microprocessor is a complex circuit built from a large number of simple circuits containing *transistors*, *diodes*, etc. made to perform *logic*. A Pentium Pro has approximately 5.5 million transistors. There are two key properties that a microprocessor has:

It can execute logical instructions in *sequence*

and

It can make *decisions*.

The instructions to carry these out (the program) are separately stored outside of the circuit in *memory*. The decisions or instructions are very modest in human terms, they usually take the form of something like 'if number A is bigger than number B then execute instruction K else execute instruction X' or 'add 6 to number A'. The logical instructions are executed in sequence by the microprocessor, each is fetched from memory then executed, one at a time. (Complex modern microprocessors can execute several instructions at once). No *single instruction* does anything really complex like 'move paragraph to the bottom of the document', they all do relatively simple tasks. Complex tasks are built from hundreds or thousands of these simple tasks, just like a town is built from thousands of bricks; the town is complex, the bricks are simple.

All the operations of the microprocessor are controlled by a *clock* which means that a constant number of pulses or 1s and 0s are fed to the circuit and each instruction is executed on each pulse. A clock in this sense has nothing to do with devices that tell the time! When you see

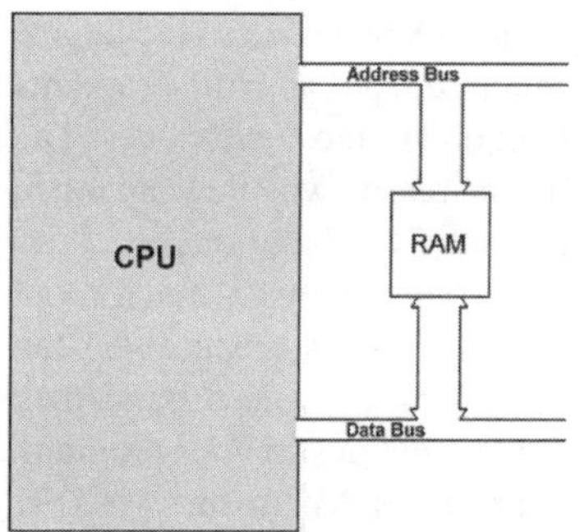

Figure 1.3.1 *Connection of a simple CPU and external RAM*

that a Pentium processor has a clock speed of 600 MHz, it means that 600 000 000 clock pulses are supplied to the circuit per second. A quick thought will tell you that if things are happening that fast, why is it that you can watch some operations take some time to execute. The answer is simple, complex tasks are made from a large number of very simple tasks, the simple tasks get executed at a speed hard to relate to human experience but there are *so* many to execute!

In Figure 1.3.1, there are two components, the CPU and the RAM. All the instructions are stored in the RAM and must be loaded one by one into the CPU. After a single instruction has been loaded, the CPU decides what it means, i.e. it *decodes* it, then *executes* the instruction. This is called the *Fetch–Execute cycle*. There is a clock input to the CPU which supplies a series of timed 1s and 0s as a square wave.

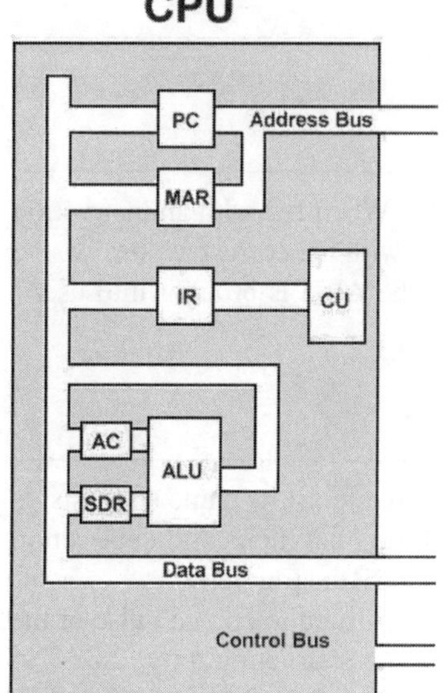

Figure 1.3.2 *Diagram of a simplified CPU*

The CPU

What follows does *not* describe a real microprocessor. It is a simplified version of the original microprocessors and is presented to demonstrate the way that these devices work. Real microprocessors are more complex but share the same basic way of working.

Registers

The CPU contains *registers*. These are circuits that can remember individual numbers for a short time. Figure 1.3.2 shows these:

- The AC register is traditionally known as the *accumulator*, it is the register where the results of calculations are held.
- The SDR is called the *Store Data Register* and is used to hold data ready for an instruction.
- The IR is the *Instruction Register* and is used to hold the latest instruction fetched from RAM.
- The MAR is the *Memory Address Register* and is used to hold addresses.
- The PC is the *Program Counter* and is used to store the location or address of the next instruction to be fetched.

Buses

The components of the CPU and those outside the CPU are connected together using *buses*. A bus is simply a collection of wires, so an 8-bit bus is just eight wires each carrying 1s or 0s. Remember that a byte is 8-bits so an 8-bit bus could carry a single byte of information. For example, the information at one moment *could* be the letter G which formed part of the data being processed by the CPU. ASCII for G is 64 + its position in the alphabet = 71 decimal or 47 hex (see page 438). If you convert this to binary you get 01000111. If each of the wires takes on the value 1 or 0 in this pattern, the bus could be said to be holding a letter G. There is no way of telling if the pattern 01000111 is a 'G' or not, the 'value' of a piece of data is only applied by the software that is using it.

Question 1.3.1

If a microprocessor has a 20-bit address bus, what is the maximum size of RAM this can address?

Question 1.3.2

How many address lines are required to address 64 Mb of RAM?

In this simple microprocessor, the data bus is 8 bits wide so the largest number it can store is $2^8-1 = 255$. If it is required, you can write programs to handle larger numbers by breaking them down into 8-bit values. The older 8-bit microprocessors did this and is one reason why they are much slower than modern microprocessors; arithmetic was laborious.

The address bus is also just 8 bits wide. This causes a much more severe restriction on operations; than an 8-bit data bus because you can only have 256 addresses. If some of the instructions need data (they usually do), you may have as little as 100 instructions in your program. When you consider that the main executable of Microsoft Word 97 comprises more than 5 million bytes and that this software needs even more support files to make it work, a 256-byte memory is very small! The width of the data bus and the address bus is an important consideration when specifying a microprocessor. The Pentium microprocessor has a 32-bit address bus and a 64-bit data bus. As 2^{32} = 4 294 967 296, a 32-bit address will allow 4 294 967 296 different addresses or 4000 Mb or 4 Gb.

Control unit

The control unit is the 'heart' of the CPU. When fed with an instruction from the IR, the microprocessor responds with the correct action, i.e. the right registers are used and if required, the ALU is brought into use.

Arithmetic and logic unit

The ALU is the *Arithmetic and Logic Unit* and, as its name suggests, is where the microprocessor actually performs additions and subtraction and logical operations such as AND and OR instructions.

In this example, the CPU will fetch an instruction on one pulse of the clock, decode it right away and execute the instruction on 1, 2 or 3 of the next clock pulses. The reason it might use 1 or 2 or 3 clock pulses is because some instructions are a little more involved than others. The instructions are held in the RAM in a sequence of numbered locations, each of which is called an address. A possible sequence of instructions is shown in Table 1.3.1.

Fetch–Execute cycle

Look carefully at Figure 1.3.3. You will see that the PC contains the value 161. The other registers have values that do not matter. Leaving out quite a lot of detail, the fetch execute sequence will go like this:

The fetch part of the fetch–execute sequence

- Instruct the RAM to give the contents of address 161 and place the number found there (3A) into the IR. This is done by putting the value 161 on the address bus and instructing the RAM to read,

Table 1.3.1 *Program for the simple CPU*

Address in RAM (numbered location)	*Code for instruction or data held in RAM*	*Meaning*
161	3A	Load the data at the next address into the AC register
162	23	Number to load, i.e. data not an instruction
163	3D	Load the data at the next address into the SDR register
164	12	Number to load, i.e. data not an instruction
165	8C	Add the numbers in the AC and SDR registers and store the result in the AC register
166	3E	Store the value in the AC register at the RAM address held at the next two addresses, low byte first
167	6E	Low byte of address
168	01	High byte of address
169	3A	Load the data at the next address into the AC register
16A	45	Number to load, i.e. data not an instruction

the value 3A will then appear on the data bus. The control unit provides all the signals for this to happen.

- Allow the IR to feed its value into the control unit.
- The control unit reacts by 'decoding' the instruction 3A which in turn has the effect of putting 162 into the MAR, i.e. the address of the next address where the data is held. The microprocessor is now ready to execute the newly fetched instruction.

Once this is complete, the instruction **Load the data at the next address into the AC register** will be in the CPU, so is the value of the next address but note that it has *not* been executed, i.e. the AC register has not been loaded with the data.

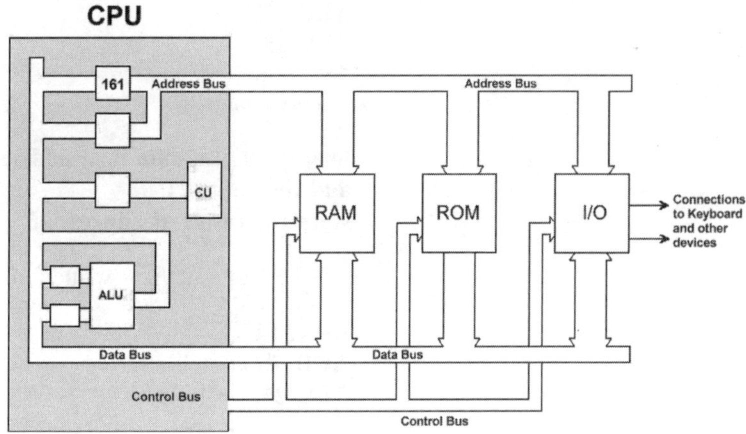

Figure 1.3.3 *The assembled microcomputer*

The execute part of the fetch–execute sequence

- Allow the contents of the MAR onto the address bus and instruct the RAM to read. This will result in the value 23 appearing on the data bus.
- Load the contents of the data bus into the AC register.
- Add 1 to the PC ready for the next fetch sequence.

The fetch execute sequence has now completed and is ready for the next cycle. Remembering this is not a real processor, we can safely ignore some practical details; in this example the fetch sequence took two 'ticks' of the CPU clock and the execute sequence took three ticks. If the clock was running at 1 MHz, i.e. 1 000 000 ticks per second (or better 1 000 000 1 s and 0 s), this would have taken 5/1 000 000 seconds or 5 millionths of a second. This is quick in human terms, but all that has happened is that a number has been loaded into a register!

The next instruction in the program is **Load the data at the next address into the SDR register** and this is fetched and executed in a similar way. The next instruction after that is **Add the numbers in the AC and SDR registers and store the result in the AC register**. You should note that this instruction does not have any data associated with it. This means it will take fewer ticks of the clock so will fetch and execute quicker because it does not have to read the RAM a second time.

In general, instructions will take the form of 'what to do' followed by the 'data to do it with' or more formally, *operation code* followed by *operand*. Other instructions will only have the operation code (often shortened to *op code*).

The actual program code and data are of course in binary but we humans do not like to see lists of binary numbers or for that matter, hex numbers. The consequence is that these programs are written down using *mnemonics* for op codes, so the instruction **Load the AC register with the contents of address 14** could be written as the mnemonic **LDA, 14** and the instruction **add 21 to the contents of the AC register** would be written as the mnemonic **ADD, #21**. The mnemonic **STA, 25** would mean **Store the contents of AC register at address 25**.

A program fragment containing these instructions is:

LDA, 14
ADD, #21
STA, 25

This means:

load whatever data is at address 14 into the AC register
add the value 21
store the result at address 25

When a program is written in the form of

LDA, 14
ADD, #21
STA, 25

it is called assembly language.

Machine code

The program and data in RAM would in reality be just a set of numbers. If you were to write them down as numbers (in hex, decimal or binary, numbers are just numbers!), the resulting code is called *machine code*. This is what is actually run in the microprocessor using the fetch–execute sequence. Everything the CPU executes is machine code; when running Windows, the .EXE or .DLL files are machine code.

Assembly code

If you write down the same program using mnemonics, the resulting program code is called *assembly code*. The reason is that the mnemonics must be converted or 'assembled' into machine code with another program called an 'assembler'. Writing a program using an assembler is much easier than writing directly in machine code. The sequence would be to use a text editor to type the assembly code then use the assembler to generate the machine code. This is then loaded into the RAM and the program run. With luck it will do what you want it to!

If the assembly language

LDA, 14
ADD, #21
STA, 25

is converted to machine code with an assembler, it might give something like

Address	*Machine code*
234	3A
235	14
236	8C
237	21
238	3E
239	25

What would be stored is just the machine code, i.e. 34, 14, 8C, 21, 3E, 25. As you can see, machine code is not easy to read.

Actually writing commercial programs using assembly code (often just called assembler) is difficult but one or two applications in computing are still written this way. An example would be very small but speed critical parts of an *operating system* or special high-speed animation sections of a game. Most programs are written using high-level languages such as C++ or Visual Basic but eventually, after all the compiling and processing of these languages, everything the CPU executes is machine code. *Absolutely* everything!

Assembly language on real processors

It is not the intention of this book or this unit of the HNC Computing to cover assembly language programming but some understanding of terms such as *16-bit operating system* will need to be explained. It is not at all clear why a 16-bit as against a 32-bit program should be different from each other but the section that follows will show there is a very large difference.

The simple processor on page 11 is not a real practical device. Several key points were ignored in order to put over the main idea of the fetch–execute sequence and what microprocessors actually do. Unlike the simple processor, real processors have a set of *general purpose registers*, the ability to multiply and divide, to handle *floating point* (real) arithmetic, but they still fetch then execute instructions in sequence. Pentium processors can fetch more than one instruction at a time, can execute whilst fetching, can store instructions in the processor chip and operate in a very efficient way but still fetch then execute instructions even if the sequence is more complex than presented above.

If you need to write assembly language, you will need to know the *architecture* of the chip that will use the resulting machine code and its instruction set, and the list of possible operations the chip will execute. Expertise in writing assembler for a Pentium chip will help your need to write for a MC68040 bit only in a general way. One will not directly transfer to the other in the same way that a C++ program would (or at least should!).

For the sake of comparison, one of the original series of Intel chips, the 8086, had four general-purpose registers called AX, BX, CX and DX so the chip could execute an instruction such as

```
MOV AX, 8000
```

which would move (or load) the number 8000 into the AX general-purpose register. This register is 16-bits wide so the largest number it can hold is $2^{16}–1 = 65\,535$. If you were to multiply 8000 by 8, then the answer of 64 000 will still fit in the AX register, so the instruction

```
MUL 8
```

will perform the multiplication and place the answer back in AX.

The problem comes when you try a calculation that results in larger numbers than will fit in a 16-bit register. The instructions

```
MOV AX, 8000
MUL 9
```

will not give the correct answer as 8000×9 is greater than 65 535. The solution is to use two registers and hold the answer in two parts but you are still limited to the size of number you can handle in this way. It is quite possible to write routines that handle larger numbers, in fact numbers of any size you choose but they require *routines*, i.e. whole sets of instructions rather than a single instruction.

A 32-bit processor can multiply two 32-bit numbers and give a 64-bit answer in a single instruction, a 16-bit processor will use a set of instructions to achieve the same result. See Program 1.3.1. It may seem that a 32-bit microprocessor is twice as powerful as a 16-bit version but in fact the 32-bit one is very much faster. Suppose you had a 16- and a 32-bit microprocessor that ran at the same clock speed and had the same complexity of instructions, the 32-bit machine would handle larger numbers a great deal quicker. Modern 64-bit machines can of course handle even larger numbers; they also execute each instruction quicker.

The assembly language program presented in Program 1.3.1 multiplies two 32-bit signed numbers and gives a 64-bit result. It is written for the 8086 processor, i.e. a 16-bit machine. It is shown here simply to demonstrate the difference between processors of different bit sizes. On a 32- or 64-bit machine, the same result is achieved using a *single instruction*. For the purposes of this unit, you should not attempt to understand how the program works. (Assembly language programmers will note that the top of the program is missing, the so-called assembler directives, etc. The program is shown here only to make the point between microprocessors, not to demonstrate assembly language itself.)

```
            PUSH   DS           ;Save caller's DS and DI
            PUSH   DI
            MOV    DI,DSEG      ;Initialise DS
            MOV    DS,DI
            MOV    NEGIND,O     ;Negative indicator 0
            CMP    DX,0         ;Multiplicand negative?
            JNS    CHKCX        ;No. Go check multiplier
            NOT    AX           ;Yes. 2s-comp. multiplicand
            NOT    DX
            ADD    AX,1
            MDC    DX,0
            NOT    NEGIND       ;and is-comp. indicator
CHKCX:      CMP    CX,0         ;Multiplier negative?
            JNS    GOMUL        ;No. Go multiply
            NOT    BX           ;Yes.2s-comp. multiplier
            NOT    CX
            ADD    BX,1
            ADC    CX,0
            NOT    NEGIND       ;and is-comp. indicator
GOMUL:      CALL   MULU32       ;Perform unsigned mult
            CMP    NEGIND,O     ;Is sign correct?
            JZ     DONE         ;Yes. Exit.
            NOT    AX           ;No. 2s-comp. product
            NOT    BX
            NOT    CX
            NOT    DX
            ADD    AX,1
            ADC    BX,O
            ADC    CX,O
            ADC    DX,O
DONE: POP   DI                  ;Restore caller's registers
            POP    DS
            RET
MULS32      ENDP
CSEG        ENDS
            END
```

Program 1.3.1 *8086 code for signed 32-bit multiplication with 64-bit answer*

1.4 More complex processors, CISC and RISC

RISC means *Reduced Instruction Set* and CISC means *Complex Instruction Set*. (The final C means Chip or Computing depending on what source material you read!)

In a RISC chip, there are fewer instructions which might lead you to believe the chip was in some way less powerful. There are several factors to consider:

- Fewer instructions mean the physical design in silicon is smaller with fewer electronic components and less complexity than a CISC chip so each instruction can execute quicker, the goal being one instruction per clock cycle.
- Analysis of actual program code written for CISC chips shows that only a small fraction of the large number of CISC instructions are actually used frequently.
- Modern 'RISC' chips have rich instruction sets.
- The Pentium series of CPUs have an architecture that gives, on average, better than one instruction per clock cycle, close to the original goal of RISC design.

In reality, modern CPUs described as RISC have little in common with the original idea of RISC. There are differences in the design approach of the chips and in the way code is written for each chip but the difference is not simple and clear cut.

Pipelining and superscalar architecture

A technique used to increase the performance of CPUs is *pipelining*. This means that the execution of each instruction is broken down into stages so when the second stage of execution is underway, the CPU can start the first stage of the next instruction *in the pipeline*. In this way, instruction execution overlaps; if an instruction takes five clock cycles to execute and there are five instructions in the pipeline, on average, it will take one clock cycle per instruction, providing a dramatic increase in performance. A CPU is *superscalar* when it has more than one pipeline.

1.5 Latest processors

Books are not the best place to have information about the latest processors, the market moves so fast that by the time a book is in print, the market has moved on. The very best way to get easy-to-understand information about the latest technology is via the internet. Have a look at the URLs below. They are not presented in any particular order nor is it claimed the list is complete.

The main developments are still in the quest for speed but recently there has been an increase in the number of application-specific CPUs for video cards, network switches and routers, etc. These chips are optimized for the particular application.

In the past, PCs had a single processor that did all the processing required to complete a task. Modern CPUs are not only very much faster but the total task is now split between the main CPU, graphics processors, CPUs on storage devices, on network cards, etc. So looked at from the viewpoint of the whole task that small computers are designed to undertake, PCs are now true multiprocessor machines.

- AMD 1.2 GHz Athlon™ processor, see www.amd.com
- Intel Pentium 4 running a 400 MHz system bus and has 20 stage pipeline, see www.intel.com
- Intel general information, including 1.13 GHz Pentium, see i-probe.com/i-probe/ip_intel_9.html
- VIA Cyrix III processor, see www.cyrix.com
- Motorola MPC7400 PowerPC, see www.mot.com
- Advanced RISC machine ARM10, see www.arm.com
- IBM application-specific processors, see www.chips.ibm.com
- UltraSPARC chips from the Sun Corporation, see www.sun.com
- General information on CPU developments, see cpusite.examedia.nl/

1.6 Motherboards and expansion buses, PCI, ISA, etc., chipsets, BIOS and the bootup sequence, POST and operating system loader, I/O ports

What happens when you turn on your PC

When you turn on a PC, it takes some time before it is ready for work. It may not seem obvious but most of the software that runs the PC is stored on a disk and when the power is turned on, this must be loaded into memory before it can be used.

With one or two exceptions, everything that happens in a PC in *controlled* by software. The hardware actually performs the tasks but is 'told' what to do by software. This includes the process whereby the software is loaded into memory, so how does the software get into memory as it is software that does the loading? This was a problem for early computers, the very first ones had people loading a *loader* program by hand. When this was run, it could load the rest of the software. In a PC, this code is always present in a chip called the *BIOS* or Basic Input Output System and this starts to execute shortly after power-up. The BIOS is stored as machine code, usually in a device that acts like a ROM but can in fact be changed. Older machines used devices like *EPROMS* (Erasable Programmable Read Only Memories) which, as the name implies, can be erased and then programmed. Newer machines use flash memory but the effect is the same, the machine code is there at start-up time.

An aside

The process of starting a computer is called 'booting' after an old philosophical problem that went something like this. *If I pull on your bootstraps, I can lift you off the ground. If you pull just as hard on your own bootstraps, nothing much happens. Why?* The problem is similar because the computer needs a piece of software (a loader) to load the problem, it is like pulling on its own bootstraps, the loader had to come from outside. For this reason, the original loader was called a 'bootstrap' loader and the process of starting a machine was called 'booting up'. It is not the same as turning on the machine; if you do that, all the electronics work but there is nothing to *control* it without software. Control is the central issue.

Experiment

With your PC turned off, pull out the keyboard connector then power up the PC. The POST will report a problem with the keyboard.

The first process to occur is the *POST* or *POwer up Self Test*. This code, stored in the BIOS chip, tries to obtain a response from each of the main components, video, RAM, keyboard, etc. As failure of the video may stop error messages appearing on the screen, success or failure of the POST is reported by sound: these are the two 'beeps' you should hear shortly after turning on the PC. Usually, if something is wrong, several beeps are sounded, either long or short beeps, the combination of which indicates what has gone wrong. Different makers use different combinations of sound but most use two beeps to mean all is OK.

The next stage is to initialize the system board and load the *interrupt vectors* into RAM (see the section on interrupts below). Having done this, a check is made for other devices and to link the BIOS information in those devices to the main BIOS code. Most devices such as video cards, disk controllers, etc. have BIOS code of their own. If you boot different PCs with various devices installed, you will see each BIOS display different text, right at the start of the process. If you have a modern power-saving monitor, it may not have started displaying before it 'warms up' so you may miss this. This is not to be confused with operating system text that appears later.

The next process is the *initial program load*. This is where the BIOS goes to a fixed place on a disk, the first sector, then loads whatever it finds there into memory and starts executing. The first sector is called the boot sector because it contains the bootstrap loader for the operating system to be used. At this point, the BIOS hands over control to the operating system stored on your disk. One of its first tasks is to configure the installed add-on boards using *plug and play*. This means that the hardware interrupts and machine addresses to be associated with each board are determined. (In the old days, this was done when the board was installed using switches on each board. It was the cause of much anguish and thankfully is now assigned to the history books!)

The operating system is now loaded using its own loader software. As much as some companies would like you to think otherwise, there are several different operating systems that work well with a standard PC (e.g. linux). From now on loading is specific to each operating system.

Once this is complete, you can start loading application software and using your PC!

What is an interrupt?

Machine code resides in RAM in a set of addresses so each instruction can be fetched then executed in sequence. Decisions made in software cause the sequence to change, so you could have a decision such as 'if A is greater than B, jump to address 3000'. If A is not greater than B, the code will continue at the next address in memory. This kind if execution is fine for small problems but is of little use when a large number of time critical tasks must be controlled. Suppose the code was running through the section that updated the video screen to place the next character in the right place. If during this process, a key was pressed on the keyboard, it would be ignored, the CPU would be busy with its video task. Remember, everything is controlled by software, even keyboard presses. A system designed in this manner (called *polling*) would be of little use.

The solution adopted very early in the life of computers is to use interrupts. This means the CPU can be signalled to stop doing the current task, give some service to the device that interrupted it, then return to the original task. Usually the interrupting task does not take too long to be serviced, so normal operations continue at a good speed.

Interrupts, an analogy

Imagine you were at home waiting for a friend to call round but were not sure of the exact time she was coming. You could do one of two things. First, you could go to the front door once every minute or so and check to see if she had arrived. That way she would never have to wait more than a minute to be let in. Alternatively, you could install a front door bell, continue with your other tasks until it rings, and when it does, you stop what you are doing and answer the door. With luck, she has arrived. The first method is called 'polling' and the second method uses an 'interrupt'. Polling implies that the software executes in a fixed sequence and that each device is looked at during regular intervals. It does mean that if busy, the CPU will not service a task, one that could be important. This is the same as your friend arriving just after you have looked out, you miss her until the next 'polling' event.

In a PC, there are many tasks the system must service, so the CPU is interrupted many times per second. Typical interrupts come from the hard drive, the serial port, network cards, etc. and mean that something has happened that needs attending to. In the analogy of you being at home, this means that while you are waiting for your friend, you put the kettle on. It may boil over if you leave it on the gas, so you choose to use an interrupt, the whistle. There is another interrupt, the telephone; another friend could ring at any time. Of course you must decide in advance which of these interrupts is the most important – what happens if the kettle boils and the front door bell rings at the same time? In a PC, interrupts have assigned priorities to cope with this problem.

When an interrupt occurs, program execution jumps to the right address in memory then returns when finished. In order to know the right address to jump to, the addresses are stored in a table. If the design of the PC was static, this table could be fixed, but every PC is configurable; you can add devices and services in a very flexible manner. This means the table of interrupt addresses must be changeable. At bootup time, a default set of addresses is copied from the BIOS chip into RAM. Later in the bootup process this can be changed to match the particular devices and programs to be used on your PC. The table of address is called the *interrupt vector*, and is situated at a low address in RAM.

Chipsets

The PC system box has three basic elements: the CPU, the memory system and the I/O subsystem.

The motherboard is a PCB (*Printed Circuit Board*) that connects these elements together. In the past, these boards were quite large as there was little in the way of integration between the circuits, indeed the very first IBM PCs were built from 'off-the-shelf' ICs (*Integrated Circuits*) available for the (then) non-PC market. As the PC market grew, the supporting chips became more specific to their task and became known as *Application Specific ICs* or *ASICs*. Since they worked in sets of chips, they eventually became known as the 'chipset'. Names have an odd way of sticking around; modern PCs may have all the functionality in one chip but it is still called a chipset. The function of the chipset is to control the flow of data around the motherboard, provide timing signals, handle DMA (see below) requests and a range of other housekeeping tasks.

The particular chipset available depends on the microprocessor socket or slot type. The main types of socket or slot are shown in Table 1.6.1. Each microprocessor has its own socket type so your choice of chipset will depend on the CPU type. Not all manufacturers make boards and chipsets to suit all microprocessors.

Most motherboards have circuits to control the mouse, keyboard, input and output from the serial ports, parallel port, floppy disks, and often the IDE hard disks.

Items not included in the chipset are video, sound, networks, NICs and expansion buses such as SCSI controllers, modems and similar devices. These are fitted as extra boards or externally.

DMA

DMA is *Direct Memory Access*, a system that allows data to be transferred in blocks. In the earliest pre-PC microcomputers, the process of moving a block of data was achieved by moving a byte at a time. The CPU would fetch the instruction, fetch the data byte, fetch the address to send it to, then send the data byte to its destination. This involved many memory operations per byte. Even the earliest PCs had DMA control, circuits that took over from the CPU and transferred whole blocks of data from devices to RAM, providing a dramatic improvement in performance.

CPU sockets

The microprocessor is fitted into a connector on the motherboard. The earliest microprocessors were built into DIPs (*Dual Inline Packages*) with a line of connecting pins down each of two sides. Modern CPUs have so many connecting pins that the package would be far too large, so the pins are now arranged in several rows or rectangular arrays. As microprocessors have developed so have the connectors, Table 1.6.1 summarizes the main kinds. CPUs made by Intel have moved to the latest designs in slots but some performance equivalent competitive designs still use Socket 7. The socket (or slot) fitted to the motherboard will affect the choice of CPU that can be fitted.

Table 1.6.1 *Main PC socket and slot types*

	Number of pins	*Voltage*	*Microprocessor*
Socket 0	168	5 V	486DX
Socket 1	169	5 V	486DX, 486SX
Socket 2	238	5 V	486DX, 486SX, DX2
Socket 3	237	3 V or 5 V	486DX, 486SX, DX2, DX4
Socket 4	273	5 V	60 or 66 MHz Pentium P5
Socket 5	320	3 V	2nd generation Pentium
Socket 6	235	3 V	486DX4
Socket 7	321	3 V	Most Pentium compatibles
Socket 8	387	3 V	Pentium Pro
Slot 1	242	3 V	Pentium II, Celeron
Slot SC242	242	3 V	Pentium III, Celeron
Slot 2	330	3 V	Xeon
Slot A (EV6)		3 V	AMD K7
Slot M		3 V	Merced

Motherboard 'form factors'

The size and shape of the motherboard is called the *form factor*. Very old 286-based PCs were called designated AT (meaning Advanced Technology!) and the board form factor was known as the AT board. This form factor was kept for the 486 microprocessors and some early Pentiums. 'Baby AT' boards were smaller than the 'full AT' boards. Most of these boards have ISA expansion slots, the old 8-bit and the slightly newer 16-bit versions. PCI expansion slots came later and are much faster than the ISA versions.

Pentium Socket 7 and the Pentium III chips use the ATX form factor and these boards will usually have PCI expansion slots, they may also have some 16-bit ISA slots to allow old (or legacy) boards to be fitted.

A newer idea is to use a *riser* where all the connectors and expansion slots are plugged in. The motherboard also plugs into this riser. These are designated NLX.

Motherboard memory sockets

Modern boards have memory slots to suit DIMM RAM chips, the older ones would use banks of either 32- or 72-pin SIMM sockets. This refers to the size and layout of the RAM chips. The reason the sockets have changed is to accommodate wider buses. Some boards allow some mixing between SIMM and DIMM chips but most set-ups avoid this complication.

ISA bus

The ISA bus is the Industry Standard Architecture. The oldest version had an 8-bit data bus and ran at 4.77 MHz, this was followed by a 16-bit version. These are the largest of the expansion slots found on all but the very latest motherboards. Old or legacy devices usually fit these slots. Because the bus runs at such a slow speed, data transfers are slow. The requirement for more and more performance has led to the development of faster buses but the ISA bus is still around to support the many legacy boards still in use. Some devices are so slow that no benefit will be obtained by connecting them to a faster bus.

Local buses

As shown in section 1.3, simple machines use a single address and a single data bus controlled by the microprocessor. This leads to a bottleneck because if one device connected to the buses is transferring data, nothing else can happen. Indeed it is odd to think that most of the time, devices in these simple machines are doing nothing at all. PCs have a much more complex architecture; many operations can and do happen at the same time. One of the means by which this can happen is to have a bus in addition to the main bus and allow the CPU to have direct access to it. This feature is called a local bus and there are different kinds available in the marketplace. One of the first was the VESA local bus but this has now been superseded by the PCI local bus. PCI is short for Peripheral Component Interconnect and was first introduced in 1993.

This original PCI was a 32-bit bus with a maximum speed of 33 MHz which means that 33 million times a second, a single piece of 32-bit data can flow along the bus to other devices. If it is set to run synchronously with the PC (the usual case), the actual speed is a set fraction of the PC bus speed. In machines that use a bus speed of 100 MHz, the PCI is running at just one-third that speed, 33 MHz.On some motherboards, the PCI bus is set to run asynchronously, i.e. not in time with the PC. Most motherboards have three or four PCI slots, and most will support *bus mastering*. This is where control of the bus is given to devices on the bus and allows data transfers to occur that are not under the direct control of the CPU. The advantage is that data can flow at the full speed of the bus when it is required. An arbitration circuit ensures that no one device can obtain complete control of the bus. The most common devices found on the PCI bus are video cards, SCSI adapters, and networking cards. Hard disk controllers are on the PCI bus but are connected directly to the motherboard rather than occupying an expansion slot.

You will see the main system bus referred to as a *front side bus*. This is because the bus has two 'sides', one connecting the CPU to the L2 cache (see page 30) and the other, the *back side bus*, connecting the CPU to the main RAM. The back side bus has a typical speed of 66–133 MHz, the front side bus runs at either one-half of the processor speed or the full processor speed.

Slower devices do not use the PCI bus, for example the serial and parallel ports. Compared with the speed of the bus, these are so slow that no advantage would be gained. They are usually connected to the old standard ISA bus which is still faster than the fastest serial devices on the market.

Compatible IDE/ATA hard disks (see section 1.10) can be bus masters. Standard IDE drives use Programmable Input/Output or PIO

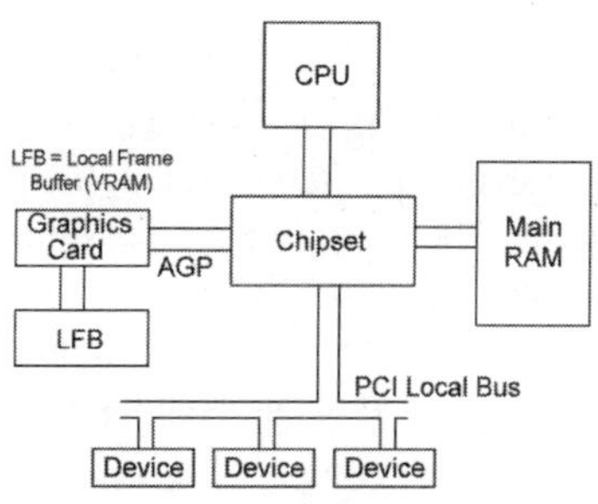

Figure 1.6.1 *Relationship of AGP with PCI local bus*

mode but bus mastering provides a performance improvement in some circumstances. It does not make everything quicker. Beware, if the hard drive you buy supports bus mastering it does not mean that it will work that way, you must ensure the operating system, motherboard and device drivers also support bus mastering.

AGP

AGP stands for *Accelerated Graphics Port* and is not really a local bus but provides similar benefits, i.e. data can be transferred to and from the AGP without other devices making demands on the circuit. The AGP is entirely independent of the PCI bus on the motherboard.

Even though the PCI bus is fast, the requirement to move very large amounts of data for 3D image effects, texturing, full motion video and ever higher resolution graphics means that the busy PCI bus cannot provide all the speed that is needed.

Graphics cards do a large amount of processing independently of the main CPU and this processing requires memory. Since VRAM is expensive, the AGP allows the graphics processor to use main memory for these calculations; this results in more data being transferred along a bus from main RAM to the video card, data that is not part of the traffic that 'belongs' to the CPU. The AGP allows this transfer of data without slowing the PCI bus or tying up the CPU.

The AGP specification is based on the PCI version 2.1 specification, it runs at 66 MHz and uses a 32-bit bus (4 bytes at once). This allows 254 Mbytes/second. It can be made to run at twice this speed by providing two two data transfers per 66 MHz clock cycle. This is done by changing the way the data is encoded, i.e. by using the rising and falling edges of the 1s and 0s. The latest AGP specification allows four data transfers per 66 MHz clock cycle, providing data throughput of up to 1 Gb/s.

Peripheral ports

USB

USB stands for *Universal Serial Bus*, a standard being worked on by Compaq, Hewlett Packard, Intel, Lucent, Microsoft, NEC and Philips.

The idea is that peripherals can be plugged in (or removed) whilst the PC is switched on, they do not need to be initialized during the bootup sequence. When a device is plugged in, the operating system recognizes the event and configures the required device driver software.

Many standard PCs are supplied with two USB ports. Attachment of more than two devices is achieved by USB hubs that allow daisy-chaining, a technique where devices are plugged in one to the next forming a 'chain' thus reducing the amount of cable required. A further reduction in cabling is achieved because USB supplies the power to the devices in the data cable, up to 2.5 watts. Hubs may be cascaded up to five levels deep providing a connection for up to 127 peripheral devices at a transfer rate of either 12 Mb/s (full speed) or 1.5 Mbs (low speed). The current USB standard, USB 1.1, is about to be superseded by USB 2.0, which will allow a claimed transfer rate of 480 Mb/s.

Firewire

Firewire is the common name for a standard called IEEE 1394. This is a serial connection aimed at very high data transfer speeds, at least high for a serial link. Speeds between 100 Mbits/sec 800 Mbits/sec are possible and a speed of 3200 Mbits/sec is promised. Up to 16 devices can be connected via a single Firewire port. It is commonly used to attach digital cameras to PCs, one reason being the very simple cable attachment and set-up that is used.

IrDA

This is an infrared serial communication standard that is intended to dispense with cables and run at a maximum of 4 Mbits/sec. IrDA will also work at standard serial speeds to mimic the old RS232-C serial standard (see below). Since there is a clear possibility of several devices in one place using IrDA and the infrared signal is 'broadcast' around that place, the standard includes techniques similar to those used in networking, to avoid device conflicts and data being sent to the wrong device. It is common to find IrDA on notebook PCs or smaller devices to allow communication with desktop PCs without cabling.

Serial ports

Serial devices have been around for many years. The earliest machines could be connected to devices such as modems or printers using just three wires, a 'send' wire, a 'receive' wire and a signal return wire. Binary 1s and 0s were sent one after the other, i.e. serially. The maximum speed was quite low. To improve speed, extra wires were introduced to allow 'handshaking', signals that allowed or disallowed the sending of data depending in the readiness to receive. These data and handshake lines and the associated timings, etc. were incorporated into a standard called RS232-C which used a 25-pin 'D' shaped connector. Since only a few of these pins were actually used, IBM introduced a similar 9-pin 'D' connector that is now common on modern PCs. Unfortunately, as a standard that has 'evolved' over the years, the 25-pin connectors are still common as are many different arrangements for interconnecting 25-pin, 9-pin old and new devices. Modern PCs with modern serial devices cause little problem but the use of legacy serial devices with any PC can prove to be problematic. The maximum speed of a serial device is currently 115 200 bits/sec. With a simple serial device link, each 8-bit byte has a 'start' and 'stop' bit added so using 10 bits/byte. 115 200 bits/sec would then give 11 520 bytes/sec. You may notice that some speeds are given as Mbytes/sec and others as Mbits/sec. This is because the number of extra bits (i.e. not data bits) is variable, depending on the application and the PC industry's common practice of quoting the largest number to look attractive in advertisements! Also you should be wary of 'standards', see note on page 49.

Serial ports under Microsoft DOS or Windows have the names COM1:, COM2:, etc. The set-up for these COM ports quotes the speed in bits/sec, number of data bits, parity and number of stop bits. A typical set-up may be 9600, 8, none, 1. This means 9600 bits per second, 8 data bits, no parity and 1 stop bit. Parity is an old error checking system now little used, it is in the set-up to allow connection with legacy devices. You may see 9600 bits/sec quoted as 9600 baud but the 'baud rate' is not the same as bits/second.

Parallel ports

Most PCs have a single port for the attachment of a local printer. This is a parallel port, i.e. it has control lines and eight data lines, one each for the 8 bits of a byte. Although designed as a single direction port for outputting to printers, some programmers have managed to allow two-way communication. The port is slow by modern standards but as the printers are even slower, no advantage is gained by using a high-speed link.

Under Microsoft DOS or Windows, the parallel port is called LPT1: (for Line Printer 1). It is possible to add more parallel ports by plugging expansion cards into the ISA bus; they would then be called LPT2:, etc.

References

Motherboards

sysopt.earthweb.com/mboard.html
www.tomshardware.com/mainboard/index.html

Buying a PC

www.pcguide.com/buy/index.htm
www.usb.org/developers/docs.html
www.agpforum.org/info.htm

1.7 Memory: RAM and ROM

Key fact

RAM

RAM is short for *Random Access Memory* and is one if the silliest names in computing! It really refers to the main memory of the PC, and is where most of the software and data are stored when the machine is in use. It is called random access because any byte can be read into the CPU in any order from any address, but this is also true of ROM. A better term would be RWM or Read-Write Memory, indeed some people do use this name.

RAM is volatile, it loses its value as soon as the power is lost. That is one reason it takes so long to boot up a machine, once the power is restored, all the software and data must be loaded.

There are many different kinds of RAM on the market, the result of intense competition to satisfy the ever-increasing demands for speed, capacity and low cost. Some of the more important types are described below but a detailed knowledge is not required to fulfil the criteria for this unit of the HNC Computing.

> **Key fact**
>
> **ROM**
>
> Unlike RAM, *Read Only Memory* cannot be written to by the CPU but it has the advantage of retaining all the data when the power is lost. It is slower than RAM, i.e. it takes longer for the circuits to present data on the data bus after a read instruction from the CPU. It is ideal for the BIOS. As explained in section 1.6, computers need software to control the loading of software, so software that is already present is very useful!

Types of RAM

For the purposes of this unit of the HNC Computing, a very detailed knowledge of memory types is not required but knowledge of how RAM works and in particular how this affects system performance is important. The points you should remember from the section below are related to this performance and they should inform your purchasing decisions when buying PCs.

Dynamic RAM or DRAM

This is the main type of RAM fitted to PCs, it is cheap but not as fast as other kinds of RAM. In technology there is nearly always a trade-off between conflicting requirements, in this case it is between cost and speed. DRAM is cheap but slow. It suffers from another problem, many times a second the memory contents need to be refreshed, i.e. the chip will forget or lose its contents unless a read or refresh operation is carried out. This means that separate refresh circuits are needed, adding to the complexity of the board.

Static RAM or SRAM

This kind of RAM holds its data without refresh signals and is faster than DRAM, but in the classic trade-off, SRAM loses on cost. It is implemented with between four and six transistors whereas DRAM is made from one transistor and a capacitor. This may not sound expensive but the six transistors are for just one bit! A byte is 8 bits, so 1 Mb of SRAM would take $6 \times 8 \times 1024 \times 1024 = 50\,331\,648$ transistors! Consider that the latest Pentium microprocessors use about a one-seventh of this, although it is really overstating it somewhat as RAM is much simpler to make than CPUs but the scale of the problem is obvious.

How is memory addressed?

In early microcomputers, RAM was addressed directly, so when an address was placed on the address bus, the RAM chips were read in one go and the data flowed onto the data bus. Modern PCs use a more complex arrangement.

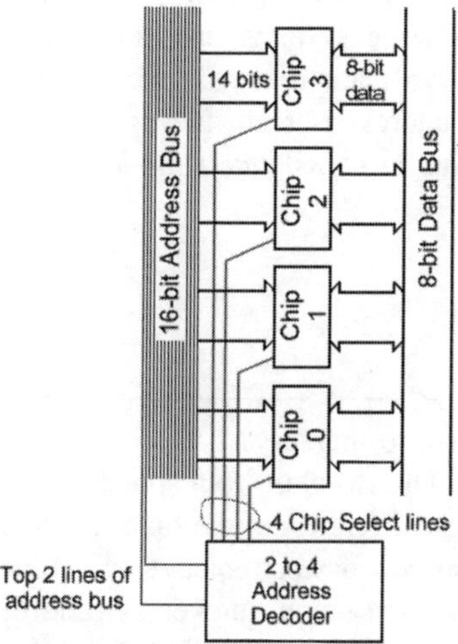

Figure 1.7.1 *Simple 2 to 4 address decoder*

Simple address decoder

If you look at Figure 1.7.1, there are four RAM chips, each holds 16 kb of 8-bit data. Since 2^{14} = 16 384 or 16 kb, this means that you need 14 address lines to address this much RAM in each chip. If 16 address lines are available from the CPU, it is easy to connect 14 lines directly to the RAM chips as shown and to connect the remaining two lines to a circuit that chooses which of the four chips to use. This way, 64 Kb of RAM is addressed.

The circuit that selects which RAM chip to use is called a *decoder*, in this case a two to four decoder. This has the property that if a 2-bit binary number is input, it outputs a logical 1 on only one of the four lines, so it is not possible to have two or more RAM chips active at the same time. Suppose you need to address location 44 650. In binary this is the number 1010111001101010 which when placed on the address bus is the pattern of 1s and 0s on the 16 address lines. This is what is meant by address 44 650. In this circuit, the top two lines are connected to the address decoder and the other 14 lines are connected directly to each memory chip. The top two lines have the values 1 and 0 respectively (the left-hand 1 and 0 from the address) so this is the pattern if fed into the address decoder. This equates to 2 in decimal so chip 2 will be active. The rest of the address, 14 bits, is already connected so the 8-bit data for address 44 650 will be inside chip number 2.

Memory control in a PC

The system described here is used in a typical PC.

Suppose you need 16 Mb of RAM, this is commonly available as 4 by 4 Mb chips on a strip. 4 Mb needs 22 address lines as 2^{22} = 4 194 304 or 4 Mb. The chips as supplied do not have 22 address lines, they have just 11, half the number. Circuits are in place for the chip to accept the high order 11 bits (called the column) and the low order 11 bits (called the row) separately in sequence. They are called *row* and *column* because logically addresses are treated like a grid with an 11-bit row and an 11-bit column address. [In reality, there is nothing grid like in this RAM.]

Ignoring detailed timing signal's etc., it works something like this:

- First the low order bits are placed on the 11 address lines.
- Time is allowed for the signals to stabilize. (Nothing in electronics is instantaneous, it might be fast but everything takes time.)
- The row address strobe line is set resulting in a read of all 2^{11} = 4096 addresses.

- The high order bits are placed on the 11-bit address bus.
- Time is allowed for the signals to stabilize.
- This results in just one of the 4096 values to be selected and fed to the memory buffer then supplied to the data bus.

This process clearly takes more time than a direct memory read as performed in early micros. The reason is one of cost; although slower, this system is cheaper.

The greatest time taken is to set up the address as row and column and wait for the chip to respond. In some systems, instead of just reading the data at one address, 32 bytes are read and stored in a buffer. It is a good guess that if one address is read, the data at the next address will be needed soon! This is called *burst mode* and is found in many modern PCs.

Memory speed

What do we mean by speed with respect to memory?

It is usually taken as the time for the DRAM chips to respond with a data request measured from the time of the request to the time the data is made available. This is quoted in nanoseconds and typical RAM chips have 60 or 70 ns ratings although some are much quicker. A time of 70 ns seems very fast but consider a 600 MHz Pentium CPU. 600 MHz means that 600 000 000 clock cycles occur each second. The time between each one is 1/600 000 000 or 1.67 ns, enough time for 70/1.67 = 42 clock cycles! Clearly, in a Pentium 600 machine, it would not be viable to have the CPU read each instruction one by one from the main memory. This is where memory cache is important (see page 30).

Mathematics in action

What is a nanosecond?

A nanosecond is 10^{-9} seconds or 1/1 000 000 000 seconds. In language, this is a thousand times shorter than a millionth of a second. In human terms, this is an impossibly short period of time but in computing terms is an 'everyday' unit of time. Table 1.7.1 shows the factors of 10 and the associated names and symbols. Table 1.7.2 shows the factors of 2; you should notice that some values, for instance 10^3, have the same name as 2^{10}, i.e. kilo. but 2^{20} = 1024 and 10^3 = 1000 so there is only an approximate equality.

It is sometimes difficult for humans to get a good mental picture of very large or very small numbers. A technique used to help with this problem is to imagine that one second is stretched out over a whole year and then to see what happens inside that year. If we take the 600 MHz clock speed as an example and imagine one second stretched out over a year. There are 60 seconds per minute, 60 minutes per hour, etc. so in

Table 1.7.1 Powers of 10 and their names

Factor of 10	*Value*	*Prefix*	*Symbol*
10^{-18}	0.000 000 000 000 000 001	atto	a
10^{-15}	0.000 000 000 000 001	femto	f
10^{-12}	0.000 000 000 001	pico	p
10^{-9}	0.000 000 001	nano	n
10^{-6}	0.000 001	micro	μ
10^{-3}	0.001	milli	m
10^{-2}	0.01	centi	c
10^{-1}	0.1	deci	d
10	10	deca	da
10^{2}	100	hecto	h
10^{3}	1000	kilo	k
10^{6}	1 000 000	mega	M
10^{9}	1 000 000 000	giga	G
10^{12}	1 000 000 000 000	tera	T
10^{15}	1 000 000 000 000 000	peta	P
10^{18}	1 000 000 000 000 000 000	exa	E
10^{21}	1 000 000 000 000 000 000 000	zetta	Z
10^{24}	1 000 000 000 000 000 000 000 000	yotta	Y

Table 1.7.2 *Powers of 2 and their names*

Power of 2	*Number of bytes*	*Symbol*	*Name*
2^{10}	1024	kb	kilobytes
2^{20}	1 048 576	Mb	megabytes
2^{30}	1 073 741 824	Gb	gigabytes
2^{40}	1 099 511 627 776	Tb	terabytes
2^{50}	1 125 899 906 843 624	Pb	petabytes
2^{60}	1 152 921 504 607 870 976	Eb	exabytes
2^{70}	1 180 591 620 718 458 879 424	Zb	zettabytes
2^{80}	1 208 925 819 615 701 892 530 176	Yb	yottabytes

one year we get $60 \times 60 \times 24 \times 365 = 31\,536\,000$ or 31.5 million seconds per real year. If 600 000 000 clock pulses occur per real second, we would get $600/31.5 = 19$ pulses per stretched-out second. In other words, even if we slowed down the Pentium by 31.5 million times, it would still be doing 19 things a second.

Question 1.7.1

Assume the average size of a hard disk drive in a PC in the year 2000 is 10 Gb. If Moore's law were applied to average hard drive sizes and continued until the year 2012, what would the average size be in that year? The answer may surprise you!)

Nanoseconds and other named fractions

Asynchronous and synchronous DRAM

The DRAM fitted to most older PCs was called *asynchronous*. This means it does not operate in time with, i.e. it is not synchronised with, the system clock signals. This worked satisfactorily with slower machines, but newer machines need better performance. SDRAM or *synchronous* DRAM has its operation tied to the system clock so the timing of what happens is under better control. DRAM chips have typical speeds of 60 or 70 ns whereas SDRAM chips have typical values of 10 or 12 ns, i.e. much faster. Beware of the trap often found in computing, especially regarding speeds. A rating of 10 ns does not mean a system with SDRAM is six times faster than one fitted with 60 ns DRAM. The SDRAM can deliver that much faster but since it is now under the control of system timing, it may not get access to the bus for long enough so giving a slower effective speed. The settings of the BIOS, especially those that affect system timings, number of wait states, etc. are critical if the maximum performance is to be achieved from the PC. Wait states are when the memory system is told to wait for a clock cycle or more (depending on wait state setting) before acting. The fastest is zero wait states but the RAM in the PC may not be able to keep up. It is quite possible to have all the right hardware fitted to the machine but for it still not to run as fast as it should.

There are several kinds of SDRAM but this unit of the HNC Computing does not require such a level of detail. You may see the following term with respect to RAM types: Extended Data Out (EDO), Burst Extended Data Out (BEDO), Double Data Rate SDRAM (DDR SDRAM), Direct Rambus DRAM (DRDRAM), Synchronous-Link DRAM (SLDRAM).

In several sections of this book you will see warnings about making simple assumptions regarding speed ratings. Be very careful, the actual situation is much more complicated than it appears to be at first. The only real-test of a PC is to run real life problems, the speed of subsystems can become very academic

Cache memory

As demonstrated above, even fast modern RAM chips cannot deliver anywhere near the speed required to feed a high-speed CPU with data. The solution adopted is to use cache memory. Analysis of a large number of machine code programs (remember *all* programs run as machine code in the CPU) reveals that most of the time, the next instruction to be executed is next to or very close to the instruction being executed. This means that if a block of the program is copied into a section of high-speed memory, the CPU would be able to access instructions and data very much quicker. The problem is that not all instructions are in the high-speed RAM, the cache, so a process must go on 'behind the scenes' to load the correct sections of data from main RAM to the cache. About 90% of the time or even better, the next instruction is already in the cache so only 5 or 10% of memory requests will result in a direct memory read.

On Pentium systems, there are two levels of cache known as L1 and L2. L1 is very high-speed RAM inside the processor chip, L2 is a high-speed RAM cache outside the CPU but still with a high performance. With caching, doubling the speed of the main RAM has little effect on the overall machine performance, the critical speed is how fast the CPU can gain access to the cache.

Virtual memory and the amount of RAM required

If cache memory is very fast, virtual memory is very slow! In old mainframe computers, the main memory was very expensive. It could be that only 1 kb was fitted (not A 1 Mb!). The programs to be run were much larger so techniques were evolved to have a small amount of code in memory and arrange for pieces of the main program to be loaded from disk only when required. This way programs of any size could be run but as the code pieces were loaded from disk each time, the process was quite slow. This is virtual memory, it is memory that exists 'virtually', i.e. it is not real. Microsoft use a similar technique with Windows. Windows needs a fair amount of space for itself, and each application you have running needs its own space in memory. In the original PCs there was generally not sufficient RAM, so a *swap file* was used. This means that sections of program code in memory that were not needed right away were 'swapped' onto the disk. As far as Windows was concerned, there was now enough memory, but of course, being disk bound, the process is slower. Fitting more RAM to a PC allows Windows to access the swap file less often so dramatically improving performance. A Pentium 100 with 64 Mb of RAM is quite likely to outperform a Pentium 200 with only 8 Mb of RAM, when running Windows. There is a limit to this process. Currently there is unlikely to be any speed benefit from fitting more than 64 Mb of RAM. Many systems have 128 Mb but any benefit would only be seen if you had a large number of applications all running at once, each demanding its own RAM space.

If you were to load a simple operating system (not Windows!) then load and run a single program, the amount of RAM fitted would have no effect whatsoever. The amount of RAM fitted only affects performance when virtual memory techniques are made less necessary. If everything is in RAM, the disk is not accessed to get more data; accessing any part of main RAM takes the same time so no improvement is made by fitting more.

Experiment

You can detect when the swap file is accessed quite often, just keep an eye on the disk drive LED on the front of the PC. If there is much activity when you open a new window, it is likely that the swap file is being accessed.

1.8 Video graphics

Pixels

When a graphical image is shown on a computer screen, it is made up from a large collection of dots. Each of these dots is called a *pixel*, short for *picture element*.

Pixels are arranged in rows and columns; typical numbers of rows and columns are shown in the table below.

Name	*Columns*	*Rows*
VGA	640	480
SVGA	800	600
	1024	768
	1280	1024
	1600	1200

The number of pixels per screen is known as the resolution. The higher the number of pixels the better the resolution or the finer the detail that can be shown.

Each pixel may have just one colour at a time, chosen from a set of colours. Suppose each pixel could be just one from a selection of 256 different colours. This would mean that a number must be assigned to that pixel. If bright red was colour number 37, then that one pixel would be stored as the value 37. Since 1 byte is made up of 8 bits, the largest number that can be stored in 8 bits is 255. If you include the value 0 then it is possible to store 1 of 256 different colour values in 1 byte, or the pixel can be one of 256 different colours. Another way to state this is that $2^8 = 256$.

If you use less memory than 1 byte per pixel, say 4 bits per pixel (half a byte), then you must be content with fewer colours. With 4 bits, the largest number you can store is 15, so (including the value 0) the number of possible colours is 16 or 24. (Half a byte is called a nibble!)

More generally, the number of colours that are available is given by 2^N. If you choose to use 8 bits per pixel then the number of colours is $2^8 = 256$, or with 24 bits per pixel, the number of colours is $2^{24} = 16.7$ million.

Most video graphics systems use a value of N that divides evenly into bytes, so values of 2, 4, 8, 16 or 24 are common, values such as 3, 5, 7 are not. The table below shows the number of colours available:

Bytes	*Bits*	*Number of colours*
$\frac{1}{4}$	2	$2^2 = 4$
$\frac{1}{2}$	4	$2^4 = 16$
1	8	$2^8 = 256$
2	16	$2^{16} = 65\,536$ (64 k), Hicolor
3	24	$2^{24} = 16.7$ million, Trucolor

The term *colour planes* is sometimes used to describe the power of 2 so a $2^{24} = 16.7$ million colour setting would be described as a 24-bit colour plane. This comes from the design of the original VGA graphics card.

16-bit colour is called *Hicolor*; 24-bit colour is often known as *Trucolor* and is used where the better graphical image quality is required. Some scanners are now offering 30-bit colour although you could not realistically expect the full $2^{30} = 1\,073\,741\,824$ colours!

Consider some realistic limitations of human perception of image quality. If you have 16.7 million colours, can you see all of them? There are several answers to this.

(1) Humans can perceive approximately 10 million colours.
(2) The phosphors in the monitor cannot reproduce all the colours that you can see, a really convincing brown colour is very hard to make.

(3) If you have a screen set to 1024 × 768 pixels, you have less than 16.7 million pixels. To have enough pixels to have one each of 16.7 million colours, you would need a resolution of 4730 × 3547 (maintaining the width to height ratio of 4:3).

The main reason to have 16.7 million colours is not to use them all but to have sufficient shades of each primary colour to reproduce a realistic shaded representation of an object.

Graphics cards

The original design of PCs had no facility to output graphics. The method used get around this problem was to have a separate *video card* or *graphics card* plugged into the main board. This card contained the video RAM and some ROM BIOS that contains the code required to write pixels, etc. More RAM allowed more colours or higher screen resolutions. Modern PCs may have the video card incorporated on the main board or as a separate component.

Modern video cards incorporate a CPU to speed up the graphics process. Imagine this problem: you wish to draw a single line at an angle on the screen and you know the colour and the start and end points of the line. Somehow the position of all the pixels that form the line must also be calculated. If this is done using the main CPU then that CPU is not available for calculating new graphics data so the system is relatively slow. If a CPU on the graphics card is dedicated to this task (known as *vector generation*), the main CPU is available for other calculations so speeding up the process greatly. A better enhancement is obtained when solid in-fill colours are required. A 100 by 100 pixel square needs 100 × 100 = 10 000 pixels to be coloured. When this is done by a dedicated CPU, the main CPU has only to calculate the corner positions, just four points.

Note that non-vertical or non-horizontal lines cannot be quite smooth as they are made up of pixels, a phenomenon known as aliasing. The same is true for circles, etc. and extra pixels can be added in different colours to smooth out the line; this is called anti-aliasing. There are a number of algorithms used to calculate these extra pixels which require a fairly large CPU 'overhead' and if not done by the graphics card, would seriously slow down the main tasks of the host PC. A disadvantage of anti-aliasing is that lines, etc. become wider so reducing the apparent crispness of detail in some images.

Figure 1.8.1 *Illustration of aliased and anti-aliased image*

Most PCs are now sold with at least an SVGA or *Super VGA* graphics cards giving 1024 by 768 screen resolution or better and at least 4 Mb of video RAM. If you need more colours, then you have the option to increase the amount of video RAM. A video card set to 1024 by 768 Hicolor requires at least 2 Mb, if you want this resolution and 24-bit Trucolor, you need 4 Mb as shown below.

Video RAM (VRAM) is a specialized type of RAM that allows *dual porting*, i.e. it allows the CPU to access the RAM at the same time as the video circuits. If a screen refresh of say 85 Hz is used, the video system must access the RAM 85 times a second. VRAM allows the CPU access during the same time.

Question 1.8.1

Calculate the video RAM required for a 1280 × 1024 resolution Trucolor screen.

Question 1.8.2

What is the best resolution possible on a machine with 8 Mb of video RAM and has Trucolor already set?

Video RAM required

A screen resolution of 800 × 600 pixels will yield 800 × 600 = 480 000 pixels. If each pixel needs half a byte it will allow for 16 colours so the screen will require 480 000 × 0.5 = 240 000 bytes of storage. 800 × 600 × 256 colours requires (800 × 600 × 1) = 480 000 bytes of storage because each pixel will need 1 byte. 2^8 = 256 different colour combinations. 480 000 is roughly half a megabyte of RAM.

In general, calculate the storage required for 1 pixel remembering that 2^N = number of colours, where N = the number of bits required. Next multiply by the number of pixels on the screen.

Video paging

More video RAM allows several video *pages* to be stored. This technique allows several programming tricks, one being to write to that part of the video memory that is not being displayed. The reason you would want to do this is because a problem encountered with video animation is the raster screen (see below) displaying a noticeable flicker if the item to be drawn on the screen is shown at the same time as the raster is generating a screenful of scan lines. This can be delayed until the raster scan is at the start of the screen but this will have the effect of slowing down the animation as the software must wait for the start of screen signal. As this happens typically 75 times a second, it will not be very fast.

A better way is to use video paging. Suppose you had 8 Mb of RAM fitted and you were using a video mode that displayed a 1024 × 768 resolution set at 16 bit or Hicolor. This would need 1024 × 768 × 2 bytes or approx. 1.5 Mb of RAM so you would have more than enough space for four areas of the RAM, each area allocated to a 'page' of video information. If the video card is set to display just one of these pages, you cannot see the other pages but the current page can be switched to any of the other three. The technique is for the software to write to a non-visible page and then for the hardware to switch video pages, a process much faster than the human eye can see resulting in very smooth animation.

A similar idea can be used with GUI software such as Windows. If a pull-down menu must be displayed, the screen area that the menu will occupy must first be saved to RAM so that it will be available to redisplay when the menu is closed. This means that the more video RAM available, the more sections of screen may be stored. Imagine you are using Microsoft Windows and wish to open several windows. Each time you open a window, the image of the screen underneath the new window must be saved. Each window may require 20 kb of data to be stored, so 10 open menus will require 20 × 10 or 200 kb of extra ram. The windows accelerator cards use this method (and others) to speed up Windows. When you open such a menu, it looks very much like the menu box is 'in front of' the screen you were looking at; this is of course an illusion!

Display types

The CRT

The glass screen you see uses essentially the same image forming technique as domestic television, the image is made up of several hundred lines of a glowing substance called a 'phosphor'. This substance is made to glow by being 'hit' by a beam of electrons radiating from a point source at the back of the CRT. A fairly sophisticated arrangement of components in the CRT causes the electrons being emitted from the point source to be formed into a thin beam. If the beam were to be kept still, all you would see is a single point of light where the beam hits the phosphor on the inside of the front of the screen. Other components allow this beam to be moved anywhere on the screen, either horizontally or vertically.

A picture is made up by very quickly moving or scanning the beam from one side of the screen to the other in a series of lines that cover the whole of the visible portion of the screen. The detail in the picture is provided by changing the brightness of the fast moving beam. The phosphor has a property that causes it to glow for a little while longer after the beam has passed, this gives the illusion that the screen is evenly illuminated at all times.

Raster scan screens

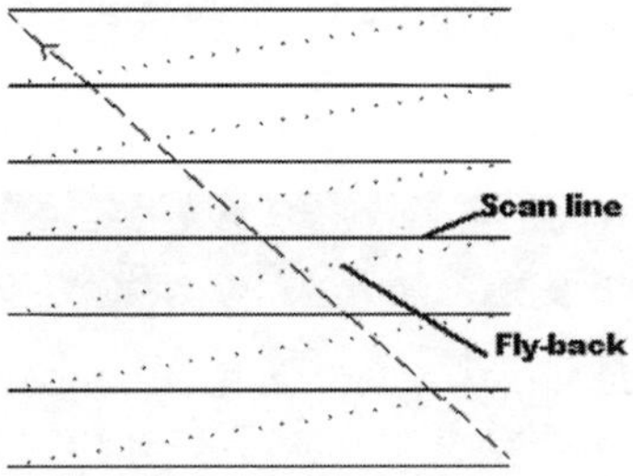

Figure 1.8.2 *Raster scan*

To display a screen image on a CRT, an electron beam is focused onto the front of the screen; this screen is coated with a material that glows when struck by a stream of electrons. The beam is scanned from left to right to form a line across the screen, a scan line. Once each line is formed, the beam is made to return (or fly back) to the side of the screen and down one line, ready for the next line. Once the bottom of the screen is reached, the beam is moved to the top and the process repeated, each screenful of lines is called a *raster*. A picture is produced by changing the intensity of the beam as it traverses the screen and synchronizing this change with the intensity of the image required.

The number of times the raster is repeated per second is called the refresh rate. Slow refresh rates are seen by humans as flickering so rates of at least 72 times a second or 72 Hz are used to display a steady image, 75 Hz is better. Normal TV screens use a raster scan but are slower than 72 Hz, a fact easily seen if you observe a TV screen in your peripheral vision where movement will be more obvious to you. This is even more obvious if you observe this at an electrical retailer's shop where you have many screens at once. If they are arranged down the side of the shop and you look down the centre of the shop slightly away from the TVs, you will see a very marked flicker in your peripheral vision.

Colour screens

Colour CRT screens use three electron beams, one each for red, green and blue parts of the image.

An electron beam does not have a colour. The achieve colour, small areas of the screen are each allocated red, green and blue parts. These small areas are called slots and each of the three electron beams is made to hit exactly the right point; the 'red' beam hits a point that glows red, etc. The distance between each one is called the slot pitch or dot pitch. Generally, the smaller the slot pitch the sharper the image because there are more points of light to make up the image. Different shades of each colour are made up by varying the relative brightness of each of the red, green and blue parts of each slot.

Slots are only visible by using a powerful magnifying glass close to the screen. They can be observed on video monitors and domestic televisions and it can be seen that different makers use different shaped slots.

Experiment

Use a magnifier to view a white portion of a monitor. You will see no white dots, only red, green and blue. All the colours you see are made of these three colours simply by mixing them in different amounts with different brightnesses. It can take some time to come to terms with the fact that there are no white portions of the screen. Most of your visual experience is concerned with your brain rather than your eyes, in this case your brain has 'manufactured' the white you see; your eyes are only receiving red, green and blue light.

Experiment

Observe the slots or dots carefully again with a powerful magnifier. Depending on the make of monitor you are using you will see dots or slots. Notice the slots have no effect on the image pixels, slots and pixels are completely different, pixels are a function of the computer graphics system and slots are fixed by the monitor maker. Move the image from side to side with the horizontal adjustments on the monitor. The slots stay still, the pixels move. You must not confuse slots with pixels; each pixel is a picture element and may take up different physical sizes on one computer by changing to different video modes. The number of slots available on one screen is fixed at time of manufacture of the screen. If you compare two video monitors with the same slot pitch but different sizes, the larger one will have more slots across the screen so will show each pixel more clearly. This is the reverse of the rule with domestic televisions, where larger screens show less sharp images.

Interlacing and refresh rates

On TV systems or old PCs, the beam cannot scan all the lines required to maintain a good number of full images per second, hence cannot provide an adequate refresh rate. To get around this, a system is used that scans only alternate lines, i.e. lines 1, 3, 5, 7, etc., to the bottom then the beam returns to the top and scans line 2, 4, 6, etc. The result is half the number of full frames per second and is called interlacing; it is the system used on domestic televisions. This is highly undesirable on video monitors as the image can be seen to

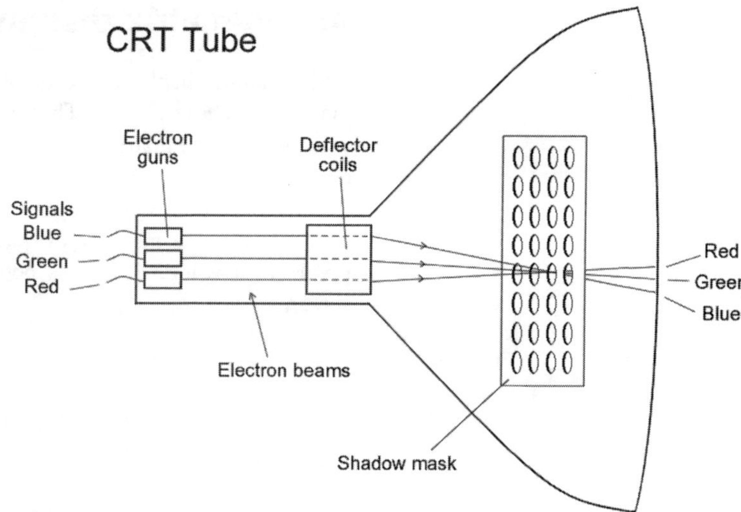

Figure 1.8.3 *Basic layout of a CRT*

vibrate slightly. The human response is for the eye to try to keep up with the moving image, a process that leads to sensations of 'tired eyes' because your eye muscles must continuously move your eyes to adjust to the slightly moving image. Better video systems use non-interlaced screens that produce very steady images. Most people now agree that screen refresh rates of 75 Hz or better are required to achieve a good quality, steady image.

Laptop screens

There are many different kinds of LCD screen on the market, but they include:

- passive supertwist Nematic displays;
- active-matrix displays.

Passive supertwist nematic displays

Passive supertwist Nematic displays make use of a material, a Nematic liquid crystal, that is able to change under the application of an electric field. The change in the Nematic liquid crystal is in the way that light is polarized when passing through it.

In its normal state with no electric field applied, the polarization of the light that passes through it follows a twisted path. If the liquid crystal is put between two polarizing filters, each one with its axis of polarization at more than 90 degrees to the other, the twisted path of the liquid crystals causes any light from one side to be transmitted out through the other side. When a voltage is applied across the polarizing screens, the light in the liquid crystals no longer travels in a twisted path and so is blocked by one of the polarizing filters. This is used to turn pixels on and off.

Active-matrix displays

Active-matrix displays incorporate a transistor to control each pixel on the screen. These TFTs or Thin Film Transistors are made into a matrix, each point in the matrix forms one pixel. Each TFT has opaque parts so not all the area assigned to a pixel is able to produce light. The ratio of the area of light production to the opaque part is called the aperture ratio and is taken as a measure of quality of the screen. A value of 30% is good but a value of 50% is better and this is achieved in the better screens.

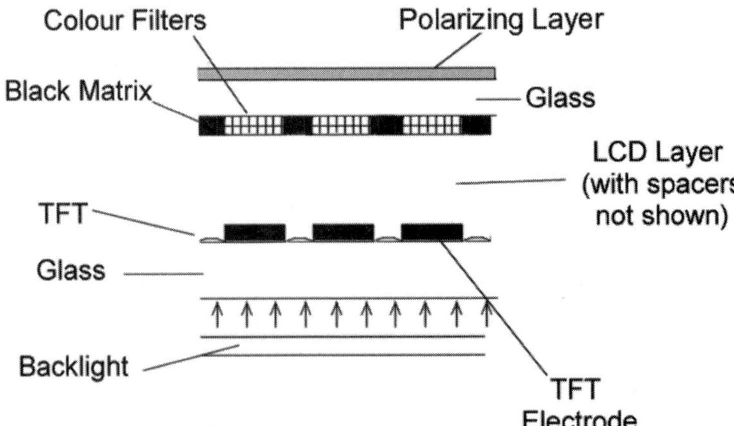

Figure 1.8.4 *Simple diagram of active LCD screen*

The backlight shown in Figure 1.8.4 is a cold cathode fluorescent light source. The light from this is attenuated by the black matrix. The higher the aperture ratio, the brighter the image.

Compared with CRTs, the LCD screens found on notebook PCs are

- physically smaller;
- have lower power consumption (allow batteries to be used);
- lighter;
- display good contrast with bright saturated colours;
- show a crisp image.

There are problems when compared with CRTs; LCD screens have a

- viewing angle;
- slow response time, they are not good for animated games, video, etc.;
- high cost. The LCD screen accounts for most of the price difference between a desktop machine and a notebook PC. Active LCD displays are more expensive than the passive type but produce a much brighter display.

Web links for LCD screens

Hewlett Packard: The First HP Liquid Crystal Display
www.hpmuseum.org/journals/hp41/41lcd.htm

Seiko LCD information
www.seiko-usa-ecd.com/lcd/html/glossary.html

Sharp LCD information
www.sharp.co.jp/sc/library-e/techn_top/top1_e.htm

LCD from Case Western Reserve University
abalone.cwru.edu/

1.9 Printers

What do you need from a printer?

The answer depends of course on the kind of business or task that you are undertaking.

Things to consider are:

- speed of text printing;
- speed of image printing;
- quality of text printing;
- quality of image printing;
- convenience;
- cost of purchase;
- cost of running.

Some of these are easy to assess, i.e. will the printer produce a good output on normal office quality photocopy paper which is cheap and available everywhere? Is it easy to use and is it supplied with software to allow your computer to communicate with it?

Other factors are not so obvious and advertisements for printers often do not show the real answer; sometimes even the technical specifications do not show the answer. The best solution is to test one or at least see it running.

Print quality

The most commonly used measure of print quality is *resolution* measured in dots per inch or dots per mm. Many laser printers have a resolution of 600 dots per inch or approximately 23.6 dots per mm. It is not sufficient to use this resolution as a measure of print quality. Figure 1.9.1 shows an image of some letters printed on a 600 dpi laser and the same file printed on a good quality inkjet set at both 360 and 720 dpi, both used the same office quality photocopy paper. You can see the problem with comparing printers just on the resolution. Other factors are also important such as how the ink 'sits' on the paper and the sophistication of the printer driver software. At least one major manufacturer of printers claims that the driver software is *more* important than a simple measure of resolution. One feature used to support this claim is marketed under various names such as 'Resolution Enhancement Technology' or similar. This takes the idea of improving the resolution of individual characters instead of the whole page. The section below shows the large amount of RAM required to store a whole page. If mathematics are used to enhance each letter in a

Roman

12 Point Times New Roman printed on a 600 dpi laser printer

Roman

12 Point Times New Roman printed on a 360 dpi inkjet printer

Roman

12 Point Times New Roman printed on a 720 dpi inkjet printer

Figure 1.9.1 *Comparison of printer resolution*

manner similar to anti-aliasing as used in video graphics, sharp letters can be produced by 300 dpi printers with a great saving in the RAM required and the associated processing. It can sometimes be difficult to tell simply by looking at a printed page, the difference between some 300 dpi and 600 dpi printers. Several reputable computer journals and magazines run tests on different printer models. These tests often show that choosing a printer on technical specification, especially the resolution alone, is not a reliable method of printer selection.

Colour reproduction (See also Appendix C – Colour)

The colour of an image on the screen will not closely match the colour of the final printed image. The reason is that one uses coloured phosphors to produce light, the other uses inks and dither patterns to simulate the same colours. Although modern printers do well in matching colours, often much experiment will be required to get the best results for your particular monitor/printer combination.

Memory required

To produce large images, printers need large amounts of RAM.

As each dot on a mono laser can be encoded in just 1 bit, 1 byte can store 8 dots.

Extending the calculation for other printer resolutions gives the results in Table 1.9.1. As you can see, if you want a 1440 dpi printer to print a mono full page image, you need a huge 20 Mb of RAM.

Question 1.9.1

For a 600 dpi printer, how many dots are there on an A4 page and how much RAM will be required to store this data? Allow a 10 mm margin all round.

Table 1.9.1 *RAM required for full A4 page with 10 mm margin*

dpi	*Dots*	*Bytes*	*Kb*
300	7 341 900	917 737	896
360	10 572 336	1 321 542	1291
600	29 367 599	3 670 950	3585
720	42 289 342	5 286 168	5162
1200	117 470 395	14 683 799	14340
1440	169 157 369	21 144 671	20649

Printer speed

This is an area where great claims are made but real printers often fail to impress. Laser printers and some inkjet printers are quoted as printing 'N pages per minute'. Eight pages per minute is pretty average for a small laser printer but can you really expect eight full pages to be finished after just one minute? Probably not. There are several reasons for this.

(1) If you are printing images, does the printer or the PC 'rasterize' the image, i.e. turn it into a set of black dots suitable for printing. If this is done in the PC, it will produce a huge amount of data to be downloaded into the printer. The answer to the question above demonstrates just how large the amount of data could be, i.e. about

30 million dots. This is the extreme case of an image the size of the page. In some cases this may take a few minutes, preventing the 'eight pages per minute' claim of the manufacturer. If done in the printer, it will probably be faster. See 'Methods used to control printers' below.

(2) Does the printer already contain all the fonts you are using? If not, each font will be downloaded, which takes time.

(3) In the case of a laser, has it warmed up yet?

If you start with a cold printer, i.e. just turned on, and have a system where the PC rasterizes images instead of this being done in the printer, the time from when you ask a page to print to the time it is in the out tray may be say 4 minutes. If the manufacturer claims eight pages per minute, it should have been in the tray after less than 8 seconds. The truth is that the speed is quoted as the 'engine speed', i.e. the maximum throughput speed of the actual printing mechanism once the data has been prepared for printing. The quoted speed is almost reached if you measure it once the printer has started producing multiple copies of the same page.

At full speed, even an eight page per minute laser printer will outperform an old dot matrix printer *but* if you time a small print job, say a single invoice, from the time of request to the finished item, dot matrix printers are often faster, they do not suffer from the start-up delay found in laser printers. If the task you must solve involves this kind of printing, especially if you need a carbon copy of every document, the old dot matrix machine still performs well.

Be very careful with claims of printer speeds.

Kinds of printer commonly used with PCs

Dot matrix	Cheap and cheerful. Used in point of sale machines or tills and in many businesses for printing invoices at point of sale because dot matrix printers will make carbon copies.
Inkjet	Cheap to buy, very popular for home use with the better models producing convincing photo quality. Will print on many different kinds of media but ink cartridge prices make it expensive to run.
Mono laser	Best quality from reasonably priced printer, makes a good crisp image at a good speed on cheap paper, good life from a toner cartridge.
Colour laser	Makes a good crisp image at a good speed on cheap paper. Machine currently expensive but prices are becoming more realistic.
Thermal wax	Good colours.
Dye sublimation	Close to photographic quality prints. Uses transparent colours allowing good colour reproduction (see Appendix C).

An aside – Hexadecimal and binary numbers

Before continuing with this section, make sure you understand hex (hexadecimal) and binary numbers; you will find these in most technical areas of computing. An introduction is included on page 433.

Another aside – ASCII characters

Also before continuing with this section, you will need to understand the ASCII character set. An introduction is also included on page 438.

Question 1.9.2

Referring to the list of ASCII codes and the example above, write down the sequence of codes that should be sent to the printer to

reset the printer,
set italic underlined font,
print the letters 'HNC',
set underline off.

Methods used to control printers

When a computer sends data to a printing device, the data may take one of several forms. This affects the way that programmers must think about how they are to format their data and how to make the best use of the printer's differing functions; it also affects the speed of response as seen by the user. More complex print formatting requires more sophisticated communication with the printer. When you install software on a machine, one task is to load a *Printer Driver*. This piece of software has the task of taking the data from an application including any mark-up that defines formatting, etc. and translating it to the form the printer will accept. Many modern printers will accept all the forms shown below.

Method 1: Send plain ASCII codes to the printer.
The simplest method of outputting data is as a stream of ASCII codes, a set of binary codes that describes each letter. A problem arises when you wish to print graphical images since each pixel must be sent as just a dot – a slow and unsatisfactory process. Another problem arises when you wish to 'control' the printer. One code will send the print carriage back to the left (a Carriage Return, ASCII character 13 decimal, 0D hex), another will advance the paper one line (a Line Feed, ASCII character 10 decimal, 0A hex), but accurate fine resolution control is difficult. Underlining or bold printing is not possible as the printer will print everything it receives. Not a useful method.

Method 2: Send plain ASCII codes to the printer with Escape sequences.
This is similar to method one but overcomes the problem of underlining, etc. by using special codes to tell the printer when to underline, print double high, etc. These codes use ASCII character 27 (1B in hex), the *escape* character. For instance, if the word 'CAT' is sent to the printer, the ASCII codes would be 67 65 84 (or 43, 41, 55 in hex), the codes for C, A and T. If you wished to have this underlined you would first send the escape sequence 27 45 1, that is 'ESC', '–','1'. The printer will not try to print these codes, it will simply print everything that comes after it underlined. To turn off the underlining you would send 'ESC', '–', '0'. The full sequence to print an underlined CAT and then to turn off underlining would then be

27, 45, 49, 67, 65, 84, 27, 45, 48 in decimal
1B, 2D, 31, 43, 41, 54, 1B, 2D, 30 in hex

Other examples of escape sequences:

ESC, 'W', 1 turn on double wide printing, ESC, 'W', 0 to turn it off
ESC, '4', 1 turn on italic printing, ESC, '5' to release
ESC, '@' resets the printer

Methods 3 and 4: Use a page description language.
The most common method used to talk to modern printers is to *describe* the page layout and contents then send that description to the printer. The printer usually contains its own computer which interprets the description and forms an image to be printed. This computer is sometimes more powerful than the one used for word processing, etc.!

The page description could be either in the PostScript language or the Hewlett Packard language called *PCL*. However the page is described, it must be *rasterized*, i.e. turned into a set of dots; this is the purpose of the computer in the printer. It is possible to do this in the main PC but this slows down the PC as far as the user is concerned and generates huge amounts of data to be downloaded to the printer, further slowing down the process.

The advantage gained by using a page description language is much better control of the printed image. For instance, the original software does not need to know how to place each dot needed to form a line, only where the line starts and ends, the printer works out the placement of each dot in the line, i.e. it generates the whole line from just the end point data. This also means that the printer can hold the shape of each letter in each size (called *fonts*), so the image of each letter does not need to be sent to the printer. If unusual letters are required, they can be sent to the printer hence allowing almost unlimited printing of characters and graphics images.

Examples of both PostScript and PCL are attached.

PCL is based on or evolved from an advanced series of escape sequences but PostScript is a stack-based computer language that may be written 'by hand' or interpreted by other software. You could if you wished write programs in PostScript. Software is available (such as Ghost Script) that will form an on-screen image of the document just by using the PostScript information. A feature of PostScript is that it is not dependent on the printer resolution. This means that if you send a PostScript file to a low-resolution printer it will be rendered according to that printer. If you send the same file to a high-resolution machine you get the same image in the same proportion but looking much sharper. This is the method of choice for many DTP operations. The image is composed on a PC and checked on a local laser printer but the file is sent to a professional typesetter who would use a printer with many times the resolution.

The use of a page description language allows much better control of the printed image and is most suitable for everyday office use but don't forget that not all printers are attached to PCs or bigger machines. The printers in point of sale machines that produce till receipts still need to be controlled as do numerous other small printing devices and many of these are still dot matrix printers. Many businesses choose to keep their dot matrix printers for printing invoices instead of using laser printers; they are simple, robust and very fast for small print jobs because they do not have a long start-up time.

Hex or ASCII dumps from four methods

The hexdumps shown below are what were output from Wordperfect 5.1 with different printers set up. The data in the word processor was just '**This is some sample text, some of it is underlined, some of it is not.**' A dump implies that a data file has been printed in a raw state as hex bytes and as readable ASCII, with no formatting or special treatment. It is used to inspect raw data and is often very useful to help understand what has gone on or gone wrong with a process. Most dumps are like these, with 16 bytes shown in hex and the same 16 bytes shown in the right-hand column in readable ASCII with CTRL characters or other non-printable characters shown as dots.

It is clear that it is *not* important to remember details shown here, just that different printers accept data in different forms to achieve similar results.

(1) As printed on a printer *with no ability to format text*. Note that all underline codes, etc. are missing, only plain ASCII is present. 0D is the Carriage Return and 0A is the Line Feed character.

```
0D 0D 0A 0D 0A 0D 0A 0D 0A 0D 0A 0D 0A 20 20 20 ............
20 20 20 20 20 20 20 54 68 69 73 20 69 73 20 73        This is s
6F 6D 65 20 73 61 6D 70 6C 65 20 74 65 78 74 2C ome sample text,
20 73 6F 6D 65 20 6F 66 20 69 74 20 69 73 20 75  some of it is u
6E 64 65 72 6C 69 6E 65 64 2C 20 73 6F 6D 65 20 nderlined, some
6F 66 20 69 74 20 69 73 0D 20 20 20 20 20 20 20 of it is.
```

(2) As printed on a Panasonic 1123 printer emulating an Epson LQ–850 24-pin dot matrix printer using escape sequence control. The escape sequences are not the same as the examples above, each printer uses its own which is why a separate *printer driver* must be loaded on your machine to work properly with your printer. A printer driver 'knows' the sequences for the relevant printer.

```
1B 40 1B 36 1B 74 01 1B 52 00 1B 32 1B 6B 06 1B .@.6.t..R..2.k..
21 02 1B 78 01 1B 43 42 1B 2B FF 0A 0D 1B 2B 95 !..x..CB.+ÿ. . .+•
0A 0D 1B 24 3C 00 54 68 69 73 1B 24 55 00 69 73 . . .$<.This.$U.is
1B 24 62 00 73 6F 6D 65 1B 24 7D 00 73 61 6D 70 .$b.some.$}.samp
6C 65 1B 24 A1 00 74 65 78 74 2C 1B 24 BB 00 73 le.$.¡.text,.$».s
6F 6D 65 1B 24 D6 00 6F 66 1B 24 E4 00 69 74 1B ome.$Ö.of.$ä.it.
24 F0 00 69 73 1B 24 FD 00 75 6E 64 65 72 6C 69 $ö.is.$ý.underli
6E 65 64 2C 1B 24 38 01 73 6F 6D 65 1B 24 53 01 ned,.$8.some.$S.
6F 66 1B 24 61 01 69 74 1B 24 6D 01 69 73 1B 24 of.$a.it.$m.is.$
7A 01 6E 6F 74 2E 1B 24 BB 00 1B 2D 01 20 20 20 z.not..$»..-.
20 20 20 20 20 20 20 20 20 20 20 20 20 20 20 20
```

(3) As printed on a Hewlett Packard LaserJet 5L printer using the page description language PCL5. Printer control languages actually send a great deal of data to the printer. The text printed was 'This is some sample text, some of it is underlined, some of it is not.' which is only 70 bytes long but the output to the printer produced 504 bytes of data. Note how each escape (1B hex) is followed by a sequence of control bytes, followed by the text to be printed.

```
1B 25 2D 31 32 33 34 35 58 40 50 4A 4C 20 52 44 .%-12345X@PJL RD
59 4D 53 47 20 44 49 53 50 4C 41 59 20 3D 20 22 YMSG DISPLAY = "
57 6F 72 64 50 65 72 66 65 63 74 20 4A 6F 62 22 WordPerfect Job"
0D 0A 40 50 4A 4C 20 53 45 54 20 52 45 53 4F 4C ..@PJL SET RESOL
55 54 49 4F 4E 20 3D 20 36 30 30 0D 0A 40 50 4A UTION = 600..@PJ
4C 20 45 4E 54 45 52 20 4C 41 4E 47 55 41 47 45 L ENTER LANGUAGE
20 3D 20 50 43 4C 0D 0A 1B 26 6C 31 6F 30 6F 31 = PCL...&l1o0o1
74 30 6C 36 64 31 58 1B 2A 72 30 46 1B 2A 63 31 t0l6d1X.*r0F.*c1
30 30 47 1B 2A 76 32 54 1B 26 6C 30 4F 1B 26 61 00G.*v2T.&l0O.&a
30 50 1B 26 6C 30 45 1B 39 1B 2A 70 30 58 1B 2A 0P.&l0E.9.*p0X.*
70 30 59 1B 28 31 30 55 1B 28 73 31 70 31 32 76 p0Y.(10U.(s1p12v
73 62 34 31 34 38 54 1B 26 6C 32 61 30 45 1B 26 sb4148T.&l2a0E.&
6C 32 68 30 45 1B 39 1B 26 6C 30 4F 1B 26 61 30 l2h0E.9.&l0O.&a0
50 1B 26 6C 30 45 1B 39 1B 2A 70 30 58 1B 2A 70 P.&l0E.9.*p0X.*p
30 59 1B 2A 70 33 33 38 59 1B 2A 70 32 32 30 58 0Y.*p338Y.*p220X
54 68 69 73 1B 2A 70 33 33 34 58 69 73 1B 2A 70 This.*p334Xis.*p
33 38 38 58 73 6F 6D 65 1B 2A 70 35 32 39 58 73 388Xsome.*p529Xs
61 6D 70 6C 65 1B 2A 70 37 30 39 58 74 65 78 74 ample.*p709Xtext
2C 1B 2A 70 38 33 34 58 1B 26 64 44 73 6F 6D 65 ,.*p834X.&dDsome
1B 2A 70 39 37 35 58 6F 66 1B 2A 70 31 30 33 39 .*p975Xof.*p1039
58 69 74 1B 2A 70 31 30 38 36 58 69 73 1B 2A 70 Xit.*p1086Xis.*p
```

```
31 31 34 30 58 75 6E 64 65 72 6C 69 6E 65 64 1B 1140Xunderlined.
26 64 40 2C 1B 2A 70 31 34 31 35 58 73 6F 6D 65 &d@,.*p1415Xsome
1B 2A 70 31 35 35 36 58 6F 66 1B 2A 70 31 36 32 .*p1556Xof.*p162
30 58 69 74 1B 2A 70 31 36 36 37 58 69 73 1B 2A 0Xit.*p1667Xis.*
70 31 37 32 31 58 6E 6F 74 2E 0C 1B 26 6C 31 68 p1721Xnot...&l1h
30 45 1B 2A 72 42 1B 26 6C 30 70 31 6C 31 68 30 0E.*rB.&l0p1l1h0
6F 30 45 1B 28 38 55 1B 28 73 70 31 30 68 31 32 o0E.(8U.(sp10h12
76 73 62 33 54 1B 26 64 40 1B 45 1B 25 2D 31 32 vsb3T.&d@.E.%-12
33 34 35 58 40 50 4A 4C 20 52 44 59 4D 53 47 20 345X@PJL RDYMSG
44 49 53 50 4C 41 59 20 3D 20 22 22 0D 0A 1B 25 DISPLAY = ""...%
```

(4) As printed on a Apple LaserWriter *PostScript printer.* Printer control languages but especially PostScript actually send a great deal of data to the printer. The text printed was 'This is some sample text, some of it is underlined, some of it is not.' which is only 70 bytes long but the output to the printer produced 13 867 bytes of data using PostScript from the word processor used, Wordperfect 5.1. When set as 10 point Courier in Word 97, this page description prints on eight A4 pages! What is shown here is only some of the data actually sent to the printer in PostScript, much of it has been left out for clarity. You can see that there is no need for a hex dump as the data is sent as a computer language in plain ASCII, i.e. a description of the results rather than the actual page.

```
%1 PS-Adobe
/wpdict  120 dict def
wpdict   begin
/bdef    {bind def} bind def

/bflg    false def
/Bfont   0 def
/bon     false def
.
.
.
```

much of the 13 867 bytes of the PostScript file removed to save space.

```
.
.
.
letter usertime 5000 add {dup usertime lt {pop exit} if} loop statusdict
/manualfeed true put usertime 5000 add {dup usertime lt {pop exit} if}
loop _bp 0 13200 10200 _ornt /HelveticaR 600 _ff
0 13200 10200 _ornt
/_r      { sflg {/_t {0 rmoveto}bdef /ron false def}
         { /_S /show load def /_t {0 rmoveto}bdef /ron false def}ifelse
     }bdef
1200 11849 _m
(This)_S 67 _t
(is)_S 67 _t
(some)_S 67 _t
(sample)_S 67 _t
(text,)_S 67 _t
_U
(some)_S 67 _t
(of)_S 67 _t
(it)_S 67 _t
(is)_S 67 _t
(underlined)_S _u (,)_S 67 _t

(some)_S 67 _t
(of)_S 67 _t
(it)_S 67 _t
(is)_S 67 _t
(not.)_S _ep
statusdict /manualfeed false put _ed end end
```

1.10 Hard drives

The hard drive in a PC employs a rotating disk or disks. These disks are coated with a material that has certain magnetic properties that are persistent, i.e. once changed they stay that way for a long period until changed again. This is all that is required to store data as 1s and 0s.

The purpose of this part of the book is to provide help with the specification of devices, so the precise details of how the various types of hard drive actually work will be ignored. The most important points to note are:

- Capacity
- Performance
- Cost
- Reliability
- Compatibility with other systems/components

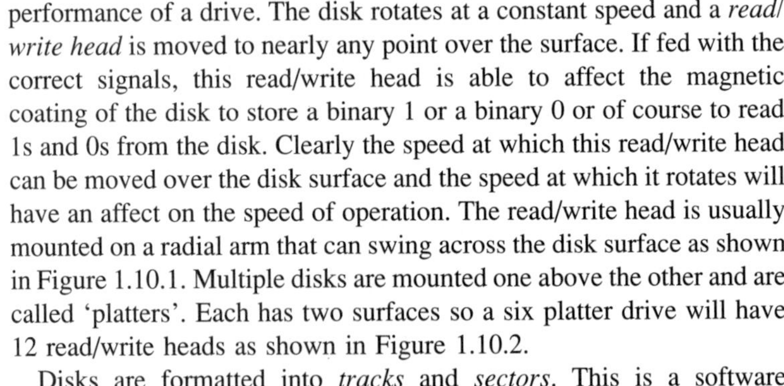

Figure 1.10.1 *Layout of simple disk drive*

Although we shall ignore the fine detail, some understanding of how a drive works is required to understand properly factors in the performance of a drive. The disk rotates at a constant speed and a *read/write head* is moved to nearly any point over the surface. If fed with the correct signals, this read/write head is able to affect the magnetic coating of the disk to store a binary 1 or a binary 0 or of course to read 1s and 0s from the disk. Clearly the speed at which this read/write head can be moved over the disk surface and the speed at which it rotates will have an affect on the speed of operation. The read/write head is usually mounted on a radial arm that can swing across the disk surface as shown in Figure 1.10.1. Multiple disks are mounted one above the other and are called 'platters'. Each has two surfaces so a six platter drive will have 12 read/write heads as shown in Figure 1.10.2.

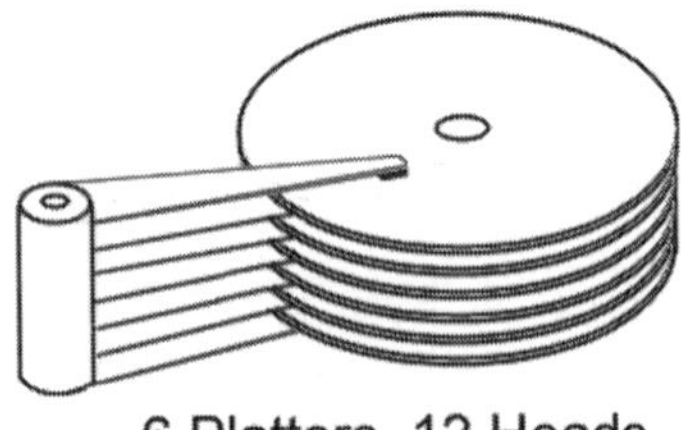

Figure 1.10.2 *Platters and heads*

Disks are formatted into *tracks* and *sectors*. This is a software controlled process that writes data onto the disk to allow control. Each track is concentric, the number of tracks depends on the bit density achievable on the disk, i.e. how much data can be stored in a small area. A sector is part of a track, it is usually numbered and it contains data and

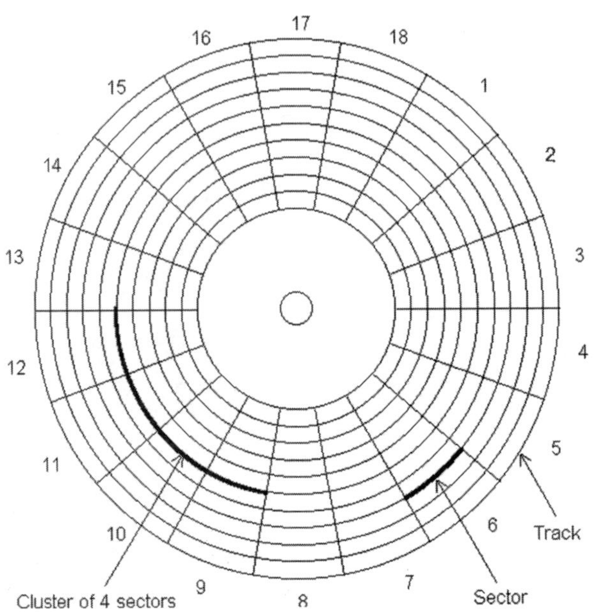

Figure 1.10.3 *Simple arrangement of tracks, sectors and clusters on a disk*

error checking code called a CRC. CRC is short for *Cyclic Redundancy Check*, it is used to test if data loaded from the disk has become corrupted in some way. If a drive has multiple disks or platters, the tracks are called cylinders, the read/write heads mounted on the actuator arm all move together so all the tracks of the same number are one above the other.

Disk performance

Amongst all the performance data for a drive that is available, there are two figures that are the most prominent, the *data transfer rate* and *average access time.*

Data transfer rate

The data transfer rate is the speed that data may be read from the drive once it is spinning, the read/write head is correctly positioned and data is flowing, i.e. it is a measure that does not take into account the time to set up the reading process. Really old drives gave values of about 0.6 Mbytes/s but newer drives can deliver 80 Mbytes/sec, about 130 times faster!

Average access time

If a request is made to the drive to supply data from a certain position on the disk, in all probability the read/write head will not be in the correct place to start the read process. It must wait until the disk has rotated to the correct sector and be placed over the correct track or cylinder. It must then wait for a short time to 'settle' or for any residual movement to stop. If you measured the time it took to complete this whole process, it would not give you a useful figure as the distance the read/write head or the disk had to travel will affect the value obtained. To get around this problem, the process is tried many times; the read/write head is positioned at a random point, a data request is made and this is repeated a thousand times or more to obtain an average time. If a drive has an average access time of say 10 ms, it simply means that on average, the time from a data request to the time the data starts to flow is 10 milliseconds or 10^{-2} seconds, it tells you nothing about how fast the data will flow after that.

To get this time in proportion, consider a disk that rotates at 3600 rev/min. 3600 rev/min = 60 rev/sec so 1 revolution takes 1/60 second or about 17 ms. Draw an imaginary line through the centre of the disk and through the centre of the read/write head; this line will cut the disk in half. Calling the halves A and B, now consider that on average, the sector that will be needed next will have a 50% chance of being in half A and a 50% chance of being in half B. It follows that the average time to access any sector will be approximately the time taken to rotate half a revolution providing the average is taken over a large number of data accesses. In this case you might expect a drive that rotates at 3600 rev/min to have an average access time of 17/2 = 8.5 ms. The actual values are slower than this because the actuator arm travel has to be taken into account as does the 'settling time'.

If a drive has a modest data transfer rate but a fast average access time, you can be sure the advertisers will concentrate on the access time.

They will say that 'drive x has a time of 8 ms which is faster than the competition value of 10 ms'. The problem you need to consider with buying or specifying drives is 'will I see a difference if I buy the 8 ms drive?' The answer depends on much more than this simple number.

In what follows, take track and cylinder to mean the same thing. Various ploys are used to improve disk performance. One is to increase the rotational speed but this is limited to the speed at which the read/write head and the associated circuits can cope with the data. Too fast and whole rotations are missed until the sector comes round again. Another ploy is to interleave sector numbering. If sector 8 is being loaded, it is a good guess that the next one that will be requested is sector 9. The trouble that once sector 8 has past the read/write head it may be just too late to request sector 9 so a complete rotation is lost. The answer is to number the sectors so they are 'interleaved', i.e. sector 9 is not next to sector 8 but is the next but one. Now when reading sector 8, after is has past, there is enough time within one rotation to request sector 9. A third ploy is called cylinder skewing. In a problem related to the need to interleave, the read/write head must change track at some point to get to the next sector. If the sector numbering goes say 0–25 then 0–25 in the same pattern on the next track, any read that needs sectors 23, 24, 25 then 0, 1, 2, etc. on the next track will result in waiting a full rotation between sectors 25 and 0 as the time it takes to move the actuator arm with the read/write head to the next track is too slow. Again, a full rotation is missed. Cylinder skewing simply aligns each sector 0 on a track differently from its closest neighbour, i.e. it is skewed. The result is a performance increase because the data can be read uninterrupted by track changes.

Disk addressing

The actual sectors on a disk are addressed according to the *cylinder* (or track of one disk), head number and sector number. This is called *CHS addressing* and is what happens inside the drive. Outside and as far as the operating system is concerned, the sectors are most often addressed by their *Logical Block Address* or LBA. The LBA is a simple number starting from 0 and counting all the available sectors. The drive hardware translates the LBA into the actual CHS. This has great advantages over the older system when the operating system itself used CHS, each drive had to be installed according to the number of heads, cylinders and sectors, the sector size (usually 512 bytes) and a few other parameters. You can see these old types listed in the BIOS of a PC as drive type 1 to drive type 46. Type 47 drives are those that are 'user definable'. Thankfully, all that is history. Logical block addressing means that drive makers are free to optimize their drives, have any combination of number of heads, cylinders, sectors, etc. and still be compatible with the PC and the operating system. Looked at another way, it places the responsibility of optimum use of the disk with the disk maker not the operating system programmer.

Disk cache

A disk can seem to be very fast if disk caching is present and active. This is a technique that copies sections of the disk into a buffer area in

RAM on the assumption that it will be needed. If there is a subsequent data request for what is already in the cache, it is loaded from there so giving a very fast response. The disk cache can be either on the hard drive itself or in main RAM. If it is on the hard drive the maximum speed it limited by the drive interface, if it is main RAM, it is only limited by the RAM system itself.

Partitioning the disk

In the past, individual physical disks were addressed directly as single devices. This is often inconvenient so modern disks can be divided into logical sections called partitions. In this way a single physical drive can appear to be several different drives. Original DOS drives had a 16-bit FAT which imposes a size limit by having $2^{16} = 65\,536$ addressable elements. As explained below, the only way to address larger disks with a 16-bit FAT is to use cluster sizes greater than 1. This results in inefficient use of disk space so partitioning a larger disk into smaller logical drives can make more efficient use of the disk space, each partition will have its own FAT. The same efficient use of the disk space can be achieved by using a 32-bit FAT. Many people find that multiple disk partitions are a convenient way of organizing their software and data.

Drive interfaces

An important factor in determining disk performance is the *interface* used to connect the drive to the PC. The two competing interfaces that dominate the PC market are *IDE/ATA* and *SCSI*. Broadly, IDE/ATA drives offer a good speed at low cost, SCSI offers higher speed and the ability to address other devices but at a higher price. For this reason, most PCs are fitted with IDE/ATA interfaces but those required for performance critical applications are fitted with SCSI drives.

Key fact

'Standards'

First a note about names and 'standards' in the computing business. A 'standard' is really an agreement usually written and published by an approved organization. International bodies such as the ISO do a great deal in this area. There exists a problem in the computing industry – there are many 'de facto' standards, i.e. standards that exist 'in fact' but have not been agreed internationally; they are simply adopted. This approach is fine except that anyone can modify the 'standard' and still claim they are conforming. This leads to an ever growing list of 'standard' names which can and often does lead to confusion. This is especially true with disk drive interfaces.

IDE/ATA interface

You will see many adverts for *IDE drives*, a term that was originally used to differentiate the old drives that used a separate controller board from the (then) new *Integrated Drive Electronics* (IDE) drives. The trouble is, other devices also have 'integral' electronics so the term is of little use. Drives that are called IDE are really using the 'AT Attachment' standard so should be called ATA, but most adverts use the term IDE. IDE/ATA is by far the most popular interface commonly available but variations are also known as ATA, EIDE, ATA-2, Fast ATA or Ultra ATA. The ATA Packet Interface or ATAPI is an extension that allows connection to CD-ROM drives, etc.

Original ATA

The original IDE/ATA supported two hard disks that worked with 'Programmable I/O' or PIO modes and DMA (see section on DMA on page 20).

ATA-2

With increasing performance demands the next standard, ATA-2, was brought out to support faster PIO, LBA and several other enhancements that need not concern us here. Ignoring a few minor details, ATA-2 is the same as Fast ATA, Fast ATA-2, or Enhanced IDE (EIDE). The differences are those between different manufactures and is an example of a 'standard' being applied differently!

ATA-3

ATA-3 is an improvement to ATA-2 that introduces Self-Monitoring Analysis and Reporting Technology (SMART). Although often confused with it, ATA-3 is not the same as Ultra ATA.

Ultra ATA

Ultra ATA (also called F, ATA-33, and DMA-33, etc.) is an even faster interface that uses a 33.3 Mbyte/sec transfer mode using DMA. Ultra ATA is backwards compatible with previous ATA interfaces, so if you fit an Ultra ATA drive to a board that does not support the faster mode, it will still work at the slower speed.

ATAPI

The original ATA would not support CD-ROM drivers or floppy disks so the *ATA Packet Interface* (ATAPI) was introduced to bring the advantage of one standard to cover all the common drives. To make this work, an ATAPI driver must be installed; this is a piece of software called a 'device driver', and it communicates with devices using 'packets' of data. This is because CD-ROMs are quite unlike hard drives in their method of working so software makes up the difference.

PIO

IDE/ATA drives support both PIO and DMA transfer modes. Programmed I/O (PIO) is performed by the main CPU, it requires no support software but ties up the CPU when I/O is in progress. There are several PIO 'modes', each newer than the last, the fastest of which is supported by the latest IDE/ATA drives. As a performance comparison these modes give maximum transfer rates of

PIO Mode 0	3.3 Mbytes/sec
PIO Mode 1	5.2 Mbytes/sec
PIO Mode 2	8.3 Mbytes/sec
PIO Mode 3	11.1 Mbytes/sec
PIO Mode 4	16.6 Mbytes/sec

DMA

Direct Memory Access or DMA achieves data transfer without the CPU, either using the old (and rather limited) DMA chips fitted as standard to all PCs or using bus mastering of the PCI bus.

DMA Mode

Single word 0	2.1 Mbytes/sec (no longer used)
Single word 1	4.2 Mbytes/sec (no longer used)
Single word 2	8.3 Mbytes/sec (no longer used)
Multiword 0	4.2 Mbytes/sec
Multiword 1	13.3 Mbytes/sec
Multiword 2	16.6 Mbytes/sec
Multiword 3	33.3 Mbytes/sec (DMA-33)

Do not think that PIO mode 4 and DMA Multiword 2 will give the same overall performance. Both achieve 16.6 Mbytes/sec but the PIO mode ties up the CPU whereas the DMA mode allows the CPU to complete other tasks at the same time, for instance if a AGP device is fitted. However, an average user will probably not see this performance improvement, it will only be when heavy demands are made on the disk that such things will be useful. The disadvantage of using bus mastering is the added complexity of getting the devices and associated software to work properly.

Small Computer Systems Interface (SCSI)

In contrast with ATA, the SCSI interface did not start in the PC world nor is it a disk drive interface; it is a standard that is used in Unix machines and others to achieve a fast and flexible means of data transfer between devices. Hard disks are only one of a range of devices that are 'skuzzy' compatible.

SCSI suffers from a similar problem to IDE/ATA, there are too many standards or names giving rise to considerable confusion in the marketplace.

There are the main standards, SCSI-1, SCSI-2 and SCSI-3, that are compatible, i.e. older devices that conform to SCSI-1 will work on SCSI-2 adapters.

SCSI-1

SCSI-1 defined a basic 8-bit bus (now called a 'narrow' bus), a 5 MHz bus and 4.77 Mb/s transfer rate.

SCSI-2

SCSI-2 is an extension of SCSI-1 giving a 10 MHz bus, an increased bus width from the original 8-bit SCSI bus to 16 bits and support for 16 devices. It also defines new higher-density connections; unfortunately SCSI has suffered from a large range of 'standard' cables. If you look at hardware suppliers' catalogues, you will see a large range of them! A 32-bit bus is defined and is called very wide SCSI but is not in common use.

SCSI-3

SCSI-3 is yet another extension giving a 20 MHz bus, improved cabling enabling 'wide' SCSI (i.e. not 8 bit!) and for the first time SCSI-3 contains the new serial SCSI, also called Firewire.

There are three different bus speeds used in SCSI, 5, 10 and 20 MHz, there is the slow and fast SCSI; all this gives rise to some confusion in the marketplace to add to the problems with cabling.

Table 1.10.1 Main SCSI parameters shows a summary of SCSI speeds.

	Bus width	*Transfer rate Mbytes/sec*	*Bus speed (MHz)*	*Number of devices per bus*
Regular SCSI-1	8 bits	4.77	5	8
Wide SCSI-2	16 bits	2 × 4.77 = 9.54	5	16
Fast SCSI-2	8 bits	2 × 4.77 = 9.54	10	8
Fast Wide SCSI-2	16 bits	2 × 9.54 = 19	10	16
Ultra SCSI-3	8 bits	2 × 9.54 = 19	20	8
Ultra Wide SCSI-3	16 bits	2 × 19 = 38	20	16

SCSI Adapters

Because SCSI is an interface standard rather than a disk drive interface, there is no point in building the SCSI interface into the drive as is the practice with IDE/ATA drives.

The interface is usually on an expansion or accessory card connected either to the (old) ISA bus or more usually to the PCI bus. This expansion card is called a host adapter. Expansion cards connected to the PCI local bus support the use of bus mastering.

Comparative performance of SCSI and IDE/ATA

Some people will say that 'SCSI is better than IDE'. Whilst it is possible to demonstrate that SCSI is faster in some circumstances, in practice the difference is harder to pin down.

- The actual disk drives spin at comparable speeds so the time to get to and access a sector should be the same.
- The fastest SCSI bus is the Ultra Wide SCSI, which has a maximum transfer rate of 40 Mbytes/sec. This is better than the best IDE/ATA rate of 33 Mbytes/sec. As 40 is only 20% faster than 33, it is unlikely the difference will be spotted except when using demanding applications and they are being timed. It must also be remembered that 40 Mbytes/sec is the maximum of the SCSI interface and not necessarily that of the drive and interface together.
- The SCSI interface has a high 'overhead', i.e. it is much more complex than the IDE/ATA interface; more processing takes place. For this reason, if you ran a comparison of a single IDE/ATA drive running simple tasks against a SCSI drive fitted in an otherwise identical machine, the IDE/ATA drive may well perform better because the interface can react quicker.
- SCSI allows multi-tasking unlike ATA, so in set-ups with multiple disks that require simultaneous access, SCSI will handle multiple tasks better.
- In PCs fitted with IDE/ATA drives that support bus mastering, the difference between SCSI and IDE/ATA is less marked. In practice, not that many IDE/ATA drives are actually using bus mastering but this situation is likely to change as better device drivers and drives become available.

In summary, for PCs with single drives for desktop use, specify IDE/ATA because it is fast and cheap. For PCs with multiple disks that run demanding tasks or are used as a server, use SCSI.

Size limits

There are various factors that limit the size of disk that can be handled in a given PC. Most modern PCs take drives that are large enough for common applications and plenty of data but if you need more information it can be found on www.pcguide.com/ref/hdd/bios/size.htm.

High-Level formatting

Operating systems must use at least one method to keep track of files on a disk. Although disks are formatted with tracks and sectors (the so-called low-level format), there is nothing about this structure that organizes files and directories (directories are called folders in Windows). This organization of files and directories is a function of the operating system, i.e. it is controlled entirely by software, the hardware plays no part at all in the *organization* although clearly it actually executes the task.

There are many different ways to arrange this organization but it is not the intention of this part of the book to describe them all. The section in Appendix D describes one of the simplest and almost certainly the most common, Microsoft DOS File Allocation Table. Operating systems like Windows NT are able to read and write to different disk filing systems whereas older operating systems use only their own. The purpose of the appendix is simply to illustrate the problems that must be solved.

1.11 CD-ROM and DVD drives

CDs work by storing large numbers of 1s and 0s as 'pits' in an optically reflective surface. Unlike hard drives, the 'tracks' are one continuous spiral and the rotational speed of the disc is adjusted to give a constant linear speed past the read head. This is called CLV or *Constant Linear Velocity*. Hard drives use CAV or *Constant Angular Velocity*, i.e. the rotational speed is constant and the nearer the outside the read/write head is, the faster the linear speed past the head. You can hear the CD-ROM drive change speed as it works, indicating that the read head is moving in or out. There are many different formats of CD, they conform to standards that are in 'books' named after colours, so you get 'orange book' for CD-R and CD-RW discs or 'red book' for audio or CD-DA discs. This unit of the HNC Computing does not cover such detail except that a drive must conform to a given standard to be useful. For instance, if you buy a CD-RW compatible drive, it will play CD-DA (audio) discs but beware, not all drives support all formats. The actual situation in the marketplace is far from standardized. Likewise, DVD is far from having common standards that are 'standard', i.e. work universally. DVD now stands for *Digital Versatile Disc* but did not start out like that, it was called a *Digital Video Disc*, an indication of the lack of standardization. The original format was for video data but now sound and data are to be found on DVD. Hopefully the 'standards' will become more standard in the near future. Older CD-ROM drives cannot read more modern formats.

Speed

You will have seen advertisements for '×32' or '×40' CD-ROM drives. This refers to the original speed of 150 kbytes/sec drive. A '40 times' or '×40' drive should deliver a data transfer rate of $150 \times 40 = 6000$ kbytes/sec or 5.86 Mbytes/sec. The drive listed below is a '×48' version so will provide $150 \times 48 = 7200$ Kbytes/sec. Do not be fooled by this number. It is the *maximum* the drive can deliver not the actual rate you will get once the drive has spun up to speed, the head has found the data you want and it has started flowing.

The average access time, just like hard drives, is the average time it takes to start delivering data after a data request has been made. Again, this figure is often misleading. Unlike hard drives, CD-ROM drives stop rotating soon after use, so if you measure the actual access time from a stationary disc, the result will be in whole seconds! [The spin-up time increases as the 'times' speed increases to a '×48' drive will take longer to spin up to the high speed it needs before the data starts flowing.] If your application accesses the CD infrequently, the spin-up time will dominate the average access time but will not figure in the specification at all.

A typical CD-ROM specification would look like this:

(1) ATAPI-IDE interface
(2) Supports Enhanced-IDE
(3) ATAPI compatible
(4) Supports ISO 9660 (High Sierra), CD-I, VCD, Multisession
(5) Photo CD, CD+, CD-extra, i-trax, CD-UDF, CD-R, CD-RW
(6) CD-DA, CD-ROM (mode 1 & 2) format
(7) Supports Multiread, CD-RW format
(8) Supports Multiread function packet writing format
(9) Supports Digital Audio Extraction
(10) High-speed audio playback
(11) Supports Ultra-DMA mode 2
(12) 48× speed drive with maximum 7200 kb/s transfer rate
(13) Average access time: less than 80 ms

Points 1, 2, 3 and 11 refer to the ATA interface that the drive can use. (See the section on hard drive.)

Points 4 to 10 refer to the format of CDs to be used. It will play audio discs, record on CD-R and CD-RW discs, play the Kodak Photo CDs, etc.

Point 12 gives the 'times' speed.

Point 13 gives the average access time in milliseconds.

DVD speeds are not the same as CD-ROM speeds, so a '×6' DVD is not slower than the '×48' CD-ROM. A '×6' DVD should be able to deliver 8100 Kbytes/sec or six times 1350 Kbytes/sec. At this rate a DVD will be 8100/150 = 54 times the CD-ROM speed. Note from the specification below that when reading CD-ROMs and not DVDs, the data transfer rate is a lot lower.

A typical DVD specification would look like this:

(1) 6× (8100 kbytes/sec) maximum speed as DVD-ROM drive
(2) 32× (4800 kbytes/sec) maximum speed at CD-ROM drive
(3) ATAPI/E-IDE interface
(4) Supports PIO mode 4/Multiword DMA mode 2/Ultra-DMA 33
(5) Compatible with CD-DA. CD-ROM/XA, Karaoke, CD/Video CD, CD-I/FMV, Single/Multisession photo CD, Enhanced CD and CD-RW
(6) Interface type: E-IDE/ATAPI
(7) Data transfer rate: 8100 kbytes/sec maximum at DVD-ROM drive, 4800 kbytes/sec maximum at CD-ROM drive
(8) Average access time: 120 ms at DVD-ROM drive, 90 ms at CD-ROM drive

(9) Disc formats: DVD single layer/dual layer, DVD-R, DVD-RW, CD-ROM, CD-ROM/XA, CD-R (CD-WO), CD-I/FMV, Single/Multisession Photo CD, Enhanced CD

Compare this specification with the one for the CD-ROM.

CD-ROMs and DVDs either use the ATAPI or SCSI interface. SCSI is better for CD-RW because it offers multi-tasking and therefore does not interfere with the flow of data to the disc. If you are recording with a CD-RW disc on an ATAPI interface, it is often better not to use the PC for any other task as the recording process is time critical. If other tasks are running that might slow down the flow of data to the writing software, *buffer under-runs* can occur. CDs need a constant stream of data when writing. This data is stored temporarily in a buffer (a piece of memory), ready to write to the disc. If this buffer runs out of data, the disc cannot be fed with a constant stream so the writing process fails. This is called a buffer under-run.

1.12 Computer performance

A human model of CPU performance

The classical model of a simple microcomputer is shown in Figure 1.12.1. The effect of this design may not be obvious from the start but the most important thing to notice is that the Central Processor (CPU) is separate from the memory (RAM). This results in the unfortunate fact that the program to be run must be fetched into the processor before the CPU knows what to do and it must be fetched in pieces. With normal programs, in no sense is the whole program ever found inside the CPU. This has quite a profound effect on the performance of the microcomputer because no matter how fast the CPU executes each instruction, the speed at which instructions are fetched from the RAM may well limit the speed at which the whole program is executed.

In this simple model, the processor fetches one instruction, decodes it, then executes it. It then fetches the next instruction, decodes and executes it and so on in an 'endless' sequence. Newer processors fetch instructions a few at a time and these can be executing whilst the processor fetches some more at the same time. Although this provides a very large increase in speed over the old designs, the fact remains that instructions in RAM must be fetched before they can be executed.

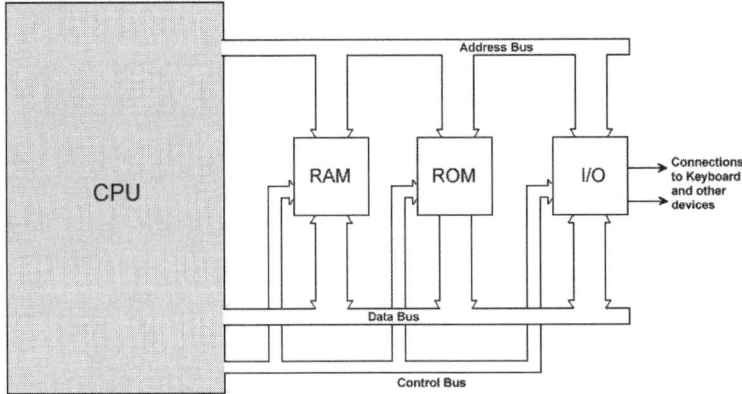

Figure 1.12.1 *A simple microcomputer architecture*

Computer performance, an analogy

Warning. Analogies such as this cannot be taken too far. For it to be of use, the humans involved are *not* using their own intelligence, they are simply following instructions blindly, acting as parts of a machine.

Imagine you were in a room with your friend, Fred, and you are to perform a calculation. You are the processor, the 'CPU', Fred is the memory or RAM. You must ignore the fact that you have intelligence and remember that you do not know what job is required of you; you can add, divide, multiply, keep a note of where you put answers, etc. but you cannot see the whole problem. Your friend Fred, in the same room, knows that a job must be completed but he does not know how to do it, all he knows is that the instructions are written down. He can read the written list of instructions from a reference book. It might go something like this.

Fred opens a tax reference book, finds the correct part then reads to you:-

(1) take the salary of £20 000;
(2) subtract £5400;
(3) remember what is left;
(4) subtract 23% of this amount;
(5) if 6% of what is left over is greater than £1250 then subtract £1250 otherwise subtract 6%;
(6) Finally add the £5400 to what is left;
(7) divide it by 12;
(8) tell me the result.

Points to note

The formal list of instructions is the program, it contains the problem.
You are the 'CPU', you do the calculating but do not have a complete picture of the problem.
The *written list* of instructions is the 'RAM'.
Your friend Fred is the connection between the RAM and you, i.e. he is the 'Bus'.

Now consider these points:

(1) On a second run through the program, you perform the individual calculations faster but Fred reads them at the same speed, would the overall problem be solved quicker? No it would not, the speed is limited by either the 'RAM' speed or the 'Bus' speed even though you, the CPU, are now quicker.
(2) On a third run through the program, if Fred reads the next instruction before you have finished the previous calculation, the speed of execution of the whole problem is now limited by the 'CPU' speed.
(3) As a reminder, do not take this analogy too far!

Simple and some more complex computers are like this, the speed of execution depends on more than the speed of the processor. The message is, when you buy a PC, do not be overawed by the processor clock speed, the speed of the whole machine relies on more than this.

Caching

In old PCs with simple processors, the speed was limited more by the RAM because the processor could run faster. Processor design far outstripped the improvements in RAM speed. Modern PCs have RAM that is not all that much faster. How can they offer such a large increase in performance? This is achieved by *caching*. In our analogy, if Fred were to write the program down on a convenient piece of paper before execution then put the main book away, he would be able to access the 'program' quicker rather than looking it up in a book. Of course larger problems would not fit on his piece of paper but most of the time a useful speed increase would be achieved. Attached to a modern processor, there is a small amount of high-speed RAM that is used for this purpose, it is much faster than the main RAM. This is called level 1 or L1 caching.

A second and even better speed increase could be achieved by copying parts of the program onto smaller pieces of paper in your hand, i.e. in the 'CPU'. These are only small pieces of paper but the execution speed is now limited by how fast you can do the calculations, you need not wait for Fred to read them. The problem is that not all the program can be on your piece of paper. Fred must ensure that the next part of the program is available when you need it by copying it whilst you are doing the actual calculations. This is level 2 or L2 caching and is one of the reasons why modern machines are so fast. Caching is what squirrels do – in autumn they hide acorns in a cache for use later on in the winter. This is a similar idea because instructions are put into a cache for use a little later on.

Clock speed

The next thing to consider is the clock speed. In our analogy, the clock speed is roughly equivalent to the time that elapsed between the execution of each simple instruction. A processor does things step by step at a constant speed so if you have a 400 MHz processor, this is doing simple things 400 million times a second. Although in human terms this seems impossibly fast, remember that each thing that is being done is as simple as 'add 3' or 'store a number', nothing as complex as 'check this spelling'. It does not matter what software is running, it is all made up of very simple machine level instructions called machine code. That includes Windows! When Windows is running, the processor cannot tell as all it does is to execute millions of simple instructions. A different analogy (as described on page 3) is one of bricks making up a building. If you imagine the detail required to understand how a single brick takes part in a building, when you consider Windows in the same analogy you would look at the design of a whole town not just a brick. Machine code, as far as the processor is concerned, is just a vast array of 'bricks'; Windows is the whole town.

What is meant by the term 'speed' in a computer?

If you look at advertisements you will find that companies selling computers quote the CPU speed and expect people to know how fast the machine is from that. For instance, you may think that a Pentium 600 PC is faster than a Pentium 500 PC. The trouble is that it is often not true. The time taken by a computer to complete a task depends on many factors.

What most non-technical people mean by speed is 'how fast the computer will do a task just for me'. Many of these people would not know or care about the CPU speed. One of these users might be using a large database in which case the main speed of the 'computer' will be limited by the disk drive and memory systems. Another user may be playing a game, the speed here is at least partly limited by the video system.

Imagine you had to describe the complete performance of a car with just *one number*, is it possible? No, in real life it is not possible to define just one such number or *performance indicator*. A Formula 1 racing car may be able to reach 200 mph but if used on a rough farm track competing in a rally it would go several yards before getting stuck in the mud, even a tractor would be faster! The problem is not just the power of the car, it is the whole design of the vehicle. One car may go very fast in a straight line but slowly around corners, a different car may do well on the corners but slow down on the straight. Could you predict which one would win a race without knowing if the race track had lots of corners? No. The problem with defining the speed of the computer is much more complex even than this; you must realize that just quoting the CPU clock speed is almost useless as a measure of speed. There is perhaps one exception to this – modern PCs with faster CPUs tend to be fitted with faster subsystems so may be faster almost by default.

The speed of the processor

If a PC has a Pentium 600 MHz processor fitted it means that the chip is *clocked* or pulsed 600 million times a second. On almost each one of these clock cycles, a low-level or machine instruction is completed. A typical instruction may be 'store number in memory' or 'add one number'. This means the number of machine level instructions performed per second is *roughly* 600 million or 600 MIPS (*Millions of Instructions Per Second*). Something complicated like putting a single character on the screen takes more than one instruction, a task like moving a paragraph in a word processor takes hundreds of machine instructions. Clearly the faster the CPU executes these instructions the better but there is a problem, the instructions are stored in memory so if the CPU needs them in a hurry, the memory system must be able to supply them at speed. The problem is, it can't! To be affordable, the RAM fitted to most machines is far too slow to supply instructions to the CPU. The solution is to copy a block of instructions to a 'cache' and the CPU looks in the cache for them. This cache is faster than the RAM and can (nearly) keep up with the CPU. Defining processor speed in MIPS is only a very crude measure of speed.

MIPS is an acronym for Million 3 of Instructions Per Second. A old measure of a computer's speed and power, MIPS measures roughly the number of machine instructions that a computer can execute in 1 second. However, different instructions require more or less time than others, and there is no standard method for measuring MIPS. In addition, MIPS refers only to the CPU speed, whereas real applications are generally limited by other factors, such as I/O speed. A machine with a high MIPS rating, therefore, might not run a particular application any faster than a machine with a low MIPS rating. For all these reasons, MIPS ratings are not used often any more. In fact, some people jokingly claim that MIPS really stands for Meaningless Indicator of Performance.

Some processors have a Complex Instruction Set (CISC) and some have a Reduced Instruction Set (RISC). You could compare the speed of two 100 MHz processors, one a RISC chip and the other a CISC chip. The problem is that such a comparison of the Millions of Instructions Per Second (MIPS) is completely meaningless unless you happen to want to sell computers to a gullible public and are happy telling straight lies! The reason is that a single instruction in a RISC processor may achieve more than a single instruction in CISC processor so you find that a 30 MHz RISC machine executes a whole program faster than a 100 MHz CISC machine. The lesson is, don't compare clock speeds unless the processor has more or less the same design, i.e. a P500 to a P600.

The speed of the internal buses

The computer uses *buses* to communicate between devices. These are simply collections of wires that transmit the pattern of 1s and 0s that represent the data and instructions. These buses operate on a clocked system, i.e. many times a second a signal is generated in the chipset that sets off one operation at a time. The buses in modern PCs all operate slower than the CPU, even the latest machines use 'only' 100 MHz or 100 million times a second. The result is that only a certain amount of data can be transmitted per second no matter how fast the CPU. This data may be on its way to the disk drive or the video system and hence some tasks are limited by the bus speed.

The speed of the disk drive system

Discs spin at a fixed speed so the maximum rate at which data can be delivered to or from a disk is partly the result of this speed. If you fit a faster CPU, the rate at which the data comes from a disk drive is not affected.

The speed of the video system

To view the result of running a program, the video system must display a large collection of dots called *pixels*. A screen with a resolution of 1024 by 768 is showing over three-quarters of a million pixels, each one must be handled by the video system. If you increase the screen resolution to 1280 by 1024 you will now have over 1.3 million pixels or 66% more so it must take more time to compute the colour of each one. The video systems in modern machines have their own dedicated set of chips to do this but some video systems are faster than others, this is not affected by the speed of the CPU.

The speed set in the power save system

If you have ever worked with a laptop computer you will have noticed that to save battery life the disk slows down after a short period of inactivity. If you want your machine to do a task, the disk must then spin up to speed before it starts. This will give the impression that the machine is quite slow, regardless of the speed of the CPU.

Summary

The only effective measure of speed is to run tasks that you require of the computer and to compare one machine with another. Some performance charts in computer journals demonstrate this technique. They would typically run these tasks:

- A large spreadsheet that requires loading and recalculation.
- Transformation of a large graphics image.
- Running a standard database enquiry on a large database.

The results are then displayed as a table. It is often the case that one machine will outperform the others in one task but not others.

Beware of adverts!

Other terms found in describing speed

- FLOPS = *Floating-Point Operations Per Second*, a common benchmark measurement for rating the speed of microprocessors. As we have seen, the CPU speed alone does not tell you everything about the performance of a whole computer.
- MFLOPS = Mega FLOPS or Million FLOPS, GFLOPS = Giga FLOPS or 1000 Million Flops, (1 000 000 000), TFLOPS = Tera FLOPS or Million Million Flops (1 000 000 000 000). Floating-point numbers are those with decimal fractions. Integers whole numbers only.

Floating-point operations include any operations that involve fractional numbers. Such operations, which take much longer to compute than integer operations, occur often in some applications. Most modern microprocessors include a *Floating-Point Unit* (FPU), which is a specialized part of the microprocessor responsible for executing floating-point operations. The FLOPS measurement, therefore, actually measures the speed of the FPU. One of the most common benchmark tests used to measure FLOPS is called Linpack. Many experts feel that FLOPS is not a relevant measurement because it fails to take into account factors such as the condition under which the microprocessor is running (e.g. heavy or light loads) and which exact operations are included as floating-point operations. For this reason, a consortium of vendors created the Standard Performance Evaluation Corporation (SPEC), which provides more meaningful benchmark values. Their Web URL is www.specbench.org/contents.html but many of the ideas shown are very technical and are not part of this unit.

The Intel Corporation keep a list of benchmarking websites on their website at www.intel.com/procs/perf/resources/benchmark.htm and a more independent site is at cpusite.examedia.nl/sections/benchmarks.html

Chips are getting ever quicker. Figure 1.12.2 is a graph of Millions of Instructions Per Second (MIPS) against year of first introduction. Remember, MIPS is a very crude measure of chip performance as

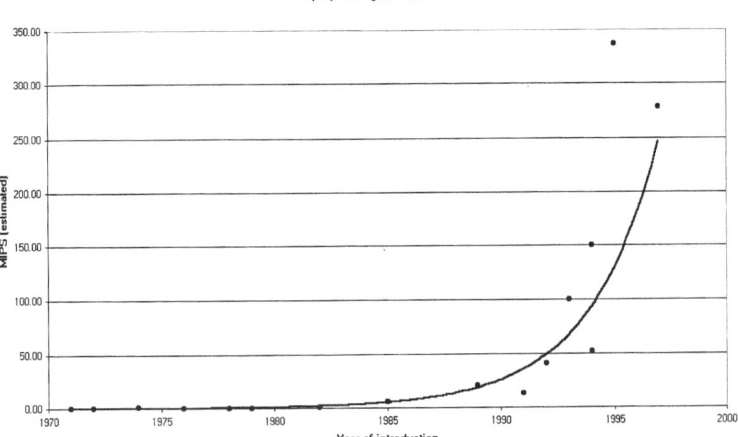

Figure 1.12.2 *MIPS against year of introduction*

individual instructions in modern chips do as much as several instructions in old chips. This really means the speed increase in real life is better than that shown on the graph.

1.13 User requirements

When considering the specification of PCs and associated equipment, there is more to consider than the machine itself. How do you know if you need the wonderful model on sale for £2000 or the lesser model selling for £500? A very large reason for the ever increasing power of computers being purchased is caused by 'upgradeitus'. Some people will buy the latest computer/software simply because it is available. Operating systems like Windows are very hungry for disk space and RAM and work very slowly unless run in a very powerful machine. People often lose sight of the fact that Windows and many Windows applications offer features most do not even realize are present let alone use or need. In a competitive commercial environment, a sound knowledge of why computers and software are specified is very important. There is no real point in upgrading a system just because it becomes available. As an example, if an application in one office is running perfectly well using an old 80286 PC running MSDOS and a dot matrix printer, why change it? What *need* is there to change. Simply upgrading the computer is very easy as is upgrading the software but successfully running and paying for the change in work practice and staff training is often very expensive and can be difficult.

Cost of ownership

In order to own and run computers in a business for a period of time, the following items of value must be considered:

- Hardware
- Software licences
- Staff training
- Installation and maintenance
- Business specific data and documents
- Staff experience and knowledge

Which of these is higher? After working for some time, much data is generated in the normal course of the business and much knowledge and experience of the computer systems is built up in the staff. After a very short time, this data and staff knowledge is much more valuable than the costs of the computers. Although the ongoing cost of IT support and maintenance is high, the value of the staff knowledge is probably greater. The cost of the hardware is often the lowest of these and its value falls to zero in a very short time.

It is not sensible to upgrade unless there is a clear business need.

Over the last few years, companies like Microsoft, Lotus, Corel, etc. have put more and more features into their software. This has resulted in the perceived 'need' to upgrade the machines and staff training, often without any real thought. It is interesting to note that the 'cost of ownership' issue has become very prominent in recent times and that these software companies have started to change their policies, making their software easier to use rather than having more features that require ever more powerful machines.

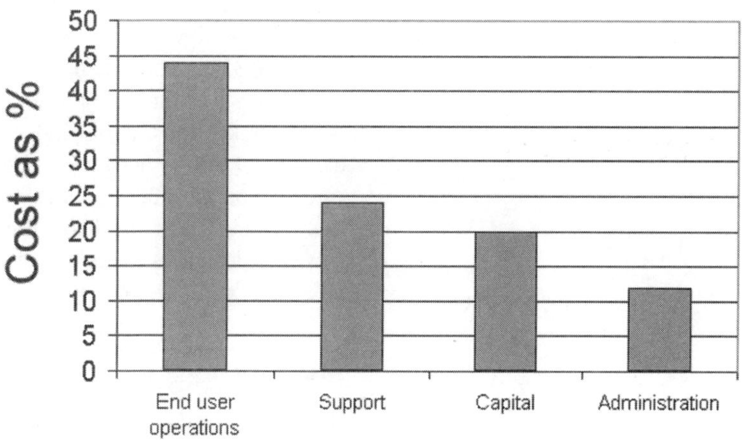

Figure 1.13.1 *An analysis of the cost of ownership*

The graph in Figure 1.13.1 shows typical proportions of the cost of ownership found in many companies. The cost of the machines themselves is just a fifth of the total. Simply upgrading machines, then the software often causes grief for no real benefit to the organization because the extra training required and the cost of data conversion outweigh any benefits of newer machines. It makes sense to 'over-specify' for a new installation so the machines will perform well for a reasonable period but it does not always make sense to upgrade when new hardware or software becomes available.

General guidelines

Microprocessor

Do not get overawed by CPU clock speeds. In practice, you are very unlikely to see the difference between a 500 and a 600 MHz machine –

600 is only 600/500 = 1.2 or 20% faster and the overall speed of a machine is a result of much more than the CPU speed. A 1.1 GHz machine has only a 10% faster clock speed than a 1 GHz machine, an even smaller difference. Machines fitted with faster CPUs are generally fitted with faster subsystems at the same time so naïve users may be fooled into thinking it is all due to the heavily advertised processor 'inside'.

RAM

If running Microsoft Windows as a desktop operating system, performance improves up to about 128 Mbytes of RAM. Fitting above this is not likely to show a marked improvement unless the applications to be run all need simultaneous open windows or are themselves very demanding on memory. Running a PC as a server is very different but is not in the scope of this part of the book. You will probably not see much difference between the latest RAM types unless you enjoy running benchmark software or timing long tasks with a stopwatch.

Video

The amount of RAM fitted to the video card depends on what you need the machine for. Running standard office applications does not require animated 3D so you calculate the RAM required from the resolution you intend to set. Many people do not like the highest resolution set for office applications, they cannot see the screen fonts, so if the target is the typical 800 × 600 you will see no benefit from an 8 Mbyte video card. If you plan 3D applications and high-speed animated games, the more video RAM the better but you will only see the benefit if the software designers make use of the hardware. More memory will have no effect on older software.

Monitor

But a good one! For the overall experience of using a PC, it is better to have a good stable image with crisp resolution and well-saturated colours than something that is a few percent faster. Spend the money you save by not specifying the 'latest, fastest processor' on the monitor. Users will thank you for it. If you run a price comparison on machines with the latest CPU you will see the price rise dramatically towards the faster end of the market. If one machine is 50% more expensive but only 20% faster, spend the difference on the monitor.

Disc drive

A while ago it was thought you could not buy a disk that was too large! (also see Question 1.7.1 on page 29). This was mainly due to the ever increasing size of the software and data files. Now that MP3, graphics and video are becoming more important, it looks like the demand for disk space will now be caused more by your data than the software. At one extreme, if you are only using the machine for typing plain text and you type at a good 'office' speed of 45 words a minute all day and all night, 7 days a week without a break for 40 years, apart from being tired and hungry, you will still only generate fewer than 5 Gbytes of data! At the other extreme, you are likely to fill a 60 Gbyte drive in a few months if you store MP3, graphics and video files. One hour of full broadcast quality video can be stored on a 10 Gbyte drive. The best option is to go for size and only buy the more expensive fast drives if the applications really need it.

Floppy disk drive

Almost every PC has one, it is hardly ever used but as soon as you specify a machine without a floppy drive, someone will arrive with an important file on a floppy.

CD-ROM

Almost all PCs are fitted with a CD-ROM or DVD drive. CD-R is now cheap and is an excellent system for backups of key data. Unless the budget is very tight, specify a CD-RW compatible drive wherever possible and use it for CD-R writing. DVD drives are gaining acceptance and offer much larger capacity but most software is still distributed on CD. Speed is only an issue if you will use the drive as a continuous source of data; software installation speed is not seriously limited by CD-ROM drive speed. Do not get carried away with a '×40' drive, for most uses, a '×20' is fine; buy quality rather than speed.

Sound

Specify the cheapest possible sound if the system is for office use. Most users turn it off after a while, especially if the office is open plan. If you need good quality sound to support games or to edit music. etc., it is better to output sound to a sound system than to spend on expensive PC speakers. In this case, buy a high-quality sound card and leave the speakers in the shop.

Modem

Modems will soon be a thing of the past, at least that will be true if the promised ADSL connections become available for home use. Most offices use a direct LAN connection. Until this happens, 56K modems are adequate. Buy quality and avoid the 'plain wrapper' kind.

A modem is a 'MOdulator-DEModulator'. In English to *modulate* means to change (like modify). The old telephone system (known to some as POTS, *Plain Old Telephone System!*) could carry only analogue sound signals. It was not possible to put a digital signal through such a system. Modern digital telephone systems are very different but modems were designed for the POTS. A modem modulated a sound with digital information and demodulated this sound for received signals. The speed of a modem is given in bits/second, most are now 56 kbits/sec. As each byte is encoded in either 9 or 10 bits, this means a 56K modem will transmit about 5.6 kbytes of data per second in an ideal world. Real-world rates are nearly always slower and having CPUs that are claimed to 'speed up the Internet' will make no difference at all!

Printer

For home or SOHO (*Small Office Home Office*) use, inkjets are fine; they are expensive to run if your output is high and are not a reliable as laser printers. For office use, the only real choice is a laser printer, they are fast, quiet and reasonably cheap to run. Even for small offices, a printer with a large paper capacity will be appreciated by the users.

How to specify and buy a computer

First, clearly specify why you need a computer, what do you want to do with it and who needs to be able to share your data. Next, decide on your budget.

The next step is to decide on what software you will need to satisfy your business needs and only then to specify what hardware is required to run that software. It is a great mistake to think 'I will need a Pentium 1000' just because they are available and heavily advertised.

Due to the ever increasing efficiency of hardware production and changes in Far East economies, the actual costs of hardware are getting lower and lower. This means that the 'lowest' specification of some computer components now on sale is more than adequate for most people. For example, many machines now come with a disk drive with a 4 Gb capacity as standard. If you only need a word processor this will meet your needs for a very long time. Some people seem to think that if they specify a 10 Gb drive the machine will be 'better' in some respect. This is not true. Many machines are fast enough for normal business activities and more speed is simply not required. Many people find that to run Windows 98 and Word 97 on a Pentium 266 with 32 Mb RAM fitted is quite adequate, why specify any more. In any case, what would you mean by 'more speed' in respect of a word processor? Always assuming that a Pentium 450 is somehow 'faster', will it enable you to type faster?

Consider these typical applications running:

- Word processing
- Spreadsheets
- Databases
- Graphic arts
- Technical design

Now consider these things that would appear on a list of components when specifying a computer:

- Disk speed
- Disk capacity
- Video resolution
- Video RAM size
- Monitor size
- Monitor resolution
- Monitor slot pitch
- Monitor refresh rate
- Main RAM size
- Processor type
- Processor clock speed
- Internal bus speed
- Internal bus type
- Motherboard features, buses, expansion slots, etc.

Now write down what is required (allowing for future expansion) rather than what you might 'like' to have. You will find that if you focus more on quality than on performance, the benefits will be higher. Clearly you need a machine that has sufficient performance but you should next consider:

- Cost/budget
- Performance
- Expandability
- Ergonomics, i.e. how well the components 'fit' with the people who will use them
- Needs of specific or specialist software, e.g. Autocad

Some people are specifying notebook computers in place of desktop machines, but you should consider that notebooks:

- cost at least 50% more for the same 'power', often twice as much;
- sometimes will not run some specialist software;
- are not as reliable as desktop machines, they are easy to damage;
- are not as expandable or configurable as desktops;
- are very portable;
- have an LCD screen (that many people prefer);
- go out of date quicker because newer versions of software make ever more demands on the hardware.

Now consider the questions shown in the sample assignment below and discuss your thoughts with your lecturer and fellow students. Keep your mind focused on what is *needed* not on what is desirable or what you may see advertised as 'The Computer Deal of the Century!'

Exercise 1.13.1

Sample assignment tasks

You are asked to specify computers for the six users below. For each of the users listed, choose a suitable machine and justify your choice. You should give a detailed explanation of choices in terms of cost, capabilities, performance and upgrade path.

The simplest way is to list the items fitted or specified in your chosen machine and explain the significance of each item and how it relates to the users' requirements. Write down the machine specification as a list of components in the same way you would present it to a supplier.

User 1

This company supplies artwork, graphics, etc. to the advertising industry, especially the glossy magazine trade. Their main expertise is in photo retouching using very high-resolution images. They only need machines for five graphic artists, the management function in the company is already computerized.

User 2

A small college runs 200 standalone PCs. A network company has offered a sponsorship deal and supplied a full network with cabling and servers to support the college provided that the college upgrades the users' machines. The current 200 machines are to be scrapped. The plan is to run Windows, MS Office and similar software on each user machine but with the software stored on the servers; they have an extremely tight budget where every penny counts. You must achieve the cheapest possible machine that will run the software.

User 3

The PA to the finance director of a large shipping company requires a machine to do word processing and email. All the other computerized functions in the company are already running elsewhere.

User 4

A very experienced design engineer working on petrochemical plant designs has been on an Autocad course. The projects she works on involve 3 D drawings of very complex pipework, etc. During the course of the next year, she will employ two assistants to computerize the existing paper drawings and to use Autocad themselves, so she needs three new networked PCs to run Autocad. The application requires that large amounts of data are stored and that the hidden line removal and other performance critical functions in Autocad are used to full effect.

User 5

A local private genealogy society has computer links to help in their research, they use an old PC with a 56 kb/s modem. To reduce costs and speed up enquiries, they have decided to start a large database of family genealogy details. The eventual size of the database may be 200 Gbytes with requirements to have at least one level of backup. Funds are very tight but users will require a good service. To limit the expenditure, only one member will use the machine at a time, linked via a fixed modem on a pre-arranged time slot.

User 6

A financial accountant uses spreadsheets to model the financial behaviour of companies. The spreadsheets are very large and she is hoping to make them even larger but is impatient with the recalculation time obtained with her current computer.

1.14 Operating systems

In Unit 1 of the HNC Computing, there is a requirement to use operating systems. Although Windows is in widespread use, there are many other varieties of OS in common use so it is not considered appropriate to provide instructions for all these types here. Practical tasks should be set locally.

An operating system has a number of functions:

- To provide an interface with the user.
- To provide a range of services that are used by application software such as disk management, printer control, time/date functions, etc.
- To provide a development environment, i.e. compilers and run-time systems, etc.

It is usual in operating systems (OS) to consider a layered architecture in a similar manner to layering in networks (see page 383).

The layers in a typical OS are:

layer 4 Applications
layer 3 Kernel
layer 2 Drivers
layer 1 Hardware

Layer 1 is how the operating system communicates with the hardware rather than the hardware itself. In PCs, this is generally the BIOS, the Basic Input Output System (see page 17).

Layer 2, drivers, refers to pieces of software that 'talk' to specific device types such as disk drives. For example, in a PC, an ATAPI CD-ROM needs a device driver loaded because the operating system at layers 3 and 4 does not 'know about' CD and how the data is organized in detail. The device driver provides this service.

Layer 3, the kernel, organizes the way that processes are controlled, i.e. if an application requests service from a printer, other application requests must not interfere.

Layer 4, applications, are the programs the user wishes to run in the machine. The OS must load them into memory and start them running.

Various operating systems have a layered architecture different in detail from the one described here. No matter, the idea is that application software is supported or supplied with services by the OS. This means that an application programmer need not know how to control a printer or a disk drive, all that is needed is to ask the OS for these services. In the case of Microsoft Windows, this is done by the Windows API or *Application Programme Interface*. Application software calls for service from the Win API, the actual code for this is stored in .DLL files or *Dynamic Link Libraries*.

User interface

In the past, what the user saw was a screen prompt (or even a printer prompt!) like C:\>. This 'prompted' the user to type a command such as DIR to gain a service. (DIR requests a listing of the files on the current disk drive.) This style of user interface is called a CLI or Command Line Interpreter because the text typed at the prompt (the command line) is interpreted by the CLI and either a request made to the kernel for service or an error message is issued. In Microsoft's DOS, the CLI is called COMMAND.COM. In the Unix world there are many different command line interpreters, they are called 'shells' but do essentially the same thing, they provide a command line user interface.

More modern PC operating systems use a *Graphical User Interface* or GUI. This is what you see when you use Windows but it is *only* an interface, what underlies Windows 95 or 98 is mostly DOS. Windows NT and 2000 are very different although they look similar, the underlying kernel is not DOS but the GUI 'talks' to the kernel in a related fashion. If you run Linux on a PC, either you use a shell (the CLI) or a GUI that has a similar 'look and feel' to Microsoft Windows. There are several on the market.

Kinds of OS

Quite independent of the user interface, the OS must provide for ideas such as multi-tasking and provision for multiple users.

Multi-tasking is not quite what is seems. To the user, the machine is running multiple tasks all at once, so for instance, a download from the Internet is running at the same time as the user types into a word processor. Of course the PC only has a single CPU which can only do one thing at a time. The solution is to switch between tasks so quickly that the user is not aware of the switching. This is achieved using a number of system software techniques. (Details can be found elsewhere, especially Unit 19 of the HNC Computing.)

Multi-user operating systems must provide additional services to allow the identification of users; i.e. they must 'login'. The OS must also provide security so that malicious or careless users cannot affect the work of others.

If more than one task or more than one user needs service from the OS, it must provide memory management. This means that the physical RAM must be organized so that users and applications are not able to infringe other areas. When using Windows, you may have seen the error message 'This program has performed an illegal operation'. A common cause of this is an application that attempts to access an address in memory that belongs to a different application or process. Windows cannot resolve the problem so shuts down the errant process.

1.15 Network administration

In Unit 1 of the HNC Computing, there is a requirement to perform network administratiion. There are many network operating systems on the market and installed in colleges and universities so it is not considered appropriate to provide instructions for all these types here. Practical tasks should be set locally.

Network operating system

A *Network Operating System* (NOS) controls the network. This control entails many different tasks at different layers in the layered architecture. For instance, a major function of an NOS is to provide security but still allow easy access for legitimate users. An NOS such as

Windows NT 4 provides the network administrator with a range of tools to manage such tasks. Examples are:

- The *DHCP administrator* manages the Dynamic Host Control Protocol, a protocol that manages the DCHP servers on the network. DHCP is a TCP/IP protocol that allows client PCs TCP/IP settings to be set up remotely instead of having an IT support technician visit each machine individually.
- *RAS administrator*, this is used to manage remote users.
- The *Server manager* is used to administer the properties of other servers on the network.
- *User profile editor*, this tool defines user profiles. A profile is a collection of settings that apply to user accounts, these include the running of a script at login time.
- *User manager*, as the name suggests, manages the user properties of those allowed to use the network.
- *WINS administrator*, WINS, the Windows Internet Name Service, translates TCP/IP network addresses into human readable names and vice versa. This software tool is used to administer WINS.

You should have at least some experience of using these or similar network administration tools.

1.16 User support and training

A help desk is just that, a service to provide help to users. It should not be seen as the place just to report faults. When a user reports a problem to the help desk, it may be for one of the following reasons:

- Their hardware has a fault.
- Their software has a fault or is not correctly set up.
- They may be trying to do something that is not possible for a variety of reasons.
- They may not know how to do something, i.e. they have a training need.

Resolution of the first two points should be covered by a *Service Level Agreement* (SLA). This is a written agreement to provide service within a given time and to agreed standards. When an effective SLA is in place, the performance of the staff providing the service is monitored to ensure the service level is achieved.

A service level agreement must be agreed, it is not something that can be decided on by those who need the service nor by those who provide it. Users will naturally ask for faults to be fixed in a very short time, the IT support staff will ask that this time be extended to make their life easier and the running costs of the department lower. The actual average time to fix faults will be the result of an analysis of the buisiness needs of the organization and the resulting costs of providing the service compared with the losses that may be incurred due to faults.

Example 1.16.1

If a local bank relies heavily on their network to support the business, computers or systems out of action for say 10 minutes may be sustainable but machines out of action for most of the day would not, the loss of business and of credibility of their customers would be too high.

Now consider the cost of having someone on hand during business hours to fix all problems. The cost of having an IT specialist ready on site with 'nothing to do' if there are no faults is far too high to be realistic. In this case, having spare computing capacity on hand is much cheaper; if a PC develops a fault, spare machines are brought into action. Another possibility is to have dual purpose staff who have sufficient knowledge to fix common problems.

If the fault lies not in a local machine but in a remote computing centre then it is not unrealistic to have IT staff on hand there 24 hours a day. The SLA for this bank would have to specify the kinds of fault and their likely resolution and the 'fixing' time that is acceptable for each kind. Some faults would have to be fixed by staff 'on call' so time will have to be allocated for them to get to the site.

Example 1.16.2

A large business on one site will most likely have an on-site IT department to provide service. Staff will be employed that have sufficient knowledge and training to fix most problems. In this case, the SLA will specify the average time to fix problems but must take into account the workload of the IT staff. As most problems are not very predictable, the number of faults at any one moment will vary. Say there was, on average, 35 calls to the help desk each week requiring work on the hardware and that each job took about an hour. This would amount to the workload of one member of staff (assuming a 35 hour week). The practical result of this would be a delay of a day or more to service a job. Problems will occur at an uneven rate so that at one point there may be say six jobs waiting. If this translates to 6 hours work, then a fault reported at mid-day will not be fixed until the next day. A solution is to employ more IT staff but this is expensive. A calculation must be made that takes into account the loss caused by faults and the cost of maintaining a certain level of service. A typical set of values would be:

- 10% of problems fixed within 10 minutes
- 80% of problems fixed within 4 hours
- 10% of problems fixed within 1 week

The 'quick' problems are those such as loose power leads, lost configuration files, etc., the slow faults would be those that require the purchase of spare parts.

Each business is different so the SLA must be worked out and agreed to suit the needs of each business.

Fault log

The fault log should be seen as a tool to measure performance in relation to the SLA. In an ideal world, this log should be available on the company intranet so that users can see the progress of 'their' fault (providing the fault does not stop them seeing the intranet!). Sadly it is often the case that such logs are kept secret in the fear that they would be used to castigate the IT support staff. In a well-run business, the task of IT support adds to the overall business so this fear is groundless. The fault log is a very valuable source of information that can be used to support the business. Many items reported to help desks are not real 'faults', they are problems caused by inadequate training on the part of the reporting person. The appropriate response to this is to provide training targeted at these people, the aim being to improve the running of the business. Help desk staff must be aware of this and see these items as a valuable source of information and not see the other staff concerned in any other way.

The fault log can also be used to analyse the hardware and software in use to determine if there are recurrent faults caused by inadequate quality or specification. For example, if a certain type of printer keeps failing, it may be that the work required for the printer is too high, i.e. the duty cycle is more than the printer can cope with. Specifying different printers would then be better than replacing the current type.

Provision of training

Too many businesses are so busy that staff feel they do not have time to train adequately. Such 'training' that occurs is of the 'stand by Nellie' variety, i.e. work with someone else and watch what they do. There is a famous quote, 'If you think education is expensive, try ignorance' (attributed to Derek Bok, one time President of Harvard University). In this sense, training and education are the same because in order to use IT installations to the maximum benefit, users must be trained effectively.

The help desk should provide information to help the analysis of staff training needs and to monitor if that training has had the desired effect.

2 Systems analysis

Summary

The aim of this chapter is to give students the ability to compare the different lifecycle models. It provides a foundation of systems analysis and design by covering requirements analysis techniques for a variety of applications used within the computing industry. The unit also covers the data and functional modelling which students can be expected to use. It also provides an opportunity for students to implement a data model using a proprietary database.

Introduction

The development of modern software systems requires a through understanding of systems analysis and design methods to ensure the end product is produced efficiently on time and within budget. The concept of requirements analysis skills for both commercial and technical applications needs to be professionally implemented to ensure the product specification meets the needs of the customer. Systems analysis provides an underlying structure for developing the key skills required within the field of software engineering.

In this chapter we will be concentrating on why different software development techniques are required in the analysis/design process.

You will learn how to apply software analysis techniques for a given 'real-world' specification based on an appropriate lifecycle model.

You will learn about different approaches to analysis and make comparisons about different models that are used within the systems analysis environment today.

You will learn about the techniques involved in 'fact finding' for a systems investigation and how to record/present follow-up documentation for a prospective customer.

In order to implement the analysis model the you will learn about basic data modelling techniques, including functional modelling development and graphical representations (for example, entity-relationship diagrams) and to implement such designs into simple rational database systems.

The importance of good quality documentation is emphasized within the chapter. It looks at different ways of presenting information using text and graphical applications. The use of a commercial CASE tool application is used to demonstrate and test graphical models.

This chapter is designed to integrate analysis techniques with practical applications in order for you to use information technology to document, analyse, design and implement systems being investigated.

2.1 Introduction to the systems analysis models

It has often been a problem for software developers to produce a quality product that fully satisfies the needs of the customer. Far too often the software product is delivered late and over budget. In order to improve the production of software systems several analysis and design techniques have been developed. These range from simple graphical techniques through to formal mathematical structures.

Several problems have been associated with the development of software systems, these include:

- Complexity
- Size
- Cost
- Deadlines
- Project management
- Environment issues

Software is classified as an 'invisible medium', you do not see what you are getting until very late in the development process. This is why it is important to apply a through-analysis strategy in order to ensure that you are developing a quality product that meets its specified aims.

Traditional lifecycle

The traditional lifecycle, or the waterfall method as it is sometimes called, represents the steps a project follows from its conception through to its termination. It starts with the customers' requirements followed by several activities each resulting in a set of documents.

Figure 2.1.1 shows a typical lifecycle layout.

The initial stages, requirements analysis and specification form the overall analysis phases and specify 'what' the system is to do. Design then follows where a solution to the problem is formulated, followed by the coding and maintenance stages. Verification and validation form the quality assurance role and act over the whole lifecycle.

The requirements analysis activity receives the 'user requirements' document as input and its main aim is to analyse its contents to ensure it is correctly structured and understood by all parties. It extracts from the customer the requirements that are needed for the software system to be developed. The output of this activity is to produce a precise document, the negotiated statement of requirements, which the system can then be designed on.

Specification then follows by taking the negotiated statement of requirements as input and develops a model as to what the system is to

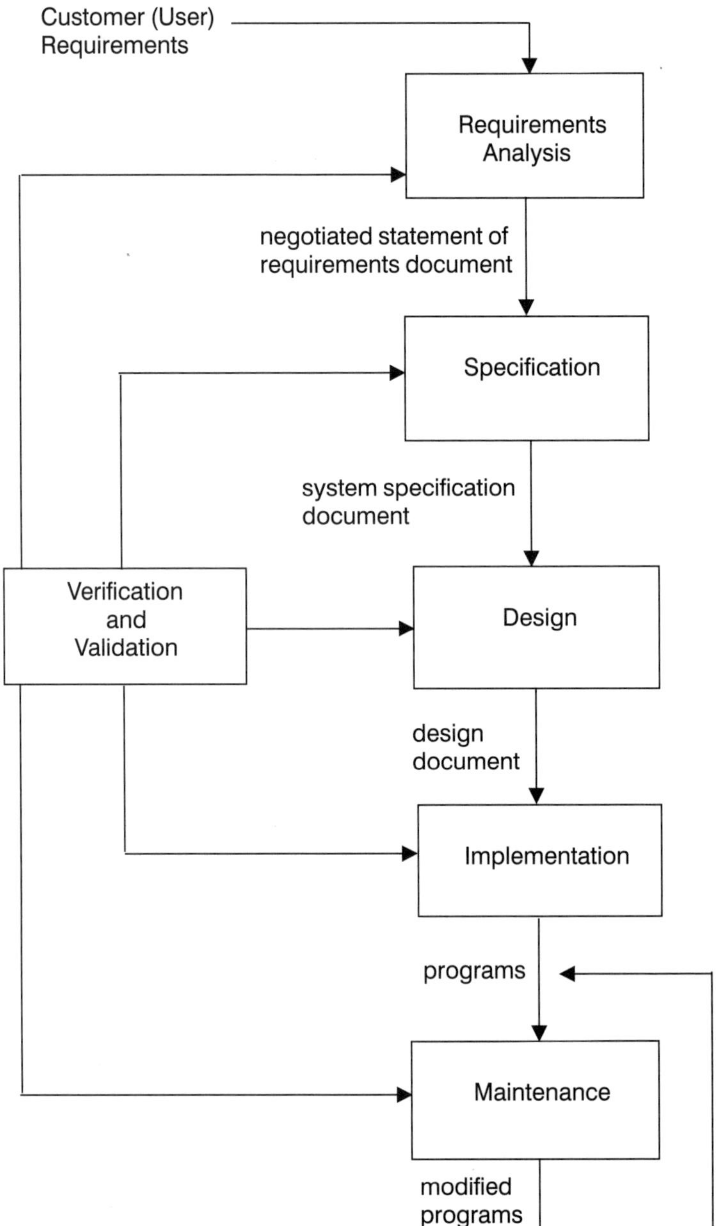

Figure 2.1.1 *Traditional lifecycle model*

do. This activity is still analysing the problem and is not concerned with providing a solution. There will still be heavy interaction with the customer during this stage to ensure the output documentation, the system specification, is accurate.

Next comes the design activity that takes the system specification as its input document and sets about providing a solution to the problem. This stage is concerned with how the system is going to operate and will use structure or class diagrams that specify components within a given programming environment. Some developers may also use a Program Design Language (PDL) with provides the code lines that can be implemented into a high-level programming language. The output of this activity is the design documentation that provides a basis for implementation.

The implementation activity takes the design documentation and codes it into a designated programming language. The output of this activity are the programs that execute the required system.

The final activity is maintenance that provides support for the developed programs. Many will contain 'bugs' that need to be rectified in order for the system to work correctly and meet the full requirements of the end user. Maintenance also provides the opportunity to upgrade software systems as the need arises. Many companies will offer software maintenance contracts which provide users with the opportunity to upgrade systems when new updates become available. The output documentation of this activity will be modified programs.

Verification and Validation provide the quality assurance activity that acts over the whole lifecycle of the project and ensures the end product reaches an acceptable level of quality. Validation ensures that the output from each activity meets the user requirements. Verification ensures the project is being built in the correct way and the output of each activity is a correct conversion as an input to the next stage.

The above description shows why the traditional lifecycle is sometimes called the 'waterfall model', this is because the output of one activity 'flows' directly into the next activity, like a waterfall.

Question 2.1.1

With reference to the traditional lifecycle model:

(1) What are the main activities associated with the traditional lifecycle?
(2) What documents result from each activity?
(3) What is the role of the Verification and Validation activity?
(4) Why is it sometimes called a waterfall model?

Prototyping

We know from the world of engineering that a manufacturer will develop a prototype model before mass producing the final product. So why not apply this concept to the development of a software product? This is what the pioneers of prototyping have set out to achieve by attempting to demonstrate how a system or a component of a computer-based information system will function in its environment.

Users find such demonstrations very helpful in visualizing what proposed systems will do for them. They often find it difficult to accurately access what they are getting from a system by reading large requirements specifications.

Prototyping can result in a set of requirements that are better understood by the user and is more likely to be complete and accurate. Its advantages are that it is dynamic, flexible and provides a collaborative methodology that both aid the end user of the product and the development team.

However, if prototyping is good why is it not used by more developers? Two main reasons are shown below:

(1) Lack of suitable prototyping tools.
(2) Lack of means of managing the prototyping process.

Some benefits of developing a prototype

- Misunderstandings between software developers and users may be identified as the system functions are demonstrated.
- Missing user services may be detected.
- Difficult to use or confusing user services may be identified and refined.

- Software development staff may find incomplete and/or inconsistent requirements as the prototype is developed.
- A working, albeit limited, system is available quickly to demonstrate the feasibility and usefulness of the application to management.
- The prototype serves as a basis for writing the specification for a production quality system.

Ince and Hekmatpour (1987) stated other uses:

- It can be used for training users before the production-quality system has been delivered.
- It can be used during system testing. The same tests can be applied to the prototype and the final system and results compared.

Boehm (1984) specified four stages in the prototype development:

- Establish prototype objectives.
- Select functions for prototype inclusion and make decisions on what non-functional functions must be prototyped.
- Develop the prototype.
- Evaluate the prototype system.

The major technical problems associated with prototyping revolve around the need for rapid software development. However, non-technical problems have meant that 'rapid prototyping' is still not widely used, except in data processing system development. Some of these management problems are:

- Planning, costing and estimating a prototyping project is outside the experience of most project managers.
- Procedures for configuration management are unsuitable for controlling rapid change inherent in prototyping.
- Management pressures to reach swift conclusions may result in inappropriate requirements.

Types of prototyping models

Exploratory programming

This method is based on producing an initial basic model that is shown to the customer for any comments, then refining the model until it reaches an acceptable system. This model may have an advantage for developers who have previously developed a similar system from which the initial model can be produced. Figure 2.1.2 shows the layout for the exploratory programming cycle.

The system uses an iterative process to refine the initial model. The success of this approach lies in how rapidly the developer can process these iterations in order to advance to model towards its end goal.

Exploratory programming tends to result in a system that is not well defined. There will be a lot of 'change' going on within the software that can lead to errors being produced. This often results in problems with maintenance that can be costly and time consuming especially for large-scale systems. Verification is also a problem as it

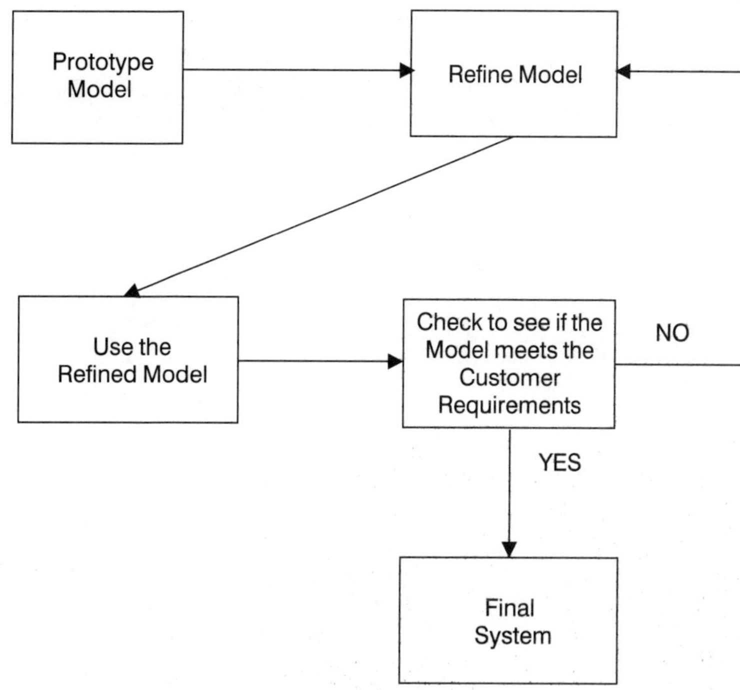

Figure 2.1.2 *Exploratory programming*

checks the project against its original specification which is not clearly defined.

Students will often start with this approach without realizing it. Given an assignment a student may start with a basic model and refine it by adding additional components until they have satisfied the requirements. More often than not this is achieved by accident and a tested analysis and design has not been adopted.

Throwaway prototyping

This method starts with an initial model, a prototype, which is checked with the customer to ascertain is correctness then developers start to build the final product from the beginning. The prototype is 'thrown away'. It is used as an aid to understanding and does not form part of the final product. Because it is only an experimental system all non-functional requirements can be ignored.

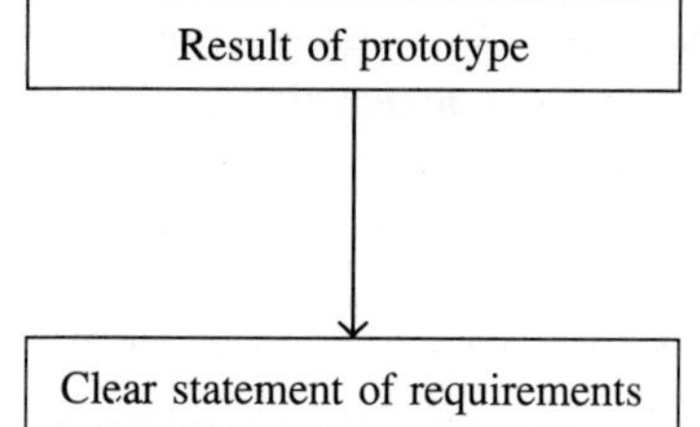

The initial model or prototype may also have some of the functional requirements missing. The use of a front end graphical user interface can be ignored and systems that handle error recovery do not need to be included at this stage.

Figure 2.1.3 shows a typical layout for a 'throwaway' prototype system. The prototype is developed from an outline specification and presented to the customer to ensure they are satisfied with its functional objectives.

The diagram starts with the prototype that is evaluated to ascertain a full system specification. Once this has been achieved the prototype is thrown away and work starts on the full version.

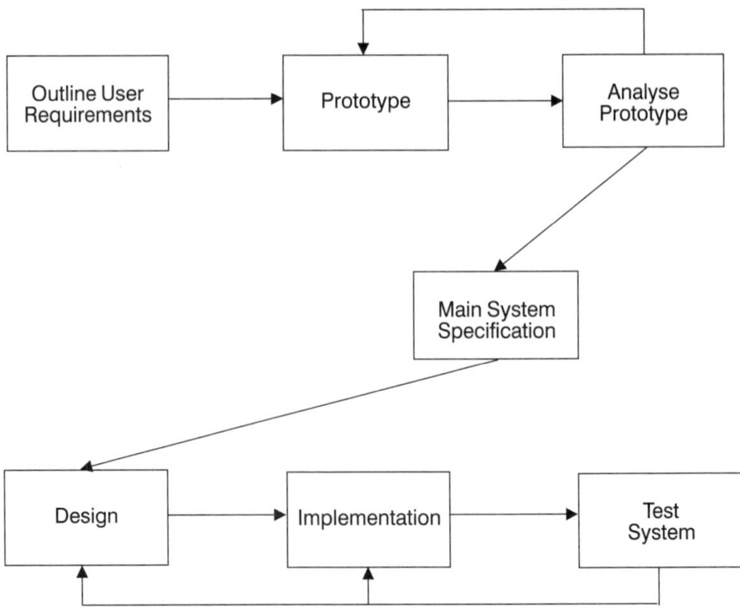

Figure 2.1.3 *Throw-away prototyping*

There are several problems with this method:

(1) Often many important functions are left out to aid the speed of the development prototype.
(2) We have seen with the traditional lifecycle that the negotiated statement of requirements can form the basis of a contract between the customer and developer. This model is incomplete at the prototype stage and therefore cannot be an adequate basis for such a contract.
(3) It does not consider non-functional requirements.
(4) The user has a restricted use of the prototype model which can lead to a false impression as to how the system will function.

Having stated these problems this method does have its advantages, for example concept of a prototype gives the customer an early view of the product. As systems grow even more complex there becomes a problem in developing a full specification from scratch. It is expected that the concepts of prototyping will grow even though they introduce problems of their own.

Reverse engineering

This is not strictly a prototype method, but often comes under that heading in many texts. It starts with some completed code (or a complete system) that may be used as a base for a current project which is developed to meet the needs of the new specification. Figure 2.1.4 shows this process in action.

The main objective of this model is to use lines of code that are already written and may be useful for the new application. The code is then reconstructed to suit the user requirements of the new system.

This activity contains the essence of code reuse that is becoming more popular in current programming paradigms, especially in the field of object-oriented designs.

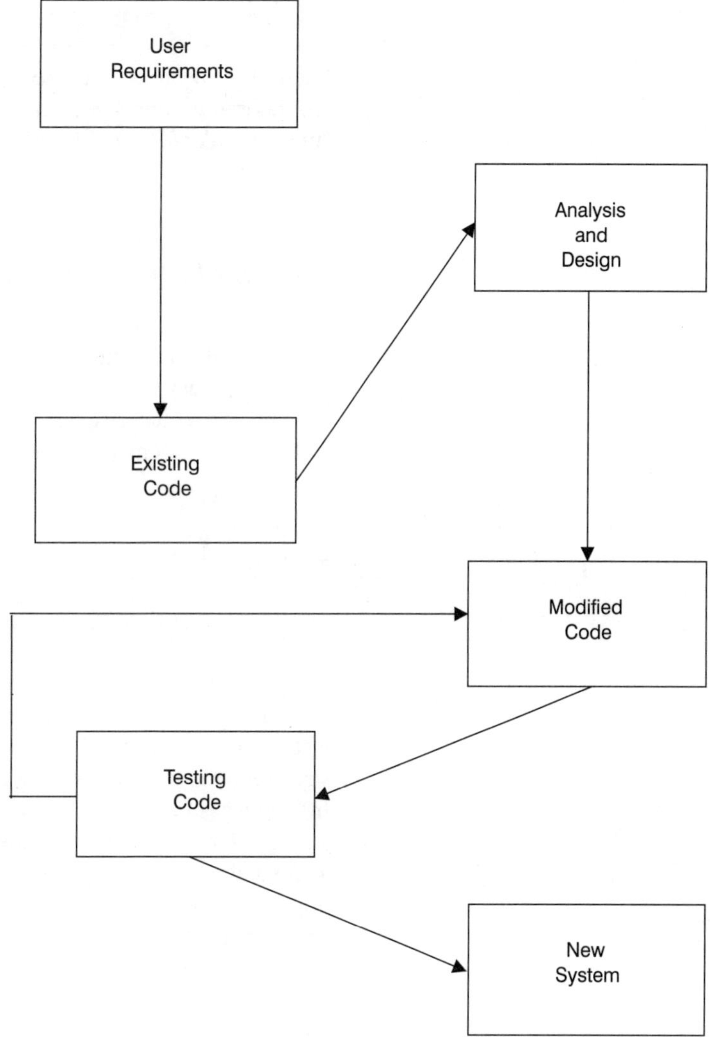

Figure 2.1.4 *Reverse engineering*

The existing code is more likely to be successful if it is properly documented and has been designed in the systematic way as the new project.

Question 2.1.2

(1) What is a software prototype?
(2) What stages are involved in software prototype development?
(3) Describe in your own words:
   (a) exploratory programming;
   (b) throwaway prototyping;
   (c) reverse engineering.
(4) Specify four problems that may arise through prototyping methods.
(5) What do you think are the main advantages of prototyping?

Object-oriented analysis

There has been a massive increase in the use of object-oriented programming languages over the last decade. Although not new, languages like C++ and Java have had a greater influence within system applications especially those associated with internet design and management.

Introduction to the world of objects

Objects model real-world or fake-world entities. Anything we can see, interact with or quantify in some way can be classified as an object. Objects are therefore real things with unique properties and each has its own set of characteristics.

The essential characteristics of objects are (Booch, 1991):

- Its STATE
- Its BEHAVIOUR
- Its IDENTITY

Characteristics within the world of objects

Encapsulation allows for certain data types and methods to be hidden from the user. This provides for a binding of data structures and methods into a class of objects. The result of this is a more efficient programming structure with a reduction in the possibility of data becoming corrupted. In languages like C++ and Java these are classified as *private* members and the *public* methods provide access into the class. Encapsulation is also known as information hiding. Encapsulation applies specifically to objects whilst information hiding can be used in any software application.

The interface between a user and a class is provided via the 'class methods' which accept the parameters (arguments) that send and receive the messages for the object to act on. This layout is shown in Figure 2.1.5.

The reason for allowing messages or arguments to have access only via their designated methods aids the process of reuse of constructed class structures. This has a benefit for the developers of systems when it comes to the concept of 'change' or designing a new system that can make use of the existing structures.

Inheritance allows for one class to inherit the characteristics of another class. Developers can exploit the property of inheritance by creating an 'ancestor' class that has attributes and behaviours that are appropriate for its own execution and reusing the ancestor class to describe new ones.

For example, if we have constructed a class called Circle and we want to create a new class called Cylinder, then Cylinder can be designed as an 'ancestor' of Circle as it describes some of the properties for Cylinder. For example, to calculate the volume of a cylinder the area of a circle is required, therefore the new class, Cylinder, can obtain this information from Circle and just add a method to multiply the length to the area in order to calculate the volume of a cylinder.

Polymorphism is the ability for a number of classes to share names of methods. The methods, that are named the same, behave appropriately to the particular class for which they were designed.

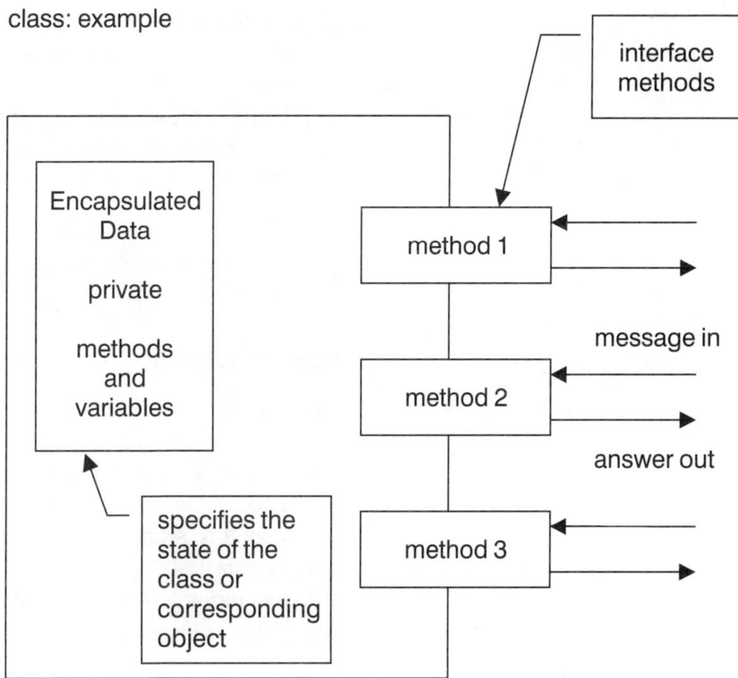

Figure 2.1.5 *Class method interface diagram*

Object analysis

This activity takes the 'negotiated statement of requirements' and analyses its contents to determine its classes and associations. This is usually achieved by constructing a class-association diagram that depicts the systems to be developed. The class-association diagram can be used as a graphical representation of the overall system or subsystem.

Classes

Object-programming languages contain class structures that represent a template for objects. A class definition is the means by which objects are designed.

For C++ we are given the definition:

> An object is an instance of a class.

Similar definitions are inherent within other object languages like Smalltalk and Java. Since the class design is a type definition for objects, an instance is a member of a class, i.e. an object.

Class structures can be classified as:

(1) **Tangible** – these represent physical entities out there in the real world. Some examples are: car, bus, house, aeroplane, college, classroom, etc.
(2) **Roles** – these represent the roles that people or other parties play in the application area. Some examples are: student, policeman, sailor, workman, etc.

(3) **Events** – these relate to particular circumstance, like a happening or an incidence. Some examples: party, enrolment, lecture, booking, etc.
(4) **Units** – these represent organizational units with the application area. For example is we are designing a college system an example of a unit would be a department.

While these classifications are useful, the overall purpose of the analysis activity is to identify classes where the behaviour of objects is significant.

Associations

An association is a connection between two classes that is significant for the application area being developed. If we take Dog and Cat as two classes then an appropriate association between them could be chases. For example, Dog chases Cat or Tutor lecturers Students. One point about syntax at this stage, it is customary to use uppercase first letters to represent classes.

Associations can be classified as one to one, one to many and many to many. These concepts will be covered in more detail later in the chapter.

Responsibilities

These describe the behaviour of an object in terms of the responsibilities that affect its overall requirements for an intended system. They can take two forms:

- Responsibilities for recording information.
- Responsibilities for carrying out a prescribed task.

The way objects work

To the user of applications objects are considered as 'black box' components. They operate by receiving a message and respond with an answer. The object that is sent a message is called the receiver. An example is outlined in Figure 2.1.6

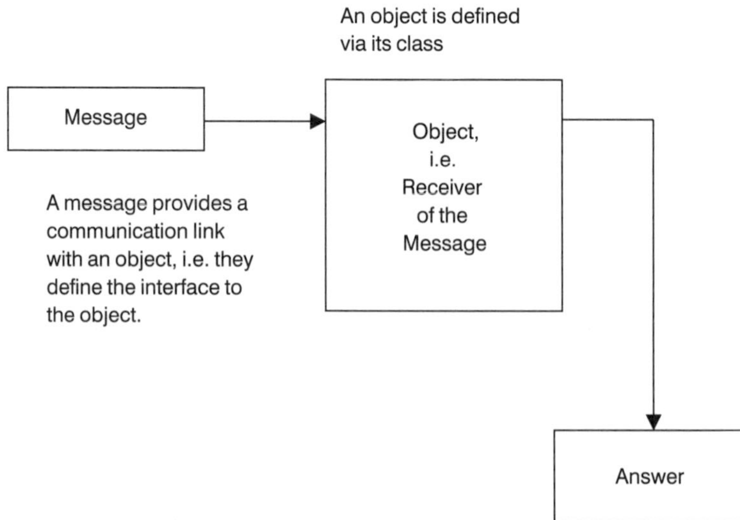

Figure 2.1.6 *Object structure*

Question 2.1.3

(1) What is the main factor why object development is popular?
(2) What is meant by the following terms:
  (a) encapsulation?
  (b) inheritance?
  (c) polymorphism?
(3) How are objects defined?
(4) What are main aims of object-oriented analysis?
(5) What provides a communication route to an object?

Evaluation of models

The use of a required model depends on a number of factors. Is the specification for a system that requires function, object or data modelling. Is the project to be implemented into a high-level language like C/C++, Pascal, etc. and if so, does it need to be structured via a visual environment. Is the application going to be developed within a database environment like Access and programmed using VB. There are so many questions and the solution often depends on what you are skilled in and what resources are available to you.

The other main factor is the availability of systems analysis tools that you need to develop the specification. A lot of these tools allow for the graphical models to be developed following set procedures and checked for syntax and semantic correctness. But they are expensive and take a lot of training to use and often you have to make do with standard graphical packages that allow the diagrams to be completed without the added advantage of in-built testing facilities.

The traditional lifecycle is gradually giving way to other models, but its inherent concepts should not be ignored. A number of software houses have been using the model, or a variation of it, for several years with very successful outcomes.

However, there is a greater emphasis on object and data modelling within industry today and these facts may provide you with the choice of which technique you use to analyse the system. You will need to provide a constructive base on which the design and implementation of the project can be developed.

Question 2.1.4

Your local college requires a management information system to handle student admissions.

From this specification extract suggest a possible method for analysis. Explain why you have chosen this method.

2.2 Requirements analysis

Introduction

The starting point for any project is a document that originates from a customer or a user of the proposed system, known as the customer or user requirements. The document, which is usually written in a natural language, can range in size from a few pages to a large booklet. It is often the case that someone who is not a computing system specialist produces this document. This results in a document that needs to be analysed to ensure the main requirements are clearly specified and fully meet the needs of the customer. The document also needs to be fully understood by the developers of the product so the resulting system can be constructed to its full potential.

The requirements analysis activity aims to produce a specification that is:

- clear
- concise
- unambiguous
- understandable to the customer or end user

The development team need to analyse the user requirements to produce the following specifications:

- functional requirements
- non-functional requirements
- hardware
- user training arrangements
- software support
- criteria for acceptability

Functional requirements

These specify the main functions that are inherent in the user requirements. They specify what the customer wants the system to do by highlighting the main aims within the document.

Non-functional requirements

These are often known as constraints that provide information about the limitation on the system. For example, 'the response time for the customer enquiry must be within 3 seconds', or 'the program is to run on the company PC network structure which operates via a Novell operating system'.

Non-functional requirements either specify the characteristics of a system, for example specifying the time it takes to receive a response or the speed of operation of a certain system, or they govern the development process by specifying a certain programming language.

Example 2.2.1

A local squash club needs a computer system to allocate the use of its courts. The players need to book in at a reception where the operator can check on the availability of the courts. The operator can type in commands to:

- Display all the courts that club owns and whether they are operational.
- Display the courts that are available to use.
- Display who is playing at the current time.
- Enter data for people who want to play currently.
- Enter data for people who need to pre-book a court.

The system also needs to inform the operator when the time is up for players on a particular court. The system is to be implemented on the club's existing PC network that operates using Pentium II machines running at 266 MHz with 2.4 Gb disk drives (less than 0.3 Gb available) and 32 Mb RAM running under Windows 95.

From this extract we need to ascertain the functional and non-functional requirements.

Functional requirements:

(1) Display all the courts that club owns and whether they are operational.
(2) Display the courts that are available to use.
(3) Display who is playing at the current time.
(4) Enter data for people who want to play currently.
(5) Enter data for people who need to pre-book a court.
(6) Inform the operator when the time is up for players on a particular court.

Non-functional requirements

(1) System to run on Pentium II machines.
(2) Machines restricted to a processor speed of 333 MHz.
(3) Limited disk drive space as only 0.3 Gb is available.
(4) Restricted RAM memory of only 32 Mb.
(5) Operating system is running under Windows 95.

It can be seen from the functional requirements that the use of bullet points helps in the finding of the main objectives, but in most cases this is not the case and the text has to be thoroughly examined to these items. This is the case in the next example where an extract from a user specification is given with no obvious indication of the functional or non-functional requirements. This unfortunately is the norm for most user requirement documentation.

Question 2.2.1

Examine the fragment from a user requirements document shown below and identify the functional and non-functional requirements.

> A system needs to monitor and display the temperatures in all the cold store units within the company. It needs to detect any adverse change in temperature that would indicate a fault within the cold store machinery. At selected intervals the system should write temperature data to a database which the engineers can use as a check for the correct running of the cold stores. The system is to be implemented on the company computer system where only 1 Mb of memory is available. The company computer is running on a VAX VMS operating system. As memory is a problem and the data needs to be kept for an indefinite period the system should periodically archive the database files to a magnetic tape system.

It is often the case that the user requirements contain the following properties.

Functional and non-functional requirements are not obviously separated

Many user requirements documents are not structured into neat categories that are easily separated into the required specifications. The document takes a lot of analysing first to find the required functions and then separate them as required.

The user requirements document contains ambiguous statements

As the customer uses a natural language to complete the requirements it is open to ambiguities within its structure. As the specification requires a high level of precision to outline the main requirements structures like the one shown below need to clarified.

> A system needs to check on the speed and temperature of a specified mechanism. Flashing red and green lights are to be used to display this information to the user.

The second sentence is ambiguous, as it is not clear as to the way the lights should operate. Do both have two lights? Red for a warning and green for OK or is there one light for each of them that uniquely identifies them?

Such ambiguities need to be addressed by the development team and if necessary the customer needs to be involved to ensure the resulting specification meets their original aims.

From the squash club example above we find:

> The system also needs to inform the operator when the time is up for players on a particular court.

Now how is the system going to inform the user, is it going to be an audible signal or visual message or both? This again needs to be clarified to satisfy the requirements for the squash club.

The user requirements may contain omissions

As many systems are very large it is more likely that the user requirements may contain omissions. If we take the squash club example above there is mention of the operator entering several commands, but what happens if the operator enters a wrong command? A suitable warning message should be given and the option of re-entering the command should be offered to the operator.

Platitudes need to be clarified

These relate to meaningless statements, for example:

> The system should be easy to use and help should be given to the operator.

This does not mean anything to the developer. It needs to be expressed in concrete terms to include facts like a graphical user interface or a menu driven interface is to be used to supply helpful information to the user.

Remove any extraneous detail

Remove any unnecessary statements that are not directly part of the final requirements.

For example, a supermarket database system does not need to contain details about precise input sequences that need to be entered when checking the database for certain stock items. This level of detail can be left to the design and implementation activities.

Properties that are important to both the developer and customer should not be hidden under unnecessary data. So remove any 'waffle' that is not essential to ensure only precise statements remain.

The output documentation from the requirements analysis activity should be presented at the same level of detail throughout. At this stage the document should be at a level that is still understandable by the customer but contains precise detail to build the next phase of analysis. It should not contain any design detail at this stage, for example it can contain statements like student file of pressure control, but not terms like direct access file system or a recursive loop structure.

It provides the written component for the system specification and a base to develop the documentation further using appropriate graphical or mathematical modelling tools. The end product of these activities, which comprise the system analysis components, is clear concise set of documents backed up with precise models that are both semantically and syntactically correct.

To sum up, the negotiated statement of requirements should contain, in an unambiguous way, what the proposed system is to do, its functions and what the limitations on the developer are. It is a description of 'what' a system is to do in application terms. It is the key document on which all subsequent activities in the software project depend. In legal terms it may provide a basis for a contract between the customer and the developer.

Question 2.2.2

(1) What is a platitude?
(2) What is meant by an omission? Give an example.
(3) Why is it important to remove ambiguous statements?
(4) What is extraneous detail?
(5) What is the final objective of the requirements analysis document?

Techniques used within the requirements analysis process

In order to ascertain what is required from a system, there needs to be a lot of interaction with the customer or end user of the product. This interaction can take on many forms, for example interviews, observations, investigations, questionnaires and meetings. These need to be carefully planned in order to make the most efficient use of the time spent during the analysis and produce the desired results.

Interviews

All interviews need to be carefully planned in order to ensure that all the required information is obtained in the most efficient time from the customer or potential end user of the product. The interview needs to be formal and conducted to a carefully thought out agenda that contains checklists and questions that are to be put to the interviewee. The questions need to draw out issues like the functional objectives, completion deadlines and acceptability criteria.

In order to get a full picture of what is required it may be necessary to conduct interviews with several members of the organization. This ensures that points that may have been forgotten by one interviewee may have been specified by another. It is always important for an interviewer to step back from an interview and to apply his/her experience in order to fully evaluate the responses.

The interviewer should provide feedback in terms of his/her own understanding to clarify concepts in order to ensure the conclusions are reached.

The main objectives of an interview are:

- Ascertain the customer needs and desires.
- Clarify the priorities for the proposed project.
- Find out about the current system and associated personnel.
- Determine the environment which the system must be interfaced to.
- How staff will accept change when implementing the new system.
- Support requirements for installing and using the new application.
- Staff responsibilities within the organization.

The interviewer must always show interest in, and thoroughly listen to, what is being said by the interviewee.

Interviews allow users to make their experiences and feel part of the analysis process. This is an essential characteristic of analysis and one that should be continued throughout this stage.

Observations

This allows for the developer to spend time in the environment in which the system is to be implemented. This practice familiarizes the developer with the needs of the system and provides an opportunity to pinpoint problems and additional requirements that may need to be added. It provides a basis for a conceptual model which can be used as a design for the final product. An example of an observation could involve the system developer travelling to a North Sea oil rig to look at the environment for a proposed 'safety warning system'.

Investigations

These involve the developer actually functioning as part of the system. It has the advantage that the developer gains a clearer insight as to what the proposed system is to do, but can have the disadvantage that the investigation may move into the area of how things should be as opposed to how they are now. The developer at this stage does not want to move away from the concept of analysis, i.e. ascertain what the system is to do, into the areas of design and implementation.

Questionnaires

This activity needs to determine the same objectives as the interview. The questionnaire or survey needs to be carefully structured so that it is easy to complete and provides all the necessary feedback that is required. A good questionnaire will be laid out so the person completing it just has to tick a box in response to a question. If it is being sent to a large market then the developer of the product could consider having the returned forms computer analysed. There should be a place for additional information so the potential user can insert additional requirement details as necessary to complement the rest of the form.

Example 2.2.2

Extract from a questionnaire

In order for us to ascertain your requirements for the proposed 'Shirt Packing System' kindly **tick** the response box **to the right** of the question.

Do you want the system to display the number of shirts packed? ☐ 01

Do you want the system to state when a target number is reached? ☐ 02

-
-
-

If you have any additional information please indicate below:

____

____

Meetings

In most cases a proposed project will start with a 'kick-off' meeting. The meeting will be attended by all parties associated with the system to be developed and it should be formally structured to a specified agenda. Below is a preparation list for setting up a meeting:

- Has a venue that is convenient for all parties been booked?
- Are the rooming facilities appropriate for the needs of the meeting?
- Have all parties been sent an agenda and location guide?
- Has tea/coffee or lunch been booked as required?
- Does the venue provide other facilities, toilets, telephones, etc?

A suitable chairperson needs to be appointed, this will normally be a company manager of the systems house appointed to develop the product. Other people from the company should include the project

Question 2.2.3

(1) What are the main objectives of an interview?
(2) Why is it necessary to use a questionnaire?
(3) What is the main disadvantage of an investigation?
(4) What members should attend a typical progress meeting?
(5) What should an agenda contain for a specified meeting?

manager, team leaders and appropriate analysts responsible for the systems analysis of the project. The rest of the members should be made up from company staff who proposed the product and should include the IT manager, senior staff and end users of the application. It may be necessary in some cases to bring in a third party to provide an independent view and give advice on external issues if the need arises. An example could be a representative of the Tax Office if a payroll system was being proposed.

Further meetings will follow this format as the development lifecycle progresses. They provide a fundamental structure for quality standards to be maintained by interactive feedback to project members and the end user of the product.

Exercise 2.2.1

College management information system

This exercise requires you to work in groups in order to carry out a simulation of a complete requirements analysis.

Below is an extract of a user requirements document:

A college admissions system is to be specified. Details for new students are entered by the operator and then stored on a student file. The required course is then checked against the course database to ensure it is available. If the required course is available the enrolment proceeds with details entered into a registered file; if the course is not available a suitable message is displayed on the operator's console. An invoice for the appropriate fees is to be produced for the students whose course is available.

The system needs to produce partially completed enrolment forms for continuing students at the start of each academic year.

Information about existing college courses should be printed for students who were not able to find an appropriate course during the previous year's enrolment.

The system is run on the existing college Apple network system where only 300 Kb of disk space is available. In order to speed up events the system should respond in less than 1 second and be easy for the operator to use.

Required steps:

(1) Within your allocated groups organize and carry out a meeting to analysis the information. The meeting should have a specified agenda and minutes written.
(2) Ascertain from the information the following:
    (a) Functional requirements
    (b) Non-functional requirements
    (c) Any obvious omissions
    (d) Platitudes
(3) Construct a suitable set of questions that can provide a basis for an interview with the customer.

2.3 Systems analysis models

Yourdon data flow diagrams

The Yourdon Structured Method or YSM has been in use for several years and like most of the analysis models on the market today – it primarily uses graphical techniques to structure the 'negotiated statement of requirements' into a coherent framework. This framework still needs to be understood by the customer so the basic structure is simple in its presentation and has the advantage that a single diagram can show what is on several pages of written text.

The Data Flow Diagram or DFD is the first graphical technique used to analyse what the system is to do. Figure 2.3.1 contains the symbols used within the analysis process.

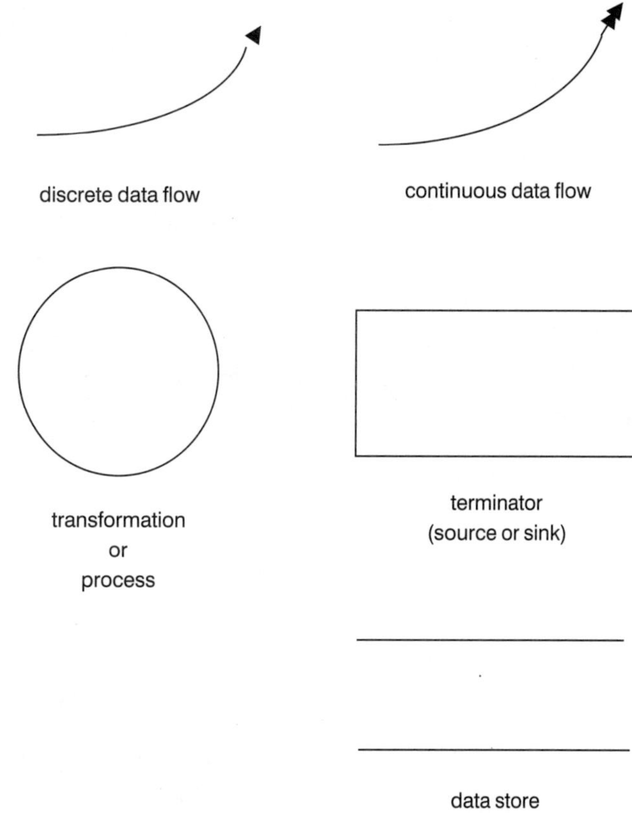

Figure 2.3.1 *Yourdon DFD symbols*

It is hierarchical in structure and all diagrams start with a 'top-level' design called a 'context diagram'. This diagram contains one process only that represents the whole of the system. Its main objective is to show where the main data sources are coming from and where the output data is going. The input data originates from a 'source' terminator(s) and the output data is sent to a 'sink' terminator(s).

Example 2.3.1

Construct a context diagram for a system that calculates the standard deviation for a given set of examination grades. The grades should be in the range 0 to 100 and entered through the keyboard via an operator. If the operator enters an incorrect value a suitable message is to be displayed on the monitor. The standard deviation values are to be printed out so the operator can send the results to the appropriate person.

Suggested solution:

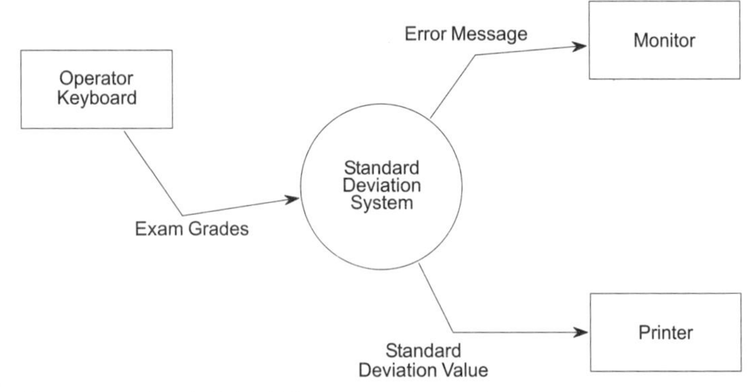

Figure 2.3.2 *CONTEXT mean and standard deviation system*

The solid directed lines represent the flow of data. A single arrow at the end depicts a discrete flow of data that arrives at its destination at discrete intervals in time.

A continuous data flow continually sends data to its destination. The process or transformation uses the data that arrives and processes it in some way to produce an output.

Some basic rules:

(1) Context diagrams contain one process only.
(2) A process must have at least one input and one output.
(3) All data flows are named with a noun.
(4) Processes must be labelled with text which suggests how the data is transformed.
(5) Data flows and processes should be uniquely named.
(6) A process can not originate data.
(7) Data flowing to a terminator can only come from a process.
(8) A diagram should be numbered and contain an explanatory caption.

Question 2.3.1

With reference to the context diagram:

(1) How many processes can a context diagram contain?
(2) What is the minimum number of input and output data flows to a process?

(3) What are the types of terminators used in a DFD?
(4) What is the difference between a discrete and continuous flow?
(5) What naming convention should be used for data flows?

Once the context diagram has been completed the next step is to refine it by creating a child. Children are only created through processes so there can only be one child from a context diagram. A child diagram should not contain more than seven processes to avoid complexity. If this is starting to appear likely then further children of the process would need to be created. The term for this is known as 'functional decomposition' and is achieved through data flow diagram refinement.

For a large-scale project the following steps are required:

- Create a context diagram.
- Refine the process in the context diagram to describe its component data flows, processes and stores.
- Refine each process into another data flow diagram.
- Repeat this process until the required level of detail is obtained.
- Complete a process specification for the final processes.
- Check all diagrams for consistency and syntax requirements.

Example 2.3.2

From the solution given in Example 2.3.1 refine the context diagram to produce a child that adequately models the system.

Suggested solution:

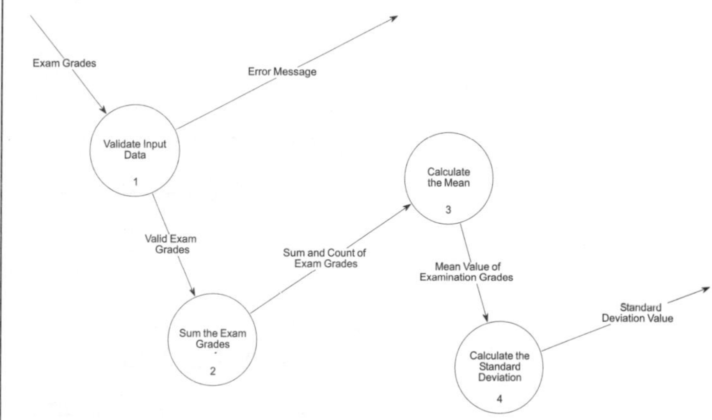

Figure 2.3.3 *Standard deviation system*

The above example required only one child to provide an analysis model of the system. Note that it is not necessary to show the original terminators in the child diagram.

IMPORTANT RULE

The flows that go in and out of the process being refined must be the same flows that appear in the child diagram. This is classified as parent-child balancing and if the two diagrams do not match an error will be evident in the design.

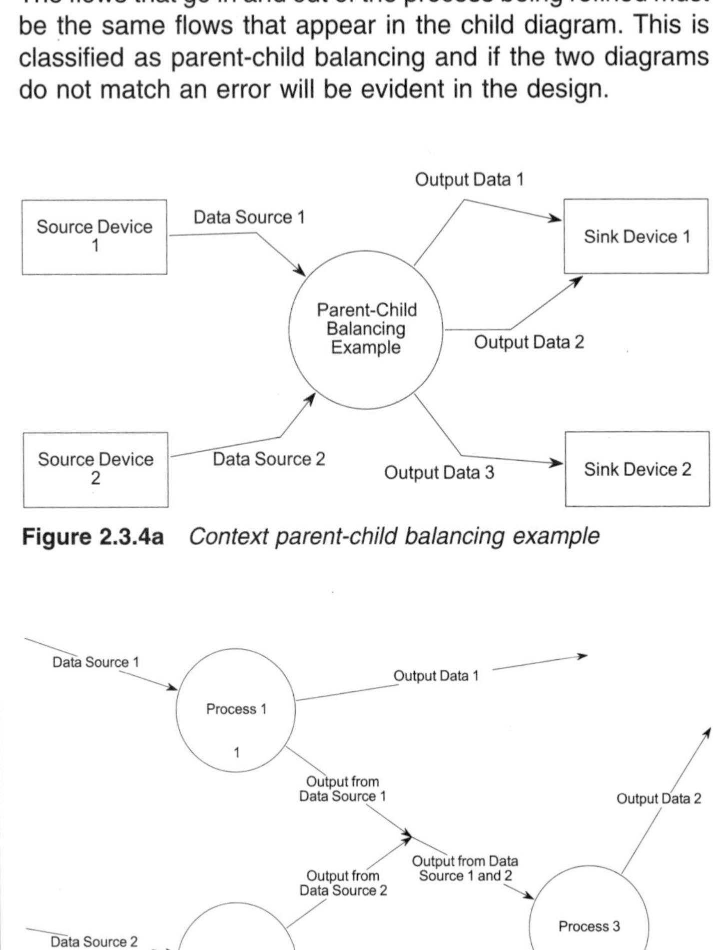

Figure 2.3.4a *Context parent-child balancing example*

Figure 2.3.4b *Parent-child balancing (child)*

Example 2.3.3

Below are the requirements for making vegetable soup.

A 'vegetable soup' is to be made with three main ingredients. These are to be potatoes, onions and broccoli. The vegetables are contained in a vegetable rack and they need to be prepared before they are ready for use. You then need to add water to a saucepan and slightly boil the potatoes first. Next you need to add appropriate condiments with the onions and broccoli. They then need to be cooked for a prescribed time and when ready the soup is to be served in a bowl.

1 Complete a CONTEXT diagram to model the specification.
2 Refine the context diagram so it fully specifies the system.

Suggested solutions:

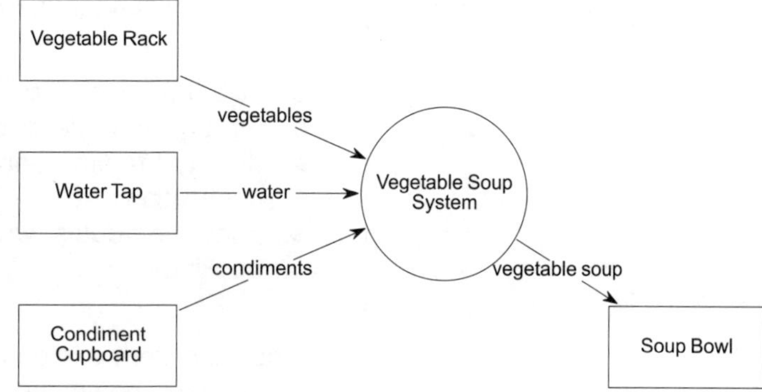

Figure 2.3.5a *CONTEXT vegetable soup*

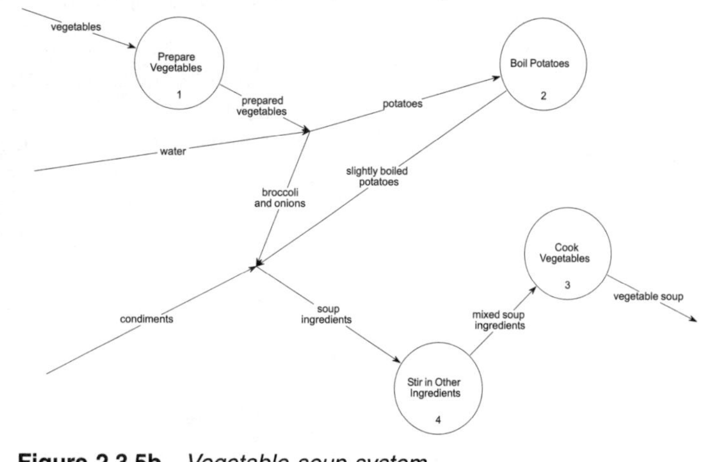

Figure 2.3.5b *Vegetable soup system*

The role of stores

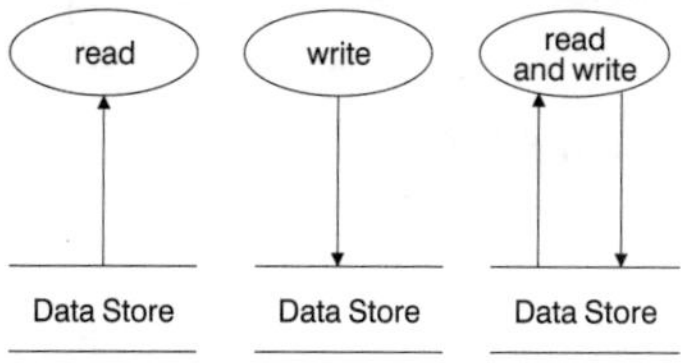

read
write
read and write
Data Store
Data Store
Data Store

Figure 2.3.6

Data stores are storage areas that are internal to a system that is being modelled. These stores often represent the basic building blocks of a database system and from which an entity-relationship diagram can be constructed. The direction of the data flow lines is important as it depicts whether the store is read only, write only or read/write. This is shown diagrammatically in Figure 2.3.6.

Example 2.3.4

Example containing stores – Bernese Coach Company

Below is an extract from a system specification

The Bernese Coach Company requires a computer-based system to handle customer enquiries. The customer enquiries that need to be answered are:

- give the travel price between any two destinations
- for a given route display the coach number
- display the time each coach leaves for a specified destination
- print the routes which are offering special party bookings

A booking clerk is to operate the system by typing in one of the four commands, the command needs to be validated to ensure it is correct. The system uses a database called 'Coach Details' that contains all the information specified above.

1. Draw a context diagram to represent the proposed system.
2. Refine the context diagram by producing a child of the main process in order to develop a solution. Keep the diagram simple, remember a good DFD should not contain any more than seven processes.

Suggested solution:

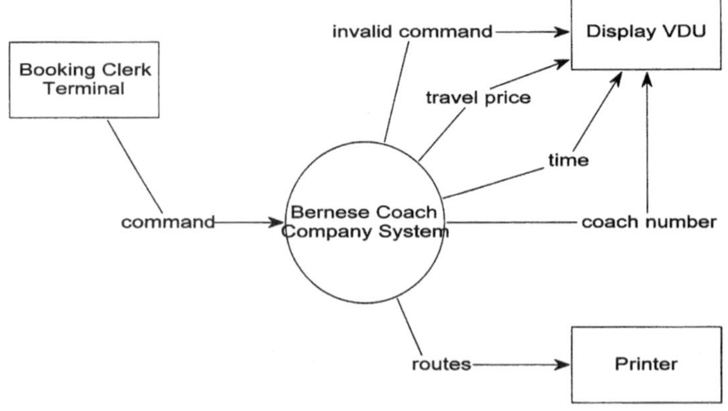

Figure 2.3.7a *CONTEXT Bernese coach system*

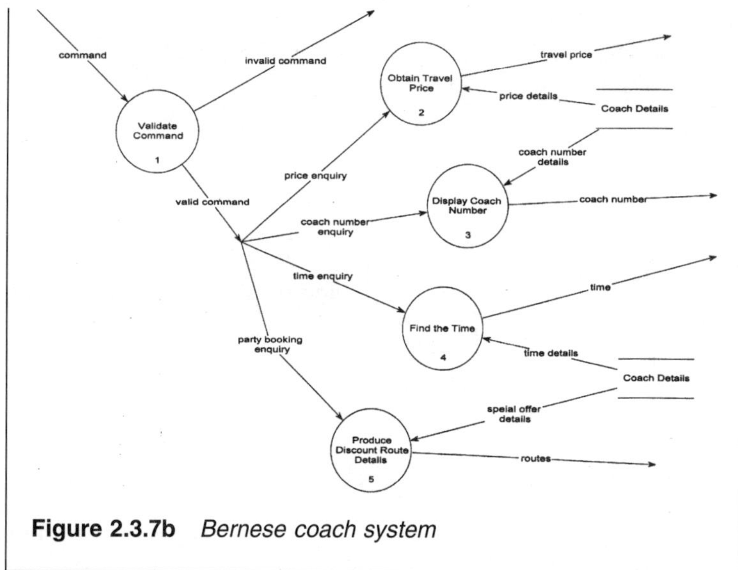

Figure 2.3.7b *Bernese coach system*

In order to ensure the developer has as much information as possible, some DFD development tools allow for a process specification to be created as a final transformation refinement. The process specification contains information about the flows in and out of the transformation and its body contains a high-level specification in structured English describing what is happening inside. An example from the Standard Deviation System is shown below.

```
@IN = Valid Exam Grades
@OUT = Sum & Count of Exam Grades

@PSPEC 0.2 Sum the Exam Grades

  On receiving the Valid Exam Grades do:
    Iterate to calculate the Sum & Count of Exam Grades
  Output these values to the next process

@
```

Note that the body is in semi-formal English and it must contain the data flow names that flow in and out of the process.

Output flows from processes

If a process produces more than one output then the way this is depicted on the DFD will give the developer information about whether all the data items are produced at the same time or if just one of them is. This 'and' and 'or' situation is shown in the diagrams below. Figure 2.3.8 shows a process where the outputs can be considered as alternatives and Figure 2.3.9 shows the outputs initially as a single flow then splitting into the output data components. The need to model the parsing of data flow into its alternative forms is a common one when modelling the essential characteristics of a system.

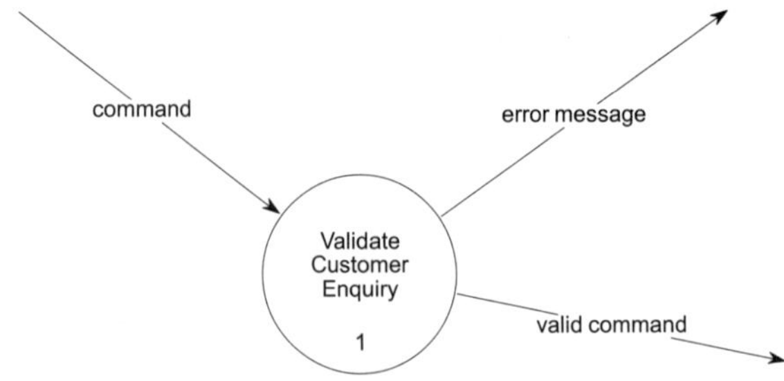

Figure 2.3.8 *Alternative output flows*

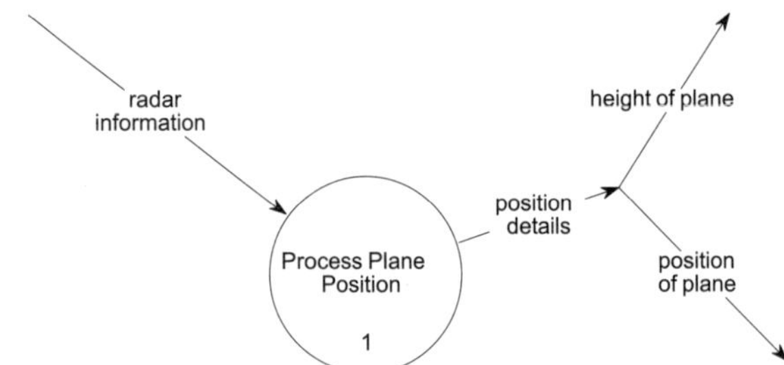

Figure 2.3.9 *Single output flow passing into two flows*

Input flows to processes

If a number of data flows are required by one process then they should merge before they reach that process. This reduces the complexity of the diagram structure and shows at a glance to the developer that all the input data items are required for the process to carry out its transformation. Figure 2.3.10 outlines this procedure.

Some graphical analysis tools allow for the splitting of flows to be carried out by 'group nodes' that need to be fully clarified via a text directive. Using Select Yourdon this is achieved by creating a BNF (Backus-Naur Format) specification. The syntax that is used is shown in the left column.

From Figure 2.3.10 a suitable BNF structure could be:

- *height of plane* + *position of plane* stating that both are outputs from *position details* stressing the **and** condition
- [*height of plane* | *position of plane*] stating that either could be outputs from *position details* stressing the **or** condition

These techniques are further refinements from those discussed above and allow a better structuring of the diagram which is both easier to read and more accurate in its content.

BNF syntax

The BNF clause is used in the data dictionary to describe the data components of data flows and stores. It uses the following syntax:

- \+ means AND
- [|] means EITHER-OR, i.e. select one of the options
- () means enclosed component is OPTIONAL
- {} means ITERATIONS OF enclosed component
- "" means enclosed component is a LITERAL value
- \\ encloses a textual description

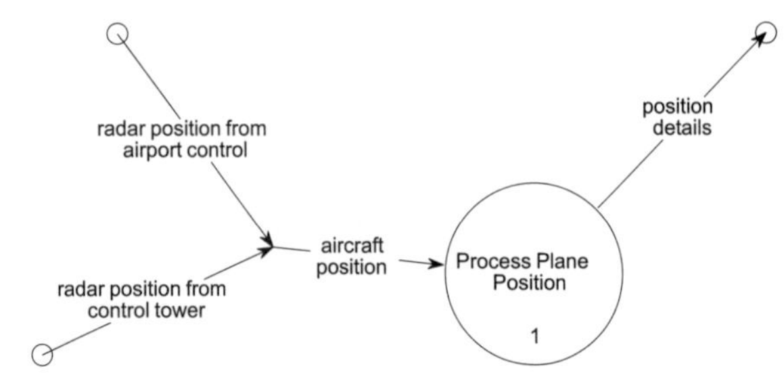

Figure 2.3.10 *Merging of input data flows*

Validating the DFD

The following list highlights the important points for validating a DFD system:

- Does each circle or process precisely state the transformation? (make sure each process contains a verb).
- Is all the data shown? and at the correct level.
- After refinement does the net input and output data flows match those in the parent diagram?
- Can the DFD be remodelled to make it easier to follow? Remember the maximum number of processes a diagram should contain is 7.
- You should not have the same name for a data flow that enters a process and a data flow that leaves it. Remember the action of a process is to transform the data, i.e. convert it from one form to another. Also all data flows should have unique names.
- Have you refined each process as far as it will go? If so have you completed an appropriate process specification? Remember a process specification is the final child to be created.

Remember a DFD is detailed at customer level. It specifies what the system is to do by providing a graphical specification, which is still open for discussion with the customer, to ensure it is a correct representation of the negotiated statement of requirements.

Question 2.3.2

(1) If more than one data flow is coming out of a process what does this convey to the developer?
(2) What is the main purpose of a process?
(3) What is the final child of a process called?
(4) What does a store represent within a DFD?
(5) What type of data flow is acceptable to and from a store?

Exercise 2.3.1

The Bailey & Bess Dog Kennels

Below is an extract from a system specification for a computerized system to be installed in the Bailey & Bess Dog Kennels.

> A computer system is required to replace the paperwork system currently in use by the kennels. The system needs to book in dogs that come to stay at the kennels and book them out when their stay is finished. The system needs to take advance bookings so the receptionist needs to be able to know if there are kennels available for a specified period. Some of the kennels are reserved for quarantine animals and these are not available for short stay dogs. A number of options need to be available to the receptionist in order to maintain the booking system. These include:
>
> - display the available kennels for a specified period
> - display which kennels have been reserved for quarantine use
> - print a report giving details of who has pre-booked
> - display what dogs are in the kennels at the present time
> - print the names, address and telephone numbers of people who currently have dogs in the kennels

In order to ensure the reliability of the system an error message is to be displayed if the receptionist enters an incorrect command.

(1) Draw a context diagram to represent the proposed system.
(2) Refine the context diagram to produce a solution to the problem.
(3) For the final transformations produce appropriate process specifications.
(4) Check your diagrams to make sure they are syntactically and semantically correct.

Exercise 2.3.2

For the College Management Information System developed in Exercise 2.2.4 complete a DFD process to include the following steps:

(1) Draw a context diagram to represent the proposed system.
(2) Refine the context diagram to produce a solution to the problem.
(3) For the final transformations produce appropriate process specifications.
(4) Check your diagrams to make sure they are syntactically and semantically correct.

SSADM

Introduction

SSADM (Structured Systems Analysis & Design Method) is a widely used system analysis and design development too and is often specified as a requirement for government computing projects. Developed within the UK it is increasingly being adopted by the public sector throughout Europe. SSADM is in the public domain, and is formally specified in British Standard BS7738.

Objectives of SSADM

SSADM divides an application development project into modules, stages, steps, and tasks, and provides a framework for describing projects in a fashion suited to managing the project. SSADM's objectives are to:

- Improve project management and control.
- Make more effective use of experienced and inexperienced development staff.

- Develop better quality systems.
- Make projects resilient to the loss of staff.
- Enable projects to be supported by computer-based tools such as Computer Aided Software Engineering (CASE) systems.
- Establish a framework for good communications between participants in a project.

SSADM covers those aspects of the lifecycle of a system from the feasibility study stage to the production of a physical design; it is generally used in conjunction with other methods, such as PRINCE, which is concerned with the broader aspects of project management.

Outline of SSADM

In detail, SSADM sets out a cascade or waterfall view of systems development, in which there are a series of steps, each of which leads to the next step. SSADM's steps, or stages, are:

- Feasibility – Feasibility Study Module.
- Investigation of the current environment – Requirements Analysis Module.
- Business systems options – Requirements Analysis Module.
- Definition of requirements – Requirements Specification Module.
- Technical system options – Logical Systems Specification Module.
- Logical design – Logical Systems Specification Module.
- Physical design – Physical Design Module.

For each stage, SSADM sets out a series of techniques and procedures, and conventions for recording and communicating information pertaining to these – both in textual and diagrammatic form. SSADM is a very comprehensive model, and a characteristic of the method is that projects may use only those elements of SSADM

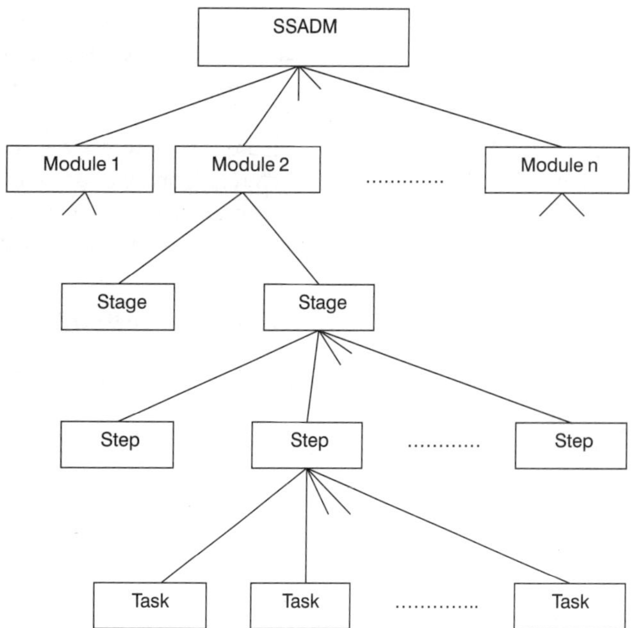

Figure 2.3.11 *Structure of the SSADM model*

appropriate to the project. SSADM is supported by a number of CASE (Computer Aided Software Engineering) tool providers.

Each stage is divided up into a sequence of numbered steps which in turn are divided into numbered tasks. For example, step 010 is specified for 'Prepare for the Feasibility Study'.

An outline of this structure is shown in Figure 2.3.11.

Diagrammatic techniques used within SSADM

- Data flow modelling.
- Logical data modelling.
- Entity/event modelling.
- Enquiry access paths.
- I/O structuring.
- Dialogue design.
- Logical database process design.

Non-diagrammatic techniques used within SSADM

- Relational data analysis.
- Requirements definition.
- Function definition.
- Formulation of options.
- Specification prototyping.

Background to the SSADM lifecycle (version 4)

Stage 0 Feasibility Study

This forms the first stage in the lifecycle and its objectives are:

- to decide whether to proceed to a full specification;
- to decide whether to proceed in a different direction from that envisaged in the initial documentation.

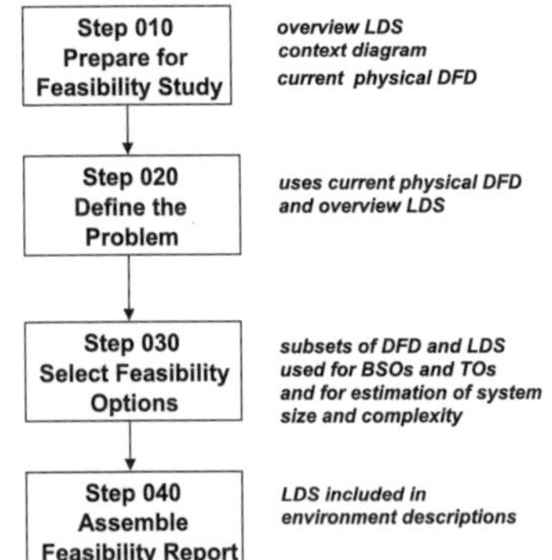

Figure 2.3.12 *Stage 0 – Feasibility*

Figure 2.3.12 shows the steps taken during this stage.

Several options for taking the project forward to a full analysis and factors like weighing benefits against cost are considered. It may be found that the project is not feasible and abandoned at this stage.

Stage 1 Investigation of the Current Environment

If the new system is intended to be a replacement for an existing system then an investigation will be carried out as a vehicle for uncovering user requirements. The following points outline what can be achieved during this stage:

- Retained functionality – what functions are still required in the new system?
- User confidence – demonstrates the developer's ability to understand the current system and their ability to ascertain the requirements for the new system.

- Identification of requirements – this is thought by many developers of systems to be the most efficient way of ascertaining the requirements of a new system. It provides opportunities for the developers to discuss problems with users of the current system and how they would like changes to be made in the new system.
- Familiarization – this gives the developer a chance to become familiar with the environment under investigation.
- Project scoping – the scope and complexity of the proposed system can often be obtained efficiently from the current system.

Figure 2.3.13 outlines the stage.

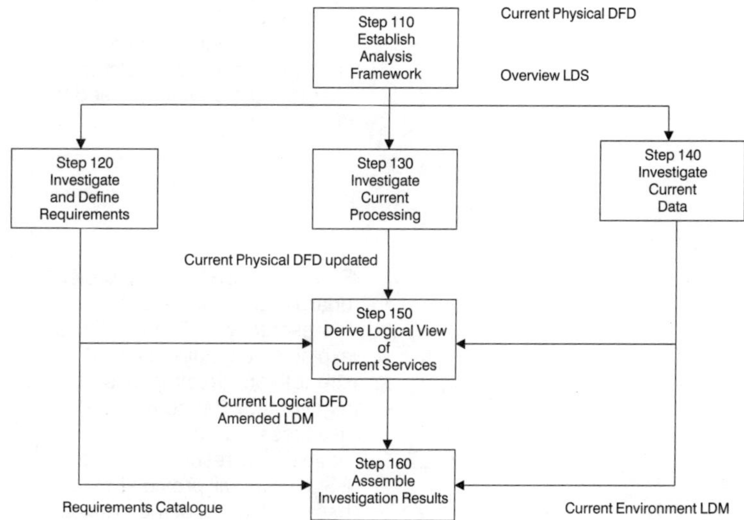

Figure 2.3.13 *Stage 1 – Investigation of the Current Environment*

The output of this stage is a comprehensive set of user requirements which provides a documentary base for developing the rest of the project.

Stage 2 Business Systems Options

Here we examine the comprehensive statement of user requirements and put together several options for solving the business problem. The objective of this stage is to define business (or logical) solutions and not to describe the technical environment.

Figure 2.3.14 shows the path taken during the Business System Option (BSO).

The SSADM tasks carried out in step 210 (Define Business Systems Options) are:

(1) Task 10 – establish minimum requirements for the proposed system.
(2) Task 20 – produce outlines for a number of BSO normally about six.
(3) Task 30 – discuss the outlines with the users to produce a shortlist.
(4) Task 40 – carry out a cost benefit and impact analysis for each short-listed BSO.

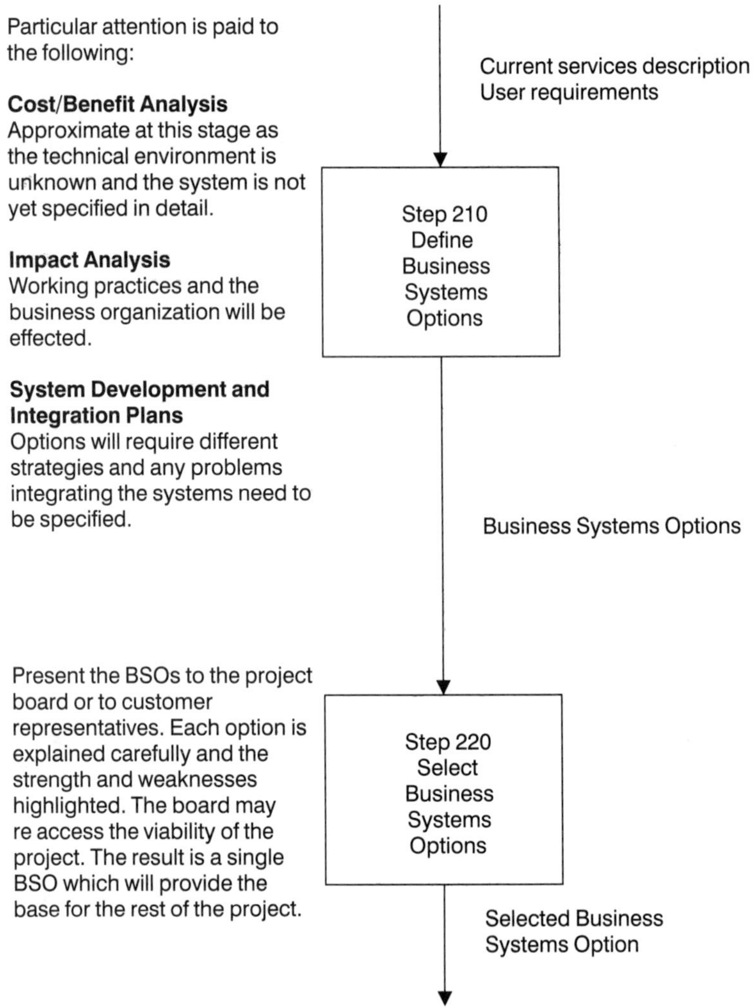

Particular attention is paid to the following:
Cost/Benefit Analysis
Approximate at this stage as the technical environment is unknown and the system is not yet specified in detail.
Impact Analysis
Working practices and the business organization will be effected.
System Development and Integration Plans
Options will require different strategies and any problems integrating the systems need to be specified.
Current services description
User requirements
Step 210 Define Business Systems Options
Business Systems Options
Present the BSOs to the project board or to customer representatives. Each option is explained carefully and the strength and weaknesses highlighted. The board may re access the viability of the project. The result is a single BSO which will provide the base for the rest of the project.
Step 220 Select Business Systems Options
Selected Business Systems Option

Figure 2.3.14 *Business Systems Options (BSOs)*

Step 220 is the remit to select the BSO to be fully investigated for the new system. This will depend on a number of factors like the internal standards and circumstances of the project. It will involve the project team and user representative body to explain each option clearly and highlight its strengths and weaknesses. The final output of this stage is a comprehensive document that specifies why the proposed option has been chosen and acts as a basis for the final system.

Stage 3 Definition of Requirements

This is the centre of the project where the user requirements are refined into a detailed and precise specification of 'what' the system is to do. Figure 2.3.15 outlines the steps taken during this stage.

The order of events through this stage needs to be carefully planned. Steps 310 and 320 can be carried out in parallel. Step 310 feeds into step 330 and step 320 feeds into step 340. Step 350 may not begin until step 310 and step 330 have been completed. Steps 330 and 340 are a trigger for step 360.

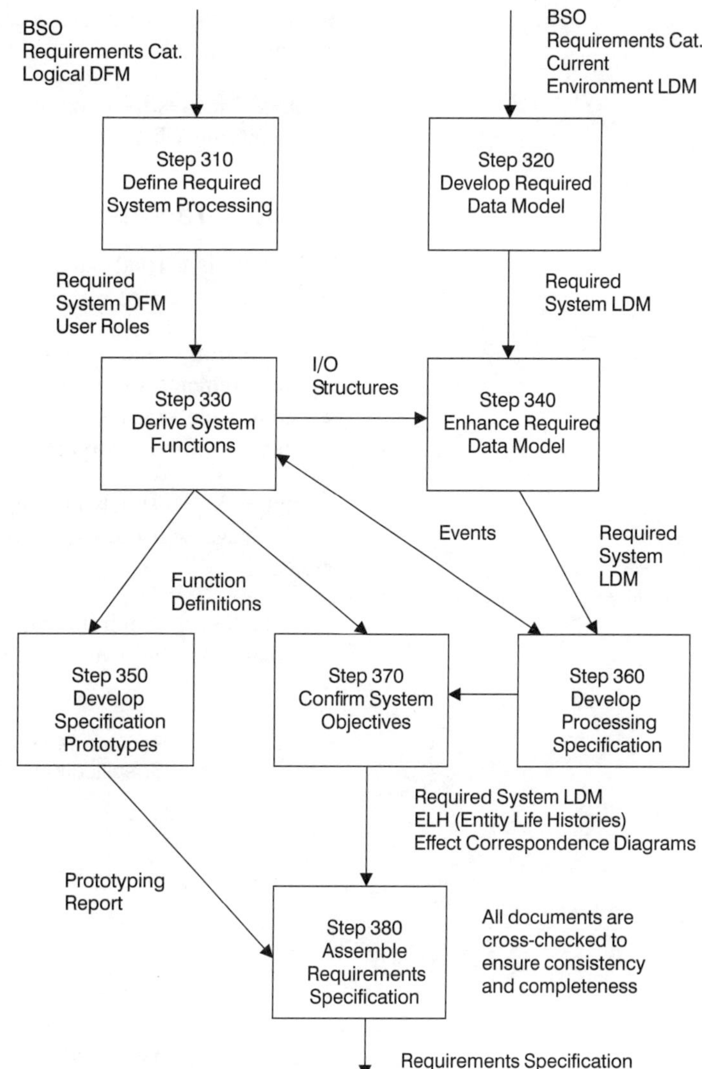

Figure 2.3.15 *Stage 3 – Definition of Requirements*

The requirements catalogue remains the centre document throughout this stage. It contains the functional and non-functional requirements which are updated as the stage develops. The Logical Data Model (LDM) is modified using the technique of relational data Analysis and will continue to provide a descriptive outline of the business rules and data requirements. The Data Flow Method (DFM) is an invaluable aid for system processing and communicating with the customer or end user of the product. It is refined up to the middle of the stage where more rigorous and detailed models are used to link the processing elements together. It will remain a useful reference document and will be included in the complete document set and used for consistency checks within the project.

The main objectives of the Definition of Requirements stage are:

- to provide a Requirements Specification Document for the development of a Logical Requirements Specification (LRS) to satisfy the needs of the customer or end user;

- to set out measurable acceptance criteria for the progress of the product.

Stage 3 moves from the process of analysis into the realms of design by specifying what the required system is to do.

Stage 4 Technical System Options

This stage is carried out in parallel to stage 5 (Logical Design). The main objectives are:

- to identify and specify ways of physically implementing the requirements specification;
- to provide a means of validation for the non-functional requirements that are to be incorporated into the proposed environment.

Figure 2.3.16 shows the steps taken during this activity.

The stage will need to plan and develop information in four main areas:

(1) Technical Environment – this will cover issues of specific hardware and software configuration and implementation.

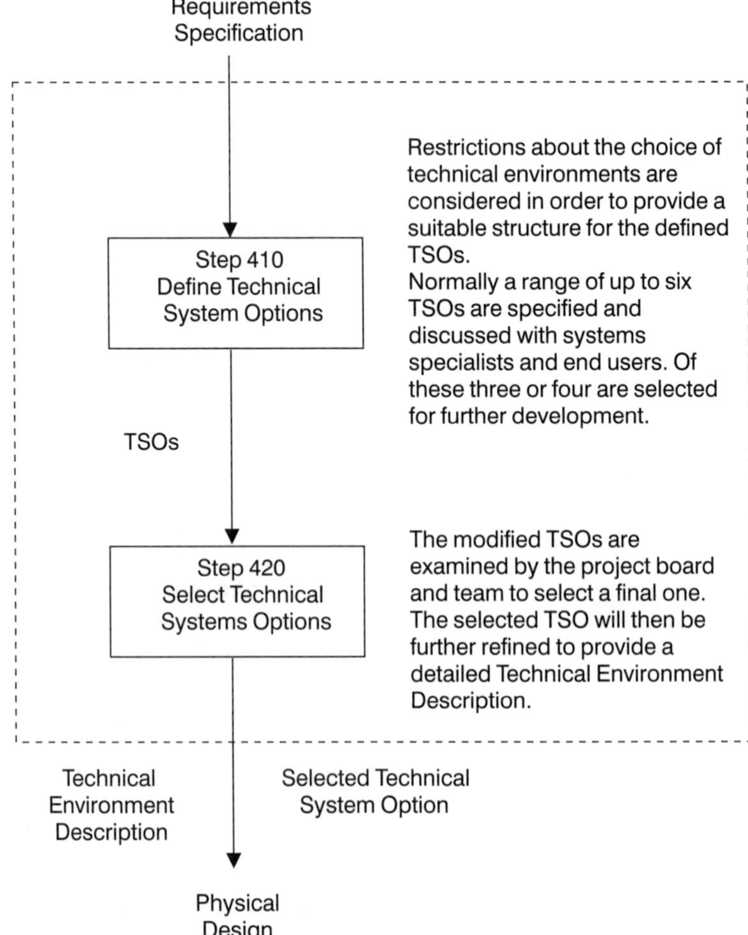

Figure 2.3.16 *Stage 4 – Technical Systems Options (TSO)*

(2) Development Strategy – who will develop the application, for example will the use of subcontractors be required or will it be developed totally in-house?
(3) Organizational Impact – this could include social issues like working practices or is it going to affect an existing project that is under production?
(4) System Functionality – this would of be handled in the BSO stage, but there may need to be some changes made in light of the technical requirements of the system.

The output of this stage is to determine the final implementation environment that the system is to run in. This includes the Technical Environment Description and the selected Technical System Option (TSO).

Stage 5 Logical Design

In this stage the developers will take the system design process as far as possible without referencing any technical environment issues. The resulting design will have a logical structure that is independent of any particular platform. It will act as a model for 'how' the system is to implement the user requirements without having any physical constraints. Figure 2.3.17 outlines the steps taken throughout this stage.

The main objectives of stage 5 are therefore:

- to create a logical specification of the system;
- to define the update and enquiry processing and the dialogues of the new system;
- to validate and ensure integrity of the processes created.

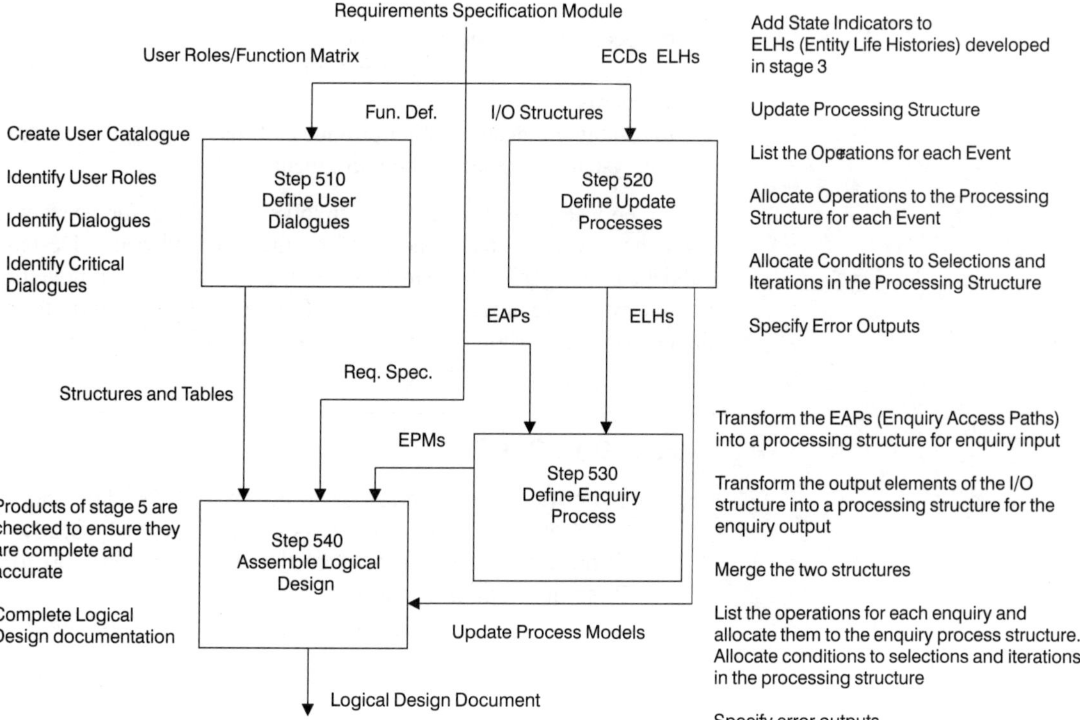

Figure 2.3.17 *Stage 5 – Logical*

The final step of this stage is to produce a Logical Design Document that will cover all the products of stage 5 and will provide an accurate base to be carried through to the Physical Design stage.

Stage 6 Physical Design

This stage translates the Logical Design method created in stage 5 and the Technical Environment Options created in stage 4 into a full Physical Design. The steps involved are outlined in Figure 2.3.18.

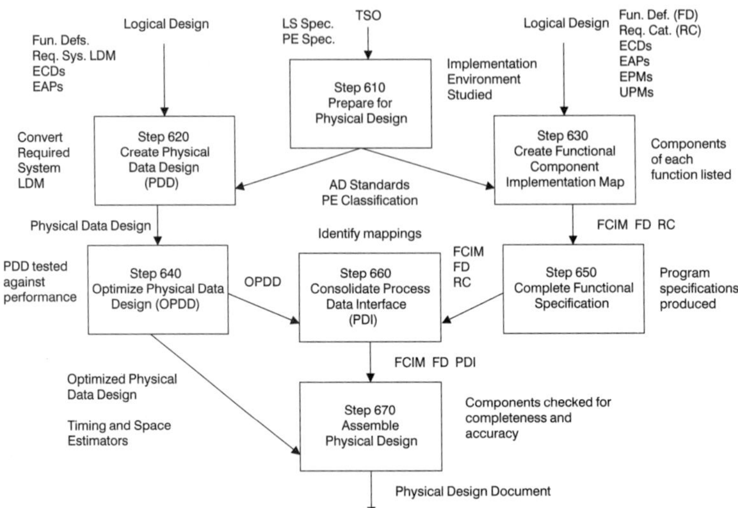

Figure 2.3.18 *Stage 6 – Physical Design*

The main objectives of stage 6 are:

- to specify the physical data, processes, input and outputs using the features of a physical environment and employing quality standards;
- to establish a design which provides all that is needed to construct the system in a specified environment.

The end step of this activity involves checking the system for completeness and consistency before the final Physical Design is published. Once this has been accepted the developers can move on to implementing the design to provide a full working application to meet the needs of the original user requirements where it all started.

Question 2.3.3

(1) State the seven stages used in the SSADM lifecycle.
(2) What are the main objectives of the Feasibility Study?
(3) Specify the requirements of the first step (210) in the Business Options stage.
(4) Specify the main requirements of stage 3 (Definition of Requirements).
(5) Within stage 4 what is a Technical Environment Description?

SSADM modelling techniques

Data flow modelling

Like other data flow diagram conventions the SSADM method is hierarchical in structure and starts with a 'context diagram'. The context diagram shows the entire system in a single process with data flowing between it and entities that represent the outside world.

Data flow modelling is used in the early stages of the SSADM model to:

- show the sources and receivers of the data into and out of the system;
- define the processes that transform or act on data;
- specify the flows of data around the system;
- show the storage requirements for the data within the system;
- provide a communication document between the developer of the system and the end user;
- outline the current environment;
- form the basis for the functional definition.

SSADM uses four main symbols to construct data flow diagrams. These are shown in Figure 2.3.19.

1. External entities

These represent real things like people and organizations, or other computer systems that supply or receive data into the system. They act as sources and sinks for the data that is required to initiate the system and receive the end result.

The name given to an external entity refers to a 'type' not an 'occurrence' of the entity. It is a generic type, for example an occurrence of College Administrator would be Sheila or Jack.

2. Processes

Processes represent the activities to be carried out and are trigged by data being passed to them. They represent a high level abstraction in user terms and do not equate directly with computer code. A process refers to the business activity that it supports.

Generally data flow diagrams that contain processes only show them transforming or changing data during the activity. There may be exceptions where the process acting on input data needs to produce enquiry information or reports.

The name given should be brief but still specify the transformation to be carried out, i.e. specify the processing to be carried out. The unique identifier is not a sequence number, like all data flow diagrams the sequence of events is not specified.

Like the Yourdon data flow diagrams the processes for the SSADM model can be refined or decomposed to produce lower level diagrams (children) containing additional data to more accurately represent the activity. This process starts with a context diagram and refinement continues until no further decomposition is possible.

The final processes are classified as 'Elementary Processes' which contain an asterisk in the lower right-hand corner of the box. For each

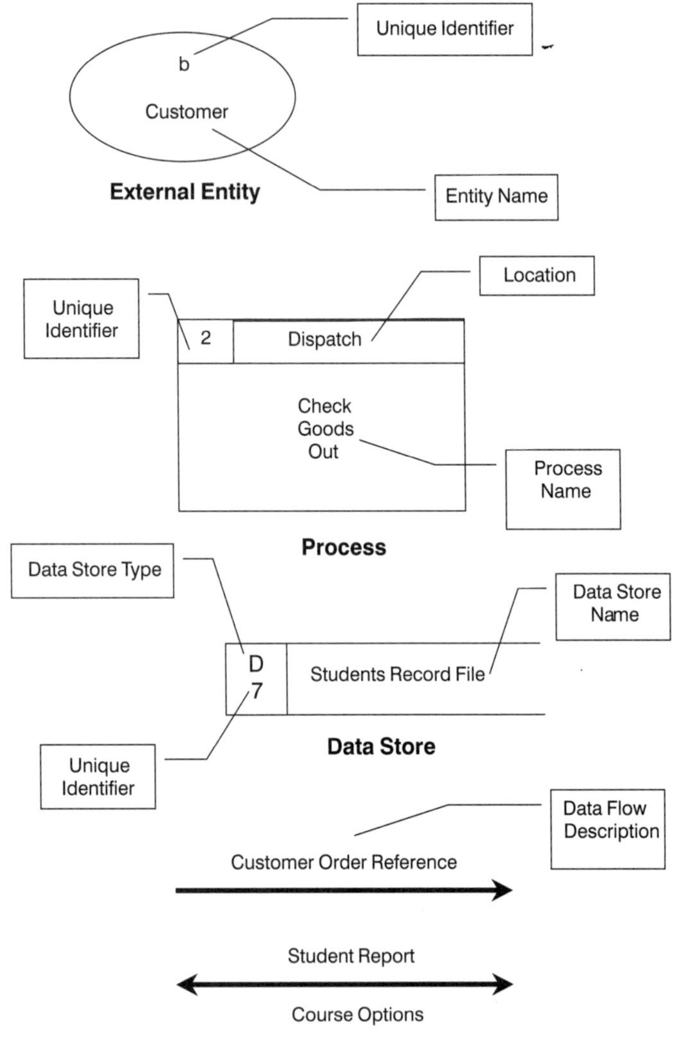

Figure 2.3.19 *Data flow diagram systems*

Elementary Process an Elementary Process Description will be completed summarizing its operations and activities. An outline of an Elementary Process Description is shown below:

Elementary Process Description
Process ID: 1
Process Name: Check Course Availability and Register Student
Description: Details about a new student are received from the college administrator for admissions. The course file is then examined to find a particular course that the student is qualified to join. Once a course is found this information along with the student details are passed on to the student file where it is permanently stored.

3. Data store

These are stores for holding data within the system. There are four types of store:

- **D:** This is a computerized data store that holds computerized data within the system being defined. For example, a computer-held purchase order file.
- **M:** This is a manual data store within the organization that the system is being developed for. For example, a filing cabinet, archive library, etc.
- **T(M):** This is a manual transient data store. This represents a temporary data store where data is held until it is read once only. After being read once the store is then removed or deleted. For example, pigeon hole, desk in-tray, etc.
- **T:** This is a computerized transient data store. This represents a temporary storage area for data passing through the system. For example, it may be necessary to temporarily save data for an input enquiry before it is fully processed. Also if searching for a number of stored items they can be temporarily stored before being displayed to the user.

The name given to a data store must reflect what it contains. There is no good just calling something 'Data Store' as this does not specify its contents. A better name would be 'Student File' as this gives a clue as to the contents of the store.

4. Data flows

Data flows use arrows to show the direction and name of the data flowing around the system. They specify the inputs and outputs to processes and data stores and highlight the information passing around the system as a whole acting as links between other objects within the DFD.

Listed below are the components that can be directly connected by data flows:

- Two processes.
- A data store and a process.
- A process and an externals entity.

What is not allowed:

- You cannot connect an external entity directly to a data store with a data flow.
- You cannot connect two data stores together with a data flow.

As shown in Figure 2.3.19 flows can be unidirectional or bidirectional and they must contain real data required to support the system. When obtaining information from a data store it is not necessary to show a flow going to the store that may contain a unique key to find a record. We only need to show data that is of interest in specifying what the business activity is to do.

All data flows should contain a unique label which clearly states the flow occurring. For example, names like Customer Order, Student Enquiry should be used, not abbreviated names like My Junk or In Data, as these do not give a clue as to the contents of the data flow.

Combining the components

By putting together the different components we can construct a picture a how data is passing through the system. The Data Flow Diagram (DFD) extract shown in Figure 2.3.20 illustrates the following activities.

(1) College Administrator sends new student details to the Admissions section.
(2) These are checked to find a suitable course which has vacancies.
(3) Student registration details are then permanently stored in the College Student File.

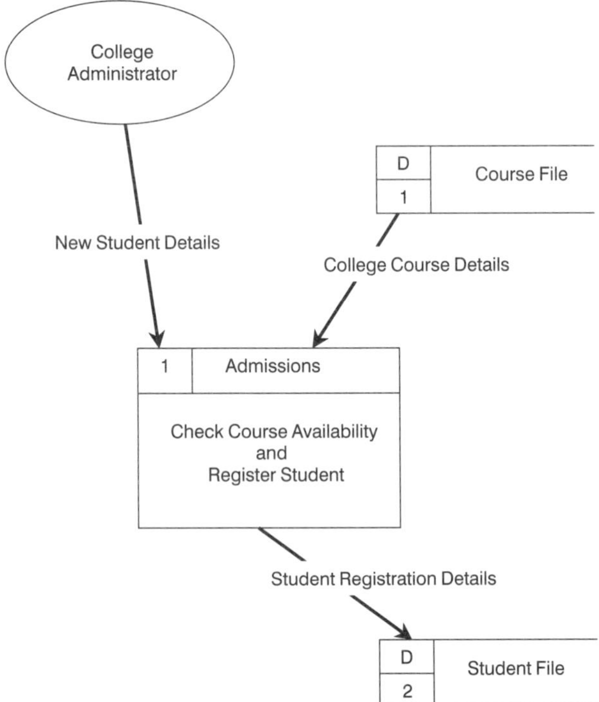

Figure 2.3.20 *College admission system*

During the early stages of the feasibility study (step 010) we are only concerned with modelling the physical flows of data in the current model, it is a high-level abstraction only. DFDs therefore provide an early representation of the system that provides a base for defining the problem along with any necessary Logical Data Models (LDM).

Logical modelling

The physical data flow diagram provides a model of how data is processed throughout the system and how data is actually stored. It does not tell the developer or user anything about the underlying meaning or structure of that data. An SSADM Logical Data Model (LDM) provides a way of graphically representing what the data information is really about, its rules and how it interacts with other information within the system.

Logical Data Modelling (LDM) consists of two parts:

- Logical Data Structure (LDS).
- Set of associated textual descriptions:
  - Entity descriptions;
  - Relationship descriptions;
  - Attribute descriptions;
  - Grouped domain descriptions.

A Logical Data Structure (LDS) is based on:

- Entities
- Attributes
- Relationships

As the concept of Logical Data Structure closely follows that of data modelling the concepts outlined above will be discussed in more detail in the data modelling section.

A Logical Data Model can be used to represent both the underlying processing of data within a current system and the required data structure of proposed new systems.

Question 2.3.4

(1) What is the function of a process within an SSADM data flow diagram?
(2) What is an Elementary Process and how is it designated?
(3) Specify what is not allowed when adding data flows to a DFD model.
(4) Name the component that acts as a source for the data flowing into a system.
(5) What are the main components of the Logical Data Model?

Example 2.3.5

The Morgan Show Company is responsible for running a series of canine exhibitions that include a number of associated seminars. A system needs to be designed that receives visitors in the foyer where a Registration Clerk checks their personal details and if they have made an advance booking. The visitor details are then added to an entry list that contains details of people who are currently in the exhibition. Once the visitors have been registered they are passed on to the Seminar Organizer who determines what seminars the visitor wishes to attend and adds the details to a seminar list. Finally visitors receive a pass from the Seminar Organizer that contains their personal details and any associated seminars that they wish to attend.

Question:
Complete an outline SSADM data flow diagram that represents the system.

Suggested solution:

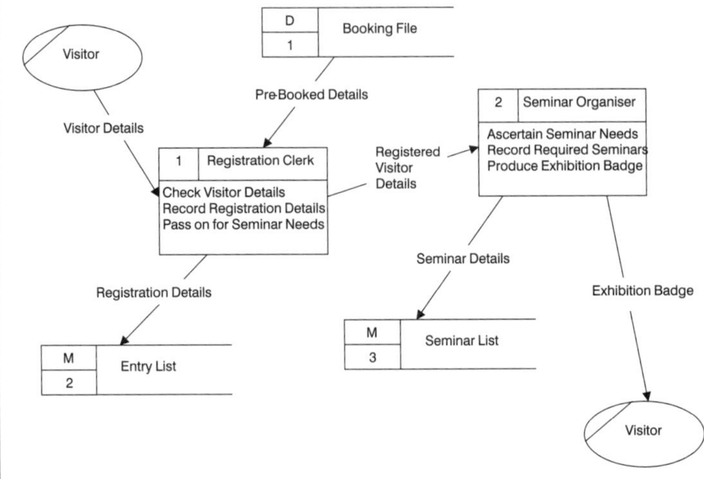

Figure 2.3.21 *Morgan Show Company*

Example 2.3.6

The Bess & Bailey Department Store has the facility to handle customers' orders 'in-house' and if the item they require is in stock it is delivered to their home. An Order Clerk is designated to attend to the customers as they enter the store. The Order Clerk assists the customer in choosing the required item and then checks via the Warehouse Manager to ascertain if it is stock. The Warehouse Manager looks up the details of the required item from the stock database and if they are available records the customer details (name and address) and raises a dispatch note which is sent to the customer's home.

Question:
Complete an outline SSADM data flow diagram that represents the Bess & Bailey Department Store system.

Object-Oriented Analysis (OOA) development

Class association diagrams

Object-oriented analysis is concerned with analysing the 'negotiated statement of requirements' to ascertain the required classes to be developed and any relating associations, responsibilities and collaborations.

Some general points:

- A class describes the behaviour of a set of objects of some kind.
- Objects are classified as instances of a class and can be associated to other objects. This is termed as an *association* between the classes for which the objects are instances.
- All classes have an internal state with an appropriate behaviour associated with them. This can be described in a set of *responsibilities* which specify a part of the overall behaviour of the intended system.
- In order to fulfil their responsibilities objects *collaborate* with other objects.

The first stage for any developer is to take the 'negotiated statements of requirements' and ascertain any classes (which represent objects) within the structure. These need to be analysed to find out if they are required in the model or not. The final list of objects then form a base for the development process to continue.

When analysing a negotiated statement of requirements we need first to identify any classes and associations that are present. There are two general issues that need to be made clear:

(1) It is difficult in the first instance to establish all the class and associations that exist within the document. It takes practice in order to become proficient in obtaining this data and analysis will improve with experience.

(2) When first establishing the classes and then the associations it must not be forgotten that both are interconnected. Considering what classes are needed helps in identifying what associations exist between the classes.

Identifying classes

Question 2.3.5

(1) What is the link between a Class and an Object?

(2) What format of class structure do Student and Library come under?

In identifying classes we are identifying the components whose behaviour is significant in the application area under analysis. It is first and foremost a requirement for a good understanding of the application area to be developed. If we take a banking cash machine system then Customer or Cash are obvious class structures that would need to be considered. Remember that class structures can come in different formats (tangible, roles, events and units, see Object-oriented analysis, page 116) which further add to the problem of class identification.

In order to analyse the requirements to determine the classes present, you should consider the 'nouns' or 'noun phrases' that occur within the text. When finding these they should be underlined in order to highlight their presence.

Take the extract below:

> In the college there are a number of rooms, some of these may be classrooms and contain students whilst others are non-teaching rooms or staff rooms. Each classroom in use contains a lecturer who is responsible for the course content being taught. Some of the lecturers are assigned course tutor roles with the responsibility of organizing the curriculum content of the subject areas.

By using the process of textual analysis the requirements can be scanned and any likely class candidates can be emphasized (or underlined).

Looking at the extract above we get:

> In the <u>college</u> there are a number of <u>rooms</u>, some of these may be <u>classrooms</u> and contain <u>students</u> whilst others are <u>non-teaching rooms</u> or <u>staff rooms</u>. Each <u>classroom</u> in use contains a <u>lecturer</u> who is responsible for the <u>course content</u> being taught. Some of the <u>lecturers</u> are assigned <u>course tutor</u> roles with the responsibility of organizing the <u>curriculum content</u> of the <u>subject areas</u>.

We can see that a number of likely candidates for classes to be developed have been underlined. But are all of these classes going to be required in the final model? This where a through understanding of the negotiated statement of requirements is essential, which is backed up with experience in developing object models.

Associations

As we have already learned an association is a connection between two objects that is significant for the application area under development.

Figure 2.3.22 shows one Lecturer object (Bailey), five Student objects (Peters, Jones, Watson, Collins and Davies) and five associations. The diagram only gives a limited view in what it is trying to express and requires what is called an *association type* to describe a group of associations with a common structure and meaning.

An association type has two important properties:

- A name which reflects the meaning of the association. This is often expressed as a verb, for example the association name between Lecturer and Class could be 'tutors' (a Lecturer tutors Class).

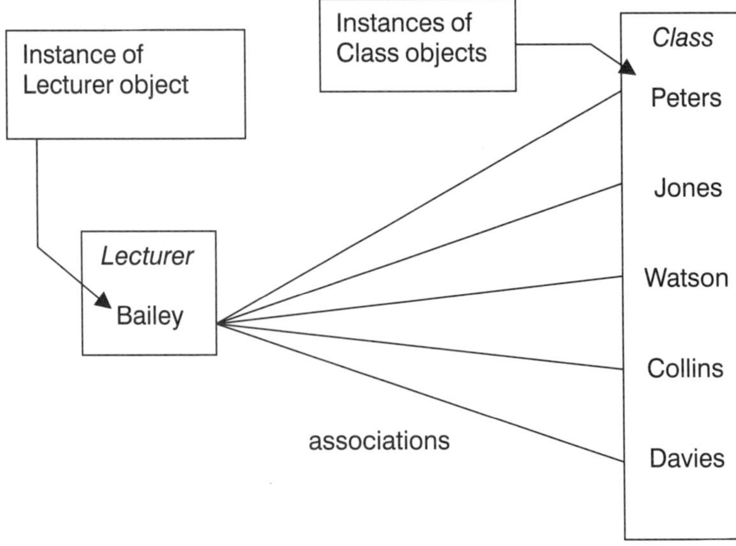

Figure 2.3.22 *Object instances and associations*

- The association will need to show multiplicity that relates to the degree between objects. These can be one to one, one to many and many to many. This is donated by the use of a block blob on the many end of the association line. The association multiplicity between Lecturer and Class is shown in Figure 2.3.23.

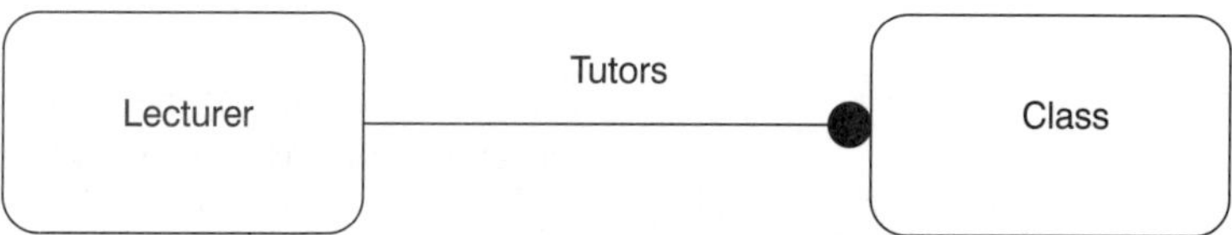

Figure 2.3.23 *The Tutors one to many association type*

When reading the diagram it stresses the multiplicity with respect to Class (i.e. there is one Lecturer object and many Class objects), but the diagram must also be considered in the other direction where Class is just concerned with one Lecturer object.

> **Question 2.3.6**
>
> Draw diagrams (similar to the one in Figure 2.3.23) by selecting objects of your own choice to represent associations that are classified as:
>
> (1) one to one;
> (2) many to many.
>
> Give a brief description for each diagram explaining the association type.

Invariants

Taking the example below:

> A Lecturer may lecture several Students and Students may be taught by a number of Lecturers that are members of the same Course Team as the Course Tutor.

This is saying that lecturers who lecture students must be from the same course team and the course tutor. This is known as an invariant and must always be true for the classes and associations being developed.

An invariant is a rule that places a constraint on the allowable instances of classes and associations.

Responsibilities

These need to be specified for the classes being developed. Shown below are two examples, one for a Student class and one for a Course class, that need to record data as part of their operational behaviour.

Class: Student
Responsibilities:
Recording the student name, enrolment number and course.

Class: Course
Responsibilities:
Recording the course name, curriculum content, formal prerequisites.

An example where the responsibility is designed to carry out a prescribed task is shown below:

Class: Sensor
Responsibilities:
To set off the temperature and pressure warning systems if they become dangerous.

Identifying associations

One way of achieving this is to use a class-association matrix which takes the classes that have been identified and pairs them together to establish if an association, which is relevant to the application area under development, exists.

For specifying small to medium size object models a useful approach for identifying associations is to use a matrix structure which is shown in Figure 2.3.24. The diagram specifies a class-association matrix for classes that are established for a typical college system.

	Principal	Vice Principal	Head of Department	Section Managers	Lecturer	Student	Administrator
Principal		X					
Vice Principal	X		X				
Head of Department		X		X	X		X
Section Managers			X		X		X
Lecturer			X	X		X	X
Student					X		X
Administrator			X	X	X	X	

The Xs signify that an association exists between classes

Figure 2.3.24 *Class-association matrix*

The wording of an association between classes plays an important role in determining its category. For example:

> A work schedule is organized by a lecturer <u>for a</u> student.

The words *for a* suggest that an association exists between Lecturer and Student which would emphasize one aspect of a one to many association. If we had a statement like:

> Work schedules are organized by lecturers and used by students.

Here the words *used by* signify a many multiplicity association with respect to the work schedules.

Inheritance

We have seen that inheritance is an important attribute of object-oriented analysis and this concept needs to be clearly specified on the class-association diagram. A college, for example, will have many employees, the principal, vice principal, senior managers, lecturers, maintenance staff, security and administration staff. They all inherit common attributes, for example they all have names, addresses, national insurance numbers, etc., but they will differ in respect to their precise roles and their associations with other class members. A graphical representation is shown in Figure 2.3.25.

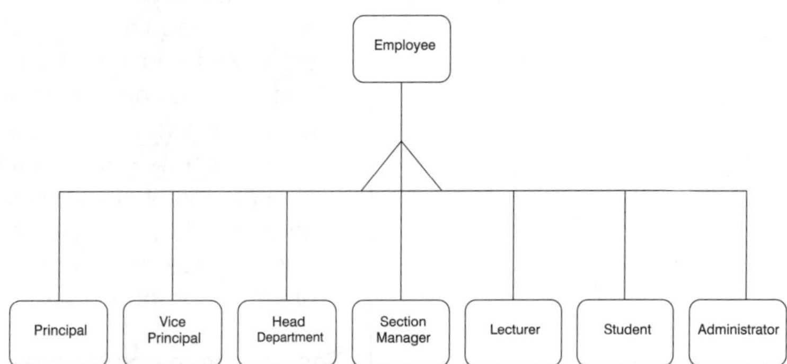

Figure 2.3.25 *Class-association diagram showing inherited classes*

In some texts this inheritance relationship is known as a 'is-a-kind-of' relationship. The semantics of this diagram specifies the behaviour of each inherited class in two ways. For example, an instance of Lecturer has its behaviour defined in two ways; the part of the behaviour that is unique for lecturers and the part common to all employees defined in the Employee class.

Developing a class-association diagram

The following example develops the concept of a class-association model by taking part of a negotiated statement of requirements, analysing its content to ascertain the classes and associations and produces a graphical representation.

Remember a class is a set of objects that share a common structure and a common behaviour. An object has state, behaviour and identity.

Example 2.3.7

Part of a negotiated statement of requirements for the Carabaz Dog Breeding Kennels is shown below:

> The kennels need to keep and maintain information about the dogs they keep and the progress of breeding when the required dogs become available. The dogs are organized into breeds; each dog belonging to a breed and a breed contains many dogs. There are two sorts of dog; a dog (males) and a bitch (female). It is important for the kennels to maintain a record for the breeding background of all the dogs. A dog (male) can mate many times a year, whereas a bitch (female) can only mate once (when they come into season). A mating will hopefully produce many puppy births.

We first need to perform a textual analysis of the requirements in order to determine the candidate objects for the classes. Possible classes are:

> The <u>kennels</u> need to keep and maintain <u>information</u> about the <u>dogs</u> they keep and the progress of breeding when the required <u>dogs</u> become available. The <u>dogs</u> are organized into <u>breeds</u>; each dog belonging to a <u>breed</u> and a <u>breed</u> contains many <u>dogs</u>. There are two sorts of <u>dog</u>; a <u>dog (males)</u> and a <u>bitch (female)</u>. It is important for the <u>kennels</u> to maintain a <u>record</u> for the breeding background of all the <u>dogs</u>. A <u>dog (male)</u> can <u>mate</u> many times a <u>year</u>, whereas a <u>bitch (female)</u> can only <u>mate</u> once (when they come into <u>season</u>). A <u>mating</u> will hopefully produce many <u>puppy</u> births.

The candidate objects are:

> Kennels, Information, Dogs, Breeds, Dog (Male), Bitch (Female), Record, Mate, Season, Year and Puppy.

From this list we need to eliminate any:

- Redundant classes – where two words mean the same thing you need to choose the one that is more descriptive.
- Irrelevant classes – those that have nothing directly to do with the problem.
- Vague classes – those that are not specific enough and need to be more closely defined before they can be developed.

The eliminated candidate objects are:

> Information, Record, Season and Year – which are not directly relevant at this stage to represent the requirements of the system.

This leaves the revised list of candidate objects:

Kennels, Dogs, Breeds, Dog (Male), Bitch (Female), Puppy and Mate.

These represent the requirements for the kennels' breeding programme and will form the basis of the class-association diagram.
Possible associations are between:

Kennels and Breed (one to many association, as each breed belongs to the kennels and the kennels have many breeds).

Breed and Dog (one to many association, as each dog belongs to a breed and breeds contain many dogs).

Dog (male) and Mate (one to many association, as a dog can mate many times).

Bitch (female) and Mate (one to one as bitches can only mate once – when they are in season).

Puppy and Mate (one to many association, as a single mating can produce several puppies).

Inheritance:

Dog (male), Bitch (female) and Puppy are all types of Dog and therefore inherit some common characteristics as well as individual ones.

Responsibilities:

Class: Kennels
'There is only one instance of this class, it is the orchestrating instance.'
Class: Breed
Responsibilities: Record the types of breed.
Class: Dog
Responsibilities: Record the name, breed, sex and age of the dogs.
Class: Dog (male)
(inherits from dog)
Responsibilities: Record the date of last mating.
Class: Bitch (female)
(inherits from dog)
Responsibilities: Record the date of last season.
Class: Puppy
(inherits from dog)
Responsibilities: Record name of new puppies.
Class: Mate
Responsibilities: Record the mating details for each litter.

Figure 2.3.26 represents an understanding of the application area to be developed. It represents the way things are related to one another and ensures that we fully understand

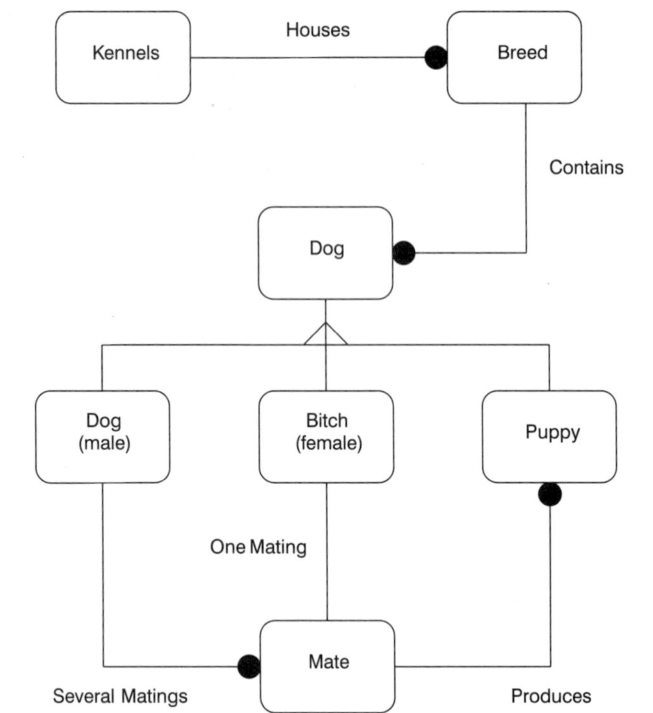

Figure 2.3.26 *Class-association diagram for the Labrador Dog Breeding Kennels*

what is required before designing a solution. It is still open for discussion with the customer, or end user, to ensure it is an accurate model for the functional requirements of the system.

Question 2.3.7

(1) What are you looking for when you carry out the process of textual analysis?
(2) Give a graphical illustration showing an example of inheritance.
(3) What is an invariant?
(4) What method can be used to identify associations?
(5) When carrying out textual analysis on a problem statement what does a redundant class mean?

Exercise 2.3.3

The following is an extract from a negotiated statement of requirements:

> An organizer needs to keep and update information on a seminar devoted to canine health. The seminar is made up of several sessions, each run by different speakers. The speakers running the sessions have to produce a

booklet for their own slot. Each session has a chairperson and that person is only allocated this role once. Information about the speakers who produce the booklets needs to be recorded; each booklet is written by one speaker only and speakers are only required to produce one booklet. For the seminar presentation purposes, a person can be a chairperson or a speaker.

(1) Perform a textual analysis to ascertain any candidate objects.
(2) Select the required classes to be presented.
(3) Ascertain any associations that exist.
(4) Specify the inheritance factors contained within the text.
(5) Produce associated text to outline the class responsibilities.
(6) Complete a class-association diagram.

UML

Introduction

The Unified Modelling Language (UML) is the industry-standard language for specifying, visualizing, constructing, and documenting the artefacts of software systems. Using UML, programmers and application architects can make a blueprint of a project, which, in turn, makes the actual software development process easier. UML was created at Rational Software by methodologists Grady Booch, Ivar Jacobson, and Jim Rumbaugh with input from other leading methodologists, many software vendors, as well as end users. Its aim is to unify the various existing systems into a best-of-breed modelling language.

The UML technique can be used to model the following processes:

- Business process modelling with use cases.
- Class and object modelling.
- Component modelling.
- Distribution and deployment modelling.

As already stated there is an increase in the use of object-oriented programming languages, so UML can provide an alternative model for analysis.

UML claims

- Is sufficiently expressive to represent and connect the concepts of abstraction within software development across a number of domains which include:
  - information systems;
  - real time systems;
  - web systems.
- It can handle the modelling of business processes:
  - their logical and physical software models;
  - provide references to their implementation.

- It is not complex:
  - the unified modelling language is built from a small number of concepts applied consistently across a number of modelling problems.

Basic components of UML

- UML specification contains a notation guide, semantics and appendices.
- UML notation and semantics describe:
  - class diagrams;
  - object diagrams;
  - use case diagrams;
  - behaviour diagrams;
    - ♦ state diagrams;
    - ♦ activity diagrams;
    - ♦ sequence diagrams;
    - ♦ collaboration diagrams;
  - implementation diagrams;
    - ♦ component diagram;
    - ♦ deployment diagram.

UML is free for all to use within their given applications. This helps to establish its usage within industry where software companies can use it within their own methods and developers of computer aided software engineering applications are free to develop associated tools.

Objects and classes

One of the main advantages of UML is that it provides an excellent foundation for object-oriented analysis and design. UML defines and object as:

> An entity with a well-defined boundary and identity that encapsulates state and behaviour. State is represented by attributes and relationships, behaviour is represented by operations and methods. An object is an instance of a class.

Question 2.3.8

(1) Where does UML originate from?
(2) What are the stated advantages of using the UML modelling process?

UML consolidates a set of core modelling techniques that are generally accepted across many current development applications. Its inherent object structure is ideally suited for implementation into modern languages like C++ and Java.

UML diagram structures

1. Use case diagram

To determine the system boundaries and the high-level requirements for the system a 'use case' diagram is constructed. It shows the 'actors' in the system and the general services that they require. Stick people normally represent the actors and the services are represented by ellipses. These diagrams originate from Jacobsen who was one of the three original developers of UML.

Definition for a use case diagram:

A sequence of actions the system performs that yields an observable result of value to a particular actor.

They are used for:

- providing scenarios that illustrate prototypical use case instances. An instance of the use case class;
- providing an overall picture of systems functionality and user requirements.

An example 'use case' model is shown in Figure 2.3.27.

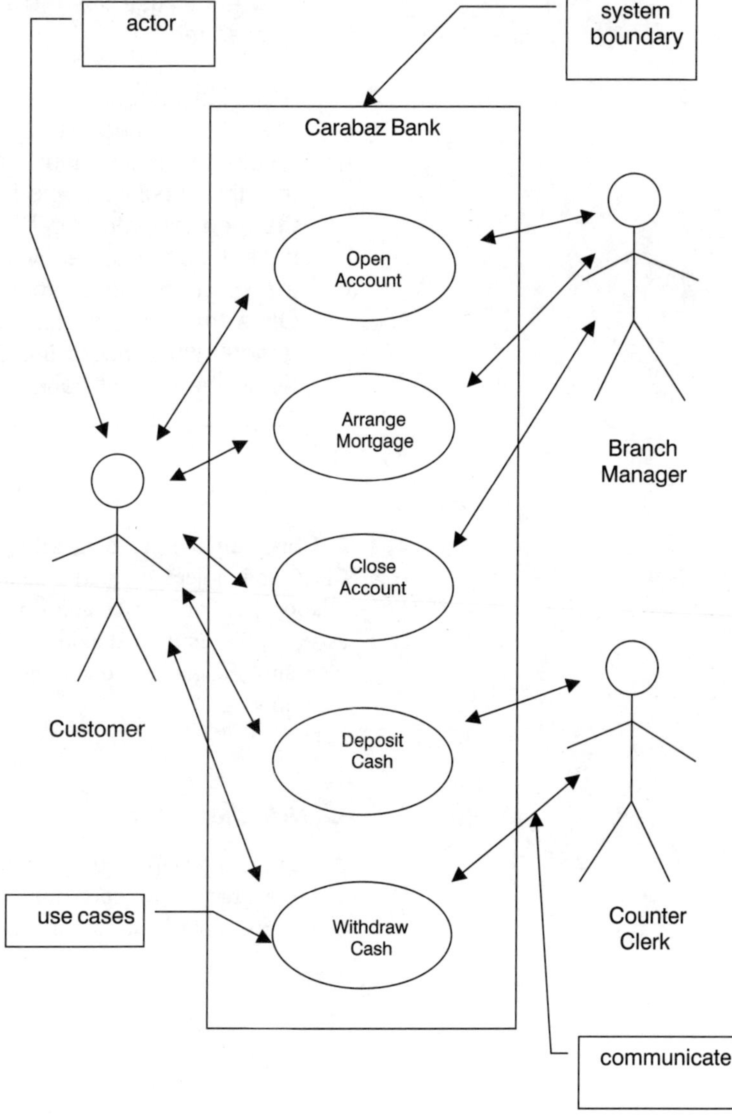

Figure 2.3.27 *A use case diagram*

A use case diagram has the following advantages:

- Captures requirements from users' perspective – it provides a diagrammatic base for user involvement and validation.
- Helps manage delivery – prioritize use cases to define processes for delivery and help estimate requirements.
- Progresses the development – can identify objects and provides a base for user manuals and test plans.
- Improves quality – aids tracing of requirements and identifies faults earlier.

Question 2.3.9

(1) Specify two advantages for creating a 'use case' diagram.
(2) Draw a 'use case' diagram to represent the following scenario:

A patient attends a consultation at the hospital and is seen by a specialist about a medical problem. This results in an operation being performed by a surgeon (not the specialist) who is also an expert in the area of the medical problem. The operation is serious and the patient needs to recover in the recovery ward where the surgeon and doctors can monitor his/her progress. Once they are satisfied the patient is transferred to a general ward where the doctors and nurses can finally nurse the patient back to full health.

2. Class and object diagrams
Class and object diagrams capture most of the static structure and relationships of classes and objects. They do not handle the dynamic aspect of their behaviour, this is modelled in either state diagrams, sequence diagrams, collaboration diagrams or activity diagrams.

Class diagram

A class is a group of things with similar attributes and behaviour. A class diagram represents 'things' that are handled in the system. A simple example is shown in Figure 2.3.28.

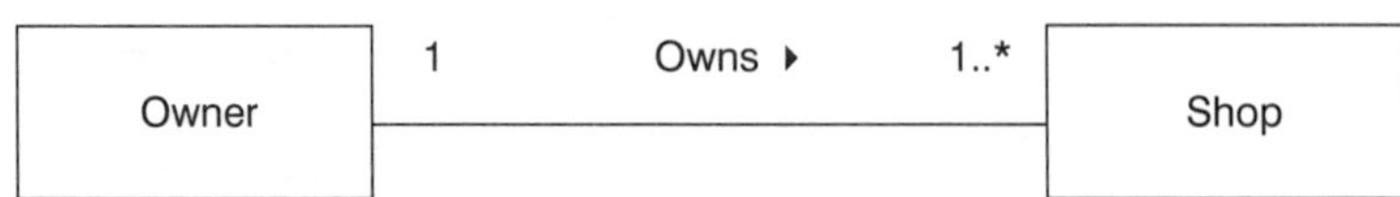

Figure 2.3.28 *Example of a class diagram*

Object diagram

This is a variation of the class diagram and uses similar notation. It differs in the fact that it shows a number of object instances of a class instead of just classes. Figure 2.3.29 shows a class diagram containing Student and Computer classes, this is then expanded to produce an object diagram which shows a Student instance 'Jones' and two Computer instances 'Library PC' and 'Room 801'.

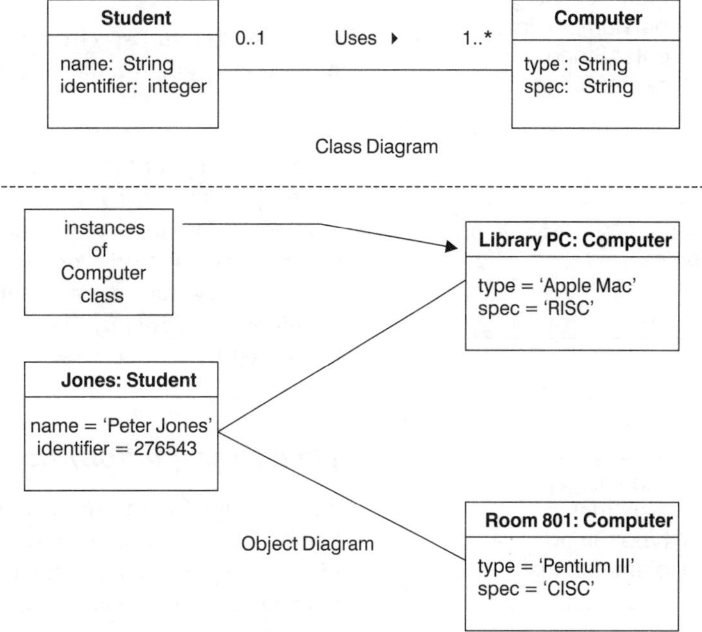

Figure 2.3.29 *Object diagram developed from class diagram*

Object diagrams are used to exemplify a complex class diagram by showing what the actual instances and relationships look like. They may also be used as part of a collaboration diagram which specifies the dynamic collaboration between objects.

Name
Attributes
Operations

Figure 2.3.30 *Class compartments*

Class diagram syntax

The class box can be split into three compartments as shown in Figure 2.3.30. The syntax used in the compartments is independent of the programming language used, although some developers like to incorporate program specific structures like Pascal, C++ or Java.

Figure 2.3.31 gives an example of this for a class Lorry with attributes Make, Model, Weight and Registration, followed by the operations start(), drive(), stop(), load(), unload(), park().

Lorry
make: String model: String weight: real registration: String
start ( ) drive ( ) load ( ) unload ( ) park ( )

Figure 2.3.31 *Lorry class example*

Name compartment

This contains the name of the class and is typed in **bold** and is centred. The name should relate directly to the class it represents and be meaningful. Often a noun is used like Customer, Student, Manager, etc.

Attribute compartment

Typical attribute types are integer, real, Boolean, enumeration and String, etc. which can be specific for certain programming languages. Attributes can be expressed as 'public' which can be viewed and used from outside the class. The encapsulated attributes are defined as 'private' and can only be viewed and accessed from within the class they are declared in. To denote the difference between these the following notation is used:

- – (minus sign) specifies a private attribute;
- + (plus sign) specifies a public attribute.

Account

- identifier: integer
- pin number: integer
+ date: String
+ name: String

Figure 2.3.32 *Visibility of attributes*

An example is shown in Figure 2.3.32 that contains two private (encapsulated) attributes *identifier* and *pin number* and two public attributes *date* and *name*.

In some variations of the model a *protected* type can also be used which is similar to the *private* type except that all inherited classes can also view and use the data. The term used for these attribute definitions is *visibility*, i.e. is an attribute visible and can it be referenced by other classes.

Operation (action) compartment

These are used to manipulate the attributes or perform certain actions. Figure 2.3.33 shows two operations *display()* and *rotate(degrees: real)*. These will look familiar to you especially if you have been programming in languages like C++ and Java where functions and methods are integral parts of the language.

The operations describe what a class can do and what services it offers.

Shape

- radians: real
+ size: real
+ type: String
+ diameter: real

display( )
rotate(degrees: real)

Figure 2.3.33 *Class operation example*

Relationships within UML

Class diagrams consist of classes and the relationships between them. The relationships can be described as:

1. *Association* – a connection between two classes or an object of those classes. An association represents a semantic link between classes that can be unidirectional or bidirectional. Graphically an association is shown as a solid line, possibly directed, with a name and showing multiplicity. An example is shown in Figure 2.3.34.
2. *Generalization* – a relationship between a more general and a more specific element. This relationship is used to define inheritance (to model derived classes from a parent class). Graphically this is shown as a solid line with an arrowhead that points to the parent. An example is shown in Figure 2.3.35.
3. *Dependency* – this specifies a relationship between two elements one being dependent and the other independent. A change in the independent element will affect the dependent element. Graphically this is shown as a dashed line and may be labelled. An example is shown in Figure 2.3.36.

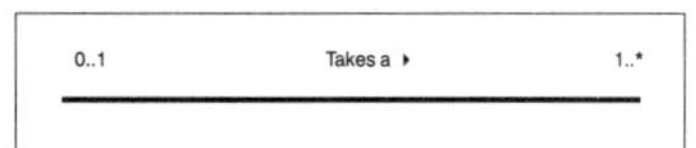

Figure 2.3.34 *An example of an association*

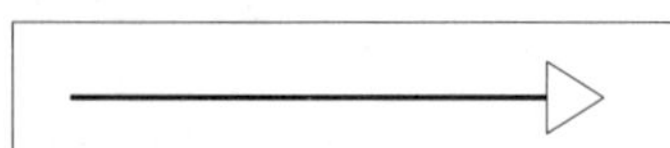

Figure 2.3.35 *An example of a generalization*

Figure 2.3.36 *An example of a dependency*

Figure 2.3.37 *An example of a refinement*

4. *Refinement* – a relationship between two descriptions of the same thing, but at different levels of development. Graphically (see Figure 2.3.37) this is shown as a dashed line with a hollow triangle between the two elements.

Association structure

An association occurs where classes depend on, or interact with, one another. They define the routes for sending messages and relate to the operations that objects must meet in order to carry out their responsibilities. An association name must be expressed so that it describes its exact relationship between classes. A filled arrow that specifies the direction of the association may also follow it. The name normally contains a verb that expresses the association, for example *Takes a*, *Placed with*, *Employs*' etc. These are found during the textual analysis process where verb and verb phrases are identified. An example of associations between two classes is shown in Figure 2.3.38.

If a class participates in the association then it has a specific role in the relationship. In Figure 2.3.39 an Assistant has the role of employee and the Shop has the role of a counter.

Most texts and the OMG (Object Management Group) UML specification outline several types of association, but for the level of work required for this 'system's analysis' unit what is classified as a normal association will generally handle its specified aims.

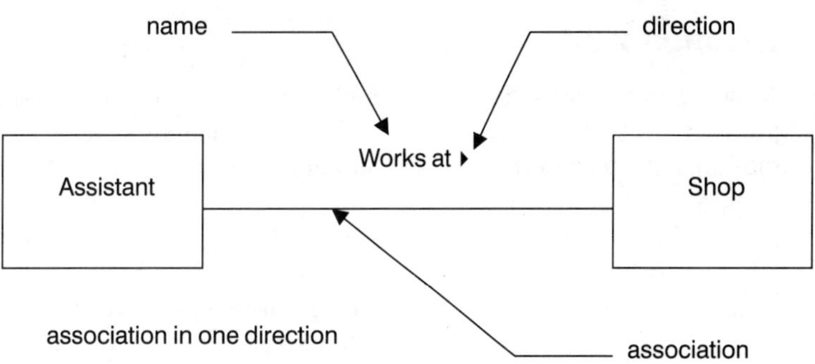

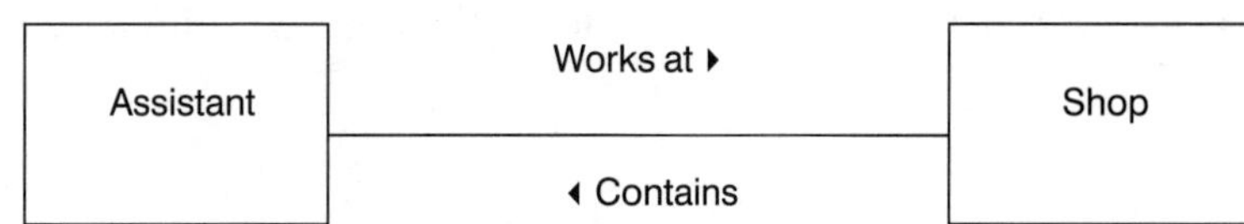

a bidirectional association

Figure 2.3.38 *Class association syntax*

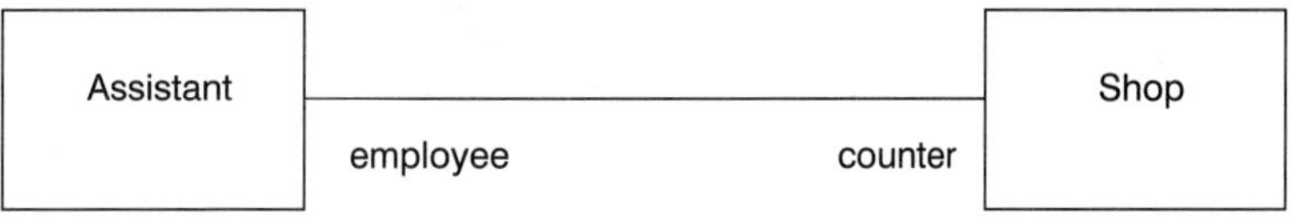

Figure 2.3.39 *Association role relationship*

Question 2.3.10

(1) What is the difference between a class diagram and an object diagram?
(2) What does *visibility* of attributes mean? Give two examples.
(3) What is the *operation* compartment of a class diagram for?
(4) Specify the four types of relationships that exist between classes.
(5) What do associations define?

Multiplicity

It is sometimes necessary to show how objects are linked across instances of an association. This is termed multiplicity (i.e. the number of objects involved in an association), examples of which are shown below:

- 0..1 (zero to one);
- 0..* or just * (zero to many);
- 1..* (one to many);
- x..y (x to y where x and y are integer values, i.e. 7..14);
- n (exact number, i.e. 5, 4, 47, etc.).

Question 2.3.11

Draw a simple class diagram to represent the relationship between a Lecturer and Tutorial group. Add a suitable name, direction and multiplicity.

Combinations of these can be used to specify more complex multiplicities which can be expressed within list structures.

If an association is shown to have a 'many' multiplicity side then an alternative way of specifying how individual objects can be found may be used. This is then termed a 'qualified association' and is donated by an identifier enclosed in a box that is applied to the class that uses it. An example of this structure is shown in Figure 2.3.40, where customers have unique identifiers that allow them to be referenced by the Accounts.

Inheritance

Inheritance is a mechanism that allows classes to inherit characteristics through a tree type structure. At the top of a tree is a superclass that

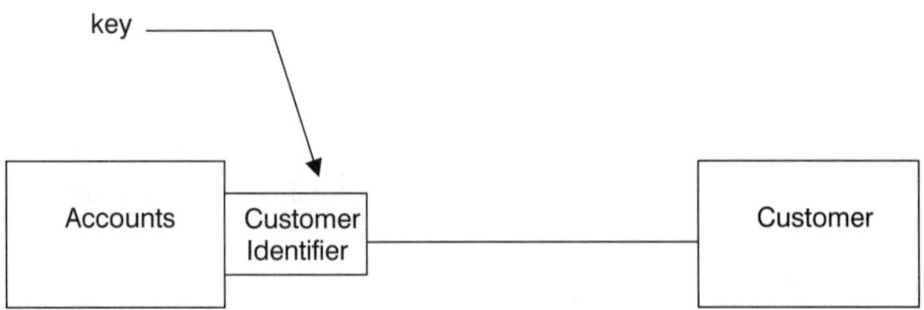

Figure 2.3.40 *Qualified association*

contains all the common characteristics required by the subclasses underneath it. The subclasses can then use the characteristics (i.e. inherit them) from the superclass plus any additional ones that they declare within themselves. Inheritance operates at class level and is the kind of relationship that centres on the activity of classification. Multiple inheritance can be shown by producing further levels, i.e. producing subclasses of subclasses.

Inheritance can be approached in two ways: through *specialization* or *generalization*. Specialization involves examining a particular class for different ways in which its member objects can be split into subclasses which have their own individual characteristics. Generalization involves searching for different classes that have the same characteristics in common and grouping those characteristics into a superclass. For example, if we wanted two classes, *Circle* and *Sphere* then they have some common attributes like radius, diameter, etc. which can be grouped in a superclass called *Shape*. Here we have used generalization to abstract common characteristics of circle and sphere into a task superclass.

Aggregation

This is split into two categories: aggregation and composition (or composite aggregation). The former is a special case of an association and signifies a 'part-of' relationship between classes or objects. Diagrammatically a hollow diamond is used at the end of the association to signify that aggregation exists between classes. For a college system a Department is part of the whole College. This representation is shown in Figure 2.3.41.

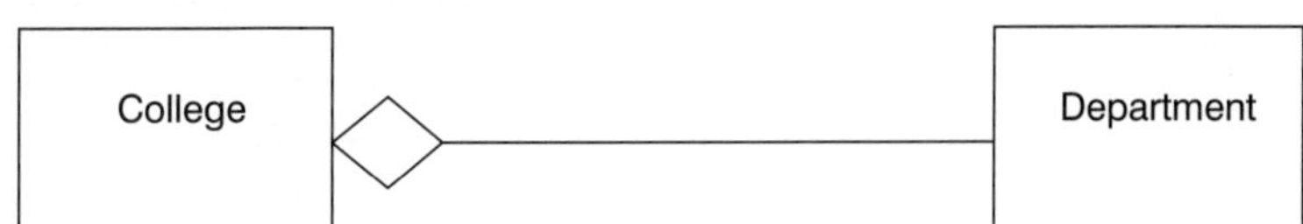

Figure 2.3.41 *Aggregation*

An aggregation operates at the object level, unlike inheritance which operates at the class level. The tree structure used is similar to that used with inheritance apart for the diamond present at the superclass end. This can lead to some confusion and you need to remember that a aggregation tree is composed of objects that are part of an aggregate object, whereas a generalization tree is composed of classes that describe a single object.

A composition (composite aggregation) indicates that any parts of an object 'live' inside a unique whole. That is, the part will live or die together with the whole. Diagrammatically this is represented by a black diamond and is shown in Figure 2.3.42 where a Statement 'lives' inside the Transaction and if the Transaction is destroyed the Statement will die along with in.

A composition owns its parts, therefore the multiplicity on its whole side must be zero or one (0..1) and the multiplicity on the part side may be any value (*).

Figure 2.3.42 *Composite aggregation*

Responsibilities

A responsibility is normally expressed in terms of obligations to other elements. It is normally expressed as a string and attached to a class in its own name compartment. Figure 2.3.43 gives an example of a classifier symbol with a list of responsibilities.

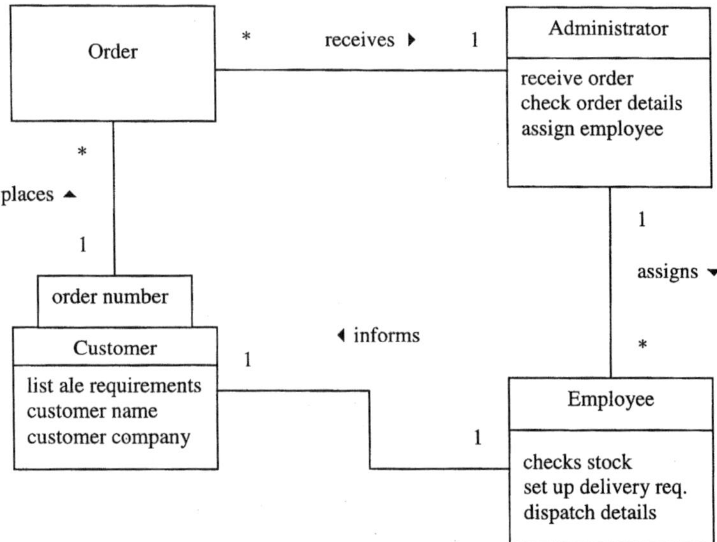

Classes with required responsibilities

Administrator	
Responsibilities	Collaborations
Receive an order from a customer	Customer
Check the order details	Order
Assign Employee to handle the Order	Employee

Associated Class-Responsibility-Collaboration Table

Figure 2.3.43 *Bailey Ale Company class diagram*

A good starting point for modelling classes is to specify the responsibilities using a natural English structure. Each class will have at least one responsibility ranging to only a few for well-structured classes. Never allow a class to have an excessive number of responsibilities otherwise it may lead to modelling problems and a complex interpretation that is difficult to validate. As you refine a class model the responsibilities can be transformed into attributes and operations.

Navigability

In more detailed diagrams it is advantageous to show the direction of the association between classes. Graphically this is shown by using an open headed arrow that points to the class that is navigable. For example, if we had two classes *Order* and *Customer* and the arrow points to the customer class then we can say that *Order* has the responsibility to tell you which customer it is for, but the *Customer* has no reciprocal ability to tell you which order it has. The lines can have the same multiplicity as ordinary associations and can be shown as unidirectional or bidirectional.

General comment

For a first-level abstraction we should not spend too much time looking for attributes and operations as these can be added as the project develops. For a general view that is understandable to the customer or end user, the responsibilities can give a clearer picture of the required behaviour for the classes. The initial class diagram should be kept simple; it does not need to fix the actual implementation, but provides a base for discussion and future development.

A class diagram only gives a static view of the classes in the system and does not give us any information about how the system behaves dynamically, i.e. what happens over time as the system is executed. In order to express these concepts UML uses the following diagrams:

- sequence diagrams;
- collaboration diagrams;
- state diagrams;
- activity diagrams.

Sequence and collaboration diagrams are different ways of specifying the messages that pass between classes over time periods. State diagrams show how objects of a class change state when acted on by certain events. Activity diagrams are similar to state diagrams but are more appropriate to systems that change state as a result of an internal event as opposed to an external one. An example of a sequence diagram is shown in Figure 2.3.44.

Question 2.3.12

(1) What is a composite aggregation? How is this symbolized on a class diagram?
(2) How are responsibilities recorded on a class diagram?
(3) What is the difference between inheritance and aggregation?

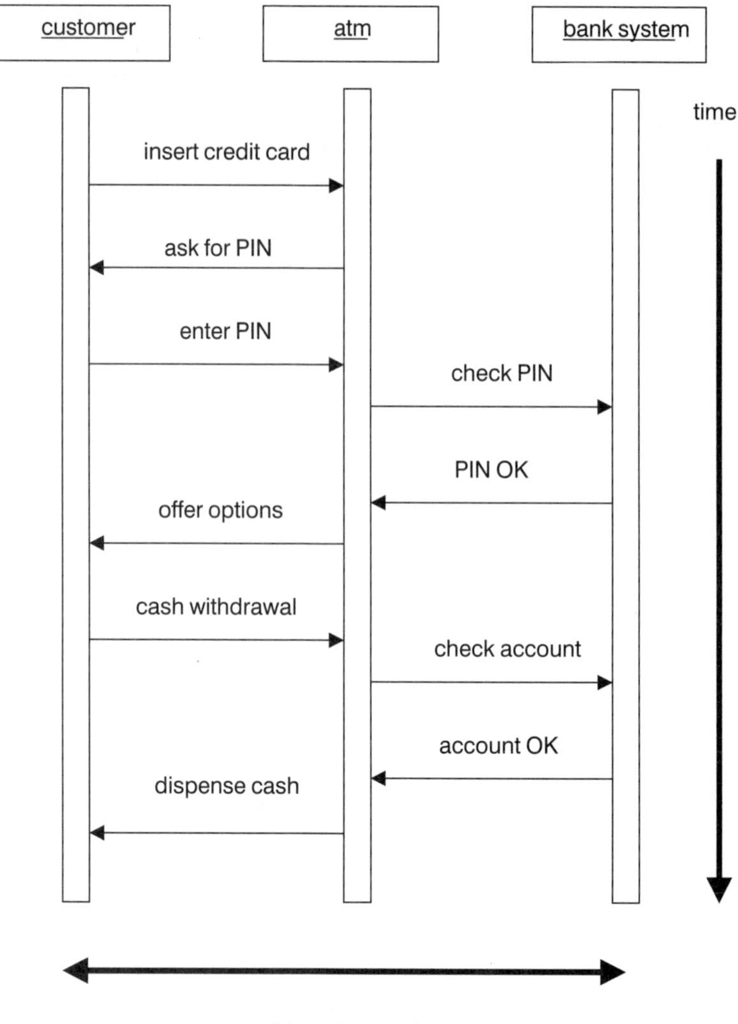

Figure 2.3.44 *Sequence diagram for an automatic teller machine system*

Example 2.3.8

The following is an extract from a negotiated statement of requirements:

> The Bailey Ale Company is a small independent brewing company that produces a selection of real ales. The company requires a system to process a customer order for a consignment of ales. The company has a designated administrator who receives the customer order and assigns an employee to check the assignment and feedback the availability to the customer.
>
> The ale supplied to the customer is part of a consignment that comes in three types:
>
> - Mild Brew – which is brewed to 3.4% alcohol with a specific gravity of 1.024 and a low sugar content;

- Vicars Tibble – which is brewed to 5.3% alcohol with a specific gravity of 1.037 and a medium sugar content;
- Bailey Gut Rot – which is brewed to 8.1% alcohol with a specific gravity of 1.098 and a high sugar content.

The management responsibilities of the administrator are to receive customer orders, check the order details and assign an employee to process the order. Each order is given a unique 'order number' by the customer and specifies the ale required for the consignment, along with the customer name and company. On receiving the cleared order the employee responsible for processing it checks the consignment details to ensure the ale is in stock, sets up delivery requirements and informs the customer that the order is being dispatched. The employee then activates the consignment requirements. The consignment responsibilities are to list the number and type of ale ordered along with the cost breakdown.

Take the following steps to analyse the requirements:

(1) Carry out a textual analysis to ascertain the classes that are relevant for the web page prospectus system.
(2) Ascertain the relationships between classes.
(3) Ascertain the responsibilities for each class.
(4) Draw a class diagram to represent the system.

Suggested solutions:

(1) Relevant classes are: Customer, Order, Administrator, Employee, Consignment, Ale, Mild Brew (Ale), Vicars Tibble (Ale) and Bailey Gut Rot (Ale).
(2) Associations come from statements like: *Administrator receives a customer Order* which specifies a *receives* association in the direction from Order to Administrator.
(3) At a high level it is a good idea to specify the responsibilities for each class, i.e. the responsibilities of Employee are to check the ale is in stock, set up delivery requirements and provide dispatch details for the Customer.
(4) See the Figure 2.3.45.

UML summary

UML is a modelling language, not a method or methodology. It defines a number of diagrams and the meaning of those diagrams. It does not describe the steps used to develop the software, who carries out certain tasks and the full implementation requirements. It is a blueprint for developers so they know exactly what they need to build and for project managers as an aid to cost estimation. It is also a bridge between technical developers and non-technical users and provides an opportunity for developers to ascertain the exact requirements the users have for the proposed system. The idea behind UML is that it is method independent.

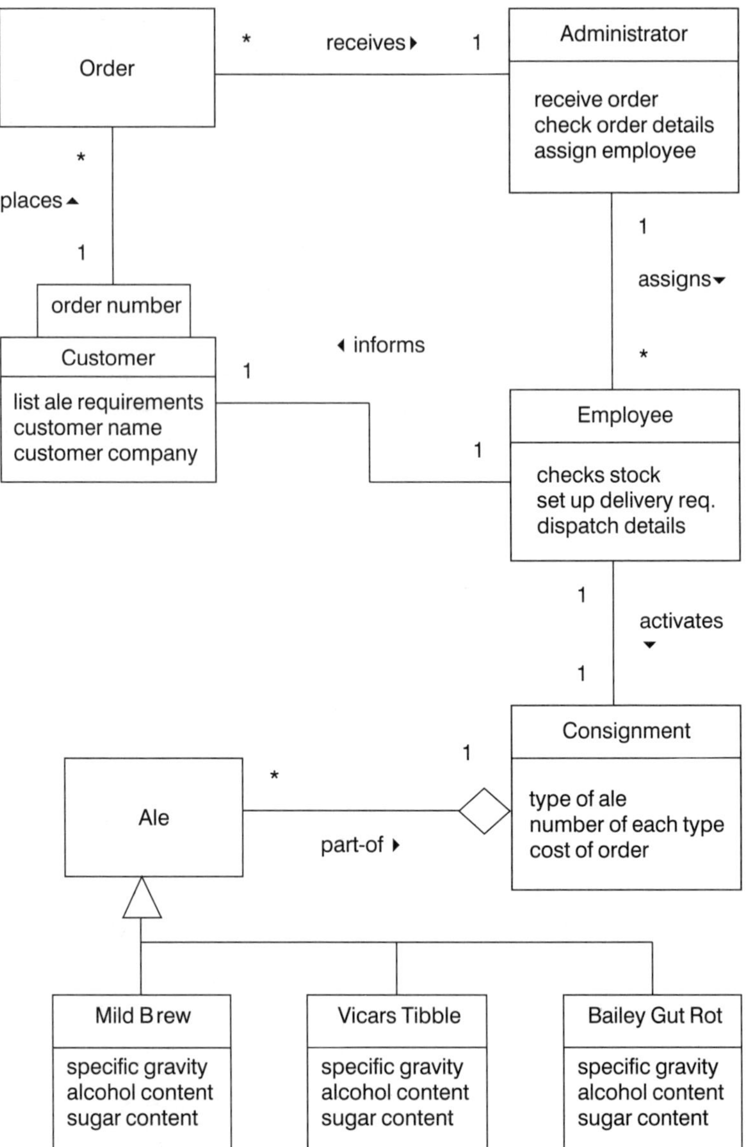

Figure 2.3.45 *Bailey Ale Company class diagram*

Exercise 2.3.4

The following is an extract of a negotiated statement of requirements:

> The Bernese College wants to improve its marketing strategy by setting up an intranet website primarily to contain a computerized prospectus. The prospectus will contain course information that can be viewed by lecturers, managers, non-teaching staff and students. The college courses are made up of modules that are classified at three different levels: foundation, intermediate and advanced. Students will take three years

(full-time) to complete the course starting at the foundation level first. Foundation modules need to be assessed by incorporating level one key skills, intermediate modules need to be assessed by directed coursework and advanced modules will incorporate 'A' level examinations.

The prospectus needs to provide a list of lecturers, courses and modules with a more detailed description of the syllabus content of the modules. Information about individual lectures should include their location, main subject disciplines and telephone extension as well as the modules that the lecturer tutors. Each course is allocated a unique identifier and is made up of a number of modules at the required level. The management responsibilities of the prospectus need to add and/or remove lecturers and courses from the system. Each course is allocated a course director, who is also a lecturer, who has the responsibility for running the course and updating the course information contained in the prospectus.

Take the following steps to analyse the requirements:

(1) Carry out a textual analysis to ascertain the classes that are relevant for the web page prospectus system.
(2) Ascertain the relationships between classes.
(3) Ascertain the responsibilities for each class.
(4) Draw a class diagram to represent the system.

Once the model has been completed it would be beneficial to check the result with other group members to ensure the classes and associations are an accurate representation of the requirements.

Data modelling

Introduction

A database is a collection of data that is required to be stored or retrieved within a specified system. The production of the data flow diagram will produce a number of stores that contain data to be used or data to be saved by the associated processes. The data flow diagram does not, however, give any further information about the precise nature of the stores and their relationships with other stores. This is where the process of data modelling comes in with the aim to provide additional graphical representations that adequately model the system to be developed.

In a number of data flow diagrams the layout of the stores is repeated to aid clarification and in some cases different stores will contain the same data items. Without any further analysis this problem will lead to implementation with a set of files that contain repeated data. This is often termed as redundant data and can lead to the following problems:

- The need for additional secondary storage that is wasteful of resources and reduces the efficiency of the final product.

- Updating becomes a problem because the system needs to ensure that if one set of data is updated then the others must also be changed to reflect this modification. This is to ensure consistency of file data throughout the system.

There may be situations where other relationships exist between data that has to be saved and acted on in the system. For example, in a college application it would be natural to keep data about courses offered, the number that have vacancies and the maximum group size for each course. In addition it would also keep information about students and employees of the college like managers, lectures and administration staff. We can see that there is a relationship between courses and students, also between lectures and students and these must be recorded. The main aim of data modelling is to further develop the data flow structure in order to produce an efficient model which reduces redundancy and shows the relationships that exist between different stores.

Entities, attributes and relationships

All data can represent items and things from the real world. Within a data model an *entity* is used to describe the objects which represent 'things' from the real world. An *entity type* represents a collection of similar properties in which we are interested. Examples of entity types are Student, Lecturer and Course and these will have their own occurrences. An example of a Course occurrence would be HNC Computing or A level mathematics and an example of a Lecturer occurrence could be Peter Brown.

All entities have underlying *attributes* that represent the associated internal properties present. The example shown below takes a 'customer entity type' from a banking system and lists some of its possible attributes.

Example 2.3.9

Customer (AccountNumber, Name, Address, Telephone Number, Balance, OverDraft) The first attribute provides a unique access route to the entity and this is sometimes termed a candidate identifier that is underlined to emphasize this point. There may be more than one candidate identifier where either, or one, of them provides unique access to the entity type they are described in. We can see that the entity can provide a bases for a *record* structure and the attributes form the required *fields.*

Finally we need to consider the way things are related and this is achieved by specifying the *relationships* that exist between entities. A relationship is an association between entities and can be based on a number of factors like ownership, structure, location and inheritance. For example, we could have entity types Student and Course and a suitable relationship could be Studies, i.e. a Student *Studies* Course. An example of relationships between entities is shown in Figure 2.3.46.

Figure 2.3.46 clearly shows examples of relationship instances, for example Bailey *Studies Intro. to Programming* is an instance of a relationship or an association between precisely two entities.

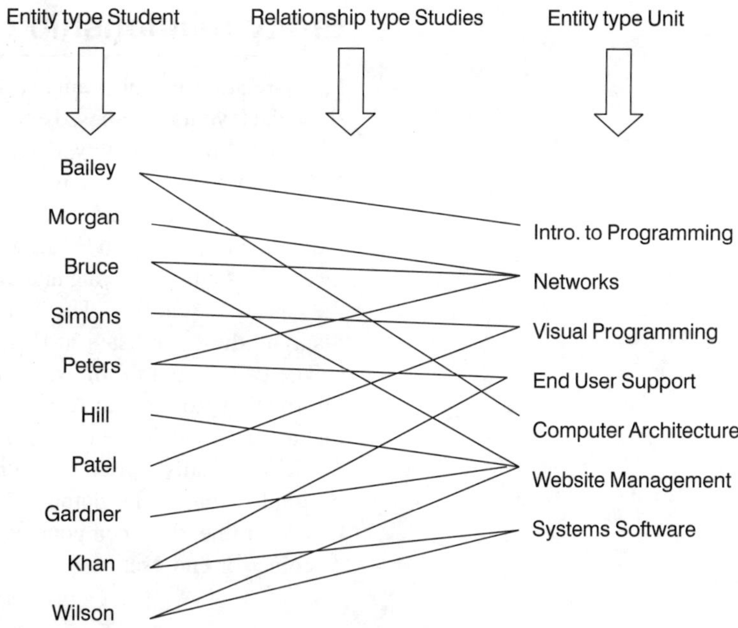

Figure 2.3.46 *A relationship between entities*

> **Question 2.3.13**
>
> Set up a table to list all the instances of the *Studies* relationship given in Figure 2.3.46.

Just like other modelling techniques discussed in the chapter entities and relationship types should be given meaningful names. Entities should be named with a noun and kept singular (i.e. it is *Student* not *Students*) and relationships named with a verb. One important characteristic of relationships is that they contain a *degree* association that can be one of the following:

- One-to-one (denoted 1:1) – each instance of one entity type is associated with one instance of another entity. For example, the entity *College* is associated with one *Principal* entity. The *College* has exactly one *Principal* and one *Principal* is appointed to exactly one *College*.
- One-to-many (denoted 1:n) – one instance of the first entity type may be associated with more than one instance of the second entity type. For example, a college *Head of Department* is in charge of many *Lecturers* and *Lecturers* have one boss, the *Head of Department*.
- Many-to-many (denoted m:n) – many instances of the first entity type may be associated to many instances of the second entity type. For example, a *Lecturer* may tutor many *Students* and *Students* will have many *Lecturers* for their course.

> **Question 2.3.14**
>
> Suggest a possible degree for the following relationships:
>
> (1) *Researches in*, between *Student* and *Library.*
> (2) *Supervises*, between *Head Teacher* and *School.*
> (3) *Takes a*, between *Passenger* and *Bus.*

Entity-relationship diagrams

Entity-relationship diagrams (E-R) provide a graphical data model to show the layout of proposed entities and their relationships. They can be constructed from data flow diagrams or directly from user requirements. Either way they provide a model which is still open for discussion with the developer and end user to ensure the components match the requirements. Most modelling tools on the market will also provide a means for syntax checking and the creation of required attribute lists for the specified entities. There are few components used in an E-R diagram, these are listed in Figure 2.3.47.

The E-R diagram forms part of a conceptual model which obtains its information from a real-world source and extracts the patterns of data that are used within the organization that the system is being developed for. It is normally carried out without reference to 'how' the system will be implemented. The output of this stage is to produce a conceptual model or the data components that satisfy the requirements of the customer or end user.

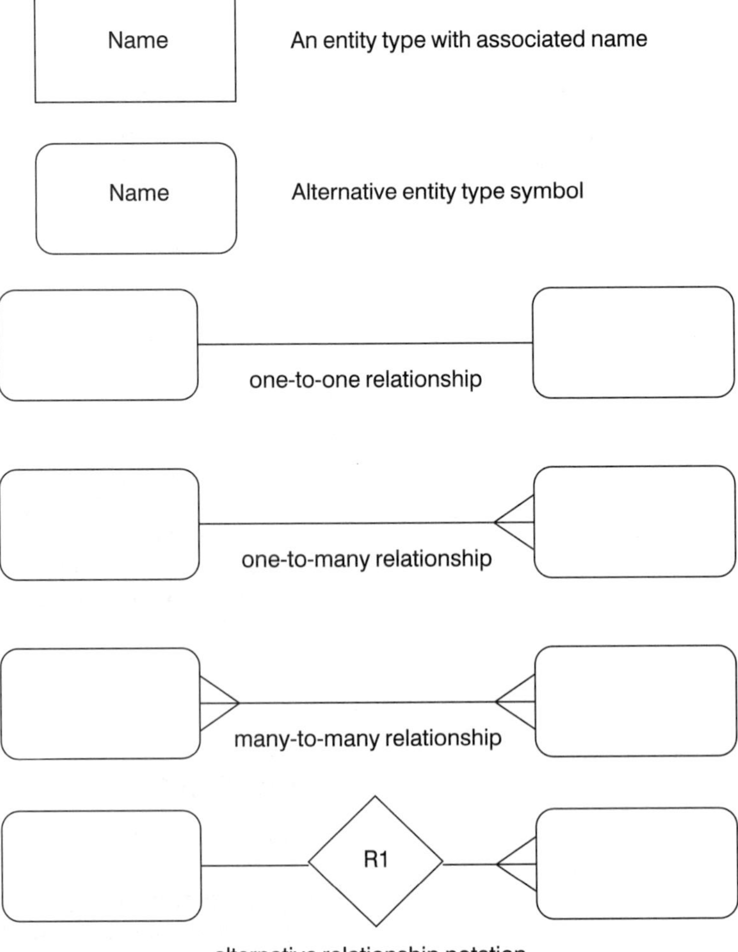

Figure 2.3.47 *Components used in entity–relationshiup diagrams*

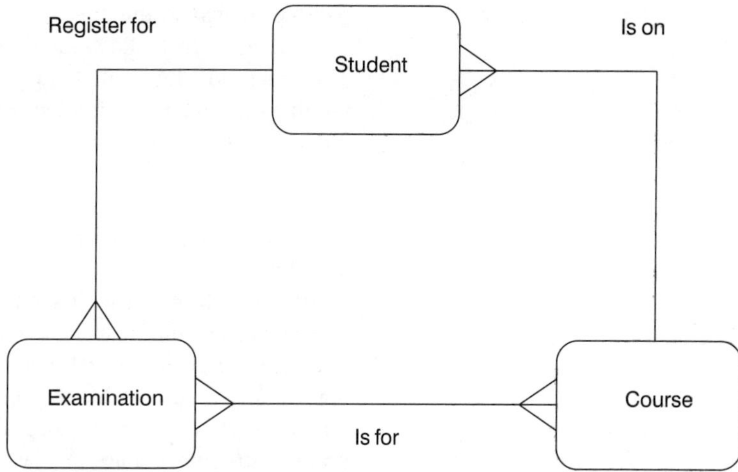

Figure 2.3.48 *An E-R diagram for a student examination course*

An example of a simple E-R relationship diagram is shown in Figure 2.3.48.

Figure 2.3.48 contains the following relations:

- *Registers for* – a student may take many examinations but each examination paper is taken by one student, hence the 1:n relationship.
- *Is on* – a course can contain many students but students can only enrol on one course, hence the 1:n relationship.
- *Is for* – courses contain many examination papers and many examinations have to be organized for each course.

Although the definition of relationships looks unnecessarily complex the description needs to be expressed from the view of each entity in order to ascertain its exact degree value.

In some cases developers will replace an m:n relationship with two 1:n relationships. This has the advantage that the implementation of the model will easily fit into the structure of a modern relational database application. An example of this procedure is shown in Figure 2.3.49.

Using CASE tools

When modelling a data system it is a good idea to use a CASE tool application for its construction. Most of these offer good checking

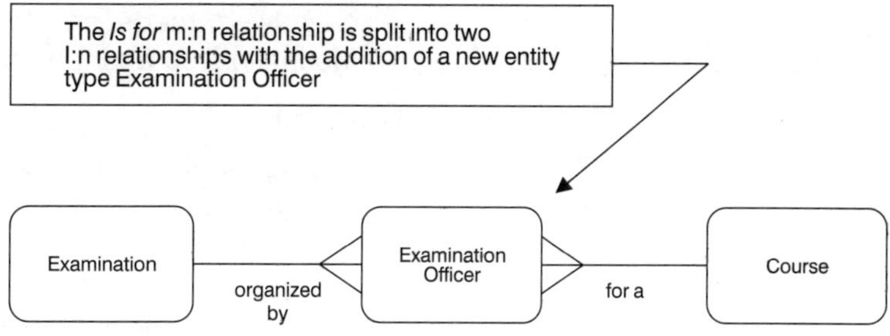

Figure 2.3.49 *Splitting an m:n relationship*

facilities which ensure they are syntactically correct and provide a range of templates which allow quick access to the required diagram symbols. They are ideally suited to implement change so correction or modification can be implemented directly across all the created diagrams. Data dictionaries allow the developer to add additional information relevant to any particular graphical component. This end result is a precise document that can easily be checked for semantic correctness and modifications can be implemented without major modifications.

The main problem with such CASE tools is that they are generally expensive, but they can be used with a number of different models. Example 2.3.10 was constructed using the Select Yourdon CASE tool application version 4.2.0. It can also be used to construct data flow diagrams, state transition diagrams, Jackson charts, Constantine diagrams, structure charts as well as associated specifications and dictionaries.

Question 2.3.15

(1) What are the main components used in an E-R diagram?
(2) What is a relationship? Specify the different degrees associated with relationships.
(3) Suggest some suitable attributes for an entity type student.

Attribute diagram

An attribute diagram shows the attributes, or data items, that are associated with a particular entity. The diagram consists of the entity in question, its attributes, and domains. A domain is a graphical representation of the set of possible values an attribute can take. For example, the attribute arrival could belong to the domain of time.

Attributes are represented as links between the entity and domains. All attribute links will have a cardinal value at either end (1:1, 1:n or m:n). Any of the attribute names may be underlined to indicate that they are prime attributes. The prime attribute(s) will represent the unique identifier field(s) that allow access to the specified entity. Most CASE tool applications will allow an attribute diagram to develop as a child of an entity.

Example 2.3.10

Below is an extract from a negotiated statement of requirements:

> As part of the new animal passport scheme the port authorities need a system to monitor the movement of animals. The system is initially to be developed as a prototype to provide information on animals of the type dog only. These are then to be classified into breeds and only two breeds are to be registered, the Bernese Mountain Dog and the Australian Shepherd Dog.

Questions:

(1) Analyse the text to ascertain the relevant entities.
(2) Establish any relationships between entities and their degrees.
(3) Complete an E-R diagram.
(4) For the Bernese Mountain Dog entity type construct an attribute diagram.

Suggested solutions:

(1) Possible entities are: Animal, Dog, Breed and Bernese Mountain Dog and Australian Shepherd.

(2) Relationships are:
- *Type of* between Animal and Dog. This is a 1:n relationship as there is only one dog animal but many dogs will go through the system.
- *Contains* between Dog and Breed. This is a 1:n relationship as a dog entity type contains many breeds but there is only one instance of each breed.
- *Are part of* between the Bernese Mountain Dogs and Australian Shepherd Dogs and Breed. This is a 1:n relationship as there is a single breed for each group of dogs and a breed contains many dogs.

(3)

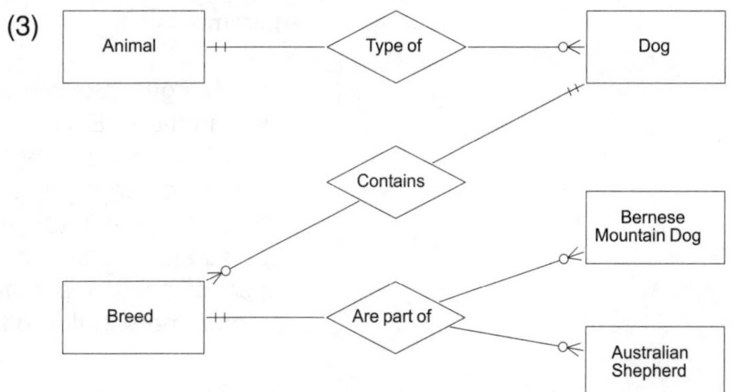

Figure 2.3.50 *E-R prototype model for animal passport system*

(4)

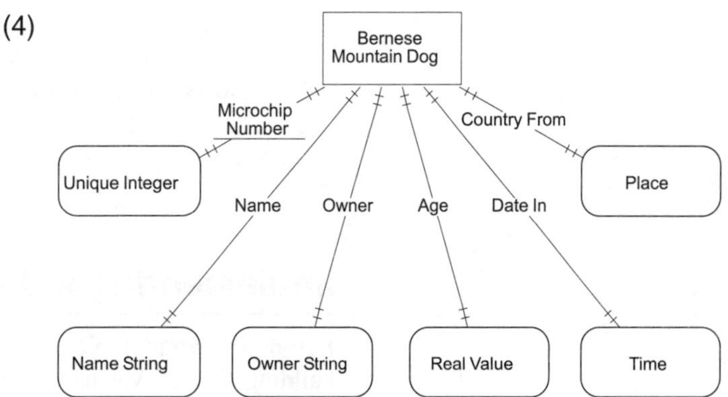

Figure 2.3.51 *Attributes for a Bernese Mountain Dog*

Note: You will notice that the diagrams are displaying some additional symbols not yet mentioned. The little circle before the many fork means a zero-to-many association (as opposed to a one-to-many). The two little dashes on the single lines indicate a strictly 'only-one' relationship. Figure 2.3.50 has been created as a child of the entity Bernese Mountain Dog in Figure 2.3.51. Both have been checked for syntax correctness, an example check report is shown below:

```
Project: C:\MYDOCU~1\SELECT\SYSTEM\DTATA1\
Title: Data Flow Example
Date: 21-Aug-2000 Time: 12:4

Checking DOG2.DAT
No Errors detected, No Warnings given.
----End of report----
```

Exercise 2.3.5

Below is an extract from a negotiated statement of requirements:

> The Morgan Software house employs a number of programmers. Each programmer is allocated their own terminal and they work on one or more systems at the same time. Each office within the company can contain up to 10 terminals and each terminal has its own operational manual as their specification is different. Each office has a manager who is in charge of the programmers in that office.

Questions:

(1) Analyse the text to ascertain the relevant entities.
(2) Establish any relationships between entities and their degrees.
(3) Complete an E-R diagram.
(4) Construct attribute diagrams for each entity selected.

Implementing a database

Before we start to implement database models we need to consider basic building blocks. We have seen the concept of entities, attributes and relationships so how do these fit into a modern database application tool? In order to answer this, we first need to start with some basic terminology and then look at the initial building blocks to create a working database application.

Relational database

A database is simply a collection of data, in our case stored electronically. It has no formal definition and is sometimes used to describe and data file made up of records and fields contained in tables.

In order to implement the real-word relationships developed in the data model a 'relational database' needs to provide a means of linking sets of table data together in order to establish the relationships. A relational database is therefore a collection of tables roughly equivalent to a collection of records that are related by the data stored jointly in their fields.

Tables

A table is a collection of data relevant to a specific entity, for example students or lecturers. A separate table is used for each topic which means the data is only stored once which improves efficiency and reduces data entries. Tables are organized into columns (these represent the field data) and rows (these represent the records).

Forms

Forms are used to help you input and manipulate data which includes:

- Data entry form to enter data into a table.
- Switchboard form to open other forms or reports.
- Custom dialog box to accept user input and carry out an associated action.

Queries

Use queries to view, use and analyse data in various ways. They can also be used as a source of records for form and reports.

Reports

A report is an effective way to present your data in a printed format. You have control over everything that is on a report, so you can display what information you want and how you want to see it.

Macro

A macro is a set of one or more actions that each performs a particular operation. Macros can help you automate tasks like opening a form, printing a report, etc. by just pressing a designated command button.

Example 2.3.11

Creating simple data tables

This exercise involves two entity types, *Customer* and *Product*. There is a relationship between them, *Orders*, which allows customers to order many products, but each product is only for one customer.

(1) Create an entity-relationship diagram to represent this system.

Figure 2.3.52 *Entity relationship between Customer and Product*

(2) Consider some suitable attributes for each entity (*Customer* and *Product*). Some examples are shown in Figures 2.3.53 and 2.3.54.

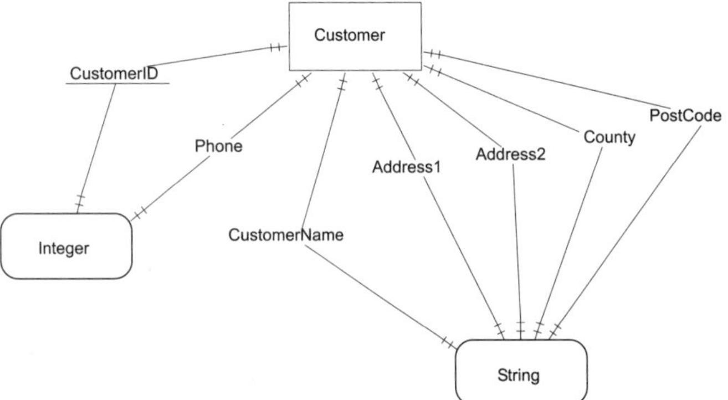

Figure 2.3.53 *Attribute diagram for Customer*

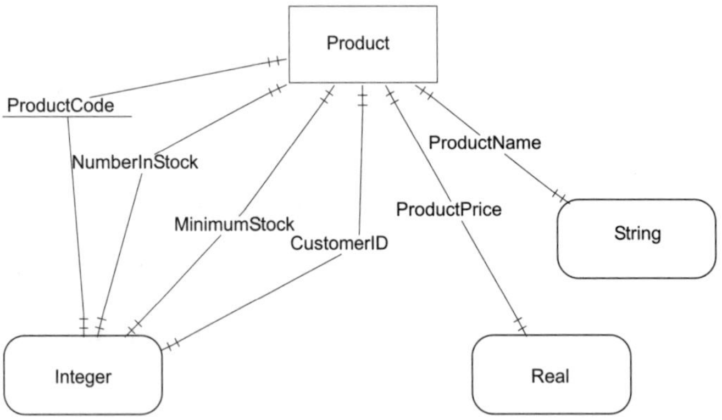

Figure 2.3.54 *Attribute diagram for Product*

(3) For each entity create database tables by entering some example field data under each specified attribute. The examples shown in Figures 2.3.55 and 2.3.56 have been created in Access 97, but the same table construction could have been implemented in any commercial database application.

Note: If you have not created database tables before then use the 'database wizard' to construct the tables with the appropriate field names. Use the 'help' option to find out more about this facility and any alternative examples.

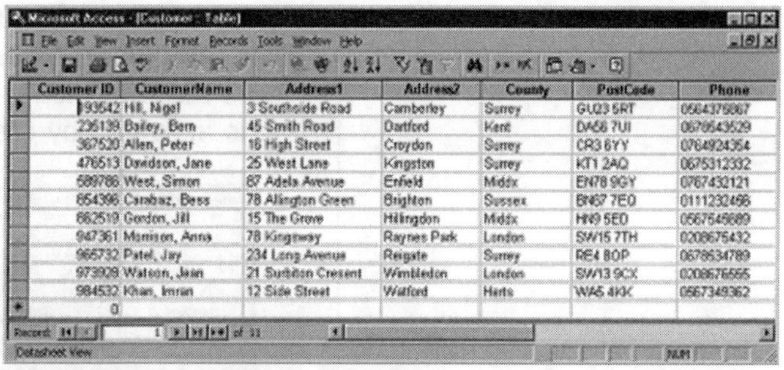

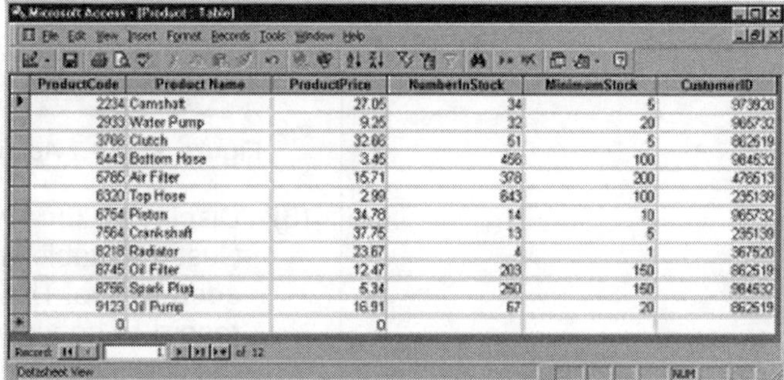

Customer ID	CustomerName	Address1	Address2	County	PostCode	Phone
193542	Hill, Nigel	3 Southside Road	Camberley	Surrey	GU23 5RT	0564375867
235139	Bailey, Bern	45 Smith Road	Dartford	Kent	DA56 7UI	0678543529
367520	Allen, Peter	16 High Street	Croydon	Surrey	CR3 6YY	0764924354
476513	Davidson, Jane	25 West Lane	Kingston	Surrey	KT1 2AQ	0675312332
589786	West, Simon	87 Adela Avenue	Enfield	Middx	EN78 9GY	0767432121
854396	Carabaz, Bess	78 Allington Green	Brighton	Sussex	BN67 7EO	0111232456
862519	Gordon, Jill	15 The Grove	Hillingdon	Middx	HN9 5ED	0567545689
947361	Morrison, Anna	78 Kingsway	Raynes Park	London	SW15 7TH	0208675432
965732	Patel, Jay	234 Long Avenue	Reigate	Surrey	RE4 8OP	0678534789
973928	Watson, Jean	21 Surbiton Cresent	Wimbledon	London	SW13 9CX	0208676555
984532	Khan, Imran	12 Side Street	Watford	Herts	WA5 4KK	0567349362
0						

Figure 2.3.55 *Customer table*

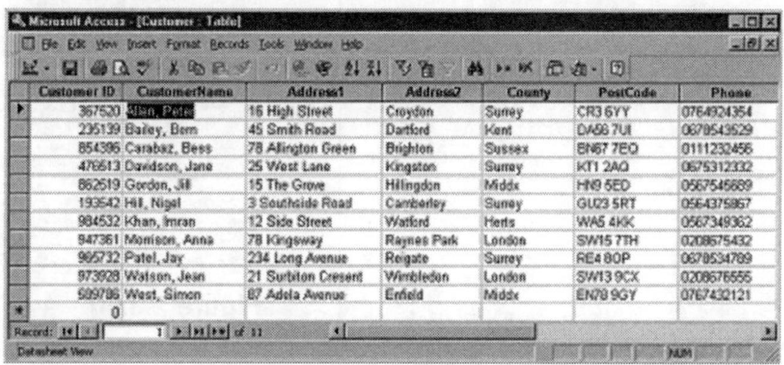

ProductCode	Product Name	ProductPrice	NumberInStock	MinimumStock	CustomerID
2234	Camshaft	27.05	34	5	973928
2933	Water Pump	9.25	32	20	965732
3766	Clutch	32.66	51	5	862519
5443	Bottom Hose	3.45	456	100	984532
5785	Air Filter	15.71	378	200	476513
6320	Top Hose	2.99	643	100	235139
6754	Piston	34.78	14	10	965732
7564	Crankshaft	37.75	13	5	235139
8218	Radiator	23.67	4	1	367520
8745	Oil Filter	12.47	203	150	862519
8756	Spark Plug	5.34	250	150	984532
9123	Oil Pump	16.91	67	20	862519
0		0			

Figure 2.3.56 *Product table*

(4) For the Customer table change the column layout so that the customers, names are shown in ascending order.

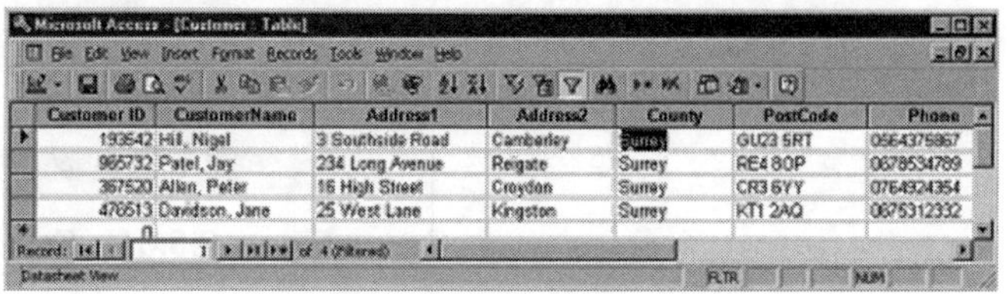

Customer ID	CustomerName	Address1	Address2	County	PostCode	Phone
367520	Allen, Peter	16 High Street	Croydon	Surrey	CR3 6YY	0764924354
235139	Bailey, Bern	45 Smith Road	Dartford	Kent	DA56 7UI	0678543529
854396	Carabaz, Bess	78 Allington Green	Brighton	Sussex	BN67 7EO	0111232456
476513	Davidson, Jane	25 West Lane	Kingston	Surrey	KT1 2AQ	0675312332
862519	Gordon, Jill	15 The Grove	Hillingdon	Middx	HN9 5ED	0567545689
193542	Hill, Nigel	3 Southside Road	Camberley	Surrey	GU23 5RT	0564375867
984532	Khan, Imran	12 Side Street	Watford	Herts	WA5 4KK	0567349362
947361	Morrison, Anna	78 Kingsway	Raynes Park	London	SW15 7TH	0208675432
965732	Patel, Jay	234 Long Avenue	Reigate	Surrey	RE4 8OP	0678534789
973928	Watson, Jean	21 Surbiton Cresent	Wimbledon	London	SW13 9CX	0208676555
589786	West, Simon	87 Adela Avenue	Enfield	Middx	EN78 9GY	0767432121
0						

Figure 2.3.57 *Customer table showing the CustomerName column in ascending order*

Note: This should be a simple operation, just click on the column to be ordered (the CustomerName field) and select the ascending order button.

(5) Apply a filter to a sort to list all the customers who live in Surrey.

Customer ID	CustomerName	Address1	Address2	County	PostCode	Phone
193542	Hill, Nigel	3 Southside Road	Camberley	Surrey	GU23 5RT	0564375867
965732	Patel, Jay	234 Long Avenue	Reigate	Surrey	RE4 8OP	0678534789
367520	Allen, Peter	16 High Street	Croydon	Surrey	CR3 6YY	0764924354
476513	Davidson, Jane	25 West Lane	Kingston	Surrey	KT1 2AQ	0675312332
0						

Figure 2.3.58 *Filter applied to show the customers who live in Surrey*

Note: In Access this is achieved by selecting the Records, Filter, Advanced Filter/Sort menu. The result is shown in Figure 2.3.59 which has its criteria set as the string 'Surrey' and is activated by clicking the **Apply Filter** button.

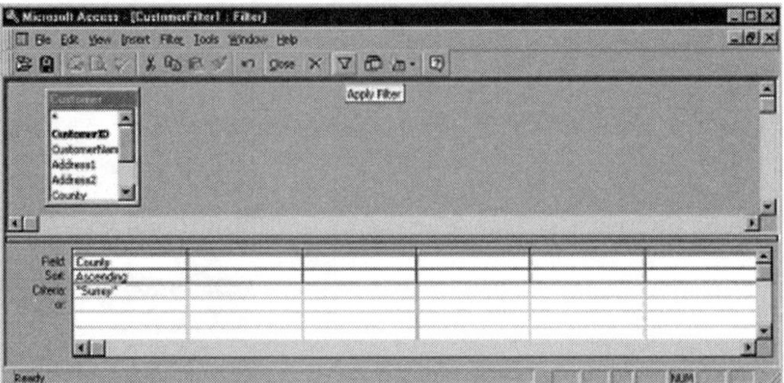

Figure 2.3.59 *Applying a filter to a sort*

(6) Display a 'form view' of a particular record from the Customer table and change a field data entry for the first address line. This is achieved in Access by selecting the record to be viewed from the Customer table and then clicking the down arrow next to the New Object button and selecting Autoform. An example form is shown in Figure 2.3.60.

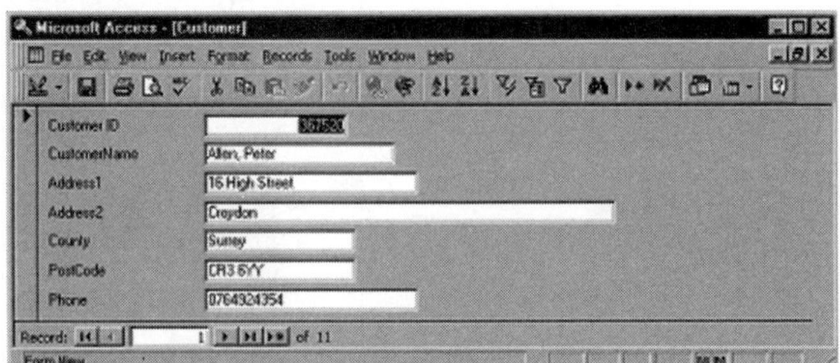

Figure 2.3.60 *A database forum*

Then view the whole table to ensure the change has taken place. Figure 2.3.61 shows the change made to the address1 field (the street number and name have been altered).

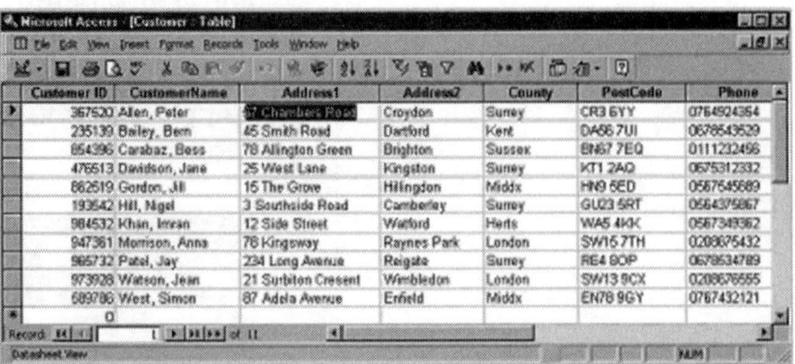

Customer ID	CustomerName	Address1	Address2	County	PostCode	Phone
367520	Allen, Peter	67 Chambers Road	Croydon	Surrey	CR3 6YY	0764924354
235139	Bailey, Bern	45 Smith Road	Dartford	Kent	DA56 7UI	0678543529
854396	Carabaz, Bess	78 Allington Green	Brighton	Sussex	BN67 7EQ	0111232456
476513	Davidson, Jane	25 West Lane	Kingston	Surrey	KT1 2AQ	0675312332
862519	Gordon, Jill	15 The Grove	Hillingdon	Middx	HN9 5ED	0567545689
193542	Hill, Nigel	3 Southside Road	Camberley	Surrey	GU23 5RT	0564375867
984532	Khan, Imran	12 Side Street	Watford	Herts	WA5 4KK	0567349362
947361	Morrison, Anna	76 Kingsway	Raynes Park	London	SW15 7TH	0208675432
965732	Patel, Jay	234 Long Avenue	Reigate	Surrey	RE4 8OP	0678534789
973928	Watson, Jean	21 Surbiton Cresent	Wimbledon	London	SW13 9CX	0208676555
589786	West, Simon	87 Adela Avenue	Enfield	Middx	EN78 9GY	0767432121
0						

Figure 2.3.61 *Customer table showing the modified for the past*

Note: Forms are used to enter, view and change data. They are usually used to improve the way that data is displayed on the screen. The arrows at the bottom of the form can be used to navigate through the table entries.

(7) Add a new record to the Customer table. There should be no problems here, just add a new record in the next available row. Figure 2.3.62 shows the new record inserted with the list still sorted in name order.

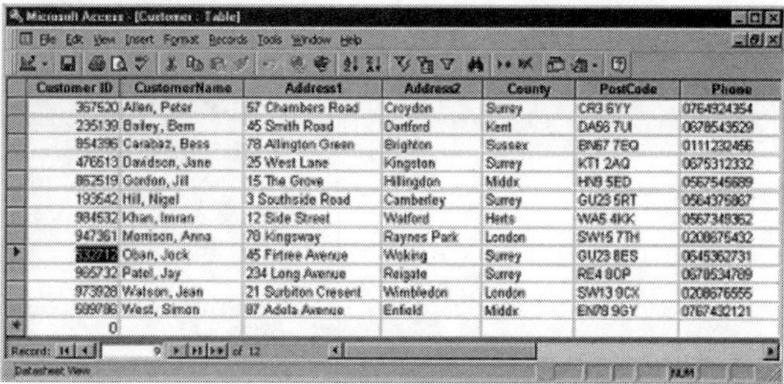

Customer ID	CustomerName	Address1	Address2	County	PostCode	Phone
367520	Allen, Peter	57 Chambers Road	Croydon	Surrey	CR3 6YY	0764924354
235139	Bailey, Bem	45 Smith Road	Dartford	Kent	DA56 7UI	0678543529
854396	Carabaz, Bess	78 Allington Green	Brighton	Sussex	BN67 7EQ	0111232456
476513	Davidson, Jane	25 West Lane	Kingston	Surrey	KT1 2AQ	0675312332
862519	Gordon, Jill	15 The Grove	Hillingdon	Middx	HN8 5ED	0567545689
193642	Hill, Nigel	3 Southside Road	Camberley	Surrey	GU23 5RT	0564375867
984532	Khan, Imran	12 Side Street	Watford	Herts	WA5 4KK	0567349362
947361	Morrison, Anna	78 Kingsway	Raynes Park	London	SW15 7TH	0208675432
[illegible]	Oban, Jock	45 Firtree Avenue	Woking	Surrey	GU23 8ES	0645362731
965732	Patel, Jay	234 Long Avenue	Reigate	Surrey	RE4 8OP	0678534789
973928	Watson, Jean	21 Surbiton Cresent	Wimbledon	London	SW13 9CX	0208676555
989786	West, Simon	87 Adela Avenue	Enfield	Middx	EN78 9GY	0767432121
0						

Figure 2.3.62 *New record added for Jock Oban*

(8) Show that a relationship exists between the Customer table and the Product table that represents the 1:n degree highlighted in the E-R model.

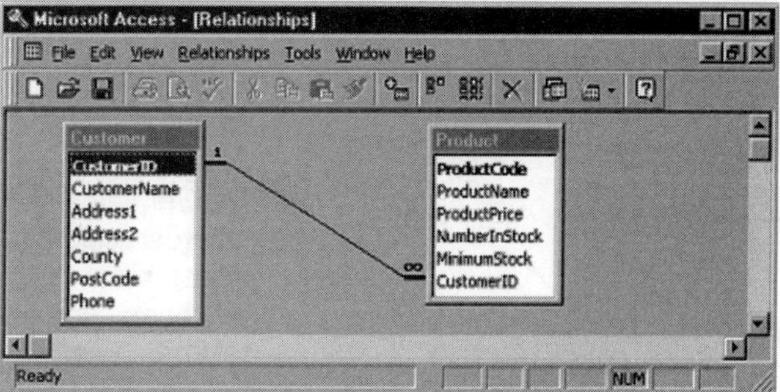

Figure 2.3.63 *l:n relationship between Customer and Product*

Note: You can build relationships between tables by *dragging* from a field in one table to another field in a second table. In our example we have dragged from the CustomerID field name in the Customer table to the CustomerID field in the Product table. This is achieved by clicking the left mouse button over the first field name in the Customer table and holding it down whilst dragging to the second table and releasing over the required field. In Access releasing the mouse button results in the dialog box in Figure 2.3.64 being displayed.

In the Join Properties dialog box you can specify the type of join that you want Access to create in new queries. Because Access is a relational database, queries can be used from more than one table at a time. As we have seen, if the database contains tables with related data, the relationships can be easily defined.

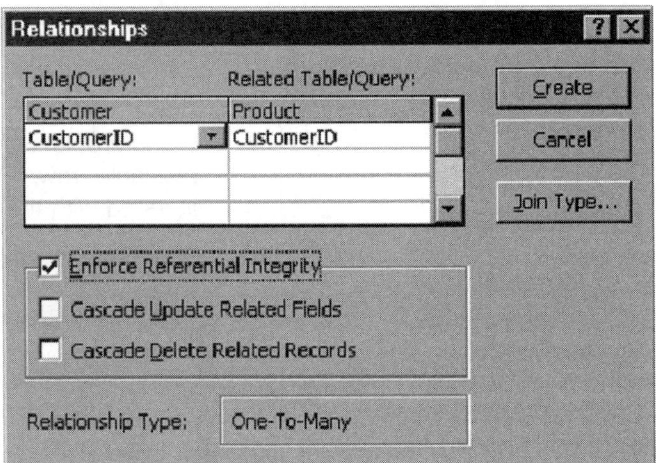

Figure 2.3.64 *Setting up relationships in Access*

It is customary for the matching fields to have the same name as in our example of Customer and Product tables. In the Customer table, the CustomerID field is the primary field and relates to the CustomerID in the Product table that is classified as a foreign key.

The various types of relationships are as follows:

- *Inherited* – for attaching tables from another Access database. The original relationships of the attached database can be used in the current database.
- *Referential* – for enforcing relationships between records according to certain rules, when you add or delete records in related tables belonging to the same database. For example, you can only add records to a related table, if the matching record already exists in the primary table, and you cannot delete a record from a primary table if matching records exist in a related table.

Note: The aim of this exercise is not to teach Microsoft Access but to provide an implementation base for the analysis example. If implementing an application within Access it is necessary to establish the relationships after setting up the tables and before any data is entered.

(9) You create a *query* so that you can ask questions about data in the database tables. By far the most common operation is to produce a subset of the data held in a table. Produce a subset from the Product table containing only the product name and price (Figure 2.3.65).

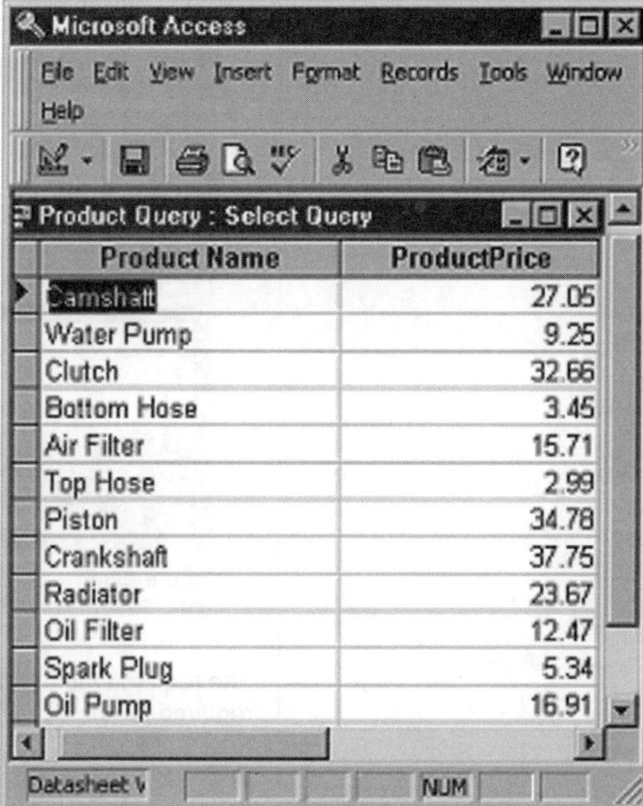

Figure 2.3.65 *Query on Product table*

To do this, load the database and in the Database window click the queries tab, followed by the New button which opens the New Query dialog box. The resulting dialog box is displayed:

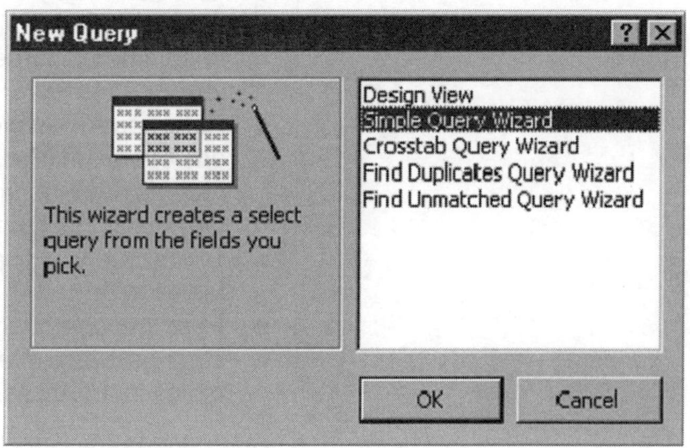

Figure 2.3.66 *New query dialog box*

Selecting the Simple Query Wizard displays the following:

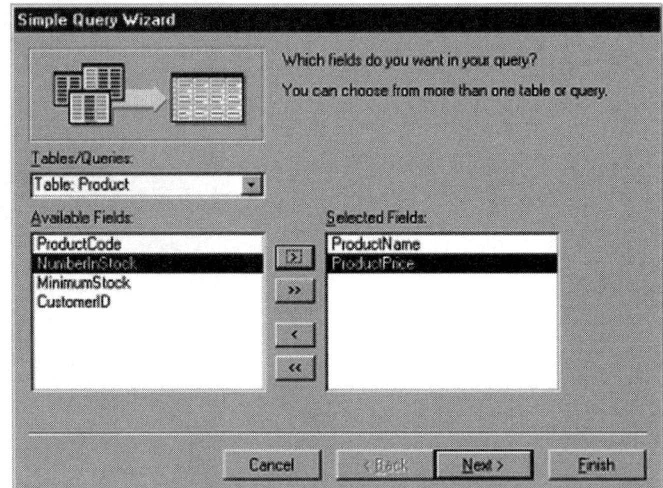

Figure 2.3.67 *Simple Query Wizard with selected fields required for the subset*

The required table is then selected with the associated fields required for the subset. On pressing the Next button another dialog box asks if you want a detailed report or a summary. Pressing Next again takes you to the final dialog box which asks you for the name of the query.

Types of queries

The query that we have created so far is known as a select query, which is the most common type of query. However, with Access you can create and use other types of queries, as follows:

- *Crosstab query* – used to present data with row and column headings, just like a spreadsheet. It can be used to summarize large amounts of data in a more readable form.
- *Action query* – used to make changes to many records in one operation. For example, you might want to remove all records from a given table that meet certain criteria. Obviously this type of query has to be used with care.
- *Union query* – used to match fields from two or more tables.
- *Pass through query* – used to pass commands to SQL.
- *Data-definition query* – used to delete, create and change tables in an Access database using SQL statements.

SQL stands for Structured Query Language, often used to query, update and manage relational databases. Each query created by Access has an associated SQL statement that defines the action of that query. Thus if you are familiar with SQL, you can use it to view and modify queries, or use it to set form and report properties. An alternative to these actions is to use a QBE (Query By Example) grid which is easier to initially structure. If you design union queries, or data definition queries, then you must use SQL statements, as these kind of queries cannot be designed with the QBE grid. Finally, to create a subquery, you use the QBE grid, but you enter SQL SELECT statement for criteria; this issue will be covered in detail in the data analysis and database design unit.

(10) Produce a *report* from the Customer table showing the customer name and telephone number. An example report is shown in Figure 2.3.68.

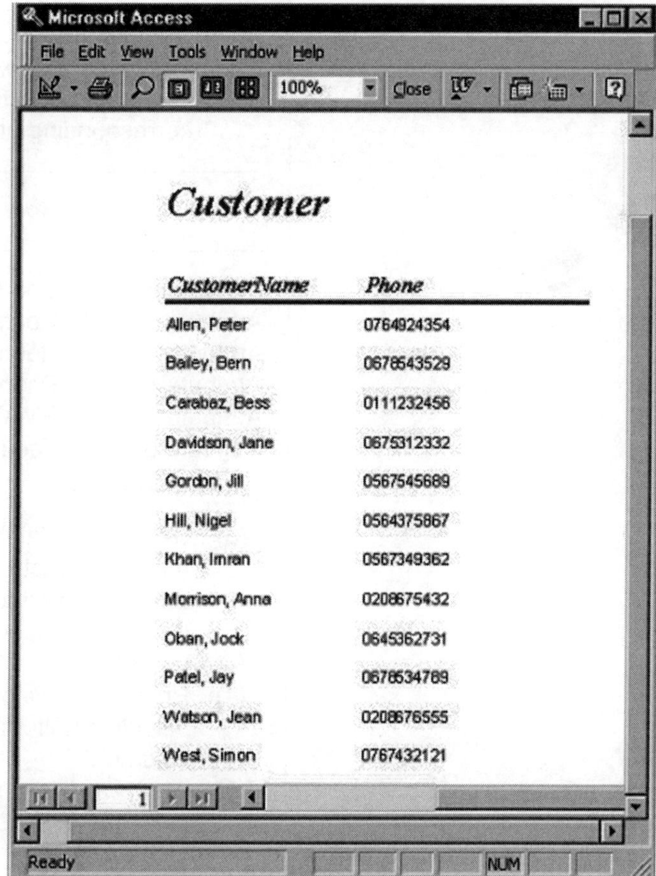

Customer

CustomerName	Phone
Allen, Peter	0764924354
Bailey, Bern	0678643529
Carabaz, Bess	0111232456
Davidson, Jane	0675312332
Gordon, Jill	0567545689
Hill, Nigel	0564375867
Khan, Imran	0567349362
Morrison, Anna	0208675432
Oban, Jock	0645362731
Patel, Jay	0678534789
Watson, Jean	0208676555
West, Simon	0767432121

Figure 2.3.68 *Report from the Customer table showing the customer name and telephone number*

A report is like a query in that it can summarize data, but its output is in a form that is more suitable for printing. In Access a basic report is set up from the Database box and selecting the Reports tab. From there you can follow the wizards (similar to queries) to set up the required report.

Exercise 2.3.6

Below is an extract from a college management information system:

> A Course Director is responsible for a number of Students and each Student is allocated a single Course Director.

Your task is to analyse and implement the scenario to produce a simple relational database for the specified entities. In order to achieve this the following steps need to be followed:

(1) Complete an entity-relationship diagram to represent this model.
(2) For the suggested attributes tabled below complete corresponding attribute diagrams.

	Course director	*Student*
Attribute(Key)	CourseDirectorID	StudentID
Attribute 2	CourseDirectorName	StudentName
Attribute 3	RoomNumber	StudentCourse
Attribute 4	PhoneExtension	StudentAge
Attribute 5	EMAIL	CourseDirectorID
Attribute 6	Faculty	

(3) Set up a database system containing two *tables* (Course Director and Student) by adding suitable data under each attribute heading. You should complete at least 10 student records and five course director records.
(4) Practice *sorting* the data into ascending order by selecting alternative columns (i.e. by the name column).
(5) Apply a *filter* to display only the records that fit a selected criteria, i.e. all the student surnames that start with an 'S'.
(6) Display a *form* view of a particular record from either table and change a field data entry. View the whole table to ensure the change has taken place.
(7) Add a *new record* to the student table.
(8) Link the two tables together to establish a *relationship* between them. Use the CourseDirectorID field from each table to set up the link and ensure the correct degree is shown (this should be the same as the original E-R diagram).
(9) Set up a *query* to summarize the student names and their corresponding courses from the Student table.
(10) Produce a printed *report* to show the Course Director's name and EMAIL address from the appropriate table.

This aim of these exercises is to provide the link between analysis, design and implementation. It only covers the basics of database implementations but provides a foundation for future development in the application area. This will be covered in detail within the data analysis and database design unit. At this stage I must stress the need for thoroughly researching and documenting the work carried out. This not only ensures a disciplined approach to the task but instils a professional ethos which is characteristic for the production of quality software systems.

Question 2.3.16

(1) In an attribute diagram the resulting domains are shown (i.e. String, Integer, Real, etc.). How are these domains specified within a database application?

(2) What is a *form* used for when implementing a database application?

(3) What are *queries* used for?

(4) What is the main difference between a *query* and a *report*?

(5) What is a *database wizard* and how does it help you implement your required database model?

3 Software constructs and tools

Summary

This chapter deals with problems and the way in which a computer can be used to solve those for which a computer solution is appropriate. It is shown that a computer solution cannot be found for all problems, but that solutions are possible for significant categories of them.

An important aspect of problem solving is the development of modelling techniques. The way in which a mathematical model can be designed is explained with the use of appropriate variables and equations. Coding a model as a spreadsheet is illustrated. It is also demonstrated how spreadsheet models can be used for the 'what if' situations so often encountered in the real world.

Spreadsheets can be used for many problems but there are also occasions when it is important to be able to design a computer program. Programming techniques are investigated and the control structures used in a program explained.

The importance of testing and documenting computer solutions is emphasized.

3.1 Problem-solving theory

A problem can be described as a situation in which there is an *initial state* and a final state or *goal state*. A set of *operations* which converts the initial state into the goal state can be regarded as a solution to the problem.

Deciding what this solution is is termed *problem solving*. Some problems may have a fairly obvious solution. Other problems may be more difficult. As an example of a simple problem, with an easily identified solution, consider the case of the driver who has run out of petrol. This situation can be reduced to an initial state, problem-solving operations and goal state.

Initial state
Car has glided to a halt and the petrol gauge reads zero. Wallet is empty.

Operations required
Walk to bank.
Cash cheque.
Walk to garage.
Buy petrol can.

Fill petrol can.
Pay for petrol.
Walk to car.
Fill tank.
Press starter several times to prime petrol pump.

Goal state
Car can be driven again.

Problems can be well defined or ill defined. In a *well-defined problem* the initial and goal states can be stated clearly and without any ambiguity or vagueness. A set of operations that convert the initial state into the goal state can also be clearly defined. In contrast an *ill-defined problem* lacks precise definitions of the initial and goal states and it is not obvious what set of operations is required to produce the goal state. A human problem solver might be able to tackle an ill-defined problem successfully but it is not suitable for computer solution.

An example of a well-defined problem is the calculation of the number of glasses of cider that can be filled from a barrel. The volume of the barrel will be known, or its volume can be found (using integral calculus if necessary), and the volume of the glass will be known as well. Calculating the number of glasses that can be filled is then simply a matter of dividing the smaller volume into the larger.

An example of an ill-defined problem is planning an interesting visit to London museums for a tourist visiting the UK for the first time. How many museums will they want to visit? How much time are they prepared to spend? What particular interests do they have? Would they also want to visit art galleries? It is important to identify those problems which are inappropriate for a computer solution before beginning to attempt such a solution.

Question 3.1.1

Decide which of the following are well-defined, and which are ill-defined, problems. You should not worry about the details of a possible solution but just whether a solution is feasible.

(a) Finding the number of people in the London telephone directories who are called 'Quatermass'.
(b) Identifying the prime numbers between 1000 and 10 000.
(c) Advising the Government on an optimum rate for Value Added Tax.
(e) Discovering how many grandchildren Anne Francis, heroine of the 1956 SF classic film *Forbidden Planet*, has.
(f) Writing down the number of times Cambridge has beaten Oxford in the Boat Race.
(g) Choosing the best Oxbridge college for a student who is keen on mathematics and pot-holing.
(h) Choosing a good time to visit the London Eye.
(i) Finding out the number of times that the London Eye rotated between 12.00 pm on 15 August 2000 and 12.00 am on 17 January 2001.

(j) Choosing the best route to drive from Winchester to Norfolk.
(k) Decoding the message '8, 14, 4,, 9, 19,, 6, 21, 14', knowing that a simple substitution code has been used in which A = 1, B = 2, C = 3.
(l) Decoding the message '8, 14, 4,, 9, 19,, 6, 21, 14', knowing that a simple substitution code has been employed.
(m) Decoding the message '8, 14, 4,, 9, 19,, 6, 21, 14'.
(n) Counting the number of times the letter 'e' appears in the novel *La Disparition* by Georges Perec.
(o) Determining the quickest route on the Underground between Richmond and Chorleywood.
(p) Calculating the interest on the National Debt.
(q) Finding out the number of times '1,2,3,4' is sung in Philip Glass's opera *Einstein on the Beach*.
(r) Discovering the name of the fattest cat in the world.
(s) Discovering the name of the heaviest cat in the *Guinness Book of Records*.
(t) Calculating the difference in height between Blackpool Tower and the Eiffel Tower.

Abstraction and generalization

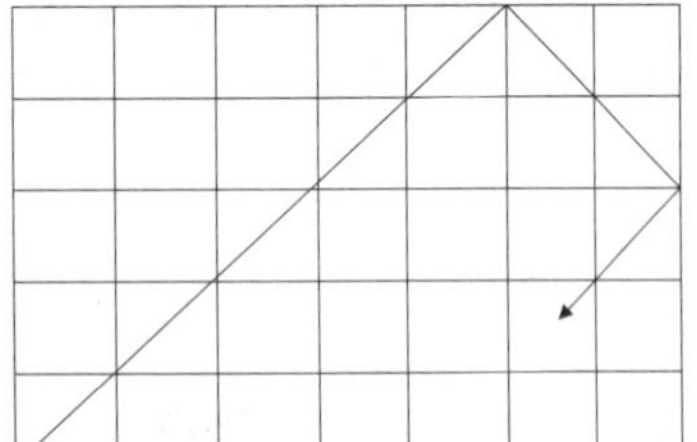

Figure 3.1.1 *The path of a mathematical billiard ball*

Two processes which can be useful in problem solving are abstraction and generalization.

Abstraction occurs when a concept is considered independently of specific situations in which it may occur. The principle can be illustrated simply by a geometric game often used as an exercise for children. The game is shown in Figure 3.1.1.

A large rectangle is divided into a set of smaller squares and a path is then traced by a line which starts at the bottom left-hand corner. This line is reflected each time it reaches a boundary of the rectangle as if it were a ray of light. The object of the exercise is to predict which corner of the rectangle the line will eventually reach.

The purpose of the smaller squares is to help this exercise to be performed by hand and also to indicate the overall dimensions of the rectangle. The rectangle here is five rows by seven columns.

If this exercise is carried out practically a pattern will be found between the final corner reached and the dimensions of the rectangle. At this point a particular property, the relationship between rows, columns and rectangle corner, is being extracted from a general situation, the set of rectangles that have been tested.

Abstraction of a particular concept from its occurrences is important because it allows thought to be focused in complex situations.

Generalization involves looking at a particular case and seeing whether the solution that has been achieved could be extended to a broader set of cases. Consider, for example, the process of scrambling the letters of a name to produce an anagram. The word 'CAR' becomes 'RAC'. It is now considered whether the method adopted to produce this anagram could be adapted to work for other words.

Examining carefully how this first anagram was created, the following steps might be observed:

- List all the letters in the word.
- Choose a letter from the list at random.
- Check whether this letter has already been chosen.
- If it has not add it to a new word.
- Continue until all the letters have been taken from the list.
- Decide whether the new word is a plausible anagram.
- If it is not repeat the process.

In this way a solution initially devised for one case can be extended to cover many.

Brainstorming

One method that can be adopted when attempting to find a solution for a problem is *brainstorming*. A group of people is encouraged to think over a problem and to suggest possible ideas to follow. These are written down immediately with no initial attempt made to filter out the less likely approaches. The rationale behind this generosity towards the unlikely is to avoid any possibility of subduing spontaneity. In contrast wide-ranging speculation is encouraged. People who might otherwise be unsure of their inspiration and guesswork feel confident in proposing the most tenuous of ideas.

The second stage of a brainstorming session does require the return of critical judgement. The large number of ideas that have been generated are now reconsidered carefully, the less relevant tactfully removed from the discussion and the more promising evaluated further. From the initial creative chaos form and direction can now emerge.

Key fact

An apocryphal instance of brainstorming was the realization that the most efficient way to land people on the moon was to have a separate lunar module which would leave, and subsequently redock, with a 'mother ship' in lunar orbit. Until this concept emerged in an early design session, the assumption had been made that the assembly of a lunar spacecraft would proceed by docking in earth orbit. This alternative, however, would have involved the use of far more fuel and heavier launch vehicles.

Although this technique is really intended to capitalize upon the imagination and intuition of a group of people it can also be a useful approach to problem solving for the individual. All that is required is a pad of paper and a pen carried around at all times. Modern technology might suggest the alternative of a 'palm top' computer or PDA. As ideas occur, in whatever location the person may be, they are jotted down quickly. Then, when an appreciable body of ideas has built up, the process continues as described above. Brainstorming oneself in this fashion has the definite advantage of tapping into the brain's unconscious problem-solving ability. Anecdotes abound of solutions suddenly appearing in the mind after an apparently fallow period in which no explicit attempt has been made to seek an answer.

Decision trees

Another problem-solving technique is the construction of a *decision tree*. Here an initial decision that has to be made is written down as a small square box (node) on the left-hand side of a large sheet of paper. From this lines show the possible routes that could follow from the decision. For example, the initial decision to be made might involve a holiday. From the first box lines might be marked 'Foreign travel', 'Day trips' and 'DIY at home'.

These lines may then terminate in either another decision or a situation in which there is simply uncertainty. The latter is represented by a small circle (also a node). A further decision is shown as another square. In the example here the DIY route might involve the new decisions 'Paint the kitchen' and 'Build new garage doors'. Again the tree could continue. The garage doors route might lead, perhaps, to 'Buy electric door kit' and 'Design traditional wooden doors'. Carrying on in this way eventually all possibilities that can be anticipated are written down.

Once the tree has been made as complete as possible it is evaluated by first assigning a numerical value to the final outcomes on the right-hand side of the tree, reflecting their worth to you. Where circles have appeared on the tree to indicate uncertainty, probabilities are assigned to each route emerging. These probabilities are 'guestimates', rather than purely arbitrary. Then values can be calculated for each node of tree by working from right to left across the tree, beginning with the values that have been assigned to the final outcomes and letting these contribute to the node on their left in the proportions determined by the probabilities. In this way a numerical value can be assigned to the original choices on the left of the diagram and permit a decision to be made.

Practical examples of problem solving

A good way of practising problem-solving techniques in design is to consider some of the children's traditional grames that were popular before computers. These offer an opportunity to study a problem in an isolated *microworld*. Here only a very restricted set of situations can appear. The absence of the extraneous details of the real world allows concentration upon a problem to the exclusion of everything else.

Key fact

Using a microworld to simplify a problem being investigated has been a traditional approach in the field of artificial intelligence. In his seminal work *Understanding Natural Language*, Terry Winograd devised a virtual 'Blocks World', the sole objects in which were the coloured wooden blocks infants play with. In this very limited universe his program SHRDLU could interpret instructions entered in ordinary English and manipulate the imaginary blocks accordingly.

The game of matches

The game of matches involves two players and 21 matches placed on the table between them. Each player takes it in turn to remove 1, 2 or 3 matches from the table. The loser is the player who has to remove the final match.

This game is an example of a well-defined problem. The player who begins first can always be forced into the losing position by the other. Call the two players Player A and Player B. Player A is the person who takes first turn. Player B can make sure that they are the winner by remembering to take matches according to the following pattern:

Player A taking 3 matches means that Player B should take 1 match.
Player A taking 2 matches means that Player B should take 2 matches.
Player A taking 1 match means that Player B should take 3 matches.

If the game is played in this way there will always be four matches fewer after each player has had their turn. The total number remaining after Player B's turn will therefore be 17, 13, 9, 5, 4, 1. This means that Player A is obliged to remove the final match, and therefore loses.

The operations Player B must follow in order to reach the goal state are:

- Count the number of matches Player A has removed.
- Subtract this number from 4.
- Remove the number of matches indicated by this subtraction.
- Repeat process until goal state is reached.

A typical sequence for the game could be:

Player A removes	*Matches remaining*	*Player B removes*	*Matches remaining*
2 matches	19	2 matches	17
1 match	16	3 matches	13
1 match	12	3 matches	9
3 matches	6	1 match	5
2 matches	3	2 matches	1
Last match!			

A guessing game

A slightly more involved game is the one in which one player, again Player A in this example, has to guess what type of object Player B has chosen. The object is often an animal but in the game illustrated here it is a vehicle, like a plane or a car. Player A asks questions which can only be answered 'Yes' or 'No'. Player B, of course, has to answer truthfully.

Although Player A will have to think of fresh questions as the game proceeds, the sequence of questions when the game is repeated with a new vehicle must remain the same. For example, if Player A's first question is 'Does it fly?' this must be the first question Player A uses for the next vehicle to guess.

The game becomes easier to understand if a diagram is drawn to show how it develops as new vehicles, and the related questions needed to identify them, are added. This type of diagram is called a *tree*, although obviously it is an upside-down tree. More precisely it is a *binary tree* because it grows as pairs of branches. The binary tree structure makes the game particularly easy to describe as a well-defined problem. (Note a nomenclature adopted here. The 'boxes' of the tree are *nodes*. If nodes are connected on adjacent levels the upper one is a *parent* and the lower a *child*.)

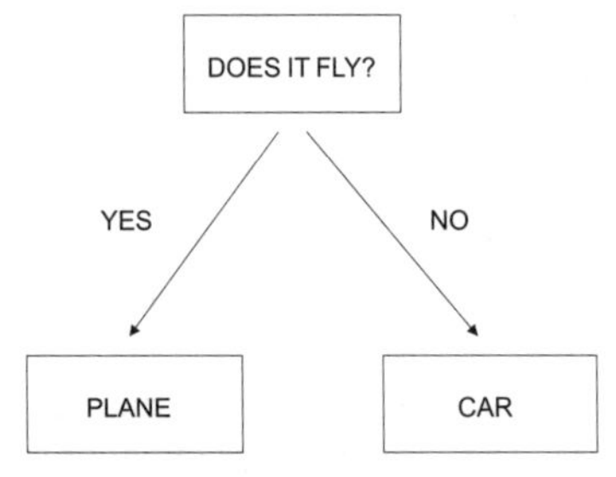

Figure 3.1.2

Suppose that Player B has chosen either a plane or a car and that the question Player A is going to ask is the one stated above. The binary tree which represents the game at this initial stage is as shown in Figure 3.1.2.

In the first example Player B has chosen a plane. The game will proceed as follows:

Player A: Does it fly?
Player B: Yes.
Player A: Is it a plane?
Player B: Yes.

In the second example a car has been chosen. This is now the dialogue:

Player A: Does it fly?
Player B: No.
Player A: Is it a car?
Player B: Yes.

Up to this point the binary tree can provide Player A with the correct answer. Suppose, however, that Player B is now thinking of a balloon.

Player A: Does it fly?
Player B: Yes.
Player A: Is it a plane?
Player B: No.

Player A has not guessed the answer and so has to ask what the vehicle is. A question must also be demanded which will distinguish between what the answer was expected to be and what it really is. This question must be one which can be answered 'Yes' or 'No' in order to preserve the binary structure of the tree:

Player A: What is the correct answer?
Player B: A balloon.
Player A: Tell me a question which shows the difference.
Player B: Does it have wings?
Player A: Thank you. I will now extend my binary tree.

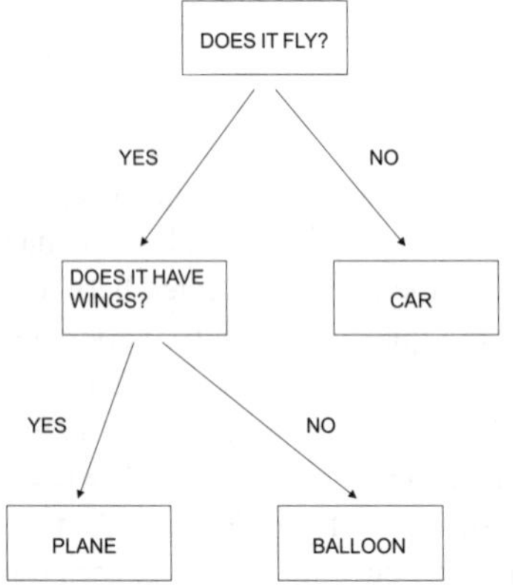

Figure 3.1.3

Player A can now modify the tree as in Figure 3.1.3 so the new information is recorded.

As the game continues the binary tree will grow until it could look as involved as this.

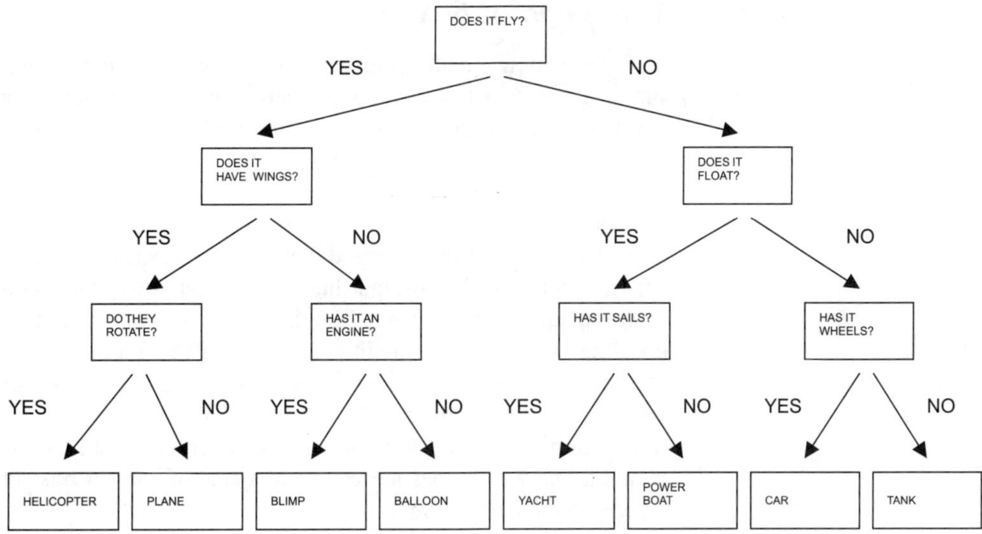

Figure 3.1.4

Although this structure may appear complicated it grows by the application of some extremely simple rules:

- Ask question in current (parent) node of diagram.
- If answer is Yes assume left-hand child node is answer.
- If answer is No assume right-hand child node is answer.
- Ask if answer is correct.
- If it is not:
  - place correct answer in left-hand child node on next level of tree;
  - place incorrect answer in right-hand node on next level of tree;
  - place new question in previous answer node.

Mathematics in action

There is an extremely simple arithmetical relationship that can be established between any parent node and the two child nodes which will be selected by a Yes or No answer to the question contained by this parent node.

The relationship is set up by first numbering all the nodes beginning with the *root node* at the top and proceeding from left to right and down the tree, level by level, until the final *leaf node* is reached. In the tree depicted here 'Does it fly?' will be numbered as 1 and 'Tank' as 15.

Consider node 2, 'Does it have wings?' The child node for Yes will be 4, 'Do they rotate?' The child node for No will be 5, 'Has it an engine?'

Similarly for node 6, 'Has it sails?', the Yes child node will be 12 and the No child node 13.

In general node N will have $N \times 2$ for its Yes child node and $N \times 2 + 1$ for its No child. This simple rule allows easy programming for this guessing game, which is possibly one of the reasons why it appeared very early in the history of personal computing!

The game of boxes

A slightly more challenging game is 'boxes', another example of a simple game which illustrates problem solving. This game should be familiar to most people as it is often played in childhood as an alternative to noughts and crosses. Like that game it only requires pencil and paper, but has the advantage that the game area can always be extended in order to increase the suspense. A rectangular array of dots is drawn on a sheet of paper and then two players take it in turn to join adjacent points with a straight line. The object is to construct as many enclosed squares as possible. The dots form the corners and the added lines the sides. Like the traditional figure of the gold prospector, each player stakes claim to territory gained by adding one of their initials to a square that they complete. When a box is won the player is allowed a further turn and these additional turns can continue until the player has to add a line which does not complete a side of another box. Play then reverts to their opponent.

An interesting feature of the game, adding to its strategy, is that a player can easily invade and capture a box that the other player has been carefully preparing as their own. They merely fill in the last side before its intended owner can. Soon it becomes necessary to plan in advance exactly what moves should be made, so that a sufficient number of partially completed squares will cover the game area. Enough of these may conceal the one to be annexed.

At first a problem like this might appear to be ill defined. It seems quite arbitrary where a player should place a line on the diagram at any stage in the game and obviously a game can evolve in a variety of ways. If it were completely predictable it would be rather boring.

However, if we consider any particular stage of the game, as shown in Figure 3.1.5, we can see that there is a method that can be adopted to maximize the possibility of winning a square at a given stage. Note that the figure shows an array of dots which can create three rows containing eight boxes each. This configuration is purely arbitrary, as the array of dots can be of any size, depending upon the enthusiam of the players and time available. Similarly the letters have been added only to identify the squares.

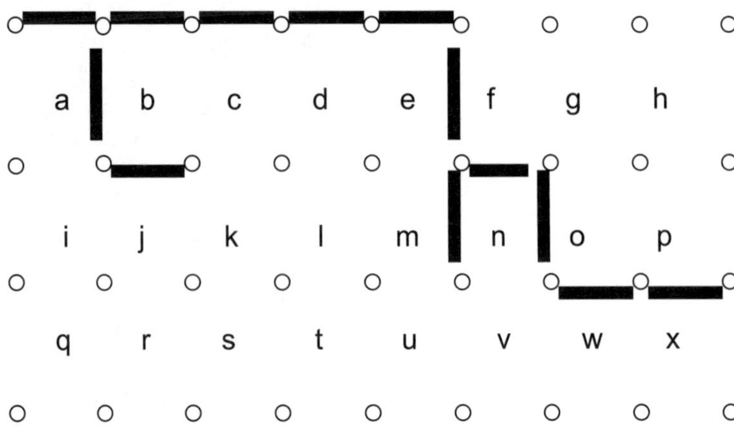

Figure 3.1.5 *The game of boxes*

At the stage of the game depicted it can be seen that there are a number of potential squares in varying stages of completion.

Some of the boxes have no sides completed at all. These are boxes g, h, i, k, l, q, r, s, t, u, v.

Other boxes have one side complete. These are c, d, j, m, p, w and x.

Four boxes have two sides completed. These are a, e, f and o.

Two boxes have three sides in position. These are boxes b and n.

A strategy which could be adopted can be described as this list of actions:

- Move methodically through the entire area of the game and examine each set of four dots in turn. Count and record how many completed sides this potential box currently has.
- Complile a list showing the number of sides for each box.
- Sort this list into order as far as possible showing groups of boxes with 0 sides, 1 side, 2 sides, 3 sides and 4 sides.
- Ignore the boxes with 4 sides. These are already won.
- If there is a box with 3 sides add the fourth side and take another turn.
- If there are no boxes with 3 sides continue searching through the list.
- Ignore any box with two sides. Adding a third side to it will only create a potential box for the other player to complete when it is their turn.
- If a box with one side is found add a side.

In practice a human being would be unlikely to play the game in such a rigid, rule-bound way. The solution suggested here is very much one for a computer to follow.

Note that some aspects of the strategy for this game are more difficult to incorporate into a well-defined scheme of play. They cannot be codified easily. Examples of these would be:

- Seeking unjoined pairs of dots which will allow a player to take their turn without any danger of passing a box over to their opponent.
- Making up a series of semi-complete boxes at the edge of the game area and facing outwards. These can be conceded later without allowing a 'chain effect' to benefit the opponent.

Testing and documentation

In later sections of this chapter it will be shown how the solution to a given problem can be coded as a spreadsheet or as a computer program written in a particular language. In either case it is important that the solution is both thoroughly *tested* and adequately *documented*.

Testing a solution requires both a *test plan* of cases which will show whether the proposed solution is complete and *test data*. The test plan will show, usually in tabular form, the range of tests that have been carried out, the expected result of the test, and what in fact occurred. The test data is chosen to permit a full evaluation of the solution by covering all possible situations.

3.2 Business models

Computers have permitted an approach to many problems that were not feasible until the possibility existed of rapidly performing a very large number of associated arithmetical calculations. For example, an engineer might want to know the cumulative effect of heavy lorries passing over a proposed new bridge. In the past he might have examined the damage that had occurred to existing bridges and attempted to extrapolate to the case of the bridge he was planning. Alternatively a small physical model might have been constructed and tested to destruction. This type of approach has now been complemented, or replaced, by the availability of computer processing which allows a numerical approach to be adopted. Instead of building a physical model a *mathematical model* is constructed instead.

This model replaces the real world with *variables* and *equations*. The variables represent aspects of the physical situation which are significant enough to merit inclusion in the model. To continue with the example above, these variables could include the length of the bridge, the tensile strength of the materials used in its construction, the number of articulated lorries crossing it every hour and many others. The equations of the model then relate the variables to each other in a way which matches the way their physical counterparts would interact in reality.

The implication is that computers have made it possible to concentrate not upon a problem itself but upon its mathematical abstraction. Although this abstraction necessarily leaves out many of the finer details which the real world contains, it represents a sufficient proportion of the original problem to permit a plausible investigation to take place. Such computer modelling especially provides the ability to ask 'what if?' questions of the real world with the confidence that the computer's version of reality will be sufficiently convincing.

When attention is diverted from the real-world situation to a model of this situation running as software on a computer, investigations can be carried out which for reasons including *cost*, *safety, time* and *feasibility*, would not be practical otherwise. As an example of a computer model saving money we could consider the advantages of simulating the construction of a new rapid transit link in a city. A realistic model running on a computer would be able to predict the benefits of a monorail upon local transport and commerce at only a fraction of the cost of building such a system in reality. A decision could then be made about whether to proceed with the monorail in the knowledge that a fair assessment had been made of what would be likely to occur.

Many situations which would be dangerous to attempt in real life can be modelled by a computer. One of the most obvious of these is the use of flight simulators for training pilots, but any situation where human life might be at risk is worth considering for initial computer modelling.

Models run by a computer have the advantage of being able to accelerate some processes which would take place more slowly in the real world. There is no need for the model to be limited by the natural progression of time. Instead the simulation *time step* can be adjusted to allow the observation in minutes of processes which might take place over a period of some years in the real world. An example here would be the use of economic models for predicting the future state of a company or even a national economy.

Perhaps one of the most exciting types of computer model is where the situation recreated by computer is completely impossible to achieve otherwise. Such an example would be the way in which astronomers have been able to draw many conclusions about the way in which the solar system formed, approximately 4.5 billion years ago, by recreating it in the computer. The impossibility of this experiment does not detract from the knowledge which has been genuinely gained from the computer model.

Computer modelling also has many applications in the business world. Below, for example, an illustration will be developed in detail of the use of time-series analysis.

Key fact

It must be stressed that the conclusion should not be drawn that there is just one model of a particular situation. A variety of models could exist depending upon what aspects of the real world are considered to be the most important. Even if these are the same for two models of a situation, the variables chosen to represent the situation may differ from one model to another. Similarly equations in the model may be formulated in different ways. Part of the modeller's creativity is to select the most appropriate model for the situation and for the computing facilities available.

Modelling and spreadsheets

Linked with mathematical modelling is the use of spreadsheets. A *spreadsheet* is not essential for the implementation of a mathematical model on a computer, but it is extremely convenient. A programmer could of course decide to code a mathematical model into a specific computer language. This would probably be necessary for a very large and complex model. One extremely complicated mathematical model which simulated the interaction of subnuclear particles even prompted the physicists involved to build a completely new computer! However, for the vast majority of situations which require modelling, spreadsheet software running on a desktop PC is quite adequate.

Key fact

Historically spreadsheets are an interesting example of a tool evolving quickly for a perceived need. Two Americans, Dan Bricklin and Bob Frankston, devised the first spreadsheet program to meet their own practical requirement for an aid which would help to automate the calculations they performed regularly. The newly available microcomputer was the obvious choice of device. The program they created to run on their Apple 2 micro soon revealed its versatility and was subsequently marketed as the commercial software 'Visicalc'. The immediate success of this program encouraged software houses to produce their own spreadsheet software and a major new type of computer application had been born.

A spreadsheet consists of a grid of *cells* displayed on the screen of a computer. The columns of the grid are identified by numbers and the rows by letters. A combination of letter and number therefore forms a coordinate pair identifying each cell of the sheet. This letter–number pair is called a *cell reference* and can be used as a variable name for any number entered on the spreadsheet.

A cell may have any one of three different types of content:

- *Text* – This allows values displayed on the spreadsheet to be identified and so makes the spreadsheet easier to use than would be the case if only numbers were shown.
- *Numerical values* – These are entered by the user and essentially permit the problem to be defined.
- *Equations* (also called formulas) – these are algebraic expressions which perform calculations and allow the spreadsheet to achieve the results intended.

These different types of cell content can be easily illustrated by a very simple example of a spreadsheet. In Figure 3.2.1 it is assumed that a child is using a spreadsheet to calculate how much pocket money remains after buying bars of chocolate.

	A	B	C
1	Pocket money	Cost of bar	Change
2	4	0.85	=A2-B2*A5
3			
4	Number of bars		
5	3		

Figure 3.2.1

She first types the identifying text 'Pocket money' into cell A1 of the spreadsheet and the actual amount, here shown as pence, into cell A2. Next she enters the cost of a bar of chocolate into B2 beneath identifying text in B1. Similarly the number of bars of chocolate are placed in cell A5 with suitable text in A4.

Finally she adds a calculation to show how much change she has. This is found by first multiplying the cost of a bar of chocolate by the total number purchased to find the total cost. The cost of a single bar is stored in cell B2 and the number of bars in A5. This means the total cost is given by the expression B2 × A5. The change is then found by subtracting this total cost from the pocket money stored in A2. The equation which calculates the change will therefore be = A2 – B2 × A5. (Note that the order of priority in a mixed calculation means that the multiplication will be performed first and that brackets are not required.) The equation is therefore added in this form to cell C2 with explanatory text 'Change' in C1.

Mathematics in action

It is important to realize that when an equation refers to the content of another cell it uses that cell's reference as a variable. The use of two characters as a variable, for example C5, should not be confusing. In mathematics compound variable names frequently occur. Spreadsheets are far more economical in the length of their variable names than tensor calculus is!

If, as shown in the Figure, she has £4.00 in pocket money and buys 3 bars of chocolate each costing 85p, she will have £1.45 in change. (For simplicity all of these amounts are shown as pence.) It is now that the spreadsheet's ability for automatic recalculation can be demonstrated, because if the content of A5 is changed to 4, the change shown in cell C2 will alter immediately to the new value of 60. It is an essential feature of a spreadsheet that all values can be automatically updated.

Note that the precise layout of the sheet is fairly arbitrary in a simple example like this. It does not matter very much where individual items are placed provided that correct cell references appear in equations. It is not necessary, for example, to place numerical input immediately beneath its identifying text, as shown here, although obviously it makes sense to adopt some convention adhered to consistently throughout the sheet in order to aid clarity.

However, the design of a spreadsheet does become very important when complicated sheets are planned. These will require ease of data entry. The spreadsheet's user will need to understand what has to be typed and where. In addition it is important to be able to maintain the software by adjusting equations and adding and deleting various cells. Care shown at the initial stage of design will reduce the likelihood of later problems.

Developing a mathematical model

It is important to stress immediately that a spreadsheet would not be used for a situation like the one outlined above. It is pointless to write a spreadsheet to use just once in a 'one-off' calculation. It would be far simpler just to perform the calculations manually, perhaps with a calculator if the numbers are awkward. Spreadsheets only present a significant saving of effort when repeated calculations are required. Then the time spent in setting up the spreadsheet is rewarded by the ease with which these calculations can be used again and again each time with different values to operate upon.

When we have to design a more complicated spreadsheet we need to adopt a more rigorous approach. Before entering Microsoft Excel, or whichever software package we have available, we have to think carefully about the problem we are attempting to solve and produce the mathematical model for it. This model defines the problem precisely and can then be coded as a spreadsheet. The model consists of variables which allow various details of the situation to be represented numerically and equations which link these variables and so provide the solution that we require.

Here is a more complicated example which will illustrate the way in which a mathematical model is constructed.

> Gareth's Gardens is a small firm that specializes in planning and laying new gardens. A particularly popular garden plan consists of a patio and lawn, together with a circular pond. Gareth's Gardens want to use a spreadsheet to calculate the cost of a new garden constructed to this design.

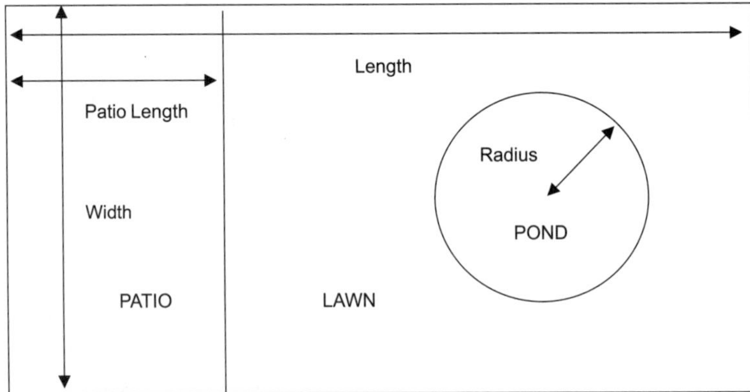

Figure 3.2.2

> ## Key fact
>
> Using a spreadsheet is plausible in this case because many separate gardens will be based upon the same layout, differing only in size. A spreadsheet model which calculates the cost of garden construction will therefore be an example of the same calculations being repeated with fresh data. This is a situation where a spreadsheet is likely to help.

Before the spreadsheet is created the mathematical model of this situation should be written. This is a particularly easy example of designing a model but is good practice in the stages involved.

First we must decide precisely what it is we want the model to do. In this case it is to produce a single *output variable*, which is the total cost of constructing the garden. A sensible variable name to choose for this is Total. So we can begin a *variable list* with:

Output variable

Total:	Cost of overall garden design

Next we make a list of all the variables which will change from one garden to another. These variables are called *input variables*, because they represent values which can be typed in to say how big the garden is, and the size of the patio and pond within it.

The variable list therefore continues as:

Input variables

Length:	The overall length of the garden
Width:	The width of the garden
Patio-Length:	The length of the patio
Radius:	Radius of pond

There are other input variables required as well which will let the user enter the cost of a square metre of paving, the cost of a square metre of turf for the lawn and the cost of the special waterproofed concrete for constructing a square metre of pond. The variable list will become:

Input variables

Length:	The overall length of the garden
Width:	The width of the garden
Patio-Length:	The length of the patio
Radius:	Radius of pond
Paving:	The cost of a square metre of paving
Turf:	The cost of a square metre of turf
Concrete:	The cost of a square metre of waterproof concrete

This completes the list of input variables.

In calculating the overall cost there are a number of stages that we have to work through. For example, there will be a calculation to determine the cost of the patio alone. This leads to the introduction of a number of *process variables* which are an essential part of the model but which are neither the final answer output nor values which are directly entered by the user. These process variables can be regarded as being 'hidden' from the user, since there is no need for the user of the spreadsheet to know all the stages of the calculation.

How far we break down the calculation into intermediate stages will be a matter for the individual modeller to decide. However, in this example we shall have the following:

Process variables:

PatioArea:	Area of patio
PatioCost:	Cost of paving patio
LawnArea:	Area of lawn
LawnCost:	Cost of laying lawn to turf
PondArea:	Area of pond
PondCost:	Cost of concrete for pond

The next part of the model to consider is the set of equations which link the variables. It should not be too difficult for you to confirm that these are the equations that are required. (The order of the equations shown below is arbitrary.)

Equations

Total	=	PatioCost + LawnCost + PondCost
PatioCost	=	PatioArea × Paving
LawnCost	=	LawnArea × Turf
PondCost	=	PondArea × Concrete
PatioArea	=	PatioLength × Width
LawnArea	=	(Length – PatioLength) × Width – PondArea
PondArea	=	3.14 × Radius × Radius

Mathematics in action

In the example here the value of π is being truncated to just two decimal places for simplicity. The true value, of course, is a never-ending string of decimal places. To the first 14 of these π is 3.14159265358949. Microsoft Excel allows π to be entered as PI().

We know that we have completed the mathematical model when:

- Each of the process and output variable(s) appears as the left-hand side of one of the equations of the model.
- The right-hand side of each equation contains only input variables or process variables which are already completely defined by one of the equations of the model.

With practice, carrying out a completeness check like this becomes very easy to do and it does provide a useful confirmation of the model's plausibility.

At this point you will have noticed that we have not included any calculation for the walls of the pond. Provided that the pond is shallow this will not be too much of a problem. In any model we create there will be necessary *simplifying assumptions* which reduce the complexity of the model and make it feasible for us to proceed with the computing facilities we have available.

Key fact

The choice of appropriate assumptions is a vital part of mathematical modelling. The need to create a model which can be coded with available computing resources should not encourage the introduction of implausible assumptions. In addition a further problem can arise if a physical situation being modelled is not fully understood. A significant example of this would be the obvious difficulty that occurred in creating effective models for global warming. The earliest models produced conflicting results partly as a result of lack of knowledge of the underlying meteorology.

Before proceeding any further the model should be now be tested by choosing appropriate data for the input variables and working manually through the equations to check that sensible answers do emerge for the process variables and the output variable. After this the model can be coded as a spreadsheet.

Coding the mathematical model

Coding a mathematical model is quite straightforward and can be stated as these stages:

- Enter the names of all of the input, process and output variables in cells on the spreadsheet.
- In neighbouring cells (perhaps immediately beneath) add test data for the input variables.
- Add the right-hand side of relevant equations (including the equals sign) in cells adjacent to the process and output variables.
- In all the equations variables should be replaced by the appropriate cell reference.

The model developed here could now be coded as a Microsoft Excel spreadsheet like the area in Figure 3.2.3.

Note that clarity of a spreadsheet is aided if it is divided into separate input, output and process regions. Sensible spacing is generally a good idea.

The way in which variable names have been replaced by cell references should be fairly obvious. For example, the equation calculating the area of the lawn was shown in the mathematical model as:

$$\text{LawnArea} = (\text{Length} - \text{PatioLength}) \times \text{Width} - \text{PondArea}$$

On the spreadsheet cell C9 has been chosen to be the location for this equation. In coding it care has been taken to identify the cells representing the input variables Length and Width and the process variables PatioLength and PondArea. These are as follows:

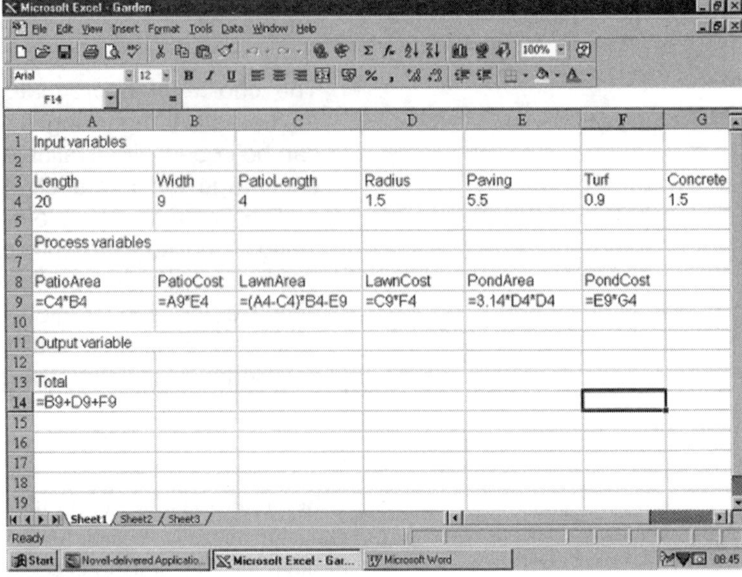

	A	B	C	D	E	F	G
1	Input variables						
2							
3	Length	Width	PatioLength	Radius	Paving	Turf	Concrete
4	20	9	4	1.5	5.5	0.9	1.5
5							
6	Process variables						
7							
8	PatioArea	PatioCost	LawnArea	LawnCost	PondArea	PondCost	
9	=C4*B4	=A9*E4	=(A4-C4)*B4-E9	=C9*F4	=3.14*D4*D4	=E9*G4	
10							
11	Output variable						
12							
13	Total						
14	=B9+D9+F9						

Figure 3.2.3

Length is placed in cell A4
Width is placed in cell B4
PatioLength is placed in cell C4
PondArea is placed in cell E9

The equation to be placed in C9 accordingly becomes:

$$= (A4 - C4) \times B4 - E9$$

All the other equations in the model have similarly been adjusted to use the cell references.

Of course it is quite arbitrary which cells should be chosen initially for the variables and so there is no unique coding of the equations into cell references. Many different spreadsheets could emerge from the same model.

The screen dump above shows the equations of the model. The calculated values will appear like those in Figure 3.2.4.

Advice on designing a model

As emphasized already, the correct approach to modelling with a spreadsheet is to begin by thinking carefully about the situation that is eventually going to be recreated using a computer and spreadsheet software. A detailed analysis will allow output, input and process variables to be identified and the equations that relate them to one another to be established. Simplifying assumptions that are required to make the model manageable are also chosen at this design stage. Then, only when the model has been demonstrated as correct by selecting suitable test data and working manually through the calculations incorporated into the model, should it be coded as a spreadsheet.

Microsoft Excel - Garden

	A	B	C	D	E	F	G	H
1	Input variables							
2								
3	Length	Width	PatioLength	Radius	Paving	Turf	Concrete	
4	20.00	9.00	4.00	1.50	£5.50	£0.90	£1.50	
5								
6	Process variables							
7								
8	PatioArea	PatioCost	LawnArea	LawnCost	PondArea	PondCost		
9	36.00	£198.00	136.935	£123.24	7.07	£10.60		
10								
11	Output variable							
12								
13	Total							
14	£331.84							

Figure 3.2.4

There are clear advantages in adopting this approach. By developing a mathematical model first and then coding as a spreadsheet, the following will be gained:

- The modelling process will have been made explicit. This will help other people to understand what you have done. Future programmers will be able to maintain and develop the model further. Assessors will be able to grade your work fairly. (A model that appears only as a spreadsheet might be a light hidden under a bushel.)
- Debugging the spreadsheet will be far easier. Error messages, possibly warning of circular references, will be far less likely!
- The model can be coded into alternative software if necessary, perhaps a Pascal or C program rather than a spreadsheet.

It has to be admitted, however, that some students approaching modelling for the first time find the rigor of this formal approach a little daunting. It can be very tempting to test out a few ideas directly, using a spreadsheet on a computer. This is not ideal, but given the frailty of human nature, or at least the human intellect, allowances should perhaps be made for those who are a little timid with algebra and who require the psychological comfort of a spreadsheet display.

Nevertheless, if you are tempted to switch the machine on first, do make sure that your experimental spreadsheet is converted at a very early stage into the prototype of your eventual mathematical model. This can be done by identifying the different types of variable that, pragmatically, you have included on your sheet, and also the equations that you have used. Type these into a text document and use them as an initial framework for the model which you then develop formally. Write this model completely before reverting to a spreadsheet and coding the new, expanded model.

Including conditions in a mathematical model

In the previous example of designing a mathematical model we were concerned only with fixed relations expressed as equations linking the variables of the model. This is not an entirely realistic approach to modelling. It is far more likely that when a real-world situation is translated into a mathematical one the equations will need to be supplemented by *conditions* which only 'fire' when particular circumstances are encountered.

For example, a trivially simple model in which the volume of a rectangular box is determined by the product of its length, width and depth will not involve any condition. However, the price of filling a similarly shaped vat will depend upon whether the contents being added will be water or whisky. A model of this situation will involve a condition like:

> If the vat is being filled with whisky then multiply its volume by the cost of a litre of whisky, otherwise multiply by the cost of a litre of water.

It can be seen that this condition involves two possible actions that can take place. The first action is followed if the condition is true. The second action is followed if it is false.

The general form of a condition is therefore:

IF {anticipated condition} THEN {appropriate action}
ELSE {alternative action}

In Microsoft Excel a condition can be written as:

= if ({anticipated condition}, {appropriate action}, {alternative action})

As a specific example of using conditions on a spreadsheet we could place this condition in cell a1:

= if (c2 > 6, b1, b1/2)

This would make the value in cell a1 equal to the value in b1 only when a number greater than 6 appeared in c2. If the value in c2 were not greater than 6 then the value of a1 would be half the value of b1.

Conditions are required in a model of the following situation.

> A small seaside firm produces greetings cards based upon local views. In order to compete with major manufacturers the firm concentrates upon a niche market, specializing in hand-tinted illustrations of local beauty spots.
>
> Two sizes of card are produced, large and small. The price charged to the customer differs for these, although the time taken to produce a card can safely be regarded as the same for either size.

Producing the cards is labour intensive and the number of staff employed by the firm as illustrators fluctuates with the demand for cards.

Each month cards which have been produced by the permanent members of staff but which have remained unsold are added to a reserve of available stock. If this total stock level drops to 300 cards or below a temporary member of staff is immediately employed at the beginning of the month to help produce additional cards. If the stock level drops to 200 or below a second temporary member of staff is employed at the same time. If it drops to 100 or below, a third temporary member is employed.

If the stock level drops to zero at the beginning of the month no further staff are employed but the time needed to produce a card is reduced to 8 minutes in order to boost production further.

Permanent staff produce equal numbers of large and small cards. Temporary staff concentrate on small cards, producing three small for every large card they hand tint.

Permanent staff work for 150 hours per month. Temporary staff work for 100 hours a month. The temporary staff are employed for a minimum period of one month. At the beginning of the succeeding month the number of staff required is recalculated according to the new stock level

The temporary staff have to attend a local college for a brief training session before they can begin work. The college charges a fixed rate of £75 per attendee, which is met by the firm.

Currently the firm employs four permanent staff and has 150 cards in stock. The price charged for a large card is £1.50 and a small card is £1.10. To retain the exclusive nature of the product orders in excess of production capacity are not accepted.

All staff are paid a flat rate of £5 per hour.

Produce a model which will allow the manager of the firm to enter monthly orders for large and small cards. The model will calculate the profit for a month, defined as the difference between income from orders and the total wages paid to all members of staff, and the value of the cards produced in a single month. Also show how the manager could decide whether employing more permanent members of staff, or altering the price charged for cards, would be advisable.

The model for this scenario is developed below.

Identifying the output variables

First the output variables required for the model must be made explicit. It is stated quite clearly how the manager will need to know the profit for a month and so a variable is created for this figure:

Profit: Profit made in a month

In addition the value of cards produced in a month is required and so a second output variable is needed:

Value: The value of the cards produced in a month

Finally the manager will want to be able to enter the current stock level. This will change from month to month and so has to be a variable in the model:

NewStockLevel: Stock held at end of month

The variable list for the mathematical model will therefore include:

Output variables

Profit:	Profit made in a month
Value:	The value of the cards produced in a month
NewStockLevel:	Stock held at end of month

Constants in a model

In the previous example we did not emphasize the role of *constants* within a mathematical model. In many ways these behave in a similar fashion to input variables. They are values which, in a slightly different situation, might have different values. However, because they are fixed for the situation being modelled they should not be entered as variables into the model.

To be more specific, in the firm considered in this example the amount staff are paid per hour is £5. It would have been possible for the firm to have paid them £4 or £6, but reading through the scenario shows that the manager is not going to consider the possibility of changing staff salaries. As a result the value of £5 can be listed as one of the constants required by the model:

Hourly rate of pay = £5

Similarly analysing the situation carefully will show that the hours worked by permanent staff, and by temporary staff will also be values that cannot be altered:

Hours worked per month by permanent member of staff = 150
Hours worked per month by temporary member of staff = 100

The training charge for temporary staff is fixed as well:

Training charge for temporary member of staff = £75

Altogether we have a constant list for the mathematical model consisting of these four fixed values. For total clarity the list indicates their role within the model:

Constants

Hourly rate of pay = £5
Hours worked per month by permanent member of staff = 150
Hours worked per month by temporary member of staff = 100
Training charge for temporary member of staff = £75

Distinguishing between constants and input variables

Deciding what should be a constant and what should be an input variable can depend upon close reading of the way a situation is worded. (If it is something in the real world which you are approaching yourself without the intermediary role of a written description, equal precision is required.) In the example here it is stated that the manager can enter the figures for monthly orders of both large and small cards. These therefore have to appear in the model as input variables:

OrdersLarge: Number of large cards ordered per month
OrdersSmall: Number of small cards ordered per month

The manager can also enter the price to be charged for both sizes of card and so input variables are required for these:

PriceLarge: Price charged for a large card
PriceSmall: Price charged for a small card

The final paragraph of the description also says how the manager can alter the number of permanent staff employed. This has to be a fifth input variable in the model:

PermStaff: Number of permanent members of staff

Note, however, that the number of temporary staff cannot be an input variable. Although not explicitly stated, the description of the situation does implicitly assume that this number will be calculated by the model and so it will be a process variable.

A sixth input variable will be the number of cards held in stock. It might at first be felt that this number would be a constant. If it were, though, it would not be possible to run the model again with a new stock level entered:

OldStockLevel: Stock held at beginning of month

The list of input variables is therefore:

Input variables

OrdersLarge:	Number of large cards ordered per month
OrdersSmall:	Number of small cards ordered per month
PriceLarge:	Price charged for a large card
PriceSmall:	Price charged for a small card
PermStaff:	Number of permanent members of staff
OldStockLevel:	Stock held at beginning of month

Identifying the process variables

The process variables are also identified by thinking about the example carefully. The time to make a card will be a process variable because it is made quite clear in the description of the situation that the time will depend upon the stock level. This value will not be input but calculated automatically. As it is not necessary for the manager to know the time specifically taken to produce a card when considering the overall profit, there is no point in making it an output variable. Hence it is a process variable within the model:

Time: Time to produce a single card

The number of cards made by the staff will have to be calculated initially as two separate quantities as a direct consequence of there being two different categories of staff, permanent and temporary, and the fact that the number of temporary staff will vary according to the stock level. This means that the model will contain two process variables to indicate the number of cards made by each group:

NumberPerm: Number of cards produced by permanent staff per month
NumberTemp: Number of cards produced by temporary staff per month

If the permanent staff and temporary staff each produced the same proportion of large and small cards then it would be extremely easy to calculate the total numbers of each type, and hence the value of the cards produced each month, simply as fractions of a combined total. However, because permanent and temporary staff produce different proportions of cards it is important to have two further process variables to represent the numbers of large and small cards made:

NumberLarge: Number of large cards produced per month
NumberSmall: Number of small cards produced per month

The total number of cards produced will be needed in order to update the stock level:

TotalCards: Total number of cards produced per month

Another process variable will be required to represent the number of temporary staff. This variable is in fact assigned the value of one or the other of two calculated variables according to the action performed by one of the embedded conditions in the spreadsheet. This be will explained in detail below, but it means that three process variables are involved altogether in the calculation of the temporary staff:

TempStaff: Number of temporary staff employed in a given month
Number1: First potential value for TempStaff
Number2: Second potential value for TempStaff

Two process variables are used to represent the wages paid to the permanent and temporary staff:

PermWages: Money paid per month to permanent staff
TempWages: Money paid per month to temporary staff

The training cost for temporary staff requires a variable:

TrainingCost: Cost of training temporary staff

Likewise a variable represents the total expense of employing the staff:

TotalCost: The wages and training cost for the staff

Finally two process variables are used to calculate the money earned from the sale of cards:

IncomeLarge: Money received from orders of large cards
IncomeSmall: Money received from orders of small cards

The complete list of process variables for the model is:
Process variables

Time:	Time to produce a single card
NumberPerm:	Number of cards produced by permanent staff per month
NumberTemp:	Number of cards produced by temporary staff per month
NumberLarge:	Number of large cards produced per month
NumberSmall:	Number of small cards produced per month
TotalCards:	Total number of cards produced per month
TempStaff:	Number of temporary staff employed in a given month
Number1:	First potential value for TempStaff
Number2:	Second potential value for TempStaff
PermWages:	Money paid per month to permanent staff
TempWages:	Money paid per month to temporary staff
TrainingCost:	Cost of training temporary staff
TotalCost:	The wages and training cost for the staff
IncomeLarge:	Money received from orders of large cards
IncomeSmall:	Money received from orders of small cards

Deriving the model's equations

The number of cards made by a permanent member of staff is found by dividing the 150 hours worked per month by the variable Time. The latter is measured in minutes and so the 150 hours needs to be converted to (150×60), or 9000 minutes. Finally the answer must be multiplied by the number of staff to give the equation:

NumberPerm = 9000/Time × PermStaff

Temporary staff work for 100 hours per month, which leads to the similar equation:

NumberTemp = 6000/Time × TempStaff

Next the number of large cards and small cards produced has to be calculated. This involves splitting the production of both permanent and temporary staff into the proportions stated in the description. Permanent staff produce equal numbers of large and small cards and so contribute 0.5 of their output to the separate totals for each. In contrast the temporary staff split their production so that a quarter of the cards are large and three-quarters small. These are the decimal fractions 0.25 and 0.75, which appear in the equations:

NumberLarge = NumberPerm × 0.5 + NumberTemp × 0.25
NumberSmall = NumberPerm × 0.5 + NumberTemp × 0.75

The total number of cards can be calculated by adding together either NumberPerm and NumberTemp, or by adding NumberLarge and NumberSmall:

TotalCards = NumberLarge + NumberSmall

The value of all the cards produced in a month (as opposed to the income from those sold) is found by multiplying together the total produced and the card price for each size of card and then adding the two products together.

Value = NumberLarge × PriceLarge + NumberSmall × PriceSmall

Two equations are required to calculate the wages paid to both sets of staff. A permanent member of staff works 150 hours per month at £5 per hour and so is paid £750. The total wages for a number of staff equal to the value of the input variable PermStaff will therefore be given by:

PermWages = PermStaff × 750

The wages for temporary staff, who work 100 hours per month, will similarly be calculated by the equation:

TempWages = TempStaff × 500

Each temporary member of staff costs the firm £75 for initial training and the total for this will be an equation involving both the £75 and the number of temporary staff:

TrainingCost = TempStaff × 75

The total cost of staff for the firm is now given by:

TotalCost = PermWages + TempWages + TrainingCost

The money the firm earns from the sale of large cards will be the number of the cards multiplied by their price:

IncomeLarge = OrdersLarge × PriceLarge

A similar equation gives the money obtained from the sale of small cards:

IncomeSmall = OrdersSmall × PriceSmall

The profit can now be found by adding the two incomes from card sales and subtracting the cost of wages:

Profit = IncomeLarge + IncomeSmall – TotalCost

It is important for the new level of stock at the end of the month to be known because the stock level is involved in future calculations of the number of temporary staff required. This stock level is determined by the old stock level plus the number of cards produced and less the number sold:

NewStockLevel = OldStockLevel + TotalCards – OrdersLarge – OrdersSmall

Mathematics in action

As already stated two separate variables are involved in deciding how many temporary staff are required. The first of these is Number1, which directly relates the number of temporary staff needed to the stock level, here represented by the variable OldStockLevel to distinguish it from the new level calculated. The detail to note is that the number of temporary staff needed increases as the level of stock drops by multiples of 100:

OldStockLevel	*TempStaff*
> 300	0
201–300	1
101–200	2
< 100	3

Expanding this table indicates an arithmetical pattern which is easy to code into an equation for the model. To simplify the notation the stock level is abbreviated to OSL:

OSL	*400 – OSL*	*(400 – OSL)/ 100*	*INT((400 – OSL)/ 100)*
500	–100	–1	–1
450	–50	–0.5	0
400	0	0	0
350	50	0.5	0
300	100	1.0	1
250	150	1.5	1
200	200	2.0	2
150	250	2.5	2
100	300	3.0	3
50	350	3.5	3
0	400	4.0	4
–50	450	4.0	4

The values shown in the table indicate that the expression:

Number1 = INT((400 – OldStockLevel)/100)

calculates the correct number of temporary staff within a certain range of values for OldStockLevel. However, if it becomes less than 1 the expression calculates too large a number of staff. The number of temporary staff must never exceed 3. Similarly the expression breaks down for large values of OldStockLevel.

Outside the range where the expression of Number1 fails a new expression is required which always evaluates as 3 provided that the stock level is less than zero. This can be achieved with a *Boolean expression* for the further variable, Number2:

Number2 = (OldStockLevel <= 0) × 3

An account will be given in a later section of this chapter of the use of Boolean expressions in writing certain code for computer programs. They can also be used, as here, in a spreadsheet. The Boolean expression for the variable Number2 relies upon the value of (OldStockLevel <= 0) being 1 when the expression is true and 0 otherwise. This means that the correct value of 3 temporary members of staff is calculated when the stock level is less than 0 and the correct value of 0 calculated when the expression for Number1 breaks down at the upper end of its range.

How these two separate calculations for the temporary staff are combined into one final value is shown below when the use of conditions in the model is discussed.

The complete set of equations for the model is:

Equations

NumberPerm = 9000/Time × PermStaff
NumberTemp = 6000/Time × TempStaff
NumberLarge = NumberPerm × 0.5 + NumberTemp × 0.25
NumberSmall = NumberPerm × 0.5 + NumberTemp × 0.75
TotalCards = NumberLarge + NumberSmall
Value = NumberLarge × PriceLarge + NumberSmall × PriceSmall
PermWages = PermStaff × 750
TempWages = TempStaff × 500
TrainingCost = TempStaff × 75
TotalCost = PermWages + TempWages + TrainingCost
IncomeLarge = OrdersLarge × PriceLarge
IncomeSmall = OrdersSmall × PriceSmall
Profit = IncomeLarge + IncomeSmall – TotalCost
NewStockLevel = OldStockLevel + TotalCards – OrdersLarge – OrdersSmall
Number1 = INT((400 – OldStockLevel)/100)
Number2 = (OldStockLevel <=0) × 3

The conditions for the model

Including 'if – then' conditions in a spreadsheet is a vital part of the modelling process, allowing 'what if' situations to be investigated. The model being developed here allows the operation of the card firm to be tested in model form by the inclusion of two such conditions.

The first condition to be included in the mathematical model will select either of the two possible values for the number of temporary staff according to the stock level, as indicated above. If the stock level is within the range for which the expression calculating Number1 is correct, this is the value given to the variable TempStaff. If the stock level is outside the range, the value given to TempStaff is the one calculated as Number2. As can be seen from the second table above the value given by Number1 has a wider validity than the range described in the original situation, but for clarity this is ignored in the coding. The condition is therefore written as:

```
If OldStockLevel > 0 AND OldStockLevel < 301
                          Then TempStaff = Number1
Else TempStaff = Number2
```

A second condition needed in the model calculates the amount of time allowed to produce a card, reducing this when the stock level is too low:

```
If OldStockLevel <= 0 Then Time = 8 Else Time = 10
```

The conditions in the model are therefore:

Conditions

```
If OldStockLevel > 0 AND OldStockLevel < 301
                          Then TempStaff = Number1
Else TempStaff = Number2
If OldStockLevel <= 0 Then Time = 8 Else Time = 10
```

The assumptions of the model

Some of the assumptions that have been made are:

- The model is concerned with labour cost rather than raw materials.
- Raising the price of cards sold does not affect sales figures.
- If a temporary member of staff is re-employed they are trained again. (They have poor retention of skills!)

Coding the card firm spreadsheet

As described previously, coding the model as a spreadsheet involves first placing all variable names on the sheet. Test data is then added for the input variables and the relevant equations for the process and output variables. Cell references are used in the equations.

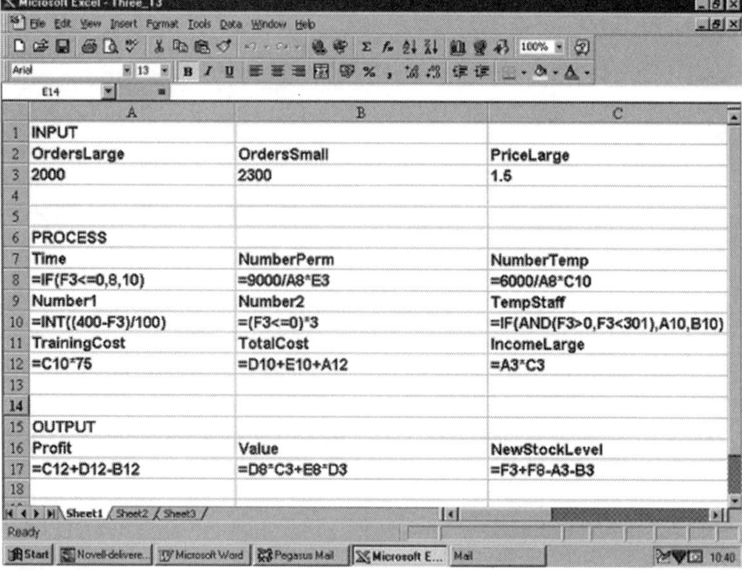

	A	B	C
1	INPUT		
2	OrdersLarge	OrdersSmall	PriceLarge
3	2000	2300	1.5
4			
5			
6	PROCESS		
7	Time	NumberPerm	NumberTemp
8	=IF(F3<=0,8,10)	=9000/A8*E3	=6000/A8*C10
9	Number1	Number2	TempStaff
10	=INT((400-F3)/100)	=(F3<=0)*3	=IF(AND(F3>0,F3<301),A10,B10)
11	TrainingCost	TotalCost	IncomeLarge
12	=C10*75	=D10+E10+A12	=A3*C3
13			
14			
15	OUTPUT		
16	Profit	Value	NewStockLevel
17	=C12+D12-B12	=D8*C3+E8*D3	=F3+F8-A3-B3
18			

Figure 3.2.5

	D	E	F
1			
2	PriceSmall	PermStaff	OldStockLevel
3	1.1	4	285
4			
5			
6			
7	NumberLarge	NumberSmall	TotalCards
8	=B8*0.5+C8*0.25	=B8*0.5+C8*0.75	=D8+E8
9	PermWages	TempWages	
10	=E3*750	=C10*500	
11	IncomeSmall		
12	=B3*D3		
13			
14			
15			
16			
17			
18			

Figure 3.2.6

Consider coding the equation:

NewStockLevel = OldStockLevel + TotalCards – OrdersLarge – OrdersSmall

Values for the variables on the right-hand side of the equation are located in cells F3, F8, A3 and B3 and so these are the references that appear in the equation placed in cell C17.

The model is shown in Figure 3.2.6 coded as a Microsoft Excel spreadsheet.

The sheet is shown in typical operation in Figure 3.2.7.

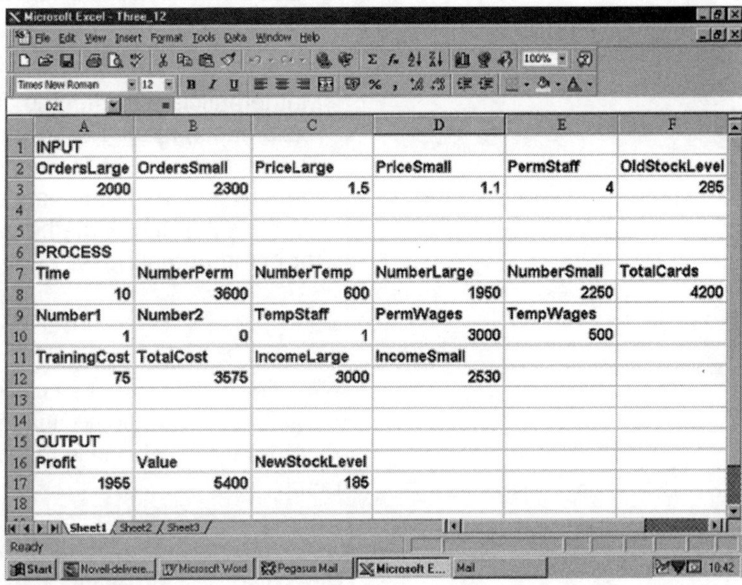

	A	B	C	D	E	F
1	INPUT					
2	OrdersLarge	OrdersSmall	PriceLarge	PriceSmall	PermStaff	OldStockLevel
3	2000	2300	1.5	1.1	4	285
4						
5						
6	PROCESS					
7	Time	NumberPerm	NumberTemp	NumberLarge	NumberSmall	TotalCards
8	10	3600	600	1950	2250	4200
9	Number1	Number2	TempStaff	PermWages	TempWages	
10	1	0	1	3000	500	
11	TrainingCost	TotalCost	IncomeLarge	IncomeSmall		
12	75	3575	3000	2530		
13						
14						
15	OUTPUT					
16	Profit	Value	NewStockLevel			
17	1955	5400	185			
18						

Figure 3.2.7

Spreadsheet functions

The mathematical capability of a spreadsheet is increased by the provision of a large number of in-built *functions* which can perform various operations on spreadsheet data. These operations take the form of a function name followed by the *argument* of the function. This is the data on which it is going to operate. The argument will usually be a cell reference or a cell range. Typical functions for a spreadsheet include the following.

ABS – this gives the absolute value of a number, which is the value of the number if it is positive or –1 multiplied by the number if it is negative, i.e. the number without its sign. A typical example might be ABS(B4).

AVERAGE – this calculates the mean of a series of numbers. If 2, 4, 7 and 3 are placed in cells C1, C2, C3 and C4 then AVERAGE(C1:C4) will be 4. Here the argument has been given as a cell range.

EVEN – a number is rounded up to the nearest even number. Even numbers are left unchanged. EVEN(5) will be 6.

FACT – The factorial of a integer is the product of all the integers from 1 to the number. For example, the factorial of 6 is $1 \times 2 \times 3 \times 4 \times 5 \times 6$, or 720. So FACT(B3) will be 720 if B3 is a cell which contains 6, or contains a formula which evaluates as 6. The function rounds down any non-integral value before calculating the factorial. This means that FACT(6.4) will also be 720.

Key fact

Mathematicians write the factorial of an integer using an exclamation mark. For example, the factorial of 5 is written as 5! This means that the conventional use of an exclamation mark within a mathematical document can be confusing. Perhaps this is why mathematicians have gained a reputation for being humourless!

INT – the integral part of a number is given by this function. INT(2.73) is equal to 2, with the decimal fraction 0.73 omitted. There are many occasions when being able to ignore the fractional part of a number is useful.

LOG – this function gives the logarithm of a number to a specified base. The syntax is LOG(number, base). For example, LOG(100,10) is 2 because 10, the base, has to be raised to the power of 2 to give 100.

MDETERM – this is a function which allows the determinant of a matrix to be evaluated. There are two ways in which the matrix can be entered. The first method is to provide the elements of the matrix directly as an argument for the MDETERM function. They are presented as a list between braces and in which individual elements are separated by commas. The end of each row of the matrix is indicated by a semicolon:

MDETERM({2, 9, 7; 3, 1, 4; 1, 5, 8})

Alternatively the matrix elements are entered into cells of the spreadsheet. The cell range for the matrix then becomes the argument for the function. This is shown in the example below.

Mathematics in action

The value of the determinant can be calculated manually first as a check. The elements are:

$$\begin{matrix} 2 & 9 & 7 \\ 3 & 1 & 4 \\ 1 & 5 & 8 \end{matrix}$$

From this the determinant will be

$$2 \times (1 \times 8 - 4 \times 5) - 9 \times (3 \times 8 - 4 \times 1) + 7 \times (3 \times 5 - 1 \times 1)$$

$$= 2 \times (-12) - 9 \times (20) + 7 \times (14)$$

$$= -24 - 180 + 98$$

$$= -106$$

The elements are entered as shown and the cell range they occupy can be seen to be A1:C3. This range is inserted into the function to give MDERTM(A1:C3). This has been placed in cell B5 (Figure 3.2.8).

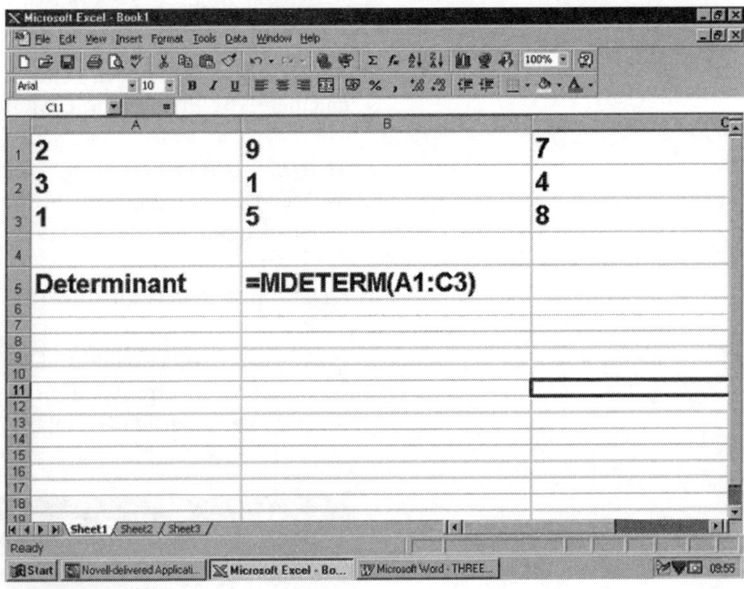

Figure 3.2.8

The second screen dump shows that the function does evaluate the determinant successfully (Figure 3.2.9).

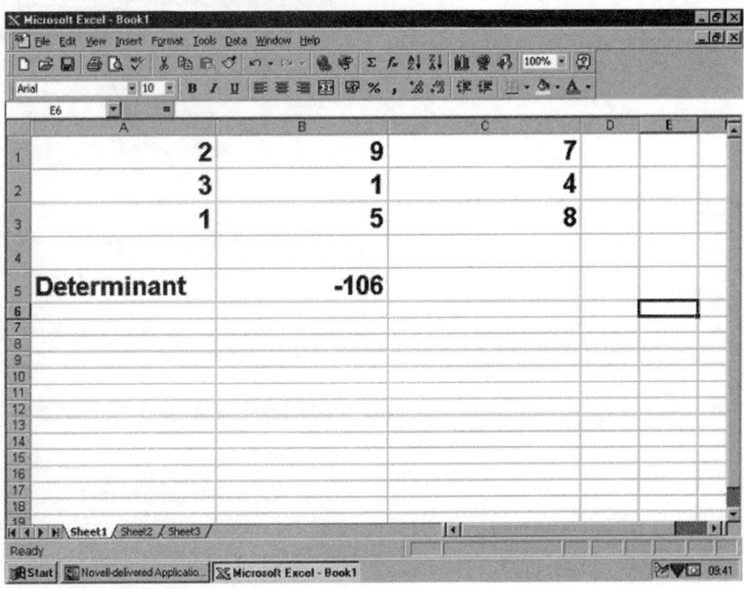

Figure 3.2.9

MEDIAN – the median of a series of numbers is given by this function. If 3, 2, 7, 1, 5 are placed in cells A1, B1, C1, D1 and E1, MEDIAN(A1:E1) returns a value of 3. Note that numbers do not need to be sorted first. This is done automatically by the spreadsheet as it performs its calculation of the function.

MINVERSE – This calculates the inverse of a matrix. The matrix elements will be placed on the sheet in the cells identified by a cell range, e.g. A1:C3. This range is then given as the argument for MINVERSE. Alternatively the matrix elements can be entered as a list as described above for MDETERM.

MOD – the remainder when one number divides into another is calculated by this function. MOD(37,5) is 2.

MODE – the most frequently occurring term in a set of data is returned by MODE. The argument for the function can again be a list of values or a cell reference.

ODD – this rounds a number up to the nearest odd number.

RAND – the function RAND() produces a random decimal fraction between 0 and 1. Frequently what is really required, though, is a random integer over a particular range of values.

Mathematics in action

Suppose that the range of integers needed is 1, 2 . . . 10. Multiplying the random decimal fraction, RAND(), by 10 will generate numbers in the range 0 to 9, together with a decimal part. Note that the product will never be 10 itself. Using INT to remove the decimal produces integers in the range 0 to 9. Finally to produce the range wanted 1 has to be added. This means that if a random throw of a dice is needed the formula would be:

INT(RAND() × 6) + 1

SQRT – the square root of a number is given by SQRT. The argument can be a number or a cell reference.

SUM – this gives the sum over a cell range.

Using look-up tables

When a spreadsheet is checked to see that it does perform all the expected calculations test data will be needed. Repeated test data will also be required when a what-if situation is being investigated. It would be tedious if the same data had to be typed repeatedly and so spreadsheets come equipped with a way of storing data in cells, ready to be used in some other part of the sheet when required. The cell references of the data allow it to be identified and retrieved for temporary insertion in various calculations. This is very similar to the use of arrays in a programming language, a topic which will be explained in a later section of this chapter.

Spreadsheets store data in *look-up tables*. This is illustrated in a brief example. Here it is assumed that the stored data is just a series of ten names: Angela, Beryl, Claudia, Denise, Edward, Fiona, Gerald, Harriet, Ian and Jennie. These are stored in a *vertical look-up* table in cells B3 to B12. An identifying number for the names has been included in cells A3 to A12 and so the whole table is defined by the cell range A3:B12.

In this example one of the names will be chosen at random. This means that a random number in the range 1–10 will be required. This is done by the calculation placed in cell C1, INT(RAND() × 10) + 1.

The selected name will be placed in cell B1 and so it is in this cell that the formula which copies data from the table has to be placed. This uses the Microsoft Excel spreadsheet function VLOOKUP. The 'V' indicates that a vertical look-up table is involved. The general form of this is:

VLOOKUP(Value, Cell range, Column)

Value is the number of the data item in the table. In this example it will be the cell reference C1.

Cell range tells the function where the look-up table is located on the sheet. The range for the table in this example is A3:B12.

Column gives the column for the data in the table. Here it will be 2.

The formula to be placed in cell B1 is therefore:

VLOOKUP(C1, A3:B12,2)

The sheet will appear as shown in Figure 3.2.10.

	A	B	C
1	Chosen	=VLOOKUP(C1,A3:B12,2)	=INT(RAND()*10)+1
2			
3	1	Angela	
4	2	Beryl	
5	3	Claudia	
6	4	Denise	
7	5	Edward	
8	6	Fiona	
9	7	Gerald	
10	8	Harriet	
11	9	Ian	
12	10	Jennie	
13			

Figure 3.2.10

The operation of the sheet is shown in Figure 3.2.11. The random number produced in cell C1 is 7. This value has selected the seventh name from the vertical look-up table, Gerald, and this appears in cell B1.

This example has used text in the look-up table. Equally well numbers or cell references could have been used as the data in the table. The latter permits great flexibility in the operation of the sheet.

	A	B	C	D
1	Chosen	Gerald	7	
2				
3	1	Angela		
4	2	Beryl		
5	3	Claudia		
6	4	Denise		
7	5	Edward		
8	6	Fiona		
9	7	Gerald		
10	8	Harriet		
11	9	Ian		
12	10	Jennie		
13				

Figure 3.2.11

Horizontal look-up tables can also be used to store data in a spreadsheet. With these the function takes the form:

HLOOKUP(Value, Cell range, Row)

Forecasting and time series

Time series analysis is an important tool in business planning. It involves recording numerical information, often sales figures, over a reasonably long period of time and then attempting to identify underlying patterns revealed by the data. If such patterns can be found, they help in extrapolating future projections.

Care has to be taken in such analysis. If past figures are to be a guide towards the future, it has to be assumed that a moderately steady, equilibrium situation exists. Numbers obtained by means of a mathematical model cannot be regarded as a complete substitute for the human expert. Nevertheless, interpreted with caution and with past experience of the practical details involved, the figures generated by a computer can be of immense help in guiding decision making.

One model which is frequently used in time series analysis assumes that the variation observed in recorded data is the result of different components added together. First there is the long-term trend. For example, the number of passengers passing through a certain sea port may gradually increase year by year. Secondly there is a cyclical variation superimposed onto the trend. To continue with the same example, certain foreign resorts with which the port is linked may undergo a fluctuating popularity among tourists. A third component is the seasonal variation. Probably fewer passengers will be travelling by sea in the winter. Finally there is a random variation which will further modify the figures. If an important sporting event occurs many more people may decide to visit the country. The overall relationship can be symbolized by this equation:

Variation = Long-term trend + Cyclical Variation +
Seasonal Variation + Random Variation

A simple list of the passengers carried by the port's ferry companies will be the result of all of these factors. Combined in an apparently complicated fashion, they will obscure the underlying trend and make planning for the companies very difficult. Fortunately the numerical analysis of such information into component parts using the methods of time series is precisely the type of number crunching for which a computer is ideally suited.

Analysing a time series

In order to introduce the concept of time series analysis we first look at the idea of a *moving average*. A moving average is a new set of numbers derived from an initial series. Suppose you have these numbers in the series:

16, 14, 12, 22, 11, 18...

Taking the arithmetic mean of the first three numbers gives:

$(16 + 14 + 12)/3 = 14$

Similarly the mean of the next, overlapping, set of three numbers is:

$(14 + 12 + 22)/3 = 16$

The average of the third set is:

$(12 + 22 + 11)/3 = 15$

In this way a second series of numbers can be created from the first:

14, 16, 15, 17...

As a result of the way in which the individual terms in this second series are calculated they are called three-point moving averages. Moving averages like these are involved in a statistical examination of financial returns which attempts to deduce long-term patterns in the fluctuation of the individual figures. The way in which data can be analysed into its component variations is best explained with a numerical example (Figure 3.2.12).

In the table the quarterly sales figures (in £ million) of an imaginary firm are recorded over a four-year period. These figures have been analysed into columns showing trend, seasonal deviation and random deviation. This has been achieved by a method involving the smoothing out process of moving averages.

The first and second columns simply show the period of four years covered by the time series and the third gives the recorded quarterly figures during this time. The fourth column gives the four-point moving

Quarterly figure	Four-point average	Centred trend	Deviation
20			
22			
	24.5		
30		27	3
	29.5		
26		28	-2
	26.5		
40			
10			

Figure 3.2.12

average. This means that the quarterly figures have been added in groups of four and the mean taken for each. The first four-point average is:

$$(28 + 34 + 36 + 30)/4 = 32$$

The second four-point average is:

$$(34 + 36 + 30 + 20)/4 = 30$$

This calculation is repeated until all the quarterly figures are analysed. These averages naturally represent a figure for the middle of the relevant period and have been placed on additional lines between the main rows of the table.

The processed information is placed back in step with the quarterly figures by calculating the centred trend. This is the arithmetic mean of the column of four-point averages, now taken in pairs. The first two centred trends will be:

$$(32 + 30)/2 = 31$$

$$(30 + 28)/2 = 29$$

All the values for the centred trend are recorded in the fifth column.

Once the centred trend has been calculated the deviation shown by the quarterly figure from this value can be found immediately by subtracting the trend from it. The first row of the table for which this can be done represents the third quarter for year one. Here the deviation, placed in the sixth column of the table, is:

$$(36 - 31) = 5$$

The second and third deviations are:

(30 – 29) = 1

(20 – 30) = –10

The deviation from the centred trend will be assumed here to be a combination of two superimposed influences, the seasonal variation and random variation, as referred to above. The time series analysis now has to attempt to separate out the seasonal deviation and random deviation caused by these.

The seasonal deviation is first found by calculating the average value of the deviation for each quarter over the years involved. There is no value for the first quarterly deviation for the first year, but the mean of the values for the first quarterly deviation in the second, third and fourth years is:

(–10 + 20 + 6)/3 = 5.33

This is the mean deviation. In the same way the mean deviation for the second quarter is calculated as:

(–7 – 8 – 1)/3 = –5.33

The mean deviation for the third quarter is similarly:

(5 + 12 – 17)/3 = 0

For the fourth quarter it is now:

(1 – 10 + 17)/3 = 2.67

The total mean deviation for all four quarters should be zero but with these figures it becomes:

(5.33 – 5.33 + 0 + 2.67) = 2.67

However, it can be reduced to zero by modifying each mean deviation with these adjustments:

5.33 – (2.67/4) = 4.67

–5.33 – (2.67/4) = –6

0 – (2.67/4) = –0.67

2.67 – (2.67/4) = 2

These values are the seasonal deviations shown in the seventh column of the table.

Finally the random deviation in the eighth column is found by subtracting the seasonal deviation from the actual deviation in the sixth column.

We can now proceed to a spreadsheet model. Again as in our previous examples we have input, process and output variables. The input variables are the series of quarterly figures and the output variables the values found for seasonal and random deviation. Process variables are the four-point moving averages, the centred trend and deviation.

Clearly we have a large number of equations linking these variables, but they belong to distinct groups. For example, the equation which calculates the first four-point moving average is:

Average_1 = (Quarter_1 + Quarter_2 + Quarter_3 + Quarter_4)/4

This equation can be seen to be very similar to the equation calculating the second moving average:

Average_2 = (Quarter_2 + Quarter_3 + Quarter_4 + Quarter_5)/4

Replication of cell content

It is here that a particular spreadsheet tool becomes important. We are able to *replicate* a particular equation, referring to a given range of cells, to provide the equivalent calculation in a different part of the sheet. The cell references are automatically adjusted to take into account the new location of each equation.

Replication becomes easier to understand if we look at a specific example. Shown in Figure 3.2.13 is the spreadsheet model for the time series analysis described above.

	A	B	C	D	E	F	G	H
1	Year	Quarter	Quarterly figures	Four-point	Centred	Deviation	Seasonal	Random
2	1	1	28					
3		2	34	=SUM(C2:C5)/4				
4		3	36	=SUM(C3:C6)/4	=(D3+D4)/2	=C4-E4	=C20-E20	=F4-G4
5		4	30	=SUM(C4:C7)/4	=(D4+D5)/2	=C5-E5	=D20-E20	=F5-G5
6	2	1	20	=SUM(C5:C8)/4	=(D5+D6)/2	=C6-E6	=A20-E20	=F6-G6
7		2	26	=SUM(C6:C9)/4	=(D6+D7)/2	=C7-E7	=B20-E20	=F7-G7
8		3	52	=SUM(C7:C10)/4	=(D7+D8)/2	=C8-E8	=C20-E20	=F8-G8
9		4	38	=SUM(C8:C11)/4	=(D8+D9)/2	=C9-E9	=D20-E20	=F9-G9
10	3	1	68	=SUM(C9:C12)/4	=(D9+D10)/2	=C10-E10	=A20-E20	=F10-G10
11		2	42	=SUM(C10:C13)/4	=(D10+D11)/2	=C11-E11	=B20-E20	=F11-G11
12		3	36	=SUM(C11:C14)/4	=(D11+D12)/2	=C12-E12	=C20-E20	=F12-G12
13		4	70	=SUM(C12:C15)/4	=(D12+D13)/2	=C13-E13	=D20-E20	=F13-G13
14	4	1	60	=SUM(C13:C16)/4	=(D13+D14)/2	=C14-E14	=A20-E20	=F14-G14
15		2	50	=SUM(C14:C17)/4	=(D14+D15)/2	=C15-E15	=B20-E20	=F15-G15
16		3	36					
17		4	46					
18								
19	1st mean	2nd mean	3rd mean	4th mean	Adjustment			
20	=(F6+F10+F14)/3	=(F7+F11+F15)/3	=(F4+F8+F12)/3	=(F5+F9+F13)/3	=SUM(A20:D20)/4			

Figure 3.2.13

Columns A and B of the sheet contain text to help the user understand what the sheet achieves. This text also indicates how information should be entered into column C of the sheet. The 16 quarterly figures for the four years are entered into cells C2–C17. The first four-point moving average is then calculated by the equation in cell D3:

= SUM(C2:C5)/4

A spreadsheet function, SUM, has been used to add the contents of all the cells in the cell range C2 to C5. This total has then been divided by 4 to give the four-point average. (The function average could have been used instead, but making the four explicit stresses the way in which the calculation is performed.)

Precisely the same calculation is required for the rest of column D. All that changes from cell to cell is the precise range of cells to be selected in column C. These equations do not have to be entered individually because they can be replicated from cell D3. In Microsoft Excel this is done using **Edit** with **Copy** and **Paste**. The equation entered into D3 is copied across the range D4 to D15.

Replication using **Copy** and **Paste** can also be used to calculate the centred trend figures required for column E. First the appropriate equation is placed in cell E4:

= (D3 + D4)/2

Copy and **Paste** is then used to replicate this equation across the range E5 to E15. After this the values for deviation in column F are obtained by first placing the equation:

= C4 – E4

into F4 and then replicating over the range F5 to F15.

Entering equations to calculate the mean deviation takes slightly longer. In A20 the equation:

= (F6 + F10 + F14)/3

calculates the mean deviation for the first quarter. Similar equations are entered into B20, C20 and D20 for the mean deviations for the second, third and fourth quarters. Care has to be taken here because the available data for the calculations is affected by 'end effects' at either end of the

Microsoft Excel - Time series

	A	B	C	D	E	F	G	H
1	Year	Quarter	Quarterly figures	Four-point	Centred	Deviation	Seasonal	Random
2	1	1	28.00					
3		2	34.00	32.00				
4		3	36.00	30.00	31.00	5.00	-0.67	5.67
5		4	30.00	28.00	29.00	1.00	2.00	-1.00
6	2	1	20.00	32.00	30.00	-10.00	4.67	-14.67
7		2	26.00	34.00	33.00	-7.00	-6.00	-1.00
8		3	52.00	46.00	40.00	12.00	-0.67	12.67
9		4	38.00	50.00	48.00	-10.00	2.00	-12.00
10	3	1	68.00	46.00	48.00	20.00	4.67	15.33
11		2	42.00	54.00	50.00	-8.00	-6.00	-2.00
12		3	36.00	52.00	53.00	-17.00	-0.67	-16.33
13		4	70.00	54.00	53.00	17.00	2.00	15.00
14	4	1	60.00	54.00	54.00	6.00	4.67	1.33
15		2	50.00	48.00	51.00	-1.00	-6	5.00
16		3	36.00					
17		4	46.00					
18								
19	1st mean	2nd mean	3rd mean	4th mean	Adjustment			
20	5.33	-5.33	0	2.67	0.67			

Sheet1 / Sheet2 / Sheet3

Ready

Figure 3.2.14

list of quarterly figures. Once all four equations for the mean deviation have been entered, however, a single equation in E20:

= SUM(A20:D20)/4

calculates the adjustments required to allow the seasonal deviations to be placed in column G.

Finally replication can be used again to calculate the random deviations for column H. Only the first equation:

= F4 – G4

has to be entered separately into H4. After this the equation can be replicated over the range H5 to H15.

The values produced by this spreadsheet model can be compared with the original table (Figure 3.2.14).

3.3 Programming methodology

Computers lack any human understanding of the world and so have to be given precise instructions in order to be able to achieve anything. No instruction can be omitted. No assumption can be made about the computer's ability to resolve ambiguity. These instructions have to be given in the form of a *program* written in a specific *computer language* consisting of a finite set of words which the computer can 'understand' and which can be used to construct a sequence of operations for the computer to perform.

However, more fundamental than any computer program is the set of underlying rules which describe the stages that have to be performed in order to obtain a solution to a given problem. This set of rules is called an *algorithm*. An algorithm has to state clearly what has to be done to solve the problem. It should be as concise as possible and unambiguous in its interpretation. Once an algorithm has been devised it is then possible to code it into whatever computer language has been selected. It is in this sense that the algorithm itself is more fundamental than any particular coding of it.

Designing an algorithm which defines a solution can be challenging. It certainly requires a degree of original thought. In contrast, once a suitable algorithm has been created, implementing it in a computer language is relatively straightforward. There is a distinction between understanding the formal rules of a system and being able to apply those rules in a creative fashion.

Key fact

Perhaps an analogy can be made with music. Many people become proficient at sight reading, playing an instrument or perhaps even orchestrating parts from a short score. Far fewer, though, become composers of original music. In a similar way producing a working computer program from a given algorithm is a moderately mechanical process.

Pseudocode

One way of stating an algorithm formally is to write down each step as a numbered statement in ordinary language. The statements are deliberately kept both simple and precise, and care is taken to make sure that no misinterpretation is possible. Examples of algorithms written as *pseudocode* are given below.

Some authorities recommend using a particular computer language, like Pascal, to show the structure of an algorithm. This has obvious advantages, but risks obscuring the fact that an algorithm is a more fundamental concept than any particular implementation of it in a computer language.

Algorithms and flowcharts

Another way of indicating an algorithm is to show it pictorially as a flowchart. This consists of boxes containing instructions and linked with arrows to show the order in which these operations should be carried out. Different shapes of box are used to represent different types of operation:

Start and stop – rectangle with rounded ends
Input and output – parallelogram
Operation – rectangle
Decision – rhombus (diamond)
Continuation – circle

The example below shows a simple algorithm as both pseudocode and a flowchart.

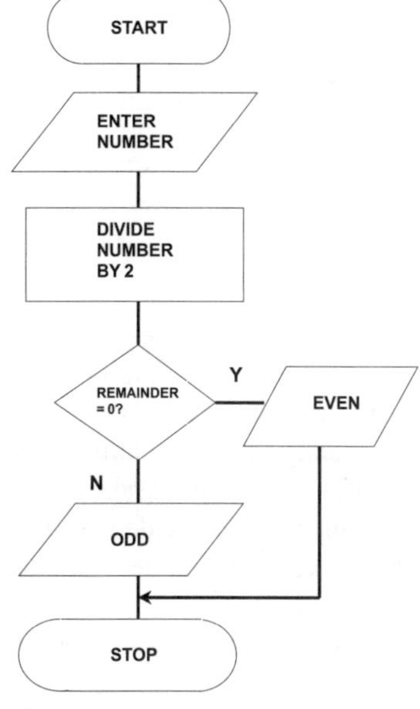

Figure 3.3.1

An algorithm for parity

The word parity is sometimes used to refer to whether a number is odd or even. An algorithm to determine the parity of a number can be used as a simple example of showing how either pseudocode or a flowchart can be used to make the systematic steps used by an algorithm clear.

The algorithm is extremely straightforward. Any even number gives a remainder of zero when it is divided by 2. An odd number gives a remainder of 1. This can be stated formally in pseudocode as:

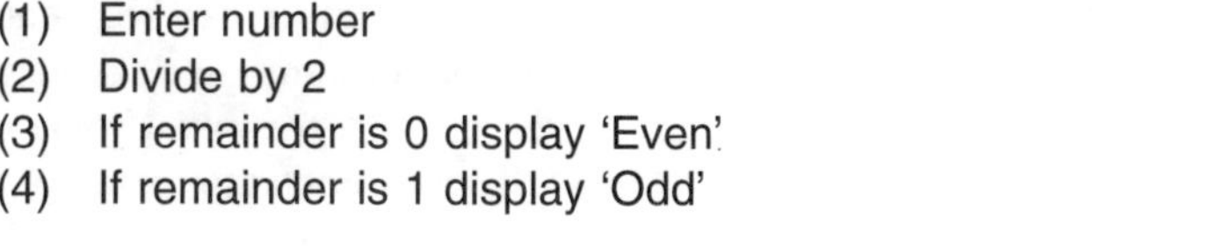

(1) Enter number
(2) Divide by 2
(3) If remainder is 0 display 'Even'
(4) If remainder is 1 display 'Odd'

Algorithms and structure diagrams

A *structure diagram* is a pictorial way of representing an algorithm. It is sometimes easier to follow the logical order in which the individual instructions of an algorithm are performed if they are shown in diagrammatic form. In a later section the programming concepts of sequence, selection and iteration will be considered in depth. Here it is possible to consider them more briefly in the context of how they are shown in a particular type of structure diagram, the *Nassi–Schneidermann diagram.*

If a series of instructions in an algorithm, or *statements* in a program, are performed in a simple sequence, one always following the same one as on a previous implementation of the algorithm, then the algorithm can be shown as a diagram as in Figure 3.3.2.

On the other hand there will be frequent situations in which either of two alternative instructions, or program statements, might follow after a decision has been made. This decision making is shown by a condition in the algorithm which will test as either true or false. Depending upon the result of the test either one statement or the other will follow. The way in which this is shown in a Nassi–Schneidermann is as in Figure 3.3.3.

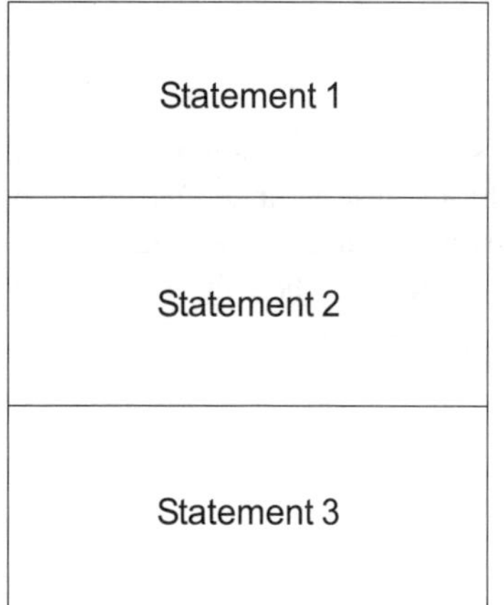

Figure 3.3.2

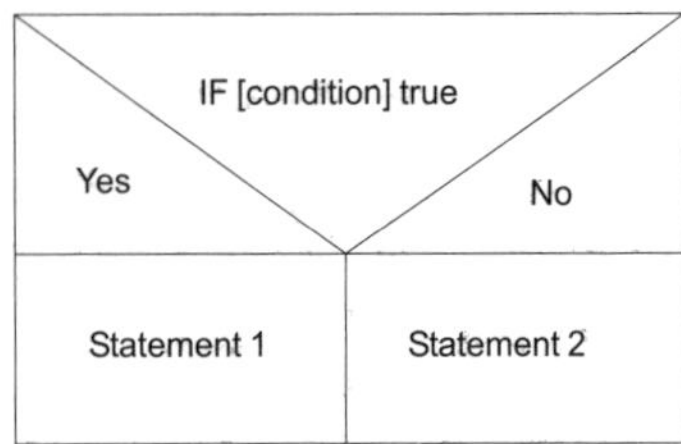

Figure 3.3.3

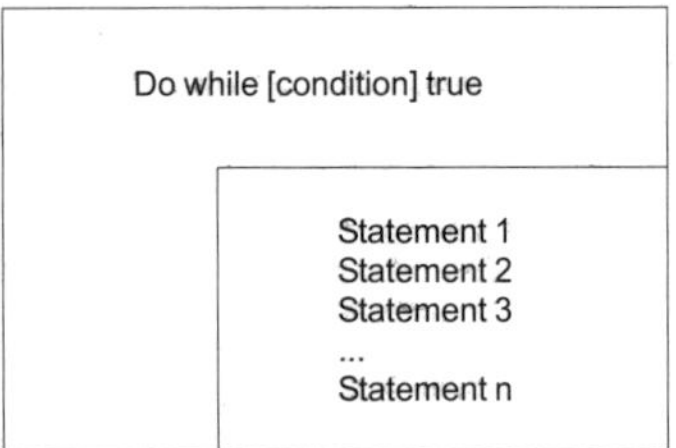

Figure 3.3.4

Note that this is the equivalent of the diamond-shaped decision box of a flowchart.

A third possibility is that a series of instructions in the algorithm will have to be repeated a number of times. The precise number can be determined by checking another condition. The instructions are repeated provided that the condition continues to test as true. Figure 3.3.4 shows how this situation can be depicted.

An algorithm for a mean

As a further example of how to design an algorithm we shall investigate how to find the *mean* of a series of numbers. The mean is the everyday sense of average. The numbers are added together and then the total divided by the total number of terms in the series. So the mean of the series:

3, 6, 8, 4, 9, 7, 2, 3, 3

is given by:

$$(3 + 6 + 8 + 4 + 9 + 7 + 2 + 3 + 3)/9 = 5$$

It is obvious how we do this, but the method has to be specified formally in a way which can be coded into a computer program without any ambiguity. The rules we specify have to make it very clear that the running total of the numbers entered is constantly updated and that the total number of terms of the series entered is also recorded. Then, when the last number has been entered the running total is divided by the number of terms. We also have to emphasize less obvious details, like the fact that the initial value of the total is zero.

If we use total to represent the running total and counter to represent the number of terms, we could devise an algorithm like:

(1) Initialize total = 0
(2) Initialize counter = 0
(3) Enter number
(4) Increment total by number
(5) Increment counter by 1
(6) If not last number, repeat from 3
(7) Divide total by counter
(8) Display result

This appears quite adequate, until it is noted that the algorithm is not sufficiently clear about what is meant by the last number. One solution would be to have a specific *sentinel value* which is not meant to be included in the calculation. Instead it indicates when the end of the series has been reached. If 999 is taken as this sentinel value, the algorithm could become:

(1) Initialize total = 0
(2) Initialize counter = 0
(3) Enter number
(4) Increment total by number
(5) Increment counter by 1

(6) If number is not 999, repeat from 3
(7) Subtract 999 from total
(8) Subtract 1 from counter
(9) Divide total by counter
(10) Display result

The way in which this algorithm works is not very different from the method a person would use to calculate a mean. The only slightly non-human detail is the rather pedantic way in which the end of the series has been detected by the use of 999. A person would just know when the last number had been reached.

Frequently, however, the algorithm designed for a computer solution will be quite unlike the way a person would tackle the same problem.

Before considering how algorithms like this can be coded as a computer program it is necessary to investigate how computer programs are organized and to look at a specific language which is able to create the code required.

High-level and low-level computer languages

This is now a good stage to think carefully about the way in which computers carry out the instructions they are given.

At the most fundamental level all operations carried out by the central processing unit involve very simple manipulation of binary numbers. Long sequences of 1s and 0s are copied from one memory location to another, or added together according to the rules of binary arithmetic, or altered in some other way, perhaps by shifting all the digits in a number one place to the left or right.

All of this is very far from the sophisticated operations that a computer is seen to perform at the everyday level. It is only because a computer can perform a vast number of simple operations per second that complexity can arise from the very simple.

Nevertheless computers ultimately have to be programmed at the binary level. In the early days of computing this was the only way in which they could be programmed. Skilled mathematicians were required to write out the long lists of *machine code* instructions needed to carry out even the very simplest of tasks. Not too long passed before simple letter codes, called mnemonics or assembly instructions, were used to represent the machine code. When the program was due to be executed the assembly code would be translated into the 1s and 0s required by the software by a special program called an *assembler* which translated the programmer's source code into the object code, or executable code that the hardware needed.

Assembly language programming was easier than machine code because the mnemonics were easier to remember. However, the translation into machine code was still on a one-to-one basis. Each machine code operation performed by the computer still had to be written down as one assembly language instruction.

High-level languages were a further development. A *low-level language*, like machine code and assembly language, is close to the level of the hardware. Program instructions are designed with the architecture of a specific CPU/processor in mind. In contrast a *high-level language* is

Key fact

Many different languages exist. The choice of a particular language will depend upon a number of factors. Ideally the nature of the problem itself should influence the choice made. In practice the availability of computing, and human resources will make a significant contribution to the decision. Even fashion has a role, as different languages gain popularity only to be replaced later by some preferred descendant which retains its better features whilst adding refinements.

oriented more towards the sort of problem the programmer is going to meet in the real world and is designed to make solving that problem as easy as possible. A high-level language is not concerned about the actual computer platform it will use. The matching of the language to the CPU is achieved by a *compiler* which converts each statement of the high-level language into the large number of machine code instructions required to realize that particular statement using the specific hardware available. There will therefore be a separate compiler for each type of computer upon which the high-level code will be executed. With a high-level language the programmer does not need to think about the platform, instead they can concentrate upon the problem.

Some high-level languages

It is useful to be aware of some of the many high level languages which have been developed.

Ada – this language is named after Augusta Ada Byron, Countess of Lovelace, who was a friend of Charles Babbage and therefore present at the very birth of computing. Although Babbage's Analytical Engine was never completed (until the recent realization by Doron Swade) Lady Lovelace is regarded as the first computer programmer. The development of the language Ada was commissioned by the United States military and involved the effort of more than a thousand computer scientists between 1975 and 1983. Emphasis was upon a reliable language in which automatic checking of programming errors was paramount. Strong data typing ensured that variables matched the data being assigned. For example, a value of 2.3 could not be given to a variable which was intended only to hold integers. Ada has become an accepted language for real-time embedded systems, used for major projects like the Channel Tunnel.

Algol – the name Algol is derived from 'ALGOrithmic Language', and only incidentally the same as the star in Perseus. It was developed between 1958 and 1968 in an attempt to produce uniformity among the increasing number of machine-specific high-level languages which were being devised by different manufacturers. The hope was that it could become a European standard. Although other languages have since eclipsed it, Algol has had a significant impact on the history of computing by placing emphasis upon the need for structured programming and also through the other computer languages which have evolved from it, like Pascal, Modula-2 and Ada.

Basic (Beginner's All-purpose Symbolic Instruction Code) was devised in 1964 at Dartmouth College by John Kemeny and Thomas Kurtz, after eight years of research into languages suitable for young students with little experience of computers, and then became widespread in the late 1970s/early 1980s with the sudden demand for home microcomputers. Early dialects of Basic were criticized for permitting poorly designed code, but this ceased to be a plausible objection with later versions. Basic remains an important educational language

C is a language which combines features of both high- and low-level languages and has been generally regarded as the language for 'real' programmers. It has been developed further into C++ and Java.

C++ is an object-oriented language derived from C.

COBOL, or COmmon Business Oriented Language, was developed in 1959/60 as a high-level language for business applications. Until then assembly language had been used. COBOL was given a number of features to suit the business world including fixed point arithmetic for accuracy, data structures called tables which can be embedded within one another to reflect the way business data occurs, more flexible file handling than was available at the time in Fortran, and arithmetical operations restricted to those needed in business.

FORTRAN (FORmula TRANslation) was the first successful high-level language, initially designed in 1954 and defeating a rival language, MATH-MATIC, in achieving popularity. It rapidly became the accepted language for science and engineering. Basic is a descendent.

Java began at Sun Microsystems during the design of a personal digital assistant intended to control domestic electronics. The device was abandoned but its language survived, achieving its current importance through its use in network programming. It *is* named after the coffee. Its principal author, James Gosling, has described Java as 'C++ without the knives, guns and clubs', commenting on the latter's difficulties in novice hands.

LISP was developed in the mid-1950s as a list processing language for artificial intelligence research and became an important tool in that discipline.

Pascal is principally an educational language intended to foster good programming practice for students who will then progress to other languages. It is named after the French mathematician, philosopher and theologian, Blaise Pascal, who also invented a mechanical calculator.

Prolog is also a computer language used in artificial intelligence and expert systems.

Variables and storage

When a computer program is written to solve a problem it is inevitable that data will need to be manipulated in some way. This might be as simple as just doubling a number that is typed in by the user, but even so it will be necessary for this number to be held in the computer's memory while the doubling takes place. A computer is like a person who cannot do mental arithmetic but is obliged instead to write everything down on paper. The computer's 'paper' is the very many memory locations it has. A programmer working at assembly level will actually have to know what the addresses of these memory locations are. This, fortunately, is not something that the high-level programmer needs to consider. Instead a variable is chosen to represent the data that will be manipulated. After that the programmer can use the name of the variable, or *identifier*, whenever the data needs to be referred to. Generally the variable is treated like an algebraic variable in mathematics.

For example, continuing the example started above, if the variable Number has been used to represent the number entered by the user and which has to be doubled, then the expression Number × 2 will be the answer required.

Data types

The data which a computer is able to operate with can be divided into a number of different *data types*. The way in which these data types are stored will involve different amounts of computer memory. As explained above, memory allocation tends to be the sort of problem that a programmer working with a low-level language needs to worry about. Programmers at high level usually just have to be aware of the appropriate data type to use with a particular variable and to declare the variable as being of this type. The compiler will take care of everything else.

Different data types are:

- Integer
- Real
- Char (character)
- String
- Boolean

Integer data is just the same as the ordinary whole numbers people use when they are counting and are not concerned about decimal places. Integer data can be zero and negative, but the range available will be restricted because computers are limited to the fixed number of binary digits that they are able to store in a particular memory location. Typically the range for integers is –32 767 to 32 767. However, this is extended in computer languages which offer a *long integer* data type.

The *real* data type permits numbers with a fractional decimal part to be represented and so can be used in calculations which do not just involve whole numbers.

Char data is individual letters, digits and other specific symbols. Char data is closely associated with ASCII code (American Standard Code for Information Interchange) which identifies particular alphanumeric characters with a numerical code. Thus capital A is represented by the decimal (base 10) number 65 or the 7-bit binary number 100 0001, and capital Z is 90, or 101 1010.

The *string* data type is related to the character type, but a sequence of characters can be stored which means that a string variable is able to represent words and text.

Boolean data can have only two values, true or false. The practical use of Boolean variables will be demonstrated in a subsequent programming example.

When a program is being designed, and again at the documentation stage, a *data table* is a useful aid to clarity. This will have three columns which specify for each variable:

- the identifier (variable name), e.g. 'Fuel';
- the role of the variable in the program, e.g. 'Number of litres in petrol tank';
- the data type used for the variable, e.g. Real.

Key fact

Syntax will vary from one language to another and the programmer must be careful. In Basic the equals sign can be used for both assignment and for testing equality, but in C a double equals sign must be used for the latter.

Programming syntax

The term *syntax* refers to the rules which a language obeys, in constrast with *semantics*, which refers to its meaning. So the English sentence 'Me Mum ain't born yesterday, yer know' suffers from poor syntax, though its semantics is perfectly clear. Computers are particularly pendantic about their syntax and the instructions in a computer program have to follow precisely the rules specified for that language. Examples abound of what goes wrong when syntax is sinned against, but one of the most spectacular was the explosion of an early European Space Agency Ariane launch vehicle.

Programming errors

Newly coded programs usually come replete with mistakes or *bugs* and a lot of the fun in programming is spotting where they are. Sometimes these mistakes are *syntax errors*, in which the programmer has forgotten the rules. These are normally quite easy to detect, especially if somebody else looks for you. More obscure are *logical errors* in which a syntactically correct piece of code does not work properly because an error has occurred at the algorithm stage. Logical errors are a consequence of rushing into coding an algorithm before testing it properly.

Using Visual Basic

A note is required at this point about the practical programming examples given in this chapter. All code shown has been written in Microsoft's Visual Basic on the assumption that the majority of students will have access to a PC on which this language (in one version or another) will have been installed. However, the intention is to illustrate general concepts in programming rather than the specific features of Visual Basic. This means that the event-driven nature of the language is deliberately ignored and instead an extremely minimal, stripped-down approach is adopted. All examples have been written to use a single Command Button, the code window for which is the presumed location of any code entered, an Input Box for all user input and a single Picture Box for output.

A brief explanation of how to establish this simple user interface in Visual Basic 6.0 is given below and should be sufficient for those using other versions of the language as well.

- Assuming that a version of Visual Basic has been installed on the machine you are using, double-click on the appropriate icon.
- At the New Project window select Standard EXE and single-click on Open. The Project1-Form1 window appears.
- Go to the Tool Box and select the Picture Box icon.
- Single-click and drag on Form1 to create a Picture Box object which will be used for display. (This needs to be reasonably large, filling a significant fraction of the form.)

- Return to the Tool Box and select the Command Button icon.
- Single-click and again drag on Form1 to create a Command Button object. This does not need to be large but just big enough to click on when required.
- You may wish to customize the Form and Picture Box to make the screen easier or more attractive to read. Background and foreground colour, together with font style and size, can all be tailored to individual taste via the Properties Window associated with the Form and with the Picture Box. When either of these is selected their Properties Window becomes accessible. Note that for the program examples given in this chapter the name of the Picture Box has been changed, via the Properties Window, to PicDisplay. The Command Button can also be captioned 'GO', or any other name which indicates that this is where to click in order to run the program.

A typical display will be like the one in Figure 3.3.5.

Program examples that you want to test using Visual Basic can be entered as code in the code window associated with the Command

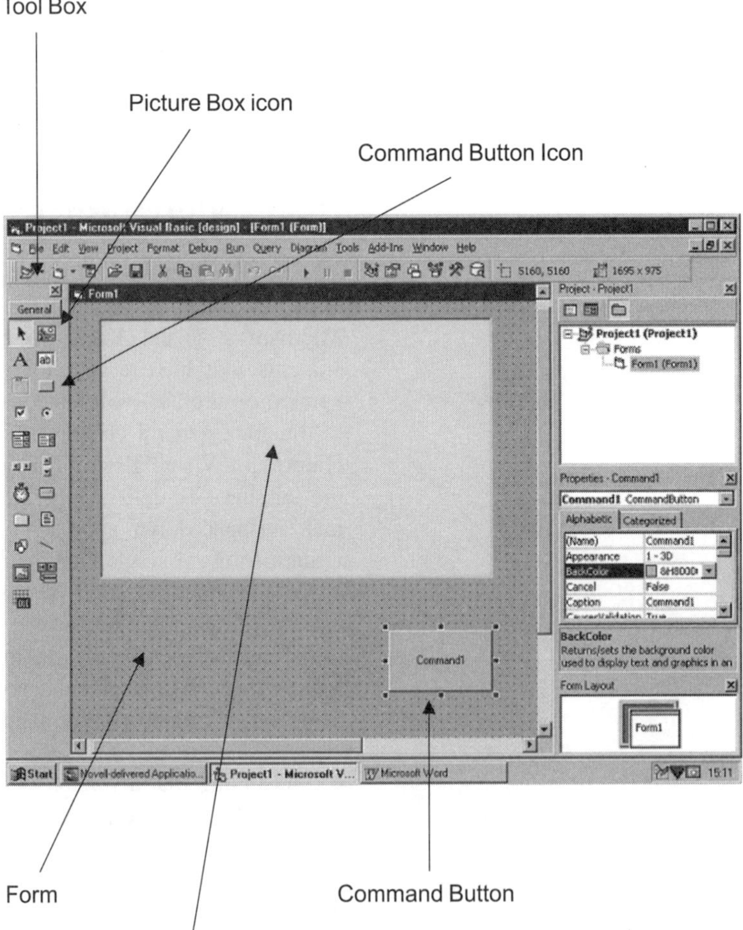

Figure 3.3.5

Button. Double-clicking on the Command Button will show this window. This will appear as:

```
Private Sub Command1_Click()
End Sub
```

Program code you wish to execute is written on separate lines between 'Private Sub Command1_Click()' and 'End Sub'. An initial program you may wish to try simply requests that the user enters some text and then confirms what has been typed. This program shows how input and output can be achieved:

```
Option Explicit
Private Sub Command1_Click()
Dim Words As String
Words = InputBox("Type a few words", , , 6500, 5500)
PicDisplay.Print "You typed"
PicDisplay.Print Words
End Sub
```

Program documentation

The program uses a *variable* called Words to hold the text that the user will enter. This has to be *declared* at the beginning of the program.

```
Dim Words As String
```

Declaring a variable allows memory to be reserved for it. It also obliges the programmer to plan in advance how the program will be coded in terms of different variables rather than producing an ad hoc creation lacking logical coherence.

The text entered by the user is *assigned* to the variable Words by using the InputBox function.

```
Words = InputBox ("Type a few words", , , 6500, 5500)
```

This is an easy method of input, though lacking the finesse of most Visual Basic code. Screen coordinates can be included, as shown in this example, and will position the Input Box at a suitable location on the display.

The output of the program is just the same text as entered by the user. It is merely redisplayed on the screen. The text appears in the Picture Box on the Form. A *print statement* does this, directing the output specifically to the renamed Picture Box, PicDisplay.

```
PicDisplay.Print "You typed"
PicDisplay.Print Words
```

The program is executed by selecting Run, then Start or alternatively clicking on the Start button. You should click on the Command Button when the Form reappears. This will lead to the program being run, with all output produced appearing in the Picture Box, PicDisplay.

The initial display will be like the one shown in Figure 3.3.6.

Once the text typed by the user has been entered the display becomes as shown in Figure 3.3.7.

Key fact

It is possible in Visual Basic to use variables without declaring them but the use of 'Option Explicit' in this example prevents this from being allowed. Option Explicit will be used in all the examples given in this chapter. It is a sensible precaution against the untidy programming habits which free use of Basic can, unfortunately, encourage. If the Option Explicit statement is included in the general declarations area of the Form (as indicated in the examples) it is not possible to use a variable in a program without first declaring it. This is common, and good, practice in most programming languages, but is something about which Basic is unduly tolerant.

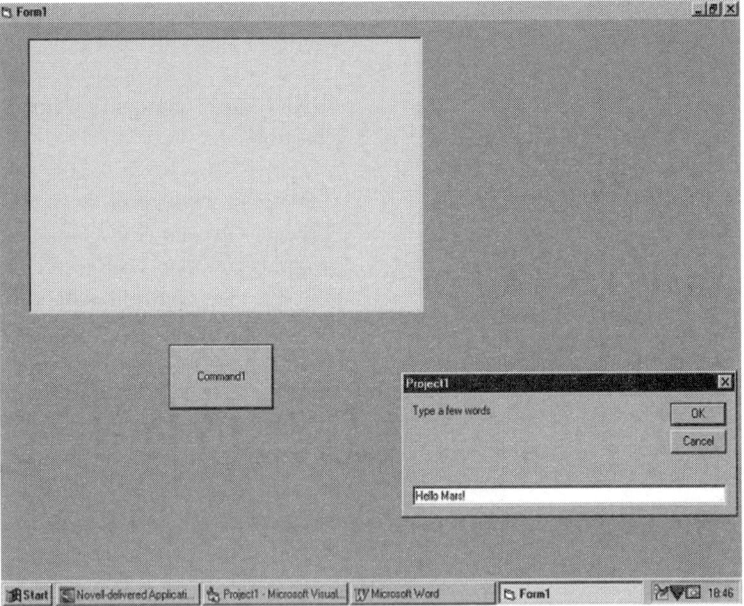

Figure 3.3.6

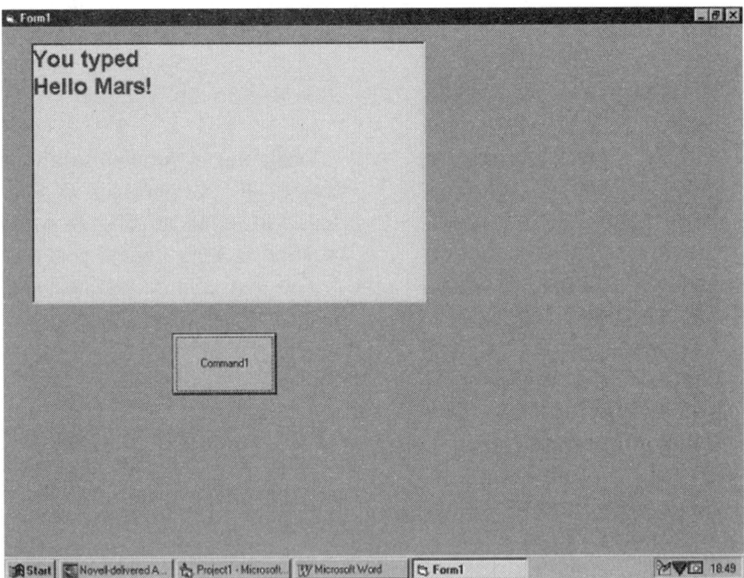

Figure 3.3.7

Programming standards

Programming is not a solitary activity. Inevitably other people will need to examine code that the individual programmer has written. This might be because the programmer is working as part of a team, or because code that has been written will need to be revised at a later date as part of general program maintenance. Even if a section of code were totally personal and never looked at by anybody else there would still be a need for the programmer to follow standard ways of working in order to understand at some point in the future how certain sections of the code actually worked.

It is therefore important to adhere to recognized guidelines for good programming practice. In particular the individual programmer should be aware of the need for comments, indentation and descriptive identifiers in all code produced.

Comments

Not all of the code included in a program will actually appear in the final executable file. Lines known as *comments* are automatically discarded by the compiler because their sole function is to make the code more easily understood by any programmer who reads through it. A comment might indicate that the lines of program code that follow are an input routine, or that a particular loop (see below) within the program is intended to display a list of names on the display.

Comments are sometimes referred to as *internal documentation*, as opposed to the external documentation which accompanies a program and helps to explain how it functions.

Different programming languages have different ways of marking a given line as a comment. In Visual Basic, the language chosen for the examples given here, a single quote, is the accepted method, although the language also supports the earlier REM statement used in traditional dialects of Basic. For example, a comment in Visual Basic might be as follows:

```
Prompt user to enter first name
```

Comments are illustrated in the first of the program examples developed below.

Indentation

Indentation in program code is very much like indentation in ordinary punctuated text. Just as the indentation at the beginning of a paragraph alerts the reader to the fact that a new topic is being introduced, so indentation of program code indicates that some specific control structure is being employed at this stage of the program. Unlike ordinary typed language, however, indentation in programming code follows a rigorous hierarchy of nesting successive levels of structure. For example, a single level of indentation will be used for the code contained within a loop, but if there is an If Then Else condition inside the loop a further indentation will occur here.

Indentation of program code is illustrated practically below.

Automatic indentation of program code is a facility offered in most programming environments.

Descriptive identifiers

Great latitude is allowed in the choice of names for variables used in a program but this freedom should not be exploited. It is essential for overall clarity that variables are given names which indicate their role within a program. For example, if a variable is required which will represent the number of students anticipated on a school educational

> **Key fact**
>
> In the early days of computing, when memory was not as freely available as it is for the contemporary programmer, there was an incentive for making variable names as short as possible. Hence if older books are consulted programming examples will be discovered in which terse, gnomic variable names abound. Thus the single letter variable names I, J and K, inherited from FORTRAN, frequently appear as loop control variables. Such memory-conserving discipline was unavoidable at the time but should not be emulated now.

visit an appropriate variable name could be intStudentNumber rather than Num, or the single letter N. Choosing the first variable name informs, even upon causal inspection, that the program involves student numbers and that an integer variable is being used to represent this number. The meaningful variable name has made this possible.

Essentially if a policy of descriptive identifiers is adopted other people can read and understand far more readily any code that they examine.

Appropriate identifier names should also be chosen when the programmer includes separate procedures in a program.

Control structures

There are a number of standard control structures which are used in programming. These are a logical concept of some generality and can be implemented in slightly different ways according to the particular programming language employed for a specific project. However, the overall principles remain the same and are not difficult to implement in a given situation.

These control structures are:

- Sequence
- Selection
- Iteration
- Subprogram
- Recursion

Iteration is frequently called *looping*. Subprogram also appears under the guise of *subroutine, procedure* and *subprocedure*. Subprogram and recursion do not appear explicitly in the specification for the Core Unit 3 of the Higher Nationals, although it is convenient in this chapter to make some reference to the use of subprocedures in Visual Basic.

Sequence

We first examine the use of sequence as a control structure in a program. Here a simple series of instructions will follow one after another, being executed in the order in which the programmer has written them in the code.

```
Option Explicit
Private Sub Command1_Click()
'Demonstration of sequence

'Clear display
PicDisplay.Cls

'Introduce topic
PicDisplay.Print "Here are some towns and"
PicDisplay.Print "cities along the south coast:"

'Leave a clear line
PicDisplay.Print
```

```
'Show town and city names
PicDisplay.Print "Dover"
PicDisplay.Print "Brighton"
PicDisplay.Print "Chichester"
PicDisplay.Print "Portsmouth"
PicDisplay.Print "Fareham"
PicDisplay.Print "Plymouth"
End Sub
```

Program documentation

The program begins by clearing the display area.

```
Option Explicit
Private Sub Command1_Click()
'Demonstration of sequence

'Clear display
PicDisplay.Cls
```

An introductory text message is shown.

```
'Introduce topic
PicDisplay.Print "Here are some towns and"
PicDisplay.Print "cities along the south coast:"
```

After a blank line the names of several south coast towns and cities are shown.

```
'Leave a clear line
PicDisplay.Print
'Show town and city names
PicDisplay.Print "Dover"
PicDisplay.Print "Brighton"
```

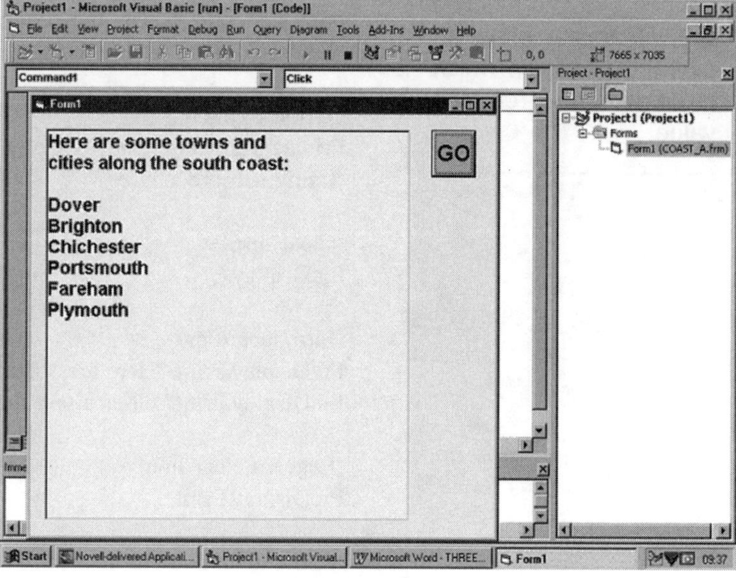

Figure 3.3.8

```
PicDisplay.Print "Chichester"
PicDisplay.Print "Portsmouth"
PicDisplay.Print "Fareham"
PicDisplay.Print "Plymouth"
End Sub
```

Running this program will produce a screen display as shown in Figure 3.3.8.

In this very simple program a direct sequence of instructions has been carried out. This can now be contrasted with the way that a similar program can use subprograms to jump out of the main sequence of execution and show more information about the places introduced.

Subprograms

> **Key fact**
>
> Subprograms take two general forms, *procedures* and *functions*. A procedure accomplishes some action required by the main program calling it, but does not necessarily have to calculate a value to be returned to the program. This means that a *call* to a procedure can just be a simple statement. In contrast a function is designed to return some relevant calculated value to the program and as a consequence of this a function call will appear within an overall expression which requires the returned value.

A simple sequence of program code can be compared with a situation in which program execution is automatically diverted to a distinct and separate section of code. This arises when a certain block of code is best regarded as an autonomous entity which has a specific role within the overall program. In particular the execution of this block of code may need to occur more than once. It would be wasteful and inelegant to duplicate the actual lines of code within the program each time the action produced by them had to be repeated. In a situation like this it is economical to place the code involved in a separate *subprogram* which is used by the main program whenever necessary.

The use of subprograms is also an inherent aspect of top-down design. When an overall problem has to be resolved into a series of distinct component tasks these can be realized as subprograms. In addition the presence of subprograms within a coded listing makes it far easier for the code to be understood by others and their distinct identity helps the discipline of internal documentation.

The elementary programming example given above can now be extended to show the way that subprocedures are coded in Visual Basic. Although the subprocedures in this new example are only called once, and therefore do not illustrate the particular advantage of breaking program code down into autonomous units, later examples in this chapter do demonstrate repeated calls to subprocedures.

```
Option Explicit
Private Sub Command1_Click()
'Using sub procedures

'Clear display
PicDisplay.Cls

'Introduce topic
PicDisplay.Print "Here are some towns and"
PicDisplay.Print "cities along the south coast:"

'Leave a clear line
PicDisplay.Print

'Show town and city names
'and additional information
```

```
PicDisplay.Print "Dover"
Dover
PicDisplay.Print "Brighton"
Brighton
PicDisplay.Print "Chichester"
Chichester
PicDisplay.Print "Portsmouth"
Portsmouth
PicDisplay.Print "Fareham"
Fareham
PicDisplay.Print "Plymouth"
Plymouth
End Sub

Sub Dover()
PicDisplay.Print "Matthew Arnold wrote a famous poem about"
PicDisplay.Print "the beach while on honeymoon here."
End Sub

Sub Brighton()
PicDisplay.Print "Graham Greene was inspired by the locale"
PicDisplay.Print "and wrote Brighton Rock."
End Sub
Sub Chichester()
PicDisplay.Print "Famed for its Cathedral and Festival Theatre"
End Sub

Sub Portsmouth()
PicDisplay.Print "The Victory, Mary Rose and Warrior are"
PicDisplay.Print "all on view in the Maritime Museum."
End Sub

Sub Fareham()
PicDisplay.Print "Located on the upper reaches of"
PicDisplay.Print "Portsmouth Harbour."
End Sub

Sub Plymouth()
PicDisplay.Print "Historical location for Sir Francis Drake's"
PicDisplay.Print "game of bowls."
End Sub
```

Program documentation

The program shares code with the previous example but displays more information about the towns and cities by the inclusion of a separate subprocedure for each. This can be illustrated by the information displayed for the first city, Dover. As before the name of the city is displayed on the Picture Box by a print statement but after this a subprocedure is called by including its name as a separate statement.

```
PicDisplay.Print "Dover"
Dover
```

The subprocedure is written as a distinct set of statements outside the code which calls it. These statements are placed between lines defining the beginning of the subprocedure, Sub Dover(), and its end, End Sub.

```
Sub Dover()
PicDisplay.Print "Matthew Arnold wrote a famous poem about"
PicDisplay.Print "the beach while on honeymoon here."
End Sub
```

Similar subprocedures are written for the other towns and cities.

If sequence and subprogram were the only control structures that were available to the programmer, programming would be a fairly unrewarding occupation as the outcome of any program code would be quite obvious from the very beginning. It is only because decisions can be made within the operation of a program, allowing branching to separate sections of code, that programs are capable of the vast range of applications with which everybody is now familiar. We will now go on to consider a control structure selection which permits these decisions to be made.

Selection

Selection is made possible in programs by the inclusion of *conditions* in the program code. You will already be familiar with the concept of conditions from the material earlier in this section which dealt with their use in spreadsheets. As you will anticipate, conditions are also an essential part of general programming. Programming languages contain commands which allow the programmer to specify a 'change in direction'. Without these it would not be possible to produce programs which could adjust their processing and eventual output according to the intermediate values created in earlier stages of processing. Programming would not be versatile.

The If Then statement

One way in which a condition can be written in a program is by the use of an *if then statement*. This creates a *condition* and an *action* which will follow if the condition is true. This is the programming equivalent of the everyday 'If the review in the *Sunday Times* is okay then I will book a ticket at the Royal Festival Hall.' It is just common sense. The use of an if then statement in Basic is shown in this short example.

```
Option Explicit
Private Sub Command1_Click()
'Demonstrating an if then statement

Dim strPerson as String

PicDisplay.Cls

'Request user's name
strPerson = InputBox("Who are you", , , 6500, 5500)

'Only say hello to Judith
If strPerson = "Judith" Then PicDisplay.Print "Hello"
End Sub
```

Program documentation

The operation of this brief example should be fairly obvious. A variable, strPerson, is declared as type String, which means that a string of characters can be assigned to it. Then the InputBox function prompts the user to enter their name, and it is assigned to strPerson.

After this the name which has been entered can be compared with the text string “Judith”. Here an if then statement is employed. The condition which is being tested is the equivalence of the input text with the string “Judith”. Only if the two are the same will the message ‘Hello’ be displayed. When this example is run the initial display will be like that in Figure 3.3.9.

Provided the correct name is typed the new display will be like that in Figure 3.3.10.

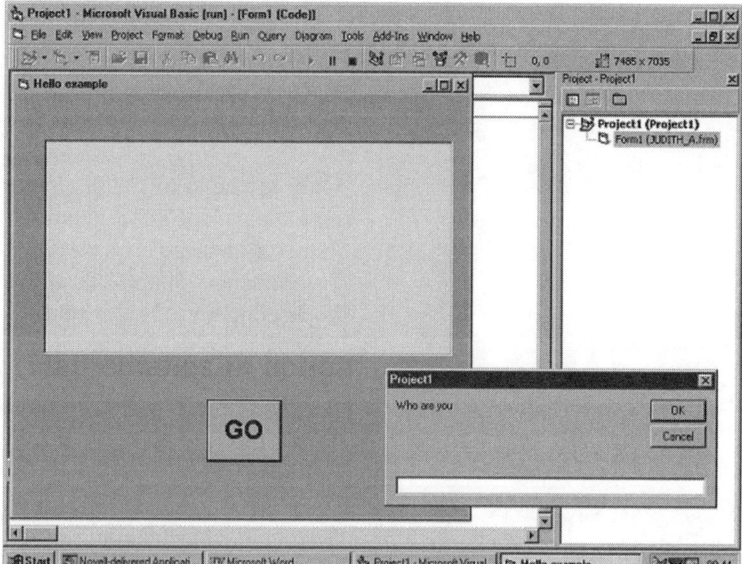

Figure 3.3.9

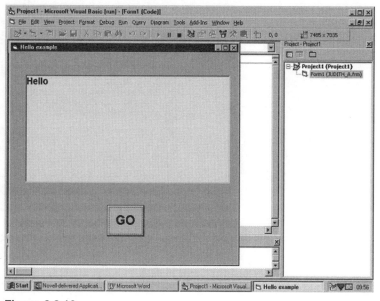

Figure 3.3.10

Using End If

It may be necessary for several lines of code to follow as the action to be implemented if the condition is true. This will require the use of the *End If statement* to indicate where the code forming the action should end. A modification to the example above will make this clear. (In this new example it is assumed that the person who runs the program is the Judith who, in the opera by Bela Bartok, meets an unfortunate fate as a consequence of her excessive curiosity.)

```
Option Explicit
Private Sub Command1_Click()
'Demonstrating an if then statement

Dim strPerson As String

PicDisplay.Cls
'Request user's name
strPerson = InputBox("Who are you", , , 6500, 5500)

'Only say hello to Judith
'and assume she's the Judith of
'"Duke Bluebeard's Castle"
If strPerson = "Judith" Then
PicDisplay.Print "Hello Judith."
PicDisplay.Print "Bluebeard says you're welcome to"
PicDisplay.Print "to visit the castle provided that"
PicDisplay.Print "you keep the doors shut..."
End If
End Sub
```

Program documentation

In the example several lines of text are displayed if the user enters the name 'Judith'. This requires the use of the End If statement to indicate

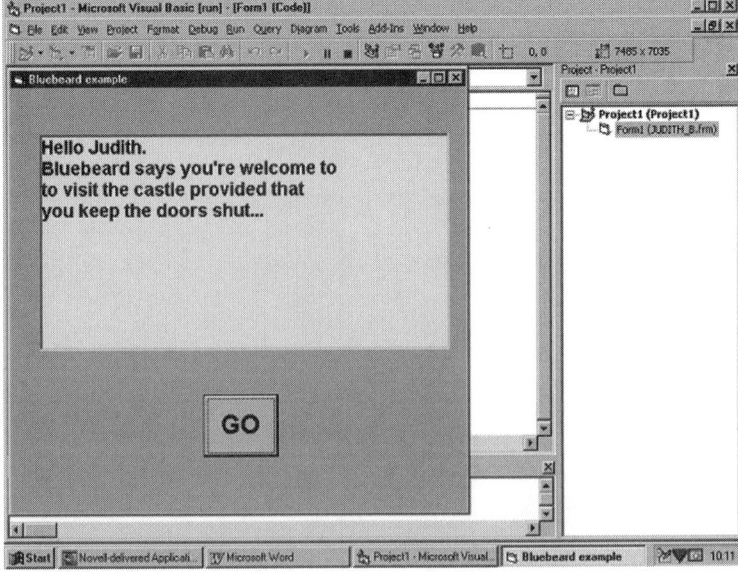

Figure 3.3.11

where the action following the condition should end. It is another illustration of the vital requirement within programming that ambiguity should be avoided at all times. Although in a simple condition like this it is obvious where the action ends, it is embarrassingly easy to misidentify the correct location for an End If in more complex code. Annoying bugs in program code can be easily created in this way.

If this program is run and the name Judith entered the display will become as shown in Figure 3.3.11.

The Else statement

Frequently two alternative actions will be the natural consequence of a condition being tested. This is the way people tend to behave in everyday life, a typical situation being the environmentally-minded 'If it is not raining very heavily I will walk to work, otherwise I will drive.' Two separate actions can be included after a programming condition by the use of the Else statement. This follows the Then in an If Then condition to create a second action which will take place if the condition tests as false.

```
Option Explicit
Private Sub Command1_Click()
'Demonstrating the use of Else

Dim intNumber As Integer
PicDisplay.Cls

'Request number from the user
intNumber = Val(InputBox("Enter a whole number", , , 6500, 5500))

'Check size of number
If intNumber < 5 Then
PicDisplay.Print "Your number was less than 5"
Else
PicDisplay.Print "Your number was more than 4"
End If

End Sub
```

Program documentation

In this example the InputBox function has been used to assign the number entered by the user to the variable intNumber. The function Val converts a string data type of the input to a properly numerical value. This value is then used in the extended If Then Else condition. (Val is not required in later versions of Visual Basic but has been employed here for those using earlier issues.)

```
If intNumber < 5 Then
PicDisplay.Print "Your number was less than 5"
Else
PicDisplay.Print "Your number was more than 4"
End If
```

Here two alternative actions, 'Your number was less than 5' and 'Your number was more than 4', will be executed according to the size of the number entered.

Using flag values

A flag is a variable which can have values of either True or False, or numerically 1 or 0. Flags can be used to distinguish between two different states in the course of program execution and are they are especially important in assembly programming. Here they monitor the progress of operations in the central processing unit and are used to determine the sequence in which these occur. They are also a useful programming technique for high-level languages, where monitoring the value of a particular flag can be used to decide when some section of code, perhaps within an If Then Else conditional structure or in a subprogram, should be executed.

```
Option Explicit
Private Sub Command1_Click()

'Illustration of using a flag
Dim strAnswer As String
Dim intFlag1 As Integer
Dim intFlag2 As Integer
PicDisplay.Cls

'Determine user's taste
strAnswer = InputBox("Do you like poetry", , , 6500, 5500)
If strAnswer = "Yes" Then
intFlag1 = 1
Else
intFlag1 = 0
End If

strAnswer = InputBox("Do you like modern poetry", , , 6500, 5500)
If strAnswer = "Yes" Then
intFlag2 = 1
Else
intFlag2 = 0
End If

'Only display poem if user likes poetry
'but not modern poetry
If intFlag1 = 1 And intFlag2 = 0 Then Poem

End Sub

Sub Poem()
PicDisplay.Print "Conceit begotten by the eyes"
PicDisplay.Print "Is quickly born and quickly dies;"
PicDisplay.Print "For while it seeks our hearts to have,"
PicDisplay.Print "Meanwhile, there reason makes his grave;"
PicDisplay.Print "For many things the eyes approve,"
PicDisplay.Print "Which yet the heart doth seldom love"
End Sub
```

Program documentation

The program requires three variables. The first to be declared is strAnswer, which will be used for the user's response to two questions. The other two variables, intFlag1 and intFlag2, are flags which will be assigned values of 1 or 0 for each of the questions in turn. A value of 1 will indicate that the user has answered Yes to the question and 0 will mean that they have answered No.

```
Option Explicit
Private Sub Command1_Click()
```

```
'Illustration of using a flag

Dim strAnswer As String
Dim intFlag1 As Integer
Dim intFlag2 As Integer
PicDisplay.Cls
```

Answers are obtained by the use of the InputBox function. An If Then Else conditional structure will make the first flag, intFlag1, either 1 or 0 according to the reply given.

```
'Determine user's taste
strAnswer = InputBox("Do you like poetry", , , 6500, 5500)
If strAnswer = "Yes" Then
intFlag1 = 1
Else
intFlag1 = 0
End If
```

A value of 1 or 0 is also assigned to the second flag, intFlag2, in the same way.

```
strAnswer = InputBox("Do you like modern poetry", , , 6500, 5500)
If strAnswer = "Yes" Then
intFlag2 = 1
Else
intFlag2 = 0
End If
```

The value of these two flags can now be used to print out a short extract from Sir Walter Raleigh. This will only happen if the value of intFlag1 is 1, which shows that the user likes poetry, and at the same time intFlag2 is 0, which indicates no liking for modern verse.

```
'Only display poem if user likes poetry
'but not modern poetry
If intFlag1 = 1 And intFlag2 = 0 Then Poem

End Sub
```

The actual poetry display is created by a call to a separate subprocedure.

```
Sub Poem()
PicDisplay.Print "Conceit begotten by the eyes"
PicDisplay.Print "Is quickly born and quickly dies;"
PicDisplay.Print "For while it seeks our hearts to have,"
PicDisplay.Print "Meanwhile, there reason makes his grave;"
PicDisplay.Print "For many things the eyes approve,"
PicDisplay.Print "Which yet the heart doth seldom love"
End Sub
```

Only if the user likes poetry, but not contemporary poets, will this display in Figure 3.3.12 be shown.

Using Boolean conditions

Programming structure can often be simplified by using *Boolean conditions* in which the value of an entire expression is evaluated as being either True or False. In many programming languages True is

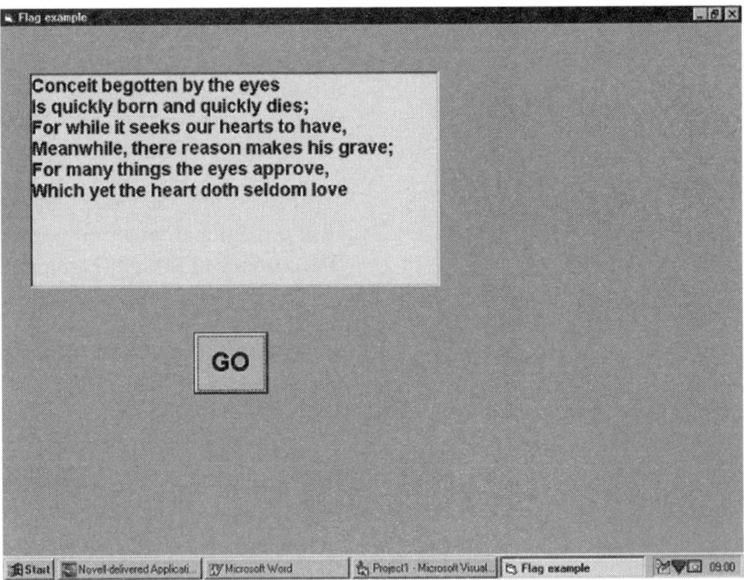

Flag example
Conceit begotten by the eyes
Is quickly born and quickly dies;
For while it seeks our hearts to have,
Meanwhile, there reason makes his grave;
For many things the eyes approve,
Which yet the heart doth seldom love
GO
Start
Microsoft Word
Flag example
09:00

Figure 3.3.12

equivalent to a numerical value of 1 and False to a value of 0. In Visual Basic True has a value of –1.

This can be applied in a simplification of the last program. The value of the flag intFlag1 can be derived immediately from the Boolean evaluation of the expression (strAnswer = 'Yes'). If the answer is Yes, this expression will be true and so it will have a value of –1. If the answer is No, the expression will be false and so its value is zero. This means that, with the addition of a minus sign, the expression is precisely the value required by the flag, as indicated here in this modification to the code.

```
'Determine user's taste
strAnswer = InputBox("Do you like modern poetry", , , 6500, 5500)
intFlag1 = - (strAnswer = "Yes")
```

In the same way the other flag could be assigned a value from the Boolean expression contained in this code fragment:

```
strAnswer = InputBox("Do you like modern poetry", , , 6500, 5500)
intFlag2 = - (strAnswer = "Yes")
```

Key fact

The concept of Boolean conditions comes from the mathematical logic developed in the nineteenth century by *George Boole* (1815–1864). Boole was an obscure elementary schoolteacher who, working entirely alone, revolutionized the study of logic, which until then had made very little progress since the Middle Ages. In Boole's system of mathematical logic whole *propositions*, like 'The Moon is made of cheese', are represented by single letters, p, q, r, etc., and assigned a *truth value* of True or False (in this case False). Different propositions can be combined and manipulated in a mathematical fashion according to the laws of logic. Boole's work, later published as 'An Investigation of the Laws of Thought' (1854), promoted him to a professorship at Queen's College, Cork, and steered logic into an entirely new direction. The work of Frege, Russell, Wittgenstein, Quine, etc. in the twentieth century would not have been feasible without the foundations created by Boole. Practically, his work underpins the whole concept of electronic computing.

Using Select Case

One way in which selection can take place in a Basic program is by the use of the Select Case program structure. In this the action taken by the program can be made to depend upon the value of a variable. Different actions will be chosen according to the circumstances specified by the Case statement. This can single out specific values for the variable or a range of values. The short program which follows demonstrates this.

```
Option Explicit
Private Sub Command1_Click()
'Simple demonstration of Select Case
Dim intChoice As Integer
PicDisplay.Cls
intChoice = Val(InputBox("Enter a number 1 -7", , , 6500, 5500))
PicDisplay.Print intChoice
Select Case intChoice
Case 1
PicDisplay.Print "You chose 1"
Case 2 To 4
PicDisplay.Print "You chose 2, 3 or 4"
Case 5, 7
PicDisplay.Print "You chose 5 or 7"
End Select
End Sub
```

Program documentation

The user is prompted to enter a number in the range 1 to 7. The number chosen is assigned to the variable intChoice, which has been declared as type Integer as the assumption is made that the user will only enter whole numbers. The value chosen is then displayed.

```
Option Explicit
Private Sub Command1_Click()
'Simple demonstration of Select Case
Dim intChoice As Integer
PicDisplay.Cls
intChoice = Val(InputBox("Enter a number 1 -7", , , 6500, 5500))
PicDisplay.Print intChoice
```

The Select Case statement then uses the value held by intChoice to permit different actions to be taken by the program.

```
Select Case intChoice
```

A single value can be selected. Here the Case statement identifies the situation when the value entered for the variable intChoice is 1. Appropriate text is displayed.

```
Case 1
PicDisplay.Print "You chose 1"
```

A range of values can also be identified. In this example if the value of intChoice lies in the range 2 to 4 text is displayed to indicate this. Note how the range is specified with the same syntax as for the control variable in a For Next loop. The permitted values for intChoice follow as part of the same program line as the Case statement.

```
Case 2 To 4
PicDisplay.Print "You chose 2, 3 or 4"
```

A third possibility is the identification of several different values which do not lie within a continuous range. Here the individual value of 5 and 7 are specified. The values are separated by commas.

```
Case 5, 7
PicDisplay.Print "You chose 5 or 7"
```

In this example the value of 6 is deliberately, and perhaps unrealistically, ignored in order to stress the way that discontinuous values can be included in a Select Case program structure.

Finally Select Case ends with the End Select statement.

```
End Select
End Sub
```

In the demonstration of the program in Figure 3.3.13 the user has chosen 2 as the number to enter.

Entering 2 produces the result shown in Figure 3.3.14.

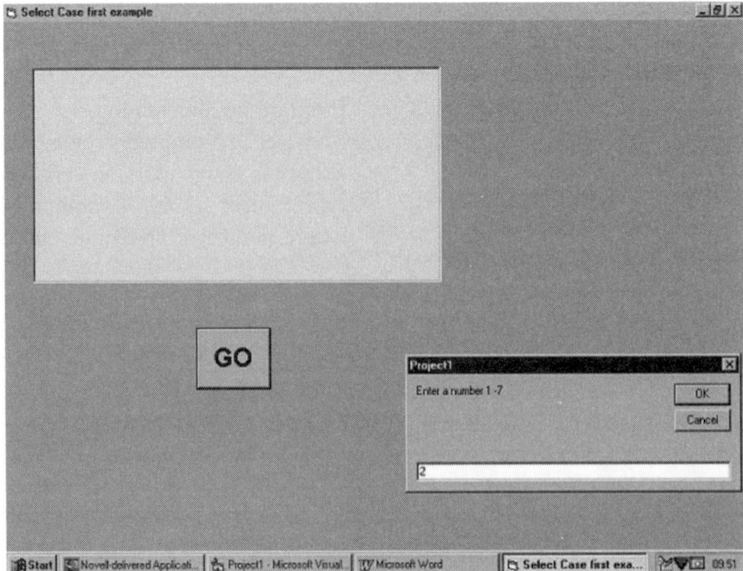

Figure 3.3.13

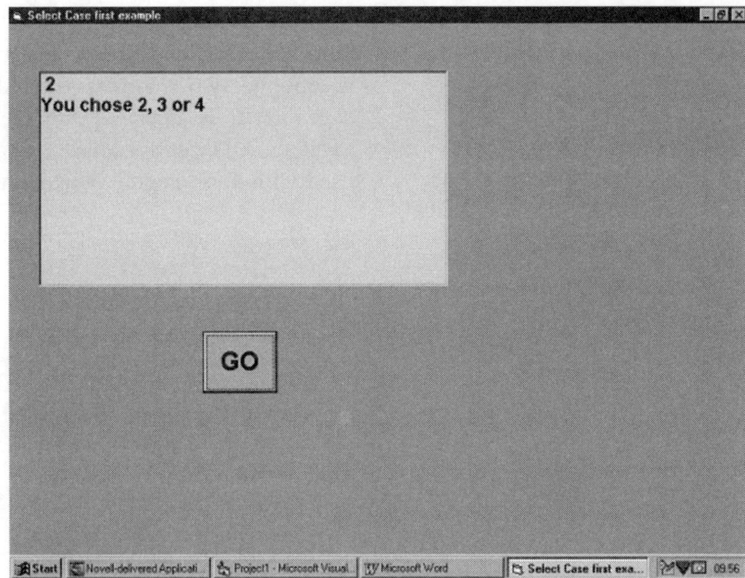

Figure 3.3.14

In this example the value assigned to intChoice has been specifically entered by the user but of course it could be a value generated within the program itself. This is demonstrated in the next example, which also shows how the Select Case can be used with expressions. In this program the user enters two numbers which are then multiplied together. Depending upon the size of the result different text is displayed, chosen using Select Case.

```
Option Explicit
Private Sub Command1_Click()

Dim sngFirstNumber, sngSecondNumber, sngProduct As Single
PicDisplay.Cls

'Request First number
sngFirstNumber = Val(InputBox("Type your first number", , ,
6500, 5500))

'Request Second number
sngSecondNumber = Val(InputBox("Type your second number", , ,
6500, 5500))

'Calculate product
sngProduct = sngFirstNumber × sngSecondNumber

'Display suitable response
Select Case sngProduct
Case Is < 50
PicDisplay.Print "Small answer"
Case Is > 50
PicDisplay.Print "Big answer"
Case 50
PicDisplay.Print "Fancy that!"
PicDisplay.Print "The answer was exactly 50"
End Select

End Sub
```

Program documentation

Two variables, sngFirstNumber and sngSecondNumber are declared to accept the two numbers entered by the user and a third variable, sngProduct, is declared for the answer when they are multiplied together. All three variables are type Single so that this example can be used with non-integral values, unlike the previous example.

```
Option Explicit
Private Sub Command1_Click()

Dim sngFirstNumber, sngSecondNumber, sngProduct As Single
```

After the Picture Box is cleared the user enters the value for the first number. It is assigned to sngFirstNumber by the InputBox function.

```
PicDisplay.Cls

'Request First number
sngFirstNumber = Val(InputBox("Type your first number", , ,
6500, 5500))
```

The second number is entered and assigned to sngSecondNumber.

```
'Request Second number
sngSecondNumber = Val(InputBox("Type your second number", , ,
6500, 5500))
```

The product of the two numbers is assigned to the variable sngProduct.

```
'Calculate product
sngProduct = sngFirstNumber × sngSecondNumber
```

Select Case is now used with the calculated value of sngProduct.

```
'Display suitable response
Select Case sngProduct
```

If the product is less than 50, the message "Small answer" is displayed.

```
Case Is < 50
PicDisplay.Print "Small answer"
```

The message 'Big answer' is shown if the answer is greater than 50.

```
Case Is > 50
PicDisplay.Print "Big answer"
```

If the answer is exactly 50 the message is slightly longer.

```
Case 50
PicDisplay.Print "Fancy that!"
PicDisplay.Print "The answer was exactly 50"
End Select

End Sub
```

This is illustrated in Figure 3.3.15 by the user first entering 8.9.

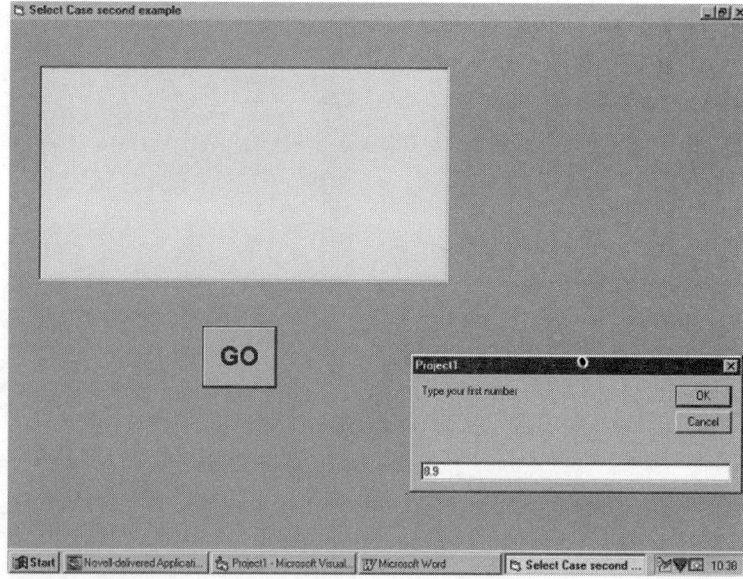

Figure 3.3.15

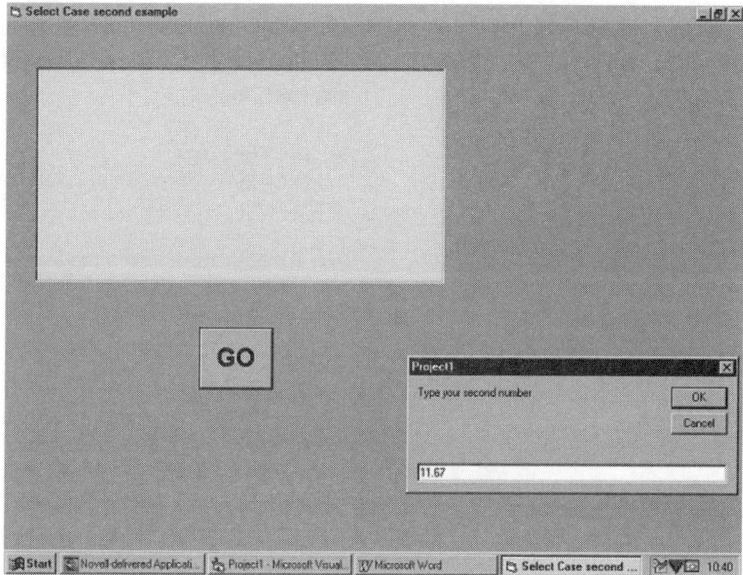

Figure 3.3.16

The second number in Figure 3.3.16 is 11.67.

This combination of numbers then produces the display in Figure 3.3.17.

Using Select Case in a menu

Select Case can be used to call entire sections of code written as functions, procedures or subroutines. This is demonstrated in this third example in which the user can request brief information on any one of three Apollo astronauts who flew in the 1960's space programme. The example shows how Select Case can be used to allow a menu-driven program, but the use of procedure or function calls in a Select Case

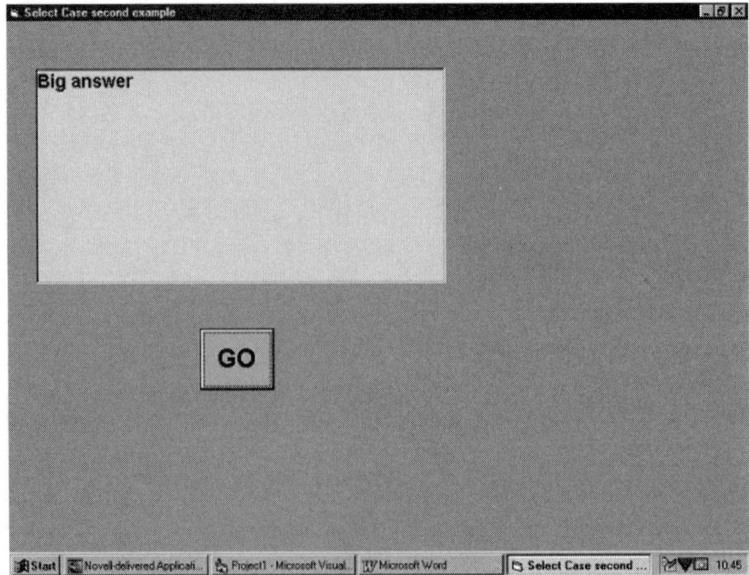

Figure 3.3.17

structure could equally well be applied to many situations in which a lengthy piece of code needs to be executed after a particular condition has been met.

```
Option Explicit
Private Sub Command1_Click()
'Astronaut program

Dim intAstronaut as Integer

PicDisplay.Cls

'Show menu
PicDisplay.Print "Astronaut Information"
PicDisplay.Print "Buzz Aldrin . . . Press 1"
PicDisplay.Print "Frank Borman . . . Press 2"
PicDisplay.Print "Michael Collins . . . Press 3"

'Request user's choice
intAstronaut = Val(InputBox("Enter 1, 2 or 3", , , 6500, 5500))

PicDisplay.Cls

'Display biographical details
Select Case intAstronaut
Case 1
Buzz
Case 2
Frank
Case 3
Michael
End Select

End Sub

Sub Buzz()
'Information about Buzz Aldrin
PicDisplay.Print "Buzz was the second man on the"
PicDisplay.Print "Moon and appears in all the"
```

```
PicDisplay.Print "photos because Neil Armstrong"
PicDisplay.Print "had the camera!"
End Sub

Sub Frank()
'Information about Frank Borman
PicDisplay.Print "Frank Borman was the commander"
PicDisplay.Print "of Apollo 8. This was the first"
PicDisplay.Print "manned spacecraft to reach the"
PicDisplay.Print "but did not land."
End Sub

Sub Michael()
'Information about Michael Collins
PicDisplay.Print "Michael Collins was the pilot"
PicDisplay.Print "of Apollo 11. He stayed in orbit"
PicDisplay.Print "when Neil and Buzz landed"
PicDisplay.Print "in the lunar module, Eagle."
End Sub
```

Program documentation

This program begins in the same way as the other examples, with output being sent to a Picture Box, PicDisplay. A single variable is required to allow the user to make a choice from the menu which will appear. This variable is the integer intAstronaut.

```
Option Explicit
Private Sub Command1_Click()
'Astronaut program

Dim intAstronaut as Integer
```

The names of the three Apollo astronauts for whom information can be provided are shown in the Picture Box.

```
PicDisplay.Cls

'Show menu
PicDisplay.Print "Astronaut Information"
PicDisplay.Print "Buzz Aldrin . . . Press 1"
PicDisplay.Print "Frank Borman . . . Press 2"
PicDisplay.Print "Michael Collins . . . Press 3"
```

The user is then prompted by the InputBox function to enter 1, 2 or 3 according to the astronaut selected. The value is assigned to the variable intAstronaut. The program does not prevent an incorrect choice being made, but later a method for preventing inappropriate input will be illustrated.

```
'Request user's choice
intAstronaut = Val(InputBox("Enter 1, 2 or 3", , , 6500, 5500))
```

As soon as a choice is made, the menu of astronaut names is cleared from the Picture Box, PicDisplay.

```
PicDisplay.Cls
```

The Select Case conditional structure can now be used with the variable intAstronaut. According to the astronaut chosen by the user,

Buzz Aldrin, Frank Borman or Michael Collins, the value of intAstronaut will be 1, 2 or 3. These values will then correspond with Case 1, Case 2 or Case 3. For each, the relevant subprocedures are called, Buzz, Frank and Michael.

```
'Display biographical details
Select Case intAstronaut
Case 1
Buzz
Case 2
Frank
Case 3
Michael
End Select
```

The subprocedures are written after the End Sub for Command1_Click().

```
End Sub
```

In this program example the subprocedures simply use Print to place a few lines of information about the astronaut chosen in the Picture Box, PicDisplay. For examples, the information shown for Buzz Aldrin is produced by this subprocedure.

```
Sub Buzz()
'Information about Buzz Aldrin
PicDisplay.Print "Buzz was the second man on the"
PicDisplay.Print "Moon and appears in all the"
PicDisplay.Print "photos because Neil Armstrong"
PicDisplay.Print "had the camera!"
End Sub
```

Similar subprocedures show information about Frank Borman and Michael Collins. As explained above, though, subprocedures called by a Select Case could instead contain complicated code and allow a program to respond in a complex way according to the value of a variable placed in a Select Case structure.

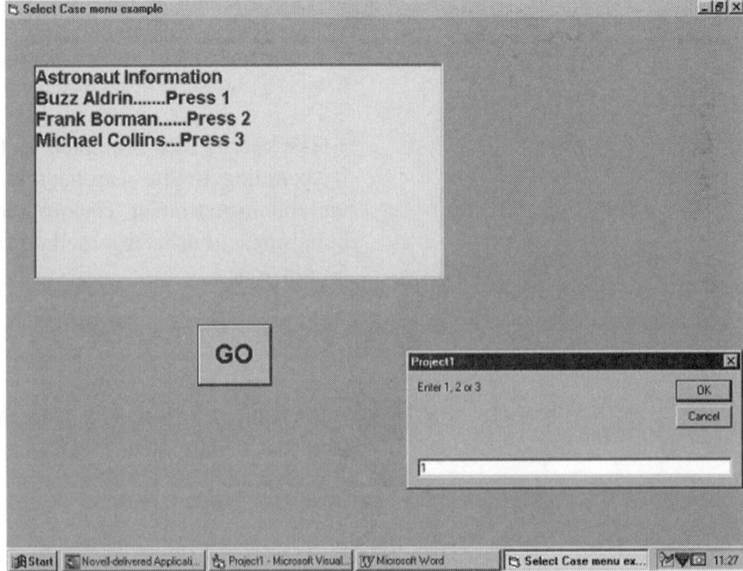

Figure 3.3.18

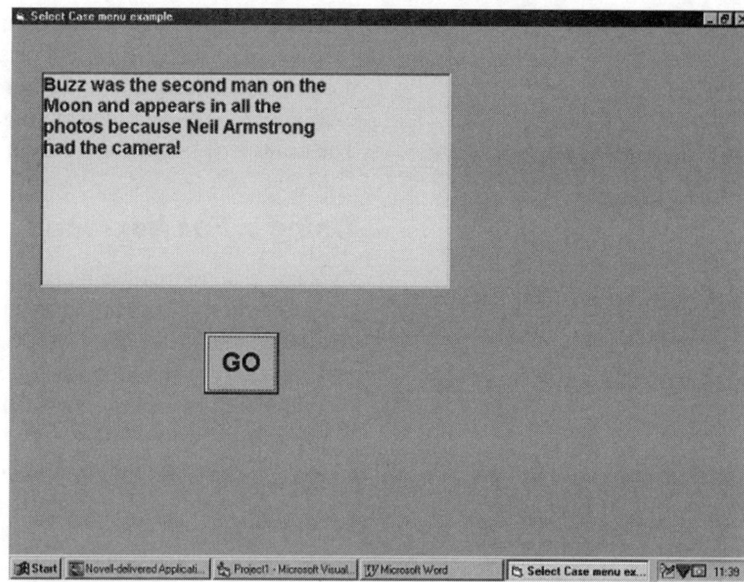

Figure 3.3.19

The initial display will be as shown in Figure 3.3.18. The user is selecting Buzz Aldrin from the menu by entering a value of 1.

When <Enter> is pressed, or the mouse clicked on OK, the information about Buzz Aldrin is as shown in Figure 3.3.19.

Iteration

Frequently it is necessary that a particular block of code should be executed a certain number of times during the operation of a program. This might occur, for example, when the same set of data is required about a number of people. It would be unrealistic to duplicate lines of program code requesting name, address, data of birth, etc., until the program had sufficient instructions to deal with a large group. Many situations within programming need the ability to execute a certain set of program instructions over and over again until a particular objective has been achieved. In fact programming would scarcely be a feasible activity at all if there were no way of employing a programming loop to repeat a selected block of code, often referred to as the loop body, the number of times required. This programming technique is referred to as *iteration*.

There are two fundamentally different types of loop. These differ in both the syntax a specific computer language uses to express them and also in their fundamental logical operation. One type is a *deterministic* loop, which will always repeat a fixed number of times decided in advance. Loops like this are also known as *unconditional*, because no additional condition is required to exit from them once the loop has begun. Another term employed is *definite*, because a definite number of repeats can be stated for the loop before it begins.

The other type of loop is *non-deterministic*. A loop of this sort includes a specific condition, similar to those employed in If Then structures, which has to be satisfied before exit is possible from the loop. For this reason these loops are also called *conditional*. The condition which allows a loop like this to end is known as the exit condition for the loop. As the number of repeats cannot be stated for the loop before it begins it can also be described as *indefinite*. Non-deterministic loops can be further divided between those which test for exit before the loop begins and those which test at the end of the loop. The latter will necessarily execute the loop body at least once.

Using a For Next loop

In Basic a deterministic loop is written using the instructions *For* and *Next*. The For statement marks the beginning of the loop and the Next statement marks the end. All the program lines in between the two statements form the loop body and therefore repeat a number of times determined in advance. How many times this should be is governed by the range given to a *loop control variable* in the For statement. This variable is given initial and final integral values, separated by the word To. The loop will then repeat the number of times required for the loop control variable to 'count up' from the initial to the final values. (See, however, the use of Step below.)

This is demonstrated by the following example.

```
Option Explicit
Private Sub Command1_Click()
'Demonstration of For Next loop
Dim intCounter As Integer

'Loop repeats ten times
For intCounter = 1 To 10
  PicDisplay.Print "This is repeat number";
  PicDisplay.Print intCounter
Next intCounter
End Sub
```

Program documentation

The loop control variable, intCounter, is declared as an integer before the loop begins.

```
Option Explicit
Private Sub Command1_Click()
'Demonstration of For Next loop
Dim intCounter As Integer
```

The For statement then requires intCounter to count from 1 to 10, which means that the For Next loop will repeat ten times.

```
'Loop repeats ten times
For intCounter = 1 To 10
```

To show that the loop body does repeat ten times two print statements are included, the second of which does actually display the incrementing value of the control variable.

```
PicDisplay.Print "This is repeat number";
PicDisplay.Print intCounter
```

The loop then ends with Next, followed by the name of the loop control variable. The variable can be omitted and the loop will still

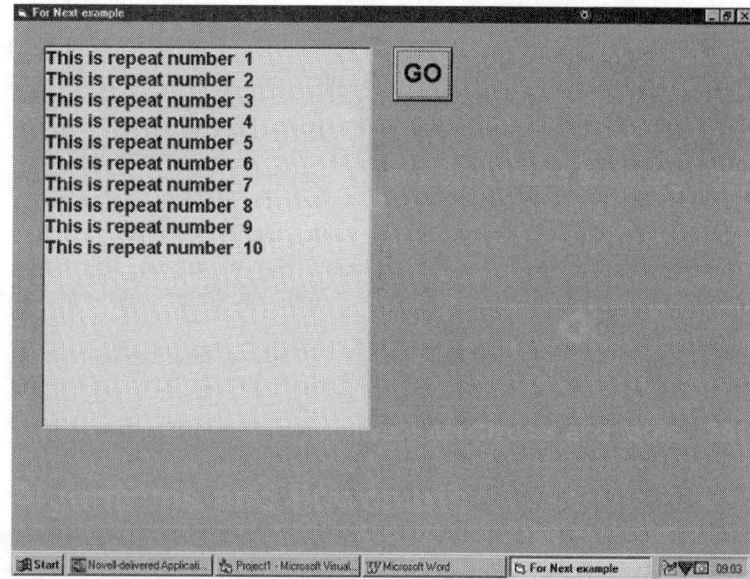

Figure 3.3.20

repeat correctly. Omitting the variable should be avoided though as program clarity is always desirable.

```
Next intCounter
End Sub
```

A typical display for this program is shown in Figure 3.3.20.

In the last example the value of the loop control variable increased by 1 each time the loop repeated. The amount by which the loop control variable is incremented can be altered, however, by including the *Step modifier* in the For statement. This is followed by the size of the increment for the variable, which can be any appropriate positive or negative integer. For example, the statement

For intCounter = 20 to 30 Step 5

will lead to the loop control variable assuming in turn the values 20, 25 and 30. The loop will therefore repeat three times before reaching the final value of 30 and stopping. Using Step is particularly important when a range of discrete values is needed for the loop control variable, for example in calculating screen coordinates for a set of points in a display.

A negative increment of –2 for Step is shown in the next example.

```
Option Explicit
Private Sub Command1_Click()
'Demonstration of For Next loop
Dim intCounter As Integer

'Loop repeats five times
For intCounter = 10 To 2 Step -2
  PicDisplay.Print "Loop control variable's value is";
  PicDisplay.Print intCounter
Next intCounter
End Sub
```

Program documentation

The program code is identical to the previous example with a few exceptions. One is the For statement.

```
For intCounter = 10 To 2 Step -2
```

Here the negative value given to the Step increment means that the values the loop control variable will assume are 10, 8, 6, 4 and 2. The loop therefore repeats five times.

Another difference is the text displayed by the statements the loop body.

```
PicDisplay.Print "Loop control variable's value is";
PicDisplay.Print intCounter
```

The display is like that shown in Figure 3.3.21.

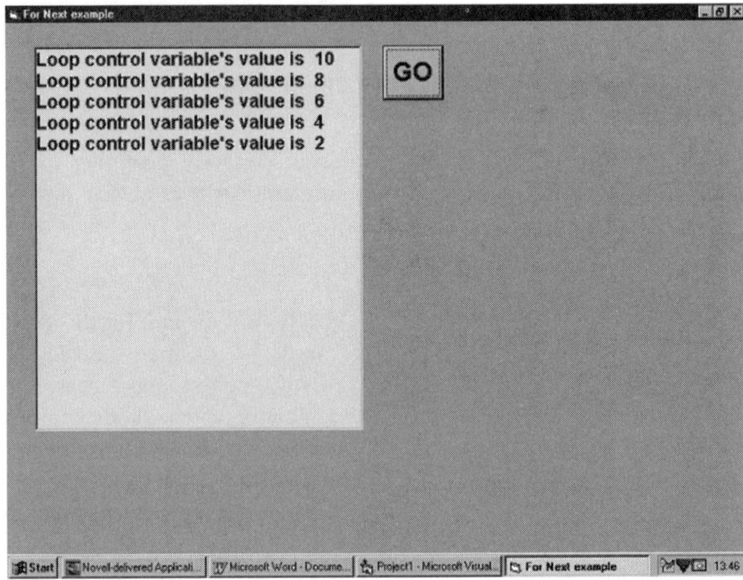

Figure 3.3.21

Using a Do Loop Until/Loop While

Conditional loops can be implemented in Visual Basic using the Do Loop Until, Do Loop While or Do While Loop structures. In each a condition is associated with the Loop statement. The condition determines when exit from the loop should occur.

Do Loop Until is illustrated by this short program which requests that the user enters a correct password before continuing.

```
Option Explicit
Private Sub Command1_Click()
'Demonstration of Do loop
Dim strPassword As String
Dim strName As String
```

```
Do
   'Request password
   strPassword = InputBox("Type password", , , 6500, 5500)
   'Display password
   PicDisplay.Print strPassword
Loop Until strPassword = "Hercules"

'Indicate password accepted
PicDisplay.Print "Access permitted."
strName = InputBox("Type your name", , , 6500, 5500)
PicDisplay.Print "Hello"; strName

End Sub
```

Program documentation

Two variables have to be declared. One, strPassword, is for the password that is entered and the other, strName, will represent the user's name.

```
Option Explicit
Private Sub Command1_Click()
'Demonstration of Do loop
Dim strPassword As String
Dim strName As String
```

The loop then begins with Do.

```
Do
```

The user has to enter a password which is then assigned to the variable strPassword.

```
'Request password
strPassword = InputBox("Type password", , , 6500, 5500)
```

For clarity the password that has been typed is displayed again in PicDisplay.

```
'Display password
PicDisplay.Print strPassword
```

This requesting a password, and then displaying it again, will continue until the correct password, Hercules, is entered. The condition following Loop Until, strPassword = 'Hercules', is then satisfied and exit from the loop takes place.

```
Loop Until strPassword = "Hercules"
```

At this point the alternative Loop While form of the loop structure could have been employed instead. This will assume that the loop should repeat while the password entered is not Hercules. The condition is written as:

```
Loop While strPassword <> "Hercules"
```

Whichever construction is chosen the rest of the program, displaying the user's name, can then be executed.

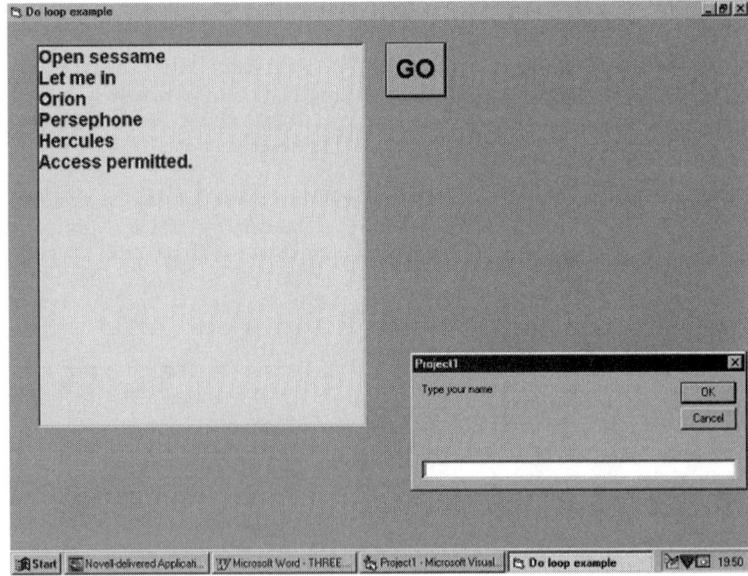

Figure 3.3.22

```
'Indicate password accepted
PicDisplay.Print "Access permitted."
strName = InputBox("Type your name", , , 6500, 5500)
PicDisplay.Print "Hello"; strName

End Sub
```

Figure 3.3.22 shows how the program appears.

Using a Do While loop

The program example above tests for exit from the loop after the loop body has been executed at least once. This is because the exit condition is placed at the end of the loop. An alternative conditional loop, Do While, tests instead at the beginning of the loop. As the next example demonstrates, this type of loop structure will not execute at all in some circumstances, perhaps reflecting an 'If it ain't broke, don't fix it' approach to programming.

The program will allow any number entered to be repeatedly decreased by 2 provided that it is initially greater than 20. The series of numbers produced is displayed, stopping as soon as 20 is approached. If the number entered is not greater than 20 the loop does not execute at all.

```
Option Explicit
Private Sub Command1_Click()
'Do While demonstration

Dim intNumber As Integer

'Request number
intNumber = Val(InputBox('Enter a number', , , 6500, 5500))

'Loop decreases number by 2 only
'if it is greater than 20
Do While intNumber > 20
```

```
'Subtract 2
intNumber = intNumber - 2

'Display result
PicDisplay.Print 'Number is now';
PicDisplay.Print intNumber

Loop

End Sub
```

Program documentation

A variable, intNumber, is declared to hold the value that will be entered.

```
Option Explicit
Private Sub Command1_Click()
'Do While demonstration

Dim intNumber As Integer
```

A value is assigned to intNumber using InputBox.

```
'Request number
intNumber = Val(InputBox("Enter a number", , , 6500, 5500))
```

The condition, greater than 20, is placed at the beginning of the Do While loop.

```
'Loop decreases number by 2 only
'if it is greater than 20
Do While intNumber > 20
```

Inside the loop 2 is subtracted from intNumber.

```
'Subtract 2
intNumber = intNumber - 2
```

The result is then shown in PicDisplay.

```
'Display result
PicDisplay.Print "Number is now";
PicDisplay.Print intNumber

Loop

End Sub
```

The result of typing in 50 can be seen in Figure 3.3.23.

Including a counter in Do loop

Unlike a For Next loop, a Do loop does not have a loop control variable acting as an automatic counter for the number of times the loop repeats. This can be inconvenient because there are situations in which the combination of a conditional loop and a counter is required. In the earlier example in which a password was requested from the user the rather unreasonable assumption was made that an indefinite number of attempts should be allowed to type in the correct word. Obviously this is not a realistic approach. There would be the possibility of the password being discovered if enough guesses were permitted. The type of program structure really required is a loop which exits when the correct password is typed, but which at the same time only allows a fixed number of attempts. Both a condition and a counter are needed.

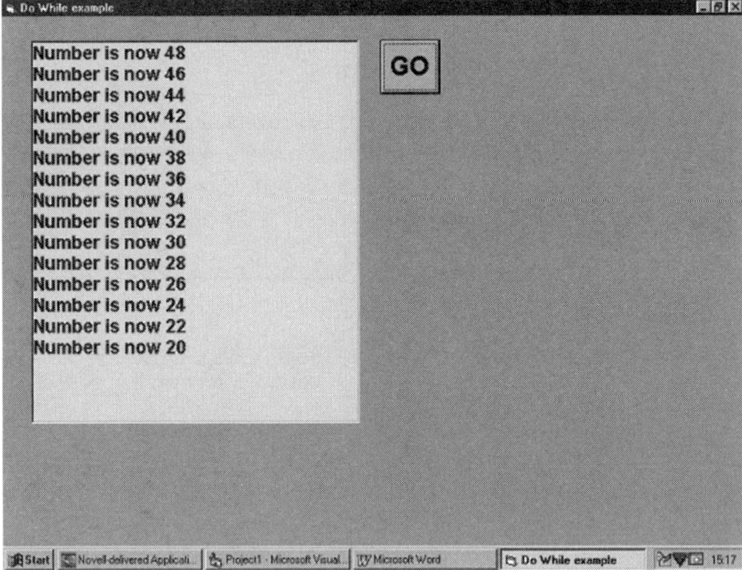

Figure 3.3.23

This can be achieved by adding a counter to a Do loop. This is a variable which is assigned a value of 0 before the loop begins and which is then increased by 1 inside the loop. Each time the loop repeats this variable will be incremented and so it acts as a loop counter.

The earlier password program is now extended to include a loop counter which will only permit three attempts to type the correct word.

```
Option Explicit
Private Sub Command1_Click()
'Demonstration inclusion of a
'counter in a Do loop

Dim strPassword As String
Dim strName As String
Dim intTries As Integer

'Initialise number of tries before loop
intTries = 0

Do

  'Increment number of tries inside loop
  intTries = intTries + 1

  'Indicate number of attempts
  PicDisplay.Print "Password...Attempt"; intTries

  'Request password
  strPassword = InputBox("Type password", , , 6500, 5500)

  'Exit loop for correct password or
  'for exceeding 3 attempts

Loop Until strPassword = "Hercules" Or intTries > 2

PicDisplay.Print
```

```
'Check number of attempts made
If strPassword = "Hercules" Then

  'Indicate password accepted
  PicDisplay.Print "Access permitted."
  strName = InputBox("Type your name", , , 6500, 5500)
  PicDisplay.Print "Hello"; strName

Else
  'Indicate too many attempts made
  PicDisplay.Print "You have exceeded three"
  PicDisplay.Print "attempts to enter the password"

End If

End Sub
```

Program documentation

The program code is developed from the earlier example and so contains the same variables. An additional variable is intTries which will be the counter for the Do loop.

```
Option Explicit
Private Sub Command1_Click()
'Demonstration inclusion of a
'counter in a Do loop

Dim strPassword As String
Dim strName As String
Dim intTries As Integer
```

The counter is first assigned a value of 0 before the loop begins.

```
'Initialise number of tries before loop
intTries = 0

Do
```

Immediately within the loop intTries is increased by 1 so that it will act as a loop counter.

```
  'Increment number of tries inside loop
  intTries = intTries + 1
```

The value of the counter is displayed to warn the user if the wrong password is entered and to give an indication of how many further attempts are possible.

```
  'Indicate number of attempts
  PicDisplay.Print "Password. . . Attempt"; intTries
```

As before the password is then requested and assigned to strPassword by the InputBox function. Unlike the earlier password example, though, the user's input is not displayed in PicDisplay. This is to create a slightly more realistic situation in which the user's personal information is not generally broadcast to anybody who might be looking over their shoulder!

```
  'Request password
  strPassword = InputBox("Type password", , , 6500, 5500)
```

An exit condition then allows the loop to end if the correct password has been entered or if three attempts have been made to type it in.

```
   'Exit loop for correct password or
   'for exceeding 3 attempts

Loop Until strPassword = "Hercules" Or intTries > 2
```

Outside the loop a blank line is added to the display for clarity.

```
PicDisplay.Print
```

The same dialogue as in the previous example, asking for and then displaying the user's name, now takes place if the correct password has been typed.

```
'Check number of attempts made
If strPassword = "Hercules" Then
   'Indicate password accepted
   PicDisplay.Print "Access permitted."
   strName = InputBox("Type your name", , , 6500, 5500)
   PicDisplay.Print "Hello"; strName
```

If the loop has ended only because three attempts at the password have been made, and it has not been entered properly for any of them, a suitable message is displayed to inform the user what has happened.

```
Else
   'Indicate too many attempts made
   PicDisplay.Print "You have exceeded three"
   PicDisplay.Print "attempts to enter the password"

End If

End Sub
```

The display for a correct password is shown in Figure 3.3.24. Here the password has (deliberately) not been entered correctly the first time.

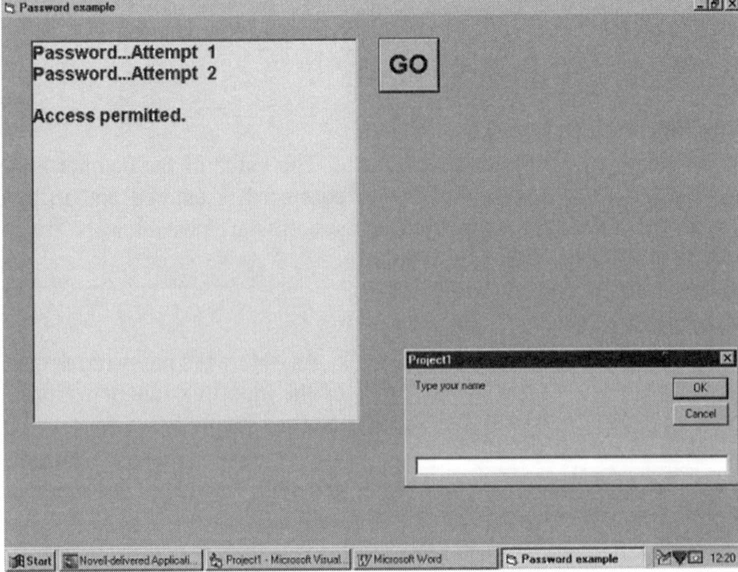

Figure 3.3.24

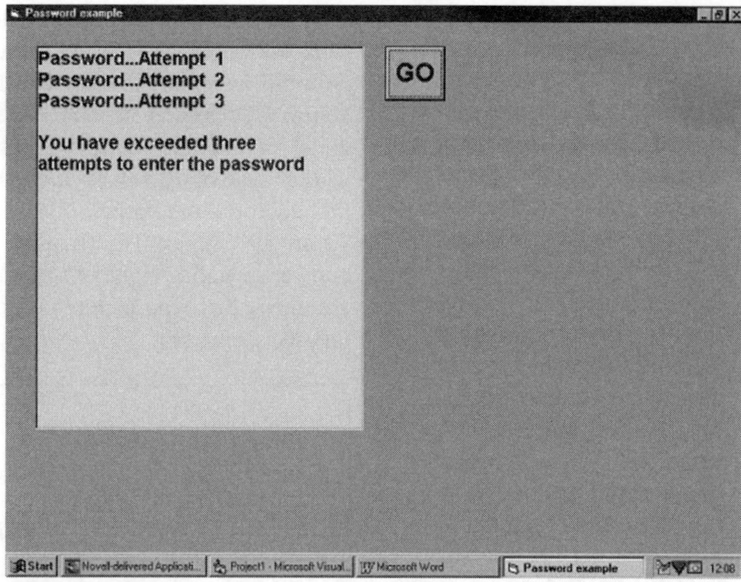

Figure 3.3.25

The next display is the one seen when three incorrect passwords have been entered (Figure 3.3.25).

Nested loops

It is possible for one loop to be placed inside another. The overall structure will have a general form:

```
For OuterLoopCounter = LowerValue1 To  UpperValue1  Step Increment1
For InnerLoopCounter = LowerValue2 To  UpperValue2  Step Increment2
{Loop body}
Next InnerLoopCounter
Next OuterLoopCounter
```

Further levels of nesting are also possible, for example with a third loop nested inside the second. It is essential that the loops are nested properly. The Next statement for the inner loop must precede, not follow, the Next statement for the outer loop. The following structure is therefore incorrect:

```
For OuterLoopCounter = LowerValue1 To  UpperValue1  Step Increment1
For InnerLoopCounter = LowerValue2 To  UpperValue2  Step Increment2
{Loop body}
Next OuterLoopCounter
Next InnerLoopCounter
```

Key fact

It is a common error with rookie programmers that loops have not been nested properly. Always be alert to this potential mishap!

In practice, programming code is likely to be simpler in structure than this general form, perhaps without the increments for Step and with the lower value for the For statements beginning at 0 or 1.

Also note that nesting is not restricted to unconditional loops as shown here. Both conditional and unconditional loops can be nested in any combination, with, for example, a Do Loop while structure nested inside a For Next or vice versa.

Key fact

Nested loops frequently provide a useful control structure in programming. In 'traditional' graphic displays, in which the programmer plans the appearance of the final screen by combining graphic primitives and simple coordinate geometry rather than relying upon the in-built facilities of a rapid applications development package, nested loops are essential. Similarly whenever a two-dimensional array is going to be used nested loops are the obvious tool to employ. In general the values taken by two loop control variables can be incorporated into statements within the loop body to produce fairly complicated processing of data.

In the example below a simple expression is shown being derived from the values of both loop control variables.

In this example there are two For Next loops each of which repeats 10 times. For each value adopted in turn by the loop control variable for the outer loop, the control variable for the inner loop cycles through its whole range of 10 values. It can be seen that the code contained inside both loops (at the centre of the 'nest') will necessarily be repeated 10 × 10, or 100, times. This is used in the example to produce a grid of numbers counting from 1 to 100, like a number square used for teaching arithmetic to young children or, more cheerfully, as a board in a game involving counting.

```
Private Sub Command1_Click()

'Demonstration of nested loops
Dim intXcoord As Integer
Dim intYcoord As Integer
Dim intValue As Integer

'Outer loop calculates X_coordinate
For intXcoord = 1 To 10

  'Inner loop calculates Y_coordinate
  For intYcoord = 1 To 10

    'X_coordinate calculated
    PicDisplay.CurrentX = intXcoord × 500

    'Y_coordinate calculated
    PicDisplay.CurrentY = intYcoord × 500

    'Number calculated for board
    intValue = intXcoord + (intYcoord - 1) × 10

    'Number displayed
    PicDisplay.Print intValue

    'End of inner loop
  Next intYcoord

'End of outer loop
Next intXcoord

End Sub
```

Program documentation

The two loop control variables, intXcoord and intYcoord, have to be declared as well as a variable, intValue, for the number which will be displayed on the 'board'.

```
Private Sub Command1_Click()

'Demonstration of nested loops
Dim intXcoord As Integer
Dim intYcoord As Integer
Dim intValue As Integer
```

The range of the outer For Next loop is from 1 to 10.

```
'Outer loop calculates X_coordinate
For intXcoord = 1 To 10
```

The range of the inner For Next loop is also 1 to 10.

```
'Inner loop calculates Y_coordinate
For intYcoord = 1 To 10
```

At this point the embedded loop body, within both loops, is reached. First the code calculates the x-coordinate at which a number will be displayed on the Picture Box, PicDisplay. It does this by multiplying the outer loop control variable, intXcoord, by 500 and assigning it to Visual Basic's CurrentX, which is used for positioning text.

```
'X_coordinate calculated
PicDisplay.CurrentX = intXcoord × 500
```

The y-coordinate for the number is found in a similar way from the value of the loop control variable for the inner loop, intYcoord, and is assigned to CurrentY.

```
'Y_coordinate calculated
PicDisplay.CurrentY = intYcoord × 500
```

Mathematics in action

The numbers, from 1 to 100, are calculated in an expression which involves the control variables for both loops. This is an example of a general technique which, as explained above, is an important aspect of programming with loop structures. The number, in a concession to junior school arithmetic, is regarded as consisting of a 'tens' component and a 'units' component. The latter is quite clearly equal to the value of the outer loop control variable, intXcoord, because the numbers displayed should count up as their position moves from left to right across the board, and this is what intXcoord also does. The tens component is slightly more devious. Moving down the display of numbers the tens component should increase by 10 for each successive row of the board. As the coordinates for Visual Basic's CurrentY also increase from top to bottom of the display this suggests just multiplying intYcoord by 10. However, this would lead to a tens figure of 10 for the very first row of the board. Instead there should be no tens at all here. The solution is to subtract 1 from intYcoord before multiplying by 10. This product is then added to intXcoord to give the final number required, intValue.

```
'Number calculated for board
intValue = intXcoord + (intYcoord - 1) × 10
```

The calculated value is then displayed.

```
'Number displayed
PicDisplay.Print intValue
```

The inner loop ends with Next intYcoord.

```
   'End of inner loop
  Next intYcoord
```

Finally the outer loop ends.

```
'End of outer loop
Next intXcoord

End Sub
```

The display created by the program is as shown in Figure 3.3.26.

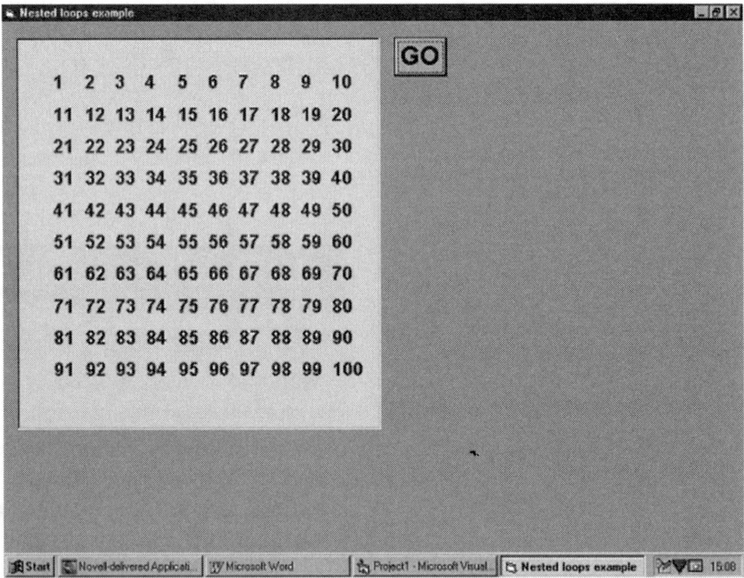

Figure 3.3.26

Arrays in programs

Data structures are not a topic in Unit 3. One data structure, however, is so useful in programming that it is quite hard to avoid. This is the *array*. An array is frequently compared with a numbered pigeon hole. If you want to know what mail has been delivered for a particular person all you have to do is find out the number of their pigeon hole. Knowing this number enables you to look at what has been placed there. In a similar way using an array in programming allows you to keep track of text or numbers which have been placed in memory. Again you have to know the number of the location at which the data has been stored. This number is called the *subscript* and another name for an array is a *subscripted variable*.

It is useful to consider the use of arrays at this point because they are frequently used in association with loops.

If an array is going to be used it has to be declared by the programmer first. In Visual Basic this is done in almost exactly the same way as with any other variable. The same instruction, Dim, is followed by the name that has been chosen for the array. The only difference is that the number of array locations required follows immediately, for example:

Dim strPerson(10) as String.

This creates a series of storage locations in which separate text can be placed. These are then identified as strPerson(1), strPerson(2), strPerson(3) . . . strPerson(10). There is also a 'zeroth location', strPerson(0). Declaring an array with a given number always creates an additional location in Basic.

Each location in an array behaves like an 'ordinary' variable. For example, an assignment could take place like:

strPerson(3) = 'Lindsay Hesselmann'

The advantage of using an array is that, in conjunction with a loop, it makes it easy to handle a large number of separate variables without the need for a large quantity of program code. Consider, for example, the difference between separate assigments like this:

```
strFirstTown = InputBox('Type town name', , , xcoord,ycoord)
strSecondTown = InputBox('Type town name', , , xcoord,ycoord)

{17 more similar lines of code}

strFirstTown = InputBox('Type town name', , , xcoord,ycoord)
```

and the equivalent code written in the form of a For Next loop:

```
For intLoopCount =1 to 20
  strTown(intLoopCount) = InputBox('Type town name', , , xcoord,
ycoord)
Next intLoopCount
```

This is now illustrated by a short example. It is a program which requests the user to enter five names. As each name is entered it is also assigned to an array. The fact that an array has been used to hold the names is demonstrated by displaying all five names again, first in their initial order and then reversed.

```
Option Explicit
Private Sub Command1_Click()

'Demonstration of an array
Dim intCounter As Integer
Dim strName(5) As String

'First loop requests names from user
'and places them in array
For intCounter = 1 To 5
  StrName(intCounter) = InputBox("Type a name", , , 6500, 5500)
Next intCounter
```

```
'Second loop displays names in same order
For intCounter = 1 To 5
  PicDisplay.Print strName(intCounter)
Next intCounter

'Leave space
PicDisplay.Print

'Third loop displays names in reverse order
For intCounter = 5 To 1 Step - 1
  PicDisplay.Print strName(intCounter)
Next intCounter

End Sub
```

Program documentation

A loop control variable, intCounter, is declared, and an array strName(). It is assumed that this will only need to store five names.

```
Option Explicit
Private Sub Command1_Click()

'Demonstration of an array
Dim intCounter As Integer
Dim strName(5) As String
```

A For Next loop now uses the InputBox function to request the five names. Each time the name entered is assigned to the next location in the array, as identified by the value of the loop control variable, intCounter.

```
'First loop requests names from user
'and places them in array
For intCounter = 1 To 5
  strName(intCounter) = InputBox("Type a name", , , 6500, 5500)
Next intCounter
```

The fact that the names have been stored in the array is demonstrated by displaying them again in PicDisplay. A For Next loop is used a second time and the sequential values of the loop control variable mean that the names are printed out in the order in which they were entered.

```
'Second loop displays names in same order
For intCounter = 1 To 5
  PicDisplay.Print strName(intCounter)
Next intCounter
```

A space is left before the names are shown again.

```
'Leave space
PicDisplay.Print
```

Another loop now displays the names in reverse by using Step. The values taken by intCounter will be 5, 4, 3, 2, 1 and the names similarly follow in this order, confirming precisely where they are held in the array.

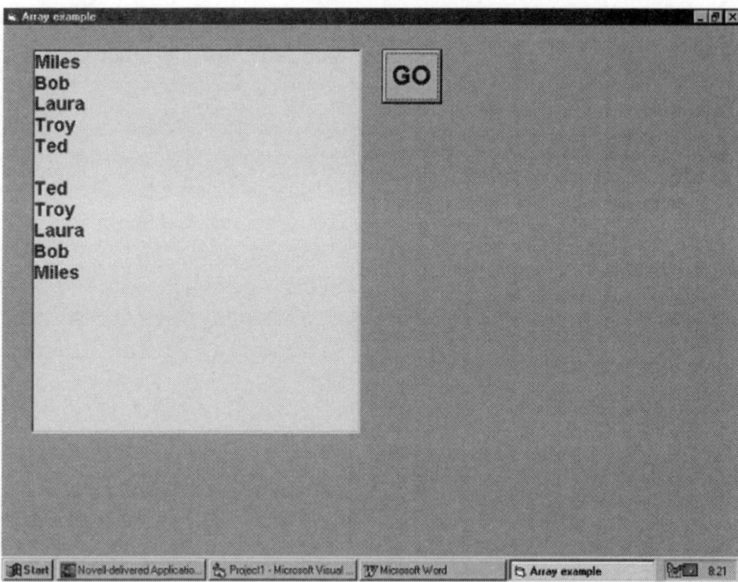

Figure 3.3.27

```
'Third loop displays names in reverse order
For intCounter = 5 To 1 Step -1
  PicDisplay.Print strName(intCounter)
Next intCounter

End Sub
```

The screen display produced is as shown in Figure 3.3.27.

Validating user input

An immediate use for conditional loops is in validating input from a user. Frequently a program needs to be protected from unwelcome values which might accidentally be entered by the person running the program. This might occur, for example, if the <Enter> key is pressed unintentionally before a numerical value has been selected. The zero then automatically assigned to an input variable could easily lead to a *division by zero error* in the subsequent program code. Alternatively the user may merely have misunderstood what response is required and entered an inappropriate value as a consequence of their confusion.

To prevent such a situation it is possible to *validate* input code. This means that the programmer first identifies a specific range of values which are permissible at a particular stage of the program's intended operation and then includes a validation routine in the form of a conditional loop enclosing the user's input. The exit condition for the loop is written to identify only those values which are relevant. If other values are entered the loop will repeat so that the user can have a further opportunity to enter again.

This technique is sometimes also referred to as *error-trapping*.

Use of a conditional loop to validate user entry is shown in the following short example. In this it is assumed that the user should enter the name of one of two countries, Australia or Brazil. The conditional loop prevents any other possibility.

```
Option Explicit
Private Sub Command1_Click()
'Use of loop to validate user input
Dim strAns As String
PicDisplay.Cls
PicDisplay.Print "Choose a country"
PicDisplay.Print "Australia"
PicDisplay.Print "Brazil"
Do
  strAns = InputBox("Enter choice", , , 6500, 5500)
Loop Until strAns = "Australia" Or strAns = 'Brazil'
PicDisplay.Cls
PicDisplay.Print "Choice accepted"
End Sub
```

Program documentation

As before a minimal use of Visual Basic is assumed, the program example being entered as code for Command_1 and output being sent to a single Picture Box, PicDisplay. A single variable, strAns, is declared to accept the user's input:

```
Option Explicit
Private Sub Command1_Click()
'Use of loop to validate user input
Dim strAns As String
PicDisplay.Cls
```

The possible choice of values that can be entered is indicated in PicDisplay:

```
PicDisplay.Print "Choose a country"
PicDisplay.Print "Australia"
PicDisplay.Print "Brazil"
```

A conditional Do Loop now follows. The InputBox function is used, as the sole statement of the loop body, to assign the user's choice to the variable strAns. The exit condition for the loop requires that the user's entry is either Australia or Brazil. Any other entry will cause the loop to repeat and so the user is forced to comply:

```
Do
  strAns = InputBox("Enter choice", , , 6500, 5500)
Loop Until strAns = "Australia" Or strAns = "Brazil"
```

Finally correct entry is confirmed by a message shown in PicDisplay:

```
PicDisplay.Cls
PicDisplay.Print "Choice accepted"
End Sub
```

Extended validation of user input

The method for validating input illustrated in the previous example can become difficult to implement if a large range of possible values is required. For example, if the number of countries that the user could enter in the program above were to be increased to ten, the exit condition for the Do Loop would clearly become impractical. Fortunately it is relatively easy to modify the program to include an array for the country names, and a flag for the exit condition. This allows the program to function as before, but with the greater number of possible input values:

```
Option Explicit
Private Sub Command1_Click()
'Use of loop to error-trap input
'including array and a flag

Dim strCountry(11) As String
Dim strAns As String
Dim intCounter As Integer
Dim intFlag As Integer

'Place countries in array
strCountry(1) = "Australia"
strCountry(2) = "Brazil"
strCountry(3) = "Chile"
strCountry(4) = "Denmark"
strCountry(5) = "England"
strCountry(6) = "France"
strCountry(7) = "Germany"
strCountry(8) = "Holland"
strCountry(9) = "Ireland"
strCountry(10) = "Japan"

'Outer loop requests choice
Do
  PicDisplay.Cls
  PicDisplay.Print "Choose a country"

  'First inner loop indicates range for choice
  For intCounter = 1 To 10
    PicDisplay.Print strCountry(intCounter)
   Next intCounter

  'Choice entered
  strAns = InputBox("Enter choice", , , 6500, 5500)
  'Second inner loop checks country is in range
  intCounter = 0
  Do
    intCounter = intCounter + 1
  Loop Until strAns = strCountry(intCounter) Or intCounter = 11

  'Flag set to 1 for choice in range
  If intCounter < 11 Then
    intFlag = 1
  Else
    intFlag = 0
  End If

Loop Until intFlag = 1

PicDisplay.Cls
PicDisplay.Print "Choice accepted"
End Sub
```

Program documentation

The program again uses a single command button in Visual Basic to run the required code. An array strCountry() is dimensioned with 11 rather than ten elements needed for the ten countries. The extra location will be required in the validation routine subsequently. As in the previous example strAns is used for the input. A loop counter, intCounter, and a flag, intFlag, are both declared:

```
Option Explicit
Private Sub Command1_Click()
'Use of loop to error-trap input
'including array and a flag

Dim strCountry(11) As String
Dim strAns As String
Dim intCounter As Integer
Dim intFlag As Integer
```

The ten country names are then directly assigned to the first ten elements of strCountry():

```
'Place countries in array
strCountry(1) = "Australia"
strCountry(2) = "Brazil"
strCountry(3) = "Chile"
strCountry(4) = "Denmark"
strCountry(5) = "England"
strCountry(6) = "France"
strCountry(7) = "Germany"
strCountry(8) = "Holland"
strCountry(9) = "Ireland"
strCountry(10) = "Japan"
```

A Do Loop then begins the validation routine. This outer loop will not exit until the user has entered a valid country name. Within the loop the user is prompted to select a country and immediately after this a For Next loop displays all the possible choices from the strCountry() array. The value of the loop variable, intCounter, selects each of the array elements in turn for display:

```
'Outer loop requests choice
Do
  PicDisplay.Cls
  PicDisplay.Print "Choose a country"
  'First inner loop indicates range for choice
  For intCounter = 1 To 10
    PicDisplay.Print strCountry(intCounter)
  Next intCounter
```

The country chosen by the user is assigned as before to the variable strAns by the InputBox function:

```
  'Choice entered
  strAns = InputBox("Enter choice", , , 6500, 5500)
```

A further Do Loop is then used to check whether the value assigned to strAns is one of the relevant countries. Within this loop reference will be made to the subscripted locations in the strCountry() array and as a result a loop counter is required. This is the variable intCounter again, but first it has to be initialized as zero. Then, within the loop, it is immediately incremented so that it counts the number of loop repeats:

```
'Second inner loop checks country is in range
intCounter = 0
Do
  intCounter = intCounter + 1
```

The loop keeps repeating until either of two conditions is satisfied. The first is simply that the country selected by the user matches one of the countries in the array. This condition is expressed as strAns = strCountry(intCounter). The other condition identifies that the end of the array has been reached without the user's selection matching any of the countries. This will occur when the loop counter reaches the empty eleventh element and so the condition is expressed as intCounter = 11. This second condition can be regarded as a default exit from the loop. The combined exit condition will therefore be:

```
Loop Until strAns = strCountry(intCounter) Or intCounter = 11
```

At this point successful exit from the loop will have been achieved but this needs to be converted into an unambiguous indication of whether the user has chosen an appropriate country or not. This will depend upon the value reached by the loop counter, intCount. If it has not reached 11 then the country entered is within the range. This is represented by a value of 1 for the flag variable, intFlag. If the counter has reached 11 then the country is not acceptable and intFlag is given a value of 0:

```
'Flag set to 1 for choice in range
If intCounter < 11 Then
  intFlag = 1
Else
  intFlag = 0
End If
```

Mathematics in action

The flag value in this program could easily be generated as a Boolean expression, assigning intFlag the Boolean value of intCounter < 11.

The outer Do Loop then only exits when intFlag is 1, indicating that the country entered by the user is within the required range. (Alternatively the value of the loop counter itself could be used directly in the exit condition, but the use of the flag variable makes the code more explicit.)

```
Loop Until intFlag = 1
```

Successful entry is then indicated to the user:

```
PicDisplay.Cls
PicDisplay.Print 'Choice accepted'
End Sub
```

Question 3.3.1

Design an algorithm to solve each of the following problems. It is suggested that you then test a coded version of the algorithm in a programming language.

(a) The price of a square metre of carpet is entered, followed by the length of a carpet and its width. The cost of the carpet is calculated.
(b) The length, width and depth of a swimming pool are entered in metres. The volume of the pool is displayed in litres.
(c) A person enters their weight in stones and pounds. It is then converted to kg. (Assume 1 lb is equivalent to 454 g. There are 14 lb in 1 st.)
(d) A sequence of numbers is entered. The smallest of these is then displayed.
(e) Read again the description of the game of 'matches' at the beginning of this chapter. Write the algorithm for this game and code it into a computer language. The user is Player A and the computer Player B.
(f) Two players compete in a computer version of 'Battleships'. The first player enters the coordinates of a battleship as a single digit (X-coordinate) followed by a second single digit (Y-coordinate). The second player then enters the coordinates of the impact of a shell. If the shell strikes the battleship, 'Hit' is displayed. If the shell is not more than 4 units away from the battleship, 'Near miss' is displayed. The second player is allowed an indefinite number of shells until the battleship is hit. (The first player is not allowed to move the ship!)
(g) Two numbers are entered and the largest number which divides into both (the highest common factor) is calculated.

The following examples may require the use of an array.

(h) A short passage of text is entered. The total number of times it contains the letter E is displayed.
(i) A short passage of text is entered. The letter which occurs most is displayed.
(j) Two separate sets of letters are entered, for example {A, C, F, H, M} and {C, H, P, Z}. The intersection of the sets, {C, H}, and the union of the sets, {A, C, F, H, M, P, Z}, are calculated. The order of the letters is not significant.

4 Computing solutions

Summary

This chapter investigates the way in which organizations use information processing tools to enhance all aspects of their operation, from the everyday tasks carried out by employees through to the highest level of decision making by executives. It will be seen that a variety of IT software can be brought to bear upon the work that has to be performed by those employed in an organization.

The nature of data and information is considered as is the way that different levels within the organization will need to utilize specialist software to cope best with the type of information processing required at that level.

Specific software tools are discussed in detail.

4.1 Information and contemporary applications

In everyday English people tend to use the words data and information to mean approximately the same thing. In computing, however, each term is distinguished from the other by being given a more specific meaning. This can be illustrated first by looking at a slightly unusual example which shows how the distinction between the two arises. After this the significance of data and information for organizations will be considered in detail.

The example is taken from astronomy, or rather from the work of one particular astronomer, Frank Drake, who suggested a way in which we on earth could broadcast our existence to potential other intelligent beings on hypothetical planets in orbit around distant stars. Drake showed how a simple picture of a stick-like human being could be coded into a radio signal. This signal could be transmitted by the then relatively new invention, the radio telescope. Although designed to receive natural radio transmissions from space, the radio telescope could also transmit artificial signals from earth. Drake wanted to use a telescope in this way and give aliens a rough idea of how intelligent lifeforms on earth looked. He was limited to a fairly simple signal consisting of only two different signs, like Morse code, sent as pulses. This limitation is useful, however, because it allows a clear distinction to be made between the *data* of the signal and the *information* content of the picture.

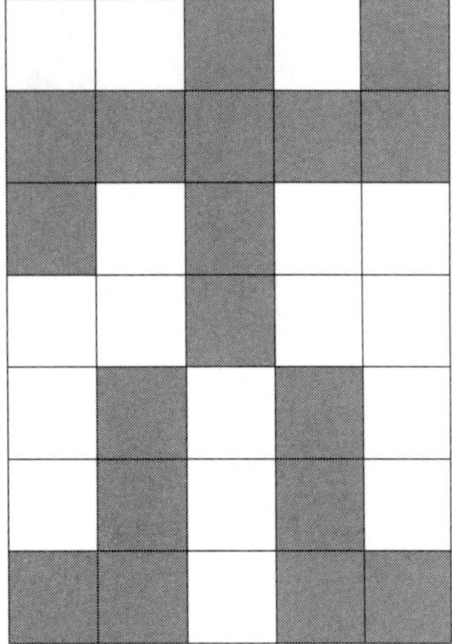

Figure 4.1.1

Frank Drake's stick man was quite detailed, and information about the solar system was included as well. It is easier to demonstrate the way the picture was transmitted if a smaller man is drawn instead. This will be on a grid of 35 squares arranged as seven rows and five columns (Figure 4.1.1).

If filled squares are now coded as a 1 and empty squares as a 0, the picture becomes:

0 0 1 0 1
1 1 1 1 1
1 0 1 0 0
0 0 1 0 0
0 1 0 1 0
0 1 0 1 0
1 1 0 1 1

The stick man can therefore be converted into this single sequence of 35 digits:

0 0 1 0 1 1 1 1 1 1 1 0 1 0 0 0 0 1 0 0 0 1 0 1 0 0 1 0 1 0 1 1 0 1 1

Frank Drake was able to transmit his larger sequence of 1s and 0s as pulses in his radio signal. He hoped that if such a message were picked up by extraterrestrial radio astronomers they would first recognize it as being a message and not some odd natural phenomenon. They would then count the 35 distinct symbols. Drake assumed that the aliens would be familiar with the concept of prime numbers and realize that 35 only factorizes into 5×7. Reassembling the picture would then be simple. Of course the signal would be transmitted repeatedly, and the aliens would have to recognize that the pattern of 35 digits was contained within the overall signal. Some additional pulse would have to indicate where one sequence ended and the next started, but this complication can be ignored here.

The essential feature of this method of coding is that the rectangular grid of squares has both a prime number of rows and a prime number of columns. The aliens count the pulses they receive. Provided that they are reasonably competent mathematicians, and know about prime numbers, they can deduce the number of rows and columns that have been used for the grid. Filling in the sequence given by the radio pulses they are able to recreate the stick man. They would of course have a choice of five rows and seven columns, or seven rows and five columns, but have a 50/50 chance of getting it right the first time.

If instead a rectangular grid of 36 squares had been employed for the initial coding of a stick man figure the following combinations would have been potential rectangular grids to use in decoding the sequence:

2 rows and 18 columns
4 rows and 9 columns
6 rows and 6 columns
9 rows and 4 columns
18 rows and 2 columns

At this point a distinction is drawn between data and information. The initial signal transmitted by Frank Drake and, it is hoped, intercepted by aliens is *raw data* which is then transformed into *meaningful information* by the decoding process of deciding what dimensions the grid should have and shading the appropriate squares. It can be seen that:

- Information is something which is obtained by processing data.
- Information is data which has had a structure imposed upon it.

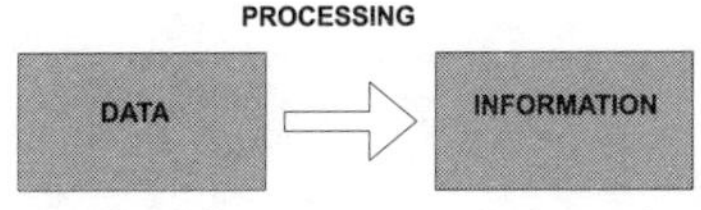

Figure 4.1.2

In the example we have used here this imposition of structure is something which is quite visual and obvious, but in any example of computer processing of data a structure of some kind is imposed.

Schematically we can think of this as shown in Figure 4.1.2.

Question 4.1.1

(a) Assume you have received this radio signal. What will processing convert it into?

0 0 0 0 0 1 0 0 0 0 0 0 0 0 0 0 1 0 0 0 0 0 0 0 1 1 1 1 1 1
1 1 1 1 1 1 1 1 1 1 1 1 1 1 1 1 1 1 1 1 1 1 1 1 1 1 1 0 1 0
0 1 0 1 0 0 1 0 0 0 1 1 0 0 0 1 1 0 0

(b) Decide what is the raw data, the processing carried out and the information obtained in the folllowing situations:

- Using a word processor.
- Downloading a web page.
- Working with a graphics package.

Sources of information

The information used by an organization can come from a wide variety of sources. Some of these will be external to the organization and others will be internal. Much information will also be obtained via the Internet. This is discussed in a subsequent chapter of this book.

The data which is actually processed by a computer must be in digital form, the 1s and 0s of binary arithmetic. However, the way in which initial information appears in everyday life is not in the form of digital raw data. A person may have filled in an A4 question sheet manually. Some of the information will be handwritten. Other information might be as shaded ovals beside printed questions. Neither is digital data at this stage and so is not immediately available for processing. Appropriate methods for entering data into a computer system so that it can be processed are essential. These methods are referred to as *data collection*.

Some data will need to be typed manually into a computer system. This is likely to involve copying from paper documents and has the danger of mistakes occurring. These mistakes are called *transcription errrors* and will lead to the computer system producing incorrect output. Wherever possible it is better to use methods of input which automatically create data in a way that a computer can interpret without manual intervention. These methods are referred to as *data capture*.

There are various techniques used in data capture including *document readers* which are devices able to convert information held on *data capture forms* into the digitized data needed for processing. Data capture forms are carefully designed to be easily understood and completed by people and, at the same time, rapidly read by the document reader. Many people will encounter data capture forms during their everyday business. A typical example might be a questionnaire or a time sheet used for data entry into a payroll system.

Typical methods for document readers include:

- Magnetic ink character recognition.
- Optical character recognition.
- Optical mark recognition.

Key fact

MICR characters have the advantage of remaining readable even if the paper they have been printed on has been roughly handled.

Magnetic Ink Character Recognition (MICR)

This is an early method of data capture adopted by banks, some of the first major commercial organizations to use computers, and therefore reflecting the technology of the period. Everybody should be familiar with MICR as the letters appear on cheques, and some other documents, as rather oddly shaped letters and digits. These are sufficiently like ordinary characters to be easily read by people but are printed using a ferric oxide ink. This can be magnetized during processing and the different shapes of the letters then create varying magnetic fields that can be read automatically by special equipment.

Key fact

OCR is frequently used for *turnaround documents.* These are used in billing systems where an invoice is produced by a computer and sent to the customer, who fills it in. The document is then returned to the organization that issued it and can be read again by the OCR input device. The respective account can then be updated.

Optical Character Recognition (OCR)

This method of data capture, like MICR, has the advantage of producing documents which can be read both by people and by input devices for computers. Note that this is not necessarily the case with data capture. The back of one credit card looks very much like another! When OCR was first introduced the characters that could be read by the input devices had to be written with a particularly distinctive font which exaggerated the differences between one letter and another. With improved pattern recognition technology this is no longer necessary, although the older equipment does survive in those organizations which adopted OCR as a method of data capture.

Optical Mark Recognition (OMR)

In this method of data capture positions on a paper document are filled in with a soft, black pencil. Because these pencil marks are in a known position they can be easily identified when the paper document is fed through a mark sense reader. OMR is used extensively for computer-marked examinations and are therefore familiar to most students.

Other methods for data capture do not require the initial data to be present in the form of a paper document. Some of these methods are:

- Bar codes.
- Magnetic strip.
- Sensors in process control.
- Voice recognition systems.

> **Key fact**
>
> An imaginative use of bar codes is in mobile robotics where an *automatic guided vehicle* (AGV) can scan large bar codes that have been attached to convenient places in its environment and use this information to update the *internal representation* of its position in its guiding software. AGVs can be used for delivering mail in offices and components in factories. They can also be employed as roving security devices on larger sites. A similar technique can be used on roads to allow the position of a vehicle carrying suitable equipment to log its position. This can be of use in highway maintenance.

Bar codes

A bar code is a familiar pattern of thick and thin lines carried on most products. This pattern holds a digitial number which can be read by a laser scanner or, less commonly, a hand-held wand. Bar codes are an essential aspect of *Electronic Point Of Sale Systems* (EPOS). By identifying a product they allow its price and description to be retrieved from a store database. The bill and an itemized till receipt can then be created. The use of bar codes also permits automatic updating of the store's stock levels. This information will be passed on, in the case of multiple stores and supermarkets, to warehouses and used to replenish the stores' shelves as part of a *stock control system.*

Magnetic strip

A magnetic strip is a short length of magnetic tape, typically attached to a credit card, store card, London Underground ticket or similar item, and which stores data magnetically in a similar fashion to a floppy disk. The tape can be read from or written to. (The latter is apparent when an Underground ticket 'knows' the end of its permitted use and does not re-emerge from the card reader incorporated into the turnstyle.)

Sensors in process control

An inportant use of computers in industry is for *process control* in which the state of some production process is automatically monitored by the inclusion of *sensors*. These measure some quantity like temperature, pressure, chemical composition, position of part of a mechanism, etc., and relay data back to a computer or microprocessor. This data may have to be passed through an *analogue to digital converter* to change a continuous signal like the number of milliamps in an electric circuit, into a digital form that the computer can accept. The signal is processed by the computer and an output signal is relayed back to actuators, which might be motors or solenoids, and used to adjust the state of the production process. In this way *feedback* from the system is used to control it. So a vat of chemicals can be maintained within a certain range of temperature and pressure, or the thickness of a sheet of molten glass can be kept within predetermined limits.

The information gathered by the sensors can also be made available for other uses. The quantity of a production can be monitored, for example, and data fed into other systems.

Voice recognition systems

In science fiction films voice recognition is always taken for granted. From Robby in *Forbidden Planet* to the later robots of *Star Wars* and *Terminator*, producers have had no difficulty with the concept of articulate mechanisms using language every bit as fluent as their script writers can mangage. This has unfortunately created the misconception for some people that laptop computers come fully equipped with software that *understands* their voice. It should be realized, of course, that voice recognition is not the same thing as understanding natural language. The latter is still a goal of artificial intelligence (see page 288).

Key fact

The difference bewteen voice recognition and understanding what is said becomes apparent when this classic example is given:

Time flies like an arrow: fruit flies like a banana.

Any future computer system which can parse that sentence correctly will be able to write SF films!

Being able to understand language is not, fortunately, a necessary or even desired capability of a computer system. Voice recognition is quite sufficient. This software, which is able to spell dictated words truly in context, is a useful method of data entry for those people who are unable, or perhaps unwilling, to use a keyboard. Executive information systems (see below) offer voice recognition as one of their facilities. IBM ViaVoice, Dragon Data Systems, and AcuVoice are all examples of commercially available voice recognition software.

Quality of information

Collecting information for use in a computer system is not sufficient. There must be sufficient safeguards in the process by which information is gathered to ensure its *quality*. A traditional saying in the world of computing is 'Garbage in: garbage out'. Although trite, this is true. How the quality of information is maintained is discussed in a later section of this chapter.

Information requirements within an organization

In order to investigate the way in which computer systems can be used to aid the use of information within organizations it is necessary to look first at how information can be classified in general terms. It is possible to view it in terms of its level, its category and its quality.

Information can be categorized according to the use to which it will be put. Three categories emerge when information is viewed in this way. These are strategic, tactical and operational information.

Strategic information will be used by top-level management in making decisions which affect the whole organization and its future. These decisions will tend to be long term and to involve high levels of expenditure. They will include issues like investment, foreign trade, exploring new markets and products, expansion of facilities, the effect of government policy on trade and many other major areas of concern. Strategic information is closely associated with strategic planning. These are the responsibilities of the most influential people within the organization.

Tactical information is involved in the day-to-day running of an organization and the decisions that have to be made by middle management. These decisions will be based upon information which rises up through the organization, as well as upon information coming from outside.

Operational information lies at the bottom of the information gathering process. Typical information here could be the number of units sold at a particular branch of a chain store, or the hours overtime worked by staff in a given department.

According to its category information will be processed with different computer software. Information at the operational, everyday level is likely to involve word processing or spreadsheet software. Tactical information might involve the use of data mining techniques. Strategic information will possibly involve the use of decision support software or perhaps expert systems. Of course it is not possible to specify precise limits to the use of any specific software tool. A word processor is fairly

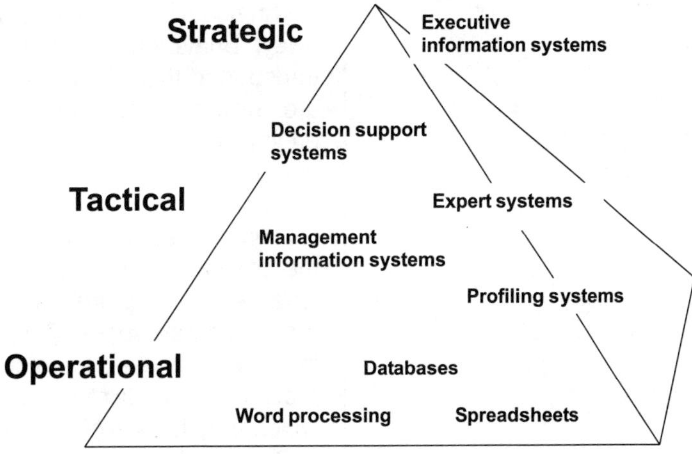

Figure 4.1.3 *Categories of information and some related software*

> ## Key fact
>
> Naturally a diagram like this presents a simplified view of organizational structure but it is a useful guide to the software that is likely to be employed. What the diagram does not indicate is that information also enters from the outside at the strategic and tactical levels. Not all the information processed at these levels has come from the bottom of the pyramid.

ubiquitous and inevitably will find a place in any office or situation. Nevertheless a trend can be discerned between category of information and type of software employed which can be indicated in Figure 4.1.3.

Three aspects of information processing within an organization are indicated by this figure.

- Information can be categorized as being appropriate for three separate levels within an organization: operational, tactical and strategic.
- According to the level different types of software will be used to process the information.
- A 'flow upwards' of information takes place from the bottom of the pyramid to the top. At each level the 'raw data' for processing is in fact the information produced by the lower level.

The way that different software is appropriate for information processing at different levels within this imaginary pyramid can be illustrated by the following scenario.

Bertrand's Boats is a family business which hires out boats to tourists on a series of small lakes surrounding a country town. The lakes are not connected and as a result there are several different fleets of boats, one on each lake.

Tourists who wish to hire boats may phone in their details before visiting. Betrand's Boats request that they state their name, address, telephone contact number and credit card details. They are then issued with a special boat hire number which they use when they visit any one of the lakes.

Each fleet has a resident 'Admiral' who wears a traditional costume and who also logs in each tourist as they arrive at a particular lake. The name of the boat hired is recorded, together with the time at which it is taken out and the time at which it is returned. This information is subsequently used to calculate the total cost of boat hire.

> The boats are serviced at a central boatyard some distance away. Boats from any of the lakes requiring service are transported there by lorry. When work is complete the boats are always transported back to the same 'fleet' at their original lake. Servicing is arranged according to the total number of hours for which the boat has been hired out since the last service.
>
> A timesheet is drawn up for every mechanic employed at the boatyard, noting which boat he/she has worked on, the type of fault repaired and the number of hours that the mechanic has spent altogether working on the repair. This information is used to calculate the mechanic's salary. Each mechanic's hourly rate depends upon the number of years for which they have worked for the firm.
>
> Persistent faults on a particular boat may be used to withdraw it completely from service.

The information used within this organization is considered in terms of the three categories described above. This can be done in the order in which information would be gathered and processed, beginning at the operational level and continuing through to the strategic.

At the operational level tourists will phone in their details. These will be typed into a computer booking system. One way in which this can be done is by the use of an on-screen form onto which relevant details for the tourist's visit can be entered. The design of the form allows different fields in an associated *database* to be updated. Confirmation of the booking, if required, can be posted to the tourist as a report from the database. This information could also be incorporated into a letter produced by a *word processor.*

Further information gathered at the operational level will involve the actual hiring of boats when the tourists visit. The name of the boat, the time of its hire and return, and the tourist's boat hire number will all be noted by the operator. This information might initially be written by hand as a paper document. The operator will probably find it easier to work this way, although it would be possible to carry a hand-held computer of the personal digital assistant type and download to a desktop PC later. If a paper document is used this should match reasonably closely the format adopted by the on-screen form used to enter the information into a database.

Further information at the operational level will include the timesheets collected for the mechanics who service the boats. Calculation of wages will depend upon hours worked, and as stated in the scenario, the length of service with the organization. A *spreadsheet* or a dedicated *payroll package* could be used for this. Boat servicing will also be used to update the service history held for the boats. This will be another example of a database.

When the boats are serviced mechanics might decide to use fault-finding software based upon an *expert system.* This allows the mechanic to follow a sequence of on-screen questions about how the engine is behaving. From this automated reasoning will suggest what the possible fault is. On the diagram expert systems are shown situated at the tactical level but they can be used at the operational level as well.

Servicing of the boats is a good example of the way information flows up from the operational level of the organization to the tactical. This occurs when there is evidence of a recurring fault on a particular boat which leads to the decision to withdraw the boat from the lake where it has been operating.

At the tactical level information that has been gathered about tourists could be processed by a *profiling system* which would create a picture of the 'typical' tourist visiting the area. This information would be useful for marketing and advertising. Information from a database held about previous tourists would be available for mail shots.

Information from mechanics' timesheets could be used in a *human resources information system* and used in planning staff training or predicting future recruitment.

At the strategic level *decision support software* could help in planning future expansion of Bertrands' Boats, while an *executive information system* would help management have an overview of the firm's viability comparing the profits made by the separate fleets of boats and examining in detail those aspects of the firm's operations which caused concern.

Structured, semi-structured and unstructured decisions

Another way of viewing the flow of information through an organization is in terms of the amount of autonomy permitted when decisions have to be made. Decisions can be viewed as:

- Structured
- Semi-structured
- Unstructured

At the operational level the type of decision that individual employees are able to make will be fairly constrained. These structured decisions will follow a pattern that has been laid down for them. A certain number of paper forms arrive on a desk. Somebody reads them and types relevant details into a form for a database. The amount of creative, free decision making allowed is not great.

At the tactical level more freedom is possible when making a decision. Perhaps a particular product line is selling less well than it has in the past. Should fewer units be displayed in store? Are there alternative brand names that could be considered? These are examples of semi-structured decisions. Imaginative contribution is possible from the middle manager, but there is still some constraint operating and decisions have to be made within the amount of freedom possible at this level.

Unstructured decisions can be made at the strategic level. Here imagination is restricted only by available finance, government legislation, the views of shareholders and other reasonably broad considerations. Apart from these, senior executives can let their thoughts rove widely.

Question 4.1.2

Read through the description of Bertrand's Boats again. How would you analyse decisions that have to be made in terms of structured, semi-structured and unstructured?

Cross-functional information systems

As well as analysing organizations in terms of operational, tactical and strategic level information processing, different functions can be identified within an overall organization. These can be classified as:

- Accounts
- Finance
- Human resources
- Marketing
- Production

These different functions or departments will tend to have their own information processing systems. For example, the central registry in a college will store details of students on a database and this information will also be of use for course administrators attempting to plan room allocation for classes.

Obviously efficiency can be enhanced if it is possible for one system to be able to access information stored in another. A cross-functional information system allows this to take place.

4.2 Information processing tools

The software used in organizations will now be considered in terms of:

- operational level software
- tactical level software
- strategic level software

Operational level software

Software that is found at the operational level in organizations includes:

- Text processing
- Spreadsheets
- Computer graphics
- Databases

Text processing

Word processing and *desktop publishing* are used at the operational level in the day-to-day running of an organization. Word processing is needed to produce letters, internal memos, email, invoices and other documents. Desktop publishing can be used to create newsletters and general information sheets for both internal and external use.

Spreadsheets

Spreadsheets can be used at the operational level within an organization to perform repetitive calculations and create tables and charts. The what-if aspect of spreadsheet modelling (see Unit 3) also makes them useful at the tactical level.

Computer graphics

Computer graphics can be used to enhance many documents and highlight the results of calculations.

Presentation graphics is described in more detail later in this chapter.

Databases

The gathering and analysis of data is a significant operation in most organizations. Early databases used a *hierarchical* tree structure which was relatively easy for programmers to design and for which efficient algorithms could be designed which were not too demanding on processing power. However, such databases did not reflect the way in which data tends to be acquired and used in real life. They were rigid, not permitting new links to be created between data items as required. *Network* data models were a little more flexible but databases did not become versatile business tools until the *relational data model* was invented by Dr Codd. A relational database stores data in a human-like way, as a series of cross-referenced, two-dimensional tables of rows and columns. One table can easily be linked with several others according to the nature of a current *query* that needs to be made about the content of the database. These queries, and the tables themselves, can be created by means of a portable *Structured Query Language* (SQL). Commercial relational databases like Microsoft Access and Oracle also allow databases to be created, queried and updated via a simple graphic user interface. Databases can be used at the operational level of an organization and also feed data upwards into data warehouses and data marts.

Tactical level software

Some of the software likely to be used in an organization at the tactical level includes:

- Data warehousing
- Data mart
- Data mining software
- Management information systems
- Telecommunications
- Human resource information systems
- Profiling systems
- Presentation graphics

Data warehouse

A *data warehouse* is a collection of databases. Unlike a typical database, which is used in everyday transactions and therefore updated frequently, a data warehouse acts more like an archive and is updated at less frequent intervals. The value of a data warehouse lies in its potential for decision making. Unlike a database used at the operational level, it can be used for tactical and strategic level decisions. It does this by aggregating data from the individual databases which supply it, allowing an overall picture to be built up. In order to create this objective view, it obtains its data from the whole of an organization and from the wide range of databases used throughout it.

As the data to be used in the data warehouse is coming from different sources there is no guarantee that it is going to fit together conveniently into an overview without some prior manipulation. In fact five distinct stages can be identified in the processing of data from individual databases to form a data warehouse.

- The data is *loaded* from the different databases.
- It is then *converted* into a common format. Perhaps some of the incoming data has been held in IBM's EBCDIC format and this might need to be translated into ASCII for the data warehouse.
- The data is *scrubbed*. This involves detecting errors and correcting them or perhaps inserting default values where values are missing and their absence would cause subsequent errors.
- The data is *transformed* by aggregation and summarizing. A whole set of figures might be reduced to a single value, just as a child's scores in a set of class examinations could be reduced to a single position, i.e. 'Jenny came second in Form 2A'.
- The data is *placed in the data warehouse*.

Data mart

A *data mart* is a data warehouse which does not extract information from the whole organization but instead from a single department, or a single function, within it.

Data mining

Searching a data warehouse or data mart for useful information is termed data mining. Recall the distinction between data and information. Identifying significant patterns in a mass of data can be extremely difficult and *data mining software* can be used to help.

Management information systems

A *management information system* is a set of integrated software packages which can be used by middle management at the tactical level within an organization. It is designed to produce:

- *Summary reports*, which give an overview of a set of regular events within the organization, like production figures for a given plant.
- *Exception reports*, which indicate some unusual circumstance, such as identical faults developing in a number of industrial robots within a short period of time.

Telecommunications

The use of telecommunications in the operation of an organization has such a significant impact that a separate account is given in Unit 9.

Human resource information systems

The term *human resources* is used to denote all aspects of the ways in which an organization's employees affect, or are affected by, the organization. The use of the word 'resource' in particular stresses how the role of people within an organization is as important as any other, physical, resource it possesses.

Within most organizations beyond a moderate size there will therefore be a human resources department, often still under its more traditional name of *personnel*. Many of the functions of the personnel department can be aided by the use of information technology. In particular a *Human Resources Information System* (HRIS) is the name given to dedicated software which helps to keep track of the wealth of personnel information which will be involved in a large organization. Examples of such software include Visual Personnel and Abra.

The use of artificial intelligence techniques (see later in this unit) can be incorporated into an HRIS to create an effective *hybrid system*.

Specific ways in which a human resource information system help a personnel department include:

- The gathering and analysis of data and its use in the production of appropriate reports.
- The creation of reports with in-built standard templates.
- Finding appropriate staff in areas where there is a shortage of specific skills.
- The provision of information for management information systems.

Specifically the personnel department will be responsible for, or have an overview of:

- Recruitment
- Staff details
- Training and appraisal
- Progression of staff
- Transfer or retirement
- Staff welfare
- Legislation

Recruitment

This will require the *advertising* of vacancies, both internally and externally. Specialist publications as well as local and national newspapers would be the location for external advertising. An overview of the organization must be produced, a definition of the *job specifications*, and an application form, all to be forwarded to those who respond to the advertising. Once completed applications are received, personnel must assemble a *short list* together with a résumé of applicants in order to guide the interviewing panel. After the interviews have been conducted personnel will be responsible for the *induction* of new staff appointed. Ideally an HRIS can help through all of these stages.

Staff details

Personal details of staff will need to be stored and work schedules and timetables provided for the employees. This responsibility might devolve to individual departments. Payroll software will be used to produce salary statements and arrange payment.

Training and appraisal

The employer needs to make sure that staff are employed effectively. This will involve providing the opportunity for *staff training*. This might take place on a voluntary basis in which the employer allows members of the organization to attend external training sessions, or part-time courses at local colleges. The staff member participating in such a scheme can be helped by being allowed time away from their post. In some cases training costs will be met as well, or a contribution made towards tuition costs by the employer. In this situation the employee will be expected to provide evidence of attending the course and the employer might even request a refund of some of the course fees paid if the employee fails to gain an agreed qualification.

Other training might be non-voluntary when, for example, a whole department closes down for a short in-service training day and external lecturers are brought in for an intensive session in which specific staff skills are tackled. Attending the training session is regarded as part of the staff's paid employment.

Employees may also be subject to *staff appraisal* in order to identify at an early stage problems which may become more serious if remedial action is not taken. Appraisal may take the form of observation, examination of records or interview and should lead on to some form of training or other support.

Progression of staff

Internal promotion may take place according to satisfactory reports and individual appraisal. Automatic salary incrememts may also occur.

Transfer or retirement

Many organizations will now expect employees who are leaving to participate in a leaving or *exit interview*. This is principally conducted to help the employer, although naturally it is made as friendly as possible and can be part of a fond farewell. Certain essential details will need to be included, like the return of keys, identity cards, etc., but the main purpose of the interview is to discover whether there is any underlying reason why the member of staff has decided to depart. Their reason might of course be obvious, perhaps increased salary or status elsewhere, or the urge for career progression. On the other hand there may be other factors like uncomfortable or inconvenient accommodation, uncongenial colleagues, an insensitive line manager, excessive workload or other factors of which the human resources department should be informed. Monitoring *staff turnover* is an important role for an HRIS.

Organizations can find themselves in circumstances in which they have to make some employees redundant. *Redundancy* is again an issue for human resources as legal commitments have to be kept.

Staff who reach *retirement* age before finding a different job, or being made redundant, will expect to have been given at an early stage in their career advice on pensions and *pension schemes*. Human resources may also give specific help with general retirement issues as well.

Staff welfare

It is vital that an organization safeguards the *health and safety* of its employees. Legal issues are involved and a health and safety officer should be aware of, and be able to seek the rapid rectification, of any situation which could compromise them. Typical problems could range from loose window catches to unsound wiring. Legal compensation to affected staff might result from neglect.

One way in which management can obtain information about the welfare of their staff is by the use of a *satisfaction survey* in which questionnaires are completed. These are, of course, anonymous and so staff who might feel embarrassed about raising issues personally can feel able to bring to management's attention matters which are causing concern. Naturally the design of the questionnaire, and selection and wording of the questions, is critical.

Staff welfare can also be monitored via *job satisfaction interviews*. These can take place on a regular basis and would be expected to occur at least once a year. Employees are interviewed on an individual basis, perhaps by a line manager or by a member of the personnel department and have the opportunity to indicate any problems they might have encountered since their previous interview. These interviews can lead to a re-evaluation of the amount and type of work expected of the employee and possibly indicate the need for counselling about *stress management*.

In a society which no longer tolerates unfair treatment on the basis of ethnicity or gender it is important that *equal opportunities* for staff are closely monitored. This is especially important when internal promotion takes place.

Prevention is always regarded as better than cure, but the need for a cure sometimes becomes inevitable. A situation can arise when the human resources department needs to be able to resolve *grievancies* and/ or participate in discussion with an employee's *union representative*.

Legislation

One role of an HRIS is ensure that the organization complies with current national legislation affecting employees. For example, the following Acts of Parliament are relevant within the UK:

- Health and Safety at Work Act (1974)
- Sex Discrimination Acts (1975, 1986)
- Disability and Discrimination Act (1995)
- Employment Rights Act (1996)
- Working Time Directive (1993)

Profiling systems

A *profiling system* allows data gathered about a group of people to be analysed in a way which will discover which of them meets a particular set of criteria.

Matching people to predetermined criteria can be illustrated by considering a situation in which only a small number of people are involved, and only a few relevant facts are known about each.

The manager of a fun fair is choosing somebody to be in charge of a new ride. This is a water flume in which large plastic rafts are dragged by machinery to the top of a high prefabricated metal tower. The rafts are then detached and allowed to slide down a long flume, carried along by a combination of gravity and the water rushing past. At the bottom the boats float across a landing pond until they can be hauled in by the ride operator, who has to stand, with a long boat hook, on the edge of a pontoon floating in the water.

The ride operator has to sell tickets to the customers and give them the correct change. This must be done quickly, of course, as the manager does not want long queues building up at the ticket booth. When the rafts land in the pool they are grabbed with the hook by the ride operator, who needs to stand on the edge of a pontoon floating in the water.

Sometimes the machinery jams and this can leave a raft and its passengers at some considerable height above the ground. Although the manager realizes that a situation like this needs the involvement of the emergency services, secretly he wonders whether a nimble-footed assistant scrambling up with a monkey wrench might save a lot of undesired media attention.

His secretary advertises the job vacancy and from the *curriculum vitae* sent in draws up this grid showing the skills and interests offered by the applicants.

1st name	2nd name	GCSE 1	GCSE 2	GCSE 3	HOBBY 1	HOBBY 2
Angela	Smith	Art	French	History	Theatre	Dancing
Bradley	Carr	Maths	English	German	Clubbing	Heavy metal
Clara	Thompson	Maths	English	History	Swimming	Rock climbing
Dean	Foreman	French	Art	Music	DIY	Swimming
Eleanor	Jansen	Latin	French	English	Walking	Knitting

Even before the interviews the manager has a pretty sure idea about who to employ. Just a quick glance at the table of information about the five applicants shows that Angela Smith, despite her various achievements, does not show any specific skill which matches the abilities which would help the ride operator in the role described above. Bradley Carr does have a maths GCSE which suggests that he would be proficient in calculating the correct change quickly. Sadly he does not match the requirements in any other way. Similarly Dean and Eleanor can be ignored. Clara Thompson, however, not only has maths GCSE but in addition her hobbies of rock climbing and swimming will be useful for a fairground ride involving great heights and water. If customers either get stuck on the way up, or fall in after coming back down, Clara is ideally suited to rise to the challenge!

This, of course, is deliberately intended as a very light-hearted introduction to profiling systems. Nevertheless it should indicate how a fairly mechanical process can sort through information about a large group of people. In the example above so little information is involved, and the necessary matching so obvious, that the best solution is mere inspection of the table. This would not be quite so feasible with a large number of candidates and a broad range of criteria upon which to judge them.

The human element is not eliminated in the creation of a profiling system. Sensible and relevant criteria have to be included in the system from the beginning if the software is to have any chance of producing plausible results. The situation for which the profile is being created needs to be analysed carefully in order to select the correct skills, qualifications, interests, personality traits and other significant distinguishing features of the individuals to incorporate into the system.

Some areas in which profiling systems are appropriate are listed below. The relevance of profiling systems to human resources will be evident.

- Selection of staff
- Employee productivity
- Organization of staff training
- Criminal investigations
- Airline reservations

Ethical issues are clearly involved in the use of profiling systems. A significant example of this is the application of *Computer Assisted Passenger Screening* (CAPS) software in airline reservation systems. The intention behind the introduction of CAPS is the prevention of terrorist attacks upon aircraft. Information obtained during ticket reservation is matched against criteria which supposedly highlights those potential passengers more likely to be terrorists. Such criteria would include:

- the passenger's last name;
- flight destination;
- the passenger's final destination;
- whether it is a one-way trip;
- purchase of the ticket by cash rather than credit card;
- whether the purchase is last minute;
- reservation of a rental car.

It is conceivable that the results of selection on such criteria would indeed have a reasonable chance of identifying a terrorist, if one were attempting to reserve a flight. It is also quite obvious that implicit discrimination is present which would place an unfair burden of suspicion on some ethnic groups. This becomes explicit when the passenger arrives at the airline ticket counter and discovers that an impersonal computer system has singled them out for embarrassing security checks on personal belongings. An ethical issue has arisen because the assumed physical security of the whole passenger list is being set against the affront to an individual.

The application of ethical standards within profiling is of considerable concern and various bodies are actively involved in encouraging a high level of integrity amongst those responsible for profiling systems. The Academy of Behavioural Profiling is one such organization. Specifically involved with the use of criminal profiling, this organization suggests guidelines that include avoiding preconceptions and biases, encouraging whistle-blowing on unethical conduct, and avoiding extrapolating results beyond their area of relevance.

General ethical considerations in the use of computer software are explored later in this chapter.

To extend the material of the previous chapter the example of a profiling system will be used as further practice in problem solving and the development of program code. The scenario at the beginning of this section is now presented as Visual Basic code followed by an account of how the problem has been solved practically.

```
Option Explicit
Private Sub Command1_Click()
'Profiling program

Dim strFirstName(5) As String
Dim strSecondName(5) As String
Dim strGcse1(5) As String
Dim strGcse2(5) As String
Dim strGcse3(5) As String
Dim strHobby1(5) As String
Dim strHobby2(5) As String
Dim intMatch(5) As Integer

Dim intCounter As Integer
Dim intMaximum As Integer
Dim intPerson As Integer

'Enter applicant details
For intCounter = 1 To 5
  PicDisplay.Cls

  'Show applicant number
  PicDisplay.Print "Applicant"; intCounter

  'Enter first name
  strFirstName(intCounter) = InputBox("Enter first name", , ,
    6500, 5500)

  'Enter second name
  strSecondName(intCounter) = InputBox("Enter second name", , ,
    6500, 5500)

  'Enter first GCSE
  strGcse1(intCounter) = InputBox("Enter first GCSE", , , 6500,
    5500)
  'Check for matching criterion
  If strGcse1(intCounter) = "Maths" Then
    intMatch(intCounter) = intMatch(intCounter) + 1
  End If

  'Enter second GCSE
  strGcse2(intCounter) = InputBox("Enter second GCSE", , , 6500,
    5500)
  'Check for matching criterion
```

```
If strGcse2(intCounter) = "Maths" Then
    intMatch(intCounter) = intMatch(intCounter) + 1
End If

'Enter third GCSE
strGcse3(intCounter) = InputBox("Enter third GCSE", , , 6500, 5500)
'Check for matching criterion
If strGcse3(intCounter) = "Maths" Then
    intMatch(intCounter) = intMatch(intCounter) + 1
End If

'Enter first hobby
strHobby1(intCounter) = InputBox("Enter first hobby", , , 6500.
```

Program documentation

Arrays are required to hold the information that will be typed in for the five applicants. These will store the first and second names, the three GCSE subjects and the two hobbies. The arrays are strFirstName(), strSecondName(), strGcse1(), strGcse2(), strGcse3(), strHobby1() and strHobby2().

```
Option Explicit
Private Sub Command1_Click()
'Profiling program

Dim strFirstName(5) As String
Dim strSecondName(5) As String
Dim strGcse1 (5) As String
Dim strGcse2 (5) As String
Dim strGcse3 (5) As String
Dim strHobby1 (5) As String
Dim strHobby2 (5) As String
```

A separate integer array, intMatch(), is declared to hold the number of 'points' each applicant will be allocated for matching one of the criteria.

```
Dim intMatch (5) As Integer
```

Three further integer variables are required by the program. These are intCounter, which will be used as a loop control variable, intMaximum, which will be used to determine which applicant achieves the closest match to the in-built criteria, and intPerson, which will indicate the location in the strFirstName() and strSecondName() arrays of the selected applicant.

```
Dim intCounter As Integer
Dim intMaximum As Integer
Dim intPerson As Integer
```

A For Next loop now repeats five times to allow all the information about the five applicants to be typed into the arrays.

```
'Enter applicant details
For intCounter = 1 To 5
PicDisplay.Cls
```

The number of the applicant is displayed to help the user enter the information.

```
'Show applicant number
PicDisplay.Print "Applicant"; intCounter
```

The first name is entered for each person.

```
'Enter first name
strFirstName(intCounter) = InputBox("Enter first name", , , 6500,
5500)
```

The second name is entered.

```
'Enter second name
strSecondName (intCounter) = InputBox("Enter second name", , ,
6500, 5500)
```

The first GCSE is entered. At this point the subject typed can be compared with 'Maths'. If the two strings are the same the corresponding array element in intMatch() is incremented by 1 to record the fact that the applicant has matched the criterion.

```
'Enter first GCSE
strGcse1(intCounter) = InputBox("Enter first GCSE", , , 6500,
5500)
'Check for matching criterion
If strGcse1(intCounter) = "Maths" Then
intMatch(intCounter) = intMatch (intCounter) + 1
End If
```

A similar check on the second GCSE is carried out as soon as the subject is typed. As the original table of information did not restrict the column in which Maths could be entered the check must be repeated at this point.

```
'Enter second GCSE
strGcse2(intCounter) = InputBox ("Enter second GCSE", , , 6500,
5500)
'Check for matching criterion
If strGcse2(intCounter) = "Maths" Then
intMatch(intCounter) = intMatch(intCounter) + 1
End If
```

The check is performed again for the third GCSE. Now if the applicant has Maths in any of the three columns on the original table it will have contributed to the value of intMatch().

```
'Enter third GCSE
strGcse3(intCounter) = InputBox ("Enter third GCSE", , , 6500,
5500)
'Check for matching criterion
If strGcse3(intCounter) = "Maths" Then
intMatch(intCounter) = intMatch(intCounter) + 1
End If
```

The first hobby is typed. The criterion for a hobby is that it should be either Swimming or Rock climbing in order to contribute to the applicant's matching score and so a double condition containing Or is used.

```
'Enter first hobby
strHobby1(intCounter) = InputBox ("Enter first hobby", , , 6500,
5500)
'Check for matching criterion
If strHobby1(intCounter) = "Swimming" Or strHobby2 (intCounter) =
'Rock climbing' Then
intMatch(intCounter) = intMatch(intCounter) + 1
End If
```

The same double condition applies for the second hobby.

```
'Enter second hobby
strHobby2 (intCounter) = InputBox ("Enter second hobby", , ,
6500, 5500)
'Check for matching criterion
If strHobby2(intCounter) = "Swimming" Or strHobby2(intCounter) =
"Rock climbing" Then
intMatch(intCounter) = intMatch(intCounter) + 1
End If

Next intCounter
```

After all the information has been entered for the five applicants the values that have been accumulating in the intMatch() array will determine which applicant has the closest match to the preselected criteria. All that is required is that the maximum value in this array is found. This can be done in a second For Next loop which displays again the information that has been entered. At the same time this loop is able to determine the greatest value in the intMatch() array by making a note of the greatest value found so far as the loop repeats. It does this by comparing each value in turn with the current value of the variable intMaximum, initially assigned a value of zero. By the end of the loop this variable will show which applicant matches the most criteria.

The loop will again repeat five times.

```
'Display results
PicDisplay.Cls
intMaximum = 0
For intCounter = 1 To 5
```

All the information is printed from the arrays, including the intMatch() array. Showing this value will help in the 'accountability' of the program.

```
PicDisplay.Print strFirstName(intCounter); " ";
PicDisplay.Print strSecondName(intCounter)
PicDisplay.Print strGcse1(intCounter); " ";
PicDisplay.Print strGcse2(intCounter); " ";
PicDisplay.Print strGcse3(intCounter)
PicDisplay.Print strHobby1(intCounter); " ";
PicDisplay.Print strHobby2(intCounter)
PicDisplay.Print "Match ="; intMatch(intCounter)
```

The value of intMatch() for the applicant currently identified by the loop control variable, intCounter, is compared with the variable intMaximum. This will hold the 'greatest value found so far'. Although intMaximum begins as 0 it will acquire the first non-zero value held in the intMatch() array. After that it will acquire any value in intMatch() which is greater than the current value of intMaximum. This means that by the end of the loop intMaximum has the greatest of all the values in the array.

```
'Find greatest match
If intMatch(intCounter) > intMaximum Then
  intMaximum = intMatch(intCounter)
```

This by itself is not sufficient. It is not the maximum value in intMatch() which needs to be displayed but the applicant associated with this value. This can be done by making a note of the loop control variable at the same time as the value of intMaximum is updated. The loop control variable's value is therefore assigned to the further variable intCounter. Obviously this will change each time that intMaximum does, but by the end of the loop intPerson will be able to identify the appropriate applicant in the strFirstName() and str SecondName() arrays.

```
  intPerson = intCounter
End If

Next intCounter
```

Outside the loop this person can be displayed.

```
'Display person chosen
PicDisplay.Print strFirstName(intPerson); " ";
PicDisplay.Print strSecondName(intPerson); " ";
PicDisplay.Print "is selected."

End Sub
```

A typical display of this program will be like that shown in Figure 4.2.1.

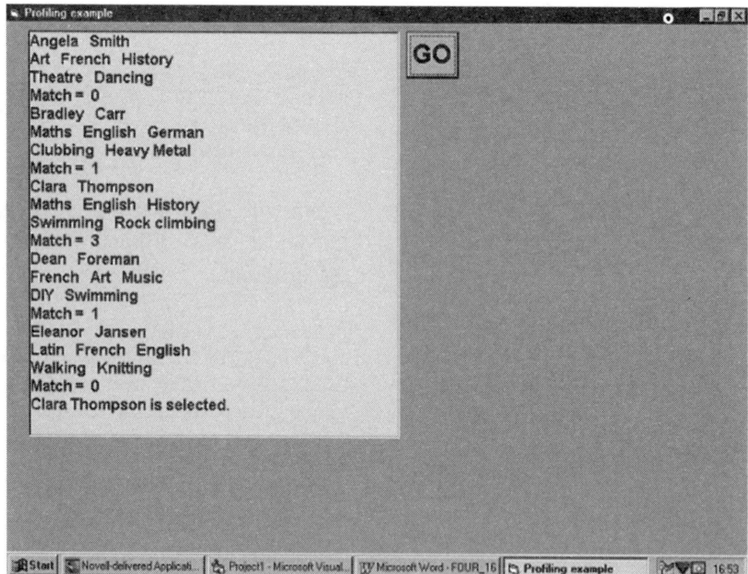

Figure 4.2.1

Presentation graphics

It is important for information to be disseminated rapidly within an organization. This might be achieved via memos or internal email on an individual basis, but if a group needs to be addressed at a meeting *presentation graphics* is an appropriate software tool to use. This has replaced the traditional white board, flip chart or overhead projector as a method for showing a large number of people prepared information. Unlike these former methods, presentation graphics has the advantage of attractive, lively displays which can even include animation. The person developing the presentation can work at their own computer,

> **Key fact**
>
> Presentation graphics frequently takes the form of a *slide show* in which individual screens created can be shown in sequence just like conventional slides, with the added attraction of various types of computer generated dissolve from one slide to the next.

taking time to edit and perfect what they are going to show. The whole presentation then fits conveniently onto a floppy disk which can be taken to a meeting far more conveniently than acetate foils or a flip chart. Also an earlier presentation can be easily updated to deal with new situations as they arise. Presentation graphics are even now expected at many interviews and unfamiliarity with the technique is a clear disadvantage for candidates.

The hardware needed for presentation graphics is a computer, ideally a laptop as meetings are likely to take place in a location some distance from the presenter's office or workstation, and a *data projector*. It is assumed that a projection screen is also available.

Features included in typical presentation graphics software are:

- Production of graphs and charts from numerical data.
- Slide show facility.
- Inclusion of output from digital cameras.
- Multimedia displays.

Typical commercial packages are Aldus Persuasion and Microsoft Powerpoint (Figure 4.2.2).

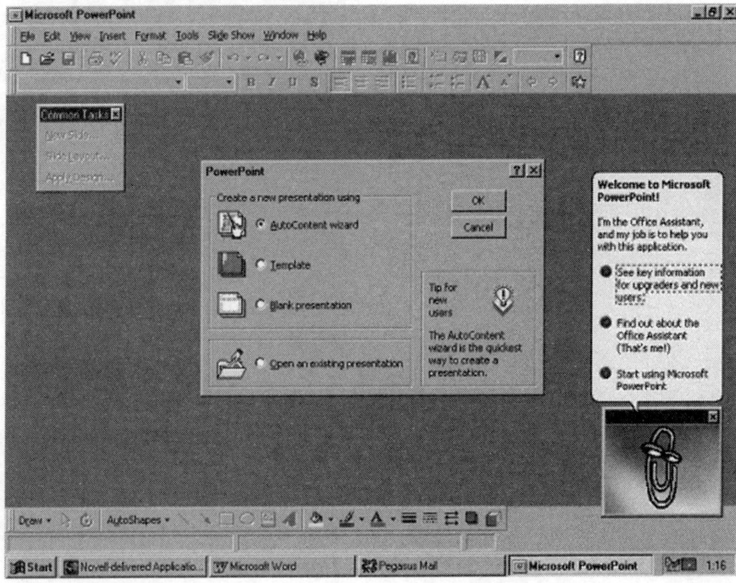

Figure 4.2.2

In order to create a simple PowerPoint slide show the user could work through the following stages, guided by the on-screen prompts:

Blank presentation
Select new slide
Apply design
Add information as a Text Box
New slide

The last two stages are repeated until sufficient slides have been made for the presentation. All the slides can then be viewed simultaneously on screen.

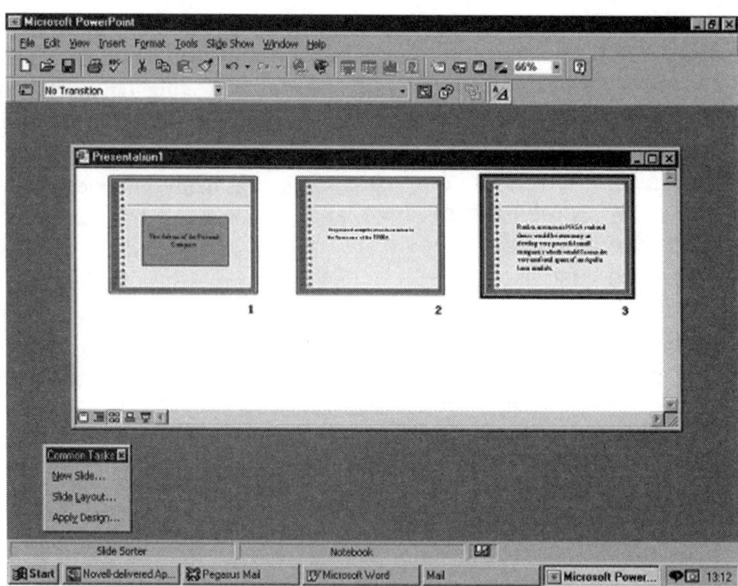

Figure 4.2.3

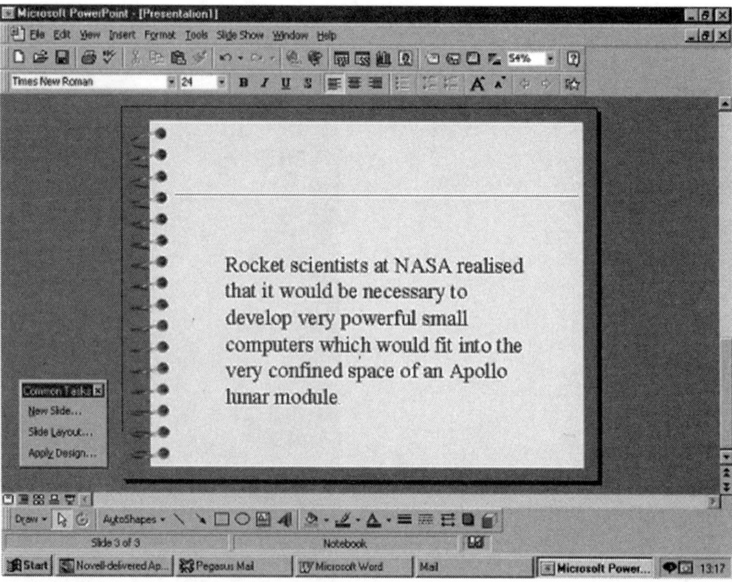

Figure 4.2.4

Question 4.2.1

Working with small groups of other students, prepare two presentations on a selected topic. One should use presentation graphics software, the other traditional methods. Compare the advantages and disadvantages of each.

Typical stages in the production of a PowerPoint presentation are shown in Figures 4.2.3 and 4.2.4.

Strategic level software

Upper echelons of management are in a position where they do not need to scrutinize every detail that their employees have to consider at the operational level. The information they receive has been suitably processed by intervening software at the tactical level and this allows management to concentrate upon decision making aided, for example, by executive information systems which provide an overview of all operations within the organization. The decisions that managers make will therefore be facilitated by information which, although ultimately based upon a foundation of commonplace events at the operational level, has been converted into a form which presents a clear picture of the organization as a whole.

Key fact

Reduction of a large amount of information to its essential details is increasingly necessary in a society which suffers from information overload. Before computers were an everyday tool, management would be have to be protected from superfluous information by the skill of secretarial staff. A personal secretary's role would involve shielding their employer from unnecessary work. They would expertly filter out the unimportant and let a manager concentrate upon managerial decisions. A similar function can now be performed by dedicated software which allows a large amount of information to be condensed into a form which permits rapid, but informed, decision making to take place.

The reason why strategic level tools are required is that senior management requires more than just the aggregated information that traditional software tools have been able to provide. It is important that executives are able to have both an overview of an organization's performance and also the ability to investigate what is occurring lower down to create the situation that they observe. Software at the strategic level therefore needs to be able to achieve both of these functions.

Here the types of software tool available at the 'top of the information pyramid' will be considered, systems which provide assistance for senior management concerned with broad long-term planning affecting the whole organization. These software tools are often referred to as *intelligent support systems*. This is because the software itself needs to be able to act in a semi-autonomous fashion and produce refined information upon which decisions can be taken. Specific types of software to be investigated are:

- Executive information systems
- Decision support systems
- Artificial intelligence

The last of these will be discussed in terms of the two specific areas of:

- Expert systems
- Neural networks

Do recall that it is not possible to pigeon hole software explicitly at a particular level and that use can be made of the same type of software at other places in the information pyramid. An example of this has already been observed in the way that expert system software is versatile enough to be used at more than one level.

Executive information systems

An executive information system allows a manager to see the results of an automatic analysis of a large amount of information. This analysis is presented in a way which aids a rapid appraisal of a situation and helps an informed decision to be made.

An executive information system contains various components to allow it to perform this role. These will include:

- Production of summary reports
- Use of graphics
- Exception reporting
- Drill-down
- Trend reports
- Access to external as well as internal information
- 'What-if' situations
- Communications

An executive information system is designed to be used by people who although experienced in the operation of their organization are not necessarily computer literate. They may have limited keyboard skills. Easy navigation through the system is therefore essential, often using touch-sensitive screens and voice commands.

The system presents information in a way which permits the overall situation to be appraised quickly. Particular areas of concern are then open to rapid investigation by the process of *drill-down.* This allows executive personnel to go to the root cause of some aspect of the organization's performance which the overview has brought to their attention. They can then quickly ascertain what precisely is present in lower level data to create the problem that they have noted. Also termed *hot spotting*, drill-down permits the manager to home in on particular areas within the organization, going right down to the operational level if necessary, and investigate discrepancies or 'blips in the data' which may be of concern.

An executive information system allows information to be timely. This is one of the traits of good information. The ability of the system to extract information rapidly from a number of separate sources within the organization, to collate it, and to produce an easily assimilated summary report, makes it particularly easy for the executive to acquire an overview of the current situation quickly enough to act effectively. Use of traditional IT systems is less likely to provide the immediate information that the executive requires to do this.

Note that the inclusion of confidential data within an executive information system can be a disadvantage since it can restrict the extent to which the system is used.

Naturally the term 'executive information system' is a generic one and there are many different applications of this software category according to the type of organization involved and the sort of decision making that is going to take place. Examples of executive information systems include:

- Human resources
- Quality management
- Productivity

Decision support systems

A decision support system allows decision making to take place in situations which cannot be clearly described in advance. It takes in information that is both internal to the organization and external to it and combines this with a variety of appropriate models. These can be financial, statistical, marketing, human resource or production. This allows 'what-if' questions to be asked. A decision support system will therefore require three major components:

- A database management system which will allow access to all relevant information.
- Models of the various situations involved.
- A user interface which can provide graphics, allow dialogues and generate reports.

Features of decision support systems are:

- They are able to perform a greater degree of analysis than is possible with software used at the operational and tactical level.
- They can deal with semi-structured decisions.
- They can combine internal and external information.
- They deal with 'what-if' situations.
- They are user-friendly.

Question 4.2.2

Williams Educational is a publishing organization which has grown considerably over the years. It began in the late nineteenth century when a tutor to Lord Williams began selling hand-copied Latin 'cribs' to students at a neighbouring public school. His success led him to opening a small bookshop and printing business, adopting his former employer's name as his own. Over the following century successive generations have been extremely successful in expanding the family business. Williams Educational now has large academic bookstores in most university towns plus a chain of smaller branches throughout the country.

The managers of these smaller stores are encouraged to monitor the popular taste in fiction and leisure interests. They sell local history books and frequently stock titles inspired by current museum displays. These shops also reflect television programmes, including 'soaps' and blockbuster documentaries and sell spin-off merchandise as well as books.

The academic shops are mainly concerned with stocking books which match reading lists provided by heads of school at the university. A gentleman's agreement also ensures that they retain one or two copies of publications by local lecturers hoping for career advancement.

Recently Williams Educational has been producing school revision textbooks published in interactive CD-ROM format, and are now keen on becoming involved in distance learning in collaboration with one university.

Management are increasingly concerned about the threat of a hostile takeover bid by a large American conglomerate, Leroy Enterprises, which controls a number of publishing and television production companies and are wondering whether to enter negotiations themselves for a merger with Electric Cat, a profitable UK publisher of electronic games.

Investigate the possible application of decision support software for Williams Educational considering:

(a) The use of database management.
(b) Internal and external sources of information.
(c) Modelling requirements.

Artificial intelligence

Artificial Intelligence, inevitably abbreviated to AI, is a branch of computer science which attempts to produce in a computer system characteristics which, if produced by a person, would be regarded as evidence for rational thought.

The major practical impact of AI upon the world, beyond pure research or future Martian robots, is in two areas of AI, *expert systems* and *neural networks*. Below the application of both of these to the commercial world will be investigated. First a short history of AI is given to indicate how expert systems and neural networks developed from AI research

Key fact

No computer has succeeded in passing an unrestricted Turing test and it is only in limited areas of discourse, where the subjects for conversation are severely restricted, that any progress has been made.

The history of AI is almost as long as that of computing itself, since *Alan Turing*, one of the major contributors to the invention of the computer, firmly believed that the creation of intelligent artefacts was simply a matter of time. He predicted that by the current century computers would exist which would be capable of passing what has since become known as the *Turing test*. In this a person tries to decide whether a conversation, carried out remotely via a 1940s teletype, is being conducted with another human being or with a computer. If it proved impossible to come to a conclusion then Turing felt the computer should be regarded as capable of a human level of thought.

The concept of the Turing test has been subjected to considerable philosophical criticism, notably by the American philosopher *John Searle*. In his *Chinese room argument*, Searle observed that a human being armed with a sufficient number of Chinese/English phrase books could conduct a plausible, though necessarily written, discussion with native Chinese speakers outside the room. This person would appear to be communicating intelligently with those outside, and yet achieve this feat merely by following rules. By analogy, Searle suggested, a computer which acted intelligently as the result of a carefully written program could not be regarded as truly intelligent. It too would only be obeying rules. Searle's reasoning has been subjected to the typical polite in-fighting to which philosophers seem unduly prone. It has been suggested that a flaw in his argument is that the system as a whole, room, occupant and phrase books, should be regarded as forming the intelligent entity, and not just the human being alone. Nevertheless the Chinese room argument remains a thorn in the flesh for AI aficionados.

Sadly Turing died before any further progress took place in AI, and the term itself was invented in 1956 when a group of enthusiastic

American computer scientists, John McCarthy, Marvin Minsky, Allen Newell and Herbert Simon, met at a Rockefeller Foundation conference at Dartmouth College. Noticing the progress that, individually, was being made in the subtlety of their programs, they decided collectively that a new discipline was being created. Initial work in AI was then conducted enthusiastically by many researchers. However, it became increasingly obvious that the relative ease with which programs could be written to solve problems in logic or calculus was not accompanied by similar progress in coding solutions for the apparently mundane aspects of human behaviour, like vision or speech recognition.

The principal problem in early AI was the failure to be able to design symbolic, rule following programs able to cope with the unexpected vagaries of the everyday world which were difficult for the programmer to anticipate. A classic example of this was a mobile robot, Terragator, built at Carnegie Mellon University and linked by radio to a controlling computer in the laboratory. The robot was designed to steer itself automatically around the university campus by using vision algorithms to follow the discontinuity in image intensity between pathway and grass lawn. However, it managed, moderately successfully, to climb a tree when its guiding program detected a similar edge between grass and trunk. This error proved typical of the problems encountered in a strictly algorithmic approach to artificial intelligence.

The development of expert systems

An encouraging potential solution was found when some computer scientists, notably *Joel Moses*, decided to include specific knowledge about the situation in which an AI program was intended to operate. Their assumption was that rational human behaviour was rarely the result of abstract thought. Instead people already knew a great deal about situations in which they found themselves. They were able to bring this prior knowledge to bear upon any decisions that they had to make. In a similar way it was felt that AI programs would also fare a lot better if they were helped by giving them access to fundamental facts about the context in which their solutions had to work.

This insight led to the development of expert systems. An expert system combines a *knowledge base* in which information about some specific subject, or domain, is stored and an *inference engine* which is able to draw upon this knowledge in order to come to conclusions. The inference engine will engage in a dialogue with the user via the *user interface* and be able to provide advice related to any queries, basing this advice upon the information held in the knowledge base.

A session with an (imaginary) expert system could, for example, take place as follows:

Does candidate have a maths score greater than 60%?
Yes
Has candidate indicated any criminal convictions for fraud?
No
Is candidate willing to work at weekends?
Yes
Recommendation: Employ for trial period of 4 months

This fictitious example should indicate very clearly that an expert system should not be regarded as 'intelligent' in any conventional sense of the word. Instead it is able to follow pre-programmed and automatic reasoning which will provide the 'right answer' only to the extent that it has been possible to program this into the system in advance. The expert system is wholly dependent upon the information which has been placed into the knowledge base in advance.

Advantages of expert systems

- Expert systems are of particular use when the area in which decisions have to be made are not straightforward. Other software can fare reasonably well when only a few factors have to be taken into account. However, when there is need for the use of 'rules of thumb' or *heuristics* an expert system is more appropriate.
- An expert system can be used to make an actual decision, unlike a decision support system or an executive information system. An expert system can control an autonomous device, like a space probe which puts itself into safe mode if it encounters excessive solar radiation from a flare.
- As already indicated, an expert system can be used at different levels within an organization.
- Expert systems can be copied as required. The same expertise has the potential to be applied simultaneously in many different places. Obviously this is not the case with the human experts from whom the knowledge has been obtained.
- Expert systems have the advantage of being able to combine the expertise of more than one human expert.
- Unlike people, expert systems have the potential for immortality. The expertise does not need to die when its human origin does.

Disadvantages of expert systems

Expert systems suffer from disadvantages as well.

- Time and difficulty are involved in creating the system.
- Concepts of position in space or sequence in time are hard to incorporate.
- An expert system does not necessarily know when it has exceeded its area of expertise.
- It is difficult for it to deal with inconsistencies.

Knowledge engineering

The content of the knowledge base will initially come from *human experts* in the relevant area. Gleaning knowledge from human experts and transforming it into the knowledge base is a particularly crucial phase in the development of a new expert system. The people who carry out this task are known as *knowledge engineers*.

A particular problem the knowledge engineer faces is the fact that human experts frequently are not clear themselves about how they solve a problem. Almost by definition an expert is somebody whose expertise has become second nature. Going back to basics and explaining to somebody else precisely how they have solved a given problem is quite difficult for a person at this level of extreme competence. Think for a moment about

> **Key fact**
>
> The knowledge engineer has to be a person who can get on well with others. It is essential that the human expert feels relaxed and able to talk happily about their skills and knowledge. Inevitably there will be a human, emotional context to the interviewing sessions. The expert must not feel threatened or patronized or simply be bored.

asking somebody for a precise set of rules that explain how to ride a bicycle. For most regular cyclists this would be quite difficult because cycling has become second nature to them. It would only be when you asked a novice (for whom success in staying on the saddle was a fairly recent memory) that you would have much chance in getting a set of rules that you could follow in your attempts to achieve the same thing:

(1) Keep your feet close to the ground either side of the bike.
(2) If you topple in one direction put that foot briefly to the ground.
(3) With the other foot push the pedal.
(4) Turn the handlebars in the direction you are swaying . . . etc.

It is also important that the knowledge engineer makes sure before the interviewing process begins that they already have a reasonable level of knowledge in the area of expertise. It is important that the expert's time is not wasted by trivial questions as the knowledge engineer attempts to learn the subject.

The interviewing process will take place in stages. Informal initial questioning will lead to a later stage of more structured inquiry as the knowledge engineer begins to focus on critical detail. 'Talking through' a specific recalled situation can also help to finalize detail that needs to be incorporated in the knowledge base. Questions asked by the knowledge engineer have to be short and to the point, designed to elucidate rather than imply the interviewer's view of things.

> **Question 4.2.3**
>
> Working with a partner, role-play being a human expert and knowledge engineer. The expert should provide information about some hobby or interest of theirs and the knowledge engineer take notes which could provide the initial information required to begin a knowledge base. Make a note of:
>
> (a) What factors improve acquiring knowledge from the expert.
> (b) What difficulties are encountered in deciding precisely what their expertise involves.

The knowledge base

The knowledge base is not restricted simply to facts about objects in the relevant domain. It can also contain concepts and theories about them. It is therefore essential that a data structure is used which can be readily manipulated by the inference engine. Different approaches have been investigated, and these divide broadly into two categories, *declarative* knowledge representation and *procedural* representation. A declarative representation involves facts and the relationships between them. In contrast a procedural representation encodes actions.

Representations include:

- propositional and predicate calculus;
- semantic networks;

- frames;
- scripts;
- production rules.

Semantic networks allow information to be stored as a combination of nodes and arcs. Initially devised by Ross Quillan in 1968 as a model of associative memory in humans, they were adopted as a method suitable for computing. In Figure 4.2.5 of a semantic network information about a student, Ashley, is shown by the content of nodes and the type of arc connecting them.

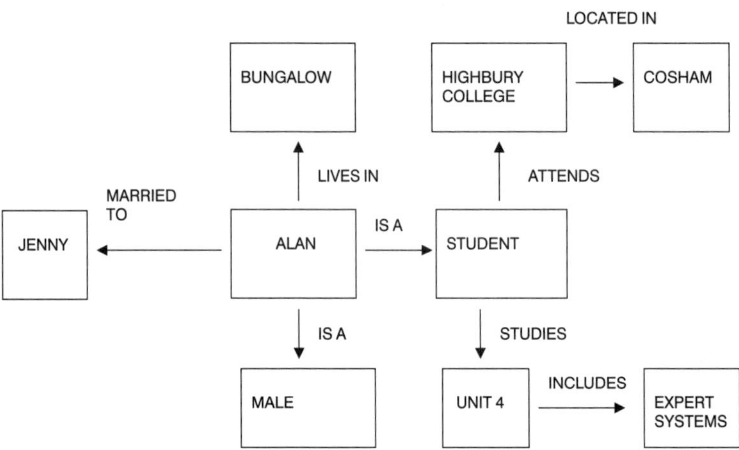

Figure 4.2.5

A *frame* is a table of information on a particular subject. Individual entries are called slots. Four types of slot can be incorporated into a frame. One type simply states a particular piece of information appropriate to the subject. Another type, a default slot, will contain an inevitable piece of information. For example, in any frame referring to an insect the slot giving the number of legs will default to six. A procedural attachment slot defines a routine or procedure needed to determine further information for the frame. Finally a reference slot links the current frame with another which contains relevant further information. Reference slots allow a hierarchy of frames to be constructed, thus building up a broad knowledge base.

A *script* is very much like a frame in that it stores detailed and fairly specific information. Unlike a frame, though, it describes a process rather than specific subjects. Variations in a script are tracks.

Production rules are a common method for storing information in a knowledge base and have the advantage of being a very natural way of storing information. They use If Then rules to represent states that will be true if a certain condition is triggered. Thus:

> If car engine is overheating And AA membership has expired Then walk.

Production rules have the advantage of making it reasonably easy to update the knowledge base when new information is acquired.

The inference engine

The inference engine combines facts that it has been given and combines these with knowledge held in the knowledge base to deduce further facts.

Suppose that the knowledge base contains the following production rules:

Rule 1: If A Then B
Rule 2: If B and C Then D
Rule: If A and D Then E

In addition assume that initial facts A and C are known and that the *goal state* is inferring the truth of fact E. Combining fact A with rule 1 allows B to be inferred. Now B and C together allow D to be inferred. Finally A and D permit the truth of E to be established. Moving from known facts to a desired goal is known as *forward chaining*. Inference engines can also use *backward chaining*, in which the deductive process begins with the goal state and attempts to match this with the known facts which would be required to establish its truth.

There are several reasons why it is sensible to keep the knowledge base distinct from the inference engine in an expert system.

- The user interface and control aspects of the expert system can be reused with other knowledge bases to create a new expert system in a fresh problem domain. This is the principle underlying the use of expert system shells.
- The knowledge engineers who have the task of placing human expertise into the system can concentrate upon this without having to be concerned with the programming required for the user interface and control of the system.
- Knowledge can be coded into the knowledge base in a fairly natural fashion which will be easy for human experts to understand and to refine further. If the inference engine were not kept as a distinct component of the expert system this knowledge would probably become embedded in a lower level of program code which would not have this advantage of ease of understanding.
- The content of the knowledge base can be modified without interfering with the operation of the inference engine.
- Similarly a distinct knowledge base permits changes to be made to the inference engine in order to improve the overall system without the risk of corrupting the knowledge held.

Expert systems shell

A shell is an expert system waiting for its knowledge base to be filled with expertise on some area. This makes it easier for organizations to build up an expert system rather than having to start at the very beginning with the design of the knowledge base structure and the inferencing mechanisms for the inference engine. Expert system shells are available commercially, one example being Crystal (Figure 4.2.6).

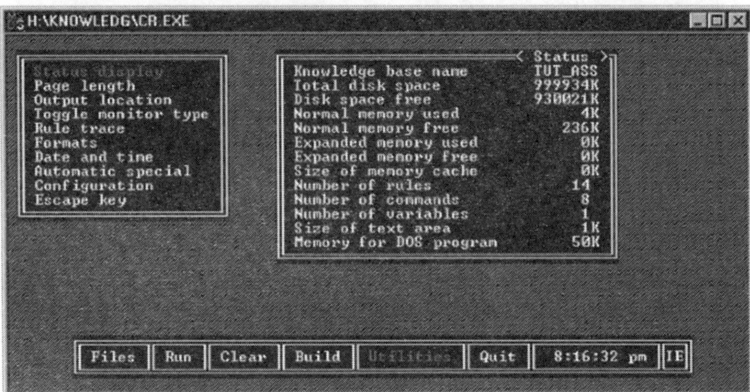

Figure 4.2.6

Question 4.2.4

'Ted's Teles' is a successful manufacturer of domestic electronic goods, mainly specializing in television production. They own two factories and a chain of retail outlets in most major cities in the UK. The managing director is very keen on expansion within the European Union and his team of senior executives are constantly looking for possible new areas in which the company can expand. In particular they study market trends and the impact of individual governments' legislation upon consumer purchases across Europe.

The company is also determined to adopt an aggressive marketing policy in the UK in order to preserve their reputation for excellent quality and low prices. This requires high sales figures. In order to sell as many sets as possible the sales department commissions a customer survey to attempt to relate potential sales to customers' general tastes, interests and possessions. Typical questions asked during this survey are:

How would you describe yourself?
(a) Unskilled
(b) Semi-professional
(c) Professional
(d) Other

How many hours of television do you watch per week?
(a) No television
(b) 0–10
(c) 11–30
(d) More than 30

Which of the following newspapers/journals do you read regularly?
(a) The Mail
(b) The Independent
(c) New Scientist
(d) London Review of Books
(e) The Tablet

Tick which of the following you own.
(a) An electric iron
(b) An electric toaster
(c) A desktop PC
(d) A mobile phone
(e) A personal digital assistant

The survey results are then scrutinized and an attempt made to plan future television set specifications according to public taste.

Customers who buy a television from one of Ted's Teles shops can sign for a special maintenance scheme. If their television develops a fault within 5 years of purchase an engineer will drive to their home and attempt to repair the set. The engineers' vans are equipped with laptop computers which enable the engineers to log their visits and also produce an invoice for the customer from a small printer attached to the dashboard. The engineers currently carry a set of manuals to help them effect repairs on the televisions.

The company purchases an expert system shell and employs knowledge engineers to develop expert systems which will help decision making within their organization.

The future of expert systems – Cyc

One of the early researchers who developed expert systems, *Doug Lenat*, is currently working on a large-scale project called *Cyc*. This is an extension of the concept of the expert system into a major software project. Its goal is a system sufficiently complex to understand ordinary language. Cyc will be a front end that allows easy interaction with other computer systems through speech. This work is an ongoing project taking place at the Microelectronics and Computer Technology Corporation at Austin, Texas, and a great deal of information about it is available on the Internet.

Key fact

Doug Lenat has made major contributions to research in AI and expert systems. AM (Automated Mathematician) was a PhD project which, working from a small set of heuristics defined as production rules, independently discovered basic concepts in set theory and mathematics including the existence of the natural numbers. AM was subsequently developed further by Lenat to create Eurisko ('Eureka Heuristic'), a system which could add to its own set of heuristics. Eurisko was very successful, but kept reinventing a particular heuristic to enhance its apparent creativity: *Add your own name as author to any useful theorem.* Lenat found it difficult to encode a concept of plagiarism!

Neural networks

Neural networks is a branch of artificial intelligence which attempts to produce a computer simulation, at a very simplistic level, of the structural organization of the human brain. Just as the neurons of a brain are connected via their axons and dendrites, so the simulated neurons of an *artifical neural network* are connected together by mathematical expressions called *weights*.

Individual neurons in the human brain can affect the way each other 'fire' by having an *excitory* or *inhibitory* effect. An artificial network tries to copy this by being able to alter the various mathematical weights between the artificial neurons. This allows the effect of one neuron upon another to be adjusted according to the training that the network is given. Eventually the initial signal presented to the *input layer* of artificial neurons will create an appropriate new signal at the *output layer*. This output is created by the way in which the neurons are connected, via a *hidden layer* of neurons. This is shown schematically in Figure 4.2.7. Here the lowest row of circles represents the input layer of artificial neurons and the top row the output layer. The hidden layer lies in between.

A neural network is usually an example of a *virtual machine*. An ordinary, although powerful, computer simulates the activity of artificial

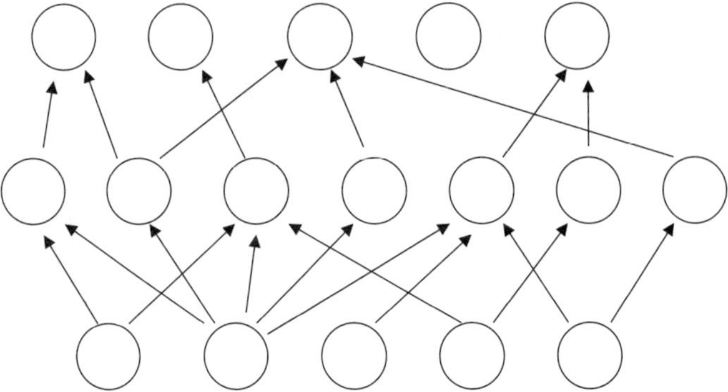

Figure 4.2.7 *Structure of an artificial neural network*

Key fact

The history of neural networks is tortuous. They actually predate the rest of AI research by over a decade but then became discredited. Only after a period of neglect were they then investigated again and are now regarded as one of the most fruitful branches of artificial intelligence.

Key fact

John Hopfield's neural networks were based on a principle of 'computational energy'. Their neurons settle into states of minimum energy a little like the way a marble rolling on a undulating surface will stop in a hollow rather than on a hill.

neurons and their connections, just as it might simulate the behaviour of a loaded bridge or the flow of traffic through a proposed motorway interchange. The individual components of the network do not have to be hard-wired together. The power and complexity of neural networks is steadily increasing. A current research project (2001) aims to simulate the 30 000 neurons of a cat brain.

The first work which contributed to the development of neural networks was carried out by *Warren McCulloch* and *Walter Pitts* and published as *A Logical Calculus of the Ideas Immanent in Nervous Activity* in 1943. McCulloch and Pitts essentially invented the concept of the neural network. A theoretical network of artificial brain cells which were allowed to have either of two states, firing or not firing, was shown to be capable of the same processes as the equally theoretical *Turing Machine* described by *Alan Turing* a decade earlier. This marked the beginning of useful research into neural networks and led to work by *Donald Hebb* (1949) in which learning in a network was associated with altering the weight of the connections.

This early stage of research culminated in the *Perceptron* built by *Frank Rosenblatt* but was later discouraged by the publication of a book, *Perceptrons: An Introduction to Computational Geometry* (1969) by *Marvin Minsky* and *Seymour Papert*. They proved that many of the claims of neural net researchers were excessive and that the approach only worked efficiently for simple problems.

A loss of confidence in the future of neural networks was the probable cause of less work being carried out, but after *John Hopfield*'s contribution (see below) enthusiasm was regained. In a paper he presented at the National Academy of Sciences in 1982, he showed that networks could be used to model associative memory, applying his theory to problems like the 'travelling salesman' (see below). Neural networks are now again an important part of AI research. It is worthwhile checking the Internet for work being done on the *Cog* project at MIT. Also note the work of *Igor Aleksander* at Imperial College, London.

Features of neural networks

Some points to note about neural networks are:

- They attempt to emulate biology.
- They have emergent properties.
- They are self-organizing.
- They are an example of machine learning.

Attempt to emulate biology – artificial neural networks are a deliberate attempt to copy the way the human brain works. This gives researchers the confidence to continue, believing that if a biological solution has been achieved already then it is sensible to probe in this direction.

A cynic or Devil's advocate might want to observe that there were many historical attempts to fly in which the would-be aviator also modelled his efforts closely upon biology. However, donning a bird costume and energetically flapping your arms proved ineffectual. When Wilbur and Orville Wright finally mastered the trick they had not been overly dependent upon Nature's solution.

A biologist could point out that in any case an artificial neural network is not a very close simulation of the brain. The more the brain is studied the more its complexity appears. Merely adjusting arithmetical weightings of connections between an excessively simplified model of neurons does not seem a convincing simulacrum of the real thing, sloppy and wet and bathed in its complex brew of neurotransmitters.

Emergent properties – a system is said to have emergent properties if its behaviour as a whole exhibits unexpected detail which could not have been easily predicted by a study of its component parts. (The 'gliders' which appear in the game of 'Life' are an example of this. They do not seem to be built into the simple rules that govern the behaviour of individual cells of the game.) The neural networks that John Hopfield designed have emergent properties.

Self-organizing – neural networks are an example of a self-organizing system. This contributes to the way that they can learn automatically.

Machine learning – neural networks are not explicitly programmed. Instead they are trained. They are given data from which they produce an output. The network is then given feedback and informed whether its output is correct or not. On the basis of such training the network learns to give the correct answer. It does this by automatically adjusting its internal weights until the feedback is affirmative. Note that this can be a disadvantage in some circumstances. It is not possible to understand how the network is arriving at its output just by looking at the changes that have taken place in the strengths of the weights. Neural networks are the ultimate black box. The creator of a neural network has difficulty in proving exactly what it is that the network has learnt. As a consequence of this a network may go on to make an unpredictable, silly mistake at a later stage.

Key fact

An example of a neural network failing to learn properly was a military application in which a net was trained to identify camouflaged enemy tanks lurking in heavily wooded landscape. Only much later, when a new set of photographs taken in different lighting conditions was presented to the network, was it realized that what actually had been learnt were patterns of light and shade cast by trees.

Neural network applications

Areas in which neural networks have been applied are:

- Assessing risk
- Pattern recognition
- Optimization

Assessing risk – neural networks have found application in assessing credit worthiness, predicting behaviour of stocks and bonds, analysing risk in business ventures, etc. They have been used by banks in currency exchange and generally by economists.

Pattern recognition – neural networks can be used in many areas where pattern recognition is required, like speech recognition, reading, handwriting, robotics and process control, military target recognition and image processing.

Optimization – the 'travelling salesman problem' considers a situation in which a commercial traveller has to visit a number of towns and tries to decide the best order in which to go to each. If there are only three towns it is easy to decide. They form the vertices of a triangle (imagine the roads pulled out to straighten them) and it makes no difference in which order he travels. However, if there are more than three towns deciding the best sequence in which to travel becomes more complicated. If the pattern is now a quadrilateral with two diagonals there is more than one way in which this network can be crossed in order to get to each vertex, or town. More towns make the problem even trickier. Finding a solution to this problem is a traditional topic in mathematics books and it is related to other real-world situations, like positioning a robot drill to cut a pattern of holes in a circuit board. The general problem is called *constraint satisfaction* and can be tackled by a neural network.

Question 4.2.5

Neural networks can be considered as 'cutting edge' technology and much of the practical information about their use can be found on the Internet.

(a) Look for examples of neural networks applied to specific organizations.
(b) Investigate other areas in which similar networks could be applied.

A mini neural network

The way in which a neural network can be trained by adjusting the weights associated with individual neurons is illustrated in this section by a short Visual Basic program. This program shows how weights change as the user answers a series of questions designed to distinguish between the two cities Edinburgh and London. When the training session is completed the final values which the weights have acquired will allow the network to be right every time.

Although this extremely slimmed down network is only capable of distinguishing between the cities Edinburgh or London, it does indicate the way a network learns through training. In particular the feedback provided during the initial session will be seen to be essential.

The principles involved can be illustrated by first considering a version of this network which has a single neuron in the input layer. As stated, there are only two possible outputs from the network. It can select either of the two possibilities:

```
The city is Edinburgh.
The city is London.
```

This decision will be made by only accepting one input, assigned as a value to the single neuron in the input layer. This input value will be the user's answer to a question which distinguishes between the two cities. This of course can be any question which is capable of making the distinction. The one selected here is:

```
Is it located in Scotland?
```

Obviously the answer will be Yes for Edinburgh and No for London. These answers will be converted to a 1 for Yes and a 0 for No. The number is assigned as the value for the single input neuron.

It is important to stress that at this point there is no explicit information contained within the network linking a value of 1 with Edinburgh and a 0 with London. After an initial dialogue of the form:

```
Is it located in Scotland?
Yes
```

the network can still make the apparently idiotic reply:

```
The city is London.
Is this correct?
```

Until it learns that this sequence receives a terse, negative retort from the user there is no reason why such an incorrect reply should not be given. The network is, after all, learning. It must be allowed to make mistakes, just as a person does when unfamiliar with the task at hand.

The learning, or training, which will take place results from two features of the system. These are the weight attached to the neuron and the feedback that the user provides, telling the network whether its output is correct or not. In this example the value that the neuron's weight can have is 1, 0 or –1. Initially the weight will be 0. Training the network consists in altering the weight to a non-zero value which permits the correct output to be obtained.

The network produces its output in a purely arithmetical way. After asking the user its single question it assigns a value of 1 or 0 to the reply entered. The product of this input value and the current value of the weight is then found. For example, if Yes has been given as the answer the following will take place:

```
Is it located in Scotland ?
Yes

Reply     Neuron     Weight     Neuron X Weight
Yes       1          0          0
```

The single-neuron network now produces its output according to the product of (neuron × weight). If this is zero or positive the network selects London as the city. If the product is negative Edinburgh is chosen. This decision making is of course purely arbitrary and would not advance the network's 'knowledge' about London and Edinburgh by the slightest amount. However, a crucial stage in the training occurs at this point. The user is asked whether the answer returned by the system is correct or not. If the answer is correct no adjustment is made to the weighting, but if the answer is incorrect the value of the weight is changed. This is where feedback occurs in the training process.

> **Key fact**
>
> Network training might be regarded as an explicit example of learning taking place from negative instances rather than positive, as a corollary of the dictum 'You only learn from defeat'.

The alteration to the weight takes place according to the product, (neuron × weight). If this product is zero or positive the value for the neuron is subtracted from the weight. If the product is negative the neuron value is added to the weight. In either case an updated value for the weight results from the user's response to an incorrect output.

This method of training can be demonstrated with the single-neuron example. The assumption is made that the user is thinking about London when answering the question each time.

```
Is it located in Scotland ?
Yes

Reply     Neuron     Weight     Neuron X Weight
No        0          0          0
```

```
The city is London.
Is this correct?
Yes
```

Although the network has given the correct answer this is deceptive and has happened by chance. No learning takes place as a result. The value of the weight remains in its zero state of ignorance. The fact that the network lacks training is seen from this alternative example in which the user is thinking about Edinburgh and not London.

```
Is it located in Scotland ?
Yes

Reply     Neuron     Weight     Neuron X Weight
Yes       1          0          0

The city is London.
Is this correct?
No
```

This is a critical stage because the negative response from the user triggers the alteration of the weight. The alteration is calculated as described above. As the product of the neuron value and the weight is zero, the training of the network consists of subtracting the neuron value from the weight. This is (0 – 1), and so the new weight is –1. This updated weight is now used when the single-neuron network answers any further question. Note that with the new weight the network can make the correct decision for either Edinburgh or London.

If the user answers Yes to the question the product of neuron and weight will be (1 × 1) or –1, and so the output identifies Edinburgh.

```
Is it located in Scotland ?
Yes

Reply     Neuron     Weight     Neuron X Weight
Yes       1          -1         -1

The city is Edinburgh.
Is this correct?
Yes
```

Alternatively if the user answers No the product of neuron and weight will be (0 × –1) or 0. Now the output identifies London.

```
Is it located in Scotland ?
No

Reply     Neuron     Weight     Neuron X Weight
No        0          -1         0

The city is London.
Is this correct?
Yes
```

> **Key fact**
>
> It is important to emphasize that no formal rules have been preprogrammed into the network, but just a method for it to train according to the feedback provided by the user.

The network is now fully trained. It has discovered that an input value of 1 for the single neuron should identify Edinburgh and a value of 0 should identify London. It does this by having a weight of –1 for the neuron based upon the (arbitrary) assumption that a negative product, (neuron × weight), corresponds with Edinburgh and a zero or positive product with London.

This single-neuron network is now extended to five neurons in the input layer and coded into a Visual Basic program. Five questions are associated with the five neurons:

```
Is it located in Scotland?
Is it fairly close to the Thames?
Was it originally a volcano?
Does it have a big Ferris wheel?
Is it a tourist attraction?
```

It can be seen that the input pattern for Edinburgh is 1, 0, 1, 0, 1 and the input pattern for London is 0, 1, 0, 1, 1. The network has to be trained so that it associates the first pattern with Edinburgh and the second pattern with London.

Again the training depends upon the output generated by the network. In this extended example with five neurons a single output value is now produced by multiplying the value of each neuron by its weight and calculating the total of all five of these products. As before if this total is negative the assumption is made that the city is Edinburgh, and if it is zero or positive that the city is London.

Initially the five weights associated with the neurons will be zero and as the network is trained the values of these weights are adjusted until the network can identify which city has been indicated by the answers entered for the five questions. The final weights will have possible values of 1, 0 or –1. More specifically the set of weights that will distinguish between the cities will be –1, 1, –1, 1, 0. This set will produce a total for Edinburgh of:

$$(1 \times -1) + (0 \times 1) + (1 \times -1) + (0 \times 1) + (1 \times 0) = -2$$

The total produced for London is:

$$(0 \times -1) + (1 \times 1) + (0 \times -1) + (1 \times 1) + (1 \times 0) = 2$$

These two totals will determine the appropriate city.

The Visual Basic coding for this neural net program is as follows.

```
Option Explicit
Private Sub Command1_Click()

Dim strQuestion(5) As String
Dim strReply(5) As String
Dim intNeuron(5) As Integer
Dim intWeight(5) As Integer
Dim intProduct As Integer
Dim intCounter As Integer
Dim intTotal As Integer
Dim intFactor As Integer
Dim strAns As String
```

```
'Questions defined
strQuestion(1) = "Is it located in Scotland?"
strQuestion(2) = "Is it fairly close to the Thames?"
strQuestion(3) = "Was it originally a volcano?"
strQuestion(4) = "Does it have a big Ferris wheel?"
strQuestion(5) = "Is it a tourist attraction?"

'Outer Loop trains network
Do
  PicDisplay.Cls
  'Show weighting for neurons
  PicDisplay.Print "Current weighting is:"
  For intCounter = 1 To 5
    PicDisplay.Print intWeight(intCounter)
  Next intCounter

  'Inner loop asks five questions in sequence
  For intCounter = 1 To 5
    'Ask question
    PicDisplay.Print strQuestion$(intCounter)
    Do
      strAns = InputBox("Yes or No", , , 6500, 5500)
    Loop Until strAns = "Yes" Or strAns = "No"

    If strAns = "No" Then strAns = "No_"

    strReply(intCounter) = strAns

    'Obtain numerical value as Boolean expression
    intNeuron(intCounter) = - (strAns = "Yes")

  Next intCounter

  'Display current state

  PicDisplay.Print "Reply Neuron Weight Neuron X Weight"
  intTotal = 0

  For intCounter = 1 To 5

    intProduct = intNeuron(intCounter) * intWeight(intCounter)
    intTotal = intTotal + intProduct

    PicDisplay.Print strReply(intCounter); "          ";
    PicDisplay.Print intNeuron(intCounter); "          ";
    PicDisplay.Print intWeight(intCounter); "          ";
    PicDisplay.Print intProduct

  Next intCounter

  'Check answer
  If intTotal < 0 Then
    PicDisplay.Print "The city is Edinburgh."
  Else
    PicDisplay.Print "The city is London."
  End If

  PicDisplay.Print "Is this correct?"

  Do
    strAns = InputBox("Yes, No or Quit", , , 6500, 5500)
  Loop Until strAns = "Yes" Or strAns = "No" Or strAns = "Quit"

  'Adjust weighting if incorrect
  If strAns = "No" Then
```

```
      If intTotal < 0 Then
        intFactor = 1
      Else
        intFactor = -1
      End If

      For intCounter = 1 To 5
        intWeight(intCounter) = intWeight(intCounter) +
          intNeuron(intCounter) * intFactor
      Next intCounter
    End If

Loop Until strAns = "Quit"

End Sub
```

The operation of the program is illustrated by screen dumps. The first of these shows the initial screen. This prints out the five zero weights for the input neurons and then the five associated questions in sequence to allow the user to enter a (validated) Yes or No. These replies are then displayed together with the neuron value, the associated weight and the product. The untrained network selects London as the city, although examining the replies shows that this is incorrect and that the user was thinking about Edinburgh instead (Figure 4.2.8).

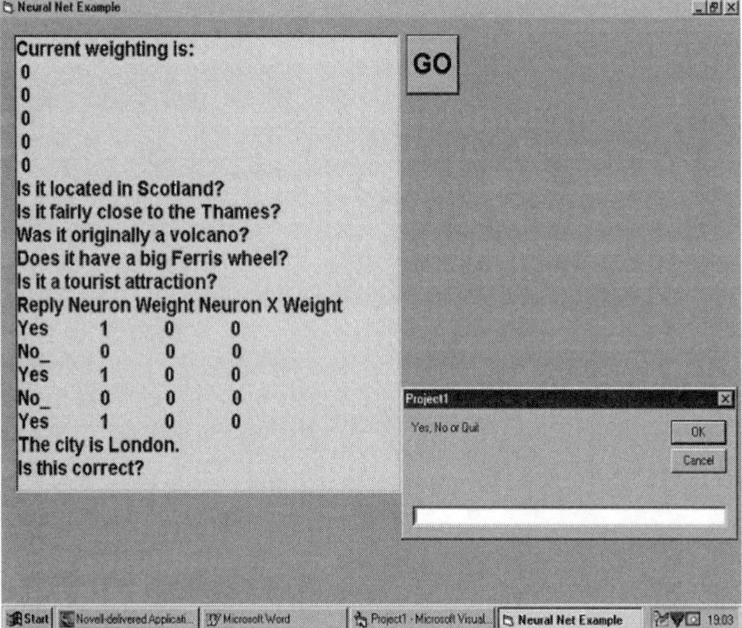

Figure 4.2.8

The next screen shows that the weights have been adjusted after the user has rejected Edinburgh. It is quite clear that the neuron values, 1, 0, 1, 0, 1, have been subtracted from the initial weights, 0, 0, 0, 0, 0, to give updated weights of –1, 0, –1, 0, –1. With the second set of questions the user replies giving the answers appropriate for London (Figure 4.2.9).

The total of the products is now negative and so the network suggests that the city is Edinburgh. Again this is wrong and so once more the

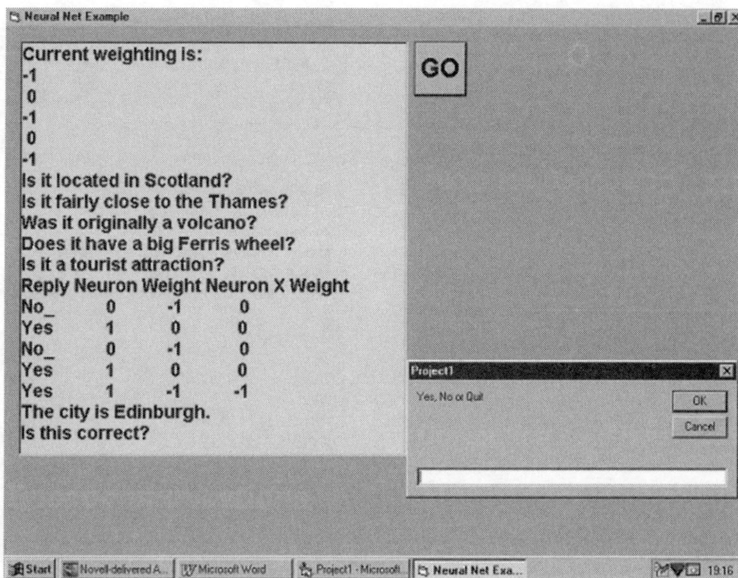

Figure 4.2.9

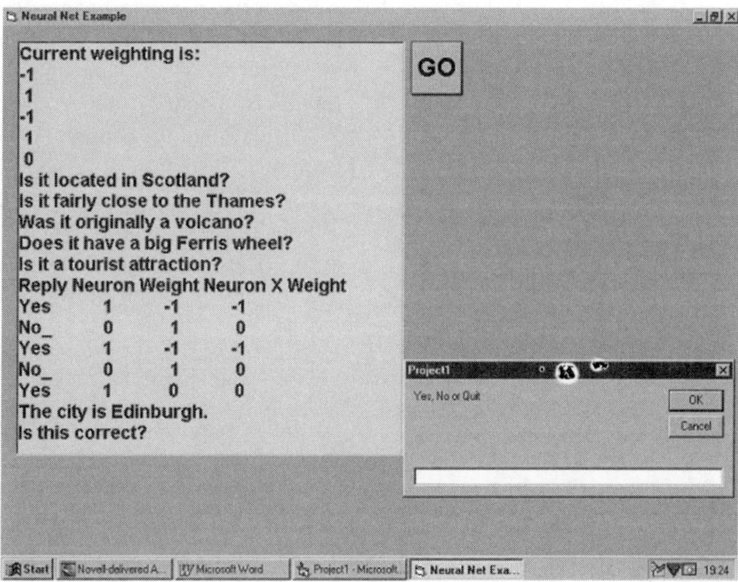

Figure 4.2.10

weights have to be adjusted. This time the neuron values have to be added to the associated weight because the total was negative. This means that the updated weights will be –1, 1, –1, 1, 0. These are precisely the values required for the network to make a correct identification of either city. The trained network can now successfully identify Edinburgh (Figure 4.2.10).

It can also identify London (Figure 4.2.11).

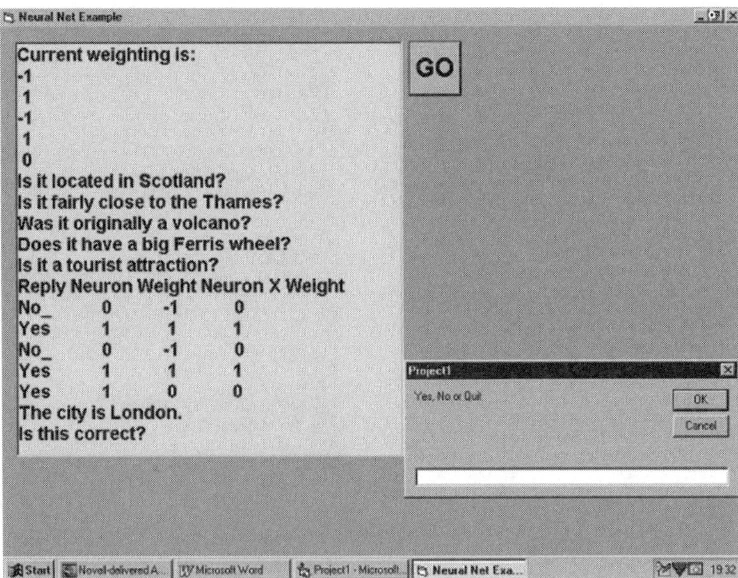

Figure 4.2.11

Program documentation

As with the program examples developed for the Unit 3 material the neural network program is written in Visual Basic but ignoring most of the features of the language. Instead user input is obtained via the InputBox function, output is printed to a single Picture Box named PicDisplay, and the program code entered into the code window for the Command 1 button. The screen dumps given here indicate how the Form and other objects can be adjusted to give a clear screen display.

Four arrays are required for the program. Two are dimensioned as string arrays. These are strQuestion(), which holds the text for the five questions, and strReply(), which allows the user's responses to be recorded.

```
Option Explicit
Private Sub Command1_Click()

'Simple neural network illustration

Dim strQuestion(5) As String
Dim strReply(5) As String
```

The two further arrays, intNeuron() and intWeight(), store the values given to the input neurons and the weights for each neuron. These arrays are dimensioned as integer type.

```
Dim intNeuron(5) As Integer
Dim intWeight(5) As Integer
```

A single integer variable, intProduct, is needed to hold the product of neuron and weight. This does not need to be an array because the separate products calculated will all be combined into the single variable, in Total. A third variable is intCounter, which will be used as a loop control variable. A fourth variable is intFactor, which is required in an intermediate calculation as explained later in this documentation. All of these variables are declared as integers.

> **Key fact**
>
> Obviously any five questions which will have an affirmative answer for one city and a negative answer for the other are preferable, although the fifth question 'Is it a tourist attraction' has been deliberately included here to shown that the associated weight will remain as zero in the trained network.

```
Dim intProduct As Integer
Dim intCounter As Integer
Dim intTotal As Integer
Dim intFactor As Integer
```

The user's response to on-screen prompts will be assigned to a string variable, strAns.

```
Dim strAns As String
```

The five questions that will be used to distinguish between Edinburgh and London are directly assigned to the five array locations in strQuestion().

```
'Questions defined
strQuestion(1) = "Is it located in Scotland?"
strQuestion(2) = "Is it fairly close to the Thames?"
strQuestion(3) = "Was it originally a volcano?"
strQuestion(4) = "Does it have a big Ferris wheel?"
strQuestion(5) = "Is it a tourist attraction?"
```

The training of the network now begins with an overall Do loop. Indentation shows that this loop occupies most of the program, exit only taking place when the user enters 'Quit'.

```
'Outer Loop trains network
Do
```

First the picture box used for display is cleared and then a For Next loop shows the current value for all five weights. These are in the intWeight() array. All five locations of the array are identified by the successive values of the loop control variable, intCounter.

```
  PicDisplay.Cls

  'Show weighting for neurons
  PicDisplay.Print "Current weighting is:"
  For intCounter = 1 To 5
    PicDisplay.Print intWeight(intCounter)
  Next intCounter
```

A further For Next loop then presents each of the five questions from the strQuestion()array in the Picture Box.

```
  'Inner loop asks five questions in sequence
  For intCounter = 1 To 5
    'Ask question
    PicDisplay.Print strQuestion  (intCounter)
```

Validation of the user's input is performed by a nested Do loop which repeats until the response, assigned by the InputBox function to the variable strAns, is either Yes or No.

```
    Do
      strAns = InputBox("Yes or No", , , 6500, 5500)
    Loop Until strAns = "Yes" Or strAns = "No"
```

In order to create a tidy display a negative response is lengthened to three characters by appending an underscore.

```
If strAns = "No" Then strAns = "No_"
```

The value of strAns is then stored in the strReply() array, the appropriate location being determined by the value of the loop control variable, intCounter.

```
strReply(intCounter) = strAns
```

As indicated earlier a numerical value of 1 for an affirmative reply, and a value of 0 for a negative one, are needed for the value given to the input neuron. This conversion of the strings 'Yes' and 'No_' is achieved by using a Boolean expression, (strAns = 'Yes'). This will evaluate as 1 when it is true, and strAns is Yes, and as 0 otherwise. These are the two values required. Whichever value is obtained, it is immediately placed in the correct location of the intNeuron() array.

```
'Obtain numerical value as Boolean expression
intNeuron(intCounter) = - (strAns = "Yes")
```

The For Next loop asking the questions then repeats.

```
Next intCounter
```

After all the questions have been asked the user is shown the status of the network. This display indicates each of the five Yes or No responses that have been made, the equivalent numerical value that has been given to the input neuron, the current weight associated with each neuron, and the product, Neuron × Weight, which will be totalled to decide which city should be identified. First headings are placed in the Picture Box to identify the columns of values that will be shown.

```
'Display current state

PicDisplay.Print "Reply Neuron Weight Neuron X Weight"
```

The value of the variable intTotal is first initialized as 0. Obviously this is necessary if a correct value for the sum is going to be found each time this section of code repeats.

```
intTotal = 0
```

A For Next loop is used to generate the display.

```
For intCounter = 1 To 5
```

Within this loop the values of each neuron and its weight are multiplied together and assigned to the variable intProduct. The value is also added to the variable intTotal. (Note that this calculation could easily have been reduced to a single line of code, and eliminate the need for the variable intProduct. The method shown here has been chosen for clarity.)

```
intProduct = intNeuron(intCounter) X intWeight(intCounter)
intTotal = intTotal + intProduct
```

The loop then shows the values held in the three arrays strReply(), intNeuron() and intWeight(), as well as the product of Neuron × Weight momentarily held in intProduct.

```
PicDisplay.Print strReply(intCounter); "         ";
PicDisplay.Print intNeuron(intCounter); "        ";
PicDisplay.Print intWeight(intCounter); "        ";
PicDisplay.Print intProduct
```

The loop then repeats until all five lines of the display have been generated.

```
Next intCounter
```

After this a simple If Then Else condition can choose either Edinburgh or London, basing the decision on whether the total of the products is less than 0.

```
'Check answer
If intTotal < 0 Then
  PicDisplay.Print "The city is Edinburgh."
Else
  PicDisplay.Print "The city is London."
End If
```

At this point the opportunity for training the network occurs. First the user is asked whether the city stated by the network is correct or not. This is also a practical stage in the execution of the program for the user to exit, and so the values accepted for strAns also include Quit as well as Yes or No.

```
PicDisplay.Print "Is this correct?"

Do
  strAns = InputBox("Yes, No or Quit", , , 6500, 5500)
Loop Until strAns = "Yes" Or strAns = "No" Or strAns = "Quit"
```

Training of the network, by adjusting the value of the individual neuron weights, only takes place if an incorrect answer has been given. In the program code this training is controlled by an If Then Else conditional structure embedded within an If Then condition, the latter triggered by a negative response from the user.

```
'Adjust weighting if incorrect
If strAns = "No" Then
```

As indicated earlier, the training will consist of adding the separate neuron values to the individual weights if the total of the products is negative and adding them otherwise. A simple way of coding this, which avoids having conditions repeated within a For Next loop, is to have a variable, intFactor, which has the positive value of 1, when the total is negative, and the negative value of –1 when the total is not negative.

```
  If intTotal < 0 Then
    intFactor = 1
  Else
    intFactor = -1
  End If
```

This variable, intFactor, can then act as a coefficient which multiplies each individual neuron value inside a For Next loop. Here it will change an addition into a subtraction when needed.

```
    For intCounter = 1 To 5
      intWeight(intCounter) = intWeight(intCounter) +
        intNeuron(intCounter) * intFactor
    Next intCounter
```

The outer, If Then Else, condition then ends.

```
  End If
```

Finally the overall Do loop will exit when the user has entered Quit.

```
Loop Until strAns = "Quit"

End Sub
```

4.3 Evaluation measures

Earlier in this unit information was described as data which has been given a structure as a result of processing. In the light of the various uses of information within organizations that have since been described, and reflecting upon the software which can be used to process it, this initial definition can now be regarded as a little too broad. It needs to be more finely tuned, according to circumstance.

Consider the following sentence.

> Tommy Jones has just married Helen Smith.

Reflect on the extent to which this statement can be regarded as information for each of the following.

- Wing Kit Kwok, who owns a fast food restaurant in Shanghai.
- The compositor who types in the sentence as part of the weddings column in the back pages of a local paper.
- The Rev. Darren O'Rourke, who had hoped to spend Saturday afternoon playing snooker.
- Jenny Jones, who is Tommy's mother.
- Samantha Burton, Tommy's fiancée.
- Narbol, an alien living on a planet near Betelgeuse, who belongs to an androgynous race which reproduces vegetatively and has no concept of marriage.

It should be clear that the concept of information needs to be made more precise. In fact the *quality* of information can be assessed according to a number of distinct criteria:

- Relevance
- Accuracy
- Completeness
- Confidence
- Appropriate recipient
- Timeliness
- Level

Relevance of information

Information which is not relevant to the needs of those who wish to use it is poor information. It must relate to what they require and omit unnecessary detail. This is an integral part of avoiding information overload.

Accuracy of information

Obviously information needs to be accurate. Nevertheless this accuracy must be related to the purpose for which the information is going to be used. The *context* for the information must be considered,

Calculating the amount of petrol required to drive from Brighton to Bristol does not require the same level of accuracy as a calculation of the volume of water needed to support the crew of the International Space Station. In the latter case overestimating the water will lead to an unnecessary increase in the fuel burnt by a Space Shuttle, or Russian Progress supply rocket. Too much petrol in the tank when cruising the M4 is a lesser issue. Similarly a major building project will not falter if raw materials are not estimated to the last pound. A pensioner double glazing her bedroom with acrylic sheet will be very aware of less money available for her weekly groceries.

Completeness of information

Good information must be complete. If a vital part of it is missing then the value of the rest is lessened. The famous 'face on Mars' is an example of this. Advocates of ancient civilizations frequently fail to add that later high-resolution photographs only showed an eroded hillside.

A comparison could be drawn with the everyday concept of lying by omission. If a child complains to her father that a dinnerlady hit her at school then she needs to add that she was choking on her lunch at the time of the apparent assault, and that it was her back that was expertly thumped.

Confidence in information

Otherwise perfect information is flawed if it is not believed. The classic case is the boy who cried 'Wolf!' Confidence in information produced by a computer system will be encouraged if the system has in place a recognized policy for enforcing the *security* and *integrity* of the data upon which the information is based. Passwords, encryption and a firewall contribute towards the former; duplicated hardware the latter.

Appropriate recipient for information

Related to the relevance of the information is the nature of the groups to whom the information is sent. Strategic level information will be of only passing interest, one hopes, to the cleaners and an efficient computer system will guard against this possibility.

Timeliness

Information which does not arrive in time for its intended use cannot be regarded as quality information. Many students have been disappointed by a distinction level assignment being marked down to only a pass as a result of missing a deadline. Their sorrow is heightened if a friend achieves a merit by being on time with their work. If an important decision is to be based on information that will be supplied by a certain date then it is essential that the information is provided in time.

Note that timely information is not necessarily the same as information that has been most recently updated. Slightly out of date is better than nothing at all, and otherwise poorer quality information gains a value by being available. Many years ago a composer working on a Hollywood film score is reputed to have said, 'Do you want it good or do you want it Monday?' Perhaps this illustrates an inevitable dilemma for the perfectionist.

Level of information

Clearly the same initial data can be processed to yield information at differing levels of complexity and detail. This has already been discussed in terms of the flow of information through an organization from operational, through tactical, to strategic level. The information which is provided for users at each level must be appropriate to their needs and therefore presented at the correct level of complexity. A geographical information system can provide broad information about land usage which is of value for government economists. The same system can also give a more detailed analysis of smaller areas appropriate for regional planning.

Question 4.3.1

Read through the following scenario and comment on the quality of information in the organization described.

Shirley Shipping is a ferry company which dominates the passenger traffic between two large islands some distance from the nearest mainland. The company owns several ferries and has an extensive organization based in a number of towns along the island coasts.

Times of sailing are displayed prominently on notice boards outside each of the ports from which ferries depart. When circumstances cause any alteration to the intended schedule, head office phones through to reception at individual branches. The sailing times are then altered by hand as soon as a member of booking staff is free.

As part of their advertising strategy Shirley Shipping devises a colourful brochure which is sent out to all inhabitants of both islands who are aged 18 or over. The managing director is especially proud of a paragraph he has contributed himself. In this he describes the propulsion system used on their latest ferry and explains how the bow thrusters can complement the rudder in conditions of extreme weather.

The advertising manager is upset a few weeks later when he receives a sarcastic letter about the brochure from the matron of a residential home for the elderly.

To reinforce their ongoing concern for health and safety, Shirley Shipping insist that all passengers sign a register which can be used by the coastguard in the event of any unfortunate incident. This register is usually kept on a table in the first class lounge, together with a biro attached on a string.

One of the ferry captains prefers using his personal hand-held GPS device to navigate into one harbour where he is uncertain about possible radar reflections from a high cliff face. His first officer takes a bearing upon the illuminated forecourt of a well-known public house as a check.

5 Quality management principles

Summary

This chapter will enable students to learn about the concepts of quality assurance through the process of analysing and designing computer systems. It will deal with the quality assurance and professional issues related to the management and implementation of computer systems. It also covers the project management aspects needed within the development of software products and introduces the legal requirements currently affecting the computer practitioner.

Introduction

The need for a 'quality product' cannot be overstated. This is especially important within the world of computing and software development. We have often heard of the product that is not produced on time and launched with a number of problems (bugs). This is why the combined techniques of project management and quality assurance need to be developed and applied over the whole lifecycle of the software product.

This chapter further develops the concepts developed in the systems analysis unit. It looks at the analysis and design tools used within the software development process and applies CASE tools to produce graphical and text-based models. The syntax and semantics of the model will be tested to ensure the quality of the product conforms to the stated requirements.

You will further develop the techniques of traditional lifecycle models and object-oriented models, and how they are developed, documented and quality assured for a simulated customer specification.

The concepts of project management are developed within the chapter to ensure the development process is planned and implemented within prescribed deadlines and checked at various milestones to ensure the verification and validation processes.

All completed systems require some maintenance to be carried out to handle any problems that may occur or update certain aspects of the software. The concept of a software maintenance contract is introduced.

You will be introduced to the basic concepts of 'quality assurance' and how it interacts across a software development project. Estimating and costing factors need to be considered along with the timing and testing issues for a software product under development. You will need to hold reviews, walkthroughs and inspections and be able to produce recognized quality assurance documents.

Legal implications surrounding the development of a product and its associated staff are addressed. For example, the software project manager needs to approach health and safety in a strictly systematic way by assessing *the risks and hazards in the workplace* and taking steps to ensure that their house is in order. Also the manager needs to be aware of the issues involving storage of data, i.e. recorded information.

Professionalism and standards are key issues developed by any successful manager. Students need to understand the importance of these issues and how they are implemented within a quality development programme. The concept of professionalism implies taking responsibility, accounting for one's work and performing work to the highest standards. Factors like ISO, British Standards, training (CPD), etc. need to be considered in the quest for producing 'quality professional software development personnel'. These issues are especially important if a professional body like the British Computer Society validates your course.

5.1 System analysis and design tools

Conventional analysis and design techniques

The aim of this section is to build on the techniques covered in Chapter 2, Systems Analysis, by expanding basic concepts and developing additional techniques that need to be established to fully represent a required system. All people involved with the development of software systems need to be aware of all the possible documentation sources that can be created during the project lifecycle. This becomes more important when aspects like quality assurance and maintenance are to be fully implemented to ensure professional standards are upheld and change requirements installed.

> My experience has shown that many people find it hard to make their design ideas precise. They are willing to express their ideas in loose, general terms, but are unwilling to express them with the precision needed to make them into patterns. Above all, they are unwilling to express them as abstract spatial relations among well-defined spatial parts. I have also found that people aren't always very good at it; it is hard to do . . . If you can't draw a diagram of it, it isn't a pattern. If you think you have a pattern, you must be able to draw a diagram of it. This is a crude, but vital rule. A pattern defines a field of spatial relations, and it must always be possible to draw a diagram for every pattern. In the diagram, each part will appear as a labelled or coloured zone, and the layout of the parts expresses the relation which the pattern specifies. If you can't draw it, it isn't a pattern.
>
> Christopher Alexander (1979)
> in *The Timeless Way of Building*

The above quote from Christopher Alexander sums up the need to express graphically the requirements of a given system. This is especially true for systems analysis and design. In Chapter 2 we saw a number of graphical techniques used; Yourdon, SSADM, UML and Data Modelling, all with similar structures and syntactical correctness. Whatever method was used by a completed system all aspects should be thoroughly understood in order for the development team to modify the requirements so the software product remains a viable product for existing and potential customers.

Mini-specifications

A *mini-specification* is a document that contains a specification of a primitive data process (a process that has not been refined). These range in the level of detail which they contain, from a simple high-level description, through to a structured table layout. There is no standard layout structure for a mini-specification and often they contain a mix of formal and informal notations. An example layout for a mini-specification is shown below.

Process Name:	
Input Data Flows:	
Name:	Type:
Input Flows from Stores:	
Name of Store:	Component:
Output Data Flows:	
Name:	Type:
Output Flows to Stores:	
Name of Store:	Component:
Process Description:	
This could be a high-level English description, a basic program design language or a formal description using pre- and post-condition syntax.	

The table contains the process name, and details of the flows passing in and out of the process within a data flow diagram. It highlights the data that is passed to and from storage devices and finally a description of what the process is to do.

Question 5.1.1

The following diagram represents part of a security system which checks the input codes to ascertain if they are correct. The codes are checked against a set of stored values and a suitable output message is displayed. For example, if the code is acceptable the output message will state 'valid code' and if it is not in the database list a message saying 'code not recognized' is produced.

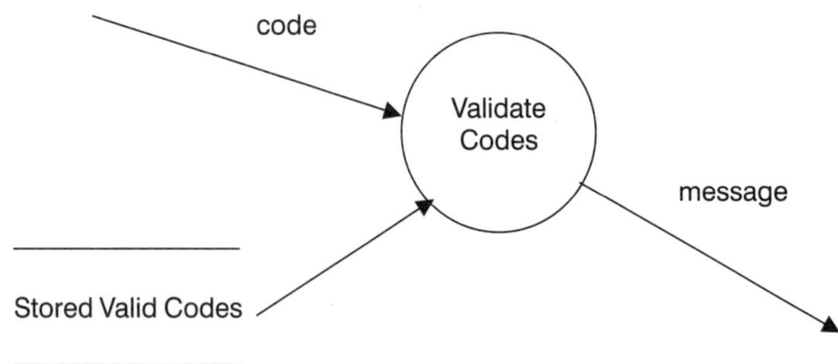

Figure 5.1.1 *Security code system*

Complete a mini-specification of the system.

Data dictionaries

This is a central repository for information flowing through a system and modelled via a data flow diagram. The information must have:

- *structure* – ascertained by looking at the converging and diverging flows and the data components held in associated stores;
- *meaning* – implied through meaningful names and documentation evidence from the negotiated statement of requirements.

A data dictionary will contain more detailed information than a mini-specification and formal notations like the BNF (Backus-Naur Format) syntax definitions can be employed. Data dictionaries vary in the way they are presented, but generally they will contain the following:

- Details of all data flows and stores for a specified set of diagrams.
- Abbreviated terms or aliases are specified. These derive on large diagrams where the developer has used an abbreviation instead of a full length word. For example, SPR could have been used instead of System Pressure Result. Technically they should be avoided, but this is not always possible as long names can sometimes overclutter the diagram.
- Extra information about the data is recorded in order to provide clarification and ensure correctness.

Data dictionaries are designed so they can easily be modified and expanded throughout the system development and maintenance process thus allowing additional information to be included when or if it becomes available.

Control aspects

Data flow diagrams give an overall picture of the system requirements but they do not convey any dynamic or time-related aspects to the developer. If the developer is to produce a complete model for a system specification then the dynamic components of the required system must be analysed and documented. The dynamic aspects can be represented by control components that are first outlined in a data flow diagram and refined as state transition diagrams.

Within the Yourdon Essential Model the main components used to represent control components in a data flow diagram are outlined in Figure 5.1.2.

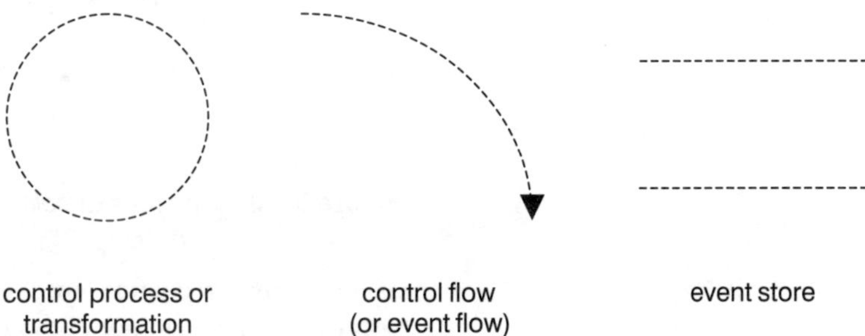

Figure 5.1.2 *Control systems used within a data flow diagram*

A *control process* represents the interface between the data flow diagram and the control specification. The name of the control process indicates the type of control activity carried out within the control specification. A control process acts on the input control flows to produce output control flows. The exact nature of the control process is documented in the control specification. The child of a control process is either a control specification or a State Transition Diagram (STD).

The main difference between a *control flow* and a discrete flow is that the latter has both an occurrence (at some point in time) and content, i.e. some data is sent down the flow line. A control flow just has occurrence and NO content, a signal is sent down the flow line to activate and deactivate a receiving process. You will find that terms like enable, disable, trigger, on, off and activator are used as control flow names. A typical control flow will be discrete-valued as opposed to continuous, it is a pipeline through which control information is sent. Its name should consist of nouns and adjectives only and may consist of a single element or a group of elements.

To enable a process means that it is activated by a corresponding data flow and will stay 'activated' until a disable signal is sent to it. When a process is not active all data flowing to it is ignored and not queued for later use. To trigger a process is to activate it so that it carries out its task and it is automatically deactivated as soon as it has finished. The processes enable, disable, trigger, etc. are called prompts and they can only originate from control transformations. Events and other control activities can originate from data transformations. Some examples of correct and incorrect syntax are shown in Figure 5.1.3.

Figure 5.1.3 shows (a) syntactically correct as control flows are allowed as activators for control processes to produce prompts as output flows. (b) is not syntactically correct because data flows are not allowed

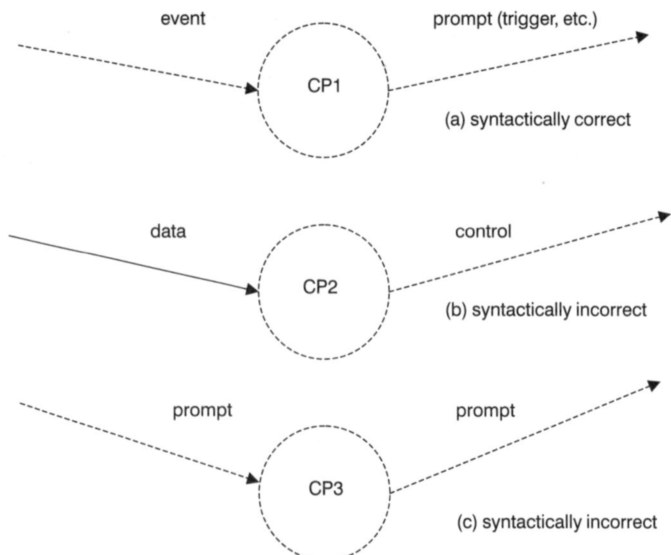

Figure 5.1.3 *Control examples*

as input flows to control processes. (c) again is not syntactically correct because prompts are not allowed as input flows to control processes.

An *event* or *control store* represents control information that has been frozen in time. The information stored may be used any time after it has been stored and used in any order. The main difference between a control (event) store and an ordinary store is that the former stores control information only. A control (event) store should be named with a noun that describes its contents.

Example 5.1.1

The following is an extract from a negotiated statement of requirements:

> The Carabaz Chemical Plant Company requires a plant control system that closes down the plant if critical temperatures are reached. The control system is initially manually activated and automatically shuts down the chemical plant when a certain (critical) temperature has been reached. The temperature is continuously read into the system via a transducer mechanism and regular readings are stored in a database. If a critical temperature reading is reached an appropriate signal is sent to the 'control plant' system and this then triggers the plant to close down. If the plant is shut down an appropriate message is displayed on the operator's console. When the chemical plant is closed down the control system is switched off. An operator can type in commands to view the latest stored temperature readings for the plant or print out a report of a series of stored temperature readings. An appropriate error message is displayed if the operator enters an incorrect command.

Use an appropriate CASE tool to:

(1) complete a CONTEXT diagram to represent the system;
(2) Complete a CHILD of the context diagram to display the main components including control aspects;
(3) produce a SYNTAX CHECK to ensure the correctness of the diagrams and their link with each other.

Suggested solutions:

(1)

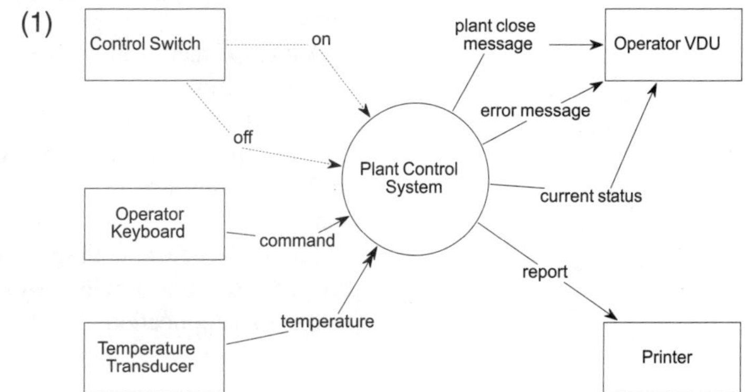

Figure 5.1.4 *Context plant control system*

(2)

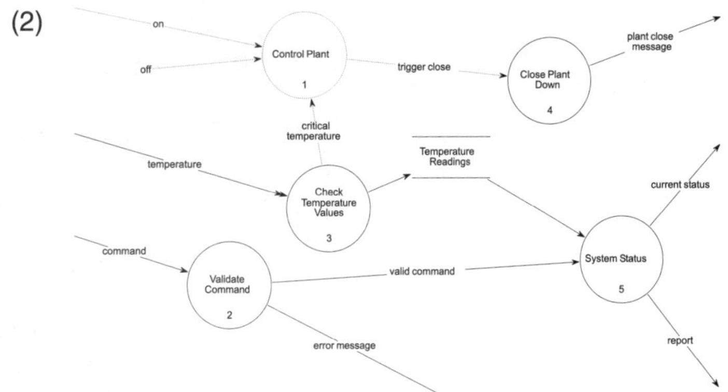

Figure 5.1.5 *Plant control system (DFD outline)*

(3) A check is shown below:

Project: C:\MYDOCU~1\SELECT\SYSTEM\CONTROL\
Title: Plant Control System
Date: 13-Sep-2000 Time: 12:0

Report: Diagram consistency checking

This report contains a consistency check of all the diagrams in the project.

Checking **CONTROL1.DAT** (CONTEXT DIAGRAM)

No Errors detected, No Warnings given.

Checking **CONTROL2.DAT** (CHILD DIAGRAM)

No Errors detected, No Warnings given.

Note: The above example would need further decomposition in order to provide a full solution to the specification. At this stage I am more interested in introducing the concepts of control (the dynamics aspects of the system) and not refining data flow diagrams that were covered in Chapter 2.

Control specifications

This document follows along the lines of a process specification (and to some extent mini-specification) and is created as a child of a control process.

A control specification is a decomposition of a control process and is used to document the time-dependent, or event-response, nature of the system. The control specification describes the relationship between control inputs and control outputs on the parent control process, either textually, using structured English, or state transition diagrams, or using state tables.

The table below highlights a typical control specification that was created from the previous example (5.1.1) using the Select Yourdon CASE tool application.

```
@IN = critical temperature
@IN = off
@IN = on
@OUT = trigger close

@CSPEC 0.1 Control Plant

        The system is activated by an on signal from the
        Control Switch
                When on the Control Plant System waits for
                a critical temperature signal.
                On receiving the critical temperature signal
                the Control Plant System outputs a trigger
                close signal to shut down the plant.
        The system is de-activated by an off signal and no
        further monitoring takes place.

@
```

Like the process specification the input and output flows are specified and the body must contain the associated flow names in order for it to be syntactically correct.

State transition diagrams

Control processes can be refined to produce a model called a *State Transition Diagram* (STD). An STD specifies how a control process is to respond to its input and output flows by specifying the states involved and their corresponding conditions and actions. An example of how a state transition diagram is structured is shown in Figure 5.1.6.

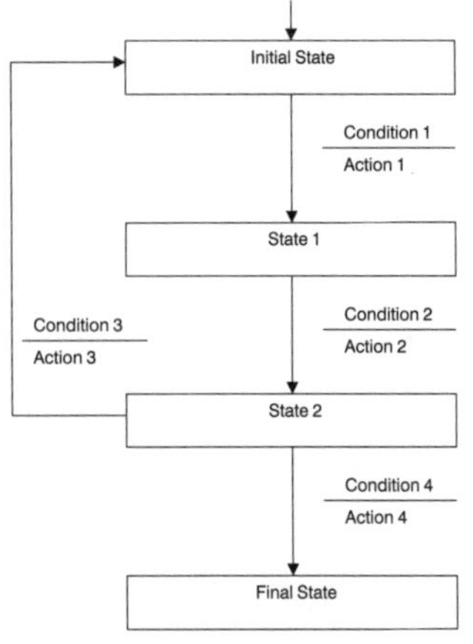

Figure 5.1.6 *Example state transition diagram*

State Transition Diagrams consist of the following objects:

- State
- Start-up state
- Transitions
- Conditions
- Actions

Diagrams normally start with a *start-up state* that has an incoming arrow above it and may contain a single action such as initialize or trigger start. The final state is signified by the fact that there is no transition line leaving it. A state can be considered as a stable condition for a system. Once in a state you have sufficient information on the system's past history to determine the next state according to input events. A state's name should be meaningful in that it should represent the real condition held by the system. States are represented by rectangles.

Transition lines are normally drawn straight either horizontally or vertically and are labelled by conditions and corresponding actions. They indicate the movement of one state to another. Transitions between states are event driven. In other words, something happens which causes the system to change from one state to another. However, it should be noted that not all events will necessarily cause a transition from a particular state and that a given event does not always cause a transition into the same state.

A condition is an event, or events, that cause a transition to occur and are displayed above the vertical line. An action is an operation that takes place as a transition occurs. The input control flows to a control process must appear as conditions on state transition diagrams. The output flows from a control process must appear as actions within a state transition diagram.

Example 5.1.2

From the data flow diagram created in Example 5.1.1:

(1) Create a state transition diagram (STD) from the specified control process.
(2) Test the resulting diagram to ensure it is syntactically correct.

Continued overleaf

Suggested solutions:

(1)

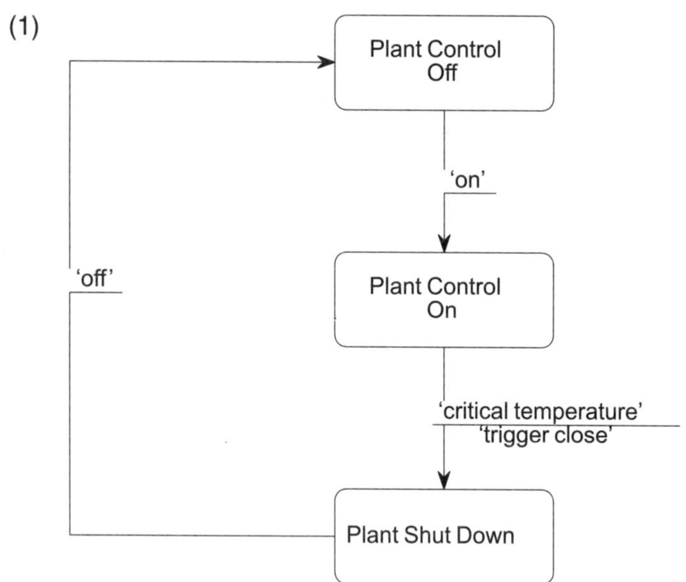

Figure 5.1.7 *State transition diagram (plant control system)*

(2) Test check shown below:

Project:
C:\MYDOCU~1\SELECT\SYSTEM\CONTROL\

Title: Plant Control System

Date: 15-Sep-2000 Time: 12:2

Checking STDCONT1.DAT

No Errors detected, No Warnings given.

----End of report----

Exercise 5.1.1

The Bailey Comfortable Room Company requires a computer system to control its air conditioning systems when installed on customers' premises. The system needs to operate three main components: a heater, a cooler and an air vent. The components can each be in one of two states:

Heater can be on or off.
Cooler can be on and off.
Vent can be open or closed.

The system will compare temperature readings at regular intervals with the requirements for operating the components. Normally this will be within 2 degrees of the target values; any change outside of this figure will instigate a change of state. To cool a room that is too warm the system goes through various stages:

(1) The heater is turned off.
(2) The vent is opened.
(3) The cooler is switched on.

To warm a room the reverse is required:

(1) The cooler is switched off.
(2) The vent is closed.
(3) The heater is switched on.

If a temperature is correct for a required component then it is left in its current state and only one change can be made at a time.

When given a problem you need to ascertain the exact number of possible states. The maximum number of states that this system can have is eight (three components each with two states). But not all are acceptable, for example it is not practical to have the heater on at the same time as the cooler or the vent open with the heater on, etc.

This can be set up as a truth table:

Components			*Possible state*
heater on	vent closed	cooler off	✓
heater on	vent closed	cooler on	✖
heater on	vent open	cooler off	✖
heater on	vent open	cooler on	✖
heater off	vent closed	cooler off	✓
heater off	vent closed	cooler on	✖
heater off	vent open	cooler off	✓
heater off	vent open	cooler on	✓

This leaves four possible states (those with a tick). Complete a state transition diagram (STD) to represent these states for the Bailey Comfortable Room Company. Test your diagram to ensure it is syntactically correct.

Question 5.1.2

(1) What are the main components of a data dictionary?
(2) What is the main difference between a mini-specification and a data dictionary?
(3) What children can be created from a control process?
(4) What is a transition within an STD and how is it labelled?
(5) What data should be contained within the body of a control specification?

System design

System design takes the functional specification from within the system specification document and provides a base for a solution of the problem. Design takes the developer from the process of defining what the system should do to how it is going to be structured. Most designs will initially use graphical techniques to specify the problem in a modular structure with communication links between them, which provides the passage of data around the system. Two important characteristics need to be inherent within any good design process:

- It must match the specification and be correctly structured by successfully undergoing both verification and validation testing procedures.
- It must be easy to maintain – a design that can reduce the amount of maintenance will result in a larger reduction in project costs.

A typical design process is shown in Figure 5.1.8.

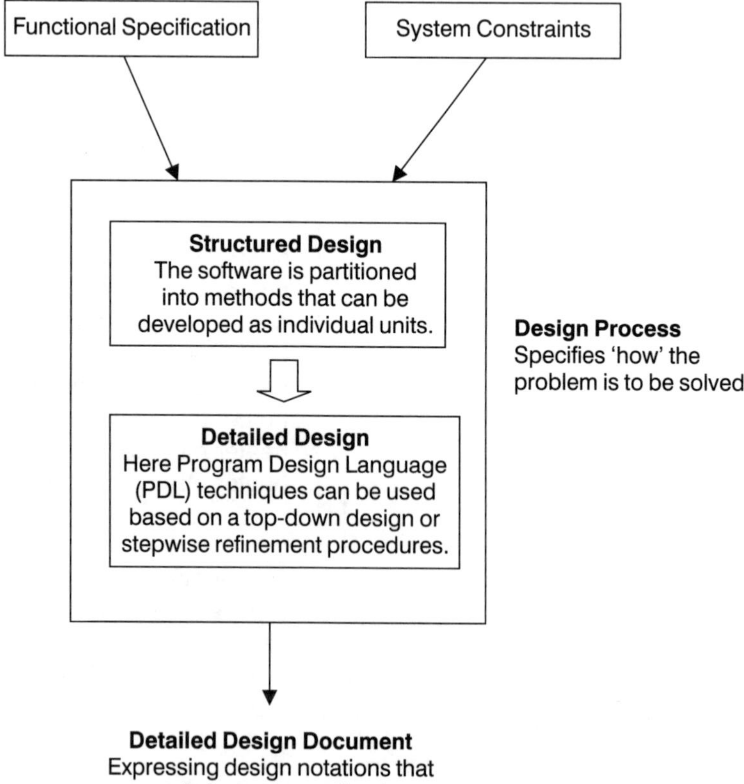

Figure 5.1.8 *System design layout*

Research has shown that systems that have been designed using a structured method are easier to understand, develop, document and modify. One of the people who originally researched this work was Larry Constantine who initially spent some ten years studying various systems before producing his diagrammatic methods to represent structured design.

Structure charts

A structure chart is a graphical representation that depicts a control hierarchy of units or modules. It is used as a tool to carry out structured design and specifies an interface between modules that have been determined from the functional requirements. The symbols used within a Constantine structure chart are shown in Figure 5.1.9.

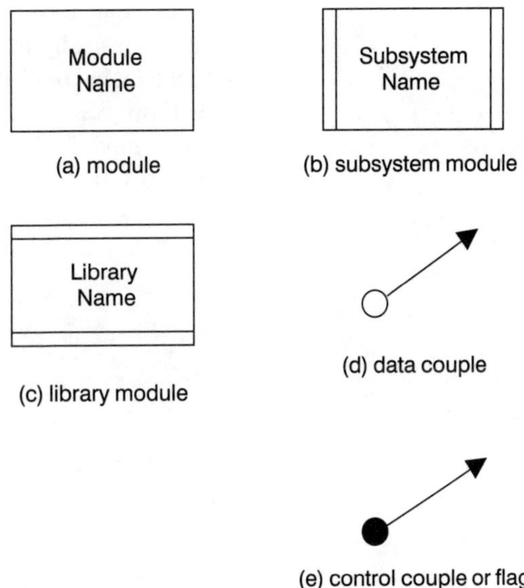

Figure 5.1.9 *Constantine structure chart symbols*

Explanation of the symbols shown in Figure 5.1.9:

(a) Modules are used to represent processing that is local to the Constantine diagram. A module is identified by a name, by which it can be referenced.

(b) Subsystems are predefined modules that are detailed through decomposition on further diagrams. Subsystem modules can be used many times by many diagrams. Here the developer uses decomposition to produce a subsystem that is made up of a structure chart in its own right.

(c) A library is a predefined module in a Constantine diagram that can be used by many different systems. The designer can take its operation for granted as its content has already been constructed and tested.

(d) Data couples are flows of data between modules. They are placed on the module-calling flows. The arrowhead indicates the direction of data flow. When implementing the structure chart they could be considered as parameters passing between code functions or procedures.

(e) Flags show control-information passing between modules on a Constantine diagram. You place flags on the module-calling flow. Examples of flags are *End of Data, Loop End, Command Entered* or *Received OK* that represent a control signal being sent between modules. The arrowhead indicates the direction in which the flag is being passed.

A structure chart describes three important areas of information:

- Shows the partitioning of information into modules.
- Shows the hierarchical relationship between modules.
- Describes the interface between modules.

Structure charts are designed to show three distinct areas of data on a diagram. These are specified as: input (sometimes called afferent) control, transform control and output (sometimes called efferent) control. Basically the afferent modules handle the input of data flowing into the main controlling module (i.e. the main part of the program), the transform control area *transforms* the data flowing into it and the efferent modules handle the output of data. A basic layout is shown in Figure 5.1.10.

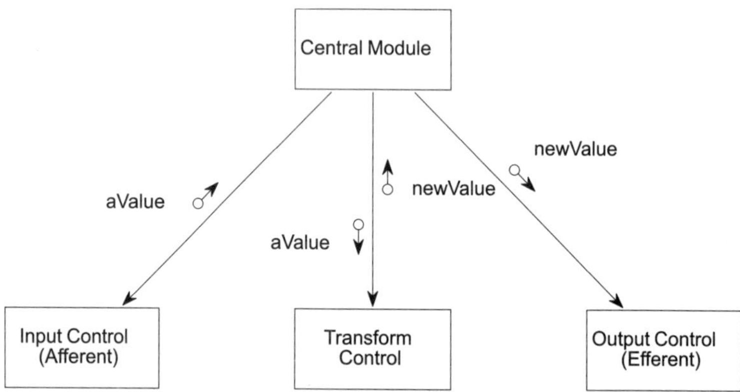

Figure 5.1.10 *Basic structure chart layout*

Note how the data flows from the input module through the central module and into the transform module where it is acted on or transformed. Likewise the *new Value* data couple flows through the central module and on the output module. This is important as the central module only controls the flow of data through the system and any processing is carried out by the subordinate modules. Note also that the subordinate modules are shown on the same level within the diagram. This is normal practice when completing structure charts because the hierarchical layout specifies to the developer the level of module processing involved with respect to the main module and the delegation of processing tasks to subordinate modules.

One of the main problems with structure charts is ascertaining which modules fit into the required categories. There is often overlap and developers need to specify a line across each boundary. This may be achieved on the original data flow diagram that outlines the main components that need to be included in the structure chart.

Example 5.1.3

A system takes a customer order number that is input from an operator's keyboard and produces a goods reference number which is transformed into a goods list. The goods list is then used to produce an invoice that is printed off and sent to the customer.

Carry out the following steps:

(1) Create a data flow diagram to represent the system.
(2) Split the data flow diagram into its three separate components (input, central transform, output) and pick out the modules required for the structure chart.
(3) Complete the structure chart.
(4) Produce a valid test procedure on the final diagram to show it is syntactically correct.

Suggested solutions:

(1)

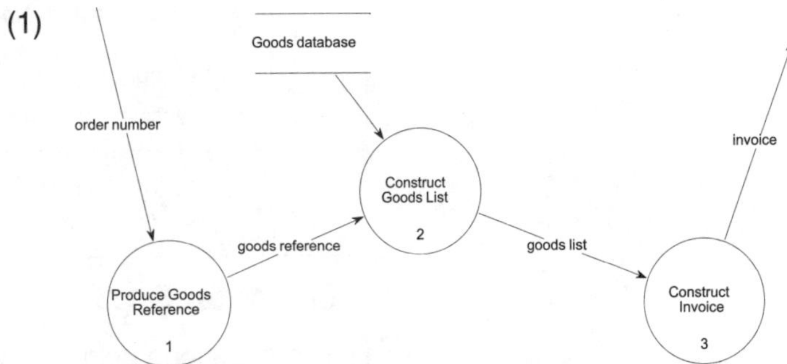

Figure 5.1.11 *DFD customer invoice system*

(2)

Components	*Module*
Input	get order number transform order number into goods reference get goods reference
Central transform	transform goods reference into goods list
Output	put goods list transform goods list into invoice put invoice

(3)

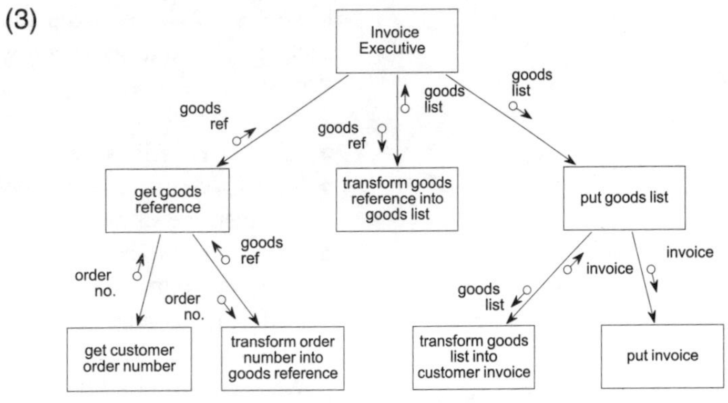

Figure 5.1.12 *Customer invoice system structure chart*

(4) A syntax check is shown below:

```
Project: C:\MYDOCU~1\SELECT\SYSTEM\INVOICE\
Title: Customer Invoice System
Date: 17-Sep-2000 Time: 12:5

Report: Diagram consistency checking

This report contains a consistency check of all the diagrams in
the project.

Checking INVOICE1.DAT          (DFD CONTEXT DIAGRAM)
No Errors detected, No Warnings given.
Checking INVOICE2.DAT          (DFD DIAGRAM Fig. 5.1.11)
No Errors detected, No Warnings given.
Checking INVOICE3.DAT          (STRUCTURE CHART)
No Errors detected, No Warnings given.

End of report
```

Question 5.1.3

The questions below relate to the development of structure charts:

(1) What is a data couple?
(2) What are the three main areas associated with a structure chart?
(3) Constantine diagrams specify three types of module. Name the modules and explain the difference between them.
(4) What is important about naming a module?
(5) What verification checks should be carried out within the system design activity?

Object-oriented analysis and design

In Chapter 2 we built up the three basic concepts of object-oriented analysis that aid the way we develop models that represent class structures. The concepts covered were:

- *Class* – describes the behaviour of a set of objects of a particular kind.
- *Associations* – the relationships between objects. Where an object is an instance of a class.
- *Responsibilities* – which describe the behaviour of a class. Responsibilities take two forms: responsibilities for recording information and responsibilities for carrying out some action.

We need to add a further component to this list in order to provide a full analysis and design specification which is ready for implementing into an object-based programming language. The fourth concept is that of collaboration:

- *Collaboration* – an object may carry out its responsibilities by collaborating with other objects. This means that an object can send a message to another object (the receiver) to obtain some behaviour characteristic(s) that are inherent within it.

Object-centred viewpoint

One method of developing an object-oriented system is to use the 'object-centred view' which gains an understanding of the system from the perspective of the individual objects that make up the application. The object-centred view leads to the analysis and design concept of CRC (Classes–responsibilities–Collaborations). CRC design focuses on:

- Classes (or abstractions).
- Responsibilities (or behaviours).
- Collaborations (the other classes that an object needs to effectively carry out its responsibilities).

An object's collaborators are those other objects that it explicitly needs access to in order for it to carry out its task. For example, if object X requires object Y to perform its function then Y is X's collaborator. The collaborators of a class generally consist of the superclass and subclasses that it has direct knowledge of and occasionally other global classes it may need to reference. Some texts use alternative terminology for collaborations, for example colleagues or helpers

Object-community viewpoint

Here the developer gains an understanding of the interactions between the individual objects that make up an application. This approach will focus on the relationships between classes and their appropriate responsibilities. The two main tools used in this area are:

- Use cases (example uses of the application that illustrates inter-object behaviour).
- Class hierarchy integration (taking classes from an existing library and determining if they are identified in the CRC design).

Walk-through

A walk-through takes some coherent piece of behaviour that the system must exhibit – like recording the enrolment of a student onto a course – and investigates how this behaviour can be constructed with the object model. The main steps taken in a walk-through are:

- Stage 1 – understanding in application area terms (or understanding in problem domain terms):
  - what information is the system provided with?
  - what must the system do with that information?

- Stage 2 – understanding in terms of instances of classes and associations. Take the action that the system must carry out and deciding for each action what classes and associations are involved. This leads to the first structural layout for classes, i.e.
  Class: Dog
  Responsibilities:
  Maintains the dog's name and age.
  Determines the group a breed of dog comes under.
- Stage 3 – understanding in terms of responsibilities and collaborations. The collaborators are often determined by reading the description of the responsibilities. The structure in stage 2 is refined as:
  Class: Dog
  Responsibilities:
  Maintains the dog's name and age.
  Determines the group a breed of dog comes under.
  Collaborators: Breed
  (this can be read as 'Breed' is a collaborator for 'Dog').

The object that makes a request for the service of another object is termed a *client* and the object that receives the request (and responds by providing a service) is termed a *server*.

Question 5.1.4

(1) What two viewpoints are often used during object analysis and design?
(2) What is a 'collaboration' between classes?
(3) What is the function a walk-through?
(4) For the example shown in stage 3 identify the client and the server.

Example 5.1.4

The following is an extract from a specification for the Bernese University:

> The Canine faculty of the Bernese University contains several lecture rooms that are uniquely named. The seating and equipment for each room allows for a maximum of 28 students to be present. The faculty administration system has the responsibility for recording information about their allocated lecture rooms, the tutors who staff them and the students that are allocated to them. The administration system will also be responsible for recording new student details and their entry to a given lecture room group. A single tutor is responsible for each lecture room group and their names and study room numbers need to be recorded by the system. Information about the pupils needs to include their name, address and emergency contact telephone number.

(1) Analyse the extract using the process of textual analysis to ascertain the classes to be developed within the system. Try to avoid any classes that are not directly relevant to the specified problem.
Suggested classes are: FacultyAdmin, LectureRoom, Student and Tutor

(2) Complete a class-association diagram to represent the system.

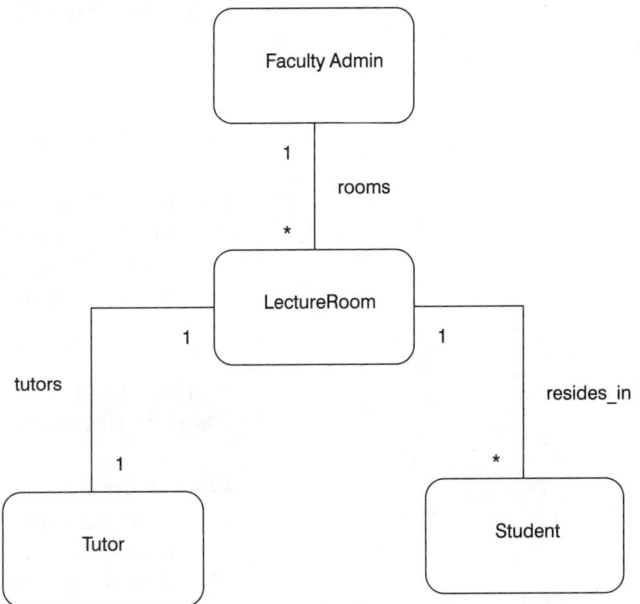

Figure 5.1.13 *Class-association for the Canine faculty*

(3) Layout the class text structure that represents the diagram outlined in part (2).

Class: FacultyAdmin
'There is only one instance of this class and it is the orchestrating instance.'

Class: LectureRoom

Responsibilities:
Records the name of the lecture room.

Class: Student
Responsibilities:
Records the student's name, address and emergency contact number.

Class: Tutor
Responsibilities:
Records the tutor's name and study room number.

Note that there is a restriction on the system that needs to be specified as an invariant.

Invariant
Any given instance of LectureRoom is associated with instances of Student via the resides_in association. The maximum number of Student instances that may be associated with any one instance of LectureRoom is 28.

This technically means that students cannot be in two lecture room groups at the same time and each lecture room has a maximum capacity of 28 students.

(4) More detail needs to be added to the class layouts in order to provide a full analysis model. This can be achieved by carrying out a 'walk-through' to ascertain the full responsibilities and collaborations.

Walk-through
Stage 1: **Understanding in application area terms**

What information is the system provided with?
(1) New student details (name, address and emergency telephone number).
(2) The lecture room group the student has joined.

What must the system do with that information?
(1) Record the new student information.
(2) Record that a student belongs to an individual lecture room group.

Stage 2: **Understanding in terms of instances of classes and associations**

Processing the admission of a new student requires the following actions:
(1) Create a new instance of Student with an associated name, address and emergency telephone number.
(2) Locate the LectureRoom instance corresponding to the named lecture room.
(3) Create a new instance of the resides_in association type.

Stage 3: **Understanding in terms of responsibilities and collaborations**

Class: FacultyAdmin
'There is only one instance of this class and it is the orchestrating instance.'
Responsibilities:
Records admissions of new students into the faculty.
Keeps track of LectureRoom instances corresponding to named rooms within the faculty.
Collaborators:
Student
LectureRoom

Note: In order for one class to collaborate with another class, a message needs to be sent to an instance of the collaborating class. For example, within C++ we could have:

```
LectureRoom newLectureRoom; //create an instance of
class LectureRoom
cout ≪ 'Enter lecture room name:';
cin ≫ newLectureRoom.name; //send name message
```

Class: LectureRoom
Responsibilities:
Records the name of the lecture room.
Keeps track of the Student instances corresponding to the students within the lecture room.
Keeps track of the Tutor instance corresponding to the assigned tutor.

Class: Student
Responsibilities:
Records the student's name, address and emergency contact number.

Class: Tutor
Responsibilities:
Records the tutor's name and study room number.

Invariant
Any given instance of LectureRoom is associated with instances of Student via the resides_in association. The maximum number of Student instances that may be associated with any one instance of LectureRoom is 28.

(5) So far we have not considered any aspects of inheritance. When we investigate the responsibilities, both the Tutor and Student have to record their respective names. This is a common factor between classes and could be represented in a parent class called Faculty Member. Technically this would be abstract as no instances would need to be directly initiated from it. Redraw the class-association diagram to represent this design modification.

At this stage the grounds for formal design are implied. The class structures have been specified but their individual components (variables and methods) need to be brought out. This would be carried out in the design stage (full details are contained in the object-oriented development unit). As an example for the Student class two private variables are required (one for the address and one for the emergency telephone number) with corresponding 'getter' and 'setter' methods. Remember nothing is required within the Student class for *name* as this is will be implemented within the superclass (FacultyMember).

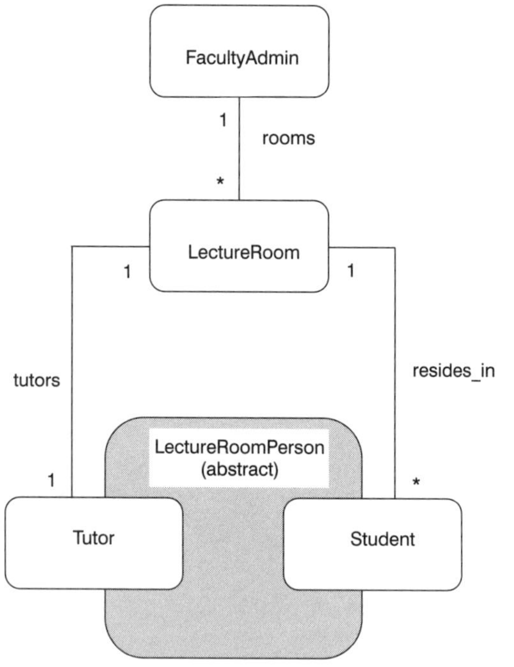

Inheritance details:

Class: FacultyMember
Responsibilities:
Maintaining the names of the faculty members (students and tutors).
Class: Tutor
is-a-subclass-of: FacultyMember
Responsibilities:
Recording the staff room number.
Class: Student
is-a-subclass-of: FacultyMember
Responsibilities:
Recording the student address and emergency telephone number.

Figure 5.1.14 *Modified class-association diagram for the Canine faculty*

(6) Use an appropriate CASE tool to design the class structures to incorporate the attributes and operations that would be required to implement the faculty model into an appropriate high-level object-oriented programming. Remember the attributes will represent the required variables (private or public) that a class will contain and the operations represent the methods that can access the variables or carry out other required functions (see Figure 5.1.15).

Case tool applications

Select CASE tools have been used to develop some of the applications within this section. The main tools used are:

Select Enterprise® for completing:

- Class diagrams
- Collaboration diagrams
- General graphics

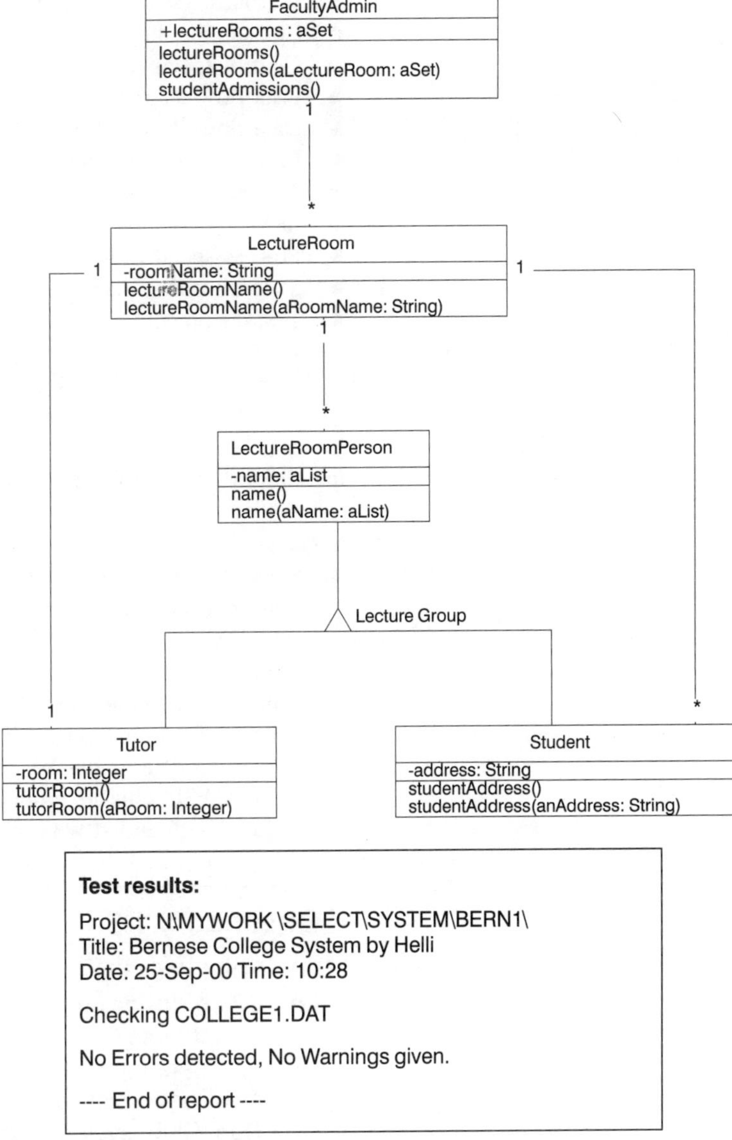

Figure 5.1.15 *Class diagram showing faculty structure*

- Interface class diagram
- Process hierarchy
- Process thread
- Sequence diagram
- State diagram
- Storage class
- Text document
- Use case diagrams

Select Enterprise® is an advanced interactive tool set for modelling, designing and building next-generation enterprise applications. It is ideally suited for developing object-oriented models by offering a component-based development with 'reuse' of designs as well as code.

Select Yourdon® for completing:

- Constantine diagrams
- Control specifications
- Data flow diagrams
- Data flow (Hartley) diagrams
- Entity-relationship diagrams
- General graphics
- Jackson diagrams
- Process specifications
- State transition diagrams
- Text documents

Select Yourdon® is designed for real-time software development projects using the Yourdon method. It incorporates full support for Yourdon methods including Jackson, Constantine techniques and both the Hartley and Ward-Mellor real-time extensions.

Other products include:

- Select SSADM® which is designed for application development projects using the Structured Systems Analysis and Design Method (SSADM). It provides support for the full range of SSADM techniques, helping development organizations realize all the benefits of adopting SSADM.
- Select SE® is a model-driven application development tool set, supporting data modelling and data management.
- Select CASE tools are produced by the Princeton Softech Company and can be found at www.princetonsoftech.com

Question 5.1.5

(1) What does the abbreviation CRC stand for?

(2) When designing class structures what is meant by:

- attribute?
- operation?

(3) Two new classes are to be added to an Agility Dog Club system. They are CommitteeMember and OrdinaryMember. Their outlines are shown below:

Class: CommitteeMember
Responsibilities:
Record the committee member name, number and role.

Class: OrdinaryMember
Responsibilities:
Record the ordinary member name, number and classification (classification relates to the classes that the members are eligible to compete in).

Note that both classes share common responsibilities, i.e. member name and member number, and therefore need to be designed as subclasses of a common superclass. Construct part of a class diagram to represent this inheritance structure, include any attributes and operations needed to implement the design.

Project management

Introduction

One of the main aims of software project management is to complete a quality product 'on time and within budget'. The end result must be a product that is fit for the purpose that was outlined in the original specifications. The product must be completed without exceeding predetermined costs that were set at the beginning of the work. Time deadlines need to be ensured in order for the completed application to be delivered to the customer or end user when they expect it to be ready.

Problems with time and budget can lead to a poor market reputation and may affect continuing projects that the organization has planned for. The aim of good software project management is to avoid these problems and ensure success in all areas of the project. The project manager needs to plan a project around the concepts of:

- Quality
- Cost
- Budget

These three characteristics are known as the 'triangle of primary objectives' and determine the priority each should play in the software development process. Project planning consists of estimating effort, scheduling tasks and monitoring their progress. The effort required to complete various activities is estimated in terms of recourses needed to implement them. Scheduling involves allocating tasks to individuals and determining the start and finish times for the associated activities. Monitoring checks the progress of a developing project against its original aims.

A *software project manager* may face the problem of directing a large development team consisting of analysts, software engineers, programmers, hardware technicians, quality assurance specialists and other related staff, where the end application will contain several thousand (or even millions) of lines of code. Research has shown that the best software products are achieved when a good manager motivates the team and they feel part of the overall plan for producing the application. It is down to the project manager to get the most from his staff in order to provide a finely tuned professional workforce that is capable of ensuring success for any given product application.

Roles of a project manager

There are no set guidelines for the tasks that a project manager has to carry out. There are many varied tasks, some of which are outlined below:

- *Controlling* – is the process of ensuring a project meets its stated objectives. The project manager will be involved in reallocating resources when a problem occurs and providing leadership by directing staff every day as to what is required and helping as necessary.
- *Planning* – this is the process of deciding what to do and will involve specifying events, cost estimates, meeting stated objectives, risk assessment and subdividing tasks.

- *Monitoring* – this involves the project manager checking the progress of a project ensuring that both internal and external milestones are met. The external milestones will be carried out with agents of the customer so they are aware of the development progress. The main objective here is to check the project is on time to meet its specified delivery date. Progress problems identified in this area may lead to new measures being put into place that come under other task headings specified in this list.
- *Organizing* – this involves the organization of staff and resources and outlining the duties and responsibilities of the people within the team. The project manager will need to ensure clear lines of communication are set up within the team in order to provide a coherent framework for information to be distributed.
- *Representing* – the project manager will need to represent the company and especially the application under development with people outside the organization. This could involve liaising with the customer, or associated agents, for which the project is being developed. The project manager will need to meet with the customer in order to report on the progress (or lack of progress) of the project under development.
- *Staffing* – here the project manager will ascertain the required staff needed to successfully complete the project. Identifying any training requirements that may be required and encouraging staff by providing promotion opportunities. This category sees the project manager playing the role of a personnel officer with the responsibility to assign staff positions from senior management down to junior and trainee appointments.
- *Innovating* – this involves the project manager developing new ideas that will improve the work being carried out on the project. An example could be a new CASE (Computer Aided Software Engineering) application that has just come onto the market which may improve the analysis and design techniques that are already in place.

Information requirements of a project manager

It is important that the project manager has information that is relevant to applications under current development. Some sources of information that should be readily available are outlined below:

- For any planning to be carried out data on earlier projects is required. This historical information is useful for estimating and costing a current project that has similar characteristics to previous projects. The project manager will be able to ascertain the possible resources required and provide a time analysis breakdown leading to a possible completion date.
- For developing any software system initial documentation is created before it starts production. Such documentation would include Project Plans, Quality Plans, Cost Estimates, Risk Estimates, etc. and should be readily available to the project manager. Documentation that is created during the software development lifecycle needs also to be available and will include the following: Requirements Analysis, Specification (both functional and non-functional), System Design, Implementation and Mainte-

nance, etc. The project manager needs to ensure that a system of 'version control' is in place in order for the information held to be the latest available.

- Data is required which helps the project manager make changes that will improve the efficiency of a project under construction. Such data would come from a number of sources, both internal and external. Within an organization any information on innovation strategies needs to be available and how the modifications can be compared across activities to ascertain their overall effectiveness. External sources may include information on existing or new tools that are available and can be implemented within the development process to improve efficiency. Above all the project manager needs to ensure that any changes made will have an economic benefit for the company.
- In order to successfully monitor the progress of a project, information including graphical data, needs to be available to the project manager. Graphical data would include Gantt charts and associated critical path networks. These would clearly show the required deadlines, stage completion dates, delivery date and any associated milestones that are required during the development lifecycle.
- If during the monitoring process it was found that the project was slipping behind schedule the project manager will need to make changes to improve the progress. This will involve rescheduling activities and documentation needs to be available that shows how any changes made in one part of the project impacts on other areas of the project.

Software project planning

All projects need to be carefully planned, failure to do so will result in an application that is difficult to manage. Large projects are generally planned in outline before development commences where the main elements are specified. These include an estimation of the project cost, required resources and how the project lines up with the company's business plan. Once the customer has accepted the project a full planning document needs to be produced. This document is called the *project plan*, and an example outline of what should be included is shown below:

Company Project Plan

Chapter 1 – Project Outline
1.1 overview of the project
1.2 overview of the development stages
1.3 customer contacts and integration
1.4 work description and product delivery

Chapter 2 – Project Planning
2.1 task lists with associated dates and people responsible
2.2 significant event points
2.3 responsibilities of the project team

Chapter 3 – Software and Hardware Requirements
3.1 software and hardware facilities required
3.2 analysis and design tools
3.3 additional support requirements
3.4 specified development strategies
3.5 required software development standards

Chapter 4 – Configuration Management
4.1 strategies for handling change during development
4.2 version control requirements

Chapter 5 – Documentation Requirements
5.1 documentation format
5.2 documentation standards
5.3 publishing and validating responsibilities

Appendices
A test strategies to be adopted
B quality plan

Question 5.1.6

(1) List the main roles of a project manager.
(2) What does monitoring involve for a project manager?
(3) Within a project plan as outlined in the previous table, explain what should be included for the following section: 3.2 analysis and design tools?

When any application has been completed the project manager should have learned something from it. Most projects involve a steep learning curve because tasks differ in complexity and new development tools come onto the market all the time. Software is increasing in complexity as the power of the hardware increases adding more challenges for the project manager. But any experience gained will be beneficial to any subsequent projects that have to be developed by the project manager.

Project management tools

Gantt charts

Gantt charts were developed by Henry Gantt, (1861–1919), an industrial engineer and have been in widespread use as planning aids within project development since. Gantt charts show various activities as blocks on the diagram that are plotted against a time base (or 'x' axis). It gives an overall outline of the scheduling of tasks throughout a given project and will be used by developers to specify the start and end dates for their associated activities. A Gantt chart is therefore a form of bar chart where activities are listed down the diagram and plotted against a horizontal time base. An example Gantt chart is shown in Figure 5.1.16.

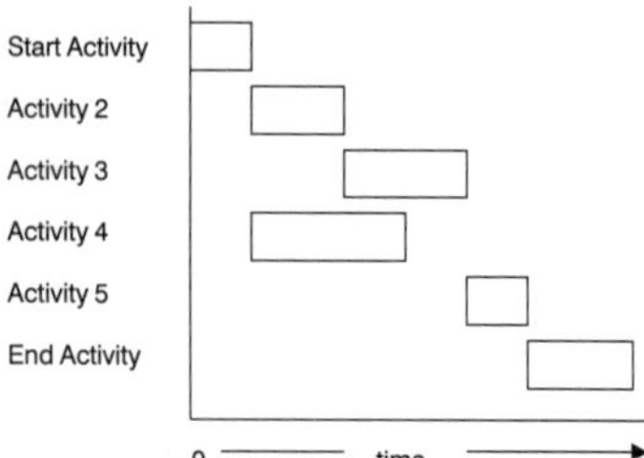

Figure 5.1.16 *Outline Gantt chart*

Within any project some activities cannot be started until other activities have finished. This means that some activities are dependent on others and this fact needs to be specified in a table before the Gantt chart is completed.

Exercise 5.1.2

From the following table create a corresponding Gantt chart.

Activity	*Estimated duration of the activity (in days)*	*Dependant*
A1	12	–
A2	27	A1
A3	10	A2
A4	29	A1
A5	21	A3, A4
A6	12	A2
A7	10	A5, A6

Suggested solution:

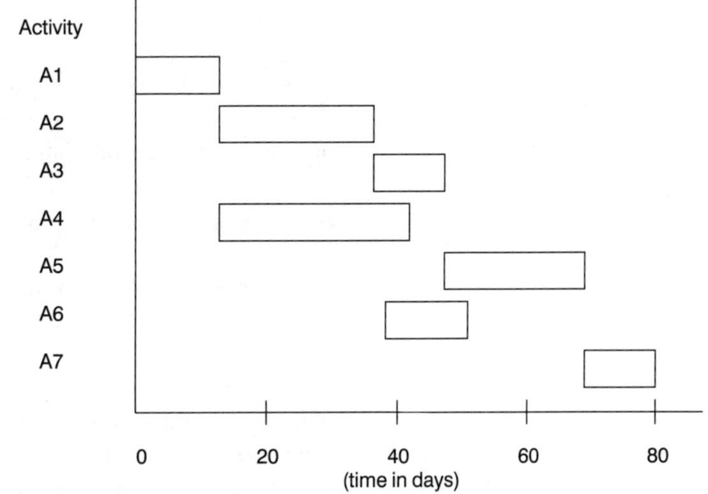

Figure 5.1.17 *Exercise Gantt chart*

Note that the time taken to the end of the project is ascertained from the activities and their associated dependencies. The final time shown in the chart will represent the end of the project and when it is ready for delivery to the customer.

The levels expressed in a Gantt chart can act as a schedule by which the progress of a project can be ascertained. If any problems occur the following actions should be employed:

- Find the critical areas of the project where any delay can affect the date the project is due to be completed.

- Check the progress of the project to ensure it is still on target to reach its planned completion date.
- If any activities need to be rescheduled ascertain what effect the changes will have on the rest of the project.

To achieve these goals the best tool available to the project manager is that of critical path analysis through network diagrams. This technique will provide a means of determining the effect changes have on the time periods allocated to each activity for a specified project. Critical path methods employ network diagrams that show the relationships between activities and their estimated durations.

Network diagrams

Network diagrams come in a variety of forms:

- CPM – Critical Path Method
- CPA – Critical Path Analysis
- ADM – Arrow diagrams
- PERT – Project Review and Evaluation Technique
- PDM – Precedence diagrams

They provide analysis of results of project progress reports and allow decisions to be made by the project manager. An outline of the objectives of a network diagram are stated below:

- Identify any possible problem areas before they are encountered.
- Provide a focus for critical activities.
- Provide a means of evaluating the relocation of resources.
- Provide a tool for monitoring the progress of a project.

In order to produce a network diagram the activities need to be stated with their estimated duration times. An example table for an engine oil change is shown below:

Activity	*Description*	*Estimated duration*
1 to 2	Empty old engine oil	10 minutes
2 to 3	Fill with new oil	5 minutes
3 to 4	Run engine and check level	12 minutes

An important point to remember here is that the duration time for each activity is kept in the same units, i.e. minutes, hours, days or months. A simple network structure to represent this table is shown in Figure 5.1.18.

The network figure contains information about the duration of each activity and the corresponding cumulative time taken over the whole project. For more sophisticated diagrams additional information may be required which includes the following terms:

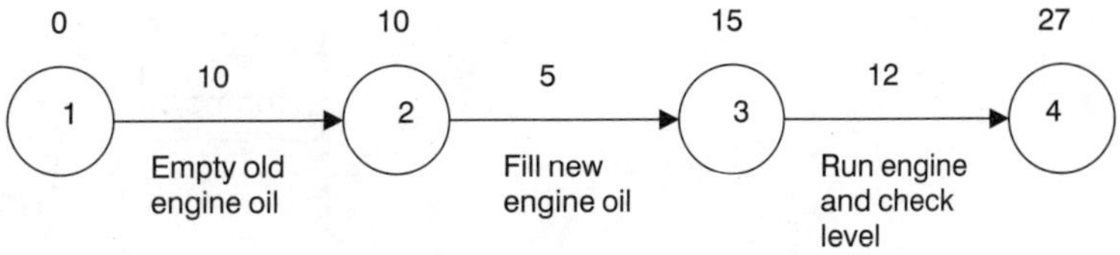

0 10 15 27

1 → 10 Empty old engine oil → 2 → 5 Fill new engine oil → 3 → 12 Run engine and check level → 4

Figure 5.1.18 *Network diagram using arrow notation*

- The earliest start time or the Earliest Expected Time (EET) which represents the earliest time that a particular activity can start to be developed within a project.
- Earliest finish which specifies the finish time for an activity that started its development at the early start time.
- Latest start or Latest Allowable Time (LAT) which specifies the latest time an activity may start in order for it to be completed on time.
- Latest finish specifies the latest time an activity may finish in order to keep the overall project on schedule.
- Maximum span is the maximum time period that an activity has to be completed in. It is calculated by subtracting the Earliest Start Time (EET) specified at the start of an activity from the Latest Finish Time (LFT) specified at the end of the activity, i.e. LAT (end of the activity) – EET (start of the activity) = Maximum span.
- Total float is calculated as the maximum span minus the estimated duration. This is very important when ascertaining the critical points within a project as activities that have a total float of zero are said to be on the critical path.

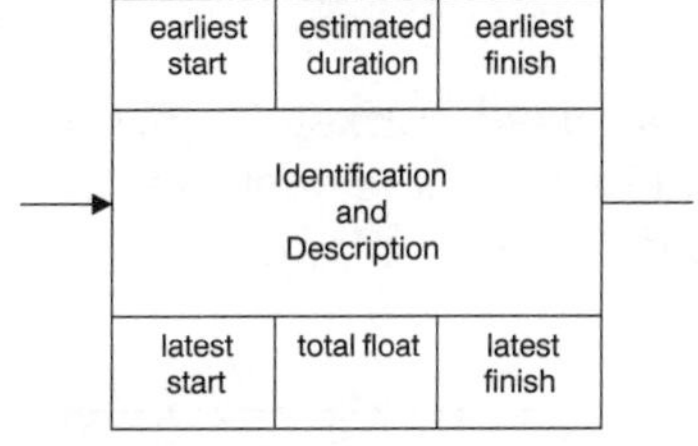

Figure 5.1.19 *Activity using a 'precedence' structure*

One way of showing this amount of data is to use a precedence diagram that provides a clear representation of the activities and their start and finish times relative to their immediate predecessors and successors. Most modern project management tools (Microsoft Project, CS Project Professional, Project Commander, etc.) support the precedence notation or a similar structure. An example of the notation used for an activity is shown in Figure 5.1.19.

Program Evaluation and Review Technique (PERT)

This technique was originally developed by the US Navy in the late 1950s and has been widely used ever since as a project management tool within education, industry and government circles. The steps taken to develop this process require the identification of all the activities and placing them in sequence. Then the timing of each activity needs to be estimated along with their associated dependencies. Once this has been established it is documented in a table from which the network diagram can be constructed and the critical path established. From then on the project manager can use the diagram for monitoring purposes. It can then be modified, if required, to take into account any rescheduling requirements and changes to the critical path.

Figure 5.1.20 shows the notation that we are going to use to develop this procedure. The figure shows an event which is used at the start or the finish of an activity and from which the estimated duration and total float can be ascertained.

When creating network diagrams it may be necessary to include 'dummy activities'. These are shown as dashed lines and are used to

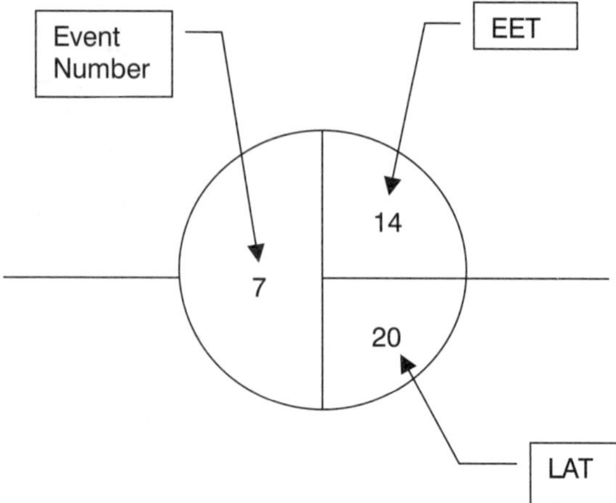

Figure 5.1.20 *Network diagram event*

specify the dependence between activities on the diagram. They do not constitute any real work and have no time allocation associated with them. They just act as a logical link to ensure the network diagram correctly represents the stated dependencies.

The following example takes you through the stages of using PERT to develop a network structure, ascertaining its critical path and tabulating the resulting information.

Example 5.1.5

This example is based on the table used in Exercise 5.1.3 and assumes the activities have already been established in their correct order for development. For your information the table is repeated below:

Activity	*Estimated duration of the activity (in days)*	*Dependant*
A1	12	–
A2	27	A1
A3	10	A2
A4	29	A1
A5	21	A3, A4
A6	12	A2
A7	10	A5, A6

Question:
From the table:

(1) Construct a network diagram.
(2) Construct a table to show the maximum span and total float.
(3) Specify the critical path and emphasize it on the network diagram.

Suggested solutions:

(1) First layout the diagram to show the activities and the event numbers. This should be achieved by looking at the activities and who they are dependent on.

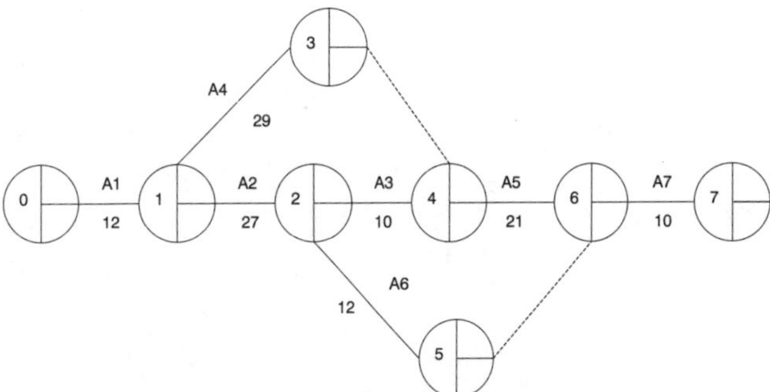

Figure 5.1.21 *Outline network diagram*

Next add the EET to each event which specifies the earliest time that a particular activity can start. This can be achieved from the table or better still the Gantt chart.

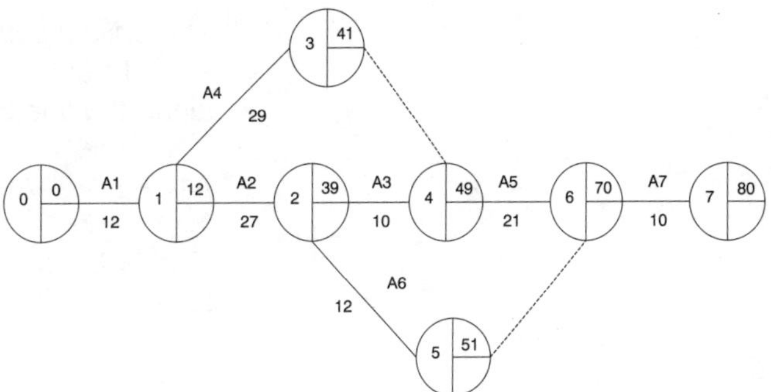

Figure 5.1.22 *Network diagram showing earliest start times*

Next add the LAT times which relate to the latest time an activity may start in order to still complete it on time. This is a little more tricky, remember that the LAT for the final event must be the same as the EET. Work back from there by subtracting the estimated duration from the final LAT (i.e. 80 – 10 = 70 and 70 – 21 = 49, etc.). Note the

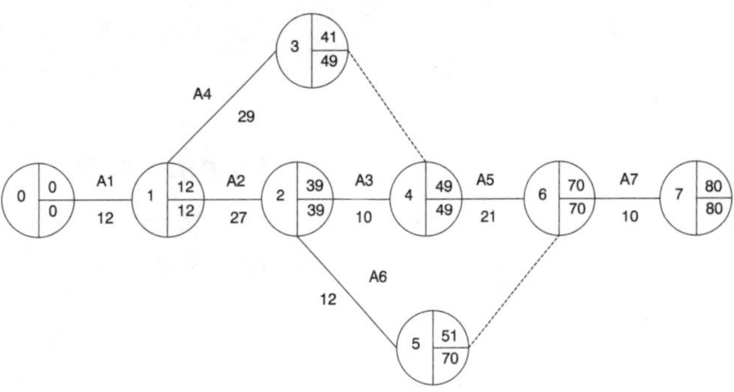

Figure 5.1.23 *Network diagram showing latest allowable times*

LATs shown for the start of the dummy activities are the same as the LATs at the end of the activity. This is because dummy activities do not have any time period associated with them.

(2) The table is shown below, remember that the total float is calculated from subtracting the estimated duration from the maximum span.

Activity	*Estimated duration*	*Maximum span*	*Total float*
A1	12	12	0
A2	27	27	0
A3	10	10	0
A4	27	37	10
A5	21	21	0
A6	12	19	19
A7	10	10	0

(3) The *critical path* lies on a line where the activities have a total float of zero. In this case the critical path lies along the line containing activities:

A1–A2–A3–A5–A7

This is been emphasized in Figure 5.1.24 (using bold lines).

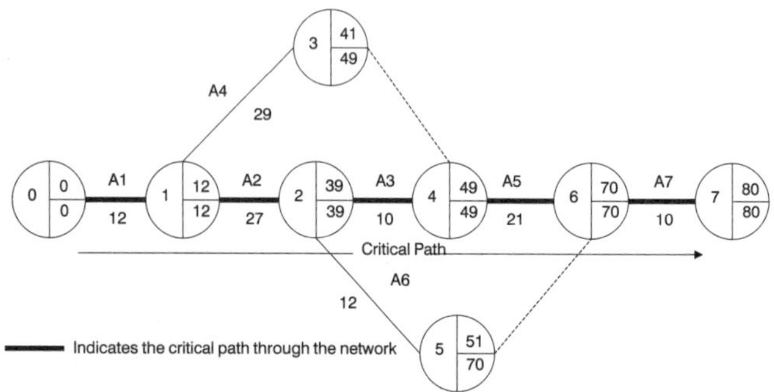

Figure 5.1.24 *Network diagram showing the critical path*

Question 5.1.7

(1) What is a Gantt chart used for?
(2) What does PERT stand for and what is its main function?
(3) What do the terms EET and LAT mean?
(4) What is important about the critical path?
(5) How is the total float calculated and what is important about its value?

Exercise 5.1.3

A partly complete network diagram is shown below:

(1) Complete the network diagram to fill in the missing EETs and LATs.
(2) Set up a table that shows the maximum span and total float.
(3) From the results obtained in (2) show the critical path on the network diagram.

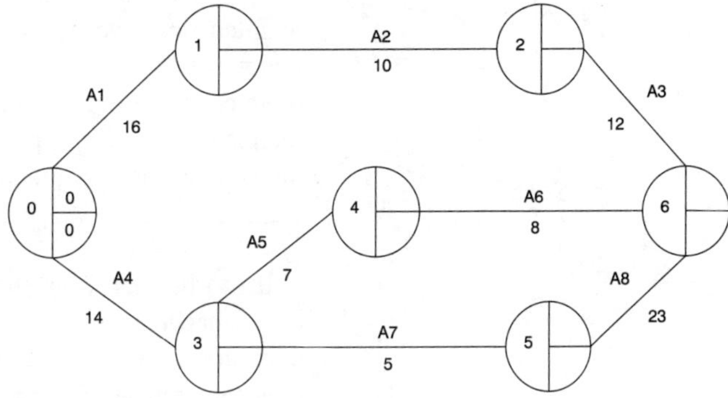

Figure 5.1.25 *Outline network diagram*

Systems maintenance

Introduction

We saw in Chapter 2 (Systems Analysis) that *maintenance* forms an activity within the software lifecycle. It has to be planned from the earliest stages and any design decisions that are made need to consider how they will affect the maintenance of the produce. A good system requires a product that is easily maintained so that its future is ensured. Remember that if a software product is not maintained it dies. If we take a word processor application the manufacture will keep maintaining the product and bring out new versions or updates in order to keep up with market requirements. If this process of maintenance does not take place the product will not be marketable and sales will fall.

Professional programmers spend a lot of time on maintenance activities. The results of a survey by Lientz and Swanson are shown below:

Activity	*% time*
maintenance	48
new development	46.1
other development	5.9

Further surveys indicate that changeability is the second most important attribute after reliability for the development of large software systems. The cost of maintenance is often over 50% and sometimes reaching 75% of the total software lifecycle costs for the development of a product.

In order for Lientz and Swanson to establish the importance of maintenance versus new software within the software development industry they surveyed several companies and the results are shown below:

Importance	*%*
maintenance is very much more important than new development	33.3
maintenance is more important than new development	21.7
maintenance is equal to new development	34.8
maintenance is less important than new development	5.8
maintenance is very much less important than new development	4.3

It can be seen from the table that 55% of the responses thought that maintenance was more important than new development. Some companies are only responsible for one major product and their existence relies on its continued success. For them new development is not a major issue because they need to ensure the existing system is thoroughly maintained. If their system does encounter problems the company needs to ensure all available effort is put into any required changes/updates, etc. The company needs to ensure that the product fully meets the requirements of the end user at all times and hence provide continued success for them as a viable software producer.

Maintenance is not always easy and encounters the same problems as those seen with an original project. But it has additional problems as often the people carrying out the maintenance activities are not the same as those producing the original software. Poor documentation can present problems; we saw a major example of this when systems underwent changes to avoid the so-called 'millennium bug' problem. Systems that had been in operation for several years required modifications, but this took time due to the lack of documentation especially in the area of internal coding and associated structures.

Lientz and Swanson surveyed nearly 500 companies to establish the distribution of effort in software maintenance. Their results are shown in the table below:

Activity	*% participation*
Emergency debugging	12.4
Routine debugging	9.3
Data environment adaptation	17.3
Changes to hardware or operating system	6.2
Enhancements for users	41.8
Improve documentation	5.5
Improve code efficiency	4.0
Other	3.4

Key fact

Unlike hardware, software products do not wear out. But they will die if they are not maintained. Dead products do not need maintenance. Therefore systems must be maintained if they are to remain a viable product in their specified environment.

The table shows that only a small percentage is assigned to emergency debugging (12.4%) and the largest maintenance activity is for enhancements to be made for the users. This would include any changes, modifications, updates, etc. that enhance the product to improve its capabilities and provide a better tool for the customer or end user.

Another survey by Lientz and Swanson looked into the types of maintenance carried out within software organizations. The types established are listed in the table below:

Type of maintenance	*% employed*
Adaptive: changing a system to work in a new operating environment	18
Corrective: changing a system to correct deficiencies, i.e. ● it will not run ● incorrect results are obtained ● does not perform as expected in order to meet the specified requirements	17.4
Perfective: changing a system to add new functionality, i.e. making it ● better ● faster ● more compact ● better documented ● easier to use ● modern	60
Other: including *preventive* maintenance which changes software to improve future maintainability or reliability or to provide a better basis for future enhancements	4.6

Question 5.1.8

(1) What are the main goals of software maintenance?
(2) Why is it important to keep on 'updating' software?
(3) From the surveys conducted by Lientz and Swanson which type of maintenance activity has the most time spent on it, and why?

The important issue resulting from these studies is that maintenance can be managed. The requirements of the adaptive and perfective types can be anticipated by the development team and measures for scheduling, monitoring and estimation can be managed in the same way as a new project. Some corrective maintenance can also be managed leaving about 10% that require special, immediate handling.

Maintenance requests

A software product that delivers large systems may take months or even years to complete. During the development process the original specification, that the system must be designed to, may become out of date so that when it is complete its lacks important functions or at worst, it may not be usable. Systems need to be developed flexibly so that modifications can be made easily through program units that have been selected to cope with anticipated changes. Such changes can be implemented during the lifecycle of the project or through maintenance procedures. The following steps outline the stages taken during the maintenance process:

- A *change request* from the customer or market requirements trigger the maintenance process.
- Often changes are implemented into a new version of the system.
- If changes are made to an installed application the corresponding documentation needs to be updated to reflect the modified structure.

The maintenance request may be activated by somebody issuing a 'change request form' which specifies all the new requirements that are to be implemented along with who issued the modification. An example of a 'change request form' is shown below.

Change request form	**Reference Number ....**
I request that this change request form be submitted to the next scheduled maintenance control meeting for discussion.	
Name:	Date:
Position:	Internal Extension:
Department:	EMAIL:
Project Title:	
Implementation Version:	
Proposed Change:	
Affected Modules/Units:	
Reasons for Change:	
Improvement Plan:	
Fallback Plan:	
Other Information:	

The *change request* is submitted and evaluated by the project manager and senior staff to ascertain its technical merit, potential problem areas, impact on other units within the project and the potential cost. The output of the evaluation process is a *change report* that is presented to the change control authority who make the final decisions about the proposed changes to the system.

The improvement plan is structured into project, group and corporate elements. The project level is concerned with the need for improved software tools that are essential for maintaining existing poor quality code. The group level issues specify the need for improved communications and roles for the maintenance team. The corporate issues focus on the creation of an environment in which the maintenance activities are seen as an integral part of the overall software development field and quality assurance issues. The main headings to be included in the improvement plan are outlined below:

- Introduction.
- Improvement process – to include overall quality issues and required needs for the proposed change. Reviews the overall process and specifies problem areas and how they can be overcome.
- Project level plan – to include required tools and training requirements for their use.
- Group level plan – ensuring who is to receive information and their status within the maintenance process.
- Corporate level plan – Communication channels and subcontract requirements. Design requirements, customer links and quality standards.
- Scheduling of the plan and progress checks.
- Summary.

Maintenance activities

The activities required to complete the maintenance work can be classified under two headings:

- Unstructured maintenance
- Structured maintenance

Unstructured maintenance takes place when the only element to work on is the source code. Documentation is often poor and the resulting maintenance process has to evaluate code sections that are difficult to ascertain and interpret.

Structured maintenance occurs if the complete software engineering documentation for the project exists. Here the activity begins with the evaluation of the design document, followed by assessing the impact of the required modification and planning a method of implementation. Finally the design is modified, reviewed, coded and tested. Figure 5.1.26 shows the layout of structured versus unstructured maintenance.

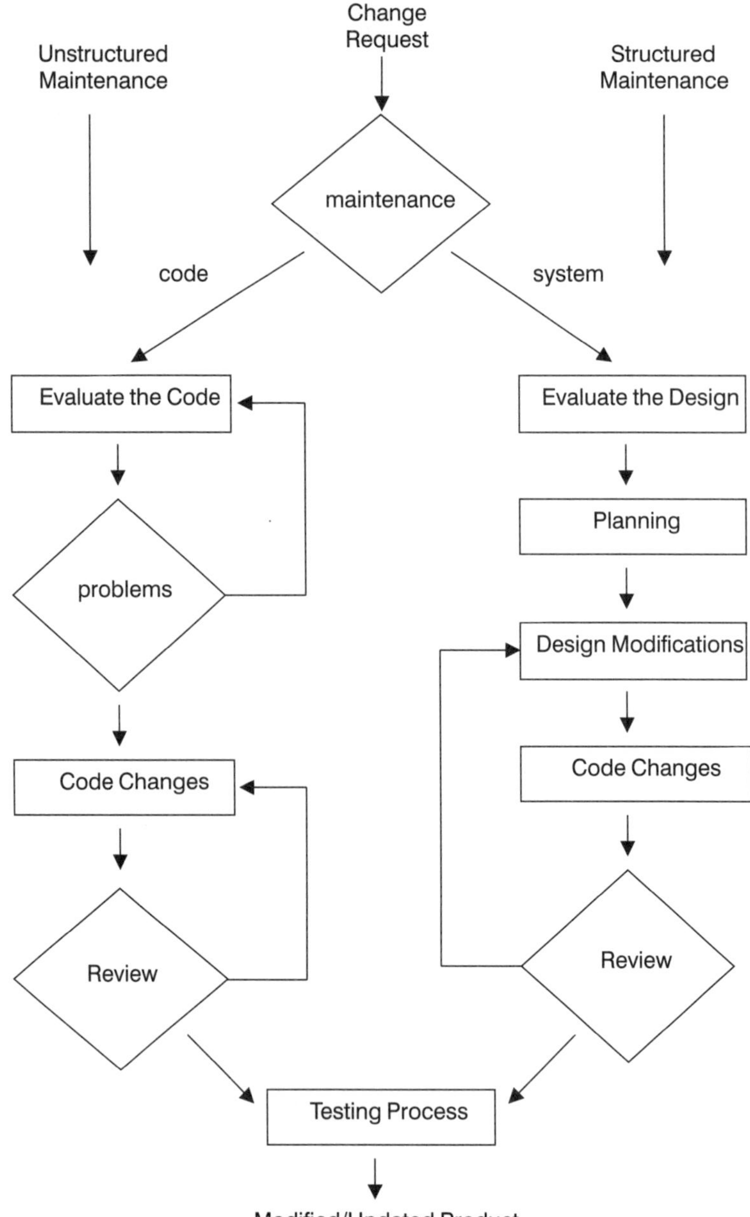

Figure 5.1.26 *Maintenance structures*

> **Question 5.1.8**
>
> (1) What is the purpose of completing a change request form and how should it be processed with an organization?
> (2) What are the two maintenance activities that are used when implementing 'change' on a software system. Which method is the least efficient?

Configuration management

The main aim of configuration management is to establish and maintain the viability of software system products throughout their development lifecycle. It involves identifying the configuration of the software at given time intervals, controlling any changes to the configuration, and maintaining traceability and integrity of the configuration throughout the development lifecycle of the project. Configuration management is about implementing and controlling change of a software system product.

The components placed under software configuration management include software products that are delivered to the customer including the requirements documents, code and any other items that have been identified to create the software product (for example, software tools, compiler, etc.). The main goals of configuration management are:

- All configuration management activities are carefully planned.
- Any affected teams or individuals are informed of the status and content of any changes to be implemented.
- The products placed under configuration management need to be identified and available to the team.
- Any changes made to the software work products need to be controlled by the configuration management team.

The table below shows some of the normal activities carried out by configuration management during the lifecycle of a product.

Lifecycle activity	*Configuration management*
Requirements analysis	expand configuration management practices from the system project plan
Systems analysis and design	control versions of documentation produced
Implementation	control versions of code and documentation produced

Software configuration management can mean many things to different people within the software development industry. For example, people see it as version control, configuration identification, status accounting, configuration control boards and modification request tracking. But the one main factor that is agreed between people working in the field is that it is seen as a crucial element in the support of software development and maintenance. As we have already stated, for software to remain successful it needs to undergo maintenance and this maintenance strategy needs to be carefully planned and implemented. A coherent maintenance strategy therefore represents one of the main aims of successful configuration management.

Configuration is therefore the discipline of coordinating software development and controlling the change and evolution of software products and their associated components.

Version control

During the maintenance phase or when an iterative activity occurs within the software lifecycle different versions of the documentation are produced. The documents that comprise all information produced as part of the software engineering process are collectively termed a *configuration*. Version control is a method used to keep track and manage changes that are carried out on a software system. For any software system to be successful a process must be put into place to ensure the development team are working on the latest version of the product. If an earlier version were to be used then the developer could be faced with repeating work that had already been carried out, or working on something that is no longer required. Either way, problems like this can hinder the development process and affect the efficiency of the product being produced.

Let's look at some issues that may occur during the lifecycle of a product:

- Customers want to modify the requirements. The project manager as part of an innovation process wants to modify the approach taken to develop the product. How are these changes going to be controlled?
- When developing part of a system the programmer notices that the listing does not match what the program is doing. The question raised is, what version of the program is this?
- Bailey the programmer is asked to modify part of a program, whilst Bess is asked to reduce its complexity. How are we going to make sure that each of them is not interfering with each other's work?

The solution is to employ the following techniques:

- Configuration Management (CM) – see the last section.
- Version Control (VC) – part of configuration management which organizes the storage of different versions of documents and controls changes to documents when new versions are produced.

Version control tools provide a means for helping multiple users to make simultaneous changes to a collection of documents or files without damaging each other's work. Most version control systems carry out the following sequence of events:

- *Connect operation* – a database is created somewhere on the system.
- *Add operation* – files need to be added to it, both existing and any new ones.
- *Checkout operation* – you are required to tell the database which files you are working on and some tools allow files to be modified at will and submitted when the developer has finished making the changes.
- *Undo checkout command* – if required you can revert to the last version of the file.
- *Checking operation* – when the changes have been made and tested they need to be put back into the database for permanent storage. This allows other members of the development team to see the files if required. The person saving the modified files will be asked to add a description and details of where the new version is.
- *Label operation* – once all the changes have been completed and the system is ready the files can be labelled to state the version number for future reference.

- *Get operation* – the developer can go back and look at earlier versions, or at latest versions that have been added by someone in the development team.
- *Rename operation* – this allows files to be renamed if required.
- *Delete operation* – this allows files to be deleted if they become obsolete.
- *Report operation* – provides reports about the files that are stored in the database.

One of the most important facilities provided with some version control systems is the ability to automatically backup copies of your work on a storage device other than your own development disk system. If changes are made by mistake on the developer's version then the checkout operation will allow you to deliberate about what changes are made and save overwriting some important work.

A document is said to be a *baseline document* when it reaches a certain stage in the development process. The project manager at the outset of the project usually determines when this will be. For example, a design document is baselined for approval or a code module is baselined once it has successfully undergone testing requirements. *Baselining* is therefore a common technique used for controlling change of documents, i.e.

- before a document is baselined, changes can be made by a member of the development team quickly and informally;
- after a document is baselined changes can still be made, but they need to follow formal guidelines to evaluate and verify the change. The changes need to be formally controlled by version control activities that track and modify the status of the document from its baseline date until the end of the project.

Version control tools

In order to implement the 'Add Operation' most tools provide a *repository* which holds the baseline documents. When a document is baselined within a repository it becomes subject to version control. This process is outlined in Figure 5.1.27.

Each team member is allocated an area known as a workspace that prevents project members from accessing the work of others. Generally the use of a workspace contains the following actions:

- In order to carry out a change on a document it is first transferred from the repository to the project member's workspace.
- Changes can then be made to the document without affecting the repository.
- Once any changes to the document have been accepted it is copied back to the repository.

The revision control system (RCS)

This is a version control system that stores all the updates of a single document in a special file called a *revision group* contained in an RCS directory. When a file is baselined a revision group for it is set up and

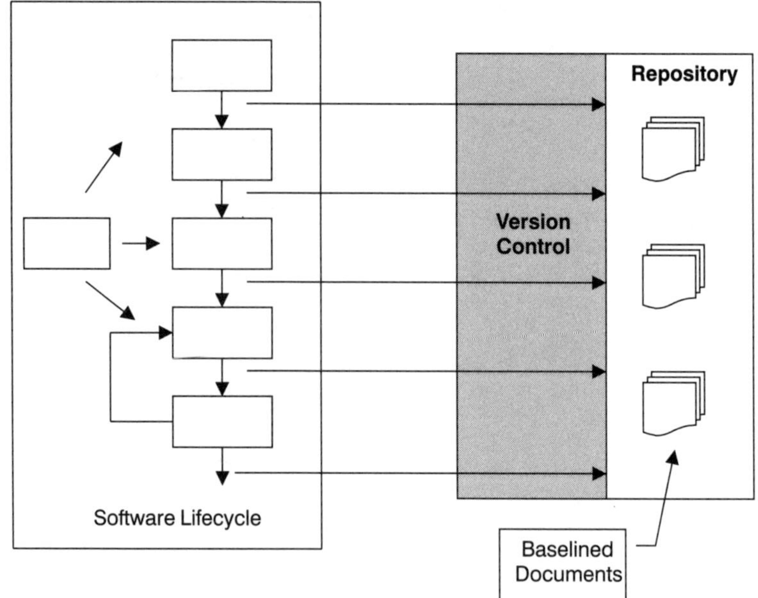

Figure 5.1.27 *Version control using a repository*

the initial version of the document is numbered 1.1. When a new version of the document is checked in a new number is allocated to it, before being added to the revision group. The numbering system is based on a hierarchical tree structure that allows branching for:

- corrections to released documents;
- development modifications;
- processing conflicting changes.

A typical tree structure is outlined in Figure 5.1.28.

The RSC system controls the changes that can be made to files by providing locks. A lock for a revision group must be obtained before a new version can be checked in. Only one user can hold a lock at a time thus allowing only one user the access to make changes to a specified

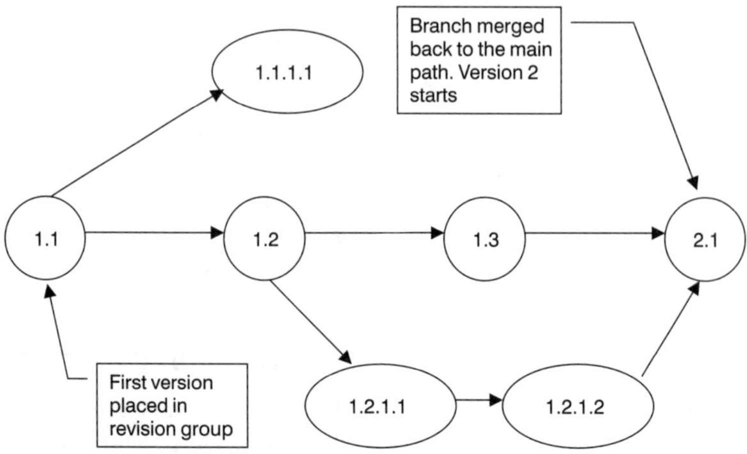

Figure 5.1.28 *Branching within revision groups*

version at a time. The RCS system has facilities for group use where each team member has a link to the central repository within their workspace.

Within the RCS environment the name and version number identifies documents. This could take the form of MYSYSTEM–1.0 allowing different versions to be grouped together in a configuration.

Specified below is an example RCS system:

ComponentSoftware Revision Control System (CS-RCS)

This is a revision control system that allows you to manage multiple versions of your documentation in an efficient manner. It is a powerful and robust document RCS that monitors changes made to files that are accessed by standalone or networked terminals. The system allows you to see how and when a file was changed or easily return to an earlier version.

CS-RCS provides the following version control facilities:

- Retrieve and revision by any criteria anytime.
- See what has changed between two revisions.
- Avoid any loss of work by backtracking.
- Save disk space.
- You know who does what and when.
- Avoids two users modifying the same document at the same time.
- Specifies when there is a modified version of a shared document.
- Operates on a variety of server applications.
- Unix and Windows users can share common files
- Conversion facilities Unix to DOS and DOS to Unix.

CS-RCS is based on the GNU RCS Revision 5.7 standard that is currently used by lots of users in the Unix field. It is based on the original command line interface, but CS-RSC has provided a modern graphical user interface application that can fully integrate with the Windows environment.

CS-RCS can be found via Component Software at:

http://www.componentsoftware.com/csrcs/swintro.htm

Other version controls systems and information can be found at:

http://www.greymatter.co.uk/gmWEB/nodes/NODE0865.htm
http://www.thefreecountry.com/developercity/version.html
http://www.cvshome.org/docs/blandy.html
http://www.systemanage.com/cff/versioncontrol/
http://www.qumasoft.com/feactures.htm
http://www.download.cyclic.com/pub/

Other systems are available, for example *shapeTools* that provides tighter integration with other configuration management requirements as well as version control. But whatever system is used the overall principle is the same, that of controlling the storage of baselined documents to ensure they come under strict version control rules. We have often heard terms like ‘I did not mean to change that file’, ‘Are we working on the latest version?’ or ‘Am I working on the same document as another project member?’ which effect the productivity of the development process. The aim of version control is to improve productivity by providing a system that keeps track, and manages changes, to the documents that are produced during the development lifecycle.

Question 5.1.10

(1) Under what management activity does version control fit into?
(2) What do you need to do in order to carry out the 'checkout' procedure for a version control system?
(3) What does the term 'baselined' mean?
(4) What is a repository?
(5) What multi-platform characteristics are specified for the CS-RSC system?

Patches and fixes

Within the software development lifecycle a *patch, fix* or *Quick Fix engineering* (QFE) are specialized cases of another version of the product. They are classified as small upgrades or modifications that are distributed to the users of the software product so they can be installed within the application. They provide an efficient method of updating software prior to releasing a new product.

Exercise 5.1.4

Download or install an RCS version control system (if one is not already available) and:

(1) Check in: create a simple text file and add it to the repository.
(2) Check when the file was last changed.
(3) Check out the latest revision of the file.
(4) Check in a new revision.
(5) View the revision history of the file.
(6) Produce a detailed report for the file.

5.2 Software quality assurance

Introduction

Software Quality Assurance (SQA) is an activity that is applied throughout the whole development lifecycle of the product. One of the main aims of SQA is to produce a product that meets the customer's requirements. Some software quality assurance definitions are shown below:

> A planned and systematic pattern of all the actions necessary to provide adequate confidence that the software conforms to established technical requirements. *ANSI/IEEE*

> Conformance to explicitly stated functional and performance requirements, explicitly documented development standards, and implicit characteristics that are expected of all professionally developed software. *Pressman*
>
> Quality consists of those product features which meet the needs of the customer and thereby provide product satisfaction. *Juran's Quality Control Handbook*

Above all a product must be fit for the purpose that it is developed for, it must be free of any deficiencies. SAQ is a term used to describe those activities that ensure a contractually acceptable product is delivered to the customer or end users. It includes good practices such as holding reviews, producing quality and project plans, precise documentation and thorough verification and validation practices.

Oakland in his book *Total Quality Management* identifies two major causes of quality problems:

- acceptance of failure;
- misunderstanding of quality.

These problems were picked up from the perspective of the customer or end user. A view that has been very strong in Japan, where customer satisfaction has been placed higher than immediate profit. This leads to the concept of Total Quality Management (TQM) where it is claimed that 'quality is free'. Adding TQM procedures to a project will add initial costs, but these will be overcome with:

- keeping customers. The company may make a larger profit one day, but this is no good if the customers do not come back. Extra effort is made with supplying a quality product, even if this initially means reduced profit margins which will be recouped at a later date.
- making concern for quality visible. This makes the associated processes and development procedures with assuring quality also visible and a new source of expenditure is not seen.

Therefore *quality management* involves taking the customer's view of quality, while Total Quality Management (TQM) involves the process of quality management being passed down the whole chain, i.e. all staff are involved in the quality process.

Within a software development company an independent QA team that reports directly to the line manager above project management level should carry out quality assurance procedures. The team should be independent of any development group but should be responsible for QA across the whole organization. A typical company layout is shown in Figure 5.2.1.

This is a general layout and there are many interpretations of this structure within modern software houses, the main point to note is that the quality manager and development manager are not too strongly associated with a specific project. It is the role of the QA team to ensure quality within the software process by:

- defining process quality standards;
- monitoring the development process to ensure quality standards are being maintained;
- providing reports to product management and the customer.

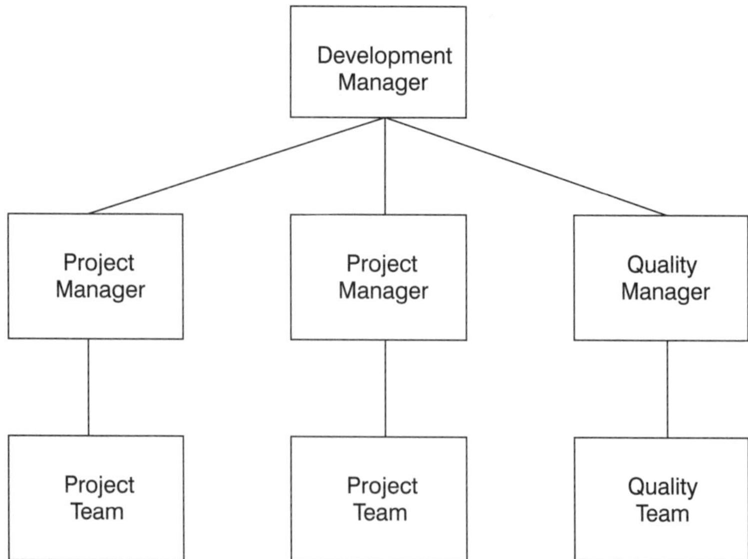

Figure 5.2.1 *Software development management structure*

Quality assurance factors

The factors that effect software quality can be divided into two categories: those that can be directly measured and those that can only be measured indirectly (for example, usability and maintainability). High-quality software can be characterized by the following attributes:

- *Efficiency*: this refers to how a system operates within its given environment. Factors like execution speed and data storage are two factors that an end user requires for efficient software.
- *Reliability*: we can see from the previous section that one aspect of software maintenance was to remove errors within software. Any error may effect the reliability of software although some may be acceptable to the customer if the product still meets its original requirements. Reliability is therefore the measure of the number of times a system fails to perform correctly.
- *Testability*: this relates to how easily a software system can be tested. We shall see later in this section that code can be structured to aid the testing process and hence aid the elimination of errors to produce an acceptable product.
- *Maintainability*: this refers to the concept of change and how it can be implemented within a system under development.
- *Usability*: this relates to how easy a piece of software is to use. We have seen a greater push towards Graphical User Interfaces (GUIs) over the past few years that have improved the way systems can be used. Usability also effects the way in which the application can be controlled, for example a user may require a quick response from the system (the keyboard input would be too slow), so some other input like a touch screen may be more appropriate.
- *Portability*: how easy is it to transfer the application to a new environment.
- *Reusability*: the concept of reuse of code is an important attribute in the development of modern software systems, especially those

developed using object-oriented concepts. Therefore reusability relates to how easy it is to reuse code sections from one system into another system. Remember this code may already be thoroughly tried and tested and so improve the quality of the new product.

Software quality assurance factors should focus on the following three aspects of a software product under development:

- its operational characteristics;
- the ability of the product to undergo change;
- how it can be adapted to a new environment.

Verification and Validation (V&V)

V&V is concerned with checking the software under development to ensure it meets the needs of the original requirements. It has two main objectives:

- to test for any faults in the system;
- to find out if the system is fully operational in its working environment.

Verification checks that a product in the software development process agrees with the product of the previous activity. The product of the system analysis phase is the system analysis document and the process of checking that it reflects the negotiated statement of requirements document is classified as verification.

Validation is the process that checks to see if a component of the software product correctly reflects the original requirements. Certain testing procedures come under this heading, for example system testing and acceptance testing.

Barry Boehm defines V&V as:

Verification: to establish the truth of correspondence between a software product and its specification.
Validation: to establish the fitness of worth of a software product for its operational mission.

or summarized as:

Verification: are we building the product right?
Validation: are we building the right product?

The testing process

During the development of a software project a number of tests are required to ensure the product conforms to its original requirements. All large software products are developed using partitioning where the product is developed using small workable units. These units will require testing in their own right before they can proceed any further. Such testing is called 'unit testing' which uses white box techniques to focus on issues like internal data structures, boundary conditions and its error handling characteristics. When all the units are complete they need to be brought together to form a complete system. The testing carried out during this phase of bringing the units together is called 'integration testing'. Integration testing involves constructing the program structure, from unit tested units, and checking for errors associated with the interfacing of the units. If, for example, you were constructing a program in C++, you would need to ensure the formal parameters from one unit matched the actual parameters to another unit. Integration testing is conducted by bringing the units together gradually and testing their interaction, as opposed to bringing them together first then testing (a technique known as the 'big bang approach'). When the program is complete a series of 'system tests' are carried out in order to validate the requirements of the system. Such tests are carried out in-house with the development team to fully test the system as if it were working in its operational environment. Finally the full system will be taken to the customer and run under its proposed operational environment. This process is called 'acceptance testing' which checks the system with the customer. Acceptance testing may form the final phase before the product is handed over and finalizes the contractual agreement between parties. The testing process over the lifecycle of a product is outlined in Figure 5.2.2.

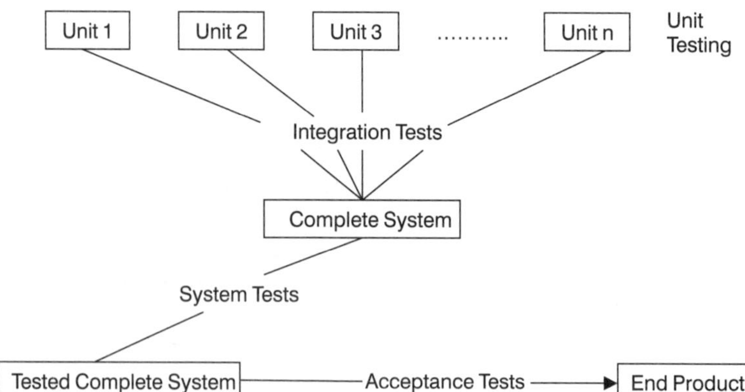

Figure 5.2.2 *Lifecycle testing processes*

Testing methods include:

- *Black box testing*: does not test the internal components of a code module but checks its operational capabilities for the input and output of data.
- *White box testing*: this closely checks the internal code structures of a module. The logical data paths through the code are examined, i.e. the conditional and iterative structures, to ensure the results obtained by the variables and data structures correspond to predicted status. We shall be looking at the work of McCabe later in this chapter which looks at methods of deriving a complexity measure by examining code sequences.
- *Alpha testing*: testing which is carried out with a customer for a specific product. Acceptance testing is an example of this method.
- *Beta testing*: a product is produced for a large market. Certain customers are sent (or they can download it from the internet) an early version of the product to use and check. This is often called a 'beta version' which can be used free of charge during the

> **Question 5.2.1**
>
> (1) What is the difference between Verification and Validation?
> (2) Why is usability a characteristic of high-quality software?
> (3) What testing strategies take place over the lifecycle of a product?
> (4) What is 'white box' testing?

testing phase and any problems encountered are reported back to the manufacturer. The manufacturer will then make any necessary modification to the product before releasing the final system.

Tests associated with Verification and Validation (V&V):

- *Statistical testing*: this provides an estimate of the run-time reliability of the system in relation to the number of user inputs.
- *Defect testing*: this provides a means of checking for faults (bugs) in the system during execution.

Software quality systems

We have seen within this book that sound engineering practices have been applied to the development of software. This broadly comes under the heading of 'Software Engineering' and the transition of standards from one discipline to another has caused some concern within the software industry. To ensure that software systems do meet the same standards that have been inherent in a number of other industries for many years, the software industry needs to conform to its own standards. Outlined below are definitions for four internationally standardized terms that are basic to any quality assurance system:

- *Quality*: the totality of features and characteristics of a product or service that bear on its ability to satisfy stated or implied needs.
- *Quality policy*: The overall quality intentions and direction of an organization as regards quality, as formally expressed by top management.
- *Quality management*: that aspect of overall management function that determines and implements quality policy.
- *Quality system*: the organizational structure, responsibilities, procedures, processes and resources for implementing quality management.

(BS 4778/ISO 8402)

Although these standards are carefully defined they are still a little hard to follow and implement. The quality system definition is perhaps a little less ambiguous and in many cases provides a starting point for planning the quality assurance procedures for a new project. It is management's responsibility to produce a quality policy for a proposed quality system. The original standard outlined for this is:

> The supplier's management shall define and document its policy and objectives for, and commitment to, quality. The supplier shall ensure that the policy is understood, implemented and maintained at all levels in the organization.
>
> (BS 5750/ISO 9001)

The *International Standards Organization* (ISO) is a non-governmental organization that was established in 1947. The main organization is based in Geneva and is the head organization for standardizations from approximately 100 countries. Its work results in international agreements that are published as international standards, over 10 000 to date (i.e. ISO 9000 series). Examples of some national standards are shown below:

AFNOR – Association Francaise de Normalisation (France)
ANSI – American National Standard Institute (USA)
BSI – British Standards Institute (UK)
DIN – Deutsches Institute für Normung (Germany)

ISO 9000–3 guidelines for applying the ISO 9001 Standard to Software. ISO 9000–3: 1997 is an expansion of the old ISO 9001:1994 standard (in fact it has been added to the original standard). The main headings associated with this standard are outlined below:

Quality management systems:

ISO 9000–3: 4.1	Management Responsibilities
ISO 9000–3: 4.2	Quality System Requirements
ISO 9000–3: 4.3	Contract Review Requirements
ISO 9000–3: 4.4	Product Design Requirements
ISO 9000–3: 4.5	Document and Data Control
ISO 9000–3: 4.6	Purchasing Requirements
ISO 9000–3: 4.7	Customer-supplied Products
ISO 9000–3: 4.8	Product Identification and Tracing
ISO 9000–3: 4.9	Process Control Requirements
ISO 9000–3: 4.10	Product Inspection and Testing
ISO 9000–3: 4.11	Control and Inspection Equipment
ISO 9000–3: 4.12	Inspection and Test Status of Products
ISO 9000–3: 4.13	Control of Non-conforming Products
ISO 9000–3: 4.14	Corrective and Preventative Action
ISO 9000–3: 4.15	Handling, Storage and Delivery
ISO 9000–3: 4.16	Control of Quality Records
ISO 9000–3: 4.17	Internal Quality Audit Requirements
ISO 9000–3: 4.18	Training Requirements
ISO 9000–3: 4.19	Servicing Requirements
ISO 9000–3: 4.20	Statistical Techniques

As you can see this is a comprehensive list and to give an example of what each heading contains details of the ISO–9001: 1994/ISO 9000–3: 1997 4.1 standard are outlined below:

ISO 9000–3: 4.1 Management Responsibilities

- Define a quality policy. This should include your organization's objectives towards quality. This should be understood, implemented and maintained at all levels within the organization.
- Define the organizational structure that is required to manage your quality system.
- Define quality system responsibilities and authority. Ensure the interactions between staff are clearly specified. Make sure all these are well documented.

- Identify and provide the resources that people will need to manage, perform and verify quality system work.
- Appoint a senior manager with executive responsibilities to:
  - establish an ISO 9001 compliant quality management system (QMS), implement and maintain it;
  - provide a link, and report to, senior management on the development and production of the QMS.
- Define procedures for use by senior managers to review the effectiveness of your QMS. This could involve interaction with the customer to:
  - obtain feedback about the system;
  - ensure the software meets the customer's requirements;
  - verify and accept any test results.

  Above all the need to conduct and document periodic reviews of the QMS.

This one area outlines some of the important requirements that should be inherent in a quality system. Standards and procedures require a lot of paperwork that has to be carefully prepared and maintained. As with a lot of software engineering concepts there cannot be too much emphasis put onto the production of quality, ordered and accurate documentation. The quality system for an organization should be documented in a quality manual that contains the following guidelines:

- Specifying the responsibilities (both internal and external to the organization) regarding the achievement of quality.
- The meetings or formal reviews to be carried out along with their composition requirements.
- The format for a corresponding quality plan that details how the developer intends to ensure the software product meets its stated quality objectives.

Standards are forever changing and the ISO has just updated its 9001 series by updating the ISO 9001, ISO 9002 and ISO 9003:1994 standards into one new standard the ISO 9001:2000 set. The 20-clause structure outlined above will be replaced with a new format containing five sections. ISO states that this produces a more logical structure and makes it more compatible with the ISO 14001 Environmental Management standard. The ISO 9004:2000 standard also deals with quality management systems but lays down guidance for performance improvements, that go beyond the basic requirements specified in ISO 9001:2000. It is intended as a guide for organizations that want to further expand and improve the QMS after implementing ISO 9001:2000. The transition from the 1994 to the 2000 standards is at a stage where registered organizations may start their transition as soon as the Draft International Standard (DIS) is available and be reassessed to the new standard, but no formal certification for ISO 9001:2000 can be issued before the final standard is published (during the last quarter of 2000).

As we have seen within this section a quality system needs to adhere to certain standards in order for it to meet its classification. We have mentioned the influence of ISO standards, but other standards also effect the quality of software system. These include the IEEE (Institute of Electrical and Electronic Engineers), BSI (British Standards Institute) and others, some dependent on the country of origin of the product. For example, the IEEE 1008 standard for Software Unit Testing or the BSI BS 7738 Specification for Information Systems Products using SSADM are alternative standards that effect the production of quality systems. There are also further ISO standards that are relevant to software development, for example ISO 5218 Representation of Human Sexes (i.e. 0 = not known, 1 = male, 2 = female and 9 = not specified to represent it as a 1 character numerical code). And so it goes on. But the application of standards to a software quality system has many advantages to the developer of the product, for example:

- customer satisfaction;
- effectiveness of budget and time requirements;
- improved management structure;
- trust in the product;
- legal compliance;
- improved product development;
- international standards help export the product.

Above all a quality product employing standards is efficient, commercially viable, credible and from both the development and customer point of view, 'safe'. Customers and end users of a system value the aspects of safety and quality that such standards install within the product. Standards install trust in a product that improve marketability and product satisfaction.

Question 5.2.2

(1) What is ANSI an abbreviation for?
(2) What is ISO and how does it influence the development of software systems?
(3) What are the management responsibilities expressed under ISO 9001/ISO 9000–3 standards?
(4) What are the advantages of implementing international standards within the software development process?
(5) What standards institution is inherent within the UK?
(6) What is a Quality Management System (QMS)?

Exercise 5.2.1

This is a research exercise. At the time of writing this section ISO 9001:2000 standards were just being published. The aim of this exercise is to investigate the latest progress of ISO standards and how they effect the development of software systems.

Costs and benefits of software quality systems

From certain perspectives it looks like developing a quality system involves a lot of extra work and costs a lot of money. On the other side software failures cost a lot of money and in some cases involve injury or loss of life. There have been several examples of severe software failure that are expensive to fix and take up valuable time.

Exercise 5.2.2

Another research exercise. Investigate a software system that has failed with severe consequence. Find out what type of software system it was, what caused the problem, how it effected the users and how it was corrected. As a guide the London Ambulance Service installed a new system in 1992; after a short period it suffered severe failure which resulted with problems dispatching ambulances to emergency situations. It was said that this resulted in a number of unnecessary deaths. Two major problems were identified: (1) A small piece of test code was left in the system which took up available memory every time a call was made until the storage area was full and (2) a backup system was recommended during development but was never implemented. Research a similar case.

Software failures cost money and take up valuable time to put right. This process can be made harder if the software was not developed using sound quality standards. As we have already seen, working to improve quality can cost money in the short term, but is beneficial in the long term. Often a contract is produced without fully considering the costs of maintenance activities. Figure 5.2.3 outlines the costs over the whole lifecycle of a project.

It can be seen that there are high costs during the maintenance phase for a system developed without using sound quality system principles. If a little extra capital is spent on activities prior to the handover date then the quality of the system should be significantly improved. A careful balance needs to be maintained by the project manager to ensure savings during maintenance are significantly larger than the extra costs incurred prior to the handover date. If this is not the case the law of diminishing returns will arise and the profits will vanish.

It may be in certain cases that a developer may enter into a 'lost leader' situation for one product, but hope to regain the initiative by selling the product to other clients. This is all right if there is a ready

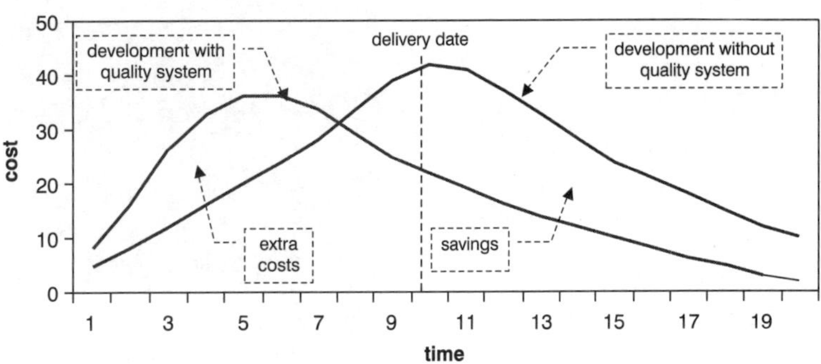

Figure 5.2.3 *Cost comparisons for software projects*

market for the product, especially a quality system, that has undergone severe quality standard procedures prior to its release. But care needs to be taken if the product is for an individual client with unique requirements, as any financial loss may not be acceptable to the business.

Estimating Quality Factor (EQF)

Deriving from the work of DeMarco the *Estimation Quality Factor* (EQF) sets out to provide a graphical and numerical measure on how successful the estimating process has been over the life of the project. The quality of an estimate is a function of how the estimating value over certain stages of a project converges to the actual cost. The result is a unitless number between zero and infinity. From the studies carried out by DeMarco, the cost estimating process over the life of a project can be deemed to be successful if the resulting numerical value is a high number. He states that given a standard error of 25% or less an EQF of 4 or higher in 68% of projects can obtain a better than average estimating process. Note that the time can be in days, weeks or months as long as it is kept standard throughout the analysis. The following essential rule outlines the estimator's motivation expectations:

> Success for an estimator must be defined as a function of convergence of the estimate to the actual cost of the project and of nothing else.

Mathematics in action

To obtain the EQF you need first to complete a graph of the estimating costs plotted against the time taken during which the estimate is relevant. The actual cost line is inserted first and is represented by a horizontal line across the graph. The other estimates, starting from the original one, are then added as blocks to represent the time period that they are active.

$$\text{EQF} = \frac{\text{total area under the actual cost line}}{\text{sum of the areas calculated from the top of the bars to the actual cost line}}$$

if: EQF >= 4 and applying the criteria laid down by DeMarco the quality of the estimating process of the life of a project can deemed to be successful.

Example 5.2.1 outlines this process.

Example 5.2.1

From the table below:

(a) Complete a graph that represents this data contained in the table.

(b) Form the graph calculate the EQF (Estimating Quality Factor).

(c) Comment on the results (i.e. are they acceptable or not).

Estimate	*Date*	*Cost (£m)*
1	1-1-98	1.3
2	1-3-98	1.8
3	15-6-98	2.5
4	15-7-98	2.2
Actual	1-10-98	2.1

Suggested solution:
estimate (£m)

(a)

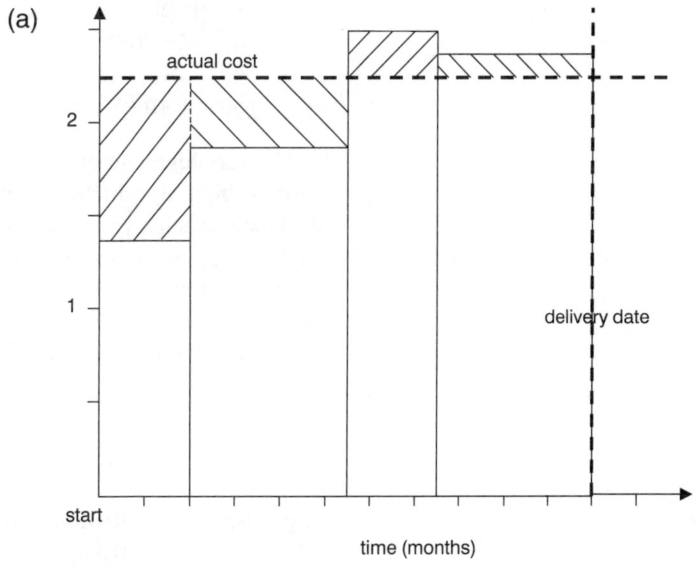

Figure 5.2.4 *EQF graph*

(b) First we need to calculate the sum of the areas that are shown hatched on the graph. For example, if we take the first estimate, the cost difference between it and the actual cost is 2.2 – 1.3 = 0.9 and the time period is from 1–1-98 to 1–3-98 a total of 2 months, therefore the area for this shaded section is 2 × 0.9 = **1.8**. For the second hatched section we have time = 3.5 and the cost difference = 2.2 – 1.8 = 0.4, therefore the area = 3.5 × 0.4 = **1.4**. Third hatched section = 2(months) × 0.3(£m) = **0.6** and the fourth hatched section = 3.5(months) × 0.1(£m) = **0.35**. Total shaded area = 1.8 + 1.4 + 0.6 + 0.35 = **4.15**. Area under the actual cost line = 2.2 (actual cost) × 11 (total time) = **24.2**.

Therefore the EQF = 24.2/4.15 = 5.83.

(c) For the criteria specified by DeMarco an EQF of 5.83 can be accepted as a good estimating process (because 5.83 > 4 which is the minimum figure specified by DeMarco as an acceptable quality factor).

Risk hierarchy

We can look at the concept of risk in two ways. First when applying it to the completed project, i.e. is the software safe and second how risky is it building a product in order to complete it on time and within budget?

From the British Standards 'Risk' is specified as:

> Risk may be specified as a quantified probability or a combination of quantified probabilities but it is not possible to specify the software safety integrity in the same manner. Software safety integrity is specified as one or more of five levels:
>
> 1. Very High
> 2. High
> 3. Medium
> 4. Low
> 5. Normal

The very high end of the range deals with safety critical systems that carry a high risk in terms of 'time and budget' constraints for the developer. Such a system must be made 'faultless' as any problems may cause injury or loss of life to people who depend on it.

In general the risk (i.e. the risk of completing the project on time and within budget) can be specified under three broad headings. This is outlined in the table below:

Risk hierarchy	*Example systems*
High risk	Real time or safety critical systems, for example fly-by-wire aircraft systems, weapons guidance systems, patient monitoring systems, etc.
Medium risk	Commercial data processing, banking and insurance systems, etc.
Low risk	Mathematical and statistical applications, etc.

From his book on risk analysis and management, Charette outlines three underpinning concepts that are always present during the development of a software system:

(1) risk concerns future happens
(2) risk involves change
(3) risk involves choice

From a developer's point of view risk is an everyday occurrence. We have already looked at the concepts of change, so 'risk' needs to be carefully considered at the start of every new project. Risk analysis is a software engineering discipline that combines four separate activities:

- risk identification
- risk projection
- risk assessment
- risk management

Risk analysis can take a lot of planning and once in place will need to be monitored. But if you can foresee problems then any areas that may present a risk to the developer's time and budget predictions can be planned for.

Question 5.2.3

(1) Discuss the cost issues of developing a quality system as opposed to a system that is built not using quality methods.

(2) Below is a table which includes the estimating costs for a completed project:

Estimate	*Date*	*Cost (£m)*
1	1-3-97	2.7
2	1-6-97	2.9
3	15-10-97	3.8
4	15-1-98	3.6
Actual cost	1-5-98	3.5

(a) Complete a graph that represents the data contained in the table.

(b) From the graph calculate the EQF (Estimating Quality Factor).

(c) Comment on the results (i.e. are they acceptable or not).

(3) What does a developer need to carry out risk analysis during the early stages of project development?

Quality assurance tools

Quality plan

The quality plan is specified in the project plan and gives details of how the quality measures are to be implemented. It provides information on how the software developer is to implement the standards and measures outlined in the company quality policy. The main aim of the quality plan is to show to the customer or the end user how the developer will ensure the requirements of the system are met. Below is an extract from the ISO 9001 standards on quality system requirements:

ISO 9000–3 4.2 Quality System Requirements

- Establish a quality system and document it in a quality manual.
- Develop and implement quality system procedures that are consistent with the quality policy.
- Define and document quality plans that show how the quality system requirements are to be implemented. Quality plans should be developed for products, processes, projects and customer contracts.
  - Develop quality plans to control software development projects.
  - Develop a quality plan whenever there is a need to control the quality of a specific project, product or contract
    - The quality plan should explain how the company intends to tailor the quality system so that it applies to a specific project, product or contract.
    - Develop detailed quality plans and procedures to control configuration management, product verification, non-conforming products and corrective actions.

There is also an earlier ANSI/IEEE standard that outlines a series of headings on how to structure a project plan. It includes areas like management, supplier control, documentation, reviews and audits, standards, etc. The project manager should document the intentions of the software development process within the quality plan. Like every other public domain standard they should be adopted critically and customized to meet the needs of the company business plan.

Outlined below is an example extract for a quality plan:

2.1 Requirements Analysis

A number of reviews are to held during this phase. Two basic types are to be conducted. Internal Reviews and External Reviews.

Internal Reviews: To check a component part of the customer's requirement document to ensure it is clear, concise and unambiguous. The reviews will be held for each partitioned section of the system and will contain the following personnel:

- Chair: The Project Manager
- Software Engineer involved with developing the component part of the system
- Software Engineer with experience in the field that is under development
- Quality Assurance representative

The meeting will be formally minuted and any unresolved matters need to be documented as actions. The unresolved matters will be resolved before the next scheduled meeting. The minutes will be available for team members to see and if required the customer.

External reviews: This review will involve the customer (or customer's representative) who will check that the resulting specification meets the needs of the original requirements. The following people will be present at the review:

- Chair: The Project Manager
- The Customer (or representative)
- Software Engineer involved with the sub-system under development
- The team leader (or line manager)

This review will normally be 1.5 hours long and arrangements for any unresolved matters will be the same as for the internal reviews. Further details will be found in the Project Plan section 2 paragraph 2.4.3.

Another example of information contained in the project plan involving testing issues:

Integration Test Requirements

Once unit testing has been completed and the partitioned units are brought together series of integration tests will be implemented. The integration tests will check the units link together and they are brought together. Each test will be carefully documented and contain the following headings:

- Test name
- Explanation of the test
- System Units to be integrated
- Where the system units are stored
- Test Data to be used (or its location)
- Expected output from the tests
- Actual test results
- Location of the integrated system
- Additional Information

At this level the tests are carried out internally with the development team under control of the team leader. Information about the results of the tests must be made available to the customer (or representative).

The quality plan needs to be understandable to all parties concerned with the project. This must include the customer who will view the document and ascertain whether the developer is going to conduct techniques that will produce a product to fully meet the requirements. If correctly documented the quality plan can inspire confidence in the customer who will be able to see the quality measures that will be adopted. For the developer they need to carefully assess the plan to ensure it defines clearly the methods to be adopted for achieving the desired quality objectives. All development activities including validation and verification requirements need to be included in the quality plan. Producing a high-quality software system relies on planning and monitoring techniques to ensure its success. The quality plan is one of the techniques that aids the development process and inspires confidence in the customer.

Question 5.2.4

(1) What is the quality plan?
(2) How should a quality plan be structured?
(3) Why is early acceptance of the quality plan by the customer important?

Test plan

Testing is a validation activity and if carried out correctly provides valuable evidence that the system (or subsystem) performs as it should. A test plan provides a basis for specifying tests that are to be carried out during the development of the project. We have already seen that a number of tests are carried out over the lifecycle of a project. Each test will require a different set of criteria, for example a unit test will need to conform to its detailed design structure, while an integration test will need to ensure the interfacing between units is correct. Below is an extract from a negotiated statement of requirements:

> When the school administrator types in an STUDENT_ID command the system will respond with the student name, course and registration details. The STUDENT_ID must be unique and made up of alphanumeric characters (two letters representing the student's initials and a six number code), for example SM123214. If the student is new the administrator adds the details to the file.

When implementing this section the developer would assume that data validation was important for the end user. This could result in the following tests being applied:

> STUDENT_ID command
>
> Test 1
> The system should show that if an incorrect identifier was entered by the user, a suitable error message is displayed and the system does not crash.
>
> Test 2
> The system should demonstrate that if a correct identifier is entered and the student has withdrawn a suitable message should be displayed.
>
> Test 3
> The system should demonstrate that if a correct identifier for a student is entered and the student is currently active the name course and registration details should be displayed.
>
> Test 4
> If an identifier was accepted but no matching file is found a suitable message should be displayed. For example the ID may not yet be allocated.
>
> Test 4
> The system needs to ensure that all identifiers are unique. If a new identifier is added and the same one already exists a suitable error message should be displayed.

> Test 5
> The system should accept three fields for each new student. IF the operator forgets to fill in one field then a suitable warning message should be displayed. This is not an error, as a student may not be allocated a course yet.

The test plan is part of the quality plan and relates directly to the testing activities being carried out. Separate sets of tests are to be specified for each test activity outlined in the original plan. Testing is about demonstrating the correctness of a system or subsystem. It is about finding errors and correcting them to produce a quality piece of software. An extract from Myers outlines this concept:

> Testing is the process of executing a program with the intent of finding errors.

When to stop testing is difficult; this again comes down to time and money. You can never assume that all errors have been detected. A thorough approach to testing procedures and documentation will improve the run-time capability of the product providing an efficient and sound application that is marketable in the real world.

Reviews

A review is a managerial activity that is used in both verification and validation processes. It involves a meeting of a number of team members and other interested parties with the view of analysing part of a document or code section produced within the system. A review will determine the correctness of a product with respect to the original requirements. They are used continually throughout the development process and are conducted under strict guidelines. They are formal meetings that are scheduled at regular intervals throughout the lifecycle and need to run to a preset agenda, be formally minuted and resulting actions carefully documented. As we have seen the quality of a product depends on whether the final product meets the customer's requirements. A review provides a simple but effective method for checking the process of development and providing feedback to interested parties. There are many types of review ranging from informal meetings through to a Formal Technical Review (FTR). The guidelines for a formal technical review are outlined below:

- the meeting should contain between three and five people and contain a chairperson;
- it should be prepared in advance and an agenda produced and distributed;
- the meeting should not be too long, a maximum of two hours is sufficient;
- minutes should be taken and distributed;
- any suggested actions should be carried out before the next meeting.

It has to be remembered that it is the product that is under review and any noted faults need to be pointed out to the developer carefully. Any comments should be constructive to ensure the morale of the development team and help should be provided where possible. A review is an essential tool in the development of modern software products, but its success is dependent on how it is conducted and how resulting actions are implemented.

Software metrics

Software metrics provide numerical methods for measuring quality issues associated with the development of software systems. Numerical measures give the project manager a clear and concise indication of how a project is progressing. Numerical measures deal in facts that are accurate as opposed to people's opinions which might not be so precise. There are two main categories of software metrics, they are:

- *Results metric*: this measure is normally implemented at the end of a project or at the end of a particular stage of the project.
- *Predictor metric*: these are applied during various stages of the project and provide numerical feedback as to the structure and complexity of code sections. They may be used to ascertain the program size (number of lines of code) which is useful for estimating the final resources needed when the program goes live.

Question 5.2.5

(1) What is the test plan and what overall plan is it part of?
(2) What is a software metric and what is its main categories?

The following models have been developed over the years to put into practice the measurement techniques for the quantitative assessment of software quality. They are all indirect techniques that do not directly measure quality but some aspect associated with it.

- Software Quality Indices.
- Halstead's Software Science.
- McCabe's Cyclomatic Complexity Metric.

Cyclomatic Complexity (McCabe)

In order to test the relationship between the control structures inherent in a section of program and the amount of testing required, Thomas McCabe developed his Cyclomatic Complexity Measure. Although a little dated by modern standards it does make the developer think about the code structures under development. Complex sections of code are difficult to test and can affect the run-time efficiency of the program if they are unnecessarily complex. His method uses a graphical technique to represent the code structure and a resulting formula to ascertain the complexity.

We shall start this process by looking at the diagram structures used to represent the flow of the program code. The diagram, or directed graph as it is sometimes called, is constructed using arcs and nodes. A node represents the start or end point of some processing activity (normally a line of code, or code structure), i.e. a point where a decision is made, and is represented by a small circle. An arc represents the processing that occurs within a program or code section and is represented by an arrowed line (or arc) indicating the direction of the data flow. The three main structures used within a directed graph are outlined in Figure 5.2.5.

McCabe's Cyclomatic Complexity

(1) Linear Sequence

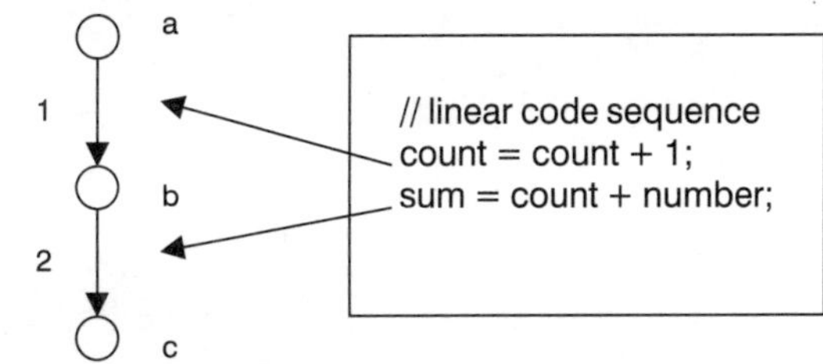

(2) Conditional Structure

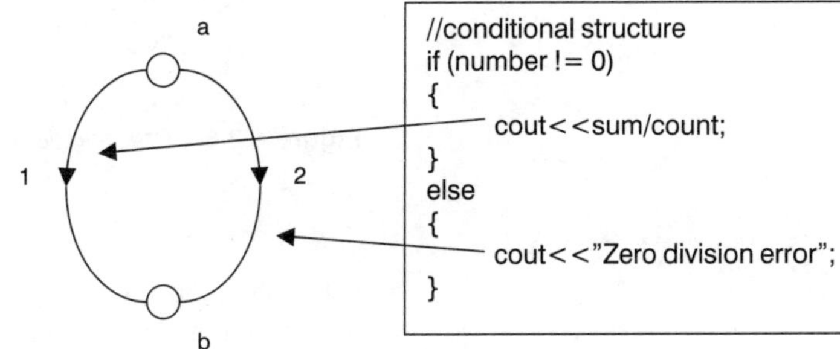

(3) Iterative Structure (post-conditioned loop only)

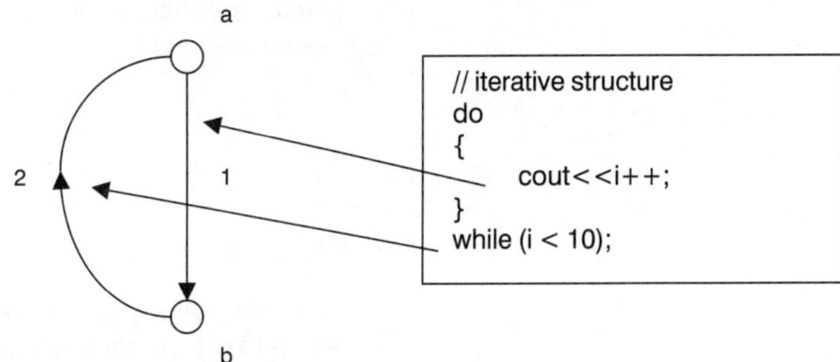

Figure 5.2.5 *Directed graph components*

Within a directed graph the arcs are labelled with numbers and the nodes with lower case letters. Figure 5.2.5 shows the three main components of a directed graph that are accompanied by program code. In this case C++ has been used, but the method could easily be applied to a Program Design Language (PDL) in the detailed design stage of development. Note how each line of code matches an arc containing the direction of the flow. The conditional statement always assumes an 'else' option even it is not used with both arcs moving down the diagram. The iteration statement provides two structures, Figure 5.2.5 shows the post-conditioned loop example with an arc that moves back up the graph every time iteration occurs. Figure 5.2.6 shows the sequence for a preconditioned loop.

Remember with a preconditioned loop it is possible that the condition is false when the loop is encountered, this would mean that the loop was never entered into and the flow of the program moves onto the data

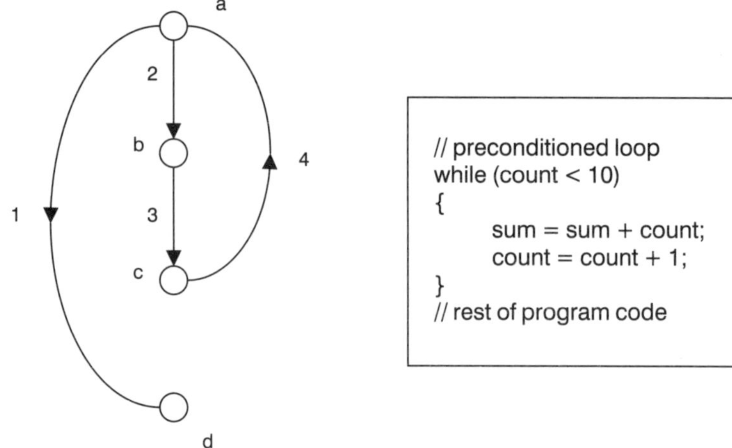

Figure 5.2.6 *Preconditioned loop structure for a directed graph*

below the loop. This is shown in Figure 5.2.6 where the outer arc (1) jumps from node 'a' to node 'd' and the loop is never executed. If the condition is true the loop is entered, the sequence of code lines executed and the flow returns ('c' to 'a') to check the loop condition again. Please note that in some texts a directed graph is known as a *flow graph* or a *program graph*. Example 5.2.2 outlines an example directed graph for a C++ code section.

Example 5.2.2

From the following section of C++ code complete a directed graph to represent the logical control of the data components.

```
// code fragment
float sum = 1;
int index = 1;
do
{
  sum = sum/index;
  if (sum < 0.5)
  {
    cout << sum + 1;
  }
  else
  {
    cout << sum - 1;
  }
  index++;
}
while (index < 10);
sum = sum + index;
```

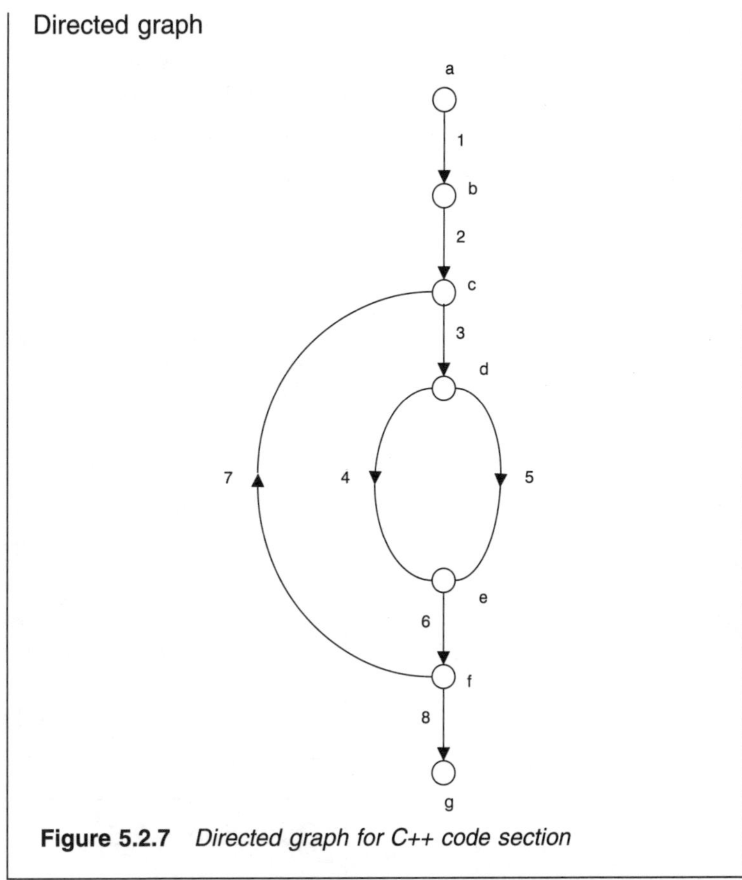

Figure 5.2.7 *Directed graph for C++ code section*

So what has a directed graph got to do about complexity measures? Directed graphs have been used for many years by mathematicians within engineering circles and provide a sound base for measuring data. McCabe's Cyclomatic Complexity Measure is based on the following equation:

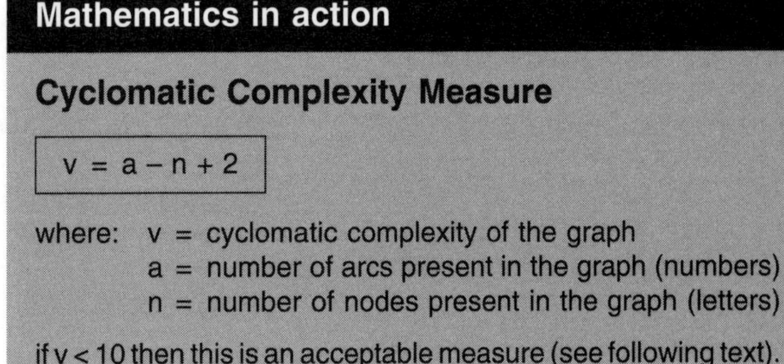

Mathematics in action

Cyclomatic Complexity Measure

$$v = a - n + 2$$

where: v = cyclomatic complexity of the graph
a = number of arcs present in the graph (numbers)
n = number of nodes present in the graph (letters)

if $v < 10$ then this is an acceptable measure (see following text).

Research by McCabe established that the higher cyclomatic complexity of a directed graph representing the PDL or code the more difficult the program is to read, understand, implement and test. In a paper containing his work McCabe suggested that a cyclomatic complexity of a value greater than 10 was not acceptable and the code should be redesigned. This is a reasonable hypothesis because to obtain a figure like this the code needs to be extremely complex containing a large amount of nested structures which affect the efficiency of design.

Example 5.2.3

Question:
From the directed graph obtained in Exercise 5.2.2 (and shown in Figure 5.2.7)

(1) calculate the cyclomatic complexity;
(2) comment on the resulting value (is it acceptable or not?).

Answer:

(1) We can see there are 8 arcs and 7 nodes

therefore

$$v = a - n + 2$$
$$v = 8 - 7 + 2$$
$$v = 3$$

(2) From the research of McCabe we can see that the cyclomatic complexity is smaller than 10 (i.e. $3 < 10$) so the code can be accepted as not being too complex and hence does not need to be redesigned.

Question 5.2.6

From the following code section:

(1) complete a directed graph;
(2) calculate the cyclomatic complexity;
(3) comment on the results.

```
// C++ code extract
int space = 0, index = 0, question = 0, count = 0;
strcpy (line, ‘Is Bailey a dog? is he large? where does
he live? please check’);
do
{
  count = count + 1;
  while (line[index] = ‘ ‘)
  {
    space = space + 1;
    index = index + 1;
  }
  if (line [index] ==’?’)
  {
    question = question + 1;
  }
  index = index + 1;
}
while (line [index] != ‘/0’);
cout ≪ ‘The % of question marks to characters is’
≪ question/count × 100;
```

Dynamic analysis

The cyclomatic complexity method used for testing code is said to be a static analysis method. Dynamic analysis occurs during the execution of a program where the number of structural elements is monitored to produce summary information. The information obtained will normally be stored in a database called an execution history. Some examples of the type of information stored are outlined below:

- values of variables at certain points in the program;
- minimum and maximum value of variables;
- the most executed statements;
- information on statements that are not used at all;
- information on branching;
- paths taken by the test data.

One way of collecting this information is to insert special code sections either manually or automatically using a dynamic analyser. Entering test data into a program is not new, in fact is has almost been around as long as computer programs themselves. We have often inserted printout lines inside code sections to find out the value of variables, to see if an array goes out of range, or to see what is happening inside a loop, etc. Dynamic analysis does this in a more efficient way on larger code sections. Once the execution history data has been stored during dynamic analysis it needs to be analysed. The tools used for this analysis can be independent of the program code. This means that programs written in different languages can be analysed by the same tool as long as they write the same information to the database. Full use of dynamic analysis is beyond the scope of this chapter, but the end result of dynamic analysis will be compared with the end result of static analysis to obtain a measure of the extent to which the program has been tested. This is known as the percentage coverage that is used as a measure to quantify test effectiveness.

5.3 Professional standards

Legal requirements

We have seen over the last two decades a revolution in the use of IT within a number of organizations and for home use. The UK government has committed to 100% electronic delivery of its services by 2008. A recent survey showed that over 95% of ISO 9000 registered companies have access to the Internet. As more and more data is now stored electronically some control must be put into place to ensure the data is correct, safe and easily accessible for the user. Establishing and managing a secure, controlled and *legal* environment is a challenge facing many organizations in the new millennium. The risks are always increasing as more undesirable practices are uncovered, such as hacking or planting viruses. There are also a number of risks that can arise internally from within organizations such as deliberate or accidental misuse of systems by employees.

As part of risk management in an organization there should be a variety of distinct business functions involved in IT legal compliance. These should include:

- personnel department – recruiting the right staff and applying the appropriate work practices;
- IT department – set up Internet and Email policies;
- management board – set up appropriate management structures to ensure all legal risks are covered.

There are independent standards that enable companies to undertake a legal risk assessment of their IT provision. Companies need to hold risk assessment reviews that investigate the legal, financial and managerial implications of risks associated with the IT provision. Many organizations have to pay fines and legal costs because they do not meet the legal requirements set by the government. Independent surveys have shown that up to 29% of UK businesses may be using illegal software that increases to 50% in smaller businesses. The ideal solution is for every UK organization to review its IT strategy on a regular basis and ensure the correct management policies are in place to ensure any bad practices or misuses are resolved quickly and efficiently. UK laws governing IT use and potential penalties are outlined below:

Question 5.3.1

(1) What are the main risks facing the use of IT within organizations?
(2) What analysis has been obtained about organizations within the UK reference planning for major IT business risk?

- Data Protection Acts (1984 and 1998)
- Copyright, Designs and Patents Act (1988)
- Computer Misuse Act (1990)
- Companies Act (1985)
- Electronic Communication Bill (2000)

Data Protection Acts (1984 and 1998)

The new 1998 Act mainly implements the provisions of the EU Data Protection Directive in the UK, where the Directive seeks to balance the needs of the IT users with the rights of the individuals. It contains greater rights for the individuals that were present in the 1984 Act. The 1998 Act came into force on 1 March 2000 and any business operating in the UK that holds information about individuals (employees, customers or other people) will be affected by the change. Outlined below are the eight data protection principles of the 1998 Data Protection Act:

- Personal data must be processed fairly and lawfully.
- Personal data must be obtained only for specified lawful purposes and not further processed in a manner incompatible with those purposes.
- Personal data must be adequate, relevant and not excessive in relation to the purposes for which it was processed.
- Personal data must be accurate and kept up to date.
- Personal data must not be kept any longer than is necessary.
- Personal data must be processed in accordance with the rights of data subjects under the Act (i.e. the right to be told what information the Data Controller holds and to have it rectified if inaccurate).
- Appropriate technical and organizational security measures must be put into place to prevent unauthorized or unlawful processing of personal data, or accidental loss of, or damage to, personal data.
- Personal data must not be transferred out of the European Economic Area (EEA) which includes the EU, Norway, Liechtenstein and Iceland, unless it can be shown that the recipient country has an adequate level of data protection, e.g. the USA and Japan do not currently have adequate legislation.

Penalties associated with the Act:

- Processing personal data without notification or failing to notify changes in data use – £5000 in a magistrates' court, or an unlimited fine in the Crown Court.
- Obtaining or disclosing data without consent of the data subject or unlawful selling of personal data – £5000 in a magistrates' court, or an unlimited fine in the Crown Court.
- Knowingly or recklessly making a false statement to the Data Protection Commissioner or failing to comply with an enforcement or information notice – £5000 in a magistrates' court, or an unlimited fine in the Crown Court.

An example of an infringement under the Data Protection Act is outlined below:

> The Data Protection Registrar has ruled that Local Authorities searching staff payrolls in an attempt to detect benefit fraud were acting illegally. Although the 1997 Social Security Fraud Act allows records held by Local Authorities and Government departments to be contacted, the Registrar has decided that under the Data Protection Act, wholesale data matching should be conducted on a case by case basis only.

Here you can see a genuine error as local authorities were trying to carry out one Act and in doing so infringed another Act. The problem arose because wholesale data matching constitutes an invasion of privacy of people who are *not* suspected of any wrongdoing.

Copyright, Designs and Patents Act (1988)

Many legal proceeding for infringements of copyright in software are based on provisions of this Act. If any legal proceedings are brought because an organization is using illegal software adverse publicity will certainly follow. This will give the company a 'bad name' and affect possible sales as well as incurring a large fine. In the BSA and Price Waterhouse software piracy report it estimated that the average percentage of software that is pirated or unlicensed for the purpose for which it is being used is 43% across Europe and approximately 27% in the USA.

Exercise 5.3.1

Carry out research to find examples where an infringement of the Copyright, Designs and Patents Act have occurred for:

(1) organizations;
(2) individuals.

In each case specify the background, infringement and resulting penalties.

The penalties for an infringement of this Act range from confiscating or destruction of the illegal software, damages awarded to the software supplier along with an account of any profits made and in some severe cases directors may be subject to imprisonment.

Computer Misuse Act (1990)

This Act generally covers more serious and malicious actions that may occur to an organization's IT systems. Under the Act, it must be proved that the alleged offender gained unauthorized access knowingly and with intent. This Act requires organizations to have adequate procedures in place to prevent individuals from accessing unauthorized data. Depending on which section of the Act is implied the penalties for infringements range from £5000 fines to up to 5 years in jail.

Companies Act (1985), section 722

This Act relates to protecting your organization adequately against falsification or loss of computerized accounting records when held within a computer system. The Act is similar to the Data Protection Act for corporate data and relates to the need for most organizations to hold and protect their account information for the last 7 years of commercial activity. Section 722 applies to all limited companies (but not partnerships or any government departments). Penalties for infringements range from the company or every officer within being liable for a fine (and a daily default fine if the problem is not corrected), the shareholder can sue the directors and if proved guilty the resignation or dismissal of the board of directors could result.

Electronic Communication Bill (2000)

The Government's commitment to making the UK the best place in the world for 'ecommerce' took a major step when the Electronic Communications Bill received Royal Assent on 25 May 2000. The Government's policy is to facilitate electronic commerce. It has also set itself targets for making government services available electronically: 25% by 2002, 50% by 2005 and 100% by 2008. The Government has also set a target for 90% of its routine government procurement of goods to be done electronically by 2001.

The main purpose of the Bill is to help build confidence in electronic commerce and the technology underlying it by providing for:

- a statutory approvals scheme for businesses and other organizations providing cryptography services, such as electronic signature services and confidentiality services;
- the legal recognition of electronic signatures; and
- the removal of obstacles in other legislation to the use of electronic communication and storage in place of paper.

We can see that it is essential for all organizations to increase their IT provision and be involved with electronic trading and tendering, but they must be aware of the risks associated with the management of such a system. They must above all be aware of the risks of prosecution due to misuse of their systems.

Question 5.3.2

(1) What are the principal Acts relating to information technology?
(2) What are the main implications of the 1998 Data Protection Act?
(3) Are organizations insured against computer misuse that involves hacking and fraud (this may require a little research)?

Other Acts that need to be considered, but do not directly relate to IT systems, include the following.

Health and Safety at Work Act (1974)

The Health and Safety at Work Act 1974 provides a wide, embracing, enabling framework for health, safety and welfare in the UK. The Act places specific duties on:

- employers;
- employees;
- occupiers of premises;
- designers, manufacturers, importers and suppliers.

It is the duty of every employer, so far as is reasonably practicable, to ensure the health, safety and welfare at work of all employees. Under the section on 'Statutory Duties to Employees' an employer must:

- produce and distribute a statement of 'safety policy' and its implications to all employees;
- consult with employees' representatives on matters relating to health and safety and establish safety committees if sought by representatives. Such consultation is guided through published codes of practice;
- ensure that those who are not employed by the organization are informed of safety and hazards for when they work or are present on employer premises and use equipment or materials.

The Act is backed up by the criminal law. Offences under the Act stem from failure to discharge duties, breach of specific sections or non-compliance with the inspector's requirements as authorized by the Act. As a project manager within a software development environment you have personal responsibilities for health and safety under the Act. If senior management have carried out their responsibilities and failure is traceable to a local operations manager (i.e. software project manager) who is responsible for the care of others, then they may be liable under civil proceedings.

Disability Discrimination Act (1995)

This is a far-reaching Act that covers employment, education, training, the provision of goods and services, property, equipment and facilities. With some 8.6 million people in the UK classified as disabled, catering for their needs and disabilities has become an increasingly important consideration in every aspect of the work environment. A number of disabled people are able to operate IT equipment, especially if it has been specially adapted. They can provide a valuable asset to an employer if the correct facilities are in place. An employer needs to be aware of the issues of failing to comply with the Act by discrimination or victimization. The Act, like the Health and Safety at Work Act, needs to be carefully studied by all management to ensure they are implementing the correct procedures and avoid incurring any unforeseen penalties.

Professional requirements

In order to ensure staff within a software development team reach a required *professional standard* during their employment, the company needs to ensure they develop certain inherent skills. Such skills will not only improve the performance of the staff, but enhance the status of the team by having a more professional and competent workforce. Such skills should include:

- interpersonal skills;
- written communication skills;
- verbal communication skills;
- presentation skills;
- project leadership skills;
- management skills;
- budgeting and control techniques;
- legal legislation requirements.

These skills can be developed in a number of ways, through line management, training programs, in-house seminars, college/university courses, etc. Whatever method is adopted the progress of developing staff needs to be carefully monitored to ensure the skills have been obtained. This could be checked by the line manager carrying out a yearly review that is designed to aid the development of the staff member, as well as checking their progress.

Professional bodies

1. British Computer Society

The BCS is a professional institution for everyone who is concerned with information system engineering. It offers IT professionals the opportunity to participate in the development of their profession. The aim of the society is to provide a structure to support you in developing and maintaining professional skills through your entire career. Member services include:

- professional qualifications;
- professional information;
- professional network;
- BCS examinations;
- accreditation of university courses;
- professional development;
- industry skills model;
- other benefits.

The BCS stresses the importance of *professionalism* that implies taking responsibility and accounting for one's work and performing the work to the highest possible standards. In order to achieve this it is important that the individual is trained to the highest possible standards and is thoroughly up to date with the latest techniques, theories and standards. Two important issues are specified by the BCS for HE courses that require accreditation:

- Project standards are maintained.
- Professional elements are embedded within the course.

Obtaining skills does not finish with a college or university qualification. New skills need to be developed to meet the ever-changing requirements of the computer industry. This can be achieved through *Continued Professional Development* (CPD) with the aim of creating an environment that enables you to remain professionally competent throughout your working life. The BCS provides an excellent guidance outline of how to carry out a continued professional development programme, which includes how it can be measured, use of log books, mentoring, the behavioural skills, etc.

The benefits of CPD are basically:

For individuals:

- improved job performance and satisfaction;
- enhanced career development;
- potentially more earning power.

For employers

- more capable, motivated staff;
- improved business performance;
- better recruitment, retention and deployment of staff.

Continued professional development may be achieved by attending or undertaking:

- short courses;
- conferences or exhibitions;
- symposia and society meetings;
- private study/self-directed learning;
- distance learning;
- further education studies;
- higher education studies;
- post qualification studies;
- imparting knowledge;
- committee work;
- official meeting or reviews;
- relevant voluntary work;
- on-the-job training.

All activities should be recorded in an official CPD log book which is specially designed to include all continuing education, on-off-the-job training courses, etc. and should be presented at the next professional review.

2. Engineering Council

The mission of the Engineering Council is to enhance the standing and contribution of the UK engineering profession in the national interest and to the benefit of society. The Council, together with its partner institutions, work together to maintain a world-class engineering profession for the benefit of the nation. The organization of the Council is made up of a senate that comprises of elected members for the supporting institutions and privy council nominees. It is supported by two executive boards, the Board for Engineering Profession (BEP) and the Board for Engineers' Regulation (BER). As an example the British Computer Society is a supporting institution.

The Engineering Council sets the standard for registration as a professional engineer or technician as:

- Charted Engineer (CEng).
- Incorporated Engineer (IEng).
- Engineering Technician (EngTech).

Details of the requirements for membership of the above classifications are contained in SARTOR (Standard and Routes to Registration). The third edition (SARTOR 3) came into force on 1 September 1999. Most of the provisions are being phased in over a period of several years. The main impact at the moment is within higher education where universities are now offering courses that have been accredited under SARTOR 3, like 4 year MEng or 3 year BEng courses for potential Charted Engineers.

An educational base requirement for an Incorporated Engineer (IEng) is:

- a 3 year programme comprising either an engineering, technology or science bachelor degree (not necessarily honours), which has been accredited for IEng registration under the criteria given in SARTOR 3 Part 2 section 4.1.2; or
- 'HND' – a programme accredited for IEng plus an accredited or approved matching section or
- 'HNC/HND' – a programme accredited for IEng plus an accredited or approved matching section.

The requirements of *Matching sections* could be met through:

- Edexcel–BTEC Professional Development Qualification programmes (full-time, part-time or modular), particularly those which integrate technology and engineering business management, or which lead to a specialist subdiscipline.
- Programmes designed by a university or college as a bridge between its accredited HND and its own degree programmes which are accredited for IEng. Ideally, the total package of such provisions should be accredited together.
- Edexcel–BTEC programmes which provide for progression from the 10 unit HNC to the 16 unit HND, as the first stage of this process for those progressing from an HNC base.
- Equivalent schemes appropriate to SQA-SCOTVEC Higher National and Professional Development Awards.
- Education, training and development programmes operated by private and public sector employers such as consultants, industrial companies, the civil service and armed forces. These schemes often include the equivalent of an academic year of 'educational development' in technology, management, personal skills, etc. in addition to 'training and experience'.
- Integrated Development Schemes and College–Business Partnerships (Teaching Company Schemes for FE).
- Distance learning packages aimed at particular graduate employment opportunities in specialist fields or at those in remote locations or mobile jobs.

- Employment-based or institution-based schemes leading to a particular form of employment. Whilst statutory or NVQ/SVQ certification of competent performance may be involved, it is the development of the knowledge, understanding and transferable skills which is key to matching sections. An NVQ/SVQ used for this purpose would have been recognized by the institution concerned, in accordance with the Engineering Council's 'Guidance to Institutions and Awarding Bodies on Occupational Standards, N/SVQs and Registration'.

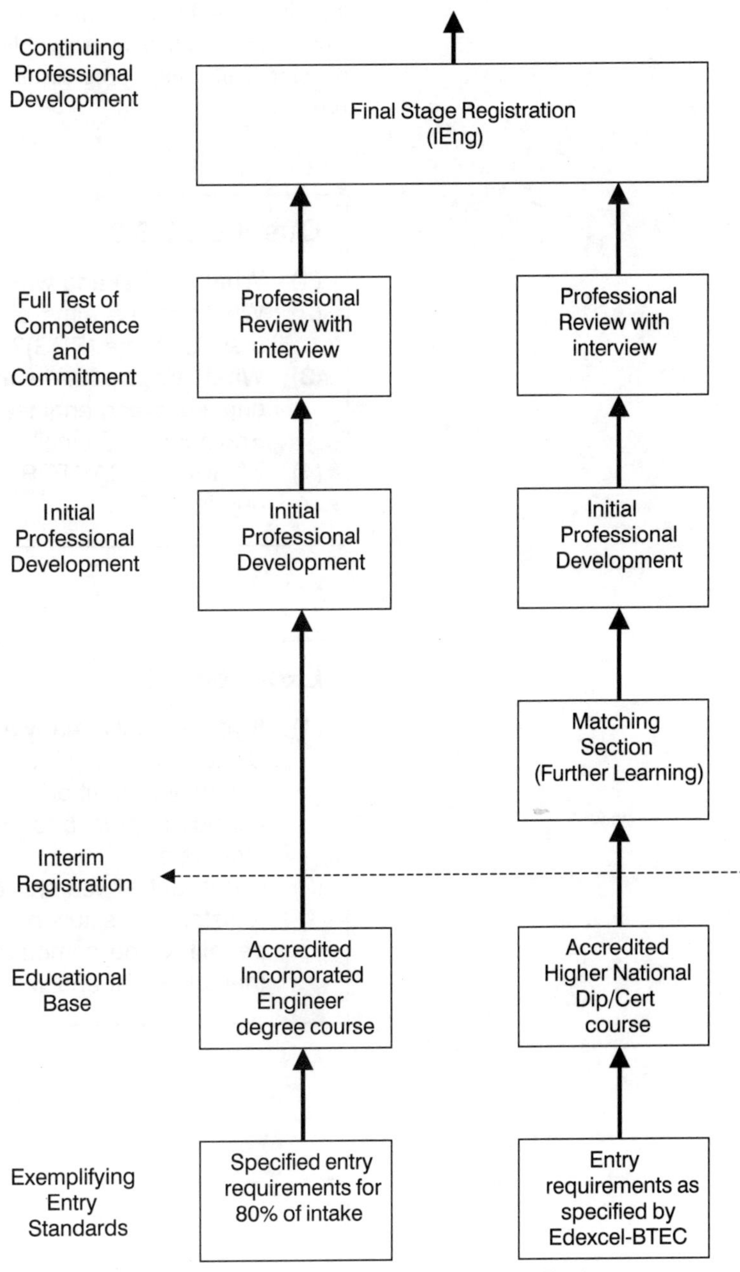

Figure 5.3.1 *Bench mark routes for Incorporated Engineers*

Educational base for Incorporated Engineer, full details are contained in SARTOR 3 and the following sections are included.

- standard and expectations;
- educational preparation for Incorporated Engineers (IEng);
- admission guidelines;
- personal and professional development;
- route to IEng from cognate courses.

Figure 5.3.1 outlines the routes for Incorporated Engineers.

There are other professional institutions that carry the status required by SARTOR, these include the Institute of Electrical Engineers (IEE) and the Institute of Incorporated Engineers (IIE). But they all carry the same code of ethics reference the professional issues that surround the development and progression of people within the computer profession.

Question 5.3.3

(1) What is CPD and who should undertake it?
(2) What are the aims of the BCS Professional Development Scheme (PDS)?
(3) What are the three main grades of membership for engineers and engineering technicians specified by the Engineering Council?
(4) What does SARTOR stand for and what are its main objectives?

Exercise 5.3.2

(1) If you are not already a member of the British Computer Society, find out what the requirements are for joining as a 'student member' and if possible, join! Write a report on their approach to professional development for their members.
(2) Carry out research to establish if there are other registered institutions within the UK that may be of benefit to the computer professional. Who exactly are they aimed at and what is their mission statement?

6 Networks

Summary

The aim of this chapter of the book is to provide sufficient technical information to enable users to make informed purchasing or specification decisions without becoming over involved with detail. Each heading will present the information from the users point of view and where necessary, ignore or gloss over the most technical details. The focus will be on providing sufficient knowledge to communicate with network specialists during network specification and installation.

Introduction

Computing is one of the worst of all subjects when it comes to jargon and networking is the worst part of computing for confusing and often contradictory jargon. Network specialists may refer to a *layer 3 switch* or *cat 5 cabling* and assume that all around understand. The aim of this part of the book is to provide sufficient knowledge to communicate effectively with these specialists.

When specifying a network, the detail is best left to a specialist, it is not an easy task to get all the details correct so the network runs problem free, however, an understanding of what is required is important when agreeing specifications.

6.1 Layering in networks

Once you have PCs connected together and there is a need for them to communicate, a whole set of new problems arise that must be resolved. The components are designed and made by different manufacturers as is the software both at the operating system level and applications.

In the past single companies have tried to dominate the network market so a user would be 'locked in' to a single supplier. This situation no longer really exists (although some companies still try!). The way that software and hardware is made to work together is by a 'layered' approach.

It is absolutely vital that before continuing with your study of networks you understand this idea of layering. The section below is written as an analogy with human communication because many of the problems of network communication are shared by humans.

As with many ideas in computing, there is a published standard that lays down an ideal specification. In the case of networks, this is called the OSI 7 layer model. It is an idealized layered architecture, manufacturers generally choose their own often simpler layers, the Internet uses a five layer model.

The reason a layered approach is so effective in network design is that any layer can be changed without changing the overall aim – to communicate.

The seven layers of the OSI model are:

- Application
- Presentation
- Session
- Transport
- Network
- Data link
- Physical

A set of communication rules between humans is called a *protocol*. You would not for instance speak to your family using exactly the same type of language you would use to your friends. People address children differently from the way they speak to old people, etc. Humans have a whole range (of very complex) protocols 'installed' in their brains that are used to communicate.

Computer networks use protocols and because they are layered, the use of the word stack (to refer to layers) has become common, indeed one hears of a 'protocol stack'. The OSI 7 layer model is not always adopted completely; you may find descriptions of, say, the TCP/IP protocol stack, a 5 layer stack used for the Internet. In this sense, a protocol is a set of rules that defines aspects of communication. The *Internet Protocol*, IP, is a set of rules.

OSI 7 layer model: an analogy

Set out below is an analogy between the layered approach to network design and communication within a group of humans. As with all analogies, you must not take it too far, it is intended as a guide only.

Imagine a group of people having a discussion and consider the rules they use to communicate, how they speak, who speaks at any one moment, what language they speak, how loud their voice is etc. Success or failure to communicate is all that concerns us here. Consider what happens if they break the rules; communication fails to take place.

Layer	Approximate meaning
Application	Speak about the subject you wish to communicate. 'Tell me about the weather today', 'who will win the election', 'how are you feeling today?'
Presentation	Do you use jargon or plain language. Does everyone communicating know the meaning of the jargon? Speak in French or English or any other human language.
Session	Start or end the conversation, possibly with 'Good Morning' or 'May I speak now?' 'That's all for today, thanks and goodbye'. Not concerned with subject only the establishment of communication.
Transport	If the hearer has not heard, how do you know they have not heard? They may send back a message: 'Pardon?' or 'I didn't quite catch what you said', i.e. message has arrived but not completely received. This is a form of error checking.
Network	Look or point at the person to whom you wish to speak, engage eye contact. Establish a path to someone you wish to speak to.
Data Link	Syllables of speech, separate sounds, not speaking if someone else is speaking. (Collision detection.)
Physical	Sound over the air or over a telephone line, megaphone or radio link.

Consider these points:

(1) What happens between the same layers between people. For example at the session layer, what happens if you miss these important social points of etiquette. At the network layer, what happens if you do not get a person's attention. The general result is that communication does not take place, at least not effective communication. (Remember, do not take this analogy too far!)

(2) What happens vertically, i.e. between, say, the transport and session layers, it is no use saying 'Good morning' if the hearer does not hear! Each layer 'talks to' or supports the layer above and below.

(3) Can you change the design of one layer without affecting the other layers? Can you for instance replace French with English in the presentation layer without affecting communication? In terms of computers, presentation layer software would be installed (on the PC). In terms of humans, as long as French is 'installed' (i.e. learnt) by all people communicating, it will have no effect – communication still takes place.

OSI 7 layered network model

Each OSI layer has a particular function and set of behaviours. Each layer provides services to the layers above it, and layers communicate directly only with the same layer on other machines. Each OSI layer provides services that can be ordered and used to describe any arbitrary network implementation. Here is a short synopsis of what each layer is responsible for doing.

Note: Most protocol stacks do not use all seven layers of the OSI model; it is an idealized model and is designed as a guide for future designs. The TCP/IP protocol stack has been included here as a comparison.

OSI/ISO 7 layer model (not every layer is used in every network implementation).	TCP/IP protocol stack
Layer 7. The application layer implements application-specific behaviour, such as the ftp protocol or http (web) session.	TCP/IP sockets
Layer 6. The presentation layer controls formatting and data exchange behaviour, such as byte order conversions, data compression, and encryption. It's in charge of how the data is reformatted for presentation to the application layer. Often not used.	Not used in TCP/IP
Layer 5. The session layer encapsulates network transmissions into 'conversations' and controls synchronization and mode switching between the session's two end points. Coordinates movement of data from client to server.	Not used in TCP/IP
Layer 4. The transport layer provides data delivery. It can also split data into packets and reassemble those packets on the receiving side.	TCP (Transport Control Protocol) UDP (User Datagram Protocol)
Layer 3. The network layer provides the services we think of as network services: routing, flow control, and so on.	IP (Internet Protocol) ICMP (Internet Control Message Protocol) IGMP (Internet Group Message Protocol)
Layer 2. The data link layer controls transmission and retransmission of data. The data is formatted in accordance with the physical layer's requirements, and higher layers may reformat or modify it.	ARP (Address Resolution Protocol) RARP (Reverse Address Resolution Protocol)
Layer 1. The physical layer actually moves bits to and from some kind of network medium, whether it's a 10 Base-T cable, a satellite link, or a modem connection.	Hardware interface

Layering in present day networks

Since the OSI 7 layer model has not been implemented fully, it should be noted that a 5 layer model that closely fits the TCP/IP model is becoming very common. It may well be the case that no network ever uses the complete 7 layer model. As mentioned elsewhere in the book, 'standards' in the computing business are often defined by first becoming popular then being adopted by official bodies later.

The exact descriptions of the layers are different from the ISO model as are the layer numbers. The key idea to grasp is that of layering itself rather than the details of each layer. Each layer 'talks' to the one above or below in a way that allows hardware or software from different makers to be used but the way the equipment or software works internally can be very different from maker to maker.

The layers in this 5 layer model are:

- Application (Layer 5)
- Transport (Layer 4)
- Routing (Layer 3)
- Switching (Layer 2)
- Interface (Layer 1)

- Layer 1, the interface layer, defines the way devices are connected. This is where network standards such as *ATM, token ring, FDDI*, etc. belong, as do the *Ethernet* standards more properly called IEEE 802.3, examples being 10Base-T, etc.
- Layer 2, the switching layer, uses hardware to forward packets of data according to their MAC address. The MAC address is the *Media Access Control*, a number appended to the packet by the NIC, the Network Interface Card fitted in each PC. The MAC address in each NIC is unique across the world.
- Layer 3, the routing layer, allows the network to be partitioned into logical pieces. With the TCP/IP protocol stack, the IP part of the stack is the layer 3 protocol. Each IP packet contains the source and destination address so routing decisions can be made. If a network is split into logical parts, the routing decisions allow packets only into parts of the network where they 'belong' so saving bandwidth. If a network is not split into logical parts, each packet travels to all parts of the network, wasting bandwidth. See TCP/IP frame on page 389.
- Layer 4, the transport layer, is concerned with the way that user applications are handled on the network. This is the TCP part of the TCP/IP protocol stack and involves things such as the retransmission of packets that were lost in layers 2 or 3 for any reason. Some layer 4 protocols such as *Real Time Protocol* (RTP) are concerned with the sequence of packets and their timing, important when packets must arrive in order and in time to support a real-time multimedia application.
- Layer 5, the application layer, is where applications supply data to layer 4 for transmission. Layer 5 applications are what the users see. Rather than writing the code to communicate directly with layer 4, software such as Microsoft's Winsock is used. A web browser such as Netscape would communicate using Winsock.

6.2 Virtual circuits in local area networks

Packets

The data that travels through networks does so in small groups of bytes called packets. This happens in both Ethernet and token ring networks and the whole thing is controlled by a set of rules called protocols. Packets contain transport protocol information depending on the network protocol in use such as Novell's IPX or the internet protocol stack, TCP/IP. This information is handled by the network operating system. A protocol is simply a set of rules that controls communication.

Frames

As the packets must find their way around the network, they must have information attached that gives the address of the destination and of the source of the data together with other information. When packets are wrapped up with this data, the result is called a frame. Frames are made by the network interface card in the PC.

When sending packets over networks the process is called packet switching and differs from older types of network. The old fashioned POTS used a physical circuit which was maintained without a break throughout the call. If you phoned Edinburgh from London, there would have been a single continuous circuit all the way. In these telephone networks, switching equipment establishes a physical unbroken connection. (Modern telephone systems do not use this technique.)

Networks use logical connection computers. In order to start a communication session, both sender and user exchange information to establish this logical connection. The user does not need to know the physical path taken by the data.

Below is a table that shows the make-up of two typical frames. You do not need to remember this level of detail, they are shown to illustrate the idea of a packet and of a frame. Different networks have their own frame design. Each frame contains a single packet of data. See the section on Ethernet for more detail.

Ethernet frame.

Preamble	Destination address	Source address	Type	Data (packet)	FCS
8 bytes	6 bytes	6 bytes	2 bytes	46 to 1500 bytes	4 bytes

FCS = Frame Check Sequence

IEEE 802.3 frame.

Preamble	SOF	Destination address	Source address	Type	802.2 header and data	FCS
7 bytes	1 byte	6 bytes	6 bytes	2 bytes	46 to 1500 bytes	4 bytes

SOF = Start Of Frame

Token ring data frame.

Start delim	End delim	Frame ctrl	Dest address	Source address	Information	Frame check	End delim	Frame status
1 byte	1 byte	1 byte	6 bytes	6 bytes	0–18 000 bytes	4 bytes	1 byte	1 byte

The source address and destination address of each frame are often called node addresses but are also called MAC addresses, short for Medium Access Control. Every Ethernet card made has a unique MAC address built into the card.

Segmentation and reassembly of messages

Unlike physical circuits, packets of data (in their frames) do not follow the same path in an unbroken stream.

To send some data, this needs to happen:

- Each message is divided into segments.
- Each segment is turned into a packet by adding transport protocol information.
- Each packet is placed in a frame.
- Each frame is sent over the network.
- On receipt, the packet is extracted from the frame.
- The packet header is read for protocol instructions.
- The data segments are reassembled into a completed message.
- An acknowledgement is sent back to the sender.

The 5 layer protocol stack shown on page 387 is closely related to TCP/IP, the Transport Control Protocol/Internet Protocol. In order that data can travel over other network types, frames, packets, etc. are *encapsulated*, i.e. become data for the next lower layer in the stack. To illustrate this, the TCP/IP systems shown in Figure 6.2.1 are encapsulated into an Ethernet frame.

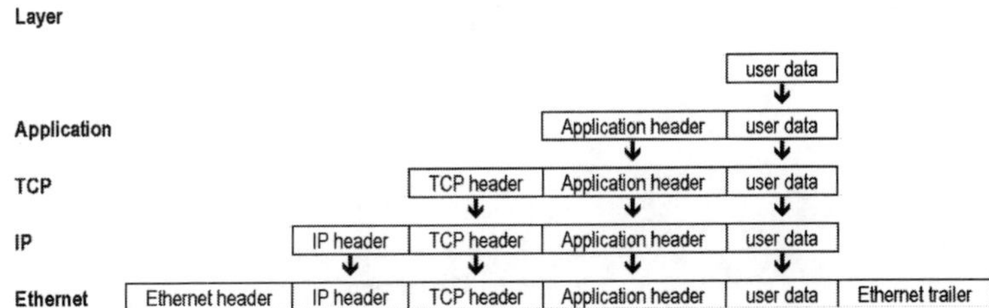

Figure 6.2.1 *TCP/IP frame encapsulated in Ethernet frame*

The maximum distance that data can be sent in a small LAN and the maximum rate at which data can flow are limited by a number of factors. To increase this distance, several different devices are used: *bridges, routers* and *switching hubs.*

Bridging

A bridge is used to join two LANs together. It works by reading the address information in each frame and only sending those frames that need to be sent, ignoring the others. Overall traffic in the LAN is therefore reduced making better use of the available bandwidth.

Routing

Routers work in a similar manner to bridges except they work on the packet transport protocol information not the MAC address. This means that each packet must have this information; packets that do not have this information come from non-routable protocols such as NetBEUI. In a routable protocol such as TCP/IP the logical address is contained in the packet header. A router is a computer in its own right and builds a table of logical addresses that map to network cards.

Switching hubs

A switching hub is a kind of multiport bridge. The software running in the hub can make 'intelligent' decisions to make bridges between ports so making what is in effect even smaller individual LANs. This reduces the traffic flowing all over the LAN so better use can be made of the bandwidth.

Comparing bridging with routing

Bridging

Good points	*Bad points*
Simple to install	Limited configuration options
Needs little or no configuration	Lacks flexibility
Cheap	Does not work well with routers
Is available from many vendors	Is limited to servicing same type of LANs only

Routers

Good points	*Bad points*
Can join dissimilar LANs because they process packets not frames	Can be expensive
Can create better data paths dynamically	Do not work with non-routable protocols such as NetBIOS or NetBEUI
	Are often more difficult to configure and administer
	Do not make good routing decisions when used with bridges

6.3 Some fundamental ideas, bandwidth, decibels, etc.

Bandwidth

This term is much used in networking; unfortunately it is also misused a great deal.

The nature of language is that meanings of words change over time, sometimes developing several meanings. It seems this is happening to the word *bandwidth*. This is a very important concept in networks and data communications so two definitions are presented here.

The informal definition

Some people use the word bandwidth to refer to the speed at which data can be *downloaded*. This is measured in bytes/second so a 4 kbyte/sec link would be considered a low bandwidth and 100 Mbytes/sec would be seen as high bandwidth.

The formal definition

The bandwidth of real communication channels is limited by physics. Some channels can transmit high-power signals, others cannot and most suffer from *noise*, i.e. random signals caused by outside interference. This interference has many causes such as:

- other electrical devices, e.g. fluorescent lighting, 'dirty' switches as found in refrigerators and central heating systems, electric motors, etc.;
- background radio frequencies from space;
- random activity of the electrons in the wires and electronic components themselves.

In an analogue channel, the bandwidth is the difference between the lowest and highest frequency that can be transmitted.

For example, in the POTS (Plain Old Telephone System) the lowest frequency that could be transmitted was about 300 Hz and the highest was about 3300 Hz so the bandwidth is 3300 – 300 = 3000 Hz or 3 kHz. You can make experiments with the POTS. If you have an alarm watch that makes a high pitched alarm, it is quite likely that the frequency is at or above 3300 Hz. If you call a friend and play the alarm down the phone, it is quite likely that your friend will not hear it, i.e. it is not transmitted right through the telephone communication channel. As telephone systems improve so will the bandwidth, so with a modern phone system your friend may be able to hear it! It still makes the point – a channel has a physical limit to the frequencies it will transmit, i.e. it has a limited bandwidth.

If we use the symbols:

- P for the power of a signal sent through the communication channel, measured in watts;
- N for the power of the noise coming out of this channel, also isn watts;
- W for the bandwidth measured in Hz;
- C for the capacity of the channel in bits/second;

then the digital capacity of the channel will be

$$C = W \log_2(1 + (P/N)) \text{ bits per second}$$

This is called *Shannon's law* after Claude Shannon, the first to prove the equation. The ratio P/N is called the *Power to Noise ratio* and is often used as a measure of quality in data and sound transmissions.

Extending the example, with the POTS, the bandwidth is 3 kHz, if we use a signal of 10^{-4} Watts and suffer noise of 4×10^{-7} watts then we get a capacity of

$$C = 3000 \times \log_2(1 + (10^{-4}/4 \times 10^{-7})) = 3000 \times \log_2(251)$$
$$= \text{approx. } 25\,000 \text{ bits per second}$$

This is maximum for the channel and is rarely achieved because the equation itself models an ideal channel; real communication channels suffer all sorts of other problems. To increase the bandwidth you can increase the power P or decrease the noise N, unfortunately there is an upper limit to P and noise is very difficult to reduce.

(If your calculator does not have a $\log_2$ key you can find log2(x) with the formula $\log_2(x) = \log_{10}(x)/\log_{10}(2)$ or more generally for logs of any base, $\text{logbaseN}(x) = \log_{10}(x)/\log_{10}(N)$.)

Here is the language problem. The POTS has a bandwidth of 3 kHz yet can transmit 25 000 bits/second. These values are not the same but in common language, the POTS has a 'bandwidth' of 25 kbits/sec.

Modems are rated at 56 kbits/sec but this speed is achieved using data compression, the actual number of 1s and 0s sent using a 56K modem is lower than the capacity of 25 kbits/sec because this speed is based on an idealized model.

In some ways it does not matter if the academically correct meaning of the word bandwidth is misused as long as people know what you are speaking about, i.e. you still have effective communication; it does matter when ideas of bandwidth are confused between analogue and digital channels.

Decibels

What is a *decibel*? A decibel is a tenth of a bel!

What is a *bel*? A bel is simply the log of the ratio of two numbers, log(number1/number2) therefore a decibel is (log(number1/number2))/10.

Suppose Fred can throw a javelin 50 metres but Joe can throw one 75 metres. The ratio of their best efforts is 75/50 = 1.5. If we take the log of this we get log(1.5) = 0.176 so we can say that Joe's best efforts are 0.176 bels better than Fred's.

The reason we use bels instead of simple ratios, i.e. we use a log scale not a linear scale, is that for very large numbers, a linear scale becomes unusable. The effect of the log scale is to reduce the size of the numbers. Even so, a bel is not a useful unit because a difference of 1 bel means that one value is 10 times the other. It is more common to multiply the ratio given in bels by 10 to give decibels.

In the javelin example, Joe's throw is 0.176 × 10 = 1.76 decibels or 1.76 dB better than Fred's.

When you see any measurement given in dB, it is *always* a ratio. If you do not know the 'other number', i.e. the value that is used to calculate the ratio, the measurement is of no use to you. Sound levels are usually quoted in dB, so a sound of 100 dB is high and a sound of 30 dB is very quiet. These sound levels are ratios to a fixed standard sound level that can be found in reference works on acoustics. dBs are *not* a measurement of sound. In the equation given above, the ratio P/N is the *signal to noise ratio*. This is usually quoted in dB as it is just a ratio of two numbers.

Example 6.3.1

A signal has a power of 2.5 watts and the channel has noise on it with a power of 0.005 watts. What is the signal to noise ratio, S, expressed as dB?

If the noise could be reduced to 0.00025 watts, what would the signal to noise ratio be then?

Answer

$S = 10 \log(P/N) = 10 \times \log(2.5/0.005) = 26.989$ or 27 dB.

For a noise of power 0.00025 watts

$S = 10 \times \log(2.5/0.00025) = 40$ dB.

Example 6.3.2

A communication channel is quoted as having a signal to noise ratio of 97 dB. Is this a good value?

Answer

97 dB means 9.7 bels. The number that has a log of 9.7 is the antilog of 9.7 which is 5 011 872 336.273 or approximately 5000 million times. This means the power of the signal is 5×10^9 times higher than the power of the noise. Pretty good!

This shows why it is better to use dB for the ratio of large numbers. It is better to quote 97 dB instead of 5 000 000 000:1!

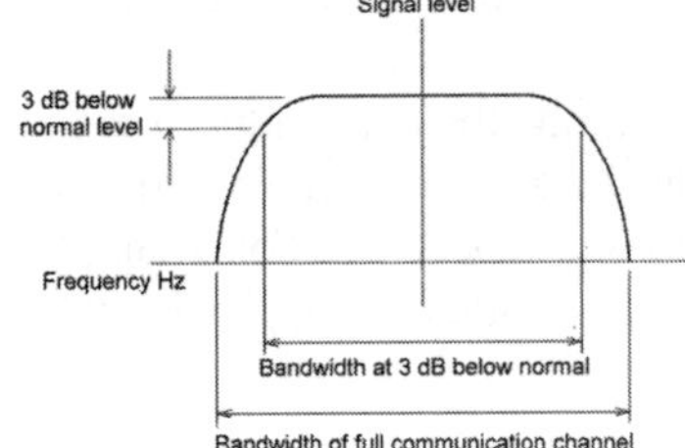

Figure 6.3.1 *Bandwidth at −3 dB*

When a signal is transmitted though a communication channel, the level drops off at some point due to the physical nature of the channel. You can see from Figure 6.3.1 that bandwidth is not a fixed value, it really depends on how you measure it or at which point on the signal drop-off you choose to measure it.

In Figure 6.3.1, the complete bandwidth is shown as the point when the signal level goes down to zero. At or near this level, the signal to noise ratio is unacceptably high so a point is taken at some arbitrary point below the maximum level and the bandwidth is taken from there.

In this example, this point is taken as 3 dB below normal. This results in a narrower bandwidth but in reality this value is a better guide to bandwidth than if the whole channel width as quoted.

If you see a bandwidth quoted as 100 MHz (3 dB) you will know what it means, the ratio 3 dB is the ratio of the level at which bandwidth is measured against the full signal level.

Baseband and broadband

Baseband it when a cable carries one complete information signal at a time, i.e. the cable is used exclusively for one message at a time and the whole of the physical bandwidth of the cable is used for that signal. Most computer communication is baseband, i.e. PC to printer, PC to modem. Except for the latest designs, most networks use baseband.

Broadband is where two or more signals are present on the cable at the same time so that the bandwidth is shared between them. This requires more complex equipment at both ends of the cable. The TV signal that is in the aerial lead to your television is broadband, it contains all the available TV channels at the same time. Circuits in the TV select or tune into just one, discarding the other signals. Broadband signalling can be achieved using frequency division multiplexing. This is where the digital signal is used to modulate a fixed frequency and this modulated signal is sent down the wire at the same time as other modulated signals of different frequencies. It is often used to mix signals of different types, e.g. voice, data, video, etc.

6.4 The physical communication media

Cabling

The bandwidth of the cable used to transmit data is limited. Several designs are available but all attempt to obtain the same thing, high bandwidth with low power loss.

Problems to be overcome:

(1) If you operate a simple radio, you may put up an aerial made up of a piece of wire. It may not work as effectively as a well-designed aerial but it will pick up radio signals. The wire connecting parts of a network is no different, it picks up radio signals as well as electrical interference from common electrical devices. These are known as *Radio Frequency Interference* or RFI and *Electromagnetic Interference* or EMI.

(2) Cables have a power limitation. The signal to noise ratio can be improved by increasing the power but this cannot be extended too far.

(3) Bandwidth. The design of the cable limits the bandwidth. It is no use trying to send a high-frequency signal down a cable with low bandwidth, it will not come out of the other end! For a simple twisted wire pair, the bandwidth is limited to approximately 1 MHz.

If a cable is made with two or more conductors or wires, the electrical properties are different depending on:

- whether they are laid side by side or are twisted together;
- the distance that separates the wires;
- the diameter of the wire;
- the purity of the copper conductor;
- if they are contained inside a 'screen' of braided copper;
- the length of the wire.

Common cable types

The two common cable designs to be found are *Unshielded Twisted Pair* (UTP) and *coaxial*. Coaxial has a single copper conductor surrounded by a braided copper sheath. This sheath is connected to ground so that any unwanted signals picked up are run to earth instead of interfering with the signal being transmitted. If you look at the cable that connects your home television to the aerial, you will find that it is coaxial in design.

UTP is simpler and cheaper to make and being more flexible than coaxial cable, is easier to install. The use of UTP is very attractive but ways must be found to make more use of its effective bandwidth. These ways include special signal processing to reduce the effects of noise in the cable, the bandwidth of UTP is therefore not just a function of the cable itself, it also comes from the devices that connect each end of the cable.

Cabling standards

As is common in the computing industry, cabling is made to conform to standards designed by commercial companies and supported or adopted

Table 6.4.1 *EIA/TIA building cabling standards*

EIA/TIA Category	*Uses*
1	POTS, the Plain Old Telephone System Analogue Voice Digital Voice
2	ISDN (Data) 1.44 Mbps T1, 1.544 Mbps Digital Voice
3	10Base-T Ethernet 4 Mbps token ring ISDN Voice
4	10Base-T Ethernet 16 Mbps token ring
5	10Base-T Ethernet 100Base-T Ethernet 160 Mbps token ring 100 Mbps Distributed Data Interface 155 Mbps Asynchronous Transfer Mode
150 ohm STP	16 Mbps token ring 100 Mbps Distributed Data Interface Full Motion Video

by official bodies. In the case of networks and cabling in particular, these standards are published by such organizations as the EIA/TIA or the IEEE. The EIA/TIA is the *Electronic Industries Association* and *Telecommunications Industry Association*, a group founded in the USA. The IEEE (known as the I triple E) is the *Institute of Electrical and Electronics Engineers*, a non-profit, technical, professional association of more than 350 000 individual members in 150 countries.

Many Local Area Networks (LANs) are cabled with what is called 'cat 5'. This refers to the EIA/TIA category 5 UTP cables. Various categories are shown in Table 6.3.1. Explanation of the terms will be found in other sections of the book.

Fibre

Fibre optic cables have an enormous bandwidth. They are made from glass of extreme purity drawn down into small diameter fibres. It is said that if a block of glass of this purity was made a kilometre thick, it would transmit as much light as a normal window pane. (You should not take such comparisons too literally, they are simply a way of illustrating an idea.)

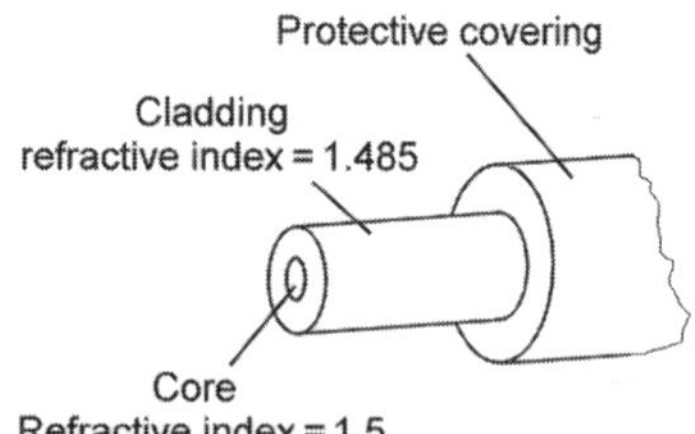

Figure 6.4.1 *Basic construction of fibre optic cable*

The fibre is constructed as Figure 6.4.1. The core is made of glass with a typical refractive index of 1.5 and is clad with a layer of glass with a refractive index that is 99% of 1.5 or $1.5 \times 0.99 = 1.485$. If the fibre was always kept perfectly straight, the light would travel right down the centre. Of course the fibre is never straight so the two layer construction is used to cause the light that enters the core to be totally refracted back into the core as shown in Figure 6.4.1.

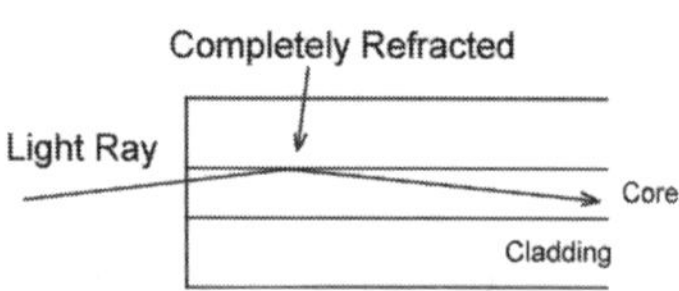

Figure 6.4.2 *Simple light path in a fibre*

It would be a great waste of fibre bandwidth to use baseband signalling unless the signal itself had an enormous bandwidth requirement. Normally this is not the case so broadband techniques are used. This usually involves *multiplexing,* i.e. sending many signals down the fibre at one time. Fibre cables can carry many simultaneous television channels, data and voice signals all at once. Fibre is quite expensive to install but the high bandwidth more than offsets this high price. It is generally used to provide the *backbone* of networks where large amounts of data flow.

Radio or wireless

Until recently, wireless LAN connections have been too slow, but the IEEE have now brought out the standard 802.11b (High Rate) that defines an 11 Mbit/sec trasmission rate which will provide performance equivalent to 'standard' Ethernet.

IEEE 802.11b requires two pieces of equipment, a PC with a wireless NIC and an access point. The access point is wired to the main network via its own bridge. Roaming is possible, i.e. just like a mobile phone, the user can take the PC anywhere in range of the set of access points and remain connected to the network. Use of different protocols will also allow peer to peer connections. For more information, see 3Com Corporation at www.3com.com/technology/tech_net/white_papers/503072a.html or Intel at www.intel.com.

6.5 Network protocols

This is a term that applies to a wide range of network standards. In the early 1970s, a network was designed by the Xerox Corporation to connect their Altos workstations together. After some time and after joining company with DEC and Intel, the first *Ethernet* specification was published. Since then, the IEEE published a network standard that was based on Ethernet but is not quite the same. This standard is called IEEE 802.3 and in common language is also called Ethernet although it is not an accurate description – another example of where words slowly change their meaning. Ethernet is now used to cover any network that uses CSMA/CD.

Network contention

CSMA/CD

This stands for Collision Sense Multiple Access/Collision Detection. As many network stations are connected to the same wire and this wire uses baseband signalling (see page 394), only one station must be transmitting at once. When a station wishes to transmit over the network, it waits until the line is quiet. If two stations start to transmit data at exactly the same time, each waits a random amount of time before retransmission, a system that ensures that one will start before the other so avoiding another collision. Humans use this system; imagine you were with a group of people, all having a conversation. Providing you are not arguing, only one person speaks at once, if two start to speak at the same time, both wait for a suitable moment to speak again.

Token passing

On a token ring network, including FDDI, a *token* is sent through the network. The token is used to communicate the busy or free state of the network. If the previous token indicated the network was free, a PC that wishes to transmit sends out a 'busy' token, stopping other machines from sending. The data sent out travels around the ring and arrives back at the sending PC which then responds by sending out a 'not busy' token, allowing access to other machines. Token passing is better than CSMA/CD under heavy traffic conditions.

In *Ethernet* networks, the individual standards are known as 10Base-2, 10Base-5, etc. In this coding, the 10 refers to the data rate of 10 Mbits/sec, 'base' refers to baseband and the number is the cable media type and approximates to one-hundredth of the segment length in metres. Using this scheme, 10Base-5 is a 10 Mbits/sec baseband system with a maximum segment length of 500 metres. Some of the specifications are summarized in Table 9.5.1. There are many more. 1000Base-LX is just one from a set of specifications that are called gigabit Ethernet.

You will see references in the marketplace for 10, 100 and 1000 Mbits/sec Ethernet. This reflects the enormous rate of progress from the

Table 6.5.1 *Details of some of the Ethernet physical layer specifications*

	Original Ethernet	*10Base-5*	*10Base-2*	*10Base-T*	*100Base-T*	*1000Base-LX*	*10Broad-36*
Signalling	baseband	baseband	baseband	baseband	baseband	baseband	broadband
Max segment length, metres	500	500	185	100	100	5000	1800
Cable	50 ohm coaxial	50 ohm coaxial	50 ohm coaxial	UTP	UTP	Fibre	75 ohm coaxial

original 10 Mbits/sec Ethernet in 1972. To be more precise, Ethernet and IEEE 802.3 runs at 10 Mbits/sec over coaxial cable, 100 Mbits/sec Ethernet is known as Fast Ethernet and operates at 100 Mbps over UTP and 1000 Mbits/sec Ethernet is known as gigabit Ethernet that operates at 1000 Mbits/sec using fibre and twisted-pair cables.

You should notice that each type has a maximum cable length for each segment of the network. The length restriction is due to the timing required for the particular Ethernet standard. If you were to fit longer cables, the signal timing would no longer conform to the standard and communication would not be reliable.

For more information, see www.3com.com/technology/tech_net/whitepapers, www.cisco.com/univercd/cc/td/doc/cisintwk/ito_doc/ethernet.htm or www.brother.com/european/networking/.

FDDI

This is the *Fibre Distributed Data Interface*, often used to provide a network backbone rather than service to individual PCs.

FDDI is a 100 Mbits/sec network standard that runs over a ring topology. It uses token passing rather than the CSMA/CD used in Ethernet and is designed to run over fibre optic cables. A related standard called CDDI runs over copper cables; it was introduced to avoid the high cost of fibre cabling.

Fibre optic cables are more secure than copper as they do not emit an electromagnetic field that can be picked up by unauthorized users. For related reasons, it does not suffer from electrical interference from outside and has a very high bandwidth. Unfortunately, it is expensive to install. FDDI uses two rings, the primary ring and the secondary ring. This means that if one fibre is broken, communication can continue over the other. Each FDDI has two ports (called A and B) that attach to the primary and secondary rings. Up to a 1000 stations can be connected but a practical limit of 500 exists because if a fibre breaks, the 500 stations would become 1000 stations. This is due to the way the signals interact in each station.

Some types of network traffic must have data that arrives in time and in sequence. An example of this is real-time video. Other data can arrive without strict timing, such as email or file transport. FDDI supports both kinds of traffic by providing synchronous and asynchronous transport. Time critical applications would use synchronous transport that can use a fixed part of the 100 Mbits/sec bandwidth; other asynchronous traffic takes what is left.

ATM

ATM is *Asynchronous Transfer Mode*, a network standard that specifies data packet format and network switching. It was designed for use by telephone companies to provide wide area data transport.

It is characterized by being a high-speed packet switching system that uses very short fixed length data packets (48 data bytes + 5 control = 53 bytes). The problem it attempts to solve is the carriage of mixed types of data. The packets for video and other time critical applications must arrive in time, other data such as email does not have this need. ATM can define the quality of service to give Constant Bit Rate (CBR), Variable Bit Rate (VBR) and Available Bit Rate (ABR) depending on the type of traffic to be carried. The speed of ATM varies with the quality of service but values of 155 Mbits/sec over copper and 622 Mbits/sec over fibre are common.

6.6 Network architectures

There are many network architectures, all with their own benefits, the descriptions below are the most common. When networks are called 'small' or 'large', remember the old problem: 'what is the difference between a ship and a boat'. There is no *definition*!

- Small networks with a few users normally use Ethernet or token ring networks with one or two servers or no server at all if peer to peer is in operation. See below.
- Medium-sized networks with a few hundred users will have the need to segment the network into logical parts. Client server is common with medium-sized networks. See below. There may be 10 or more servers and hardware such as routers or switches to provide the segmentation. Ethernet or token ring is still common with this size of network.
- Large networks usually involve many floors or areas in a building and serve a large organization with diverse needs. This results in a network that must be segmented into logical parts for security, to share the load on servers and the need to balance bandwidth for best performance. High-speed backbones are used, possibly FDDI, ATM or gigabit Ethernet.

A critical choice about the specification of a network is the level of traffic, where the traffic is heavy and how can it be reduced. Factors to consider:

- Is the application software on a server or on local PCs?
- Is part of the PC operating system on the server or local PCs (particularly the Windows swapfile – see page 3)?
- In the business of the organization, do users need to access large centrally stored databases?
- Is there a requirement for bandwidth hungry applications such as video conferencing?

If software is held locally and the Windows swapfile is held locally, the network traffic is likely to come from transfer of whole files so the total load on the network will vary a fair amount but still be quite light, most of the time only small demands are made on the available bandwidth. The IT support department now has a larger job as maintenance of the system will require visits to each machine on the site. (One reason for centralizing application software is to reduce this workload.) If software is held centrally or there is a need to access large central databases, use video, etc. the traffic rises and therefore you must either provide higher bandwidth or take care in the architecture of the network to maximize the available bandwidth.

Peer to peer

Peer to peer means that each machine is treated as a 'peer' or equal. On a peer-to-peer system, you will be able to see devices on other machines such a disks, printers, etc. It is a network that is very good for small organizations. Microsoft Windows from version 3.11 onwards is capable of providing a peer-to-peer network with no additional network operating system.

Client server

Client server means the PC is (usually) a *client* to services provided by the *server*. If everything is provided by the server, traffic is high, if some functions are locally based, traffic is reduced. The decision is how to split local and server-based services, e.g. do you have all network-based printing so all print jobs travel via the network or do you have some local printing? Most, but not all medium or large networks use the client server model.

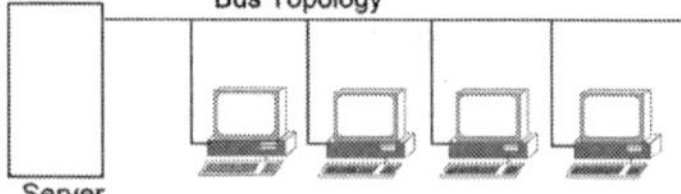

Figure 6.6.1 *Bus topology with a single server*

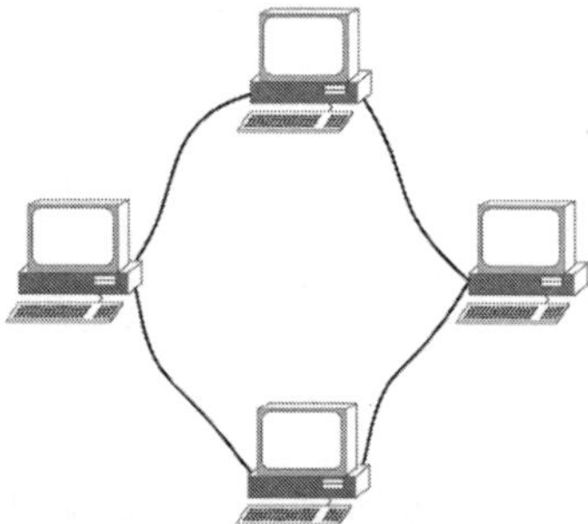
Figure 6.6.2 *Ring topology*

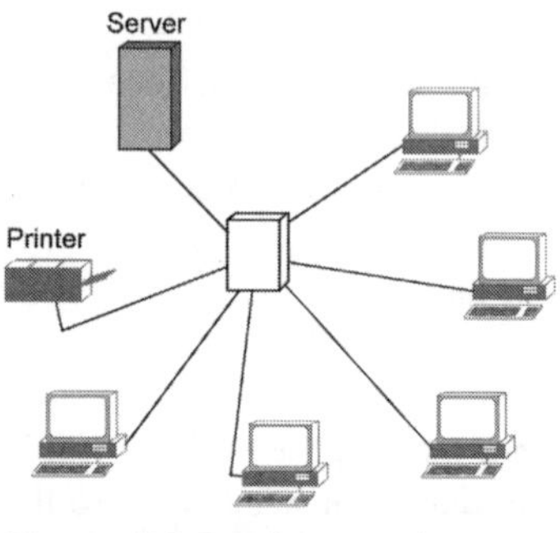

Small networks

Possible topologies for small networks

The device in the centre of the star topology of Figure 6.6.3 is most likely to be a switch. A switch is a kind of multiport bridge, i.e. it treats each arm of the star as a separate network, sharing the available bandwidth. Typical values are 10 Mbits/sec per PC.

Figure 6.6.3 *Star topology*

Medium-sized networks

Figure 6.6.4 shows a possible topology for a medium-sized network. The figure shows a router but this could be a switch. The choice depends on how the network is to be segmented.

- Routers allocate segments by use of individual ports, i.e. it is done by the hardware.
- Switches allocate segments by software control, so source and destination addresses can be physically anywhere on the network.

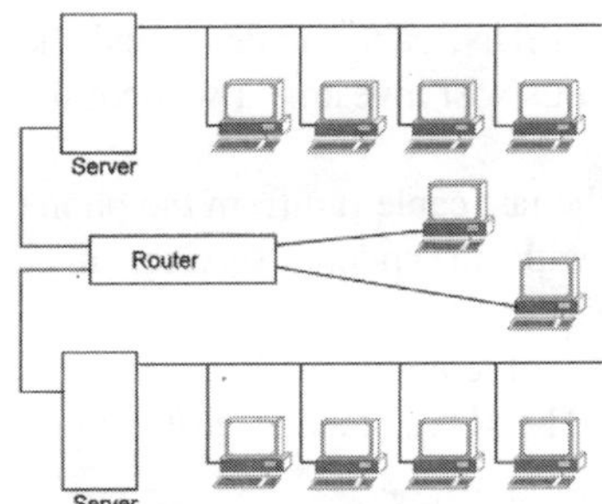

Figure 6.6.4 *Medium-sized network with collapsed backbone*

This arrangement allows for a VLAN or Virtual LAN (see page 406). If the segmentation is being done to suit an organization department by department then routers are fine but VLANs allow for greater flexibility either as the organization changes or as accommodation changes.

A collapsed backbone is a strange name, it simply means there is no longer one single backbone.

Large networks

An important difference between medium and large networks is in the management of the bandwidth. It is easy to design a system that has a bottleneck, a part of the system that slows things down, because it is running at full speed but this speed is not sufficient to cope with demand. The solution in existing networks is to use traffic analysis software to determine the exact point of the trouble. In the design of a new network, it is important analyse the bandwidth needs before any design decisions are made. The choice of backbone between FDDI, ATM, gigabit Ethernet, etc. is not an easy one to make, there are many factors to consider. It is the not the intention of this unit of the HNC Computing to consider all these in detail.

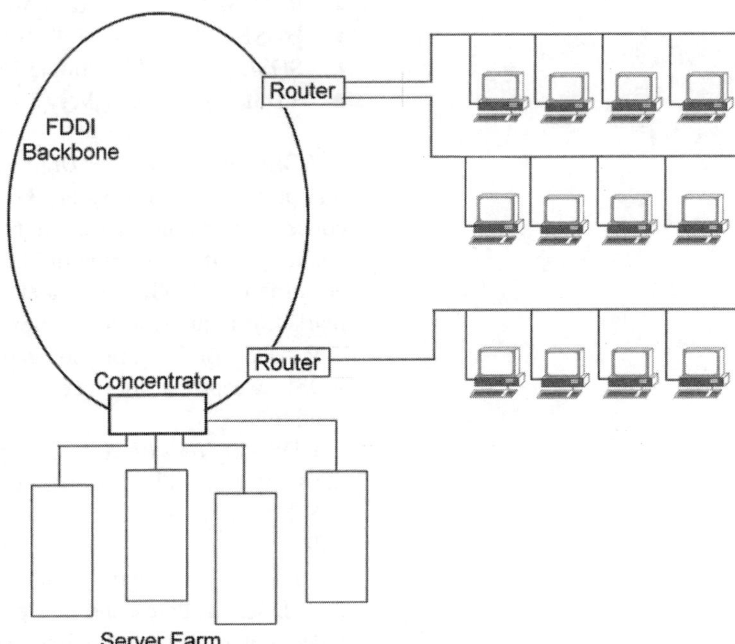

Figure 6.6.5 *Possible topology of a large network using FDDI*

6.7 Connecting to networks from remote sites

xDSL

A major problem for Internet or networking companies is the cost of providing connections to large numbers of remote users. There exists a huge investment in the local loop, cabling to houses and offices that already carry voice telephone services. ISDN, cable modems and the xDSL standards were developed to use this vast investment without the need to recable the world.

The local loop is the name given to the last cable run from the phone company to the buildings supplied with the phone service. It is sometimes referred to as the 'last mile'.

xDSL is the name given to a range of communication standards designed to carry voice and data traffic. The xDSL standard just coming into use in the UK is ADSL.

Data connections are not the only reason that higher bandwidth is required. Better voice telephone services are also required so digital systems are being installed that provide added value services to the user such as caller identification, call waiting, etc.

The xDSL standards are

- ADSL/ADSL-lite Asymmetric Digital Subscriber Line
- R-ADSL Rate-Adaptive Digital Subscriber Line
- HDSL High Bit-Rate Digital Subscriber Line
- SDSL Single-Line Digital Subscriber Line
- VDSL Very High Bit-Rate Digital Subscriber Line

ADSL or *Asymmetric Digital Subscriber Line* is a digital standard that provides an 'always on' service to a remote network. There is no concept of making a call, it behaves to the user more like a LAN connection. It is 'asymmetric' because the upload and download speeds are different. ADSL-lite is a slower version intended for the domestic market, it requires less complex equipment at the user end.

R-ADSL or *Rate-Adaptive Digital Subscriber Line* is very similar to ADSL except that the speed can be adjusted to suit cable lengths and conditions.

HDSL or *High Bit-Rate Digital Subscriber Line* is symmetric, it has the same bandwidth for uploads and downloads.

SDSL or *Single-Line Digital Subscriber Line* is similar to HDSL but will work with single copper wires over restricted distances.

VDSL or *Very High Bit-Rate Digital Subscriber Line* is the fastest of the xDSL standards and can provide sufficient bandwidth to support video but over shorter distances. The standard can be extended by providing a fibre optic link from the telephone provider to a local distribution point but this defeats part of the reason for the xDSL standards, i.e. to use the installed local loop.

Table 6.7.1 shows the speed in either kbits/sec or Mbits/sec for up- and download of data for various standards together with approximate maximum distances in km. The abbreviation T1 refers to a US standard for a 1.55 Mbits/sec telephone connection and E1 is the faster European equivalent.

ADSL modems use a technique that is related to traditional modems but introduce more complexity.

A traditional modem modulates a 'sound' with digital data to make it compatible with the POTS. The POTS was originally designed as a voice only analogue system and as such will not transmit digital 1s and 0s. There is an exception to this, in the very oldest POTS, opening and closing the lines was used to dial the number, the 'dial' itself was speed controlled to open and close the lines at a set rate to match the speed of the switches in the exchange. This was called 'loop disconnect' dialling.

Table 6.7.1 *Speeds of local loop connection standards*

Standard	*Upload*	*Download*	*Distance*
56 kbps analogue modems	28–33 k	56 k	
ISDN	128	128	5.5 km
Cable modem	128 k–10M	10–30M (over shared lines)	50 km
ADSL Lite	512 k	1M	5.5 km
ADSL/R-ADSL	1.544M	1.5–8M	5.5 km
IDSL	144 k	144 k	5.5 km
HDSL	1.544M (T1) 2M (E1)	1.544M (T1) 2M (E1)	4.5 km
SDSL	1.544M (T1) 2M (E1)	1.544M (T1) 2M (E1)	3 km
VDSL	1.5 = 2.3M	13–52M	0.3–1.3 km

For backwards compatibility, some phones and most modems will still execute loop disconnect dialling. On a phone, you may see a switch marked 'LD' and 'Tone'. LD is Loop Disconnect, and 'tone' is the system used now to dial numbers, a set of tones of different frequencies. Because of this history, the POTS could not transmit 1s and 0s so modulated sounds were used instead.

The ADSL modems modulate signals of higher frequency resulting in the ability to provide a higher bandwidth. (The actual system of modulation used is quite complex but of no interest here.) As ADSL is asymmetric, one frequency is used for upload and another for download with the higher bandwidth being assigned to download. This is called frequency division multiplexing, which means different signals are carried using different frequencies on the same broadband line. A technique called *echo cancellation* allows the frequency bands to overlap so using the available bandwidth more efficiently. A filtering device called a POTS splitter is used to split off 4 kHz of bandwidth to provide a simultaneous voice channel that works at the same time as data transmission. As is usual with broadband transmissions, the cost and complexity of the equipment at both ends of the line offsets the saving made by using cheap cabling, but the cost of providing high bandwidth cable to support baseband signalling would be prohibitive. This is the whole purpose of ADSL.

xDSL can deliver ATM (Asynchronous Transfer Mode) services to the home.

ISDN

ISDN means *Integrated Services Digital Network*. It is a switched service designed originally to provide high-quality voice telephone connections to PBXs, Private Branch Exchanges. ISDN 30 provides 30 64 k lines to support PBXs but a domestic version is available called ISDN 2 and, as the name implies, provides two 64 k lines that can be combined to give a bandwidth of 128 k. In the UK there has been a slow take-up of ISDN lines and the newer ADSL lines seem to offer better bandwidth. ISDN requires a call to be set up in a similar manner to a modem used over a voice line whereas ADSL is always on service; for this reason, ISDN attracts call charges.

Cable modems

Cable Modems do not really belong in this section as they do not use the local loop, they must use the cable provided for cable TV services. They do provide a high-bandwidth broadband connection. Once connected, cable modems use a LAN protocol to transport data over the network, so issues of security become more of a concern. One of the first cable modem installations had a fault that allowed each user's C: drive to be visible over the network! Download to the user is via the cable modem but many installations rely on the POTS with a traditional modem to upload data at a much lower bandwidth.

6.8 Network security

Hackers attack networks for profit, to be malicious or just 'because it is there'. They do not need any special knowledge because hacking tools are easily obtained from the Internet as is advice on how to attack networks and lists of the latest hacks. Some hackers just do it for kicks but some are very proficient people bent on criminal or at least immoral gain. These people are all a real nuisance.

Why should you protect a network?

You need to keep your intellectual property from the eyes of your competitors. Much of your data is very expensive to generate, loss or damage can put you out of business.

Consider that when a hacker gains access to a network, they may have just had a 'look' at what is there and gone elsewhere. If you cannot be very sure that nothing is modified, your loss is still potentially very large as you must now examine every part of every file to make sure no damage has been done. Even if you have a complete system backup, you must be sure the backed-up data was secure before the backup was created. As many hacks are only discovered later on, you may well find that backups several generations old may now be compromised.

The kinds of damage that hackers do are:

- stealing your data;
- fraudulent use of your data or funds;
- denial of Service attacks that stop you using the network;
- changing your data for any reason including fraud;
- politically motivated acts.

Firewalls

A *firewall* is a piece of software usually but not always running on a dedicated computer or piece of hardware such as a router. It acts by controlling access to your network from the outside. A firewall defines which parts of the internal system can be seen from the outside and can also act in reverse; it can control what outside services are visible from inside.

Firewalls block incoming hacker attacks; they also use Network Address Translation (NAT) to hide much of the detail in the network traffic so it looks like it all comes from one machine.

The software can be set to screen traffic from:

- a predefined set of addresses;
- a predefined set of users;
- traffic that contains certain kinds of data.

One of the tools used by hackers is the port scanner. This is a piece of software that looks at the structure of a network. Hackers can use this information to target one or more of its parts.

Denial of service attacks are launched by a hacker sending large amounts of data to an address so tying up the machine. To do this the hacker needs the IP address. If a firewall is in place, the IP address is not available as it is hidden. In this case the firewall can react by ignoring the incoming data and even detect to some extent the origin of the attack. Hackers, however, are aware of this and take steps to hide themselves. Hackers have firewalls of their own.

Firewalls come in different types such as:

- packet filter;
- application-level proxy servers;
- statefull packet inspection.

A *Packet Filter Firewall* works with IP packets in the TCP/IP protocol stack. Packets are examined for their IP address, TCP/IP port number and the type of data. The system administrator can set the controls to many different levels. Although a powerful means to protect data, this method is difficult to set up and small errors can leave a system open to attack. Hackers are adept at what is called 'IP spoofing' that makes the IP address seem as though it has come from a reliable source.

An *Application Level Proxy Server* works on the top-level layers of the protocol stack, i.e. at the application that is using the data. This means that a different proxy server must be set up for each application, e.g. one for the web's http protocol, another for email and a third for ftp, the file transfer protocol.

A firewall that uses *Statefull Packet Inspection* examines every aspect of data packets. Data that was not requested is rejected (because unrequested data may be unreliable). Data that was requested is also checked. This type of firewall is said to be the most reliable.

Some firewalls must work to protect networks where non-requested data packets will arrive. Public servers that provide Internet connections, email servers, etc. get non-requested data as part of their normal work. Firewalls that have the rather oddly named feature the *demilitarized zone* allow access to certain parts of the system but lock users, even registered users, out of most of the system. Such firewalls also provide a measure of anti-virus protection and support for encryption.

Virtual private networks (VPN)

VPNs or VLANs (*Virtual Local Area Networks)* are those networks that use a publicly available system to physically attach to a network but one set of users are kept private from all others by firewalls. Systems like this are used by people such as employees of one company who can login from anywhere in the world using public telecommunication systems but the network will 'look' like a private one. Clearly the systems are prone to hacker attacks as the physical connection is there. VPNs benefit from the use of data encryption as any hacker who succeeds in getting data from the system will not be able to read it. This does not mean that total security has been achieved because you will not be able to tell what has been deleted and encryption will not prevent denial of service attacks.

The other side of the security issue

Legislation

It should be noted that some governments have already made data encryption illegal and other governments are looking to follow their example. Other governments allow encryption provided that a way in for the government is allowed via a *trusted third party.* The reasons given are that police forces need to be able to detect crimes such as illegal drug dealing, sex offenders or terrorists. Whatever the validity of this argument, many people are of the opinion that the chief government concern is their lack of power of taxation over international business transactions. Consider that if you obtain services such as the supply of software from an international source, your home government will not be able to tax you. This has the potential to 'lose' very large amounts of revenue for the home government.

People

Firewalls and related security are administered by one or two individuals in a company, or at the very least, a single department. In most cases this is fine except that these people must be trusted absolutely, they have the security key for the whole business. These people will be in a position to do much more damage than a hacker attack, indeed many hackers have been found to have insider information.

The issue of data security will become more and more important as countries move toward the 'information society'. Information is power and those who hold the key to power must be trusted.

There is an often overlooked feature of security, that of the loss of usefulness of the system if it is overprotected. It is an unfortunate fact that some humans like locking things away. An IT manager may decide that a given feature on a network is at risk so then decides to set the network operating system security features to prevent some (or all) users from seeing it or using it. This is fine if this manager actually understands the business needs of the organization but can cause real problems when systems are locked or hidden for no good reason.

An example is when networked printers are set for use by a restricted group of people. For example, if person A wishes to print, they are only allowed to print in their own office. This looks fine as it prevents accidental printing in other parts of the building; the 'reason' to lock things away like this is to prevent confidential documents being seen by others accidentally. On the other hand, it may well be that a particular job requires another printer (it may produce colour or print on special paper, etc.). In this case, person A will have to approach some other person to print their work. If the system is locked up, this may be quite inconvenient so person A may well shy away from such efforts and work in a different and less advantageous way, losing some of the benefit of the network. Had the IT manager properly understood the situation, the locking may not be so widespread.

A fact that compounds this situation is the lack of knowledge on the part of many network users about what is or is not possible; they will assume that if a system is not provided, it must not be possible to provide. This is another reason why those in charge of networks must be trusted absolutely; they have an important part to play in the profitability of the organization but equally may well be preventing better use of the investment put into their care.

6.9 Network specification

Required bandwidth

Many people suffer from 'upgradeitus' – they must have the latest, fastest system because it is available. Some IT specialists are not immune to this. In an era of tight financial budgets and the push for ever higher savings and productivity, it does not pay to suffer from this unfortunate complaint!

When specifying PCs or networks, a realistic assessment must be made about what performance is required rather than what is available or what someone may 'like'. In the case of networks, the big performance issue is bandwidth.

Providing that application software is on local PCs and that most of the work of the organization uses normal office applications such as word processing, spreadsheets, email of text, etc. the bandwidth requirement will be low. There will be peaks in demand as large files are sent or large print jobs are sent to a central printer, but most of the time, work is local and does not add to network traffic. The bandwidth demand rises dramatically when applications such as Video Conferencing (VC) are required. If the network can provide for VC, most other traffic will flow without much trouble. The protocols used must be able to support VC. So how much bandwidth do you need for VC?

A possible 'worst case' bandwidth requirement

Assuming you plan to use video conferencing, what bandwidth is required? Assuming you have a 1024 × 768 screen resolution set on a PC, start by deciding what size video image is best. This resolution has a ratio of 1:0.75 so if you choose video images with the same ratio, typical sizes are represented to scale as shown in Figure 6.9.1.

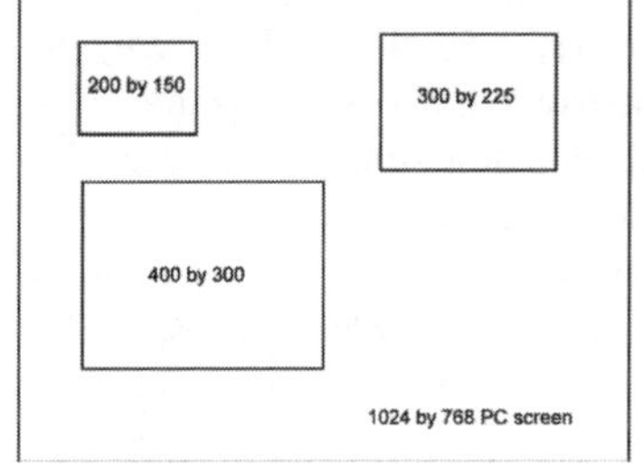

Figure 6.9.1 *Image sizes in proportion 0.75:1*

Example 6.9.1

Problem

If the video has 256 colours and gives, say, 25 full frames/second, the same speed as a domestic television, what bandwidth is required?

One answer, without compressing the data

An uncompressed video image size of 400 × 300 has 400 × 300 = 120 000 pixels. At 256 colours that means 1 byte per pixel or 120 000 bytes/second. At 25 frames a second this gives 120 000 × 25 = 3 000 000 or 3 million bytes per second. As digital bandwidth is quoted in bits/sec, we would need a minimum of 3 × 8 = 24 Mbits/sec, ignoring any control data. A typical 10Base-T network connection to a PC gives 10 Mbits/sec, clearly not enough.

To fix this, either a higher bandwidth connection to the PC is required (assuming the backbone can supply it), use is made of video compression or a compromise made on the picture quality. The frame rate could be reduced, so could the number of colours and the image size.

To take the other extreme, use could be made of the 200 by 150 size image, 16 colours and 10 frames/sec. This would give a very poor, jerky image, a little hard to see but the bandwidth required would be:

200 × 150 = 30 000 pixels

30 000 pixels at 16 colours = 15 000 bytes (½ byte per pixel)

15 000 bytes at 10 frames/sec = 150 000 bytes/sec

150 000 bytes/sec = 1.2 Mbits/sec

Clearly 10 Mbits/sec is now fast enough, but would users want such a poor quality image?

Compression

One possible solution is to use mathematical techniques to compress the image, thus reducing the bandwidth required. There are several standards common in the marketplace but the one that looks like being most common is MPEG (from *Motion Picture Experts Group*). This compression works in a number of ways, one of which is only to transmit frame pixels that are different from the previous frame. If a video scene shows a fixed background with something moving in the foreground, only the moving parts are transmitted.

The problem with MPEG is that either software is used to compress and decompress at each end of the transmission or hardware is used. The software is slower than the hardware, defeating some of the advantage of compression, the hardware is fast but currently not cheap. MPEG is being used in digital television distribution over high-bandwidth channels.

The bandwidth required for video therefore depends on the quality of image that is seen as acceptable. Compression helps but a fast PC is required if decompression is done with software. MPEG cards to decompress the image provide a high-quality image but are still relatively expensive.

Further informtion on MPEG can be seen at www.mpeg.org/MPEG/video.html.

6.10 Impact of communications technology

In the 1960s defence computers in the United States were organized in a hierarchical structure. This meant that the systems were vulnerable to attack. A Soviet warhead striking a computer near the top of the hierarchy would effectively disable all those that were beneath it in the network. In order to create a more robust defence which would be able to survive limited loss of machines American computer scientists developed an alternative system. The *Advanced Research Projects Administration* (ARPA) devised a computer network in which no single machine held a critical role. Instead if a particular military base and its associated computers were lost through enemy attack, vital defence information could still be routed automatically through the surviving machines in the network. Considerable redundancy was built into the system. This computer network, *ARPANet*, became the ancestor of the *Internet*. Gradually it was extended. It was made available for university research. Then, as the Cold War ended and the Soviet Union was replaced by Eastern European friends, the computer network slowly became available to everybody. Now anybody with a personal computer, a modem and an *Internet Service Provider* (ISP) has access.

The *World Wide Web* began at the European nuclear physics research centre, CERN, as a way for scientists to exchange information easily but soon developed into a tool adopted by anybody using the Internet. Basically it adds a graphics user interface to the Internet to make its use almost intuitive. It also adapts the earlier concept of *hypertext* to link one document, or web page, to another. Similar to the way the human mind readily associates one idea with another, without necessarily moving logically through all the logical steps in between, so *links* in a hypertext document allow the user to jump from one document to another. It is rather like the contrast between the scrolls used in classical times and the folded pages of a modern book. The latter allows the reader to skip quickly from one section to another. The links are shown on screen as a change in font, different from the rest of the text by being a distinct colour, by highlighting or by being underlined. Clicking at this location informs the *browser* software that the fresh page is required.

Hypertext as it was originally designed only linked documents on the same standalone computer. The Web by extending the concept to computers connected across the world by the Internet has made it almost infinitely more powerful.

All web documents have a *Universal Resource Locator* (URL) which gives the address at which the document is located. The URL consists of the computer name, the directory in which the document is to be found and the document name. The URL is proceeded by the *hypertext transfer protocol command* http://

Key fact

The author Arthur C. Clarke (yes, the one who invented the communication satellite) wrote as an almost incidental detail in one of his many novels that in the future the ability to search for information on internationally networked computers would be an essential skill for any student. This particular novel predated the Internet and the World Wide Web by many years. Clarke's prediction has come true. Today there is a vast amount of information available on the Web. The difficult part is accessing it easily.

Once you know of a particular website which is likely to hold the information you require it is simply a question of entering its address. It is also possible to navigate from one site to another following plausible links to home it on what you want. Commonsense plays a part as well. If you are trying to find a list of novels written by a particular author then a reasonable move is to look first at the on-line catalogue of a large university bookshop. The shop sets up its site in order to encourage sales, but you do not necessarily have to buy. It is rather like window shopping, and on the Internet there are many windows.

Key fact

Valiant attempts are made to provide guidance for Internet surfers. An example would be *The Rough Guide to the Internet*, regularly updated, which adds clarity to the chaos!

However, if these methods fail you are faced with the fact that there is a colossal amount of information on the World Wide Web but that this information is clearly very difficult to classify. There cannot be a universal index for something which is in a state of flux and constant alteration and addition.

The solution to this problem is to use a *search engine*. The trouble is that it is not an ideal solution. A search engine is capable of matching a query to a vast number of sites but this matching does not involve a human level of understanding of the query itself. Computer pattern matching is not yet the equivalent of human semantics.

Typical search engines are:

- Alta Vista
- Ask Jeeves
- Excite
- Google
- InfoSeek
- Lycos
- Yahoo

Searching can take place as a *key word search* or as a *menu search*, in which successive menus give the user the opportunity to narrow the search down to the topic required.

The impact of communications technology on society, and on the way that organizations conduct their business, can be investigated as a number of overlapping topics:

- Electronic mail
- Electronic commerce
- On-line and distance learning

- Web TV
- Digital broadcasting
- Multimedia
- Video conferencing
- Convergence

Key fact

The growing use of the derisory term *snail mail* for conventional postal services reflects the enthusiam for the electronic variety.

Electronic mail

One impact of the Internet upon society that seems to have affected a large proportion of the population is the way in which *electronic mail* can be sent from one computer to another. Manufacturers have even produced domestic email devices which do not require a computer or for the sender to have specific computer skills. The popularity of modified televisions, and dedicated 'emailers', indicates the importance many people attach to being able to send and receive email.

Every person who uses email has their own unique address. This consists of their user identity, the @ symbol, and the domain name of their internet service provider. When the email is sent it will contain this address together with the time and date and of course the email address of the recipient.

It has been suggested, in *The New Hacker's Dictionary*, that the word 'email' is actually derived from the French 'emmailleure', or 'network'.

Email facilities are possible without access to the Internet. A computer might be linked to a bulletin board system which has an email gateway.

Advantages of electronic mail

Electronic mail allows *rapid communication* with other organizations. It combines the speed of telephone communication with the precision of printed text. This enables rapid decision making, with the resultant benefits to the organization. Orders can be placed quickly or sales confirmed.

Email is *less expensive* than other methods for sending the same information.

Email documents are soft, unlike the hard copy of a letter or a fax. This means that the recipient can modify the email, or embed it in a document they are working on. This could lead to plagiarism but has the obvious benefit of facilitating *group working*.

Worldwide communication is available. People can keep in touch readily wherever they are. There is a distinct contrast with the situation only a few years in the past where the delay in overseas post could lead to friendships or business contacts withering.

Important documents can be forwarded as email *attachments*. Emails are not restricted to brief memos.

A group of people can be sent copies of the same email. This permits fast dissemination of information, especially via an organization's intranet. For example, a warning to evacuate offices after sudden flooding has created an electrical danger can be sent to all those logged on to the network.

The *paperless office* has been a widely advertised benefit of computers ever since they began to appear in the commercial world. Email has actually begun to reduce the amount of paper generated by memos, reports and letters, although in many cases filing a hard copy of emails received is an advantage.

Scientific research can be facilitated by email. Astronomers have been alerted to sudden supernovas or comets by email from other observatories.

Historians have often commented on the fact that the invention of the telephone led to a lack of *source documents* for the study of vital periods in which important issues were debated by phone rather than by the exchange of written documents. Before the phone all communication between politicians (unless both present in a meeting) would have been by letter. This meant that later historians could gauge accurately the way in which various decisions were made. All the intermediate stages of debate would be present, provided that the documents had survived. However, after the telephone became ubiquitous many decisions resulted from unrecorded telephone conversations. Historians therefore were denied access to records which would help them evaluate what had actually occurred 'behind the scenes'. Now with the ever-present email, many telephone conversations will be replaced by emails. Unlike the ephemeral phone message, an email is far more likely to survive, perhaps as an automatic backup to a mail folder, more likely as a deliberate decision to save, maybe even as the result of third-party monitoring. Historians will therefore have a far greater chance of understanding the course of late twentieth century policies than of those a century earlier.

This access to past documents will also be likely to have an impact upon organizations. It will be relatively easy to look back and investigate precisely what was happening at some stage in the organization's past. Data mining of an (even accidental) email archive has the potential to facilitate future decisions.

Disadvantages of electronic mail

Electronic mail does not have the equivalent of a comprehensive telephone directory. Attempts have been made to compile lists of individual email addresses but the situation is still at the stage of the enterprising businessmen who first created street directories by wandering around looking at names above doorways. No central authority exists which knows the identity of all those who use email. The only reliable way to find a person's email is to ask them, although often an intelligent guess will strike lucky, e.g. Joe.Cool@snoopy.com.

Key fact

One disadvantage of email results from the fact that it is too new a development to have acquired an accepted 'correct form'. Etiquette has yet to evolve. This can create problems in the office environment in which the ease of sending an internal email to a colleague can exceed the individual's awareness of polite form. Unintentional criticism, or even threat, is a distinct possibility when overworked staff attempt to contact another in an urgent situation. In this context it is significant that personnel officers, when conducting exit interviews, frequently ask whether unfortunately worded emails have been a contributory factor to the decision to leave. Note that some software, for example Eudora, now incorporates embedded AI to detect accidental unpleasant wording.

Electronic mail is open to the same abuse of *junk mail* to which conventional mail is subject. Unrequested material can be forwarded to people whose addresses have been acquired by an advertiser. A sensible policy is to delete according to the address shown.

Spamming is an email attack in which a recipient is inundated with multiple copies of a message. The name comes from a 1970s *Monty Python* television sketch in which a cafe offers increasingly absurd amounts of the pressed meat, spam, in successive menus.

Deliberately abusive emails are referred to as *flame mail* and can obviously be extremely upsetting.

The ease with which electronic mail can be sent can lead to an unnecessary amount of correspondence taking place. Time can be lost and people distracted from their work, especially by the way that message boxes announcing a new email will readily pop up in the middle of something more serious on screen.

The readiness with which an email can be sent can also have the disadvantage of a reply being forced before its author has time to reflect upon the best possible wording or content.

There is a potential negative impact on language from email. The wording of messages is frequently terse. Spelling and punctuation become strange. There is a possible danger of this carrying over into other use of language, especially with the young whose use of language is still maturing.

Question 6.10.1

Astronauts and scientists manning the International Space Station have access to email via standard laptop computers. How does this affect:

(a) the research they are able to perform?
(b) the quality of their lifestyle in orbit?

Mailing list management system

It is possible for a *mailing list management system* to send email automatically to users who have elected to subscribe to the service provided. This can be particularly useful for those who wish to read the latest information on a subject which interests them. This arrives like any other email message and has the advantage of alerting users to news items 'as they break'. Using this facility also allows access to the source of the information, and not having to rely upon the editing skills, and inherent bias, of newspaper, magazine or journal staff. It is another example of the way that the Internet has made information far more freely available than it was in the past.

Naturally a suitable mailing list must be known in advance. These are frequently provided by newspapers and by organizations which want to maintain a high public profile, like the Johnson Spaceflight Center. Their JSC mailing list can be found at:

Majordomo@vesuvius.jsc.nasa.gov.

A mailing list is an automated system. Emails are dispatched in reply to queries made by users without any human intervention being required. For example, such a system can guide users through the initial stages involved in subscribing.

Features of a mailing list management system include the following.

The ability to subscribe to mailing lists. This is done by typing a command like *subscribe* in the body of an email sent by the user to the mailing list management system. The name of the list or lists required is also included, e.g. subscribe mail list. It is possible to request that the emailed information is *redirected* to another email address different to the one from which the command is sent.

As a precaution against being deliberately subscribed to an unwanted list as a practical joke by somebody who knows your email address, when you first subscribe you will usually be asked for an *authorization key*. This will have been sent to the email address given. In that way somebody attempting to add you to a mailing list without your knowledge will fail. The authorization key will not have been sent to that person. This is an important protection against spamming.

When you subscribe you are forwarded an *introductory message* outlining details of the system and policies adopted by its designers.

Mailing lists also provide the ability to *unsubscribe* again!

Retrieval of *archived files* on the system is possible. The *index* command shows which files are archived and the *get* command retrieves them.

The user can inquire which separate mailing lists are available on the system by typing a simple command, e.g. lists. This will lead to an email being returned which names the lists available and which gives an outline of the type of information each list will provide.

More specific information about the content of a given list can be found by using the command *info*, together with the name of the list.

The command *which* will show to which lists you are currently subscribed. Some mailing lists also allow the use of *who* to show the email addresses of other subscribers, although this command is often disabled to ensure privacy.

A human site manager can be contacted by including *-Owner* in the mailing list address, e.g. Majordomo-Owner, followed by the rest of the address.

Electronic commerce

The use of the internet to allow commercial transactions to take place is known as *electronic commerce*, or ecommerce. It is one aspect of the rapidly changing world which is emerging from the merging of computing and communication technology, although in its earliest phase it predates the Internet in the form of *electronic funds transfer*.

The history of electronic funds transfer

An essential concept underlying electronic funds transfer (EFT) is that money can be regarded as data about individuals and organizations.

This use of electronic data to replace hard cash is merely the latest incarnation of a long process of abstraction. Wealth originally would have

> **Key fact**
>
> Electronic commerce first began to appear in the banking world. Banks were one of the earliest organizations to use computers. The use of magnetic ink character recognition (see Unit 4) was introduced in 1962 in the UK. Banks had the need to process large quantities of data, and were also in a position to afford the large mainframe computers of the period.

been in the form of physical objects, sheep, cattle, corn, etc. The introduction of tokens, or coinage, to represent wealth was the first stage in moving away from the actual goods in the real world to a more abstract quantity. A certain number of coins would represent an agreed quantity of goods, and could be exchanged far more easily than permitted by the previous arrangement of barter. The flexibility permitted economic growth otherwise unattainable, but did, of course, require faith in the system. Coins eventually came to represent a physical wealth unrelated to the metal from which they were minted. Paper money followed, and then figures written in bank accounts. Moving to an electronic representation is just the inevitable consequence of current society and its computing facilities. Regarding wealth as data residing in information systems has many advantages as described below.

One task facing banks is the problem of *central clearing*. Every day cheques and automatic payments have to be processed and money transferred from one account to another, matching the very large number of financial transactions that have taken place during the day. The use of MICR allows automatic identification of customer account number and bank sort code. The amount handwritten by the customer is also added in MICR format to the cheque. If everybody used just the same bank the siuation would then be relatively easy, but instead cheques have to be physically transported to each major bank's central clearing department. Here they are sorted and transferred via the Bankers' Clearing House to the other major banks. From there they can be taken to individual branches and checked manually. The whole of the sequence described here takes the familiar 'three days clearing'.

This clearing process involves moving large quantities of paper documents around the country and was an obvious area in which the use of banks' computers could be extended. Organizations which had to present a large number of paper documents (salaries, direct debit payments, etc.) simultaneously would clearly benefit from a direct transfer of electronic data from their computer system to the bank's. This led to the creation of the *Bankers' Automated Clearing Services* (BACS). This was not subject to the three day delay.

A further use of computing technology, the *Clearing House Automated Payments System* (CHAPS) was introduced in 1984. This allowed London banks to clear large amounts between each other in a single day.

> **Key fact**
>
> Telex should not be compared with contemporary computing. The messages exchanged were not processed in any way. They were merely transferred from one location to another.

Computers also played a significant role in international banking. Before computing facilities were available, banks were obliged to conduct long-distance communication via telex, a traditional technology which allowed typed messages to be transferred via telephone lines.

This transfer was quite slow. Messages could be lost and if communication were from one country to another there was the further problem of translation. The *Clearing House Interbank Payments System* (CHIPS) was introduced as an organization to facilitate electronic funds transfer via standardized formats and similarly the *Society for Worldwide Interbank Financial Telecommunication* (SWIFT) allowed international transfer of funds. This system began operating in 1977.

Electronic point of sale

Another precursor of electronic commerce was the introduction of *Electronic Point Of Sale* (EPOS) terminals in stores. These are the familiar supermarket checkout tills. Bar codes on purchases are scanned by laser. The information obtained is then used to search a database to obtain the identity and price of the item.

The system allows the production of an itemized receipt, updating of the store's stock level and of any database associated with a store 'loyalty card'. An EPOS terminal can also be combined with a customer's credit or debit card to create an *Electronic Fund Transfer at Point Of Sale* (EFTPOS) system.

The advent of electronic commerce

Full electronic commerce did not become practical until the further developments of both hardware and software in the last decade of the twentieth century. Retailers who wish to benefit from electronic commerce need to be able to create an extensive website with various links to pages detailing their products. Similarly their potential customers have to have access to the Internet with modems capable of downloading extensive data and computers with sufficient memory and processing power to browse electronic commerce sites effectively. This degree of computing sophistication did not exist for the first 20 years or so of domestic computers, and so the full impact of EFT and the 'cashless society' remained speculative at that time.

The need for powerful facilities cannot be underestimated. One electronic commerce retailer subsequently atrributed its failure to the excessive quality of its site. So much data had to be downloaded that those visiting lost interest. Screens took too long to appear and people worried about the amount of time they were obliged to spend on- line.

A distinction has to be made between simply *advertising* on the Internet and providing full facilities for *on-line sales*. The latter is far more complicated for the retailer to establish and maintain. Advertising could just provide details of products and then give a phone number on which orders could be placed. This would have the advantage that the person accepting the order would be able to confirm the validity of the card number given immediately, in the usual way used in any shop. If, however, a full ordering service was going to be provided there would be associated potential problems with stock control. A sudden rush of on-line purchases could overwhelm supply, and sophisticated software would be required to indicate on the website what precisely was still available. The stock level would need to update the site.

Visiting a typical electronic commerce site

The best way to appreciate what electronic commerce is like is to do some electronic window shopping on the Internet. You can always quit without buying! However, the typical stages in a visit to an electronic commerce site are as follows:

- First locate a suitable site, either one already known or found via a search engine or from advertising.
- From the website link with the on-line catalogue.
- Browse through the catalogue and choose the items required.
- Go to an electronic checkout and complete an invoice.
- State the address for the purchased items to be delivered, and the address for the paper invoice if different.
- Give credit card details.

Points to notice about the experience are:

- Navigation around the catalogue is made as simple and encouraging as possible.
- An icon can be clicked on to acquire a shopping basket or trolley (called 'cart' in American English).
- Buttons on the catalogue allow items to be added to the basket or removed from it.
- The contents of the basket can be viewed whenever required.
- Prices of items, and the current total of items selected, are displayed.
- Size, colour and other specifications can be chosen where appropriate.
- Clicking on small icons of items brings further details. More detailed pictures are given and further text descriptions.
- Screen prompts are given, such as 'You currently have no items in your basket'.
- Links are provided to other related sites, for example a manufacturer of an item considered.
- Home pages give a friendly image of the firm, designed to encourage customer loyalty.

Advantages of electronic commerce

The advantages of electronic commerce can be considered for both the customer and the retailer. (The term 'retailer' is perhaps unfortunately also used for the latter.)

Advantages for the customer include:

- Purchases can be made immediately. The customer does not have to check whether they actually have money in their purse. Of course, this advantage applies to any purchase made with a card whether via the Internet or in a conventional store.
- The customer can visit one electronic commerce site after another to compare prices or availability of merchandise. This can be quite difficult in the real world, where competing stores will probably be quite some distance apart.
- Customers do not have to queue, or cope with inclement weather, or fight through Christmas crowds. Shopping can be done at any time during the day. Generally time is saved and the experience is more convenient. Note, however, that the 'any time during the day' has to be realistic. The Internet works better when Americans sleep!

Advantages for the retailer include:

- Electronic commerce eliminates the need for large buildings and numerous employees. Theoretically less money has to be invested in setting up the IT systems required and the small staff to service them.
- The Internet allows a far wider area from which customers can be attracted. A local shop will tend to do business only with local people. Likewise even multiple stores will have a finite catchment area. In contrast customers for electronic commerce are limited only

by Internet access. Note here that the more specialized a particular business is the likelier will be its potential to expand over a wide area.

- Some electronic commerce sites are proud of the 'personal' relationship that they can establish via email with their customers. Customer loyalty can be an important factor in their success. Staff can, in fact, involve themselves more with customer service and less upon the administrative aspects of sales as this will be dealt with by the software used.
- Small businesses can compete with large organizations in a way which would not be possible if the customer could physically appraise a corner store and compare it with a large unit in a glamorous, state-of-the-art shopping centre. Electronic commerce appears to have permitted some small organizations to grow rapidly in terms of sales.

Disadvantages of electronic commerce

Again these can be considered in terms of the disadvantages for the customer and for the retailer.

Disadvantages for the customer include:

- Internet access is required. This will become less of a disadvantage as Internet access continues to grow.
- A credit card is also required. Not everybody has a card and some cultures are not credit-oriented.
- Customers may have uncertainties about the nature of the product they are buying. They cannot touch and examine closely goods in the way they can in a conventional store.

Disadvantages for the retailer include:

- A website has to be constructed. This will involve time and expense as it is unlikely that the average businessman will have the enthusiasm or opportunity to immerse themselves in FrontPage or JavaScript.
- The site will have to be advertised, perhaps purchasing advertising on a search engine or via a *website directory.*
- There may be a need to employ a webmaster to keep the site monitored and answer email inquiries.
- There is the possibility of customers being reluctant to commit card details to the Internet.
- Customers might be worried about purchasing from an 'unknown name'. This will not be a problem for large organizations entering electronic commerce.
- There might be an unfortunate mismatch between customer expectation, derived from the quality of the product as seen on the site, and the reality of the purchase when it is delivered. How will the retailer deal with returned items?
- If trade is conducted over a large area there will be increasing difficulty in delivering the goods that have been ordered.
- A decision will need to be made about whether the business should combine a physical store and a web presence or just be the latter.

Exercise 6.10.2

'Maine Coone Moggies' is a small firm specializing in products aimed at cat owners. It sells a wide range of cat-related commodities, like cat toys, baskets, scratching posts, flea collars, gourmet cat food and various medicinal items.

The firm also publishes a cat newsletter carrying adverts for pet magazines, requests for homes for stray cats, zany short stories featuring cats, and other items that are likely to appeal. Currently this magazine is given away to customers who buy any item from the shop.

Although Maine Coone Moggies is only a one-shop, family-owned business, the attraction of electronic commerce is great and Jeremy and Diane Derwent are enthusiatic about developing in this direction. Discuss how the business could utilize the Internet in their plans for expansion.

On-line and distance learning

Another impact of the Internet on society is the likely increase in on-line learning and distance learning.

Distance learning has a long history in the UK, where the Open University established by Harold Wilson's Government in the 1960s has led to a large number of highly qualified people achieving success which would otherwise have been denied to them. The Open University, of course, relied upon conventional technology. Lectures were (and are) delivered by television or radio, learning materials were supplied through the post, human contact was established with tutors and other students through summer schools and examinations were taken in formal centres.

The Internet has provided the opportunity for a more disembodied form of education. Already qualifications, like those awarded by Cisco, can be achieved purely electronically. Tuition and examination can both take place on-line. Obviously an extension of such programmes of study will allow far wider participation in education and already (2001) various universities are being approached for their cooperation.

How this will develop is an open question. Possibly distance learning for the mature student, and especially for those wishing to seek a second degree or other further qualification, will become an important part of society in the future. Perhaps also it would be sad if young students were denied the experience of maturing in the company of peers and in a traditional university environment.

Indeed it has been suggested by some science fiction authors that we could be threatened by a future educational dystopia in which schools and universities all but disappear. Broadcast lessons would pay but passing reference to a token 'class' of students, posed like cinematic extras before the televised lecturer, while the real students studied alone at home. Experiencing only distance learning package and machine-marked assignments, they would, nevertheless, yearn to be part of the fictional class then envied on screen.

Web TV

Television receivers can be equipped with an Internet unit which then enhances the services viewers enjoy. Instead of being a one-way medium in which the viewer can only play a passive role, an interactive service is available. With a web-enabled television it is possible to:

- Take part in television game shows.
- Vote in ballots on a variety of subjects presented via the television service.
- Engage in 'on-line chat' with other viewers.
- Watch two television programmes simultaneously.
- Record one television programme while watching another.
- Obtain listings of television programmes.
- Actively search through programme listings.
- Send emails.
- Access Internet services.

Web TV is a service to which viewers have to subscribe, a typical provider being the Microsoft Web TV network.

Web TV receivers will often also have a satellite receiver as well to extend access to programmes.

Digital broadcasting

Radio is now broadcast in digital format as well as in its traditional AM and FM analogue form. The advantages of digital broadcasting include:

- Clear reception of radio signals.
- Near CD quality sound.
- A greater number of radio stations available.
- Short text messages to accompany radio programmes, appearing via simple alphanumeric or LCD displays on the receiver. The technique is referred to as *Programme Associated Data* (PAD).
- Transmission of (still) pictures to accompany radio programmes.
- Automatic retuning of car radios to the nearest transmitter.
- The potential to send traffic data directly to navigation systems in vehicles. For example, maps could be downloaded to help a driver. A protocol for such systems is currently being developed by the *Transport Protocol Experts Group* (TPEG).

Digital radio is provided via a multiplexed signal which combines the various individual strands of the service, audio, text, other data services, into a single stream for broadcasting. The *multiplex* consists of a *synchonization channel* which provides frequency and timing data, a *fast information channel*, which provides receivers with decoding instructions and the *main service channel*, which carries the audio and data for the service.

Key fact

Data compression is used in digital broadcasting. The Eureka 147 standard employs a data compression system called Masking Pattern Universal Sub-band Integrated Coding and Mulitiplexing (*MUSICAM*) which can compress a signal to as little as a twelfth of its initial length. This system involves eliminating those parts of the signal which would not be audible to the human ear, even if transmitted.

A standard has been agreed upon for digital broadcasting. This is the Eureka 147 Digital Audio Broadcasting system developed in Europe but promising to become accepted globally.

Multimedia

The Web was initially limited to handling only text. This was a result of the wide bandwidth required for any form of graphics. The modems possessed by the majority of home users were only 14.4 k and this made it unrealistic to attempt anything more than simple text. People are unwilling to wait too long to download overelaborate sites, a reason frequently given for the failure of some early ecommerce businesses. The arrival of 28.8 k modems made it possible for websites to become more adventurous. The Web is now the location for much *multimedia* in which it is possible to see, in addition to simple text, graphics and animation, and to hear sound.

Key fact

A typical package used to generate multimedia sites is Macromedia's Flash, which goes beyond the facilities of typical HTML, allowing designers to create colourful and animated pages which also include sound. Material developed in other packages can also be incorporated into Flash productions, which adds to its appeal.

Mathematics in action

A vital aspect of successful design software for multimedia is the inclusion of *vector graphics*. Unlike a typical *bit-mapped* graphics file, in which the attributes of an image are precisely determined at its creation, vector graphics involves a set of mathematical instructions for creating the image.

This can be illustrated by some basic coordinate geometry. Suppose you had drawn a right-angled triangle on a sheet of graph paper and wanted (for obscure personal reasons!) to send a copy of this triangle to a friend. One way of doing this would be to send the coordinates of each of the three vertices of the triangle, (2, 2), (6, 2) and (6, 5). By plotting these three points on another sheet of graph paper your friend could recreate the triangle. This is rather like sending a bit-mapped file, because the precise numerical values are given.

However, there is a second way in which a copy of the triangle could be transmitted. Instead of giving the actual coordinates of the vertices you send your friend the three equations which define the three sides of the triangle. These are:

Equation 1: $x = 6$

Equation 2: $y = 2$

Equation 3: $y = 3x/4 + 0.5$

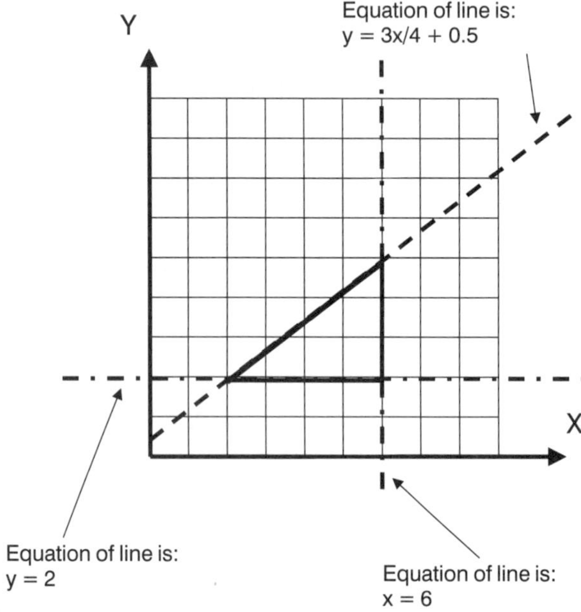

Figure 6.10.1

Now your friend has to plot each of these equations. They will intersect at the three vertices of the triangle and hence recreate an image of it. This method is similar to vector graphics, in which calculations have to be performed by the computer which is creating an image.

Key fact

The advantage of vector graphics is that images can be resized and rotated by fairly straightforward mathematical calculations. This has obvious application in animation, where altering the size of an image can make it appear to move closer or further away. Similarly rotation can imply a change of direction. The mathematics required for rotating 3D coordinates is standard 'textbook material'. Historically it was used by Ivan Sutherland in the 1950s to demonstrate the real-time processing capabilty of the Whirlwind computer at the University of Illinois.

Multimedia design packages usually include a tool known as *tweening*. This allows a designer to create just the initial and final images for a short sequence of animation with the software determining all the frames required to move from the first image to the second.

These packages will also be multi-platform, which means that different operating systems can use them, like Windows, Solaris, Linux or Macintosh.

Multimedia developments in the Web have enhanced its appeal for many users. The inclusion of video clips with sound can have educational benefits as well as commercial. (A typical site which offers educational animated material is at http://www.nasa.gov, where many video clips of Nasa launches, and from various space probes, can be viewed.)

Naturally there are potential disadvantages to avoid in the design of a multimedia site:

- The fact that the ability to include animation exists in a design package can lead some creators astray. Unnecessary animation is probably a threat to the success of a site and just a pointless distraction. Many surfers have sat groaning through some particularly silly cartoon sequence. Humour is a very personal thing and also culture-dependent, a fact which is significant given the 'World Wide' aspect of the Web.
- Designing an exciting site, with features which appeal instinctively to the designer, can actually detract from the user's ability to navigate rapidly through various links to the desired web page.
- The effort put into a glamorous presentation can lead to insufficient attention being paid to updating the factual content of a site.
- Excessive machine resouces can be demanded.
- Exotic packages have the potential to reduce compatibility across the Web. Various *plug-ins* are needed if the user's web browser is incapable of handling the material being downloaded.

Video conferencing

The use of video conferencing techniques on the Internet permits meetings to take place even when the participants are separated by considerable distance. The development of inexpensive CCD cameras and advanced software has allowed ordinary office computers to become the equivalent of a television studio.

A video conference has obvious advantages:

- A video conference can be set up very quickly, in far less time than would be required to arrange a conventional meeting.

- Money and time are saved by not having to travel.
- Those participating in the video conference are not tired as a consequence of travelling to the location for the meeting.
- Less time is taken away from other duties.
- Standard human cues are still available. Expression and body language are transmitted allowing people to understand one another more intuitively. (Yawning is harder to disguise.) Video conferencing is a far more personal and natural way of communicating than using a phone or an email.
- Many people can communicate simultaneously. Two groups of people can sit in front of the computer/camera at either end.
- If required the session can be recorded.

Convergence

In the middle decades of the twentieth century it would have been obvious to anybody that there were quite distinct ways in which the (then) modern science and technology were contributing to the welfare of society. If you wished to listen to the King's abdication speech you would switch on your wireless set. If you were keen to see the latest Hollywood movie you would take a bus to the nearest Odeon. If you had to convey urgent news to your brother in Australia you would send a telegram. If you wanted to work at home without going into the office you would get the sack.

Such distinctions are now becoming increasingly difficult to make. The PC that sits on your desktop, and even the mobile phone in your pocket, are becoming general-purpose devices that bring you everything, entertainment, information, and perhaps your salary if you are one of the increasing number of people who are able to work from home as a result of the Internet. Different technologies are converging into an integrated world of communications and leisure, the future of which we can only vaguely anticipate.

Network costs

The implementation and financial management of a network does not have to be something which is carried purely in-house. Organizations can use external suppliers to maintain a network, even to the extent of setting up local area networks for specific sites. It is important therefore for managers to be aware of the competing services available and the possibility of costs varying according to the provider approached.

The likely costs of implementing a network will include charges from the service provider such as:

- A *network connection fee*. This will be a one-off charge relating to the cost of hubs and switches.
- A *network access fee*. This will be an ongoing charge for the duration of the service provided, typically billed per month.
- The cost of *workstation cards*.

Evaluating the overall cost of providing an organization with networked facilities must take into account various factors like:

- *Maintenance* and replacement of equipment.
- *Depreciation.*
- Monitoring *staff use* of workstations. Some organizations turn a blind eye to the personal use of corporate facilities. Email is treated as an incentive for employees, and similarly access to the Internet. The principle is that if staff spend extra time on-site because the facilities offered are attractive to them, then they are also going to be available for extra, unexpected duties that may arise. Somebody who has stayed late at work to catch up on personal email might well be able to deal with an unexpected request from a client. In other words the dividing line between home and office life becomes blurred and probably in favour of the employer. Nevertheless this sort of thing could get out of hand if too much time is spent in leisure use of facilities. There are also possible legal consequences for the firm itself from improper use of email or the Internet. Administrators generally have to be aware of the costs per employee of the use of local and wide area networks and of voice mail.

The cost of hardware implementation of a network is only part of its overall value to an organization. It is essential that an estimate is made of the financial worth of the services provided by the network both in terms of the internal functioning of the organization and the external revenue it earns from the organization's clients and customers.

The cost of downtime will therefore involve not only lost revenue but also the additional technical support that may be needed to restore the network.

Internal security

The security of data on a network can be protected by a number of methods:

- Passwords and access to network
- Backups
- RAID
- Mirroring
- Simple Network Management Protocol

Passwords and access to network

Not everybody in an organization is going to have the right to access all of the information stored within its computer networks. A system of passwords allows different levels of access to data held according to the status of the user within the organization. For example, in a college students will be given the opportunity to look at lecturers' course notes but not examination grades.

Backups

The ease with which electronic copies of documents can be made automatically means that in theory data should never be lost. Regular back up copies should be made of all documents and separate and distinct physical devices for holding the copies ensured. This extends from the individual to the corporate level. It is foolish to back up files from your laptop to floppy disk, and then keep both on the back seat of your car. Similarly an organization should make sure that data is copied to other sites via a WAN.

RAID

The acronym RAID refers to *Redundant Array of Inexpensive Disks*, a technology in which in excess of 100 disk drives are combined into a single overall unit with its own controller and software. This permits data to be delivered over multiple paths simultaneously. Advantages of RAID systems are that very large amounts of memory are available, in excess of 10 terabytes. In addition RAID implies in-built redundancy. If one disk fails others can replace it.

Mirroring

A method which minimizes loss of data is *disk mirroring*. Here the data is written simultaneously to two separate disk drives. Should one of the drives develop problems the system will automatically change to the other drive without loss of data This can be particularly important in database systems. An extension of disk mirroring is *remote disk mirroring* in which data is written simultaneously to additional hardware devices, perhaps provided by a separate commercial organization, at another location completely. Such organizations specialize in data recovery techniques.

Mirroring can also be used to provide *server mirroring* in which a backup server is present to duplicate all the operations of the primary server. This precaution, though expensive in terms of hardware resources, will prevent any downtime in a network.

An alternative to server mirroring is *clustering*. Here a number of computers are connected in a way which allows them to operate like a single machine.

Simple network management protocol

Simple Network Management Protocol (SNMP) is an application layer protocol used in TCP/IP networks. It allows network administrators to monitor and control performance and attend to problems which may arise.

The management system includes:

- Network elements – these are hardware devices like computers, routers, etc.
- Software agents – software which monitors management information.
- Managed objects – 'object' can be confusing here as managed objects are states rather than physical entities. For example, a managed object could be the number of active circuits in a physical device at a given time.
- Management Information Base (MIB) – this is a set of managed objects held in memory of individual devices.

SNMP gathers information about a network by a process called *MIB collection*. This involves polling separate devices in the network and requesting copies of each MIB encountered. In this way problems can be detected without any need for individual devices to sense themselves that errors are occurring. However, a disadvantage of SNMP is that it can add excessive network traffic.

External security

The Internet has enhanced the possibilities of work, research, social interaction and entertainment for a vast number of people worldwide. Unfortunately its very freedom and ease of access also allows tremendous opportunity for those who prefer to hinder others. Like any newly tiled platform on the Underground, the Internet is vulnerable to the unhelpful attention of the less well intentioned. As a consequence various ways of protecting data transmission are necessary. These include:

- Firewalls
- Anti-virus software
- Encryption

Firewalls

The role of firewalls in security has been examined above. Do note that installing a firewall should not be an excuse for complacency as there are other ways in which an organization's data can be attacked. An attack will not be necessarily through the firewall. A floppy disk innocently introduced by a member of staff may be a source of danger. There is also the possibility of deliberate attack from the inside by a disaffected employee.

A firewall can have other functions besides security. As it acts as an interface between an organization and the world outside it can be used as an obvious place for general information about the organization, rather like a mesh fence surrounding a factory yard that can support notices advertising the product! In addition a firewall will allow monitoring of all system traffic for administrative purposes.

Anti-virus software

A *computer virus* is a program which has been maliciously designed to embed itself into other programs or the boot sector of a floppy disk. A computer which has become infected with a virus can then spread it to another machine, either by running an infected program or by booting a machine with an infected disk.

Viruses can also be transmitted as email attachments or as macros in a word processed file or spreadsheet. With the growth of the Internet this has become the major threat as the virus can spread almost exponentially via email address books. These viruses are referred to as *worms*.

A *Trojan* is a program which is intended to allow a hacker a backdoor into a computer system, just as the Greeks captured Troy via their Trojan Horse. A firewall is the best protection against this type of attack.

Encryption

One way in which the security of data transmitted over a network can be enhanced is by coding signals in a way that only the intended destination can interpret them. This is called *encryption.* There is nothing particularly original in the concept of coding a message so that if it falls into the wrong hands nothing is revealed. For example, a simple substitution code is often used by children when they are playing at being spies. Here an additional piece of information, known as a *key*, allows the coded message to be understood. In a child's game the key could be the rule 'Count forward one letter', so that HAL becomes IBM. More sophisticated codes will have a more complicated key to unlock the message.

A similar principle applies in the encryption of data transmitted over a network. A *cryptosystem* is an algorithm which can convert a message into a form which cannot be understood unless the recipient has the appropriate key. There are two types of cryptosystem. A *symmetric* system uses the same key both to encrypt and decrypt a message. This is the *secret key.* In contrast an *asymmetric* cryptosystem uses two different keys to encrypt and decrypt. Encryption uses a *public key* and decryption uses a *private key* which is not public knowledge.

A well-established public key cryptosystem uses the *RSA algorithm.* This derives its name from the three MIT academics who devised it, Ron Rivest, Adi Shamir and Leonard Adleman. It relies for its security upon the difficulty in factorizing large numbers. For example, if you are asked to deduce which two prime numbers have been multiplied together to give the product 21 it is fairly easy to discover that they are 3 and 7. If, however, you were asked to determine the two prime numbers which had a product of 10 961 it would be much more difficult to find out that they were 97 and 113. The prime numbers used in the RSA algorithm will be typically far, far larger than these.

Mathematics in action

The stages of the RSA algorithm are as follows:

(1) Choose two prime numbers, p and q. These are deliberately chosen to be very large.

(2) Calculate the product p multiplied by q. This is called the *modulus*, represented here by N.

(3) Calculate the second product (p –1) multiplied by (q – 1), represented here as m.

(4) Choose an exponent, d, which should be an odd number which has no factors (other than 1) in common with m. The *public key* is now the values of d and N, (d, N).

(5) Calculate a second exponent, e, from the values of d and m by using the equation:

$$e = (1 + n \times m)/d$$

The value of n is an integer which is chosen to permit an integral value of e. The *private key* is the values of e and N, (e, N).

(6) The message, as a series of numbers like ASCII codes, can now be coded using the public key. The expression which calculates the encrypted value, M′, of a number M is:

$$M' = (M^d) \text{ MOD } N$$

This expression means that the number M is first raised to the power of d and then the remainder found when this calculated value is divided by the modulus N. The encrypted value M′ is now safe for transmission.

(7) The encrypted value M′ can be decoded using the private key, which as stated above contains the exponent e. The expression which does this is very similar to the first expression:

$$M = (M'^e) \text{ MOD } N$$

Note that the number which is going to be encrypted must be smaller than either of the two primes, p and q, for the algorithm to work. This is not a problem in practice because p and q will be deliberately chosen to be very large so that the private key cannot be discovered.

Also note that the two original prime numbers themselves are not revealed. This is because if they were known it would be possible for an unauthorized recipient of the message to calculate the private key and then decode the encrypted signal. For example, if small values were chosen for p and q it would be relatively easy to factorize the modulus (the product of p and q) and hence discover what the two prime numbers were. The value of m, $(p-1)(q-1)$, would follow immediately and then anybody could use the equation for e above to calculate the private key.

The very nature of encryption makes it rather inconvenient to illustrate the algorithm by simple numerical examples. Realistic values for p and q and d will lead rapidly into difficult mental arithmetic! However, the algorithm can be demonstrated here with 'toy' values that keep the calculations simple. Do remember, however, that big numbers are used in practice simply because they are difficult to handle; improbable, in fact, for computers to crack the code!

In this gentle illustration the values chosen for p and q are:

$$p = 3$$

$$q = 5$$

This leads to a value for the modulus of:

$$N = p \times q$$

$$= 15$$

The value for m will be:

$$m = (p-1)\times(q-1)$$
$$= 2\times 4$$
$$= 8$$

The exponent d must be an odd number which does not have any factors (except 1) in common with 8. The choice here will be 3. The value of the second exponent, e, now has to satisfy the equation:

$$e = (1 + n\times m)/d$$
$$= (1 + n\times 8)/3$$

A value of n = 1 will allow an integral value of e:

$$e = (1 + 1\times 8)/3$$
$$= 9/3$$
$$= 3$$

Having identical public and private keys, each (3, 15), would hardly be suitable in a real situation but will be acceptable in a simple demonstration like this one. To illustrate how the system works, a number, the 'message', has to be selected for encryption. Remember that a number which can be encrypted must be less than either of the values p and q. This limits the current illustration to encoding the number 2. The encryption expression is:

$$M' = (M^{d}) \text{ MOD } N$$

Inserting the values of M = 2, d = 3 and N = 15 gives:

$$M' = (2^{3}) \text{ MOD } 15$$
$$= 8 \text{ MOD } 15$$
$$= 8$$

This encrypted value can now be checked using the decryption expression:

$$M = (M'^{e}) \text{ MOD } N$$

Inserting the values M' = 8, e = 3 and N = 15 gives:

$$M = (8^{3}) \text{ MOD } 15$$
$$= 512 \text{ MOD } 15$$

As 512 is equal to $(34\times 15) + 2$, this means that 512 MOD 15 is the original message of 2. It can be seen, with this very simple example, that the RSA algorithm does work.

Of course, the example shown here has been kept deliberately simple. With even slightly more awkward numbers the process of encryption and decryption involves massive arithmetic. This is illustrated below with values for p and q of 7 and 13.

$$p = 7$$

$$q = 13$$

This gives a value for the modulus of:

$$N = p \times q$$
$$= 91$$

The first exponent, d, is selected by initially calculating m:

$$m = (p - 1) \times (q - 1)$$
$$= (7 - 1) \times (13 - 1)$$
$$= 6 \times 12$$
$$= 72$$

An odd value for d is now chosen which does not have any factor in common with 72. As $72 = (2 \times 2 \times 2 \times 3 \times 3)$ and obvious choice is:

$$d = 5$$

The public key is therefore (5, 91).
The second exponent, e, is found from the equation:

$$e = (1 + n \times m)/d$$
$$= (1 + n \times 72)/5$$

A value of $n = 1$ gives:

$$e = (1 + 72)/5$$
$$= 73/5$$
$$= 14.6$$

This clearly is unsuitable because e must be an integer. However, choosing $n = 2$ gives:

$$e = (1 + 2 \times 72)/5$$
$$= 145/5$$
$$= 29$$

The private key will therefore be (29, 91).

The public key, (5, 91) can now be used to encrypt the single digit message 6. This means that 6 is the value assigned to M as the encryption expression:

$$M' = (M^d) \text{ MOD } N$$

Remember that the other values from the public key are d = 5 and N = 91:

$$M' = (6^5) \text{ MOD } 91$$

$$= 7776 \text{ MOD } 91$$

As 7776 is equal to $(85 \times 91) + 41$, this gives:

$$M' = 41$$

Now consider the difficulty of decryption:

$$M = (M'^e) \text{ MOD } N$$

$$= (41^{29}) \text{ MOD } 91$$

The security afforded by the RSA algorithm is evident! Do bear in mind, of course, the fact that very large values are actually chosen for p and q in real applications of the algorithm.

Appendix A Hexadecimal and other number bases

If you remember the arithmetic lessons in your primary school days, you were shown hundreds, tens and units, often written as h t u. The sum 137 + 15 would be set out like this:

h	t	u
1	3	7
+	1	5
1	5	2

The meaning here is that 3 refers to 3 tens or 30, the 1 refers to 1 hundred because we use numbers by position, you know the 3 refers to 30 and not 3 because it is in the tens column, i.e. its position tells you more that just the digit.

As $1 = 10^0$, $10 = 10^1$, $100 = 10^2$, $1000 = 10^3$ and so on we could head the columns like this instead of using h t u; it all means exactly the same.

10^2	10^1	10^0
1	3	7
+	1	5
1	5	2

The fact that we use 10 as a number base is due only to the fact that humans were born with 10 fingers; there is nothing 'natural' about numbers to the base 10. If we were born with 8 fingers, we would use numbers to the base 8 (called *octal* numbers) and think that numbers to the base 10 very odd indeed! We can use any number we please as a base; 10 is the 'everyday' value but bases of 2, 8 and 16 are common in computers.

Hexadecimal means 16, hex for 6, decimal for 10, and we can use 16 as the number base in just the same way as we use 10. Numbers to base 10 use 10 symbols, i.e. 0–9, so hex numbers must have 16 symbols. The problem is that we run out of symbols past 9 so the letters A to F are used in addition. This means that numbers in hex run 0–F, equivalent to

0–15 in decimal numbers but of course 15 uses 2 symbols, 1 and 5. Counting in both looks like this:

Dec	Hex	Dec	Hex	Dec	Hex
0	0	16	10	32	20
1	1	17	11	33	21
2	2	18	12	34	22
3	3	19	13	35	23
4	4	20	14	36	24
5	5	21	15	37	25
6	6	22	16	38	26
7	7	23	17	39	27
8	8	24	18	1000	3E8
9	9	25	19	1024	400
10	A	26	1A	1025	401
11	B	27	1B	1026	402
12	C	28	1C	2048	800
13	D	29	1D	4096	1000
14	E	30	1E	65536	10000
15	F	31	1F	1048576	100000

The columns in a hex sum would be headed 16^2, 16^1, 16^0 using the same system as above; each column uses the next greater integer as a power.

16^2	16^1	16^0
1	3	7
+	1	A
1	5	1

The mechanics of the sum are just the same.

Note that hex 19 + 1 = 1A not 20! Hex 19 converted to decimal equals $(1 \times 16) + 9 = 25$ because the 1 is in the 16^1 column, the 9 is in the 16^0 column, i.e. numbers by position.

Examples

Hex 1B $= (1 \times 16^1) + (B \times 16^0) = 27$

Hex 5D $= (5 \times 16^1) + (D \times 16^0) = 93$

Hex 2A7 $= (2 \times 16^2) + (A \times 16^1) + (7 \times 16^0) = 512 + 160 + 7 = 679$

Working the other way:

Decimal 68 $= (6 \times 10^1) + (8 \times 10^0)$, converting this to hex, $68 = 64 + 4$ and $64 = 16 \times 4$ so decimal 68 = 44 hex

A simple way to convert decimal to hex is to:

divide the number by 16 and write down the remainder,

679 DIV 16 = 42 remainder 7

divide the quotient 42 by 16 and write down the remainder,

42 DIV16 = 2 remainder 10

divide the quotient 2 by 16 and write down the remainder,

2 DIV16 = 0 remainder 2

and repeat until the quotient is zero.

The number in hex is now in the set of remainders 2, 10, and 7 but of course 10 is written as A so 679 decimal = 2A7 hex.

Set out in a table it looks like this:

Dec	Base	Quotient	Rem base 10	Rem base 16
679	16	42	7	7
42	16	2	10	A
2	16	0	2	2

so 679 decimal = 2A7 hex

Here are some more examples:

Dec	Base	Quotient	Rem base 10	Rem base 16
1329	16	83	1	1
83	16	5	3	3
5	16	0	5	5

so 1329 decimal = 531 hex

397	16	24	13	D
24	16	1	8	8
1	16	0	1	1

so 397 decimal = 18D hex

Binary

The same rules apply to using numbers to the base 2 or binary numbers. Numbers to base 10 need 10 symbols so binary numbers only need 2 symbols, 0 and 1. We still use numbers by position so all the normal arithmetic operations apply.

In decimal $1 = 10^0$, $10 = 10^1$, $100 = 10^2$, $1000 = 10^3$ and so on and these form the column headings in our numbers by position system. In binary, the same rule applies but the column headings will be 2^0, 2^1, 2^2, 2^3, etc. translating to 1, 2, 4, 8, etc., i.e. each column is double the previous one.

If we write the decimal number 9 it is made up of 8 + 1. The binary number 1001 equates to 9 decimal because we have 1 in the 2^3 (or 8s) column, none in the 2^2 or 2^1 columns and 1 in the 2^0 (or 1s) column as shown below

2^7	2^6	2^5	2^4	2^3	2^2	2^1	2^0
				1	0	0	1

By the same system, the decimal value 65 = 64 + 1 or 1000001 in binary as below:

2^7	2^6	2^5	2^4	2^3	2^2	2^1	2^0
	1	0	0	0	0	0	1

Any leading zeros are ignored.

The same system as used above can be used to convert decimal to another base, in this case the base 2. In the example below, the decimal number 38 is divided by the new base, 2, and the remainder placed in the remainder column. The quotient is copied to the next line down and the process repeated until the quotient is zero. The binary number is then read off the remainder column from the bottom, i.e. 100110.

Decimal	Base	Quotient	Remainder
38	2	19	0
19	2	9	1
9	2	4	1
4	2	2	0
2	2	1	0
1	2	0	1

so 38 decimal = 100110 binary

Another example, decimal 297:

Decimal	Base	Quotient	Remainder
297	2	148	1
148	2	74	0
74	2	37	0
37	2	18	1
18	2	9	0
9	2	4	1
4	2	2	0
2	2	1	0
1	2	0	1

so decimal 297 = 100101001

Converting binary to decimal is easy. The number 100110 = 32 + 4 + 2 = 38

	2^7	2^6	2^5	2^4	2^3	2^2	2^1	2^0
Decimal equivalent	128	64	32	16	8	4	2	1
			1	0	0	1	1	0

Hex to binary and binary to hex

You may be wondering why we use hex numbers at all. One reason is that converting hex to binary and binary to hex is very easy. The trick is to realize that each hex digit can be encoded by 4 binary digits, so hex A = 1001. If you split a binary number like 101100100100010 into groups of 4 digits starting from the right like this:

101 1001 0010 0010,

you can encode each group of 4 into a hex digit directly so

101 1001 0010 0010 = 5922,

similarly, 10 1010 = 2A. This is shown in the table below.

101	1001	0010	0010
5	9	2	2

and

10	1010
2	A

The process is just as easy to reverse, the hex number 41= 0100 0001 in binary, each digit is written as a 4-bit binary number and the results joined together.

Question AppA.1

Practise conversion to and from binary. Fill in the blanks in this table.

Decimal	*Hex*	*Binary*
69		1000101
193		11000001
200		11001000
255		11111111
254		11111110
	2DC	1011011100
	200	1000000000
	377	1101110111
	8D	10001101
	31E	1100011110
410		
416		
685		
153		
350		
		1000101111
		1001101001
		1011100111
		1000110011
		11000110

Appendix B
ASCII character set

Before the days of computing, communication systems required each character to be sent as a code. Simple systems used 1s and 0s for transmission just like today so binary numbers were used to encode characters. You could not send an 'A' character directly but you could send binary 1000001 in its place. This eventually lead to a 'standard' set of characters that were used to control printing devices before the widespread use of VDUs. ASCII stands for American Standard Code for Information Interchange but there are other character encoding systems around like EBCDIC and LICS and they work in a similar way but ASCII is the most widespread.

In ASCII, the codes from 0 to 31 were called 'control characters'. These were used to control the movement of the old mechanical printers so we have terms like 'Carriage Return' (now known as Enter or just Return) that actually caused the carriage that held the paper to return to the left-hand side. Understanding this historical basis of the control characters helps you to understand the names they are given which now seem a little odd. If a control character (written as CTRL A, etc.) is sent to a printer or screen, it usually results in an action rather than a printable character. Because some of the codes only have real meaning for mechanical printers, some modern uses do not always make sense of the original name.

Before the widespread use of Microsoft Windows, most machines responded directly to these control characters. As an experiment, try opening a DOS window and type a command. Instead of pressing the Enter key, press CTRL M instead, you should find it does the same thing as pressing Enter. The Enter key is just a CTRL M key in DOS. If you try this using Microsoft Word, CTRL M has a different effect. If you are using Unix or Linux, try using CTRL H in place of the backspace key, it should work unless it has been remapped on your machine.

The ASCII control characters

Dec	*Hex*	*Keyboard*		*Binary*	*Description*
0	0	CTRL @	00000	NUL	Null Character
1	1	CTRL A	00001	SOH	Start of Heading
2	2	CTRL B	00010	STX	Start of Text
3	3	CTRL C	00011	ETX	End of Text
4	4	CTRL D	00100	EOT	End of Transmission
5	5	CTRL E	00101	ENQ	Enquiry
6	6	CTRL F	00110	ACK	Acknowledge
7	7	CTRL G	00111	BEL	Bell or beep
8	8	CTRL H	01000	BS	Back Space
9	9	CTRL I	01001	HT	Horizontal Tab
10	A	CTRL J	01010	LF	Line Feed
11	B	CTRL K	01011	VT	Vertical Tab
12	C	CTRL L	01100	FF	Form Feed
13	D	CTRL M	01101	CR	Carriage Return
14	E	CTRL N	01110	SO	Shift Out
15	F	CTRL O	01111	SI	Shift In
16	10	CTRL P	10000	DLE	Date Link Escape
17	11	CTRL Q	10001	DC1	Device Control 1
18	12	CTRL R	10010	DC2	Device Control 2
19	13	CTRL S	10011	DC3	Device Control 3
20	14	CTRL T	10100	DC4	Device Control 4
21	15	CTRL U	10101	NAK	Negative Acknowledge
22	16	CTRL V	10110	SYN	Synchronous Idle
23	17	CTRL W	10111	ETB	End of Transmission Block
24	18	CTRL X	11000	CAN	Cancel
25	19	CTRL Y	11001	EM	End Medium
26	1A	CTRL Z	11010	SUB	Substitute or EOF End Of File
27	1B		11011	ESC	Escape
28	1C		11100	FS	File Separator
29	1D		11101	GS	Group Separator
30	1E		11110	RS	Record Separator
31	1F		11111	US	Unit Separator

Characters in ASCII are easy to remember, they run from A = 65 to Z = 90. This may look like an odd choice of numbers until you convert the 65 into binary and get 1000001, i.e. 64 + 1. This means that any letter is easy to calculate, it is 64 plus the position in the alphabet. M is the 13th letter in the alphabet so in ASCII, M = 64 + 13 = 77. To make it lower case, just add 32. This is a good choice as 32 encodes as a single binary digit. Lower case m is then 64 + 32 + 13 = 109. Of course it would be better to use hex, so A = 41, M = 4D, a = 61, m = 6D, etc. Numerals are just as easy, '0' encodes as 48, '1' encodes as 48 + 1 = 49, etc.

The full set of 7-bit printable ASCII characters is shown here.

Char	*Dec*	*Hex*	*Binary*	*Char*	*Dec*	*Hex*	*Binary*	*Char*	*Dec*	*Hex*	*Binary*
Space	32	20	100000								
!	33	21	100001	A	65	41	1000001	a	97	61	1100001
″	34	22	100010	B	66	42	1000010	b	98	62	1100010
#	35	23	100011	C	67	43	1000011	c	99	63	1100011
$	36	24	100100	D	68	44	1000100	d	100	64	1100100
%	37	25	100101	E	69	45	1000101	e	101	65	1100101
&	38	26	100110	F	70	46	1000110	f	102	66	1100110
'	39	27	100111	G	71	47	1000111	g	103	67	1100111
(	40	28	101000	H	72	48	1001000	h	104	68	1101000
)	41	29	101001	I	73	49	1001001	I	105	69	1101001
*	42	2A	101010	J	74	4A	1001010	j	106	6A	1101010
+	43	2B	101011	K	75	4B	1001011	k	107	6B	1101011
'	44	2C	101100	L	76	4C	1001100	l	108	6C	1101100
–	45	2D	101101	M	77	4D	1001101	m	109	6D	1101101
·	46	2E	101110	N	78	4E	1001110	n	110	6E	1101110
/	47	2F	101111	O	79	4F	1001111	o	111	6F	1101111
0	48	30	110000	P	80	50	1010000	p	112	70	1110000
1	49	31	110001	Q	81	51	1010001	q	113	71	1110001
2	50	32	110010	R	82	52	1010010	r	114	72	1110010
3	51	33	110011	S	83	53	1010011	s	115	73	1110011
4	52	34	110100	T	84	54	1010100	t	116	74	1110100
5	53	35	110101	U	85	55	1010101	u	117	75	1110101
6	54	36	110110	V	86	56	1010110	v	118	76	1110110
7	55	37	110111	W	87	57	1010111	w	119	77	1110111
8	56	38	111000	X	88	58	1011000	x	120	78	1111000
9	57	39	111001	Y	89	59	1011001	y	121	79	1111001
:	58	3A	111010	Z	90	5A	1011010	z	122	7A	1111010
;	59	3B	111011	[	91	5B	1011011	{	123	7B	1111011
<	60	3C	111100	\	92	5C	1011100	|	124	7C	1111100
=	61	3D	111101	]	93	5D	1011101	}	125	7D	1111101
>	62	3E	111110	^	94	5E	1011110	~	126	7E	1111110
?	63	3F	111111	_	95	5F	1011111	del	127	7F	1111111
@	64	40	1000000	‘	96	60	1100000				

You will notice that the codes only extend to 127. This is because the original ASCII only used 7 binary digits and was referred to as a 7-bit code. Whilst there is some standardization of the codes 128 to 255, some machines will give different characters for codes 128 to 255, for instance older machines will give an é for code 130 whilst more modern machines will give an é for code 233.

Whilst it is not important to remember ASCII codes, it is often useful, especially when writing text or string handling parts of programs. If you remember that ‘A’ = 64 + alphabet position (40 in hex) and that ‘a’ = ‘A’ + 32 (‘A’ + 20 in hex) you can work out all of the alphabet. The ‘0’ character is 48 and the digits are 48+ their value. If you also remember that a Carriage Return is 13 (0D hex) and that Line Feed is 10 (0A hex) you will be able remember about half of the codes and be able to interpret some hex-dumped files.

Question AppB.1

Write down the ASCII values in decimal and hex for the string 'HNC Computing 2000'. Try to work it out so you should not look at the code table. Don't forget the spaces are ASCII characters as well.

Text	H	N	C		C	o	m	p	u	t	i	n	g		2	0	0	0
Decimal																		
Hex																		

Unicode

ASCII characters, although universally accepted, present one serious problem, there are not sufficient characters to cover all symbols and characters from different languages. The solution adopted until the introduction of *Unicode* was to set up each computer to have its own character set according to country or language. This makes it harder to communicate files between computers set up for different countries; try finding the pound sign on an American keyboard! Unicode uses 16-bit characters so there are $2^{16} = 65\,536$ possible characters, more than enough to cover all the world's main languages. The ASCII character set has been incorporated so character 65 is still an 'A' but the 65 is a 16-bit value. The Unicode standard is developing all the time, the latest situation is presented on their web page at www.unicode.org/unicode/standard/standard.html. This describes the current version 3 which defines 49 194 different characters and the work in progress to add more.

Conversion of ASCII to Unicode is very easy as the codes are simply changed 8 bit into 16 bit. Conversion from Unicode to ASCII may result in the loss of data as ASCII cannot support more than 256 different characters. Some operating systems will work with both character sets; the more modern ones will use Unicode as the native code.

Unicode is developing all the time with new characters being added, etc. See the latest information on the website www.unicode.org.

Appendix C Colour

The amazing human ability to perceive colour comes from a complex interaction between the eyes and the brain. What we 'see' is not always exactly what is in front of us! An example of this is the 'white' area of a monitor. If you look with a magnifier, you will see only red, green and blue dots, nothing 'white'.

Light is part of the electromagnetic spectrum. The wavelength of visible light is between approximately 400 and 700 nanometres, the shorter wavelength being perceived as violet, followed by blue, green, yellow and finally as red at the longer wavelength. Light is detected in the human eye by two sorts of cell in the retina, these are known as rods and cones. The rods are not colour sensitive but can detect low-level light. There are three kinds of cone cell, one each that detects red, green and blue. This explains why at night, colours seem much less intense, the rods are more active and the cones less so. In very dark conditions, colour disappears altogether. It is not that the colour is not there, it is the way we 'see' it.

For an ordinary object, the colour we see depends on the light that is used to illuminate it and the object itself. As sunlight contains 'all the colours of the rainbow', a blue object will appear blue in sunlight because it absorbs the other colours and reflects blue light. If the light did not contain blue, the same object would appear to be black.

Additive colour system

Blue is one of the primary colours of light, the others are red and green; if areas of equal intensity of these colours are made to overlap, the result is white light. Different colours are made by changing the 'amount' of each in different combinations.

Red and blue combine to make magenta
Green and blue combine to make cyan
Yellow is made by combining red and green

The colours, cyan, magenta and yellow are the 'complementary' colours of red, green and blue respectively. Blue is complementary to yellow, i.e. if sunlight had all the blue filtered out, it would look yellow. It is this effect that makes sunsets change colour, some of the colours in the sunlight no longer reach your eyes (due to refraction in the atmosphere) so you no longer 'see' white light. The way that coloured light can be combined in this way is called the additive colour system and applies when you consider colour RGB (Red Green Blue) monitors.

Subtractive colour system

Providing that a printed page is illuminated with white light, the colour of dyes or pigments you see depends on the amount of each colour absorbed by the ink. Cyan is complementary to red, it looks cyan because it absorbs all the red light and reflects the other colours. Cyan, magenta and yellow (known as the secondary colours) are used in combination to make different colour inks. This is called the subtractive colour system.

In theory, cyan, magenta and yellow inks will combine to make black ink. In practice, you get a muddy brown colour. To counteract this effect, printers use a black ink when black is needed, leading to the minimum requirement of four ink colours. This is known as CMYK for *Cyan, Magenta, Yellow and blacK* (B is already used for Blue).

Dithering

If you use opaque inks applied unmixed to make colour combinations, the colour achieved is the colour of the last ink applied. Clearly this does not give the required result. The solution is to use patterns of coloured dots where the combination of the colours gives the impression of a new colour. These combinations of different coloured dots are called 'dither patterns'. Dithering is the technique used on lasers, thermal wax and inkjet printers because the inks are opaque. Dye sublimation printers use transparent inks so the photographic quality is better, i.e. dot free.

Experiment

Use a magnifier to examine the colour printed images in a magazine or the coloured images on the front cover of this book. Most use dithering techniques and the patterns of dots are very clear. When viewed from normal reading distance, the dots appear to blend into each other to form 'solid' colour. As was stated at the above, what we 'see' is not always exactly what is in front of us!

Appendix D Case study: DOS File Allocation Table

Data stored on DOS disks is organized into 512 byte pieces to fit on the 512 byte sectors. Unless very small, each file will fit on more than one sector or cluster so the system must also keep track of which sectors are being used for each file. DOS, Windows 3.x and 95/98 use a system called a File Allocation Table or FAT, other operating systems like Unix use different systems but more modern operating systems like Windows NT can use several types of disk management.

DOS formatted 1.44 Mb floppy disks have

- two sides;
- 80 tracks on each side;
- each track split into 18 sectors.

Each sector contains 512 bytes of data, so $80 \times 512 \times 18 \times 2 = 1.44$ Mb. (Remember 1 MB = $1024 \times 1024 = 10\,485\,576$ bytes, not 1 000 000.) Hard disks are formatted with a large number of tracks and sectors, depending on their size.

The structure of a floppy will be

- The boot sector.
- Two copies of the FAT.
- A root directory.
- The data area.

With a DOS formatted floppy disk, the first part contains the *boot sector*, which is a piece of code used to initialize the disk, two copies of the *FAT* (or File Allocation Table) and a fixed size *root directory*. This is followed by the *data area*. A hard disk has a similar structure except that the boot record contains the *partition table*, that is data that defines how many 'logical' disks the real disk is divided into. You may have worked on a PC that has drive C: and drive D:. These may have been the same physical disk just partitioned into two logical disks.

A FAT is a linked list of sector addresses, i.e. each entry in the FAT points to or addresses one area of storage. A root directory is simply a list of filenames with the address of the first sector of where the file is stored. This in conjunction with the FAT enables the operating system to find every sector for a file. The root directory can only hold a fixed number of entries so to increase the number of filenames stored on disk, the writers of DOS copied the system used in Unix, i.e. subdirectories. These are effectively files of filenames, the only difference is that the operating system treats or reads them differently. With appropriate utility software you can open them as a file and read the list of file data, which is very similar in format to root directory entries.

File Allocation Table

The FAT is a fixed size and each entry refers to one *allocation unit* on the disk. This allocation unit is one sector for a floppy disk or one cluster for a hard disk. A cluster is simply a group of sectors. If a hard disk has a cluster size of 4 it means 4 sectors are referred to in one go instead of each sector on its own. It has the advantage of being able to be used on larger disks but it results in very wasteful disk storage.

The language of computing can be confusing at times but you may see the term 'allocation unit' used with regard to disks. This term simply means a sector or a cluster and is the smallest piece of disk that can be addressed. If you were to save the words 'Mary had a little lamb' as a file on a disk, it would use all of one allocation unit of storage, not just the 22 bytes of the file. One allocation unit on a 1.44 Mb floppy is one sector so the file would use 512 bytes of storage. If you had a hard drive with a cluster size of 64 sectors = 1 cluster (or one allocation unit), the 22-byte file would then use $64 \times 512 = 32\,768$ or 32 Kb of storage!

The reason that cluster sizes are fixed is that the FAT is fixed in size so will only address or point to a fixed number of items. Older DOS hard drives had a 16-bit FAT and no concept of a cluster so could point to only $2^{16} = 65\,536$ sectors. As each sector is 512 bytes, this meant the hard drive could only store 32 Mb of data, extremely small by modern standards. The same FAT with 64 sectors per cluster can store 64 times as much data, i.e. 2 Gb.

An example format calculation

Figure 1.10.3 shows a disk formatted with 11 tracks and 18 sectors. (Clusters are only used on hard disks.) If each sector contains 512 bytes of data and there are two sides, there are $11 \times 18 \times 2 = 396$ sectors, so the disk should hold $396 \times 512 = 198$ Kb of data. In fact it will hold less *user* data as one sector will be the boot record, more will be used to hold the FAT and root directory.

The minimum size of the FAT can be calculated from the number of sectors reserved for user data. Each sector will require one entry in the FAT so will need 396 entries. As $2^8 = 256$, 8-bit values will not be enough. At least 9-bit values are required because $2^9 = 512$, more than the 396 required. Although 9-bit values would be impractical, if we use 396 9-bit values we would need $(396 \times 9)/8 = 446$ bytes or one sector to hold the FAT. If we used the DOS idea of two FATs and a root directory of two sectors, that would leave $396 - 1 - 2 - 2 = 391$ sectors left for data or 195.5 Kb.

The root directory stores filenames or subdirectory names in a fixed format. In DOS this is:

- filename
- size of file
- date
- time
- address of first sector
- file attributes

If our 11 track disk used this structure and allowed 32 bytes per entry, a two sector root directory would allow $(2 \times 512)/32 = 32$ filenames.

A DOS 1.44 Mb floppy uses 14 sectors for the root directory so the maximum number of filenames or subdirectory names possible is $(14 \times 512)/32 = 224$. This format uses a 12-bit FAT, i.e. 12-bit entry for each sector (allocation unit as it is sometimes called), older hard disks use a 16-bit FAT and more modern ones use a 32-bit FAT.

$2^{12} = 4096$ so the maximum number of entries in a 12-bit FAT = 4096, more than required on the floppy disk. As $2^{16} = 65\,536$, there are a maximum of 65 536 possible entries using a 16-bit FAT, each entry is 16-bits or 2 bytes long so the FAT will occupy $65\,536 \times 2$ bytes or $65\,536 \times 2/512 = 512$ sectors of storage space.

Similarly, as $2^{32} = 4\,294\,967\,296$, there are that many possible entries. The problem is that each entry will be 32-bits which is 4 bytes for each entry so the space to hold a full 32-bit FAT is 17 179 869 184 bytes or 16 Gbytes of storage, i.e. more than many hard drives can hold! In fact FAT32 only uses 28-bits, the top 4-bits are reserved for future use.

DOS 1.44 Mb disk sector usage

Boot sector uses 1 sector
FAT number 1 uses 9 sectors
FAT number 2 uses 9 sectors
root directory uses 14 sectors
data uses 2847 sectors, a total of 2880 sectors

This gives $2847 \times 512 = 1.4235$ Mb. Less than the advertised 1.44 Mb!

The boot sector is always the first sector on a DOS disk. It contains details of the disk format, number of sectors per track, etc. The boot sector is often where a computer virus can be found. Both the FATs come after the boot sector. These are used to keep track of the sectors on the disk for each file. The second copy of the FAT exists but does not seem to be used by DOS, if you corrupt one, DOS reports the disk unreadable as it cannot tell which FAT is corrupted! The root directory holds details only of files in the root directory; some of these entries will be subdirectories but the contents of these subdirectories are held elsewhere.

How the FAT works

Suppose the root directory stored the following data for the file FRED.DAT:

FRED DAT 3478 27 12/12/1998 12:34

This means the file is 3478 bytes long, the first sector is stored in sector 27, and it was last modified on 12/12/1998 at 12:34. The size 3478 bytes needs 3478/512 = 7 sectors (each sector holds 512 bytes) as you cannot use part sectors. To follow all the sectors used for this file, note the first one is in sector 27 so *go to* position 27 in the FAT to find the sector address of the next one stored there. Then go to this new position in the FAT for the next one and repeat until you get to EOF or End of File. For FRED.DAT, this gives 27, 28, 29, 61, 62, 106 and 109. Trace this through the FAT as shown here. The numbers down the left indicate FAT positions counting in tens and the numbers across the top refer to counting in ones.

Table AppD.1 *Part of the File Allocation Table of a disk*

	0	**1**	**2**	**3**	**4**	**5**	**6**	**7**	**8**	**9**
0	x	x	3	4	5	6	7	8	9	10
10	11	12	13	14	15	16	17	18	19	20
20	21	22	23	24	25	26	EOF	28	29	61
30	31	32	33	34	35	36	37	EOF	39	40
40	65	42	43	44	45	46	47	48	49	50
50	51	52	53	54	55	56	57	58	59	60
60	63	62	106	64	68	66	67	107	69	70
70	EOF	72	73	EOF	75	76	77	78	79	80
80	81	82	83	84	EOF	86	87	105	89	90
90	91	EOF	FFFF	94	95	96	97	98	99	100
100	101	102	103	104	EOF	110	109	108	EOF	EOF
110	111	112	113	114	115	116	0	0	0	0
etc.	0	0	0	0	0	0	0	0	0	0
	0	0	0	0	0	0	0	0	0	0

etc. down to 2847

Position in FAT shown in bold (they are not stored)

Question AppD.1

If an entry in the root directory had an entry BURT TXT 3796 38 12/12/1998 12:17, list all the sectors required to store this file. Use the FAT in Table App D.1.

This file is *fragmented*, i.e. the sectors are not all one after the other. This can be remedied by using a defrag program which simply moves data on the disk until all the sectors are in order for each file; this will result in faster load times. It would probably load faster if the data were in sectors 38, 39, 40, 41, 42, 43 and 44.

The entry FFFF means a bad sector. As the format program tries to format each sector, it writes a value to the disk then immediately tries to read it back. If the same value is not read back or is unreadable, an entry of FFFF is placed in the FAT to prevent that sector being used. The sectors marked with a 0 mean they have not been used and are available for new data. The first two positions in the FAT are placed there by the format program to mark the FAT start point.

The root directory of a real disk is shown in Table App D.9 and contains an entry for a file called PTR.EXE, the first sector where the file is stored is 2 as shown in the root directory. If you now look at the FAT below in Table AppD.11 and find position 2, you should find the value 3. Now look at position 3 and find the number 22, etc. Follow this along until you find an End Of File EOF marker.

The first seven sectors of this file are therefore 2, 3, 22, 23, 24, 41 and 48.

Questions

AppD.2 What are the next five sectors?
AppD.3 Where is the 15th sector?
AppD.4 How many sectors are used to store this file?
AppD.5 How many sectors are available on this disk for use by data?

Now look at the file called LIB2.ASM in the root directory and the FAT then write down all the sector numbers where this file is stored.

Track/sector layout of 1.44 Mb floppy disk

To make things more efficient, data is stored on both sides of the disk at once so a single file will have parts on both sides. This is because the read/write heads in the drive for both sides do not move independently, but move together, the result being a difference between the physical and logical numbering of the sectors/heads and tracks. This is further compounded by the classic computer problem of counting from 0 or

Table AppD.2 *Logical and physical sector numbering*

Logical sector	*Head*	*Track*	*Sector*	*Name*	*Logical sector*	*Head*	*Track*	*Sector*	*Name*
0	0	0	1	Boot sector	39	0	1	4	Data
1	0	0	2	1st FAT	40	0	1	5	Data
2	0	0	3	"	41	0	1	6	Data
3	0	0	4	"	42	0	1	7	Data
4	0	0	5	"	43	0	1	8	Data
5	0	0	6	"	44	0	1	9	Data
6	0	0	7	"	45	0	1	10	Data
7	0	0	8	"	46	0	1	11	Data
8	0	0	9	"	47	0	1	12	Data
9	0	0	10	"	48	0	1	13	Data
10	0	0	11	2nd FAT	49	0	1	14	Data
11	0	0	12	"	50	0	1	15	Data
12	0	0	13	"	51	0	1	16	Data
13	0	0	14	"	52	0	1	17	Data
14	0	0	15	"	53	0	1	18	Data
15	0	0	16	"	54	1	1	1	Data
16	0	0	17	"	55	1	1	2	Data
17	0	0	18	"	56	1	1	3	Data
18	1	0	1	"	57	1	1	4	Data
19	1	0	2	Root Dir	58	1	1	5	Data
20	1	0	3	"	59	1	1	6	Data
21	1	0	4	"	60	1	1	7	Data
22	1	0	5	"	61	1	1	8	Data
23	1	0	6	"	62	1	1	9	Data
24	1	0	7	"	63	1	1	10	Data
25	1	0	8	"	64	1	1	11	Data
26	1	0	9	"	65	1	1	12	Data
27	1	0	10	"	66	1	1	13	Data
28	1	0	11	"	67	1	1	14	Data
29	1	0	12	"	68	1	1	15	Data
30	1	0	13	"	69	1	1	16	Data
31	1	0	14	"	70	1	1	17	Data
32	1	0	15	"	71	1	1	18	Data
33	1	0	16	Data	72	0	2	1	Data
34	1	0	17	Data	73	0	2	2	Data
35	1	0	18	Data	74	0	2	3	Data
36	0	1	1	Data	75	0	2	4	Data
37	0	1	2	Data	76	0	2	5	Data
38	0	1	3	Data	etc.	etc.	etc.	etc.	etc.

etc. to include all the sectors on the disk

from 1. In normal everyday counting we start at 1 but of course our number system actually starts with zero. You will find this throughout the subject of computing, some will count 8 as 0–7 others as 1–8. You can see from the numbering below that logical sector number 33 is actually head 1 and track 0 physical sector 16.

Hex dumps

The hex dumps below show 24 bytes of data per line, the left-hand columns being displayed in hex and the right-hand column being the same data displayed as readable ASCII. Dots are shown in place of control codes.

Boot sector of a 3.5″ disk

It shows that it was formatted using MSDOS version 5.0 and uses a 12-bit FAT. If you have ever tried to boot a PC with a non-bootable floppy in place, you will have seen a message similar to the one here. As you will appreciate, it is simple to personalize your error messages!

Table AppD.3 *Boot sector of a 3.5″ disk*

```
Side 0, Cylinder 0, Sector 1 .................................... Hex format
                                                              Offset 0, hex 0
EB3C904D 53444F53 352E3000 02010100 02E00040 0BF00900 .<.MSDOS5.0........@....
12000200 00000000 00000000 000029E5 1D511C44 4953435F ..............)..Q.DISC_
4F4E4520 20204641 54313220 2020FA33 C08ED0BC 007C1607 ONE   FAT12   .3.....|..
BB780036 C5371E56 1653BF3E 7CB90B00 FCF3A406 1FC645FE .x.6.7.V.S.>|.........E.
0F8B0E18 7C884DF9 894702C7 073E7CFB CD137279 33C03906  ....|.M..G...>|...ry3.9.
137C7408 8B0E137C 890E207C A0107CF7 26167C03 061C7C13 .|t....|..  |..|.  &.|...|.
161E7C03 060E7C83 D200A350 7C891652 7CA3497C 89164B7C ..|...|....P|..R|.I|..K|
B82000F7 26117C8B 1E0B7C03 C348F7F3 0106497C 83164B7C .    ..&.|...|..H....I|..K|
00BB0005 8B16527C A1507CE8 9200721D B001E8AC 0072168B ......R|.P|...r......r..
FBB90B00 BEE67DF3 A6750A8D 7F20B90B 00F3A674 18BE9E7D ......}..u .. .....t...)
E85F0033 C0CD165E 1F8F048F 4402CD19 585858EB E88B471A ._.3...^....D...XXX...G.
48488A1E 0D7C32FF F7E30306 497C1316 4B7CBB00 07B90300 HH..    |2.....I|..K|......
505251E8 3A0072D8 B001E854 00595A58 72BB0501 0083D200 PRQ.:.r....T.YZXr.......
031E0B7C E2E28A2E 157C8A16 247C8B1E 497CA14B 7CEA0000 ...|.....|..      |..I|.K|...
7000AC0A C07429B4 0EBB0700 CD10EBF2 3B16187C 7319F736 p..  .t).........;..|s..6
187CFEC2 88164F7C 33D2F736 1A7C8816 257CA34D 7CF8C3F9 .|....|3..6.|..%|.M|...
C3B4028B 164D7CB1 06D2E60A 364F7C8B CA86E98A 16247C8A .....M|....  60|......  |.
36257CCD 13C30D0A 4E6F6E2D 53797374 656D2064 69736B20 6%|...   Non-System  disk
6F722064 69736B20 6572726F 720D0A52 65706C61 63652061 or disk error Replace a
6E642070 72657373 20616E79 206B6579 20776865 6E207265 nd press any key when re
6164790D 0A00494F 20202020 20205359 534D5344 4F532020 ady  .IO        SYSMSDOS
20535953 000055AA                                      SYS..U.
```

Boot sector with a virus

The boot sector shown here contains a virus. The code in the boot sector is executed at bootup time so it is simple to add code that corrupts your data or simply writes harmless characters to the screen. A 5.25″ floppy is here infected with the stoned virus.

The virus code is in the body of the boot sector where the inevitable message is easily read.

Table AppD.4 *Boot sector of a 3.5″ disk with a virus*

```
Side 0, Cylinder 0, Sector 1 ........................................ Hex format ..
                                                                      Offset 0, hex 0 .
EA0500C0  07E99900  001AAF00  F0E40080  9F007C00  001E5080  ..................|...P..
FC027217  80FC0473  120AD275  0E33C08E  D8A03F04  A8017503  ..r....s...u.3....?...u..
E8070058  1F2EFF2E  09005351  52065657  BE0400B8  01020E07  ...X......SQR.VW.........
BB000233  C98BD141  9C2EFF1E  0900730E  33C09C2E  FF1E0900  ...3...A......s.3........
4E75E0EB  359033F6  BF0002FC  0E1FAD3B  057506AD  3B450274  Nu..5.3.........;u..;E.t.
21B80103  BB0002B1  03B6019C  2EFF1E09  00720FB8  010333DB  !.................r....3..
B10133D2  9C2EFF1E  09005F5E  075A595B  C333C08E  D8FA8ED0  ..3......._^.ZY[.3.......
BC007CFB  A14C00A3  097CA14E  00A30B7C  A1130448  48A31304  ..|..L...|.N...|...HH....
B106D3E0  8EC0A30F  7CB81500  A34C008C  064E00B9  B8010E1F  ........|....L...N.......
33F68BFE  FCF3A42E  FF2E0D00  B80000CD  1333C08E  C0B80102  3......... ......3.......
BB007C2E  803E0800  00740BB9  0700BA80  00CD13EB  4990B903  ..|..>...t...........I....
00BA0001  CD13723E  26F6066C  04077512  BE89010E  1FAC0AC0  ......r>&..l..u..........
7408B40E  B700CD10  EBF30E07  B80102BB  0002B101  BA8000CD  t........................
1372130E  1FBE0002  BF0000AD  3B057511  AD3B4502  750B2EC6  .r..........;.u..;E.u....
06080000  2EFF2E11  002EC606  080002B8  0103BB00  02B90700  .........................
BA8000CD  1372DF0E  1F0E07BE  BE03BFBE  01B94202  F3A4B801  .....r............B......
0333DBFE  C1CD13EB  C507596F  75722050  43206973  206E6F77  .3........Your PC is now.
2053746F  6E656421  070D0A0A  004C4547  414C4953  45204D41   Stoned!. LEGALISE MA.
52494A55  414E4121  00000000  00000000  00000000  00000000  RIJUANA!.................
00000000  00000000  00000000  00000000  00000000  00000000  .........................
00000000  00000000  00000000  00000000  00000000  00000000  .........................
00000000  00000000
```

First two sectors in first copy of FAT, shown as a linked list

This disk is unfragmented, i.e. each sector address follows in sequence.

Table AppD.5

Side 0, Cylinder 0, Sector 2 .... FAT format

Sector 1 in 1st copy of FAT   Cluster 2, hex 2

3	4	5	6	7	8	9	10	11	12	13	14
15	16	17	18	19	20	21	22	23	24	25	26
27	28	29	30	31	32	33	34	35	36	37	38
39	40	41	42	43	44	45	46	47	48	49	50
51	52	53	54	EOF	56	57	58	59	60	61	62
63	64	65	66	67	68	69	70	71	72	73	74
75	76	77	78	79	80	81	82	83	84	85	86
87	88	89	90	91	92	93	94	95	96	97	98
99	100	101	102	103	104	105	106	107	EOF	109	110
111	112	113	114	115	116	117	118	119	120	121	122
123	124	125	126	127	128	129	130	131	132	133	134
135	136	137	138	139	140	141	142	143	144	145	146
147	148	149	150	151	152	153	154	155	156	157	158
159	160	161	162	163	164	165	166	167	168	169	170
171	EOF	173	174	175	176	177	178	179	180	181	182
183	184	185	186	187	188	189	190	191	192	193	194
195	196	197	198	199	200	201	202	203	204	205	206
207	208	209	210	211	212	213	214	215	216	217	218
219	220	221	222	223	224	225	226	227	228	229	230
(Continued in next sector)											
231	232	233	234	235	236	237	238	239	240	241	242
243	244	245	246	247	248	249	250	251	252	253	254
255	256	257	258	259	260	261	262	263	264	265	266
267	268	269	270	271	272	273	274	275	276	277	278
279	280	281	282	283	284	285	286	287	EOF	0	0
0	0	0	0	0	0	0	0	0	0	0	0
0	0	0	0	0	0	0	0	0	0	0	0
0	0	0	0	0	0	0	0	0	0	0	0
0	0	0	0	0	0	0	0	0	0	0	0
0	0	0									

The same FAT but only the first sector, shown in HEX (12-bit FAT)

A 12-bit FAT means each entry is stored in 1.5 bytes. This makes a little more work when you need to decode the 8-bit bytes given here. As this disk is not fragmented, you can still see the sequential nature of the FAT, 4, 5, 6, etc.

Table AppD.6

```
Side 0, Cylinder 0, Sector 2 .......................................... Hex format

 Sector 1 in 1st copy of FAT

                                                                          Offset 0, hex 0

F0FFFF03  40000560  00078000  09A0000B  C0000DE0  000F0001  ....@..'........... .....
11200113  40011560  01178001  19A0011B  C0011DE0  011F0002  . ..@..'................
21200223  40022560  02278002  29A0022B  C0022DE0  022F0003  ! .#@.%'.'..)..+..-../..
31200333  40033560  03FF8F03  39A0033B  C0033DE0  033F0004  1 .3@.5'....9..;..=..?..
41200443  40044560  04478004  49A0044B  C0044DE0  044F0005  A .C@.E',G..I..K..M..O..
51200553  40055560  05578005  59A0055B  C0055DE0  055F0006  Q .S@.U'.W..Y..[..].._..
61200663  40066560  06678006  69A0066B  F0FF6DE0  066F0007  a .c@.e'.g..i..k..m..o..
71200773  40077560  07778007  79A0077B  C0077DE0  077F0008  q .s@.u'.w..y..{..}.....
81200883  40088560  08878008  89A0088B  C0088DE0  088F0009  . ..@..'................
91200993  40099560  09978009  99A0099B  C0099DE0  099F000A  . ..@..'................
A1200AA3  400AA560  0AA7800A  A9A00AAB  F0FFADE0  0AAF000B  . ..@..'............
B1200BB3  400BB560  0BB7800B  B9A00BBB  C00BBDE0  0BBF000C  . ..@..'...............
C1200CC3  400CC560  0CC7800C  C9A00CCB  C00CCDE0  0CCF000D  . ..@..'................
D1200DD3  400DD560  0DD7800D  D9A00DDB  C00DDDE0  0DDF000E  . .@.'..  ..  ..  ..  ...
E1200EE3  400EE560  0EE7800E  E9A00EEB  C00EEDE0  0EEF000F  . ..@..'................
F1200FF3  400FF560  0FF7800F  F9A00FFB  C00FFDE0  0FFF0010  . ..@..'................
01211003  41100561  10078110  09A1100B  C1100DE1  100F0111  .!..A..a.......... .....
11211113  41111561  11178111  19A1111B  C1111DE1  111FF1FF  .!..A..a................
00000000  00000000  00000000  00000000  00000000  00000000  ........................
00000000  00000000  00000000  00000000  00000000  00000000  ........................
00000000  00000000  00000000  00000000  00000000  00000000  ........................
00000000  00000000
```

Root directory, shown as text

Each entry takes up 32 bytes and stores the 8.3 format filename (not the dot!), the size, date and time of last modification, address of first sector (one sector = one cluster here), and the file attributes, i.e. if the file is hidden, read only, archived or is a system file.

The volume name is stored as a filename but with its attributes set the Vol.

Table AppD.7

```
Side 1, Cylinder 0, Sector 2 ................................. Directory format

                                                                    Offset 0, hex 0
                                                                    Attributes
Filename  Ext    Size      Date      Time    Cluster    Arc R/O Sys Hid Dir Vol
........ ..... ........ ........ ....... .......  ...........................
DISC_ONE                 23/11/94  22:27              Arc                   Vol
FILE1           26625  23/11/94  22:18         2    Arc
FILE2           26625  23/11/94  22:19        55    Arc
FILE3           32563  23/11/94  22:20       108    Arc
FILE4           59305  23/11/94  22:24       172    Arc
              unused directory entry
               unused directory entry
                unused directory entry
                 unused directory entry
                  unused directory entry
                   unused directory entry
                    unused directory entry
                     unused directory entry
                      unused directory entry
                       unused directory entry
                        unused directory entry
```

The same root directory, shown in HEX

The information is the same, the only difference is in the method of display.

Table AppD.8

```
Side 1, Cylinder 0, Sector 2

                                                                        Offset 0, hex 0

44495343  5F4F4E45  20202028  00000000  00000000  00006DB3  DISC_ONE   (..........m.
771D0000  00000000  46494C45  31202020  20202020  00000000  w.......FILE1       ....
00000000  000050B2  771D0200  01680000  46494C45  32202020  ......P.w....h..FILE2
20202020  00000000  00000000  00006DB2  771D3700  01680000      ..........m.w.7..h..
46494C45  33202020  20202020  00000000  00000000  000087B2  FILE3       ............
771D6C00  337F0000  46494C45  34202020  20202020  00000000  w.1.3...FILE4       ....
00000000  00000DB3  771DAC00  A9E70000  00000000  00000000  ...... .w...............
00000000  00000000  00000000  00000000  00000000  00000000  ........................
00000000  00000000  00000000  00000000  00000000  00000000  ........................
00000000  00000000  00000000  00000000  00000000  00000000  ........................
00000000  00000000  00000000  00000000  00000000  00000000  ........................
00000000  00000000  00000000  00000000  00000000  00000000  ........................
00000000  00000000  00000000  00000000  00000000  00000000  ........................
00000000  00000000  00000000  00000000  00000000  00000000  ........................
00000000  00000000  00000000  00000000  00000000  00000000  ........................
00000000  00000000  00000000  00000000  00000000  00000000  ........................
00000000  00000000  00000000  00000000  00000000  00000000  ........................
00000000  00000000  00000000  00000000  00000000  00000000  ........................
00000000  00000000  00000000  00000000  00000000  00000000  ........................
00000000  00000000  00000000  00000000  00000000  00000000  ........................
00000000  00000000  00000000  00000000  00000000  00000000  ........................
00000000  00000000
```

After many file additions and deletions, the same directory, shown as text

The starting clusters are no longer in size order indicating disk fragmentation. Note, one file is marked as deleted, it is the file that *was* called THING5. It is now shown as µHING5, the µ character denoting a special marker that has overwritten the first character of the filename showing that it is marked as deleted, the space occupied is now available to other files. Deleting a file simply overwrites the first character in the directory with a special character and the space made available. The entire file is still on disk and it is a simple task to retrieve it. If you have a file that must remain confidential after deletion, it must be *overwritten* with one of the same size or larger.

Table AppD.9

Side 1, Cylinder 0, Sector 2 .... Directory format

Offset 0, hex 0

Attributes

Filename	Ext	Size	Date	Time	Cluster	Arc	R/O	Sys	Hid	Dir	Vol
DISC_ONE			23/11/94	22:27		Arc					Vol
PTR	EXE	232788	1/08/91	15:16	2	Arc					
JUNK345		19180	13/11/92	12:00	450	Arc					
THING35		674	24/11/94	20:08	4	Arc	R/O		Hid		
THING36		755	24/11/94	20:08	8	Arc					
THING37		836	24/11/94	20:08	10	Arc	R/O		Hid		
EGA	SYS	4885	9/04/91	5:00	333	Arc		Sys			
OLDJUNK			24/11/94	20:23	12					Dir	
OLDFILE		18976	13/02/90	13:59	2446	Arc					
THING39		999	24/11/94	20:08	14	Arc					
ANSI 40	SYS	1080	24/11/94	20:08	16	Arc	R/O	Sys	Hid		
THING41		1162	24/11/94	20:08	19	Arc					
NEWJUNK			24/11/94	20:23	13					Dir	
THING43		1324	24/11/94	20:08	25	Arc					
A		776	22/06/92	20:17	5	Arc					
THING1		1327	24/11/94	20:06	28	Arc					
(continued in the next sector)											
DECPATH		11894	8/08/92	4:00	488	Arc					
THING2		1408	24/11/94	20:06	31	Arc					
LIB2	ASM	1750	24/11/92	9:26	168	Arc					
THING3		1490	24/11/94	20:06	34	Arc					
PROCTYPE	ASM	1942	4/02/92	11:43	172	Arc					
THING4		1571	24/11/94	20:06	37	Arc					
KEYB	COM	14986	9/04/91	5:00	408	Arc					
MENU	ASM	1764	17/11/92	18:51	176	Arc					
µHING5		1652	24/11/94	20:06	41	Arc					
EQUATION	WPK	2983	29/09/92	11:17	1704	Arc					
THING6		1734	24/11/94	20:06	51	Arc					
THING7		1815	24/11/94	20:06	55	Arc					
SHORTCUT	WPK	11963	5/08/91	10:31	1750	Arc					
KEYBOARD	SYS	34697	9/04/91	5:00	438	Arc					
MSLANMAN		10583	8/08/92	4:00	537	Arc					
EDIT	WPM	10826	5/08/91	10:31	1845	Arc					

The FAT after many file additions and deletions

This disk is now fragmented. First sector in first copy of FAT, shown as a linked list (12-bit FAT). Note, the fragmentation is obvious because the numbers (sector addresses) are no longer in sequence.

Table AppD.10

```
Side 0, Cylinder 0, Sector 2 ........................................ FAT format

 Sector 1 in 1st copy of FAT                                       Cluster 2, hex 2

 2      3     22      7      6  {EOF}  {EOF}      9  {EOF}     11  {EOF}  {EOF}  {EOF}
       15  {EOF}     17     18  {EOF}     20     21  {EOF}     23     24     41     26
       27  {EOF}     29     30  {EOF}     32     33  {EOF}     35     36  {EOF}     38
       39     40  {EOF}     48     43     44     45     46     47     64     49     50
      129     52     53     54  {EOF}     56     57     58  {EOF}     60     61     62
    {EOF}    105     65     66     67     68     69     70     71     72     73     74
       75     76     77     78     79     80     81     82     83     84     85     86
       87     88     89     90     91     92     93     94     95     96     97     98
       99    100    101    102    103    104  {EOF}    106    108    160  {EOF}    110
      111    112    113  {EOF}    115    116    117    118  {EOF}    120    121    122
      123  {EOF}    125    126    127    128  {EOF}    130    131    132    133   1035
      135    136    137    138  {EOF}    140    141    142    143  {EOF}    145    146
      147    148    149  {EOF}    151    152    153    154    155  {EOF}    157    158
      159    161  {EOF}    162  {EOF}    164    165    166    167    180    169    170
      171  {EOF}    173    174    175  {EOF}    177    178    179  {EOF}  {EOF}    182
      183    184    185    186  {EOF}    188    189    190    191    192  {EOF}    194
      195    199    197  {EOF}    200    247  {EOF}    202  {EOF}    233    205    206
    {EOF}    208    209    210    211    212    213    214    215  {EOF}    217    218
      219    220    221    222    223  {EOF}    225    226    227    228    229    230
(Continued in next sector)
      231    232  {EOF}  {EOF}    235  {EOF}    240    238    239  {EOF}  {EOF}    242
    {EOF}    244  {EOF}    246    288    267    249    250    251    252    253    254
      255    256    257    258    259    260    261    262    263    264    265    266
    {EOF}    297    269    270    271    272    273  {EOF}  {EOF}    276    277    278
      279    280  {EOF}  {EOF}    283    284  {EOF}    286    287    445  {EOF}    290
      291  {EOF}    293    294  {EOF}    296    317  {EOF}    299    300    301    302
      303    304  {EOF}    306    307    308    309    310    311  {EOF}    313    314
      315    316    319  {EOF}    343    320  {EOF}    322    323    324    325    326
      327  {EOF}    329    330    331    332    602    334    335    336    337    338
      339    340    341
```

The same FAT interpreted and shown as a simple linked list

This is the same information as above but shown as a linear list with the FAT positions numbered. These are for your convenience, but are not stored on the disk.

Table AppD.11

P= Position in FAT
N= Next position in FAT

P	N	P	N	P	N	P	N
2	3	92	93	182	183	272	273
3	22	93	94	183	184	273	{EOF}
4	7	94	95	184	185	274	{EOF}
5	6	95	96	185	186	275	276
6	{EOF}	96	97	186	{EOF}	276	277
7	{EOF}	97	98	187	188	277	278
8	9	98	99	188	189	278	279
9	{EOF}	99	100	189	190	279	280
10	11	100	101	190	191	280	{EOF}
11	{EOF}	101	102	191	192	281	{EOF}
12	{EOF}	102	103	192	{EOF}	282	283
13	{EOF}	103	104	193	194	283	284
14	15	104	{EOF}	194	195	284	{EOF}
15	{EOF}	105	106	195	199	285	286
16	17	106	108	196	197	286	287
17	18	107	160	197	{EOF}	287	445
18	{EOF}	108	{EOF}	198	200	288	{EOF}
19	20	109	110	199	247	289	290
20	21	110	111	200	{EOF}	290	291
21	{EOF}	111	112	201	202	291	{EOF}
22	23	112	113	202	{EOF}	292	293
23	24	113	{EOF}	203	233	293	294
24	41	114	115	204	205	294	{EOF}
25	26	115	116	205	206	295	296
26	27	116	117	206	{EOF}	296	317
27	{EOF}	117	118	207	208	297	{EOF}
28	29	118	{EOF}	208	209	298	299
29	30	119	120	209	210	299	300
30	{EOF}	120	121	210	211	300	301
31	32	121	122	211	212	301	302
32	33	122	123	212	213	302	303
33	{EOF}	123	{EOF}	213	214	303	304
34	35	124	125	214	215	304	{EOF}
35	36	125	126	215	{EOF}	305	306
36	{EOF}	126	127	216	217	306	307
37	38	127	128	217	218	307	308
38	39	128	{EOF}	218	219	308	309
39	40	129	130	219	220	309	310
40	{EOF}	130	131	220	221	310	311
41	48	131	132	221	222	311	{EOF}
42	43	132	133	222	223	312	313
43	44	133	1035	223	{EOF}	313	314
44	45	134	135	224	225	314	315
45	46	135	136	225	226	315	316
46	47	136	137	226	227	316	319
47	64	137	138	227	228	317	{EOF}
48	49	138	{EOF}	228	229	318	343
49	50	139	140	229	230	319	320

Table AppD.11 (*Continued*)

P	N	P	N	P	N	P	N
50	129	140	141	230	231	320	{EOF}
51	52	141	142	231	232	321	322
52	53	142	143	232	{EOF}	322	323
53	54	143	{EOF}	233	{EOF}	323	324
54	{EOF}	144	145	234	235	324	325
55	56	145	146	235	{EOF}	325	326
56	57	146	147	236	240	326	327
57	58	147	148	237	238	327	{EOF}
58	{EOF}	148	149	238	239	328	329
59	60	149	{EOF}	239	{EOF}	329	330
60	61	150	151	240	{EOF}	330	331
61	62	151	152	241	242	331	332
62	{EOF}	152	153	242	{EOF}	332	602
63	105	153	154	243	244	333	334
64	65	154	155	244	{EOF}	334	335
65	66	155	{EOF}	245	246	335	336
66	67	156	157	246	288	336	337
67	68	157	158	247	267	337	338
68	69	158	159	248	249	338	339
69	70	159	161	249	250	339	340
70	71	160	{EOF}	250	251	340	341
71	72	161	162	251	252	341	342
72	73	162	{EOF}	252	253	342	{EOF}
73	74	163	164	253	254	343	344
74	75	164	165	254	255	344	{EOF}
75	76	165	166	255	256	345	346
76	77	166	167	256	257	346	347
77	78	167	180	257	258	347	{EOF}
78	79	168	169	258	259	348	349
79	80	169	170	259	260	349	350
80	81	170	171	260	261	350	{EOF}
81	82	171	{EOF}	261	262	351	352
82	83	172	173	262	263	352	353
83	84	173	174	263	264	353	{EOF}
84	85	174	175	264	265	354	355
85	86	175	{EOF}	265	266	355	356
86	87	176	177	266	{EOF}	356	{EOF}
87	88	177	178	267	297	357	358
88	89	178	179	268	269	358	359
89	90	179	{EOF}	269	270	359	360
90	91	180	{EOF}	270	271	360	{EOF}
91	92	181	182	271	272	361	362

Appendix E
A brief network glossary

Mnemonic	*Meaning*	*Comment*
API	Application Program Interface, e.g. Windows API	
ARP	Address Resolution Protocol	Part of TCP/IP
DLC	Data Link Control	
FTP	File Transfer Protocol	Internet layer 7 protocol
HTTP	HyperText Transport Protocol	Internet layer 7 protocol
ICMP	Internet Control Message Protocol	Part of TCP/IP
IEEE	Institute of Electrical and Electronic Engineers	For the setting of standards, e.g. IEEE 302
IGMP	Internet Group Message Protocol	Part of TCP/IP
IP	Internet Protocol	Part of TCP/IP
IPX	Internetwork Packet Exchange	IPX/SPX is Novell's routable datagram protocol
ISO	International Standards Organization	
LLC	Link Layer Control	
LSL	Link Support Layer	
NBT	NetBEUI over TCP	Microsoft
NCP	Netware Core Protocol	Novell
NDIS	Network Device Interface Specification	Microsoft's answer to ODI

Mnemonic	*Meaning*	*Comment*
NetBEUI	NetBIOS Extended User Interface	Microsoft native transport protocol, not routable
NetBIOS	Network Basic Input Output System	From old Microsoft LAN systems, not routable
NIC	Network Interface Card	The actual network card
ODI	Open Data Link Interface	Novell
OSI	Open Systems Interconnect	7 layered model from the ISO
RARP	Reverse Address Resolution Protocol	Part of TCP/IP
RIP	Routing Information Protocol	
RPC	Remote Procedure Calls	Novell
SMB	Server Message Blocks	Used in all Microsoft networks for file and print service
SMTP	Simple Mail Transport Protocol	Internet layer 7 protocol
SNMP	Simple Network Management Protocol	Part of TCP/IP
SPX	Sequenced Packet Exchange	IPX/SPX is Novell's routable datagram protocol
TCP	Transport Control Protocol	Part of TCP/IP
TLI	Transport Layer Interface	
UDP	User Datagram Protocol	Part of TCP/IP

There are many glossaries available free on the Internet.

For networks, a 'standard' version can be found in a file called a 'request for comments', an odd sounding name for what amounts to an Internet standard. The network glossary is called rfc1983 and it can be found all over the Internet. The main link page to find it is at

www.rfc-editor.org/rfc.html

and a typical site where it can be found is

ftp://ftp.isi.edu/in-notes/rfc1983.txt

or you can search for the word glossary at

www.rfc-editor.org/rfcsearch.html

which will point to sources of rfc1983 and other standard network glossaries.

Mapping of outcomes

Chapter 1

Outcome	Topic	Pages	Reference material
1	Computer performance	56	Winn L Rosch, Hardware Bible, *Que*, General description of PC component parts, systems and performance. Websites for computer performance:- cpusite.examedia.nl/sections/benchmarks.html i-probe.com/i-probe/ip_intel_9.html www.usb.org/developers/docs.html www.specbench.org/contents.html
1	User Requirements	62 and 4–62	Lacy, M. Understanding Computer Systems Architecture, *DP Publications* Mano, Morris M, Computer Systems Architecture, *Prentice Hall*, sysopt.earthweb.com/mboard.html www.pcguide.com/buy/index.htm www.pcguide.com/ref/hdd/bios/size.htm www.agpforum.org/info.htm www.tomshardware.com/mainboard/index.html www.tme-inc.com/html/service/general.htm
2	Operating Systems	69	Maddix F and Morgan G, Systems Software, *Ellis Horwood*
3	Upgrade a computer system	8–16	Minasi, Mark, PC Upgrade and Maintenance Guide, *Sybex,* detailed descriptions of components and their compatibility. Brooks, Charles, Microcomputer Systems Theory and Practice, *Marcraft International*, Tischer M and Jennrich, B, PC Intern, *Abacus* Dick D, The PC Support Handbook, *Dumbreck Publishing*
3	Microprocessors		Microprocessors www.amd.com www.amd.com/products/cpg/cpg.html www.arm.com www.chips.ibm.com www.chips.ibm.com/products/powerpc/

Outcome	Topic	Pages	Reference material
3	Microprocessors *continued*		www.cyrix.com www.cyrix.com/products/cyrindex.htm www.hpmuseum.org/journals/hp41/41lcd.htm www.intel.com www.intel.com/intel/museum/25anniv/ www.intel.com/intel/product/index.htm www.intel.com/procs/perf/resources/benchmark.htm www.mot.com www.mot.com/SPS/MMTG/mp.html www.sun.com www.sun.com/microelectronics/products/microproc.html www.zilog.com/products/zx80.html
All	General	All	itri.loyola.edu/displays/c4_slb.htm www.seiko-usa-ecd.com/lcd/html/glossary.html www.sharp.co.jp/sc/library-e/techn_top/topl_e.htm Search Engine www.go.com Search Engine www.metacrawler.com/ Unicode www.unicode.org/unicode/standard/standard.html unicode website www.unicode.org MPEG Video www.mpeg.org/MPEG/video.html

Chapter 2

Outcome	Topic	Pages	Reference material
1	Compare **different lifecycle models**	75–86	Pressman R *Software Engineering* (McGraw-Hill) Sommerville *Software Engineering* (Addison–Wesley) EDEXCEL Tutor Support Material Core Units (Code: B004666)
2	Perform a **system investigation**	86–94	Layzell & Loucopoulos *Systems Analysis & Development* (Chartwell-Bratt) Texts listed under outcome 1
3	Perform **functional and data modelling**	94–156	Weaver P *Practical SSADM 4* (Pitman Publishing) Goodland & Slater *SSADM Version 4* (McGraw-Hill) SSADM web sites Various sites containing introduction through to advanced examples, tutorials, glossaries, articles etc. (search under SSADM) Also the International SSADM User Group at: www.cscs.wmin.ac.uk/~ssadm/main.html Yourdon INC *Yourdon Systems Method* (Prentice Hall) Booch G *Object-oriented analysis and design* (Addison-Wesley) Schmuller J *Teach yourself UML in 24 hours* (SAMS) Booch, Rambaugh & Jacobson *The UML User Guide* (Addison–Wesley) Booch, Rambaugh & Jacobson *The UML* *Reference Manual* (Addison–Wesley)

Outcome	Topic	Pages	Reference material
			Booch, Rambaugh & Jacobson *The complete UML training course* (Addison–Wesley)
			UML Zone at www.uml-zone.com For articles, modelling tips, tools, links to other UML sites etc. (also links to other zones like SQL, C++, Java, XML etc.)
			Coles & Rowley *Access 97 Basic Skills* (Letts Educational)
			Whitehorn and Marklyn *Inside relational databases* (Springer)
			Rock-Evans *Data Modelling & Process Modelling* (Butterworth-Heinemann)
			Texts listed under outcome 1

Chapter 3

Outcome	Topic	Pages	Reference material
1	Investigate problem-solving theory, applications and techniques	158–167	1. How To Solve It G Polya 2nd ed., Princeton University Press (1957) ISBN 0–691–08097–6 2. The Art and Craft of Computing Stefano Ceri, Dino Mandrioli and Licia Sbattella Addison-Wesley ISBN 0 201 87698 1 3. A useful Web site is: http://www.hawaii.edu/suremath/howTo.html
2	Develop business models using spreadsheets	167–200	1. Learn Microsoft Excel 2000 VBA Programming Korol, Julitta Wordware Publishing, Inc ISBN 1556227035 2. Designing and Building Business Models Using Microsoft Excel Robson, Andrew J. McGraw-Hill ISBN 0077090586
3	Design and develop code using an appropriate programming methodology	200–252	1. An Introduction To Program Design David Sargent McGraw-Hill ISBN 0 07 707246 4 2. The Art and Craft of Computing Stefano Ceri, Dino Mandrioli and Licia Sbattella Addison-Wesley ISBN 0 201 87698 1 3. Visual Basic Made Simple Stephen Morris Made Simple Books ISBN 0 7506 3245 3 4. C Programming Made Simple Conor Sexton Made Simple Books ISBN 0 7506 3244 5

Chapter 4

Outcome	Topic	Pages	Reference material
1	Examine the nature of information and contemporary applications	253–262	Management Information Systems Kenneth Laudon and Jane Laudon Prentice Hall ISBN 0 13 015682 5
2	Examine the tools available to organizations for information processing	262–302	1. Information Systems Uma Gupta Prentice Hall ISBN 0 13 010857 X 2. Electronic Commerce Ravi Kalakota and Andrew Whinston Addison-Wesley ISBN 0 201 88067 9 3. The Essence of Expert Systems Keith Darlington Prentice Hall ISBN 0 13 022774 9 4. The Essence of Neural Networks Robert Callan Prentice Hall ISBN 0 13 908732 X
3	Evaluate the information systems within an organization	302–304	Management Information Systems Kenneth Laudon and Jane Laudon Prentice Hall ISBN 0 13 015682 5

Chapter 5

Outcome	Topic	Pages	Reference material
1	Employ **systems analysis and design tools** to maintain an existing system	306–350	Pressman, Roger *Software Engineering – A Practitioner's Approach* McGraw-Hill Sommerville, Ian *Software Engineering* (Addison–Wesley) Lock, Dennis *Project Management* Gower Thaver, Richard *Software Engineering Project Management* IEEE Computer Society Higgins, David *Data Structured* *Software Maintenance* Dorset House Jacobson, Ivar *Object-Oriented* *Software Engineering* Addison-Wesley EDEXCEL *Tutor Support Material* *Core Units* (Code: B004666) Longstreet, David *Software Maintenance and Computers* IEEE Computer Society Software Engineering Institute www.sei.cmu.edu/about/about.html *Software Project Management* *Videotape Courses* www.sei.cmu.edu/products/videos/sw.proj.mgmt.html see also www.sei.cmu.edu/products/videos/video.html
2	Apply **quality assurance** procedures	350–373	Schulmeyer & Mackenzie *Verification & Validation of Modern Software Systems* Prentice Hall Ginac, Frank *Customer Oriented* *Software Quality Assurance* Prentice Hall

Outcome	Topic	Pages	Reference material
			ASQ Quality Press *Software Quality Assurance* ASQC Quality Press Darrel, Ince *An Introduction to Software Quality Assurance and its Implementation* Macmillan Educational
3	Review the **professional standards** of a computer practitioner	373–382	HMSO The Stationary Office www.itcompliance.com British Computer Society www.bcs.org.uk The Engineering Council www.engc.org.uk The Institute of Electrical Engineers www.iee.org.uk Data Protection Act 1998 www.hmso.gov.uk/acts/acts 1998/19980029.htm see also www.dataprotection.gov.uk Health & Safety at Work Act www.healthandsafety.co.uk/haswa.htm see also www.hse.gov.uk/pubns/hsc13.htm see also www.bbc-safety.co.uk/HSE/hasawa.htm Institute of Incorporated Engineers www.iie.org.uk Institute of Electrical Engineers www.iee.org.uk[/ub] Institute of Analysts and Programmers www.iap.org.uk

Chapter 6

Outcome	Topic	Pages	Reference material
1	Network specification	407	Held, G, Understanding Data Communications, *SAMS Publishing* Hodson, P, Local Area Networks, *Letts* Black, Uyless D. Data Communications and Distributed Network, *Prentice Hall.* www.3com.com/technology/tech_net/white_papers/ www.3com.com/technology/tech_net/white_papers/503072a.html www.brother.com/european/networking/ www.cisco.com/univercd/cc/td/doc/cisintwk/ito_doc/ethernet.htm
2	Analyse the impact of communications technology	409/425	Information Systems Uma Gupta Prentice Hall ISBN 0 13 010857 X
3	Describe and evaluate the cost and security of communications systems	425–432	http://www.cisco.com
4	Network specification	407	Held, G, Understanding Data Communications, *SAMS Publishing* Hodson, P, Local Area Networks, *Letts*
4	Network Architectures	399	Black, Uyless D. Data Communications and Distributed Network, *Prentice Hall.* ISO 7 layer network model www.3com.com/technology/tech_net/white_papers/ www.3com.com/technology/tech_net/white_papers/503072a.html www.brother.com/european/networking/ www.cisco.com/univercd/cc/td/doc/cisintwk/ito_doc/ethernet.htm
4	Connecting to networks from remote sites	401	Sant'Angelo R and Chagtai N, Windows NT Server Survival Guide, *SAMS Publishing*,

Index